New Testament Commentary

New Testament Commentary

Exposition
of the
Epistle to
the Hebrews

Simon J. Kistemaker

Baker Book House

Grand Rapids, Michigan 49506

Copyright 1984 by
Baker Book House Company

ISBN: 0-8010-5460-5

Library of Congress Catalog Card Number: 84-71166

Printed in the United States of America

Unless otherwise noted, all Scripture references are from the Holy Bible: New
International Version. Copyright © 1978 by the International Bible Society.
Used by permission of Zondervan Bible Publishers.

Contents

Abbreviations

ASV	American Standard Version
ATR	*Anglican Theological Review*
BA	*Biblical Archaeologist*
Bauer	Walter Bauer, W. F. Arndt, F. W. Gingrich, and Frederick Danker, *A Greek-English Lexicon of the New Testament*, 2d ed.
BASOR	*Bulletin of the American Schools of Oriental Research*
BF	British and Foreign Bible Society, *The New Testament*, 2d ed.
Bib	*Biblica*
BibLeb	*Bibel und Leben*
Bov	Jose M. Bover, *Novi Testamenti Biblica Graeca et Latina*, 4th ed.
BS	*Bibliotheca Sacra*
CBQ	*Catholic Biblical Quarterly*
CTJ	*Calvin Theological Journal*
I Clem.	First Epistle of Clement
Dial.	Justin Martyr, *Dialogue with Trypho*
Epid.	Irenaeus, *Epideixis*
EvQ	*Evangelical Quarterly*
ExpT	*Expository Times*
GNB	Good News Bible
Heresies	Irenaeus, *Against Heresies*
HTR	*Harvard Theological Review*
Interp	*Interpretation*
JBL	*Journal of Biblical Literature*
JB	Jerusalem Bible
JETS	*Journal of the Evangelical Theological Society*
JTS	*Journal of Theological Studies*
KJV	King James Version
LB	The Living Bible
LCL	Loeb Classical Library edition
LXX	Septuagint
Merk	Augustinus Merk, ed., *Novum Testamentum Graece et Latine*, 9th ed.
MLB	The Modern Language Bible

Moffatt	The Bible: A New Translation by James Moffatt
NAB	New American Bible
NASB	New American Standard Bible
NEB	New English Bible
Nes-Al	Eberhard Nestle; Kurt Aland, rev., *Novum Testamentum Graece*, 26th ed.
NIDNTT	*New International Dictionary of New Testament Theology*
NIV	New International Version
NKJV	New King James Version
NovT	*Novum Testamentum*
NTS	*New Testament Studies*
Phillips	The New Testament in Modern English
4Q *Florilegium*	Collection of biblical texts from Qumran Cave 4
1QSa	Rule of the Congregation *(serekh hayaḥad)* from Qumran Cave 1
RefR	*Reformed Review*
RSV	Revised Standard Version
RV	Revised Version
ScotJT	*Scottish Journal of Theology*
SB	H. L. Strack and P. Billerbeck, *Kommentar zum Neuen Testament aus Talmud und Midrasch*
StTh	*Studia Theologica*
Talmud	The Babylonian Talmud
TB	*Tyndale Bulletin*
TDNT	*Theological Dictionary of the New Testament*
TR	Textus Receptus: The Greek New Testament According to the Majority Text
Tyn H Bul	*Tyndale House Bulletin*
TS	*Theological Studies*
TZ	*Theologische Zeitschrift*
WH	B. F. Westcott and Fenton Hort, *The New Testament in the Original Greek*
WTJ	*Westminster Theological Journal*
ZNW	*Zeitschrift für die Neuentestamentliche Wissenschaft*
ZPEB	*Zondervan Pictorial Encyclopedia of the Bible*
ZTK	*Zeitschrift für Theologie und Kirche*

Preface

When Dr. William Hendriksen died in January 1982, he had completed commentaries in the New Testament Commentary series on the four Gospels and on all of Paul's epistles with the exception of I and II Corinthians. He set the goal of writing as many commentaries as he was able.

I have been given the challenge to continue this task. Although my style may differ somewhat from that of Dr. Hendriksen, the format, design, and purpose are those of my predecessor. My commentary on Hebrews has been written for the benefit of the pastor and the lay person.

The commentary on the text itself is free from technical terms and phrases, so that the lay person can read the explanation of a text without difficulty. For the student who knows Greek, I have placed the explanation of Greek words, phrases, and constructions at the conclusion of each section of the text.

Introductory statements, comments about doctrinal considerations, and a summary are part of every chapter. And throughout the commentary the reader finds numerous practical helps and applications. Last, a Scripture index in the concluding pages proves to be of great value for quick reference and consultation.

Spring 1984   Simon J. Kistemaker

Introduction

Outline

A. What Are the Characteristics of Hebrews?
B. Who Wrote This Epistle?
C. What Is the Message of Hebrews?
D. Why Was This Letter Rejected in the Early Centuries?
E. When Was Hebrews Written?
F. Who Were the First Readers?
G. How Can Hebrews Be Outlined?

If there is one book of the New Testament that exhorts the Christian to remain faithful "in the last days," it is the Epistle to the Hebrews. This epistle has a special message for a day marked by apostasy; it addresses the believer who, facing unbelief and disobedience, must stand firm in the faith. The letter to the Hebrews, then, is an exhortation to faithfulness. Granted that Hebrews teaches the superiority of Christ over angels, Moses, Joshua, Aaron, and Melchizedek, the exhortations that are freely interspersed among the doctrinal sections set the tone. The admonitions reveal the warm heart and deep concern of the pastor-writer.

Constantly in the epistle the author pleads with the reader to remain faithful to the gospel and not to drift away (2:1; 3:12; 4:11; 6:11–12; 10:22–25; 12:25). He stresses corporate responsibility: fellow believers are exhorted to take care that not one believer is allowed to turn away from the living God (3:12–13; 4:1, 11). The consequences of falling away are indeed unimaginable, for, says the writer, "It is a dreadful thing to fall into the hands of the living God" (10:31).

The writer of Hebrews counsels the believer to listen obediently to the Word of God (4:2–3, 6, 12). He exhorts the believers to "worship God acceptably with reverence and awe" (12:28). And he concludes that "our God is a consuming fire" (12:29)—in case this exhortation is disregarded.

In an age in which apostasy is commonplace and "the secret power of lawlessness is already at work," as Paul puts it in II Thessalonians 2:7, the message of Hebrews is most relevant. We simply cannot ignore the warning that accompanies "such a great salvation" (2:3), because we are unable to escape if we do. Therefore, we do well to listen attentively.

A. What Are the Characteristics of Hebrews?

Many translations of the Bible call Hebrews "the Epistle to the Hebrews." But is this New Testament book really an epistle? If we compare it with the epistles of Paul, James, Peter, Jude, and John, we must say that it is not. Greetings customary in these letters—with the exception of I John—are absent in Hebrews.

1. Letter or Epistle?

In the letter itself, however, the writer includes a few references to the conduct and possessions of the readers (6:10; 10:32–34). And in chapter 13

3

he becomes rather intimate with the recipients. He calls Timothy "our brother" and mentions that Timothy, having been released from prison, will accompany him to visit the readers (13:23). The letter ends with greetings (13:24), and therefore in view of this last chapter Hebrews is indeed a letter.

The beginning of Hebrews has something in common with the First Epistle of John. Both have an introduction that in many respects serves as a summary statement for the succeeding chapters. The name of the author is absent in Hebrews and in I John. Also, specific mention of the addressees, greetings, and prayers are missing. These elements are characteristic of the rest of the New Testament epistles.

To say that Hebrews is a treatise in order to avoid the use of the words *epistle* or *letter* is not too satisfactory. A treatise consists of an exposition of or discourse on one topic, but Hebrews teaches a number of doctrines and intersperses them with pastoral exhortations. We admit that whatever word is used to describe this book of the New Testament, difficulties remain. One solution to the problem is to call the book Hebrews, as some of the more recent translations do. Yet Hebrews itself is one of the general Epistles of the New Testament.

As an epistle Hebrews is similar to some of the writings of Paul; it contains doctrine and exhortation. Paul's custom, however, is to set forth doctrine first; toward the end of his epistles, Paul gives his exhortations. Hebrews differs in this respect. The writer mingles doctrine and pastoral admonition; for example, in the midst of his teaching on the Son's superiority to the angels, the author exhorts the reader to "pay more careful attention" to the Word of God (2:1–4).

2. Pastoral or Doctrinal?

Is Hebrews a pastoral or doctrinal epistle? We can easily answer, "It is both." Yet we admit that on balance the purpose of the writer of Hebrews is to convey a pastoral exhortation to the recipients. He strengthens his admonitions with doctrines about Christ's superiority, the priesthood, the covenant, and faith.

Nowhere in the entire New Testament except in the letter to the Hebrews are the doctrines of Christ's priesthood and the covenant explained. We find but a passing reference to the priesthood of Christ in Romans 8:34, "Christ Jesus, who died—more than that, who was raised to life—is at the right hand of God and is also interceding for us." Paul merely mentions the intercessory work of Christ and thus implies Christ's priesthood. But in all his epistles Paul refrains from writing about this doctrine. Although Paul's theological training included the doctrine of the covenant as an integral part of Old Testament teaching, he mentions the word *covenant* nine times (Rom. 9:4; 11:27; I Cor. 11:25; II Cor. 3:6, 14; Gal. 3:15, 17; 4:24; Eph. 2:12). In Galatians 4:24 he is somewhat specific: "These things may be taken figuratively, for the women represent two covenants. One covenant is from Mount Sinai and bears children who are to be slaves: This is Hagar." Yet even in this setting, Paul's treatment is rather scant. The writer of Hebrews, on the other hand, teaches the doctrines of the priesthood and the covenant in full.

3. Revelation and Inspiration

The author gives the reader God's revelation. For him the primary author of Scripture, namely, the Holy Spirit, is all important, for God addresses the reader through his Word. Thus, not the secondary author but God is the speaker in the introductory phrases to the numerous quotations from the Old Testament. In chapter 1, God is the One who utters the citations from the Psalms, the Song of Moses (Deut. 32:43, LXX), and II Samuel 7:14. With variations the phrase *God says* occurs constantly (1:5, 6, 7, 8, 10, 13; 2:12, 13; 3:7; 4:3; 5:5, 6; 7:21; 8:8; 10:5, 15, 17; 13:5). And because the secondary author is unimportant for the writer of Hebrews, his own name also has been deleted, perhaps purposely, in this letter. By focusing attention on the Triune God as speaker, the author teaches that Scripture is divinely inspired. He has heard not the voice of man but the voice of God.

Interestingly, however, when the author quotes from the Old Testament he uses the Greek translation (the Septuagint) of the Hebrew text. And this translation in places differs from the original. Here are two examples. First, Psalm 8:5 has: "You made him a little lower than the heavenly beings [or: than God]," and Hebrews 2:7 reads: "You made him a little [or: for a little while] lower than the angels." Second, the wording of Psalm 40:6 is: "Sacrifice and offering you did not desire, but my ears you have pierced." However, Hebrews 10:5 gives this reading: "Sacrifice and offering you did not desire, but a body you prepared for me."

Why did the author use a translation that differed from the Old Testament text? Possibly the writer did not know Hebrew, had learned the Scriptures through a Greek translation, and wrote to readers who themselves used this translation. Does this mean that the so-called Septuagint translation was inspired? Of course not. The Hebrew text of the Old Testament, not the translation, was inspired by God. But this does not mean that the writer of Hebrews was forbidden to quote from a translation, even from one that showed some variation. However, at the moment the author wrote his letter, the inspiration of the epistle, including the Old Testament quotations, took place. Guided by the Holy Spirit, the writer was free to take his material from a translation that differed from the Hebrew text; he did not have to correct the translation to make it conform to the reading of the Hebrew original. He wrote to Hebrews who were familiar with the Septuagint; that, for them, was the Bible.

4. The Old Testament

We who are accustomed to owning personal copies of the Bible should not think that this was true for the readers of Hebrews in the second half of the first century. Copies of the Old Testament books were kept in the local synagogue and church. These were used during the worship services for the instruction of the people. But the people attending the worship services did not possess these books. They treasured the Word in their hearts and minds by committing the psalms and hymns to memory. Also they learned messianic passages of the Old Testament by heart. They sang the well-known psalms and hymns in church or at home, and they recited particular verses from the Old Testament.

The author of Hebrews chose his citations carefully. For instance, in chapter 1, five quotations are from familiar psalms, one from the Song of Moses, and one from a messianic passage. The author appeals to the memory of his readers and thus communicates the Word clearly and effectively.

5. Style

A final characteristic of Hebrews is the choice of words, the balanced sentences, the rhetorical rhythm in the original Greek, and the excellent style. Even in translation the reader today perceives something of the magnificence of the author's literary ability. Take, for example, the author's pithy definition of faith: "Now faith is being sure of what we hope for and certain of what we do not see" (11:1). Or analyze this sentence for balance: "If we deliberately keep on sinning after we have received the knowledge of the truth, no sacrifice for sins is left, but only a fearful expectation of judgment and of raging fire that will consume the enemies of God" (10:26–27). The author reveals himself as an educated person who chose his words carefully and who was thoroughly familiar with the teaching of the Old Testament.

B. Who Wrote This Epistle?

When questioned about the authorship of Hebrews, the third-century theologian Origen said, "But who wrote the epistle, to be sure, only God knows." And that was in A.D. 225. If scholars at the dawn of the Christian era did not know who wrote Hebrews, we certainly will not rise above them.

1. Apollos

Of course, scholars have suggested possible candidates, but they must resort to hypotheses. Martin Luther, for example, thought that Apollos was the author of Hebrews. He based his hypothesis on Acts 18:24–26, "Meanwhile a Jew named Apollos, a native of Alexandria, came to Ephesus. He was a learned man, with a thorough knowledge of the Scriptures. He had been instructed in the way of the Lord, and he spoke with great fervor and taught about Jesus accurately, though he knew only the baptism of John. He began to speak boldly in the synagogue. When Priscilla and Aquila heard him, they invited him to their home and explained to him the way of God more adequately."

Luther pointed out that Alexandria was a great educational center, where Apollos learned to express himself masterfully in the Greek language. Apollos used the Septuagint translation of the Old Testament because the Septaugint was first published in Alexandria.

Apollos had become acquainted with the Christian faith, had heard Paul preach in Ephesus, and had been instructed "in the way of God more adequately" by Priscilla and Aquila. He possessed a "thorough knowledge of the Scriptures," "taught about Jesus accurately," and became an outstanding speaker. For Martin Luther, Apollos was most qualified to write the Epistle to the Hebrews.

The hypothesis is attractive indeed and answers many questions. However, the silence of the centuries is telling. We would expect that Clement of Alexandria, about A.D. 200, says something about this matter, but he omits the name *Apollos*. Instead Clement ascribes Hebrews to Paul.

2. Paul

Was Paul the author of Hebrews? For centuries numerous people have accepted the Pauline authorship of this epistle. From the first publication of the King James Version in 1611 to the present, many people have taken the title verbatim: "The Epistle of Paul the Apostle to the Hebrews." But in the margin of some Bibles of this version the reader is told: "Authorship uncertain, commonly attributed to Paul."

The uncertainty of Pauline authorship stems from the difference between the epistles of Paul and Hebrews. To begin with the language of Hebrews, we see a distinct difference. Nothing in Hebrews reminds us of the style, diction, word choice, and material of Paul's letters. The language in Hebrews simply is not that of Paul.

The doctrines expressed in Hebrews find no echo in any of Paul's epistles. Usually in these letters cross-references to major doctrines are evident. Not so in Hebrews. The doctrines of Christ and the covenant are prominent in Hebrews, but absent from the letters of Paul.

The use of names referring to Jesus in Hebrews differs from that of Paul. In his earlier epistles Paul refers to the Lord as Jesus Christ, but in his later epistles this combination is reversed: Paul calls him Christ Jesus. He seldom writes *Jesus* (II Cor. 11:4; Phil. 2:10; I Thess. 4:14). The author of Hebrews, by contrast, repeatedly calls the Lord by his given name *Jesus* (2:9; 3:1; 4:14; 6:20; 7:22; 10:19; 12:2, 24; 13:15). Three times the author of Hebrews uses the combination *Jesus Christ* (10:10; 13:8, 21), and only once he says *Lord Jesus* (13:20). The Epistle to the Hebrews, however, lacks the combination *Christ Jesus*.

The most significant point in considering whether Paul wrote the Epistle to the Hebrews has to do with Hebrews 2:3. The writer, who includes himself in his warning to pay attention to the Word of God, says, "This salvation, which was first announced by the Lord, was confirmed to us by those who heard him." In schematic form, we have the following sequence:

This salvation which
1. was first announced by the Lord
2. by those who heard him
3. was confirmed to us

The conclusion may be drawn that the writer had not heard the Lord personally but had to rely on the reports of others. Paul, of course, states categorically that he did not receive the gospel from anyone but Jesus Christ (Gal. 1:12). Paul heard the voice of Jesus on the Damascus road (Acts 9:4; 22:7; 26:14). And Jesus spoke to him afterward (Acts 18:9–10; 22:18–21). Paul, therefore, could not have written the words of Hebrews 2:3.

3. Barnabas

Tertullian, around A.D. 225, suggested that Barnabas was the writer of Hebrews. He did this in light of Barnabas's credentials given in Acts 4:36–37: "Joseph, a Levite from Cyprus, whom the apostles called Barnabas (which means Son of Encouragement), sold a field he owned and brought the money and put it at the apostles' feet." As a Levite, Barnabas was fully acquainted with the Levitical priesthood. Besides, he came from the island of Cyprus where he presumably learned the Greek language well. He was familiar with the church and its needs. Thus, he was eminently qualified to write the Epistle to the Hebrews, according to Tertullian. The weakness of this position is that it has not found any support in the history of the canon. Tertullian has not gained any followers and his suggestion has been viewed as a curiosity.

4. Priscilla

Last among the names that have been proposed for solving the question of authorship is the name of Priscilla. She with her husband Aquila instructed Apollos (Acts 18:26). But Priscilla could not have written Hebrews because in the original Greek of Hebrews 11:32, the writer uses a participle with a *masculine* ending when he refers to himself: "I do not have time to tell about Gideon. . . ."

What is the conclusion of the matter? We simply say with Origen, "But who wrote the epistle, to be sure, only God knows." In the final analysis, authorship is not important. The content of the epistle is what matters.

C. What Is the Message of Hebrews?

A cursory glance at the Epistle to the Hebrews tells the readers that its content is strengthened by numerous quotations from the Old Testament; next, the author constantly exhorts the readers pastorally; and last, the development of the doctrinal part follows a logical sequence. We begin our survey of the content with a discussion of the Old Testament citations in Hebrews.

1. Old Testament Quotations

Estimates of the number of direct quotations in the Epistle to the Hebrews vary. For example, some scholars count all the direct citations and come to a total of thirty-six.[1] Others find twenty-four direct quotations from the Old Testament and add another five passages "which are used verbally though not formally quoted." They recognize twenty-nine citations.[2]

Although we realize that the author of Hebrews did not have to provide introductory statements for each Old Testament quote, we still think that a direct citation is one with an introductory formula. We find twenty-six quotations, to which we add five that lack an introduction. This brings the total to thirty-one passages.

The Psalter was a favorite book for the writer of Hebrews. One-third of his direct quotations have been taken from the Book of Psalms. Most of them are located in Hebrews 1. One citation comes from the Hymn of Moses, Deuteronomy 32, in the Septuagint version.

Direct Quotations

Old Testament	Hebrews
1. Psalm 2:7	1:5a; 5:5
2. II Samuel 7:14	1:5b
3. Deuteronomy 32:43	1:6b
4. Psalm 104:4	1:7
5. Psalm 45:6–7	1:8–9
6. Psalm 102:25–27	1:10–12
7. Psalm 110:1	1:13
8. Psalm 8:4–6	2:6–8a
9. Psalm 22:22	2:12
10. Isaiah 8:17	2:13a
11. Isaiah 8:18	2:13b
12. Numbers 12:7	3:2, 5
13. Psalm 95:7–11	3:7–11
14. Genesis 2:2	4:4
15. Psalm 110:4	5:6; 7:17, 21
16. Genesis 22:17	6:14
17. Genesis 14:17–20	7:1–2
18. Exodus 25:40	8:5
19. Jeremiah 31:31–34	8:8–12
20. Exodus 24:8	9:20
21. Psalm 40:6–8	10:5–7
22. Deuteronomy 32:35a	10:30a
23. Deuteronomy 32:36a; Psalm 135:14a	10:30b
24. Isaiah 26:20; Habakkuk 2:3–4	10:37–38

1. Ceslaus Spicq, *L'Épître aux Hébreux*, 2 vols. (Paris: Gabalda, 1952), vol. 1, p. 331.
2. B. F. Westcott, *Commentary on the Epistle to the Hebrews* (Grand Rapids: Eerdmans, 1950), pp. 469–74.

25. Genesis 21:12	11:18
26. Proverbs 3:11–12	12:5–6
27. Exodus 19:12–13	12:20
28. Deuteronomy 9:19	12:21
29. Haggai 2:6	12:26
30. Deuteronomy 31:6	13:5
31. Psalm 118:6	13:6

The writer of Hebrews appeals to his readers by quoting familiar passages from the Old Testament. These passages presumably had been memorized by the readers, so that when they heard the Epistle to the Hebrews read to them in a worship service, they could relate to its content. The Old Testament Scriptures, therefore, were of great importance to the author and the readers of this epistle. In the words of the writer, "the word of God is living and active. Sharper than any double-edged sword" (4:12). And that Word has been quoted, alluded to, and used in Hebrews more than in any other New Testament book.

2. Pastoral Admonitions

Repeatedly the author admonishes his readers to "pay more careful attention" to the Word of God (2:1). He calls that word preached to the Israelites in the desert "the gospel" (4:2), and he states that these rebellious people died in the desert because they failed to combine the Word they had heard with faith.

Is the epistle predominantly pastoral? Or is it doctrinal? Differently stated, the question is whether the author's admonitions result in theological teaching or, vice versa, whether doctrines lead to admonitions.[3] If we look at the numerous passages that exhort the readers, we see a remarkable consistency in approach. The author writes pastorally and encourages the Hebrews to remain faithful to God and his Word. "See to it, brothers, that none of you has a sinful, unbelieving heart that turns away from the living God" (3:12). This admonition is the key to understanding the pastoral concerns of the writer. It is basic to the warnings that precede and follow. In sequence, here are a number of admonitions that make up the content of the Epistle to the Hebrews:

2:1–4	"We must pay more careful attention, therefore"
3:1	"Therefore, holy brothers, . . . fix your thoughts on Jesus"
3:12–19	"See to it, brothers"
4:1–3	"Therefore, . . . let us be careful"
4:11	"Let us, therefore, make every effort"
4:14–16	"Therefore, . . . let us hold firmly to the faith"

---

3. F. W. Grosheide, *De Brief aan de Hebreeën en de Brief van Jakobus* (Kampen: Kok, 1955), p. 43.

10

6:1–3	"Therefore let us leave the elementary teachings"
6:11–12	"We want each of you to show this same diligence"
10:19–39	"Therefore, brothers, . . . let us draw near to God"
12:1–28	"Therefore, . . . let us throw off everything that hinders"
13:1–25	"Keep on loving each other as brothers"

The appeal of the writer comes to the readers in phraseology that borders on repetition. The message is clear: keep the faith, be obedient, remain strong, come to God, and claim your salvation. The author warns the reader against the sin of unbelief that eventually takes its toll and ends in apostasy.

As the writer exhorts so he teaches. He expresses his concern that the readers obey the Word of God, and thus he exhorts them. He also wants his readers to know the Word, and thus he teaches them.

3. Doctrinal Sequence

In the opening verses of his introduction (1:1–2), the author defines the extent and the range of the Word of God: in the Old Testament era God spoke through his prophets; in New Testament times, he has spoken through his Son. He expected his people to obey his Word when it was communicated to them "by angels" (2:2), for disobedience resulted in "just punishment." How much more, then, are the people of the New Testament era to obey God's Word that was proclaimed not by angels but by the Son of God. And this Son is far superior to the angels because he is the Prophet who spoke the Word (1:2), the Priest who "provided purification for sins" (1:3), and the King who "sat down at the right hand of the Majesty in heaven" (1:3). Furthermore, this Prophet, who is Priest and King as well, demands strict obedience to the Word that proclaims salvation (2:3).

The superiority of the Son of God in relation to the angels is confessed in psalm and song. The psalm and hymn writers portray the Son as King, God, Creator, and one whose "years will never end" (1:12). In distinction from the angels, the Son took upon himself man's human nature (2:14) and is not ashamed to call his people brothers and sisters, for he and they "are of the same family" (2:11–12). Because of this close identity with his brothers and sisters, Jesus became their "merciful and faithful high priest in service to God," and thus he made "atonement for the sins of the people" (2:17). For this reason, says the writer of Hebrews, I exhort you to "fix your thoughts on Jesus, the apostle and high priest whom we confess" (3:1).

Jesus is greater than Moses. Moses was a faithful servant in God's house; Jesus is a faithful son over God's house (3:5–6). In the time of Moses the Israelites refused to obey God's Word and consequently perished in the desert (3:17). The believer today is exhorted to listen to "the gospel" and to make every effort to enter the rest God has promised (4:3, 6, 11). Take the living and active Word of God to heart, counsels the author, because it may be compared with a double-edged sword (4:12).

Also, Jesus is far greater than Aaron. Aaron was a high priest, but a sinner; Jesus is the great high priest, yet without sin (5:3; 4:14–15). Jesus became high priest in the order of Melchizedek (5:10). The readers should have known this fact by searching the Scriptures. Therefore, the author of Hebrews reproves them for their indolence (5:11–13). He exhorts them to advance in the "teachings about Christ" (6:1); refusal to advance leads to spiritual death (6:4–6, 8). He encourages the believers with the reassuring word that God is true to his promise. That promise God confirms with an oath, so that his word is unchangeable (6:17–18).

The writer shows the readers from the Old Testament Scriptures that Jesus, belonging to the high-priestly order of Melchizedek, is superior to the Levitical priests (chap. 7). Priests in the Aaronic order were appointed by law, were sinners, and were subject to death (7:23, 27–28). When God swore an oath, Jesus became priest and thereby indicated the unchangeableness of his priestly office (7:21). He is sinless and is priest forever.

Jesus is priest-king, but he does not serve in an earthly tabernacle; he has gone to serve in "the true tabernacle set up by the Lord, not by man" (8:2; see also 9:11, 24). There in the Most Holy Place he obtained eternal redemption for his people, and there he serves as "the mediator of a new covenant" (9:15). Christ offered himself once for all and thereby "made perfect forever those who are being made holy" (10:14) and have the law of the new covenant in their hearts and written on their minds.

The second part of the epistle begins with 10:19 and is pastoral throughout. The writer encourages the readers "to draw near to God," to meet together for worship, and to await the coming Day (10:22, 25). Once more he stresses that deliberate sin cannot be forgiven (6:4–6; 10:26–29). The result of willful sin is that one "fall[s] into the hands of the living God" (10:31).

Chapter 11 is a consideration of the heroes of faith depicted in the Old Testament. The author has been selective and devotes most of the discussion to Abraham the father of believers (11:8–19). He exhorts the readers to fix their attention on Jesus, the "author and perfecter" of their faith (12:2), to strengthen their "feeble arms and weak knees" (12:12), and "to live in peace with all men and to be holy" (12:14). Chapter 12 concludes with an exhortation to "worship God acceptably with reverence and awe" (12:28). The last chapter of Hebrews is a series of concluding exhortations with an eloquent benediction (13:20–21) and personal greetings (13:22–25).

D. Why Was This Letter Rejected in the Early Centuries?

1. First Century

The history of the Epistle to the Hebrews in the Christian church of the first few centuries is rather varied. The letter was accepted in the West and quoted by Clement of Rome in his epistle, known as I Clement, to the church of Corinth. First Clement was written about A.D. 96 and contains segments from Hebrews (see especially I Clem. 36:1–5; 17:1, 5; 19:2; 27:2; 43:1;

56:2–4). Clement's use of Hebrews in the last decade of the first century is sufficient evidence that the Epistle to the Hebrews circulated widely.

2. Second Century

Irenaeus, about A.D. 185, quotes from Hebrews. He was bishop of the churches of Vienne and Lyon in southern France. Tertullian, a North African writer who died in A.D. 225, quotes Hebrews 6:4–8. He introduces the lengthy quotation as follows:

> For there is extant withal an Epistle to the Hebrews under the name of Barnabas—a man sufficiently accredited by God. . . . Warning, accordingly, the disciples to omit all first principles, and strive rather after perfection, and not lay again the foundations of repentance from the works of the dead. . . .[4]

The church of the West (Italy, France, and Africa), during the latter part of the second century, had reservations about the place of Hebrews in the canon of the New Testament. For example, the list of New Testament books known as the Muratorian Canon that presumably dates from A.D. 175 does not include the Epistle to the Hebrews.

The reason for these reservations can be traced to the doctrinal controversies of the second and third centuries. In A.D. 156, Montanus, a self-proclaimed theologian from Asia Minor, practiced asceticism and expected his followers to live a life of holiness. He applied Hebrews 6:4–6 to anyone who indulged in worldly matters and thus denied such a person the possibility of repentance. Then in A.D. 250 Emperor Decius instigated persecutions against the Christians, many of whom under duress denied the Christian faith. Novatian, a native of Phrygia in Asia Minor, used Hebrews 6:4–6 against all Christians who had fallen away because of these persecutions. Novatian was of the opinion that it was impossible for them to come to repentance; they were cut off from the church and denied readmission. The application of this Scripture passage in the rigorous manners of the Montanists and the Novatians did not meet with approval in the church. Because of these schismatic movements and their abuse of this particular passage, the Epistle to the Hebrews was not placed among the canonical books of the New Testament in the West.

3. Third Century

The church of the East (Egypt and Syria), however, applied the rule that for a New Testament book to be canonical it had to be apostolic. The Epistle to the Hebrews was thought to be written by Paul, who was an apostle, and therefore Hebrews was accepted as canonical. Already in A.D. 175 Pantaenus said that Paul omitted his name in the epistle for several reasons: his mod-

---

4. Tertullian, "On Modesty," *Ante-Nicene Fathers* (Grand Rapids: Eerdmans, 1965), vol. 4, chap. 20, p. 97.

esty, his respect for the Lord, and the superabundance of his writing.[5] Although these reasons are unconvincing, they indicate that Pantaenus harbored a degree of uneasiness about Pauline authorship.

His successor Clement of Alexandria, in approximately A.D. 200, expresses the same uneasiness.

> And as for the Epistle to the Hebrews, [Clement] says indeed that it is Paul's, but that it was written for Hebrews in the Hebrew tongue, and that Luke, having carefully translated it, published it for the Greeks. . . . The [words] "Paul an apostle" were naturally not prefixed. For, says he, "in writing to Hebrews who had conceived a prejudice against him and were suspicious of him, he very wisely did not repel them at the beginning by putting his name."[6]

An Alexandrian papyrus manuscript, listed as P^{46} and dated approximately A.D. 200, places the Epistle to the Hebrews among those of Paul. In fact, Hebrews comes after Romans and before I Corinthians. And Athanasius, bishop of Alexandria, writes in A.D. 367 about Hebrews and places it between II Thessalonians and I Timothy.

In the Western church, Hebrews was eventually accepted in the fourth century. Some scholars ascribed it to Paul, but others doubted whether Paul was the author. At any rate, the councils of that century placed Hebrews in the canon. The Council of Hippo Regius in A.D. 393 provides this interesting note: "Thirteen epistles of Paul, and one by the same to the Hebrews." And the Council of Carthage in A.D. 397 includes Hebrews in the epistolary of Paul and simply ascribes fourteen epistles to Paul.

E. When Was Hebrews Written?

Because of I Clement, we can say that Hebrews was composed before A.D. 96. In that year Clement of Rome wrote his epistle to the Corinthian church and incorporated a number of quotations and allusions from Hebrews in his epistle. The outer limit of dating the Epistle to the Hebrews is sure: sometime before A.D. 96. To determine a starting point for the composition of the epistle is difficult.

1. Internal Evidence

In Hebrews 2:3, the author places himself among the readers as second-generation Christians. That is, he himself had not heard the gospel from the lips of Jesus but with the readers had to rely on the preaching of those who had heard Jesus. The author, then, was a follower of the apostles, many of whom could still be alive at the time the writer composed his epistle. Numerous passages in Hebrews reflect a time in which the Christians' ardent love for Christ had waned and the enthusiasm of a former period had disappeared.

---

5. Eusebius, *Ecclesiastical History*, 6.14.4 (LCL).
6. Eusebius, *Ecclesiastical History*, 6.14.2–3 (LCL).

The readers of Hebrews were in danger of drifting away from the gospel they had heard (2:1). Some of them might run the risk of being hardened by the deceitfulness of sin (3:13). Some were in the habit of no longer attending the worship services (10:25). Others were faltering in their spiritual zeal (12:12).

The author rebukes the readers for having failed to learn the doctrines of Scripture. "In fact, though by this time you ought to be teachers, you need someone to teach you the elementary truths of God's word all over again" (5:12). Also their leaders who had taught the Word of God had died (13:7).

In earlier days the readers had endured persecution after they "had received the light" (10:32). They had experienced suffering, insults, and confiscation of their property (10:33). The author fails to provide an indication when the persecution took place. Although we are inclined to think of the time following the burning of Rome in A.D. 64—after which the Neronian persecutions were instigated—the author says nothing more than "remember those earlier days."

The frequent exhortations—to pay attention (2:1), to encourage one another (3:13), to persevere (10:36), to run with perseverance (12:1), and to resist sin (12:4)—leave the impression that the recipients of the epistle lived in a period of religious peace. They no longer seemed to suffer for being Christians, as they had on earlier occasions. And because of the peaceful times, religious backsliding had become a distinct threat to the people to whom Hebrews was addressed.

2. Historical Setting

If we look at the historical setting of the second half of the first century, we note that Nero acceded to the imperial throne in A.D. 54. A decade later the persecutions against the Christians began; they lasted until Nero committed suicide in A.D. 68. Within a year in short succession, Galba, Otho, and Vitellius ruled the Roman empire. But in A.D. 69 Vespasian, who at the time functioned as general of the Roman army that surrounded the city of Jerusalem, became emperor. He loved peace and stability; he was a virtuous man, upright in character.[7] During his ten-year rule, peace returned to his worldwide domain, and consequently persecutions against the Christians belonged to history.

Vespasian's son, Titus, who took his father's place as general of the army in Judea, also followed in his footsteps as emperor in A.D. 79. His brief reign of two years was marked by the same desire for peace and tranquility. When Titus' brother, Domitian, began to rule the empire in A.D. 81, the peaceful trend established by Vespasian and continued by Titus endured for the next decade. Toward the end of his reign, Domitian introduced persecutions that may have caused the exile of John to the isle of Patmos (Rev. 1:9).

---

7. Michael Grant, *The Twelve Caesars* (New York: Scribner's, 1975), p. 219.

History verifies that a decline of religious fervor occurs more often in a period of peace and prosperity than in times of persecution and hardship. I venture to say that the Epistle to the Hebrews reflects a period of sustained peace during which the Christians had relaxed spiritually. The writer of the epistle, then, felt obliged to write words of exhortation and occasional rebuke. His reference to the persecution the readers had endured in "those earlier days" may refer to that of Nero in the years A.D. 64–68. The epistle probably was written in the early 80s.

3. Religious Context

However, a much more weighty consideration relates to the author's discussion of the high priesthood of Christ. When the writer is about to discuss the topic of Jesus as high priest in the order of Melchizedek, he says that this subject "is hard to explain because you are slow to learn" (5:11). The word *hard* had overtones that reverberated in the Hebrew community. For the Jew, the Aaronic priesthood was sacrosanct because God had ordained it by law (7:11–12). No Jew would dare suggest that the Levitical priesthood ought to be "set aside because it was weak and useless" (7:18) and assert that "the law made nothing perfect" (7:19). Should he say such a *hard* thing, he would bring the wrath and indignation of the Hebrew community on his head.

The fact that the author of the epistle boldly writes about the setting aside of the Levitical priesthood can best be understood when we place the time of composition a decade or more after the destruction of the temple and the cessation of the Aaronic priesthood. The writer, therefore, had the freedom to express himself on this matter without incurring the anger of the Jewish people. Perhaps this is one of the reasons that the other New Testament writers refrained from discussing the priesthood of Christ. For example, in spite of the vow of purification that Paul took to show the Jews in Jerusalem that he was living in obedience to the law (Acts 21:22–26), he was accused of teaching doctrines against the Jewish people, the law, and the temple (Acts 21:28). What Paul could not do regarding the priesthood, the writer of Hebrews was able to do in a time in which the priesthood and the law concerning it belonged to the past.

Nowhere in the Epistle to the Hebrews do we find any mention of the temple in Jerusalem. The writer discusses the tabernacle and priesthood of the forty-year period in the wilderness. Because he deletes any reference to the temple or the destruction of Jerusalem, he may imply that the priestly services had come to an end. And for that reason, he turns his attention to the initial stages of the Levitical priesthood and the construction of the tabernacle.

The conclusion to these observations is that a date for Hebrews of a decade after the destruction of the Jerusalem temple and the cessation of the priesthood is not at all improbable. Perhaps Hebrews was composed between A.D. 80 and 85.

F. Who Were the First Readers?

The recipients of the Epistle to the Hebrews were Jewish Christians. Where these Hebrews lived, the author fails to say. If he had only given some indication as to the epistle's place of destination, we would not need to work with a hypothesis. Many place names have been suggested: Jerusalem, the Qumran settlement near the Dead Sea, Alexandria, Rome—to mention no more.

1. Israel

If we accept a date of composition after A.D. 70, automatically Jerusalem and the Qumran community are ruled out. After the Romans destroyed the city of Jerusalem, they eventually renamed it Aelia Capitolina and forbade the Jews from resettling there. Also, the Qumran community evacuated during the years of Roman occupation.

2. Alexandria

Scholars who favor Alexandria as the place where the Hebrews lived base their supposition on the fact that Alexandria for centuries had been the home of many Jewish people. Here the Septuagint originated to aid the Greek-speaking Jews in their Scripture reading. And according to Acts 18:24, Alexandria was the place from which Apollos came. But no writer of the first few centuries testifies to an Alexandrian destination or to a possible authorship of Apollos. We need to look elsewhere for a place of destination.

3. Rome

Many factors point to Rome. The final greeting of the epistle mentions Italy. "Those from Italy send you their greetings" (13:24). Granted that the preposition *from* can be interpreted to mean *in*—that is, "those who are in Italy send you their greetings"—the commonly understood meaning *away from* Italy seems to be preferred. Christians from Italy who were away from their homeland conveyed greetings to their loved ones in Italy, presumably Rome.

Did the writer of Hebrews address his letter to the same congregation that received Paul's letter to the Romans? Not necessarily. Many congregations flourished in the imperial city in view of the early beginnings of the church in Rome. (For example, archaeologists have unearthed a funerary inscription in Rome that bears the name of a Christian lady, known as Pomponia Graecina, who was buried in A.D. 43.) We assume that in the course of time the church continued to increase in numbers. The author of Hebrews makes a distinction between "leaders" and "people" when he writes, "Greet all your leaders and all God's people" (13:24). He seems to leave the impression that he addresses his epistle to a particular congregation in Rome.

Next, Clement of Rome quoted from the epistle soon after it was written. Although the letter could have been composed elsewhere and in time brought to Rome, a letter addressed to the Hebrews in Rome would circulate among the congregations in that city and thus be available to Clement.

And last, Jewish people were most numerous in the imperial city, as Roman historiographers and Flavius Josephus attest. An inscription bearing the word *Hebrews* and dating from the second century after Christ has been found in Rome.

We feel comfortable with the choice of Rome, although we admit that we can only use a hypothesis. And yet the accumulated facts seem to point to this choice. Perhaps the intention of the author of Hebrews in omitting the place of destination may have been to indicate that his epistle has a message for the church universal. Especially in our day in which we hear the expression *the end time* repeatedly, the message of the Epistle to the Hebrews is most relevant.

G. How Can Hebrews Be Outlined?

A concise outline of Hebrews can easily be committed to memory with the following seven points:

1:1–4	1. Introduction
1:5–2:18	2. Jesus Is Superior to Angels
3:1–4:13	3. Jesus Is Greater Than Moses
4:14–7:28	4. Jesus Is the Great High Priest
8:1–10:18	5. Jesus Is the Mediator of a New Covenant
10:19–12:29	6. Jesus' Work Is Applied by the Believer
13:1–25	7. Conclusion

Here is a more detailed outline:

1:1–2:18	Jesus' Superiority and His Role as Savior and High Priest	
	A. Introduction	1:1–4
	B. Jesus' Superiority to Angels	1:5–14
	C. Jesus, Savior and High Priest	2:1–18
3:1–4:13	Jesus' Superiority to Moses	
	A. A Comparison of Jesus and Moses	3:1–6
	B. A Warning Against Unbelief	3:7–19
	C. An Invitation to Enter God's Rest	4:1–13
4:14–5:10	Jesus' High Priesthood	
	A. Encouragement for the Readers	4:14–16
	B. Enablement of the High Priest	5:1–3
	C. Fulfillment of the High-priestly Office	5:4–10

18

Commentary

1

Jesus' Superiority and His Role as Savior and High Priest, *part 1*

1:1–14

Outline

1 1 In the past God spoke to our forefathers through the prophets at many times and in various ways, 2 but in these last days he has spoken to us by his Son, whom he appointed heir of all things, and through whom he made the universe. 3 The Son is the radiance of God's glory and the exact representation of his being, sustaining all things by his powerful word. After he had provided purification for sins, he sat down at the right hand of the Majesty in heaven. 4 So he became as much superior to the angels as the name he has inherited is superior to theirs.

A. Introduction
1:1-4

The writer of Hebrews dispenses with the usual greetings and salutations that are typical of Paul's letters and those of James, Peter, John, and Jude. (The First Epistle of John does not give any greetings in the introduction nor in the conclusion, and for that reason is technically not an epistle.) In the conclusion of Hebrews, however, the author uses the first person pronoun *I* a few times; mentions that if Timothy, who has been released from prison, arrives soon, he will accompany the writer on a visit to the recipients of the epistle; and conveys greetings to all God's people.

Why would the writer not address the readers in the customary way by making himself known, specifying the addressees, and pronouncing a salutation of grace, peace, and mercy? The answer must be that the author wants to focus attention primarily on the ultimate revelation of God—Jesus Christ, his Son. This revelation is contrasted with the piecemeal revelation that God, through the prophets, gave to the forefathers for many centuries. The author stresses the theme of the person, offices, and function of Jesus, the Son of God.

The writer does not address the original readers by name or place even though he intimately uses forms of the first person pronoun ("we," "us," and "our") throughout his epistle. The title of the epistle may have been added later, for the writer nowhere in his letter refers to Hebrews. We may assume that the epistle, although written to a specific congregation originally, was intended for the church universal. The message conveyed is addressed to the church of all ages and places. To put it differently, if there is any epistle in the New Testament that addresses the church universal in the days prior to Jesus' return, it is the Epistle to the Hebrews.

25

The failure of the author to identify himself at all in his writing is in keeping with the time in which he lived. It was customary for a writer to display modesty by omitting his name; for example, the Gospel writers do not refer to themselves by name, and among the writers of epistles, John refrains from using his name in the three letters attributed to him.

The author of Hebrews does not call attention to himself or to the recipients of his epistle, but to Jesus, who completed through his appearance the revelation of God to man.

1. In the past God spoke to our forefathers through the prophets at many times and in various ways.

In sonorous tones and in a somewhat musical setting, the author begins his epistle with an introductory sentence that is elegant in style, diction, and word choice. Some translators have tried to convey the dignity and alliteration of the original, but most of them have been ineffectual in capturing the exact intonation of the opening sentence of Hebrews.[1]

God spoke to the forefathers in the ages preceding the birth of Jesus and communicated to them his revelation. God is the originator of revelation. He is the source, the basis, the subject. God used the prophets in the Old Testament era to make his Word known to the people. But he was not limited to speaking through the prophets; this first verse states that God brought his revelation to his people at many times and in various ways. The words *times* and *ways* have a prominent place in the original Greek: they stand first in the sentence. Among the forefathers who received God's revelation were Adam, Abel, Enoch, Noah, Abraham, Isaac, Jacob, Joseph, and Moses. God spoke to Adam "in the cool of the day" (Gen. 3:8); to Abraham in visions and visits—in fact, Abraham was called God's friend (James 2:23); to Jacob in a dream; to Moses "face to face" (Exod. 33:11) as a man speaks with a friend.

Through the prophets, from Moses to Malachi, God's revelation was recorded in written form as history, psalm, proverb, and prophecy. The prophets were all those saints called by God and filled with his Spirit to speak the Word as a progressive revelation that intimates the coming of Christ. In his first epistle, Peter refers to them:

> The prophets, who spoke of the grace that was to come to you, searched intently and with the greatest care, trying to find out the time and circumstances to which the Spirit of Christ in them was pointing when he predicted the sufferings of Christ and the glories that would follow. It was revealed to them that they were not serving themselves but you, when they spoke of the things that have now been told you by those

---

1. Among the translations that most successfully reflect the emphasis and the alliteration of the original are the Dutch translation of 1637, *Staten Vertaling* ("God, voortijds veelmaal en op velerlei wijze tot de vaderen gesproken hebbende door de profeten, heeft in deze laatste dagen gesproken door de Zoon") and the Spanish translation of 1602 ("Dios, habiendo hablado muchas veces y en muchas maneras en otro tiempo á los padres por los profetas, en estos postreros días nos ha hablado por el Hijo").

who have preached the gospel to you by the Holy Spirit sent from heaven. [1:10–12]

The prophet did not bring his own message, his own formulation of religious truth. Inspired by the Holy Spirit, he spoke the Word of God, which did not have its origin in the will of man (II Peter 1:21) but came from God (Heb. 3:7).

2a. But in these last days he has spoken to us by his Son.

Although the contrast between the times before the coming of Christ and the appearance of Christ as the completion of God's revelation is striking in verses 1 and 2, the continuity of this revelation is also significant. Both parts of God's revelation form one unit because there is but one Author. There is but one God who reveals, and there is but one revelation. The Word spoken by God to the forefathers in the past does not differ basically from the Word spoken to us by his Son.

Yet in many ways the contrast between the first and the second verse is obvious. We may show the contrast graphically:

God has spoken
in the

	OLD TESTAMENT ERA	NEW TESTAMENT ERA
how?	at many times and in various ways	
when?	in the past	in these last days
to whom?	to our forefathers	to us
by whom?	through the prophets	by his Son

The figure appears to be incomplete: the "how" on the Old Testament side does not have a New Testament counterpart. The phrase "at many times and in various ways" lacks a parallel. The writer is pointing out that the fullness of revelation is unique, final, and complete. He is not implying that the piecemeal revelation given through the prophets was inferior and that the revelation provided by the Son was without variation. Not at all. The many-sided revelation of God that came repeatedly to the forefathers in the ages before the birth of Christ was inspired by God. It was a progressive revelation that constantly pointed toward the coming of the Messiah. And when Jesus finally came, he brought the very Word of God because he *is* the Word of God. Therefore, Jesus brought that Word in all its fullness, richness, and multiplicity. He was the final revelation. As F. F. Bruce aptly remarks, "The story of divine revelation is a story of progression up to Christ, but there is no progression beyond Him."[2]

---

2. F. F. Bruce, *The Epistle to the Hebrews,* New International Commentary on the New Testament series (Grand Rapids: Eerdmans, 1964), p. 3.

Jesus himself did not write a single verse of the New Testament; men designated by him and filled with the Spirit wrote God's revelation. Jesus, the living Word, speaks to us because no one else possesses equal authority; "for there is no other name under heaven given to men by which we must be saved" (Acts 4:12). By his Son, God addresses all believers. In these last days God has spoken to us by his Son. The phrase *in these last days* is set over against the phrase *in the past* and refers to the age in which the fulfillment of the messianic prophecies has taken place. This age waits for the liberation "from its bondage to decay" to be "brought into the glorious freedom of the children of God" (Rom. 8:21).

In the first two verses of Hebrews there is a contrast between the prophets, who were a distinct group of people chosen and appointed by God to convey his revelation, and the Son of God, who surpasses all the prophets because he is Son. In fact, all the emphasis in verse 2 falls on the word *Son*.[3] There is, strictly speaking, only one Son of God; all others are created sons (angels) and adopted sons (believers). As God has spoken by his Son, so the Son has spoken by the apostles who, inspired by the Holy Spirit, wrote the books of the New Testament. The new revelation that God has given us in his Son is a continuation of the revelation given to the forefathers. God's revelation, completed in his Son, is a unit, a harmonious totality in which the Old is fulfilled in the New.

2b. Whom he appointed heir of all things, and through whom he made the universe.

To express the excellence of the Son of God, the writer of Hebrews describes what God has done.

God appointed his Son heir of all things. An heir rightfully inherits whatever the father has stipulated in his will. As the one and only Son, Jesus thus inherits everything the Father possesses. Incomprehensible! Unfathomable!

The time when God appointed the Son heir of all things cannot be determined. The Son may have been appointed heir in God's eternal plan. Or Jesus may have been appointed heir when in the fullness of time he entered the world, or when he pronounced the Great Commission: "All authority in heaven and on earth has been given to me" (Matt. 28:18).

The writer of Hebrews immediately clarifies the term *all things* by saying that God made the universe through his Son. The phrase obviously refers to the creation account in the first chapters of Genesis. Many people think that the New Testament, which speaks about redemption, has nothing to say about creation. However, the New Testament is not entirely silent on this subject; both Paul and the writer of the Epistle to the Hebrews teach that Jesus was active in the work of creation. In his discussion about the supremacy of Christ, Paul teaches: "For by him all things were created . . .; all things

---

3. The RSV gives the literal translation *by a Son*. But the noun is used in an absolute sense of the word and is equivalent to a proper name. See John Albert Bengel, *Gnomon of the New Testament*, ed. Andrew R. Fausset, 7th ed., 5 vols. (Edinburgh: Clark, 1877), vol. 4, p. 339. The definite article in the Greek is omitted, as it is in Heb. 1:5; 3:6; 5:8; and 7:28.

were created by him and for him" (Col. 1:16). And John in his Gospel confirms the same truth: "Through him all things were made; without him nothing was made that has been made" (1:3).[4]

Through his Son, God made the universe. It is impossible for man to understand the full import of this statement, but complete understanding is not the objective at this point. However, it is important to recognize the majesty of the Son of God, who was present at creation and is the sovereign Lord of all created things. He is God.

The word *universe* signifies primarily the cosmos, the created world in all its fullness, and secondarily all the stars and planets God has created. But the meaning is much more comprehensive than this, because it involves all the events that have happened since the creation of this world. It concerns the earth and its history throughout the ages. The word has been interpreted as "the sum of the 'periods of time' including all that is manifested in and through them."[5] It refers not to the world as a whole but to the entire created order that continued to develop in the course of time.

3. The Son is the radiance of God's glory and the exact representation of his being, sustaining all things by his powerful word. After he had provided purification for sins, he sat down at the right hand of the Majesty in heaven.

a. "The Son is the radiance of God's glory." The word *radiance* is to be preferred to variations of the word *reflection,* which many translations provide.[6] The moon receives its light from the sun and simply reflects these light beams to the earth. The moon itself does not possess nor emanate light, because it does not produce light. The sun as a heavenly body radiates its light in all its brightness and power to the earth. By way of comparison, we may see Christ as the radiant light coming from the Father as sunlight emanates from the sun.[7]

Jesus said, "I am the light of the world" (John 8:12); he is light, and in him there is no darkness. He radiates the light of God's glory, perfection, and majesty. Philip Edgcumbe Hughes observes that Jesus' radiance "is not so much . . . the glory of the Son's deity shining through his humanity, but . . . the glory of God being manifested in the perfection of his manhood completely attuned as it was to the will of the Father."[8]

Jesus' radiance is derived from the Father, even though he himself is the light. The Son causes the radiance of the Father to shine forth. As John writes in the prologue to his Gospel, "We have seen his glory, the glory of

---

4. See also Ps. 33:6; Rom. 11:36; I Cor. 8:6; Rev. 3:14.

5. B. F. Westcott, *Commentary on the Epistle to the Hebrews* (Grand Rapids: Eerdmans, 1950), p. 8.

6. GNB, MLB, *Moffatt,* NAB, RSV.

7. Gerhard Kittel, *TDNT,* vol. 1, p. 508; Ralph P. Martin in *NIDNTT,* vol. 2, p. 290, writes, "On balance, the act[ive] sense of 'radiance' is to be chosen in preference to 'reflection.' "

8. Philip Edgcumbe Hughes, *Commentary on the Epistle to the Hebrews* (Grand Rapids: Eerdmans, 1977), pp. 41–42.

the One and Only, who came from the Father, full of grace and truth" (1:14). The Son's radiance, therefore, is an extension of God's glory.

b. "And the exact representation of his being." The Son is the perfect representation of God's being. That is, God himself stamped upon his Son the divine imprint of his being. The word translated as "exact representation" refers to minted coins that bear the image of a sovereign or president. It refers to a precise reproduction of the original. The Son, then, is completely the same in his being as the Father.[9] Nevertheless, even though an imprint is the same as the stamp that makes the impression, both exist separately. The Son, who bears "the very stamp" (RSV) of God's nature, is not the Father but proceeds from the Father and has a separate existence. Yet he who sees the Son has seen the Father, as Jesus explained to Philip (John 14:9).

The word *being* is really a parallel of the word *glory*, for both terms describe the essence of God.[10] Although existing separately, the Son, as the exact representation of the Father's being, is a perfect copy of God's nature. The Son is the mediator who possessed God's glory by nature before he assumed his mediatorial role. The Son bears the exact imprint of the Father's being from eternity.

c. "Sustaining all things by his powerful word." The Son is not only the Creator of the universe (1:2); he is the upholder of all things as well (1:3). The two passages complement each other and reveal the divine power of the Son. He speaks, and by his word all things are sustained, preserved, upheld.

This part of the verse in the original is closely connected to the preceding portion by means of the particle *and*,[11] which unfortunately many translations omit. It directly ties the participial phrase to the verb *is* in the first part of the sentence.

The first part of the verse stresses the person of Christ; the second, the work of Christ. From a discussion about the being of the Son, the writer proceeds to an explanation of the Son's activity, which involves caring for all things. In fact, the word that has been translated as "sustaining" basically means carrying. That word in itself signifies a forward motion, although not in the sense of an Atlas whose movement is torturously slow because the weight of the globe nearly crushes him.

The Son carries "all things" to bring them to their destined end. And he does this by a mere utterance ("by his powerful word"). Christ, the ruler of the universe, utters a word, and all things listen in obedience to his voice. No other motions are necessary, for the spoken word is sufficient.

d. "After he had provided purification for sins, he sat down at the right

---

9. The writer of the Wisdom of Solomon says of wisdom: "For she is a breath of the power of God, and a pure emanation of the glory of the Almighty; therefore nothing defiled gains entrance into her. For she is a reflection of eternal light, a spotless mirror of the working of God and an image of his goodness" (7:25–26, RSV). *The Apocrypha of the Old Testament*, ed. Bruce M. Metzger (New York: Oxford University Press, 1965).

10. Helmut Köster, *TDNT*, vol. 8, p. 585.

11. Westcott, *Hebrews*, p. 13.

hand of the Majesty in heaven." This sentence indicates a sequence in the redemptive deeds of Christ.

He performed his mediatorial work by completing and yielding his earthly life as a sacrifice on the cross for the removal of sins. In a rather pithy phrase the high-priestly work of Christ is summarized: Christ himself "provided purification for sins." According to the Mosaic law the high priest had to make atonement on the Day of Atonement to cleanse the people of Israel of all their sins (Lev. 16:29–34). The Aaronic high priest was a sinner and therefore did his work imperfectly, whereas Christ as the sinless One and the true High Priest completed the work of purification perfectly. The high priest in the Old Testament era needed animal sacrifices, first to cleanse himself and afterward to remove the sins of the people. Christ was simultaneously the High Priest and the sacrifice when he offered himself for the purification of the sins of his people. The Son once for all offered himself up on the cross in order to atone for our sins. The plural is used for the concept *sin* (see Eph. 1:7; Col. 1:14; II Peter 1:9).

After his mediatorial work was completed, the Son ascended to heaven and took his rightful place of honor next to God the Father. In typical Hebraic style, perhaps to avoid offending any of his Jewish readers, the author refers to God as the Majesty in heaven. Of course, elsewhere in the epistle he freely uses God's name.

e. "He sat down at the right hand of the Majesty in heaven" (cf. Rom. 8:34; Eph. 1:2; Col. 3:1). The expressions *sat down* and *the right hand* must not be taken literally, but rather symbolically. The idea of sitting at the right hand of someone signifies a privilege granted to a highly honored person. In this instance it means that the Son now has authority to rule his worldwide kingdom on earth and is enthroned above all spiritual powers "in heavenly places." The kingdom belongs to him and God has given him "the name that is above every name, that at the name of Jesus every knee should bow, in heaven and on earth and under the earth, and every tongue confess that Jesus Christ is Lord, to the glory of God the Father" (Phil. 2:9–11).

4. So he became as much superior to the angels as the name he has inherited is superior to theirs.

The writer of Hebrews has portrayed the Son as

1. the Prophet through whom God has spoken
2. the Creator who made the universe
3. the Heir of all things
4. the Representation of God's being
5. the Upholder of all things
6. the Priest who provided purification for sins
7. the King who sat down at his place of honor

Now the author compares the Son with angels, those created beings that constantly surround the throne of God. They of all creatures are closest to

31

God; they serve as his messengers; they are appointed to be busy in the work of providing man with God's revelation and in the work of redeeming fallen man (Acts 7:38, 53; Gal. 3:19; Heb. 2:2). In many respects, angels are higher than man, who was crowned with glory and honor as king in God's creation (Ps. 8:5).

Even if angels are in a certain sense higher than man, they are in no sense superior to the Son, because "he has inherited" a name that is superior to theirs. Thus far the Son has not been introduced by name, either as Jesus or as Christ. The name of the Son does not refer to a specific personal name but to his designation as the Son. He is known as the Son of God, the one and only Son. He is also Lord and Savior. The prophet Isaiah calls him "Wonderful Counselor, Mighty God, Everlasting Father, Prince of Peace" (9:6). By contrast, angels are referred to as "messengers" (Ps. 104:4); they are designated "ministering spirits" (Heb. 1:14).

The name of the Son came to him by inheritance, because the Father appointed him heir (Heb. 1:2). The angels have been created to be servants and are excluded from being heirs. They minister to those who shall inherit salvation (Heb. 1:14), but they themselves do not share in any inheritance.

Angels may be called "sons of God" (Job 1:6; 38:7), "mighty ones" (Ps. 29:1), or "holy ones" (Ps. 89:6), but remain created beings, in contrast to the Son, who is their Creator.

Christ inherited the name, which was foreordained in the counsel of God; and when he completed his mediatorial work on earth, he received the inheritance so that he could say, "All authority in heaven and on earth has been given to me" (Matt. 28:18). The permanence of his inheritance can be seen in Paul's description of the resurrection and the ascension of Christ, who is seated at the right hand of God "in the heavenly realms, far above all rule and authority, power and dominion, and every title that can be given, not only in the present age but also in the one to come" (Eph. 1:20–21).

Doctrinal Considerations in 1:1–4

The revelation that God had given to the believers in the Old Testament era was completed in the New Testament era by the Son of God. There are not two revelations, one for the Old Testament believers and one for New Testament believers. God's revelation is one, although given in two phases. During the first phase God's revelation came often and in a variety of ways. The second phase constitutes the fulfillment of God's revelation in the person of his Son. The Old Testament is the promise of the coming of the Son; the New Testament is the fulfillment of that promise. These familiar lines summarize the unity of God's revelation in the Scriptures:

> The New is in the Old concealed,
> The Old is in the New revealed.

The writer of Hebrews demonstrates his high regard for the Scriptures by stating unequivocally that God is the author of his revelation. God spoke in the past and has now spoken in his Son. And because it is God who has spoken, no one ought to question the authority of his written Word. God has spoken last of all in his Son, and that revelation is final.

The threefold office of prophet, priest, and king is spelled out in the first few verses of this brief introduction. The Son is the Prophet, for God in these last days has spoken in him; he is the Priest who has provided purification for sins; and he is the King who sustains the world by his powerful word and is seated at the right hand of God in heaven. These few introductory verses are a summary of what the writer is about to teach in the remainder of his letter.

The author's teaching about the supremacy of Jesus Christ (Heb. 1:4) is preceded by three verses that stress the divinity of the Son. The theme in Hebrews 1:3 is similar to that which Paul develops in Colossians 1:15, 17, 20.

Hebrews 1:3	*Colossians 1:15, 17, 20*
The Son is the radiance of God's glory and the exact representation of his being, sustaining all things by his powerful word.	He is the image of the invisible God, the firstborn over all creation.
	He is before all things, and in him all things hold together.
After he had provided purification for sins, he sat down at the right hand of the Majesty in heaven.	and through him [God was pleased] to reconcile to himself all things, whether things on earth or things in heaven, by making peace through his blood, shed on the cross.

The construction of Hebrews 1:3–4 indicates that the verses were an early Christian confession, perhaps used for liturgical and catechetical purposes. The short participial phrases in the original remind the reader of similar confessions that are recorded in Philippians 2:6–11 and I Timothy 3:16.

Greek Words, Phrases, and Constructions in 1:1–4

Verse 1

λαλήσας—aorist active participle, which may denote concession.

ἐν τοῖς προφήταις—the preposition ἐν is followed by the instrumental dative. Because of the definite article, the word προφήταις should be taken in its broadest possible sense.

Verse 2

ἐπ᾽ ἐσχάτου τῶν ἡμερῶν τούτων—although translated as "in these last days," the Greek literally says, "at the end of these days." The adjective ἐσχάτος is singular.

ἐλάλησεν—aorist active, to be taken in the culminative sense. Note that, as in verse 1, the verb λαλεῖν is used instead of λέγειν to indicate that the emphasis falls on the act of speaking and not on the content.

ἐν υἱῷ—the preposition ἐν implies a locative and an instrumental meaning. The definite article is lacking because the absolute sense of the noun is stressed: Jesus Christ is the one and only Son.

κληρονόμος—the word is a combination of κλῆρος (lot) and νέμομαι (I possess) with the meaning *one who received by lot*. The word occurs fourteen times in the New Testament, three of which are in Hebrews (1:2; 6:17; 11:7).

Verse 3

ὤν—present active participle of εἰμί, denoting time.

ἀπαύγασμα—the noun is derived from the verb ἀπαυγάζω (I emit brightness). A related noun is αὐγή (brightness). The ending -μα in ἀπαύγασμα generally indicates the result of an action.

χαρακτήρ—from χαράσσω (I engrave, inscribe). The noun refers to the exact expression, the precise reproduction of an original. See I Clement 33:4. A related noun is χάραγμα (a stamp or imprinted mark); this word is used in Acts 17:29; Revelation 13:16, 17; 14:9, 11; 15:2; 16:2; 19:20; 20:4.

ὑπόστασις—the word finds its root in ὑφίσταμαι (I stand under). The meaning of the noun includes the idea of substance, nature, or essence.

φέρων—present active participle denoting time.

τε—an adjunct particle that links this clause closely to the preceding one.

τὰ πάντα—note the definite article used to emphasize the concept by making it all-inclusive.

τὸ ῥῆμα—the use of τὸ ῥῆμα instead of ὁ λόγος stresses the act of speaking more than the content of the spoken word.

ποιησάμενος—aorist middle participle. The aorist is used to show that the Son accomplished the task of purification; the middle indicates that he himself was the agent.

Verse 4

τοσούτῳ—the dative of degree of difference, followed by ὅσῳ. See Hebrews 7:20–22; 10:25. The word is a pronoun of degree referring to size and quantity.

κρείττων—comparative adjective.

γενόμενος—aorist middle participle that may have a causal or a temporal meaning.

τῶν ἀγγέλων—genitive of comparison. The definite article points to the class or the category of angels.

διαφορώτερον—comparative form from διάφορος (excellent, surpassing). The word is derived from the verb διαφέρω (I bear or carry through).

κεκληρονόμηκεν—perfect active indicative to state that the inheritance has been, is, and will be in effect.

---

5 For to which of the angels did God ever say,
> "You are my Son;
>> today I have become your Father"?

Or again,
> "I will be his Father,
>> and he will be my Son"?

6 And again, when God brings his firstborn into the world, he says,
> "Let all God's angels worship him."

7 In speaking of the angels he says,
> "He makes his angels winds,
>> his servants flames of fire."

8 But about the Son he says,

"Your throne, O God, will last for ever and ever,
and righteousness will be the scepter of your kingdom.
9 You have loved righteousness and hated wickedness;
therefore God, your God, has set you above
your companions
by anointing you with the oil of joy."
10 He also says,

"In the beginning, O Lord, you laid the foundations
of the earth,
and the heavens are the work of your hands.
11 They will perish, but you remain;
they will all wear out like a garment.
12 You will roll them up like a robe;
like a garment they will be changed.
But you remain the same,
and your years will never end."
13 To which of the angels did God ever say,

"Sit at my right hand
until I make your enemies
a footstool for your feet"?
14 Are not all angels ministering spirits sent to serve those who will inherit salvation?

B. Jesus' Superiority to Angels
1:5–14

5. For to which of the angels did God ever say,

"You are my Son;
today I have become your Father"?

Or again,

"I will be his Father,
and he will be my Son"?

The reader of Hebrews is immediately struck by the numerous citations from the psalms that the author uses to strengthen his teaching about the superiority of Jesus Christ. In the first chapter alone he includes five quotations from the Psalter and two from other books. And in the following chapter, quotations from the Psalms occur rather frequently; they almost become the hallmark of this epistle.

The recipients of the letter had become familiar with the Psalms in the local worship services in which the congregation sang "psalms, hymns and spiritual songs" (Eph. 5:19; Col. 3:16). They possessed a store of knowledge that had been communicated orally in the worship services and committed to memory. "It is not surprising at all that the author [of Hebrews], in an attempt to reach perfect communication, strengthens not only his whole Epistle with quotations from the Psalter known in the liturgy of the Church: indeed in his first chapter he avails himself of five passages from the Psalms and one from the Hymn of Moses (Deut. 32)."[12] The quotations are from Psalm 2:7 and II Samuel 7:14 in verse 5; Deuteronomy 32:43 (according to the readings in the Dead Sea Scrolls and the Septuagint) in verse 6; Psalm 104:4 in verse 7; Psalm 45:6–7 in verses 8–9; Psalm 102:25–27 in verses 10–12; and Psalm 110:1 in verse 13.

1. Psalm 2:7
1:5

For to which of the angels did God ever say, "You are my Son; today I have become your Father"? The writer obviously links this verse to verse 4, in which he introduces the teaching of the Son's superiority to angels. He does not intend to by-pass the significance of the first three verses, but in verse 4 he makes the point of comparing the Son with the angels and stating his superiority. With the help of quotations from the Old Testament, specifically from the Book of Psalms, the author indicates that the Son has fulfilled the Scripture passages that he quotes.

One of these passages, Psalm 2, is probably of Davidic origin. This assumption is predicated on information in Acts 4:22–26, which indicates that the Jerusalem church handed down an ancient tradition concerning the authorship of this psalm.[13] The Jewish people understood Psalm 2 to be messianic, and their use of the psalm in the synagogue reflected that understanding.[14] The individual writers of the New Testament also interpreted messianically all the quotations and references from the second psalm. For example, when Paul preached in Pisidian Antioch, he said, "What God promised our fathers he has fulfilled for us, their children, by raising up Jesus. As it is written in the second Psalm: 'You are my Son; today I have become your Father'" (Acts 13:32–33). Quotations from Psalm 2 are given in Acts 4:25–26; 13:33; Hebrews 1:5; 5:5; Revelation 2:26–27; 19:15. Allusions to verses 2, 7, 8, and 9 can be discerned in Matthew, Mark, Luke, Acts, Hebrews, II Peter, and Revelation.

As Psalm 2:7 asks, did God ever say to any of the angels, "You are my son; today I have become your Father"? The answer to this rhetorical question obviously is negative, even though angels are called sons of God (see especially Job 1:6; 2:1; 38:7). The status described in this verse has never been conferred on the angels, and no angel has ever been given the title *Son of God* anywhere in the Scriptures.[15]

In the same way, Solomon, the son of David, never completely fulfilled the words of the psalm. Why, for example, would a son of a king receive the

---

12. Simon J. Kistemaker, *The Psalm Citations in the Epistle to the Hebrews* (Amsterdam: Van Soest, 1961), pp. 14–15.

13. Jan Ridderbos, *De Psalmen,* 2 vols. (Kampen: Kok, 1955), vol. 1, p. 21.

14. SB, vol. 3, pp. 675–77; 1QSa 2.11.

15. Westcott, *Hebrews,* p. 20. The title *Son of God* is never given to a person in the Old Testament. Only the nation Israel is called "my son" (Hos. 11:1) and "my firstborn son" (Exod. 4:22).

title *son*? It would be more fitting to call him king at the time of his accession to the throne (as in Psalm 2:6, "I have installed my King on Zion, my holy hill"). This son is a type of the Son of God. The believers in the Old Testament era, then, were given a representative who foreshadowed the Messiah.

Obviously the earthly king, called Son, was unable to fulfill the words of Psalm 2, for the passage referred to the Messiah who in the fullness of time gave the psalm its ultimate significance. (In the prophecy of Isaiah, the Messiah is revealed as a Son: "for to us a child is born, to us a son is given" [9:6]). The words of Psalm 2 apply ultimately to the Son of God. His appointment to the office of Son—specifically, his appearance in the flesh—is reflected in the clause "today I have become your Father." (The word *today* ought not be taken literally but should be understood generally to refer to the time of Jesus' work on earth.) But the clause does not say that at the moment of Jesus' birth he became the Son or at the time of his resurrection (Acts 13:33) God became his Father. Rather, the words *I have become* indicate that God the Father from eternity has begotten and continues to beget the Messiah, his Son. The Athanasian Creed of the fourth century summarizes this succinctly in its twenty-first and twenty-second articles:

> The Father is made of none, neither created nor begotten, the Son is of the Father alone; not made nor created, but begotten.[16]

The words of Psalm 2:7 could have been fulfilled by neither David nor Solomon but only by Jesus Christ.

Or again. The writer uses a second selection from the Old Testament to show that God has never been called Father of angels and that no angel ever addressed God as Father. Archangels, including Michael and Gabriel, never experienced that honor.

2. II Samuel 7:14
1:5

I will be his Father, and he will be my Son. The context of the quotation reflects David's desire to build a house for the Lord God. The word of the Lord is given to Nathan the prophet, who informs David that not he but his son is to build God's house. Declares the Lord, "He is the one who will build a house for my Name, and I will establish the throne of his kingdom forever. I will be his father, and he will be my son" (II Sam. 7:13–14; I Chron. 17:12–13). The words of the Lord were directed to David's son Solomon, who indeed built the temple in Jerusalem. But through his mediatorial work the Son of God completely overshadowed Solomon.

The author of Hebrews evidently chose this Old Testament passage be-

---

16. The Nicene Creed states, "[I believe] . . . in one Lord Jesus Christ, the only-begotten Son of God, begotten of the Father before all worlds." And the Belgic Confession says, "We believe that Jesus Christ . . . is the Son of God, not only from the time that he assumed our nature but from all eternity" (art. 10).

cause of its messianic significance. The allusions to II Samuel 7 in the New Testament (especially in Luke 1:32–33; and in John 7:42) indicate that the passage was applied to the Messiah.[17]

3. Deuteronomy 32:43
1:6

6. And again, when God brings his firstborn into the world, he says, "Let all God's angels worship him."

From a well-known messianic psalm and a similar passage from a historical book the writer of Hebrews turns to the Hymn of Moses, recorded in Deuteronomy 32 and used in temple services and local synagogues. The Jews considered the concluding verses of this hymn to be messianic.[18]

This quotation is introduced by the phrase *and again*, which is followed by the clause "when God brings his firstborn into the world." The subject is God the Father, who brings his Son into the world. But when did or will this take place? The question remains: should the translation from the Greek read, "And again, when God brings his firstborn into the world" or "But when God shall bring again his firstborn into the world"?[19]

The first translation is a reference to the birth of Jesus, when a multitude of the heavenly host praised God in the fields near Bethlehem (Luke 2:13). The second translation is an amplification of Jesus' discourse on the end of the age. At the end of time "he will send his angels with a loud trumpet call" (Matt. 24:31); that is, the angels of God will worship the Son when he returns at the close of this age. However, why does the writer of Hebrews speak of a second coming of Jesus when he has not said anything in the immediate context about Christ's first coming? It seems more appropriate to prefer the first translation, for it logically follows the quotations in verses 5 and 6.

The word *firstborn* in verse 6 (see also Luke 2:7; Rom. 8:29; Col. 1:15, 18; Heb. 11:28; 12:23; Rev. 1:5) qualifies the word *Son* and is a title given to Jesus. We cannot determine when that title was given, because the writers who use the term apply it to creation, resurrection, dignity, and honor. The psalmist records a blessing upon David when God said, "I will also appoint him my firstborn" (Ps. 89:27). The Son, as the firstborn, enters the inhabited world of men. The word *world* is Hellenic and was used in ordinary speech to refer to the populated world.[20]

a. The quotation itself shows that "not only is the Son greater than angels,

---

17. In 4Q *Florilegium,* II Sam. 7:14 is quoted and interpreted in a way that calls attention to the Messiah.

18. F. W. Grosheide, *De Brief aan de Hebreeën en de Brief van Jakobus* (Kampen: Kok, 1955), p. 69.

19. See ASV, NASB. A number of commentators, including Westcott, Grosheide, Franz Delitzsche, and R. C. H. Lenski, feel that the Greek word order should be followed. Scholars who think that the adverb *again* modifies the verb *bring* interpret the clause as a reference to the return of Christ; others think that the clause refers to the resurrection.

20. *TDNT,* vol. 5, p. 157; *NIDNTT,* vol. 1, p. 519.

but He is worshipped by angels."[21] The Son is the Creator of the angels, and God orders these creatures to show homage to his Son. The angels, because they are created, must serve the Son and "those who will inherit salvation" (Heb. 1:14).

b. The origin of the quotation seems to be a Greek translation of the Hymn of Moses (Deut. 32:43). The translation based on the Hebrew text is rendered:

> Rejoice, O nations, with his people,
> for he will avenge the blood of his servants;
> he will take vengeance on his enemies
> and make atonement for his land and people.

The Septuagint and the Dead Sea Scrolls show an addition to the first line of the verse.

> Rejoice, O nations, with his people,
> and let all the angels worship him,
> for he will avenge the blood of his servants.

In the Septuagint version of Psalm 97:7 (Ps. 96:7, LXX) we read the exhortation: "Worship him[,] all you his angels." The translation based on the Hebrew text reads, "Worship him, all you gods!"

c. The Hymn of Moses is quoted and alluded to more than any other portion from the Book of Deuteronomy. The writer of Hebrews quotes twice from this hymn (Heb. 1:6; 10:30). In his letter to the Romans, Paul cites the hymn three times (Rom. 10:19; 12:19; 15:10). Allusions to this hymn are found in Matthew, Luke, John, Acts, Romans, I Corinthians, II Corinthians, Ephesians, Hebrews, I John, and Revelation. John records in Revelation 15 that the victorious saints were given harps by God and "sang the song of Moses the servant of God" (Rev. 15:3). This reference to the heavenly use of the Hymn of Moses reflects its liturgical use in the church on earth. And in the church on earth the hymn was sung in languages other than Hebrew. The Jews living in dispersion used the Greek rendition of this song, from which the author of Hebrews quoted a line that describes the superiority of the Son over the angels.

The addressee in Deuteronomy 32:43 is the Lord God, who must be worshiped by his angels. This homage the writer of Hebrews (having clearly established the divinity of Jesus) transfers to the Son. The quotation reinforces the author's teaching about the deity of Christ.

Doctrinal Considerations in 1:5–6

Angels do not share in God's promises; they have no part in the inheritance that is accorded to believers ("we are heirs—heirs of God and co-heirs with Christ"; Rom. 8:17). Scripture does not say that any angel is God's Son; therefore an angel,

---

21. Bengel, *Gnomon,* vol. 4, p. 344.

although exalted by being in the presence of God, is in no way equal to, nor can in any way be compared to, the Son of God.

The writer of Hebrews quotes from the Hymn of Moses as it was rendered in the Septuagint. The Greek translation of Deuteronomy 32 was well known to him and his audience because in the dispersion the Jews used the Septuagint in the synagogues. The early Christians adopted the liturgy with variations to express the Christian emphasis.

The author's use of a quote from the Septuagint that is without an exact equivalent in the Hebrew text in our possession does not mean that the doctrine of inspiration has been undermined. The Holy Spirit, who is the primary author of Scripture and inspired every human writer, directed the author of Hebrews to select a quote from the Hymn of Moses in the Greek. When the author incorporated the line into his epistle, that line became inspired Scripture.

The word *today* (v. 5) is not limited to designating a specific time but ought to be understood in a broader sense. For example, the declaration of Christ's sonship was effective not only on the day of his resurrection, but also on the day of his ascension and his session at the right hand of God the Father (Heb. 1:4).

Greek Words, Phrases, and Constructions in 1:5–6

Verse 5

οἱ ἄγγελοι—in the Septuagint the phrase ἄγγελοι θεοῦ occurs frequently. The definite article points to the angels as a class.

υἱός—without the definite article the noun is to be understood in the absolute sense: "My Son you are"; not "You, too, are my son."

μου . . . σύ, ἐγώ . . . σε—the use of the personal pronouns shows the emphasis the writer wishes to express in this rather short sentence.

γεγέννηκα—the use of the perfect of γεννάω conveys the idea of a completed state, constitutes a declaration of sonship, and relates an action that continues perpetually and eternally.

Verse 6

εἰσαγάγῃ—the aorist active subjunctive of εἰσάγω. The aorist signifies single occurrence of an action but says nothing about the time itself.

προσκυνησάτωσαν—the verb προσκυνέω means "to bow down, to show respect, to worship by falling down." The verb form is the aorist active imperative, which implies command as well as consent.

---

4. Psalm 104:4
1:7

7. In speaking of the angels he says,
   "He makes his angels winds,
     his servants flames of fire."

The contrast between the Son of God and the angels is evident to the writer. Nowhere in Scripture are angels given a title that indicates they are equals of the Son. Instead, as creatures they are servants of God and stand ready to do his bidding.

Psalm 104 is a nature psalm, well known to Jewish and early Christian worshipers, who sang the psalm in synagogues and churches. In the liturgy of the synagogue the psalm was sung on Friday evenings and Saturday mornings.[22] The synoptic Gospels quote Psalm 104:12 (Matt. 13:32; Mark 4:32; Luke 13:19). The great multitude that praises God in heaven makes use of Psalm 104:35 (Rev. 19:1, 3, 6). In the early church the psalm was not unknown.

The writer of Hebrews quotes from the Greek translation of this psalm because of the key word *angels*. In most translations of Psalm 104:4, the word *angels* does not appear. The verse is translated

> He makes winds his messengers,
> flames of fire his servants.[23]

The psalmist ascribes splendor and majesty to God, who as the Creator "stretches out the heavens like a tent and lays the beams of his upper chambers on their waters" (Ps. 104:2–3). Clouds and winds stand at his call because they are (figuratively) his means of transportation. Winds are his messengers; bolts of lightning, his servants. God is in perfect control of his creation.

However, in the Septuagint, the word *angels* is predominant because it is the first of two direct objects (that is, the word *angels* comes before the term *winds,* not vice versa). For the writer of Hebrews, who had the Greek translation at his disposal, the text read: "He makes his angels winds," not "He makes winds his messengers."

The writer uses the quotation from Psalm 104 to emphasize the subservient state of the angels. They are like winds and bolts of lightning, which are part of God's creation and completely obedient to his will. The text compares angels to winds and flames of fire to indicate that their deeds are as transient as changes in nature.

God uses angels to execute his will, and they serve him in a mighty way, forceful as the wind and destructive as a streak of lightning. When their task is completed, however, they return to him as humble and obedient servants. Although they perform mighty deeds, they remain lowly attendants.

The comparison between the Son and the angels is a further elaboration of the first four verses of chapter 1. God appointed the Son "heir of all things, and through [him] made the universe" (Heb. 1:2). The words *he makes* in the sentence *he makes his angels winds* point to the Creator who made all things and who by implication relegates angels to the status of created beings.

---

22. Ernst Werner, *The Sacred Bridge* (London: D. Dobson, 1959), p. 150.

23. English translations have the reading *messengers,* although footnotes may give the word *angels* as an alternative. The LXX as well as the Targum Jonathan and the ancient rabbis read Ps. 104:4, "He makes his angels winds." See SB, vol. 3, p. 678.

5. Psalm 45:6–7
1:8–9

8. But about the Son he says,
   "Your throne, O God, will last for ever and ever,
   and righteousness will be the scepter of your kingdom."

The contrast between angels and Son is expressed most characteristically by means of the two quotations from the Psalter.

The first quoted psalm (104) is a nature psalm that extols the works of God in creation and in the fourth verse, according to the Greek translation, speaks about the angels' role as servants.

The second psalm (45) portrays an earthly king who celebrates his wedding. After the introduction (v. 1), the psalmist describes the excellence and grace of the king (vv. 3–4), his victory in battle (v. 5), his rule of justice and righteousness (vv. 6–7), and his joy in his palace and in the daughters of kings (vv. 8–9). The second part of this psalm (vv. 10–15) concerns the bride and her companions. The conclusion follows in verses 16–17.[24]

The psalm is typological of the Messiah. Only in the advent of the Son of God is the description of the king's wedding completely fulfilled. The Jewish rabbis understood this psalm as a nuptial hymn composed for the occasion of the marriage of a king of Israel.[25] An Aramaic translation or paraphrase, Targum Jonathan (which dates from the first centuries of the Christian era), gives this rendition of Psalm 45:2: "Your beauty, O king Messiah, is greater than that of the sons of men."[26] That Christians of the first and second centuries considered that Jesus Christ fulfilled the words of the psalm is obvious from the context and the application in Hebrews 1 and from such writers as Justin Martyr and Irenaeus, who quote Psalm 45:6–7 numerous times.[27]

The person addressed in the first chapter of Hebrews is called the Son; thus far no other name has been given to him. The author of the epistle writes, "But about the Son he [God] says." The Son, divine and eternal (as the author has shown earlier), is the king seated at the right hand of the Majesty in heaven.

The writer selects verses 6–7 of Psalm 45 and applies them to the Son to emphasize the deity of the Son. These particular words form the core of

---

24. Ridderbos, *Psalmen,* vol. 2, p. 32.

25. John Calvin and other scholars have interpreted the psalm as describing a wedding of King Solomon. The Jerusalem Bible, in a footnote to Ps. 45, states, "According to some scholars, this psalm may be a secular song to celebrate the marriage of an Israelite king, Solomon, Jeroboam II, or Ahab (whose bride was a Tyrian princess, 1 K 16:31). But Jewish and Christian tradition understand it as celebrating the marriage of the messianic King with Israel. . . ."

26. For further details consult SB, vol. 3, pp. 679–80. Franz Delitzsch, in his *Commentary on the Epistle to the Hebrews,* 2 vols. (Edinburgh: Clark, 1877), vol. 1, pp. 76–77, "regards the forty-fifth Psalm as a not merely typico-Messianic, but as a directly prophetico-Messianic Psalm."

27. Justin, *Dial.* 63, 56, 86; and Irenaeus, *Heresies,* 3.6.1; 4.33.11; *Epid.* 47.

Psalm 45 because of their message to the king: "Your throne, O God, will last for ever and ever" (v. 6). The reference to the perpetual stability of the king's throne may point to the Davidic line.

Of much greater importance is the appellation *O God,* which teaches the divinity of the Son. The question raised by translators of Psalm 45:6 and Hebrews 1:8 is whether the word *God* is an address or a predicate construction that should be translated "Your throne is God."[28] According to ancient translations of Psalm 45:6, the address *O God* makes excellent sense, and the author of Hebrews uses this address to express the deity of Christ.[29]

To reveal the stability of the king's throne—that is, the throne of the Son—the writer of Hebrews quotes the rest of the verse: "and righteousness will be the scepter of your kingdom." The scepter in the hand of the Son is a scepter of righteousness to administer justice and equity. Says John Calvin, "But righteousness in the kingdom of Christ has a wider meaning; for he by his Gospel, which is his spiritual scepter, renews us after the righteousness of God."[30]

9. **"You have loved righteousness and hated wickedness;**
   therefore God, your God, has set you
   above your companions
   by anointing you with the oil of joy."

The divine kingship could not be assumed by any Israelite monarch; only the Son of David, Jesus Christ, fulfilled the words of the psalm. He has loved righteousness and hated wickedness, as he demonstrated during his earthly ministry. The question, however, is whether the words of the quotation can be applied to a particular event or period in Jesus' ministry. We ought not limit the verse to designating any particular moment in the life of Christ, but rather understand it as a description of his nature. Jesus loves righteousness and desires that the people in his kingdom also love righteousness and hate wickedness. Righteousness is the foundation of his kingdom. Thus he exhorts his followers to seek first the kingdom of God and his righteousness (Matt. 6:33).

It is because of Christ's love for righteousness that God has anointed Jesus with the oil of joy. Obviously, Jesus Christ is the Anointed of God from eternity to eternity. There is no particular moment at which Jesus began his love for righteousness and after which he was anointed.

We do well to understand the phrases *scepter of righteousness* and *oil of joy* as Hebraic idioms that were translated literally into Greek.

---

28. Some translations apparently wish to avoid reference to the divinity of the king. Examples are NEB ("Your throne is like God's throne, eternal"); GNB ("The kingdom that God has given you will last forever and ever"); and *Moffatt* ("Your throne shall stand for evermore").

29. These ancient translations include the Sahidic and the Vulgate. Refer to James Moffatt, *Epistle to the Hebrews,* International Critical Commentary series (Edinburgh: Clark, 1963), p. 13.

30. John Calvin, *Epistle to the Hebrews* (Grand Rapids: Eerdmans, 1949), p. 46.

a. Thus, the phrase *scepter of righteousness* actually means that the king holds in his hand a scepter, which symbolizes royal authority. The king can hold out the scepter to invite someone to approach his throne, or he can sway his scepter to demand silence. By means of this instrument the king rules. How does the king execute his rule? Justly!

b. Likewise, the phrase *oil of joy* is not a symbolic description of either the baptism of Jesus in the Jordan River or his ascension and session at the right hand of God; rather, it describes the constant administration of his just rule. The application of his justice fills him with joy and happiness, and constitutes his anointing. It is the anointed Son who, set above his companions, shares his happiness with them (Isa. 61:3).

c. The word *companions* implies that the companions of Jesus share in his righteousness and joy. The word is used not of angels but of Jesus' followers, who "share in the heavenly calling" (Heb. 3:1).[31] "Hence he is the Christ, we are Christians proceeding from him, as rivulets from a fountain."[32] Therefore Jesus is not ashamed to call his companions brothers (Heb. 2:11). They, too, "have an anointing from the Holy One," says John in his first epistle. And he continues, "As for you, the anointing you received from him remains in you" (I John 2:20, 27).

A sixteenth-century catechism asks the penetrating question, "But why are you called a Christian?" and gives the revealing answer:

> Because by faith I am a member of Christ
>   and so I share in his anointing.
> I am anointed
>   to confess his name,
>   to present myself to him
>   as a living sacrifice of thanks,
>   to strive with a free conscience
>   against sin and the devil in this life,
>   and afterward to reign with Christ
>   over all creation
>   for all eternity.[33]

Greek Words, Phrases, and Constructions in 1:7–8

Verse 7

πρὸς μέν . . . πρὸς δέ—the contrast between verse 7 and verse 8 is clear and unequivocal because of the particles μέν and δέ. The contrast is between the angels on the one hand and the Son on the other. The preposition πρός followed by the accusative case conveys the idea *with reference to.*

τοὺς ἀγγέλους αὐτοῦ πνεύματα—the two accusatives are double, depending on

---

31. Moffatt, in *Hebrews*, p. 14, understands the term *companions* to refer to "angels (Heb. 12:23) rather than human beings (Heb. 3:14)."
32. Calvin, *Hebrews*, p. 46.
33. Heidelberg Catechism, question and answer 32.

the present participle ποιῶν, which conveys the thought that God is constantly using and sending them. Of the two direct objects, ἀγγέλους has the definite article and therefore comes first in translation.

τοὺς λειτουργοὺς πυρὸς φλόγα—the double accusative gives priority to the word λειτουργούς because of the definite article; φλόγα, therefore, takes second place. The singular accusative φλόγα (from φλόξ) is used collectively. The reading πυρὸς φλόγα seems to be an integral part of the New Testament wording; the combination of πῦρ and φλόξ occurs six times (Acts 7:30; II Thess. 1:8; Heb. 1:7; Rev. 1:14; 2:18; 19:12).

Verse 8

τὸν υἱόν—the definite article preceding υἱόν is balanced by the definite article in the introduction of verse 7, καὶ πρὸς μὲν τοὺς ἀγγέλους.

σου/αὐτοῦ—the reading αὐτοῦ is supported by excellent witnesses, although the text of Psalm 45:7 (Ps. 44:7, LXX) reads σου. The word αὐτοῦ is preferred by some commentators: F. W. Grosheide, Ceslaus Spicq, and B. F. Westcott. "Thus, if one reads αὐτοῦ the words ὁ θεός must be taken not as vocative (an interpretation that is preferred by most exegetes), but as the subject (or predicate nominative), an interpretation that is generally regarded as highly improbable."[34]

---

6. Psalm 102:25–27
1:10–12

10. He also says,
   "In the beginning, O Lord, you laid the foundations of the earth,
   and the heavens are the work of your hands."

The sixth quotation from the Old Testament is taken from Psalm 102:25–27. The psalm, actually a prayer of a believer who is grieving for Zion, ends with a song of praise about the unchangeableness of God. The writer of Hebrews applies this song of praise to Christ, the eternal Son of God. The author needed the words of this psalm to explain the introduction to his epistle: "But in these last days [God] has spoken to us by his Son, whom he appointed heir of all things, and through whom he made the universe. The Son is the radiance of God's glory and the exact representation of his being, sustaining all things by his powerful word" (Heb. 1:2–3). The sixth quotation therefore was prompted by the introduction, in which the writer set forth the doctrine of the eternity of the Son, through whom everything was created and through whom all things are sustained. What formerly was said of Israel's God has now been applied to Jesus Christ. The Son of God is Creator and Upholder of the universe and as such is far superior to angels. For that reason, the writer of Hebrews emphasizes the pronoun *you* to express the contrast between the "Lord, [who] laid the foundations of the earth, in the beginning" and the angels, who serve only as God's messengers.

In the original Hebrew text of Psalm 102:25, the address *Lord* is lacking;

---

34. Bruce M. Metzger, *A Textual Commentary on the Greek New Testament* (London and New York: United Bible Societies, 1975), p. 663.

the Greek translators supplied the word, which was used as a title of respect by those who addressed Jesus. The author of Hebrews, who relied on the Greek translation of the Old Testament, understandably applied this section of Psalm 102 to the Christ, because the title *Lord* appeared in the Greek text.

The phrase *in the beginning* immediately calls to mind the creation account in Genesis. And the words "laid the foundations of the earth" are a figure of speech, a synonym for creation.[35] The creation of the heavens and the earth is recorded in Genesis 1. It is but natural that for reasons of balance and completion the psalmist says, "And the heavens are the works of your hands." Paul summarized all of these comments by saying of the Christ that "by him all things were created: things in heaven and on earth" (Col. 1:16).

11. **"They will perish, but you remain;**
    they will all wear out like a garment.
12. **You will roll them up like a robe;**
    like a garment they will be changed.
  But you remain the same,
    and your years will never end."

The message of this portion of the psalm is the unchangeableness of God, a characteristic that the writer of Hebrews ascribes to the Son. Everything changes, deteriorates, passes away—except the Creator. Henry F. Lyte captured the thought when he wrote:

> Change and decay
>   in all around I see;
> O Thou who changest not,
>   abide with me.

Although heaven and earth have been created by the Son who is eternal, they do not share his eternity. They are and will remain temporal. The heavens and certain parts of the earth (for example, the mountains) seem to exhibit timelessness. Yet they are subject to change, as Isaiah prophesies: "Lift up your eyes to the heavens, look at the earth beneath; the heavens will vanish like smoke, the earth will wear out like a garment and its inhabitants die like flies. But my salvation will last forever, my righteousness will never fail" (51:6).

Everything the Creator has made bears the mark of time. The psalmist uses the illustration of a garment that changes, gradually deteriorates, is eventually rolled up and discarded. The Creator, however, lives forever; he is the same because his years never end. His years never end inasmuch as they never began. The Son has no beginning and no end. Certainly this can never be said of angels, who may live eternally in the presence of God. Their beginning dates from the moment the Son created them.

---

35. Job 38:4; Ps. 24:2; 89:11; 104:5; Prov. 8:29; Isa. 24:18; 48:13; 51:13, 16; Mic. 6:2; Zech. 12:1.

The citation from Psalm 102 teaches the distinguishing characteristics of the Son: he is the Creator, almighty, unchangeable, and eternal. The pre-existence of the Son is indicated by the phrase *in the beginning*; his permanence, by the clause *you remain the same*; and his eternity, by the words *your years will never end.*[36]

Doctrinal Considerations in 1:10–12

The comparison in verses 10, 11, and 12 is between the Creator and his creatures. That which is created shall perish, but the Creator transcends time and space and therefore remains forever.

He who is unchangeable is far superior to that which is changeable.

The contrast between the Son and the perishable heaven and earth is intensified by means of the frequent use of personal pronouns (for instance, "*they* will perish, but *you* remain"; italics added).

Greek Words, Phrases, and Constructions in 1:10–12

Verse 10

σύ—the first word in the sentence receives the emphasis. The author has deliberately taken this second person pronoun from its original place and has given it prominence by putting it first in the sentence.

κατ' ἀρχάς—the phrase *in the beginning* (ἐν ἀρχῇ; John 1:1) differs from κατ' ἀρχάς in number. The former, in the singular, denotes a point in time; the latter, in the plural, seems to refer to periods of time.

Verse 11

διαμένεις—some manuscripts accent the verb as a future active indicative διαμενεῖς, but this tense does not suit the context. The present tense, referring to the permanence of the Son, is contrasted with the passing nature of heaven, earth, and the objects of the earth (robe and garment) expressed in future tenses. The verb διαμένεις is a compound with a perfective connotation, denoting the Son's eternity.

Verse 12

ἑλίξεις—the word is the future active indicative of ἑλίσσω (I roll up; Rev. 6:14). A few manuscripts have the reading ἀλλάξεις, the future active indicative of ἀλλάσσω (I change), most likely because of ἀλλαγήσονται, the second future passive indicative, which occurs shortly thereafter.

ὡς ἱμάτιον—although the phrase is omitted in some manuscripts, its inclusion receives strong support from early and varied witnesses. Says Metzger, in his *Textual Commentary*, p. 663, "The absence of the words from most witnesses is the result of conformation to the text of the Septuagint."

---

36. Ceslaus Spicq, *L'Épître aux Hébreux*, 3d ed., 2 vols. (Paris: Gabalda, 1953), vol. 2, p. 20.

7. Psalm 110:1
1:13

13. To which of the angels did God ever say,
   "Sit at my right hand
      until I make your enemies
      a footstool for your feet"?

This introductory sentence resembles the one in Hebrews 1:5. Interestingly, the author of the epistle begins his series of seven quotations with the question, "For to which of the angels did God ever say," and ends the series with the same rhetorical question, which expects a negative answer. The first six quotations lead to the climax in the last one, taken from Psalm 110:1. No angels have ever been given the honor of sitting at God's right hand, although their work may be important. Nowhere does God ever honor an angel by giving him a reward for services performed; nowhere does God promise an angel any gift, distinction, or rank. An angel is an angel and will remain an angel. By contrast, the Son, "after he had provided purification for sins, . . . sat down at the right hand of the Majesty in heaven" (Heb. 1:3). The Son took his place of honor in answer to the Father's invitation to sit at his right hand.

Of all the psalm quotations in the New Testament, Psalm 110:1 is quoted and alluded to most often. It is quoted in Matthew 22:44 and the parallel places Mark 12:36 and Luke 20:42–43, as well as in Acts 2:34–35 and Hebrews 1:13. Writers allude to Psalm 110:1 in Matthew 26:64; Mark 14:62; 16:19; Luke 22:69; Romans 8:34; I Corinthians 15:25; Ephesians 1:20; Colossians 3:1; and Hebrews 1:3; 8:1; 10:12.

   a. Jesus himself, in discourse with the Pharisees on the identity of Christ, the Son of David, quoted Psalm 110:1 and asked the revealing question: "If then David calls him 'Lord,' how can he be his Son?" (Matt. 22:45). Obviously, Jesus is the Messiah.[37]

   b. Peter, on the day of Pentecost, quoted Psalm 110:1 and, ruling out a possible reference to David, concluded, "Therefore let all Israel be assured of this: God has made this Jesus, whom you crucified, both Lord and Christ" (Acts 2:36).

   c. And Paul, in the resurrection chapter of I Corinthians, applied Psalm 110:1 to Christ, who " 'has put everything under his feet' " (I Cor. 15:27).

The command *sit at my right hand* is addressed not to David but to Christ,

---

37. This particular citation from the psalms occupied a prominent place in the writings of the Fathers. Clement of Rome borrowed a passage from Heb. 1 and quoted Ps. 110:1 together with Ps. 2:7 (I Clem. 36:5); the verse is also mentioned in the Epistle of Barnabas (12:10). Justin Martyr cited Ps. 110:1 many times (*Dial.* 32, 33, 56, 82, 127; *Apol.* 1.45), as did Irenaeus (*Heresies*, 2.28.7; 3.6.1; 3.10.6; 3.12.2; *Epid.* 48, 85). During the first century, Ps. 110:1 was understood messianically in the ancient synagogues. (See especially SB, vol. 5, pp. 452–65.) Also, Billerbeck, in his appendix on Ps. 110:1, argues convincingly that the Jews in the first century of the Christian era interpreted the psalm messianically.

who is elevated to a place of honor, seated next to God the Father. Angels are never asked to be seated; they stand around the throne ready to do God's bidding in the interest of "those who will inherit salvation" (Heb. 1:14).

The words *sit at my right hand* are not only a symbolic description for the seat of honor; they also conjure up a picture of an oriental court in which the king, seated on his throne, is surrounded by servants. The servants stand in the presence of the king to show their deference. To be asked by the king to take a seat next to him on his right is the greatest honor one could hope to receive. "To sit near the king at any time, is the emblem of being on terms of familiarity and friendship with him, for all but his peculiar favourites *stand* in his presence; but to sit near him when on the throne, is an emblem of rank, and dignity, and power in the kingdom. A seat on the right hand and a seat on the left of the king are just other words for the two most dignified stations in the kingdom."[38] The mother of John and James, the sons of Zebedee, asked Jesus whether one of her two sons might sit at his right side and the other at his left side in his kingdom (Matt. 20:21).

Of the two seats, one on the left hand and one on the right hand, that on the right hand of the king is more honorable. This is the place Jesus received when he completed his mediatorial work:

> He ascended into heaven,
> and sits at the right hand
> of God the Father Almighty.
> —Apostles' Creed

We do not need to think of Jesus continuously seated at the right hand of the Father. Stephen, before he was dragged out of Jerusalem to be killed, said, "Look, . . . I see heaven open and the Son of Man *standing* at the right hand of God" (Acts 7:56; italics added). Jesus does not quietly spend his time sitting or standing. He is preparing a place for his followers and is subjugating his enemies. "Sit at my right hand until I make your enemies a footstool for your feet" (Ps. 110:1; Heb. 1:13).

The expression "your enemies a footstool for your feet" describes an oriental military practice. A victorious king or general would place his feet on the neck of a defeated king (Josh. 10:24; Isa. 51:23) to demonstrate his triumph over his enemy. Jesus "must reign until he has put all his enemies under his feet" (I Cor. 15:25). When the last enemy, death, has been destroyed, Jesus "hands over the kingdom to God the Father" (I Cor. 15:24).

14. Are not all angels ministering spirits sent to serve those who will inherit salvation?

From the throne of God and from the seat of honor, commands are given to angels to work in behalf of and for the benefit of the believers, who will inherit salvation. Whereas Jesus sits enthroned in majesty and grandeur,

---

38. John Brown, *An Exposition of Hebrews* (Edinburgh: Banner of Truth Trust, 1961), pp. 66–67. Italics his.

angels are ministering spirits. They must obey and serve. Not a single angel is excluded. Even archangels, including Gabriel and Michael, are sent by God to work in the interest of the saints (Luke 1:11–38; Jude 9).

Scripture teaches that angels are ministering spirits, "sent to serve those [the people of God] who will inherit salvation." Angels announce the law of God (Acts 7:53; Gal. 3:19; Heb. 2:2); deliver messages to God's people (Isa. 6:6–7; Dan. 8:18–19; 9:20–23; 10:12, 14; Luke 1:18–19); minister to the needs of the people of God (I Kings 19:5, 7; Ps. 91:11–12; Matt. 18:10; Acts 7:38; 12:15; I Cor. 11:10); are appointed guardians of cities and nations (Ezek. 9:1; Dan. 10:13, 20–21; 11:1; 12:1); and will gather the elect at the time of Christ's return (Matt. 24:31; Mark 13:27). However, the angels have not been commissioned to teach or preach to the elect. Nor are they given power to govern God's people, although the angels stand in the presence of God and share his plans (Zech. 1:12–13).

The angels constitute a numberless host, for John relates in Revelation that he "heard the voice of many angels, numbering thousands upon thousands, and ten thousand times ten thousand" (Rev. 5:11; see also Dan. 7:10). Their work continues until the time of the judgment, when Jesus, sitting on his throne, will say to the elect: "Come, you who are blessed by my Father; take your inheritance, the kingdom prepared for you since the creation of the world" (Matt. 25:34).

The reference to salvation as an inheritance that the elect will receive on judgment day ought to be understood in the broadest possible sense. When the elect are in the presence of Christ, they will no more experience death, mourning, crying, or pain (Rev. 21:4). They will enter a blessed and glorious state reserved for them and given to them for eternity. They shall be with Christ forever. That is the fullness of inherited salvation.

In this quotation the contrast between the Son and the angels has been brought to a climax: Jesus is sitting on the throne and is sending the angels to serve the believers. The contrast indeed is striking. In spite of their holiness, their status, and their dignity, the angels continue to function as ministering spirits to the inheritors of salvation. In a sense, therefore, angels are inferior to the saints.

Doctrinal Considerations in 1:13–14

In contrasting the Son with the angels, the writer of Hebrews begins and ends his set of seven quotations with rhetorical questions that expect a negative answer. The response to the question, "For to which of the angels did God ever say" (v. 5) is: to no one. The same is true of the question in verse 13. However, in the concluding verse of chapter 1, the writer poses a rhetorical question that expects a positive answer. "Are not all angels ministering spirits sent to serve those who will inherit salvation?" The answer is: Yes, all of them are.

The Son has been given the place of highest honor; that is, he is seated next to God the Father. The throne of God is the throne of Jesus, who rules until all his enemies are conquered.

All angels are ministering spirits. Obviously, the text speaks only of the angels that have not fallen into sin. Every angel, regardless of status, has been ordered to minister to the needs of the saints.

The saints do not have to doubt their salvation. Their inheritance is waiting for them when they, in the last day, stand before the judgment throne.

Greek Words, Phrases, and Constructions in 1:13–14

Verse 13

εἴρηκεν—the perfect active indicative is used here in distinction from the aorist active indicative εἶπεν in Hebrews 1:5. For the use of the perfect see Hebrews 4:3, 4; 10:9; 13:5. Also consult Acts 13:34.

κάθου—the present middle imperative, second person singular of κάθημαι indicates that the Son is indeed seated next to God the Father and is told to continue to do so.

ἐκ δεξιῶν μου—the adjective δεξιός is given in the neuter plural with the noun μέρη (parts) understood. The Greeks used this expression idiomatically, although often in the singular ἡ δεξιὰ [χείρ] (the right hand).

ἕως ἂν θῶ—the temporal construction with the aorist active subjunctive of τίθημι shows the finality of the matter.

Verse 14

οὐχὶ—the strengthened form of οὔ. It introduces a rhetorical question that expects an affirmative reply.

πάντες—because of its position in the sentence, the adjective πάντες is emphatic.

ἀποστελλόμενα—the present passive participle in the neuter plural modifying πνεύματα indicates that angels are constantly being sent out to aid the saints.

διά—the author of Hebrews could have used ὑπέρ (in behalf of). Instead he chose διά with the accusative to show cause.

τοὺς μέλλοντας—although the verb μέλλω is found with the future infinitive (Acts 12:6; Gal. 3:23; Rev. 3:2), it is generally followed by the present infinitive (eighty-four times in the New Testament). The present active participle ("those who are to inherit salvation"), in the context of Hebrews 1:14, conveys the idea of an action that must or certainly will take place.

Summary of Chapter 1

The central figure in chapter 1 is the Son of God, who is introduced not by name but rather as Creator of the universe, Redeemer of his people, and King who rules at God's right hand. The author of Hebrews formulates themes that he develops in the remainder of his epistle.

The Son of God is superior to angels, says the author of Hebrews. He writes not to discredit angels, but to direct attention to the exalted position of the Son. He proves his point by quoting from the Old Testament seven times, chiefly from the Book of Psalms. The author shows that the Son of God is eternal and unchangeable, and rules in royal splendor, seated at God's right hand. Angels, by contrast, are ministering spirits who are told to serve the elect people of God.

2

Jesus' Superiority and His Role as Savior and High Priest, *part 2*

2:1–18

Outline

2 1 We must pay more careful attention, therefore, to what we have heard, so that we do not drift away. 2 For if the message spoken by angels was binding, and every violation and disobedience received its just punishment, 3 how shall we escape if we ignore such a great salvation? This salvation, which was first announced by the Lord, was confirmed to us by those who heard him. 4 God also testified to it by signs, wonders and various miracles, and gifts of the Holy Spirit distributed according to his will.

5 It is not to angels that he has subjected the world to come, about which we are speaking. 6 But there is a place where someone has testified:

> "What is man that you are mindful of him,
>   the son of man that you care for him?
> 7 You made him a little lower than the angels;
>   you crowned him with glory and honor
> 8   and put everything under his feet."

In putting everything under him, God left nothing that is not subject to him. Yet at present we do not see everything subject to him. 9 But we see Jesus, who was made a little lower than the angels, now crowned with glory and honor because he suffered death, so that by the grace of God he might taste death for everyone.

10 In bringing many sons to glory, it was fitting that God, for whom and through whom everything exists, should make the author of their salvation perfect through suffering. 11 Both the one who makes men holy and those who are made holy are of the same family. So Jesus is not ashamed to call them brothers. 12 He says,

> "I will declare your name to my brothers;
>   in the presence of the congregation I will
>   sing your praises."

13 And again,

> "I will put my trust in him."

And again he says,

> "Here am I, and the children God has given me."

14 Since the children have flesh and blood, he too shared in their humanity so that by his death he might destroy him who holds the power of death—that is, the devil—15 and free those who all their lives were held in slavery by their fear of death. 16 For surely it is not angels he helps, but Abraham's descendants. 17 For this reason he had to be made like his brothers in every way, in order that he might become a merciful and faithful high priest in service to God, and that he might make atonement for the sins of the people. 18 Because he himself suffered when he was tempted, he is able to help those who are being tempted.

C. Jesus, Savior and High Priest
2:1–18

1. An Exhortation
2:1–4

One of the links between the first and the second chapters is the author's direct and indirect references to the threefold offices of Christ: prophet, priest, and king. In the first chapter, the writer describes the Son as the person through whom God spoke prophetically (1:2), a high priest who "provided purification for sins" (1:3), and the one who in royal splendor "sat down at the right hand of the Majesty in heaven" (1:3). The author continues this emphasis in the second chapter by portraying Christ as "the Lord" who as a prophet announces salvation (2:3), the king crowned "with glory and honor" (2:9), and "a merciful and faithful high priest in service to God" (2:17).

In chapter 1, the author introduces Jesus as "Son" (vv. 2, 5) or "the Son" (v. 8); in the next chapter he refers to Christ as "the Lord" (2:3) and "Jesus" (2:9).[1] In succeeding chapters the author uses these and other names more frequently.

Throughout his epistle the writer intertwines teaching and exhortation, doctrine and advice about practical matters. After providing an introductory chapter about the superiority of the Son, the author explains the significance of that chapter in a unique and practical manner. In the exhortation he reveals himself to be a loving, caring pastor who seeks the spiritual well-being of all who read and hear the words of this epistle.

1. We must pay more careful attention, therefore, to what we have heard, so that we do not drift away.

In this verse the author reminds us that we have been given a portrait of Christ's eminence and greatness and, therefore, ought to listen to what he says. For the higher a person stands in rank, the greater authority he exerts, and the more he demands the listener's attention. The original, emphatic and expressive, is conveyed well in the New English Bible: "Thus we are bound to pay all the more heed to what we have been told, for fear of drifting from our course." Obviously, refusal to pay attention to the spoken word has detrimental consequences that can lead to ruin. The difference between hearing and listening may be acute. To hear may mean merely to perceive sounds that do not necessarily require or create action. To listen means to pay thoughtful attention to sounds that enter the ear and then

---

1. Throughout the epistle the following names are used: Son (1:2, 5, 8; 3:6; 5:8; 7:28); Lord (2:3; 7:14); Jesus (2:9; 3:1; 6:20; 7:22; 10:19; 12:2, 24; 13:12, 20); Christ (3:6, 14; 5:5; 6:1; 9:11, 14, 24, 28; 11:26); Jesus Christ (10:10; 13:8, 21); Jesus the Son of God (4:14); and the Son of God (6:6; 7:3; 10:29). See the section on divine names in B. F. Westcott's *Commentary on the Epistle to the Hebrews* (Grand Rapids: Eerdmans, 1950), pp. 33–35.

evoke positive results. A child may be told by his parents to attend to some household chore and, if the task is somewhat disagreeable, may dawdle. He has heard his parents clearly but at the moment fails to listen. There is no response.

The author of Hebrews says that we—and he includes himself—must direct our minds toward listening attentively to the divine message.[2] The words may not immediately slip from one's mind because of sloth and failure to pay attention; yet there is always the danger that the words will fall into disuse.[3] Moses taught the people of Israel their creed ("Hear, O Israel: The LORD our God, the LORD is one," Deut. 6:4) and the summary of the Ten Commandments ("Love the LORD your God with all your heart and with all your soul and with all your strength," Deut. 6:5). He instructed the people to impress the words of the creed and the law on their children, to talk about them constantly, to tie them on hands and forehead, and to write them on houses and gates (see Deut. 6:7–9).

2. For if the message spoken by angels was binding, and every violation and disobedience received its just punishment . . .

The expression *the word spoken by angels* refers to the law that God gave to the Israelites from Mount Sinai. Although the Old Testament in general and Exodus in particular give no indication that God used angels to convey the law to the people of Israel (Exod. 20:1; Deut. 5:22), Stephen in his address before the Sanhedrin (Acts 7:35–53) and Paul in his Epistle to the Galatians (3:19) mention the instrumentality of angels. There is, of course, a reference to angels, present at Mount Sinai, in the blessing that Moses pronounced on the Israelites before he died (Deut. 33:2).[4] It is conceivable that oral tradition preserved this information for Stephen, Paul, and the writer of Hebrews.

The text indicates that God was the actual speaker, even though he made use of his messengers, the angels. The Word—that is, the Old Testament law—was binding because behind this Word stood God who made a covenant with his people at Mount Sinai. It is God who gives binding validity to his Word, for he is true to his word.[5] He is the covenant-keeping God of his people. The Word of God (Heb. 1:1–2) remains the same and constitutes one revelation that was entrusted to God's people at various and successive

---

2. The author constantly includes himself in the admonitions by using the first person plural verb forms. He recognizes his own frailty and avoids claiming spiritual superiority for himself.

3. The verb *drift away* may be a nautical term.

4. The Septuagint adds the words "on his right hand angels were with him" to Deut. 33:2. Also, the Targum, the Midrash, the Talmud, and liturgical hymns sung in the ancient synagogues reflect the view that angels mediated the law. See Franz Delitzsch, *Commentary on the Epistle to the Hebrews*, 2 vols. (Edinburgh: Clark, 1877), vol. 1, p. 96.

5. Otto Michel, *Der Brief an die Hebräer*, 10th ed. (Göttingen: Vandenhoeck and Ruprecht, 1957), p. 63.

times. That is, the law of God came to the Israelites by angels from Mount Sinai; the gospel was proclaimed by the Lord.

The Old Testament provides numerous instances that show that "every violation and disobedience received its just punishment." Instead of mentioning specific examples from Old Testament history, the author of Hebrews stresses the principle that transgressing the divine law results in righteous retribution. Every violation is evil; every act of disobedience, an affront to God.

3a. How shall we escape if we ignore such a great salvation?

The key word in this part of the sentence, which began with the preceding verse, is "salvation." The term has already been used in 1:14, in which the readers are told that all angels are ministering spirits that serve believers (the heirs of salvation). The value of salvation ought never be underestimated, for its price was the suffering and death of Jesus. He is called the author of salvation who brings many sons to glory (2:10). Therefore, the believer's salvation is immeasurably great.

As verse 2 states, the message of the Old Testament could not and cannot be violated without suffering the consequences. How much more, then (this verse says), ought we to treasure our salvation. If we ever ignore the message concerning our redemption, it is impossible for us to escape God's wrath and subsequent punishment. The more precious the gift, the greater the penalty if it is ignored.

3b. This salvation, which was first announced by the Lord, was confirmed to us by those who heard him.

The focus of chapter 2, like that of chapter 1, is Jesus, the Son of God, who is Lord even over angels. And verses 2–3 are an example of the principle of arguing from the lesser to the greater, a method the author employs repeatedly in his epistle.[6] These verses remind the readers of the teaching about the Son's superiority (1:4–14); the author's method of argument emphasizes the contrast between angels, who mediated the law, and Jesus, who proclaimed the gospel. Angels merely served as God's messengers when they were present at Mount Sinai, but the Lord has come with the message of salvation, which he proclaimed and which his followers have confirmed by the spoken and written Word.

In this verse (3b) the emphasis is on Jesus, whose word is sure. It is true that the angels brought "the message," whereas Jesus brought "salvation." The author, however, employs a figure of speech called metonymy (in which a concept is brought to mind by the use of a word that describes a related idea. An example is Abraham's comment to the rich man who wants to keep his five brothers out of hell: "They have Moses and the Prophets" [Luke

---

6. The hermeneutical principle *a minore ad maius* (from the lesser to the greater) was originally formulated by Rabbi Hillel (died c. A.D. 20) as *qal wa-homer* (light and heavy). The implication is that particulars that are applicable in the case of minor things certainly hold true for major things. See, for example, Heb. 9:13–14.

16:29]. The intent is to say that they have the Old Testament.). Thus the word *salvation* refers to the gospel of salvation proclaimed by Jesus. This single word encompasses the doctrine of redemption in Christ and in a sense refers to the New Testament. Jesus came not to annul the Law and the Prophets, but to fulfill them (Matt. 5:17). The Old and New Testaments are God's written revelation to man, although the fullness of redemption comes to expression in the New. Jesus, whose name is derived from the name *Joshua* (salvation), was first in proclaiming the riches of salvation. From the moment of his public appearance to the day of his ascension, Jesus unfolded the full redemptive revelation of God. He, who came from heaven and therefore is above all, was sent by God to testify "to what he has seen and heard" (John 3:32). His message of full and free salvation "was the true origin of the Gospel."[7]

However, perhaps the readers would say that they did not hear Jesus proclaim his message, for Jesus' earthly ministry lasted only three years, chiefly in Israel. Countless people never had the opportunity to listen to him. The author of Hebrews immediately counters this objection by saying that the message "was confirmed to us by those who heard him." He himself had not had the privilege of being in Jesus' audience; he too had had to listen to those followers who had heard the word spoken by Jesus.

This statement tells us that these followers were faithful witnesses of the words and works of Jesus. They testified as eyewitnesses to the veracity of the events that had happened and the message that had been preached (Luke 1:1–2). And the author indicates that he and the readers of his epistle belong to the second generation of followers; they had not heard the gospel from Jesus himself. This fact rules out the possibility of apostolic authorship of the letter to the Hebrews. Because the author states that he and his readers had to rely on the reports of the original followers of Jesus, it is reasonable to assume that some decades had passed since the ascension of Jesus.

4. God also testified to it by signs, wonders and various miracles, and gifts of the Holy Spirit distributed according to his will.

The writer of the epistle assumes that his readers are quite familiar with the gospel, in either oral or written form, and have a knowledge of the beginning and the development of the Christian church. For that reason he does not elaborate on the proclamation of the gospel by Jesus (1:3) and the apostles and does not specify what the "signs, wonders, various miracles, and gifts of the Holy Spirit" are. He assumes that his readers are well acquainted with the history of the church, specifically the spread of the gospel accompanied by supernatural signs and wonders. His reference to the gifts of the Holy Spirit seems to imply that the readers are aware of those gifts mentioned in I Corinthians 12:4–11.

Signs, wonders, miracles, and gifts of the Spirit supplemented the proc-

---

7. Westcott, *Hebrews,* p. 39.

lamation of God's Word in the first few decades of the rise and the development of the Christian church. The Book of Acts is replete with vivid examples of miracles: Peter healed the crippled man at the temple gate called Beautiful (3:1–10), rebuked Ananias and Sapphira (5:1–11), restored a bedridden paralytic (9:32–35), and raised Dorcas from the dead (9:36–43).

Apparently the words *signs and wonders* were somewhat of a stock phrase referring to either the end of the world (when miracles and portents would take place) or the time of the initial growth of the church. The words *signs* and *wonders* were used as synonyms, especially in Acts, where this phrase *signs and wonders* occurs nine of the twelve times it appears in the New Testament.[8] Moreover, the phrase occurs in the first fifteen chapters of Acts, which relate the early growth and spread of the church (2:19, 22, 43; 4:30; 5:12; 6:8; 7:36; 14:3; 15:12). It is found in Jesus' eschatological discourse (Matt. 24:24; Mark 13:22) and in Jesus' word spoken to the royal official of Capernaum (John 4:48).

The terms *miracles* and *miraculous* describe the supernatural deeds of Jesus as recorded especially in the synoptic Gospels (Matt. 7:22; 11:20, 21, 23; 13:54, 58; 14:2; 24:24; Mark 6:2, 14; 13:22; Luke 10:13; 19:37; 21:25 ["signs"]). Peter also used the expression in his sermon at Pentecost: "Jesus of Nazareth was a man accredited by God to you by miracles, wonders and signs, which God did among you through him, as you yourselves know" (Acts 2:22). The word *miracles* (or *powers*) occurs also in Acts 8:13; 19:11; Romans 8:38; 15:13; I Corinthians 12:10, 28, 29; II Corinthians 12:12; Galatians 3:5; Hebrews 6:5; and I Peter 3:22. Among the gifts of the Holy Spirit listed by Paul in I Corinthians 12:4–11 is the gift of "miraculous powers" (I Cor. 12:10).

And gifts of the Holy Spirit [are] distributed according to his will. It does not matter whether we interpret the phrase *according to his will* as referring to the Holy Spirit or to God the Father. The parallel verse, I Corinthians 12:11, says that the Spirit "gives them [the gifts] to each man, just as he determines." Ultimately God is the one who testifies to the veracity of his Word. If we understand the words *according to his will* to include signs, wonders, and miracles, then God himself is the agent who used these divine powers "for the distinct purpose of sealing the truth of the Gospel."[9]

Practical Considerations in 2:1–4

The author is not an ivory-tower theologian; he reveals the heart of a pastor who cares for the church. He warns the readers and the hearers of his epistle to pay close attention to the Word of God. Effectively he includes himself in the warnings and the exhortation.

This passage is a continuation of Hebrews 1:1–2. In the gospel that is proclaimed

---

8. Bauer, p. 748.
9. John Calvin, *Epistle to the Hebrews* (Grand Rapids: Eerdmans, 1949), p. 56.

by the Lord and confirmed by those who heard him, the full revelation of God has now been made known. The message, whether communicated by the angels or proclaimed by the Lord, constitutes God's revelation to man.

In Hebrews 2:1–3 the writer uses many key words that even in translation show a definite sequence:[10]

we	to us
have heard	who heard him
the message	confirmed by those
spoken	announced
by angels	by the Lord
	salvation

Repeatedly the author warns the reader not to turn away from the living God (3:12) and writes that it is dreadful "to fall into the hands of the living God" (10:31), "for our God is a consuming fire" (12:29). Neglect of the Word of God does not appear to be a great sin; yet the writer, by contrasting this sin with the disobedience of people in the Old Testament era, teaches that ignoring God's Word is a most serious offense. Because God has given us his full revelation in the Old and New Testaments, it is impossible for us to escape the consequences of disobedience or neglect.

Salvation announced by the Lord is far greater than God's law that was announced to the Israelites at Mount Sinai. Christ takes away the veil that covers the hearts of those who read the Old Testament (II Cor. 3:13–16).

Signs, wonders, and various miracles were performed only by Jesus and by the apostles who had received authority to act during the establishment and growth of the early church. The gifts of the Holy Spirit, however, are still with the church today.

Greek Words, Phrases, and Constructions in 2:1–4

Verse 1

περισσοτέρως—a comparative adverb of περισσός, which in itself is already a comparative; in effect, the idea of a double comparative is present.

προσέχειν—the present active infinitive is durative; it needs the words τὸν νοῦν to complete the thought: it is necessary to hold the mind to [a matter].

παραρυῶμεν—the second aorist passive subjunctive, first person plural, παραρρέω (παρά and ῥέω, to flow past). The passive voice may be translated "in order that we may not be carried past" or (intransitively) "in order that we do not drift away." The latter is preferred. The author does not say that the readers are actually drifting away. The aorist indicates that the danger lies before them and may at once overtake them. The possibility of drifting—hence the subjunctive—is not at all imaginary.

---

10. The diagram is from Pierre Auffret, "Note sur la structure littéraire d' HB II. 1–4," *NTS* 25 (1979): 177. Used by permission of Cambridge University Press.

Verse 2

ὁ λόγος—the word λόγος is used for the giving of the law at Mount Sinai; one would expect the term ὁ νόμος (the law). The choice of λόγος to describe the law was made, as Westcott puts it, "to characterise it as the central part of the Old Revelation round which all later words were gathered."[11]

πᾶσα παράβασις καὶ παρακοή—the adjective πᾶσα governs both nouns. παράβασις refers to the overt deed; παρακοή, the underlying motive. παράβασις, because of the -σις ending of the word, shows that the deed itself is in a state of progression. Transgressing the law is a degenerative process. Of course the lawbreaker must take full responsibility for his behavior.

μισθαποδοσίαν—a combination of μισθός (pay, wages) and ἀποδίδωμι (I recompense). The word can mean "reward" (10:35; 11:26) or "punishment" (2:2).

Verse 3

ἐκφευξόμεθα—the future middle active indicative, first person plural, translated in the active voice, expresses finality.

ἀμελήσαντες—the privative ἀ (not) and the verb μέλω (I care for) in the aorist active participial form may be rendered "neglecting, being unconcerned about something, ignoring." The participle denotes condition: if we ignore.

ἀρχήν—the Lord is the originator of the gospel. Jesus Christ is the ἀρχή (Col. 1:18) and the ἀρχηγός (Heb. 2:10; 12:2).

ἐβεβαιώθη—the verb is used twice in the epistle (2:3; 13:9); the adjective βέβαιος (firm, reliable, stable), five times (2:2; 3:6, 14; 6:19; 9:17). The aorist passive shows that an action was done once for all, and that it was done by others.

Verse 4

συνεπιμαρτυροῦντος—the compound consists of the verb μαρτυρέω (I bear witness) and two prepositions, σύν (together) and ἐπί (upon). The present active participle implies continued action. God continues to testify. The genitive case is the genitive absolute construction.

τε καί—the combination of these conjunctions is used to connect two corresponding concepts; in this verse the conjunctions connect two synonyms.

μερισμοῖς—only in Hebrews is this word used, apart from extrabiblical literature. Here it means "distribution"; in 4:12 the word is translated "division." The subject of the distribution—that is, the agent—is the Holy Spirit.

θέλησιν—in the New Testament, Hebrews 2:4 is the only place where this word occurs. The noun θέλημα (will) is the accepted term. The difference is that the -σις ending shows continued action; hence, θέλησις may be translated "willing." The noun ending -μα indicates result, that which is completed or settled.

2. Jesus Is Crowned with Glory and Honor
2:5–9

5. It is not to angels that he has subjected the world to come, about which we are speaking.

---

11. Westcott, *Hebrews*, p. 37.

After inserting a pastoral word of exhortation and admonition, the writer of the epistle continues the theme he set forth in chapter 1: the superiority of the Son. The angels are creatures subject to their Creator, the Son of God. Angels, as the writer said in 1:14, are ministering spirits sent to serve the believers who will inherit salvation. And in the world to come, not the angels, but the Son, will rule.

This reference to the world to come may surprise us, because from our perspective the Bible speaks primarily about the present world. When we think of the world to come, we imagine Jesus' return and the restoration of the earth. The author of Hebrews, however, looks at the salvation that believers will inherit in the world to come and makes it part of the messianic age in which Jesus rules supreme. This age began when Jesus took his seat at the right hand of the Majesty in heaven (1:3). That is what the author is referring to when he says, "about which we are speaking."

Why does the writer teach that the world to come will not be subject to angels? The author and the original readers were accustomed to reading the Old Testament in the Greek translation, the Septuagint. This translation differs from the Hebrew text: "When the Most High gave the nations their inheritance, when he divided all mankind, he set up boundaries for the people according to the number of the sons of Israel" (Deut. 32:8). The Greek translation relies on another Hebrew reading, which was discovered at Qumran.[12] The text in the Septuagint reads, "according to the number of the angels of God."

Moreover, in Hebrews the writer frequently used quotations from the Psalter and from hymns. By this method he reminded his readers of psalms and hymns that they had memorized during childhood. The Song of Moses (Deut. 32), most likely in the wording of the Septuagint, was familiar to them. Because his readers were accustomed to the wording of the Greek texts, the author acquainted them with the truth that the world to come will be subject not to angels but to the Son.

6a. But there is a place where someone has testified.

Verse 5 is a negative declaration that makes the reader ask to whom the world to come will be subject. The author wishes to answer by letting Scripture speak. However, instead of merely introducing the quotation from Psalm 8, he writes, "But there is a place where someone has testified." He does not reveal ignorance, for as a theologian he knows the Scriptures thoroughly. He wants to call attention not to the place from which the quotation is taken or to David who wrote Psalm 8, but to the content and meaning of the citation. For the author, the Word of God is central.

---

12. See P. W. Skehan, "A Fragment of the 'Song of Moses' (Deut. 32) from Qumran," *BASOR* 136 (1954): 12–15. The RSV, JB, and NAB have the reading *sons of God*. The footnote in the JB explains: "The 'sons of God' (or 'of the gods') are the angels, Jb 1:6+, the heavenly courtiers, cf. v. 43 and Ps 29:1; 82:1; 89:6, cf. Tb 5:4+; in this context they are the guardian angels of the nations, cf. Dn 10:13+. But Yahweh himself takes care of Israel, his chosen one, cf. Dt 7:6+. 'God' Greek; Hebr. 'Israel.' "

6b. What is man that you are mindful of him, the son of man that you care for him?

a. In Psalm 8 David first describes the glory of the heavens, the work of God in creation. He looks at the work of God's hands—the heavens, the moon, and the stars, all set in their places.

b. David then compares these heavenly bodies to man, who is nothing but a speck of dust; yet God is mindful of him and cares for him. Not size and volume but worth and value count, for man has been made in the image and likeness of God (Gen. 1:26–27). Man was given authority over the fish in the sea, the birds of the air, and all creatures that move on the ground.

c. Although this fact is not mentioned in the psalm, we know that because of Adam's fall into sin man's condition changed: he became mortal. David does not mention the mortality of man, but merely writes about the seeming insignificance of man (Ps. 8:4). Nonetheless, man's purpose ("to fill the earth and subdue it and to rule over all God's creatures") remains, even after sin entered the world.

d. Furthermore, God commanded Noah and his sons to "be fruitful and increase in number and fill the earth. The fear and dread of you will fall upon all the beasts of the earth and all the birds of the air, upon every creature that moves along the ground, and upon all the fish of the sea" (Gen. 9:1–2). Abraham also was given authority to rule. These names, then, are representative: Adam, the head of the human race; Noah, the head of post-flood humanity; Abraham, the father of many nations. Thus David, aware of the insignificance of man, can nevertheless speak of man's authority to rule God's great creation.

7–8a. "You made him a little lower than the angels; you crowned him with glory and honor and put everything under his feet."

One of the reasons that the author of the epistle chose verses 4–6 of Psalm 8 may have been that in the Septuagint, which he used, the word *angels* appeared. (The Hebrew text, in translation, reads, "You made him a little lower than the heavenly beings [or: than God]," Ps. 8:5). If the readers relied on the Greek translation, they then needed to reexamine the author's statement that the world to come will not be subject to angels, for this trans-lation meant that man had been placed on a lower level than the angelic beings.

The words *you made him a little lower* do indicate that God has brought man from a higher to a lower position. Man shared immortality with the angels until his fall into sin.[13] At the time of the resurrection, man once again will be equal to the angels: he will be immortal (Matt. 22:30).

However, the term *a little* can be understood to mean either degree (man's position in God's creation) or time (for a short while). In Psalm 8:5 (8:6, LXX) the word signifies degree, but in the context of Hebrews 2 the ref-

---

13. John Brown, *An Exposition of Hebrews* (Edinburgh: Banner of Truth Trust, 1961), p. 93.

erence to time is definitely to be preferred. By applying the text to Jesus (Heb. 2:9), the author seems to favor the temporal interpretation of the term *a little*.[14]

This interpretation means that for a little while, man is placed on a lower level than the angels. Does this indicate that angels are superior to man and have been given authority to rule? Nowhere in Scripture do we read that God has honored angels in the way that he has honored man. Only man has been crowned with "glory and honor." This expression points to man's exalted position: king over God's creation.[15]

Everything that God has made is placed "under [man's] feet." In Hebrews 2:5 the verb *to subject* was used; now, in this last line of the psalm citation, the author seeks to convey the thought that all things, including angels, are subject to man. In the world to come, the author intimates, angels do not rule man; on the contrary, they, as "ministering spirits sent to serve those who will inherit salvation" (1:14), are subject to man.

8b. In putting everything under him, God left nothing that is not subject to him. Yet at present we do not see everything subject to him.

> What is man that he should be
> Loved and visited by Thee,
> Raised to an exalted height,
> Crowned with honor in Thy sight!
>   How great Thy Name!
>
> With dominion crowned he stands
> O'er the creatures of Thy hands;
> All to him subjection yield
> In the sea and air and field.
>   How great Thy Name!
>   —*Psalter Hymnal*

Psalm 8 speaks of man's rule over God's creation. At the time man received the mandate to rule all that God had made (Gen. 1:28), nothing was left outside of man's control. He was responsible to God alone. The mandate was given to Adam as the king of creation. He stood at the pinnacle of creation, for God had left nothing that was not subject to him. Such was man before the fall into sin.

Yet verse 8 is, in one sense, ambiguous. Does the writer think of Christ or of man in this particular verse? It is possible that the author meant to say: God put everything under Christ, although at present we do not see every-

---

14. Many translations have adopted this explanation. See, among others, the NASB, NAB, NEB, JB, MLB, GNB, and RSV.
15. The clause "you made him ruler over the works of your hands" (Ps. 8:6) is omitted because of the distinct "probability that the longer reading may be the result of scribal enlargement of the quotation (Ps. 8:7 LXX)." Bruce M. Metzger, *A Textual Commentary on the Greek New Testament* (London and New York: United Bible Societies, 1975), pp. 663–64.

thing subject to Christ. Conversely, some translations of this text show that the emphasis should be on man. They read, "But in fact we do not yet see all things in subjection to man."[16]

Because of the phrase *son of man* in Hebrews 2:6 and the apparent similarity between the quotation from Psalm 110:1 in Hebrews 1:13 ("a footstool for your feet") and the last line of the citation from Psalm 8:6 in Hebrews 2:8 ("and put everything under his feet"), it is possible to interpret 2:8b messianically. However, it is preferable to interpret the psalm citation as referring first to man and second to Christ. B. F. Westcott puts it rather succinctly when he comments on Psalm 8: "It is not, and has never been accounted by the Jews to be, directly Messianic; but as expressing the true destiny of man it finds its accomplishment in the Son of Man and only through Him in man. It offers the ideal (Gen. 1:27–30) which was lost by Adam and then regained and realised by Christ."[17] Certainly Jesus Christ fulfilled the words of Psalm 8, but the original intent of the psalm was to call attention to man's rule in God's creation.

In time, Psalm 8 was interpreted messianically by Paul (I Cor. 15:27; Eph. 1:22). Jesus had quoted the psalm (8:2) when he heard the children in the temple area shout, "Hosanna to the Son of David" (Matt. 21:15–16). And the writer of Hebrews, who was fully acquainted with the Old Testament, may have used Daniel 7:13–14 (with its description of the Son of man who was given authority and dominion) and Luke 22:69 (Jesus' word to the Sanhedrin that "the Son of Man will be seated at the right hand of the mighty God") to make the theological transition from Psalm 110:1 to Psalm 8:4–6.[18]

9. But we see Jesus, who was made a little lower than the angels, now crowned with glory and honor because he suffered death, so that by the grace of God he might taste death for everyone.

a. Jesus fulfilled the message of Psalm 8: "Being found in appearance as a man, he humbled himself and became obedient to death" (Phil. 2:8). Because of his humiliation, especially his death and burial, he was made lower than the angels for a little while. Jesus, then, is portrayed as man, who in effect has accomplished what the first Adam because of sin failed to do. Jesus became man, suffered, died, and was buried. After his humiliation was completed, he was no longer "lower than the angels." His state of exaltation came to full realization when he was crowned with glory and honor; that is, when he ascended to heaven to take his seat at the right side of the Majesty in heaven (Heb. 1:3). Jesus rules supreme as king of the universe!

---

16. See the NEB, GNB, and *Moffatt.*

17. Westcott, *Hebrews,* p. 42.

18. In a perceptive article ("The Son of Man in the Epistle to the Hebrews," *ExpT* 86 [11, 1975]: 328–32) Pauline Giles writes, "The fact that the Son of Man is not used outside the gospels as a title for Jesus, except in the passage under consideration [Heb. 2:6], in Stephen's vision recorded in Acts 7:55, 56, and in the Apocalypse, does not necessarily imply that it was unknown or unimportant." See also Simon J. Kistemaker, *The Psalm Citations in the Epistle to the Hebrews* (Amsterdam: Van Soest, 1961), pp. 81–82.

Because of man's disobedience in Paradise and the curse God placed upon him (Gen. 3:17–19), sinful man could never fully experience the state that is described in Psalm 8. But, says the author of the epistle, we see Jesus. He suffered death and gained the victory. He wears the crown of glory and honor, and rules the universe. In fact, even though the author does not explicitly state it, all things are subject to Christ (see I Cor. 15:27; Eph. 1:22). Jesus said, "All authority in heaven and on earth has been given to me" (Matt. 28:18).

b. Christ is introduced as Son in the first chapter; here he is called Jesus. By using the personal name *Jesus*, the author of the epistle draws attention to the historical setting of Jesus' suffering and death. We assume that the name was vivid in the minds of the first readers of the epistle because of the steady preaching of the gospel. These readers were acquainted with the details of the life, death, resurrection, and ascension of Jesus.

c. The name *Jesus* calls to mind the concept *salvation*. Jesus, the Savior, gained glory and honor for himself and life eternal for his people. The death of Jesus was purposeful in that it provided benefits, as the author writes, "for everyone." This expression does not imply universal salvation, for the writer in the broader context mentions that "many sons" (not all the sons) are brought to glory (2:10) and that they are called Jesus' brothers (2:11–12).

Jesus accomplished the redemption of his people by tasting death, so that his people may live and rule with him. The text does not say that Jesus died, but that he tasted death for everyone. This phrase is not just a Hebraic idiom for the verb *to die,* which also occurs in Matthew 16:28; Mark 9:1; Luke 9:27; and John 8:52.[19] The words *to taste death* are "a graphic expression of the hard and painful reality of dying which is experienced by man and which was suffered also by Jesus."[20]

Jesus experienced death in the greatest degree of bitterness, not as a noble martyr aspiring to a state of holiness, but as the sinless Savior who died to set sinners free from the curse of spiritual death.

d. The phrase *by the grace of God* has been replaced in some manuscripts by the words *apart from God.* The evidence for this latter reading, although not strong, indicates that the phrase may be a reference to Jesus' death on the cross when he cried out, "My God, my God, why have you forsaken me?" (Matt. 27:46).[21] The reading *apart from God* gains support when we see that

---

19. Brown, *Hebrews,* p. 101.

20. Johannes Behm, *TDNT,* vol. 1, p. 677. Also consult Erich Tiedtke, *NIDNTT,* vol. 2, p. 271; SB, vol. 1, p. 751; and Bauer, p. 157.

21. Some translations (JB, NEB) provide an explanatory footnote on this point. And some commentators have chosen the reading *apart from God* as the original text. Among them is Hugh Montefiore, *The Epistle to the Hebrews* (New York and Evanston: Harper and Row, 1964), pp. 58–59. Gunther Zuntz, in his Schweich lectures published in *The Text of the Epistles* (London: Oxford University Press, 1953), pp. 34–35, argues cogently for the adoption of the reading *apart from God.* In his opinion, the accepted reading "yields what can only be called a preposterous sense in stating that Jesus suffered 'through the grace of God.' " Also see J. K.

twelve of the thirty-eight New Testament uses of the Greek word for "apart" occur in the Epistle to the Hebrews. On the other hand, the phrase *by the grace of God*—with slight variations—is common in the Gospels and in the Epistles.

On the basis of the author's intent, if that can be ascertained, we could defend the reading *apart from God*. And we could argue that it is easier to explain how in the original the word *grace* was substituted for the term *apart* than to explain the converse. But the fact that the earliest manuscript, dating back to A.D. 200, has the reading *grace* is significant. A solution to this rather difficult problem is often sought in conjecture. One theory is that a scribe reading Hebrews 2:8 ("God left nothing that is not subject to him") added a note in the margin that said, "nothing apart from God." He did so because of Paul's comment in I Corinthians 15:27 ("For he 'has put everything under his feet.' Now when it says 'everything' has been put under him, it is clear that this does not include God himself, who put everything under Christ"). According to this theory, then, the note eventually became part of the text when the word *grace* was substituted for the term *apart*.[22] Perhaps the conjecture ought to be taken seriously; yet the phrase *by the grace of God* needs interpretation.

e. What is meant by the phrase "tasting death for everyone by the grace of God"? The grace of God is equivalent to the love of God (by analogy to Rom. 5:15; II Cor. 8:9; Gal. 2:20–21; Eph. 1:7; 2:5, 8; Titus 2:11; 3:7). In the words of John Calvin, "The cause of redemption was the infinite love of God towards us, through which it was that he spared not even his own son."[23]

Doctrinal Considerations in 2:5–9

Angels surround the throne of God and constantly behold the glory of the Lord. They are immortal, do not marry, and in a sense are superhuman because of their power and might. Nevertheless, God has given man dominion over the works of his hands. Authority over every living creature in the world was given to man, not to angels.

In Hebrews 1, the author stresses the divinity of Christ; in the second chapter, he emphasizes Christ's humanity. Jesus Christ, in his divine and human natures, was able to fulfill the mandate originally given to Adam. *Christ shall have dominion.*

Because Christ accomplished his work of atonement and therefore claimed the

---

Elliott, "Jesus apart from God (Heb. 2:9)," *ExpT* 83 (11, 1972): 339–41; and R. V. G. Tasker, "The Text of the 'Corpus Paulinum,' " *NTS* 1 (3, 1954–55): 180–91.

22. Metzger, *Textual Commentary,* p. 664. Also consult F. F. Bruce, *The Epistle to the Hebrews,* New International Commentary on the New Testament series (Grand Rapids: Eerdmans, 1964), p. 32, n. 15. Conjectures, of course, have been proposed before. F. Bleek, in *Der Brief an die Hebräer* (Berlin: Dummler, 1828–40), suggested that the Greek text of the original was not very clear, so that a scribe who was copying the word made a mistake by reading one expression for another.

23. Calvin, *Hebrews,* p. 61.

crown of glory and honor, he is the rightful ruler of God's creation. And by his death he has obtained dominion not only for himself but also for all his followers. We have become heirs and coheirs with Christ.

The parallel between Paul's quote from Psalm 8:6 (and his interpretation in I Corinthians 15:27 and Ephesians 1:22) and the citation of Psalm 8:4–6 by the author of Hebrews in 2:6–8 (and his interpretation) is striking. A key term in both I Corinthians 15 and Hebrews 2 is the verb *to subject*. Both writers demonstrate that God is the agent, that Christ has taken the place of the first man, and that time elapsed before Christ's work came to completion.

Greek Words, Phrases, and Constructions in 2:5–9

Verse 5

οἰκουμένην—the form is actually the feminine present passive participle from οἰκέω (I dwell). The form may be completed with the noun γῆ (earth). The term refers to the inhabited world.

μέλλουσαν—the present active participle from μέλλω (I am about to, I am at the point of). As a participle it has the connotation *about to happen*. The participle has already been introduced in Hebrews 1:14.

Verse 6

μιμνῄσκῃ—the form is a second person singular, middle (deponent), indicative of μιμνῄσκομαι (I remind myself, remember, care for, am concerned about).

ἐπισκέπτῃ—a somewhat synonymous term; a second person singular, middle (deponent), indicative of ἐπισκέπτομαι (look at, visit [especially visiting sick people], look after, care for). Here it signifies "God's gracious visitation in bringing salvation."[24] The quotation is punctuated in two ways: as two questions (Bov, Nes-Al, [25th ed.], BF, KJV, RV, and ASV) or as a single question (TR, WH, Nes-Al [26th ed.], RSV, NEB, NIV, MLB, NAB, and JB).

υἱὸς ἀνθρώπου—the term is used here without definite articles, although in the Gospels and Acts it is always with the two definite articles ὁ υἱὸς τοῦ ἀνθρώπου. The phrase does not occur in Paul's epistles. In Revelation 1:13 and 14:14 it is written without the definite articles as a quote from Daniel 7:13.

Verse 8

ὑποτάξαι—the aorist active infinitive shows single occurrence.

τὰ πάντα—the definite article τά makes the earlier πάντα (2:8a) all-inclusive; it encompasses the whole of God's creation.

ἀνυπότακτον—derived from α-privative and ὑποτάσσω (I subject). It is a verbal adjective with a passive interpretation: it is not made subject.

ὑποτεταγμένα—the form is a perfect passive participle in the neuter plural accusative. The perfect points to an act of God with lasting consequences.

---

24. Bauer, p. 298.

Verse 9

τὸ πάθημα τοῦ θανάτου—the noun with the -μα ending constitutes the result of an action—in this case, suffering. It is debatable whether the genitive should be taken subjectively (suffering that is characteristic of death) or objectively (suffering that leads to death).

παντός—the adjective in the genitive singular can either be masculine (everyone) or neuter (everything). The context seems to favor the masculine usage.

χάριτι θεοῦ—the manuscript evidence is early and weighty, whereas the evidence for the reading χωρὶς θεοῦ is late and somewhat scanty—three minuscules and the testimony of church fathers.

3. Jesus and His Brothers
2:10–13

10. In bringing many sons to glory, it was fitting that God, for whom and through whom everything exists, should make the author of their salvation perfect through suffering.

In Hebrews 2:9 the author briefly states that Jesus suffered the agony of death—he tasted death—for everyone. In the next verse he explains the term *everyone* by designating those who are saved as "many sons" and by referring to Jesus as "the author of their salvation." The Son suffered the pains of death, which the sons should have experienced, and was crowned with glory and honor afterward. Because of the redemptive work of the Son, the sons are led into the glory with which the Son is crowned.

a. The subject in verse 10 is God, for whom and through whom everything exists. The wording obviously echoes Romans 11:36, where Paul in a doxology writes, "For from him and through him and to him are all things." The honor, however, is shared with Jesus, as is evident from I Corinthians 8:6: "Yet for us there is but one God, the Father, from whom all things came and for whom we live; and there is but one Lord, Jesus Christ, through whom all things came and through whom we live."[25] (See also Col. 1:16–17.)

b. Jesus is presented as "the author of their [the sons'] salvation." He is actually going ahead of them because he is the pioneer, the founder of salvation.[26] In Hebrews 12:2 Jesus is called "the author and perfecter of our faith." God made him pass through gruesome suffering to bring about perfection. It was God's will that his Son had to suffer in order to effect the salvation of many sons. And when the Son completed his suffering, he became the founder of their salvation. He received the appointment to lead

---

25. Philip Edgcumbe Hughes, R. C. H. Lenski, Ceslaus Spicq, and Westcott directly and indirectly quote or borrow from Thomas Aquinas, who describes God as the efficient cause and the final cause of all things. Says Hughes, "All creation flows from God and all creation flows to God." *Commentary on the Epistle to the Hebrews* (Grand Rapids: Eerdmans, 1977), p. 98.

26. Hans Bietenhard, *NIDNTT*, vol. 1, p. 168; Gerhard Delling, *TDNT*, vol. 1, p. 488. Translations vary: "their leader in the work of salvation" (NAB); "the leader who would take them to their salvation" (JB); "the leader who delivers them" (NEB); "the pioneer of their salvation" (RSV); and "the Leader of their salvation" (MLB).

the elect out of a life of slavery in sin to a life of eternal happiness in which they are considered sons and heirs with Christ.

c. The sequence in Hebrews 2:10 presents a transposition of four concepts, which can be put in the following scheme:[27]

many sons to glory	the author's suffering
and	and
their salvation	his perfection

But how can Jesus be made perfect? He is without sin or blemish. The word *perfect* must be understood to mean achieving the highest goal. In the context of the Epistle to the Hebrews, the term *to make perfect* signifies that Jesus removed the sins of his people from the presence of God and thus by his sacrificial death on the cross consecrated the "many sons." The perfection of Jesus, therefore, points to the work of salvation he performed on behalf of his people.[28] In 10:14, for example, the author of the epistle writes that "by one sacrifice he has made perfect forever those who are being made holy."

11. Both the one who makes men holy and those who are made holy are of the same family. So Jesus is not ashamed to call them brothers.

This verse constitutes an explanation of the preceding thought, in that the work of perfecting the "many sons" is a work of holiness. This work of holiness is performed by and through the members of God's family: Jesus, the one who makes men holy, and those who are made holy. This verse clearly teaches the *humanity* of Jesus (by implying his identification with the human race) and alludes to his *divinity* (by noting his sanctifying work).

Jesus is the one who makes men holy, and he continues to do so until the end of time. He is the one who removes the sin of the world (John 1:29) and constantly serves as high priest on behalf of his people. The sanctification of his people is not an isolated event but a lifelong process. The path of sanctification lies in obedience to doing God's will, and that obedience is out of gratitude. But, we may ask, can holy people do God's will perfectly? A sixteenth-century catechism states, "No. In this life even the holiest have only a small beginning of this obedience."[29] If we fall into sin, our holiness is soiled. However, there is no need to stay unclean, for Jesus Christ, who shares our human nature, stands ready to cleanse us and make us holy.

The bond of humanity that links the one who makes holy to those who are made holy is further defined by the word *brothers*. In this holy family the spiritual relationship supersedes the human aspect. Jesus died for his

27. John Albert Bengel, *Gnomon of the New Testament,* ed. Andrew R. Fausset, 7th ed., 5 vols. (Edinburgh: Clark, 1877), vol. 4, p. 360.
28. The group of words related to the verb *perfect* occurs in the Epistle to the Hebrews rather frequently (nineteen times). The verb *to make perfect* is used nine times in this epistle (2:10; 5:9; 7:19, 28; 9:9; 10:1, 14; 11:40; 12:23) out of twenty-four occurrences in the entire New Testament.
29. Heidelberg Catechism, answer 114.

own people; he redeemed them from the curse of sin; he forgives their sins; he leads them to glory; and, because of his sacrificial work, he is not ashamed to give them the name *brothers*. The implication is that we, in turn, may call Jesus our brother. What a privilege to be called brothers of the Son of God! He who is seated at the right hand of the Majesty in heaven condescends to sinful man and unashamedly calls him brother (Matt. 28:10; John 20:17).

12. He says,

> **"I will declare your name to my brothers;**
> **in the presence of the congregation I will**
> **sing your praises."**

To prove his bold assertion that Jesus calls his followers *brothers,* the author gleans a verse from the messianic twenty-second psalm. Interestingly, he puts the words of this particular text on the lips of Jesus and introduces the quotation with the words *he says.* In chapter 1 of Hebrews, God is the speaker; in chapter 2 Jesus utters verses from Psalm 22:22 and Isaiah 8:17–18 (quoted in v. 13) with divine authority.

The Messiah proclaims the name of his brothers in the midst of the congregation—that is, in the church. By calling attention to the place in which he will testify, the Messiah limits the appellation *brothers* to those who spiritually make up the church, the body of believers. The psalmist exhorts those who fear the Lord to praise him (Ps. 22:23), for he says:

> [The Lord] has not despised or disdained
> the suffering of the afflicted one;
> he has not hidden his face from him
> but has listened to his cry for help. [Ps. 22:24]

The Messiah is speaking not only in the first part of Psalm 22, well known because of Jesus' words spoken on the cross, but also in the last part of the psalm. This Scripture is fulfilled by the Christ, who rejoices in the midst of his people, the church, of which he is the head. He defends his brothers, upholds them, and listens to their prayers. They can put their trust in him.

13. And again,

> **"I will put my trust in him."**

And again he says,

> **"Here am I, and the children God has given me."**

At this point in the discussion, the writer turns to the prophecy of Isaiah and takes two lines from Isaiah 8:17–18. "I will put my trust in him" is the last part of verse 17; "here am I, and the children God has given me" forms the first portion of verse 18. Isaiah testifies that he "will wait for the Lord, who is hiding his face from the house of Jacob." And the children God has given him "are signs and symbols in Israel from the LORD Almighty, who dwells on Mount Zion."

The context of these two citations is quite important. Chapters 7, 8, and 9 of Isaiah are decidedly messianic in tenor. For example, the name *Immanuel* occurs in Isaiah 7:14 and 8:8, 10. And the birth of a Son is mentioned in Isaiah 7:14–17 and 8:1–4.

Also, the sentence "I will put my trust in him" was incorporated into psalm and spiritual song (II Sam. 22:3; Ps. 18:2; Isa. 12:2) and constituted part of the heritage of God's people.

Further, the words of the prophet Isaiah become the words of Christ. The prophet and the Messiah say that they put their trust in God; the prophet and his children, as well as Christ and his brothers, stand before God. (The children the Lord gave Isaiah are the remnant of faithful Israel. The brothers of Jesus form the church.) As Isaiah was surrounded by his God-fearing countrymen, so Christ is in the midst of his people. And as the faithful remnant in Isaiah's day were God's sign and symbol in a world of unbelief, so the church today functions as lightbearer in a dark and sinful world. Thomas Benson Pollock prayed:

> Jesus, with thy Church abide;
> Be her Savior, Lord and Guide,
> While on earth her faith is tried:
> We beseech Thee, hear us.
>
> May her lamp of truth be bright;
> Bid her bear aloft its light
> Through the realms of pagan night:
> We beseech Thee, hear us.

Doctrinal Considerations in 2:10–13

Throughout chapter 2 God is the primary subject: he testified (2:4); he left nothing that is not subject to man (2:8); and he makes perfect the author of salvation (2:10).

The author of salvation is Jesus, crowned with honor and glory because of his suffering and death on behalf of his people.

The world of unbelief rejects the path of suffering and death that Jesus undertook, but in the sight of God Jesus' course of action was most fitting.

Because of his sacrificial death on the cross, Jesus leads his people to glory and identifies himself with them. Together they form the family of God.

Greek Words, Phrases, and Constructions in 2:10–13

Verse 10

ἔπρεπεν—the imperfect active indicative, third person singular impersonal use of πρέπω expresses that which is proper and acceptable. The same form occurs in Hebrews 7:26. Consult Matthew 3:15; I Corinthians 11:13; Ephesians 5:3; I Timothy 2:10; and Titus 2:1 for other forms and usages.

ἀγαγόντα—the participle, in the aorist active accusative singular from ἄγω (I lead, bring), agrees with the noun τὸν ἀρχηγόν. The aorist is ingressive.

τὸν ἀρχηγόν—as a compound (ἀρχή and ἄγω), the term is related to the preced-

73

ing participle. Gerhard Delling claims that ἀϱχηγός means the same thing as τελειωτής and refers to the "crucifixion as the causative presupposition of πίστις."[30]

Verse 11

ὁ ἁγιάζων—the present tense of this participle in the active voice illustrates the work that Jesus progressively performs. The present passive participle ἁγιαζόμενοι shows that sanctification is a process whose implied agent is Jesus and whose subjects are the believers.

Verse 12

ἐκκλησίας—since the word ἐκκλησία is part of the quotation from Psalm 22:22, the author of Hebrews employs this term instead of the more familiar συναγωγή. In the Septuagint, including the Apocrypha, the word ἐκκλησία occurs 100 times; by contrast, συναγωγή, 225 times.[31]

Verse 13

πεποιθώς—the second perfect active participle in conjunction with ἔσομαι forms a future periphrastic construction.

---

4. Jesus Is like His Brothers
2:14–18

14. Since the children have flesh and blood, he too shared in their humanity so that by his death he might destroy him who holds the power of death—that is, the devil— 15. and free those who all their lives were held in slavery by their fear of death.

In an earlier verse (2:11) the author of Hebrews has demonstrated that Jesus and his people belong to the same family; the implication is that Jesus has assumed our human nature.

Now the author indicates that the necessity of delivering his people from their enemies, death and Satan, meant that Jesus had to become man. He had to have a body of flesh and blood and had to be fully human in order to set his people free. Delivering his followers from the curse of sin and the clutches of the devil demanded nothing short of taking the place of those whom God had given him but who stood condemned because of their sin.

> Bearing shame and scoffing rude,
> In my place condemned He stood,
> Sealed my pardon with His blood;
> Hallelujah! What a Savior!
> —Philip P. Bliss

---

30. *TDNT,* vol. 1, p. 488, n. 4.
31. Lothar Coenen, *NIDNTT,* vol. 1, p. 292.

a. Because Jesus is divine, it would have been impossible for him to deliver us from sin unless he himself shared in our humanity. Jesus shared our human nature and, although he was sinless, lived a full life with its weaknesses, ills, desires, needs, and temptations (Heb. 4:15).

Jesus became fully human in such a manner that he is related to us. He is our blood relative. In the original Greek the word order is reversed ("blood and flesh," rather than "flesh and blood"); possibly this is an idiom. But the prominence of the word *blood* indicates that the ties that bind us are blood ties. We can say of Jesus that he is one of us. He is our brother.

b. God the Father desired that Jesus be born of the Virgin Mary, ordained that he should suffer and die, and set him free from the bondage of death by raising him from the dead (Acts 2:23–24). Thus God expressed his love toward his people by delivering his own Son to die a shameful death. And the Son willingly suffered and died in humiliation on behalf of his brothers and sisters, the members of the household of God.

c. The result of Christ's death is twofold: he conquered Satan and set his people free from the fear of death. Satan desired the destruction of God's creation in general and man in particular. After the fall Satan had the power of death over Adam and his descendants and used death as a weapon against us. He had the privilege of coming before God in heaven to accuse the believers (see Zech. 3:1–2), and stood ready to execute the verdict pronounced upon the guilty and to destroy man, who was condemned to death. He, the murderer from the beginning (John 8:44), desired man's death in the fullest sense of the word: physical death and spiritual death (separation from God). He wanted to serve as the angel of death by wielding the power of death.

However, not Satan but God pronounced the curse of death on the human race when Adam and Eve fell into sin. And Satan, who is an angel created by God, is a servant of God. Without permission from God, Satan is unable to do anything.

Jesus, the Son of God, was present at creation, for through him God made the universe (Heb. 1:2). He alone would be able to destroy Satan, and he could do this by means of his death on the cross. That is, Jesus defeated Satan by using the weapon of death. Jesus paid the penalty of sin by giving his life and set us free from the curse of death. And by paying this penalty for us, Jesus took the weapon of death out of Satan's hands. Jesus took away the fear of death.

d. Of course, all men die, including believers, so that Satan still appears to rule supreme. However, the curse of God no longer rests upon the family of God, for Jesus removed it. All those who are his people no longer fear death, for they are free from the bondage of death. We know that nothing, not even death, can "separate us from the love of God that is in Christ Jesus our Lord" (Rom. 8:38–39). By contrast, all those who do not know Jesus as their Lord and Savior face eternal death and thus are eternally held in slavery. Only Jesus sets man free from this slavery.

Since the death of Jesus on Calvary's cross, death has lost its power and its effect. Through death the Christian enters not hell but heaven. And because Jesus' human body was resurrected, the believer's body also shall come forth from the grave in the last day. The believer knows the words of Jesus: "I was dead, and behold I am alive for ever and ever! And I hold the keys of death and Hades" (Rev. 1:18).

16. For surely it is not angels he helps, but Abraham's descendants.

The author of Hebrews is bringing his discourse on Jesus' superiority to angels to a conclusion. He does so by appealing to a self-evident truth: Jesus redeems not angels but the spiritual descendants of the father of believers, Abraham. The name *Abraham* obviously must be understood to mean that all those who put their faith in Jesus are Abraham's descendants.

The translations of this verse vary because of the main verb in the sentence. For example, the King James Version reads, "For verily he took not on him the nature of angels; but he took on him the seed of Abraham." And the Revised Standard Version says, "For surely it is not with angels that he is concerned but with the descendants of Abraham."[32] The New International Version, on the other hand, translates, "For surely it is not angels he helps, but Abraham's descendants."

If Jesus had been an angel, he would be expected to come to the aid of fellow angels. But he helps men instead, thereby giving ample proof of his identity.[33] As the God-man he has come to help Abraham's spiritual children because he has identified himself with them. Jesus is the author not of the salvation of angels, but of the salvation of Abraham's descendants. And they receive his help.

17. For this reason he had to be made like his brothers in every way, in order that he might become a merciful and faithful high priest in service to God, and that he might make atonement for the sins of the people.

In this verse the writer of Hebrews explains the necessity of Christ's identification with man. In order to be of help to sinful man, Jesus had to become like his brothers in all but one way: he was sinless. Full identification was necessary; he was under divine obligation to become like his brothers. In a sense the author of Hebrews repeats himself, for earlier in chapter 2 he has introduced the thought of identity (vv. 9, 14, 15). But now he shows that Jesus had to become man in order to assume his role as a merciful and faithful high priest.

In this verse the term *high priest* occurs for the first time in Hebrews. In no other book of the New Testament is Jesus described as high priest. Only in Hebrews is the doctrine of Jesus' high priesthood fully developed (2:17–18;

---

32. Other versions read "takes to himself" (NEB) or "took to himself" (JB). The NASB broke rank and translated, "For assuredly He does not give help to angels, but He gives help to the seed of Abraham." In Sir. 4:11 the same Greek verb is used: "Wisdom exalts her sons and gives help to those who seek her" (RSV).

33. Montefiore, *Hebrews,* p. 66.

3:1; 4:14–16; 5:1–10; 6:20; 7:14–19, 26–28; 8:1–6; 9:11–28; 10). The writer calls attention to two of Jesus' high-priestly characteristics: mercy and faithfulness (see 7:26 for additional characteristics).[34]

a. The adjective *merciful* occurs only twice in the New Testament: once in the Beatitudes ("Blessed are the merciful," Matt. 5:7) and once in Hebrews 2:17. In Matthew we read that mercy is to be expressed from man to man; those who practice mercy are promised the mercy of God. In Hebrews 2:17, Jesus is depicted as the high priest who represents man before God, averts God's wrath, heals the brokenhearted, lifts up the fallen, and ministers to the needs of his people.

b. Whereas mercy is directed to man, faithfulness is directed to God. Jesus is a faithful high priest in service to God. Westcott aptly remarks that the word *faithful* actually has two meanings: a person is faithful in performing his duties and is trustworthy toward persons who rely on him.[35] Usually the two meanings merge.

After noting these two characteristics of Christ's high priesthood, the author mentions the purpose of Christ's high priesthood: he makes atonement for his people.[36] The term *atonement* is a theological one with profound meaning; it is often explained by other, even more difficult, terms such as "propitiation" and "expiation."

In the context of Hebrews the word *atonement* means that Jesus as high priest brought peace between God and man. God's wrath was directed toward man because of his sin, and man because of sin was alienated from God. Jesus became high priest. And as the high priest once a year on the Day of Atonement entered the Holy of Holies, he sprinkled blood—first for himself and then for the people—to remove (literally, to cover) sin. In the same way, Jesus offered himself so that the shedding of his blood covered our sins. Thus we might be acquitted, forgiven, and restored. Jesus brought God and man together in inexpressible harmony. In the words of Paul, "Since we have been justified through faith, we have peace with God through our Lord Jesus Christ" (Rom. 5:1).

The marvel of it all is that in the act of reconciliation God himself took the initiative. God, although angry because of man's sin, appointed his Son to become high priest and sacrifice in order to remove sin by his death on the cross. Thus, through Christ the relationship between God and man is restored. "For if, when we were God's enemies, we were reconciled to him through the death of his Son, how much more, having been reconciled, shall we be saved through his life!" (Rom. 5:10).

---

34. R. C. H. Lenski, following Martin Luther, translates the adjective *merciful* as a predicate and the word *faithful* as an attributive. "Hence he was obliged in all respects to be made like his brothers in order to be merciful and a faithful High Priest. . . ." *The Interpretation of the Epistle to the Hebrews and of the Epistle to James* (Columbus: Wartburg, 1946), p. 92.

35. Westcott, *Hebrews*, p. 57.

36. A study on the word *atonement* by C. H. Dodd (*JTS* 32 [1931]: 352–60) elicited strong reactions from Leon Morris (*ExpT* 62 [1951]: 227–33) and R. R. Nicole (*WTJ* 17 [1955]: 117–57).

18. Because he himself suffered when he was tempted, he is able to help those who are being tempted.

That Jesus' humanity is genuine can be demonstrated, says the author of Hebrews, by the fact that Christ was tempted. He personally experienced the power of sin when Satan confronted him and when the weaknesses of our human nature became evident. Jesus experienced hunger when he was tempted by Satan in the wilderness, thirst when he asked the woman at Jacob's well for water, weariness when he slept while the storm raged on the Sea of Galilee, and sorrow when he wept at the grave of Lazarus.

As high priest, through his sacrificial work, Jesus removed the curse of God that rested on man. Because of the forgiveness of sin, God's love flows freely to the redeemed, and Jesus stands ready to help. Those who are being tempted may experience the active support of Jesus. They can expect nothing short of perfect understanding from Jesus, because he himself suffered when he was tempted.

Of course, Jesus did not share with us the experience of sin; instead, because of his sinlessness, Jesus fully experienced the intensity of temptation. He is able and willing to help us oppose the power of sin and temptation. As he said to the sinful woman in the house of Simon the Pharisee, "Your sins are forgiven. . . . Go in peace" (Luke 7:48, 50), so also Jesus shows his mercy, peace, and love to us. He is our sympathetic High Priest.

Doctrinal Considerations in 2:14–18

"Now the prince of this world will be driven out," said Jesus when he predicted his death after his triumphal entry into Jerusalem on Palm Sunday (John 12:31).

Jesus became fully human like his brothers, yet remained the Son of God. Athanasius formulated this doctrine in creedal form:

> 30. For the right faith is that we believe and confess that our Lord Jesus Christ, the Son of God, is God and man.
> 31. God of the substance of the Father, begotten before the worlds; and man of the substance of his mother, born in the world.
> 32. Perfect God and perfect man, of a reasonable soul and human flesh subsisting.
> 33. Equal to the Father as touching his Godhead, and inferior to the Father as touching his manhood.
> 34. Who, although he is God and man, yet he is not two, but one Christ.

The writer of Hebrews develops progressively the doctrine of Christ's high priesthood.[37] In 2:17 we read that Jesus "had to be made like his brothers in every way, in order that he might *become* a merciful and faithful high priest" (italics added). In 5:10 the writer says that once Jesus was made perfect, he "was *designated* by God to be high priest" (italics added). And after Jesus had entered the inner sanctuary, "he . . . *bec[a]me* a high priest forever" (6:20; italics added).

---

37. Bengel, *Gnomon*, vol. 4, pp. 367–68.

Greek Words, Phrases, and Constructions in 2:14–18

Verse 14

κεκοινώνηκεν—the perfect active indicative, third person singular, from κοινωνέω (I share, take part, contribute) shows the continued sharing of flesh and blood by every generation from the days of Adam until the present.

παραπλησίως—the form of this adverb occurs only once in the New Testament, although it is frequently used in other literature. It is translated "similarly," and "it is used in situations where no differentiation is intended."[38]

μετέσχεν—the aorist active indicative, third person singular, of μετέχω (I share, participate) is synonymous with κοινωνέω. The aorist points to a definite time in history. It is followed by the partitive genitive τῶν αὐτῶν. Also see Hebrews 7:13.

καταργήσῃ—the verb in the aorist active subjunctive, third person singular, conveys the meaning *destroy, abolish, bring to an end*. The subjunctive is expressed in a purpose clause introduced by ἵνα; the aorist indicates a single occurrence. See the parallel verses of I Corinthians 15:26; II Thessalonians 2:8; and II Timothy 1:10.

Verse 15

ἀπαλλάξῃ—the aorist active subjunctive, third person singular of ἀπαλλάσσω (I free, release) is a compound verb expressing an intensive meaning—the verb ἀλλάσσω means "I change."

Verse 16

ἐπιλαμβάνεται—the compound verb has a directive sense: ἐπί points to the goal in giving aid and λαμβάνομαι denotes the act of receiving support. The verb is translated "to take hold of, grasp, catch," but in a figurative sense it means "to be concerned with, take an interest in, help." It is used of God, who takes the hand of his people in order to help them.[39]

Verse 17

ὅθεν—this adverb occurs fifteen times in the New Testament, six of which are in Hebrews (2:17; 3:1; 7:25; 8:3; 9:18; 11:19). The word is a compound of the neuter relative pronoun referring to place or fact and the suffix -θεν, which signifies motion away from a place. It is translated "for this reason"; that is, "from the available information the following conclusion is drawn."

ὤφειλεν—the imperfect active indicative, third person singular, of ὀφείλω (I owe, must, ought) is followed by the aorist passive infinitive ὁμοιωθῆναι (to be made like). The word signifies that because of law, duty, custom, or convention, an obligation is placed on a person to attend to a matter under consideration. A distinction, then, between ὀφείλω and δεῖ is that the first expresses obligation; the second, necessity.

ἱλάσκεσθαι—the present tense of the infinitive indicates that the work of atoning

---

38. Bauer, p. 621.
39. Delling, in *TDNT,* vol. 4, p. 9, says that the verb in Heb. 2:16 means "to draw someone to oneself to help," and thus to take him into the fellowship of one's own destiny.

is a continuing activity. Man is being reconciled to God. Says Westcott, "The love of God is the same throughout; but He 'cannot' in virtue of His very nature welcome the impenitent and sinful: and more than this, He 'cannot' treat sin as if it were not sin."[40]

τοῦ λαοῦ—contrasted with τὸ ἔθνος (the nation, the people), the word generally refers to God's elect people.

Verse 18

πέπονθεν—from the verb πάσχω (I suffer), the perfect active indicative, third person singular, brings out the lasting effect of Jesus' suffering.

πειρασθείς—the author of Hebrews has a penchant for using participles describing Jesus and his people (see 2:11). The aorist passive, nominative masculine singular πειρασθείς points to the earthly ministry of Jesus in general and to his temptation in the desert in particular. The present passive πειραζομένοις (dative plural), on the other hand, points to the continued and varied temptations God's people endure.

βοηθῆσαι—in light of the immediate context (2:16), the aorist infinitive of βοηθέω (I help, come to the aid of) is a synonym of ἐπιλαμβάνομαι.

Summary of Chapter 2

The Epistle to the Hebrews is characterized by teaching and pastoral admonition—the writer is a teacher and a pastor. As a spiritual overseer he constantly admonishes his readers to listen attentively and obediently to God's Word. He shows a genuine concern for the spiritual well-being of the recipients of his letter.

One of those readers perhaps asked if Jesus, the divine Son of God, is unacquainted with human nature. The answer is given in the form of a lengthy quotation from Psalm 8. Jesus "was made a little lower than the angels" but now, because of his death, resurrection, and ascension, is "crowned with glory and honor." Jesus fulfilled the words of Psalm 8 and through this fulfillment has obtained salvation for his people. No angel could have fulfilled the task that Jesus accomplished by "tast[ing] death for everyone." He is one with his brothers because together they constitute the family of God. Jesus, the Son of God, is truly human and fully identifies with his brothers. Because of this identity, Jesus has "become a merciful and faithful high priest in service to God." He sets his people free from sin and stands with them in their times of trial and temptation. Jesus sympathetically and at the same time intimately understands the problems believers face.

---

40. B. F. Westcott, *The Epistles of Saint John* (Grand Rapids: Eerdmans, 1966), p. 87.

3

Jesus' Superiority to Moses, *part 1*

3:1–19

Outline

3 1 Therefore, holy brothers, who share in the heavenly calling, fix your thoughts on Jesus, the apostle and high priest whom we confess.   2 He was faithful to the one who appointed him, just as Moses was faithful in all God's house.   3 Jesus has been found worthy of greater honor than Moses, just as the builder of a house has greater honor than the house itself.   4 For every house is built by someone, but God is the builder of everything.   5 Moses was faithful as a servant in all God's house, testifying to what would be said in the future.   6 But Christ is faithful as a son over God's house. And we are his house, if we hold on to our courage and the hope of which we boast.

A. A Comparison of Jesus and Moses
3:1–6

In the span of two chapters, the author of Hebrews has demonstrated from the pages of the Old Testament that Jesus is superior to angels. Someone among the Hebrews who received the epistle might ask whether Jesus is greater than Moses. The Jews thought that no one was greater than Moses, for he gave the people of Israel two tablets of stone on which God had written the law (Exod. 34). The angels, by contrast, were only intermediaries at the time the law was given (Acts 7:38, 53).

In the preceding chapter the writer described Jesus as high priest (Heb. 2:17) but did not compare him with Aaron. The comparison between Jesus and Moses in this chapter in a sense parallels the comparison of Jesus and the angels.

1. Therefore, holy brothers, who share in the heavenly calling, fix your thoughts on Jesus, the apostle and high priest whom we confess.

The word *therefore* links chapter 3 to the immediately preceding discourse on the unity Jesus has with his brothers. Together they belong to the family of God. The brothers are holy because they are made holy by Jesus (Heb. 2:11), and on that account Jesus is not ashamed to call them brothers.

In 3:1 these people are, for the first time in Hebrews, specifically addressed as "holy brothers." The adjective *holy* reveals that the brothers have been sanctified and may enter the presence of God, for sin has been removed through the suffering and death of Jesus. The term *brothers* also applies to the author of Hebrews. In fact, he is one of them in the family of God (Heb. 3:12; 10:19; 13:22).

The recipients of the epistle are also sharers in the heavenly calling. This is a unique calling, a heavenly invitation to enter the kingdom of God (Rom.

11:29; Eph. 1:18; 4:1, 4; Phil. 3:14; II Thess. 1:11; II Tim. 1:9; II Peter 1:10).

The privilege of being called by God is coupled with a command. The charge is not difficult and complicated, and the brothers are able to comply with it. They are asked to fix their thoughts on Jesus and to do this diligently. Apparently the readers of the epistle are not doing this at the moment, for they seem to drift away. Already in Hebrews 2:1 the writer exhorts them to "pay more careful attention" to the gospel they have heard, for knowledge about Jesus is essential. As the author prepares to teach about Jesus, he does not call Jesus the Christ, the Son of God, the Son of man, or Lord and Savior, but calls him the apostle and high priest. Interestingly, the word *apostle* appears first in this verse, even though we would have expected the expression *high priest* to have precedence because of its use in Hebrews 2:17.

The term *apostle* refers to the one whom God has sent—a concept repeatedly used by the evangelist John in his Gospel (3:17, 34; 5:36–38; 6:29, 57; 7:29; 8:42; 10:36; 11:42; 17:3) and even in his first epistle (I John 4:10). The word *apostle* has the deeper meaning of ambassador. The apostle is not merely sent: he is empowered with the authority of the one who sends him.[1] Furthermore, he can and may speak only the words his superior gives him. He is forbidden to utter his own opinions when they are at variance with those of the one who sends him. Jesus, then, proclaims the very Word of God. He brings the gospel, the good news.

Whereas the term *apostle* relates by comparison to Moses, the designation *high priest* is reminiscent of Aaron. The separate functions of these two brothers are combined and are fulfilled in the one person of Jesus. And in his work Jesus is greater than both Moses and Aaron.

The congregation that received the author's epistle confessed the name of Jesus. I do not think that the church of that time had a standard confession apart from the saying *Jesus is Lord* (I Cor. 12:3) and a few hymns (Phil. 2:6–11; I Tim. 3:16; II Tim. 2:11–13). After all, the author of Hebrews instructs his readers about the apostleship and high priesthood of Jesus. In subsequent years, however, a carefully worded confession may have begun to circulate in the early churches.

2. He was faithful to the one who appointed him, just as Moses was faithful in all God's house.

God the Father appointed Jesus to be the mediator between God and man and to bring the good news of salvation to sinful humanity. God appointed him to be apostle and high priest and expected him to faithfully execute his task, which Jesus did.

---

1. The Hebrew term *shaliach* is an equivalent of the Greek *apostolos*. See Otto Michel, *Der Brief an die Hebräer*, 10th ed. (Göttingen: Vandenhoeck and Ruprecht, 1957), p. 94; Philip Edgcumbe Hughes, *Commentary on the Epistle to the Hebrews* (Grand Rapids: Eerdmans, 1977), p. 127; Ceslaus Spicq, *L'Epître aux Hébreux*, 3d ed., 2 vols. (Paris: Gabalda, 1953), vol. 2, p. 64; Karl Heinrich Rengstorf, *TDNT*, vol. 1, pp. 414–16; Erich von Eicken and Helgo Lindner, *NIDNTT*, vol. 1, pp. 126–28.

The translation employs the past tense, "he *was* faithful" (italics added). However, the author, by using a present participle in the original, intimates that the work God appointed Jesus to do did not terminate when his earthly task was complete, but continues in heaven. Jesus continues to be faithful in his high-priestly work of intercession and in preparing a place for his people (John 14:3). He remains faithful in loving and in perfecting the church of which he is the head. Paul states this eloquently: "In him the whole building is joined together and rises to become a holy temple in the Lord" (Eph. 2:21).

However, the first recipients of the epistle perhaps asked, "Was not Moses faithful to God?" They knew the words God spoke to Aaron and Miriam in the presence of Moses:

> When a prophet of the LORD is among you,
> I reveal myself to him in visions,
> I speak to him in dreams.
> But this is not true of my servant Moses;
> he is faithful in all my house. [Num. 12:6–7]

Observe this parallel:

> Jesus was faithful to God who appointed him
> Moses was faithful to God in all his house[2]

The parallelism takes on added meaning when we interpret the word *house* not literally but figuratively. The term *house* is a synonym for the family of God. Moses ministered faithfully to the church of God in the desert during the forty-year journey. Then what is the difference between Jesus and Moses? That question the writer answers in the next verse.

3. Jesus has been found worthy of greater honor than Moses, just as the builder of a house has greater honor than the house itself.

In this verse the author returns his attention to Jesus and deems him worthy of greater honor than Moses. Certainly both Jesus and Moses have been faithful to God, but the difference between the two goes beyond the virtue of faithfulness. Already the writer has called Jesus apostle and high priest; Moses never filled this twofold office. But that point is not under discussion at the moment. To demonstrate this truth the writer uses an illustration from the building trade, an example whose validity everyone acknowledges.

As we know, the builder of a house has greater honor than the house itself has. When a house or a building is erected, people may admire the

---

2. A number of manuscripts (among them papyri documents, Codex Vaticanus, and the Coptic versions) omit the word *all*. Conversely, leading manuscripts (including Codices Sinaiticus, Alexandrinus, Ephraemi, and Bezae, along with the Vulgate, some Old Latin versions, and all the Syriac versions) attest to the reading *all*. Understandably, a few of the more recent translations do not include the adjective *all*, either: see the RSV, NEB, and GNB. Other translations include the adjective: see the NAB, JB, NIV, and NASB.

beauty of the structure and speak words of praise, but they reserve tribute and honor for the architect and for the builder. The architect and the builder stand, figuratively, above the structure they have created. They stand on a different level. By analogy, the author says, God is the architect; Jesus is the builder of God's house; Moses is a servant in God's house.

By making the comparison between Jesus and Moses the author does not minimize the work of Moses. His faithfulness is not in question; indeed, Scripture reveals that God honored Moses in many ways. God himself appeared to Moses face to face (Exod. 33:11) and conferred on him the gift of a long life—to be precise, 120 years. And when Moses died in Moab, God buried him (Deut. 34:6). But the writer of Hebrews is saying that there is no comparison between Jesus and Moses because we really are talking about two different categories. Jesus constructs the spiritual house of God; Moses was a faithful servant in all God's house. Jesus is the founder of God's household (which has its beginning in creation) and Moses himself belongs to that household. In addition, the seat of honor at God's right hand belongs to Jesus. Jesus has been honored by God because through him God made the universe (Heb. 1:2).

4. For every house is built by someone, but God is the builder of everything.

This verse is an explanatory comment and may be placed in parentheses.[3] A house does not grow as a plant does; it is an inanimate object that needs a builder. Every house has a builder. The word *house* may be understood literally, as in verse 3; or it can be used figuratively to refer to the family living in the house.

The emphasis in verse 4 falls on the last part of the sentence. The change of subject is introduced by the conjunction *but*. God is the builder of everything. At first the meaning of this clause seems incongruous with the context, which speaks about Jesus. We would have expected a statement that Jesus builds the house, instead of the comprehensive remark that God builds everything. Of course, no one disputes the truth of the remark, and it directs our attention to God's sovereignty.

The author of Hebrews thus far has shown that he does not make a clear distinction between God and the Son. Rather he teaches that God works through the Son; for example, in creation (Heb. 1:2). Also, God makes Jesus perfect through suffering (Heb. 2:10). God the Father, then, builds everything through his Son. And because Christ constructs God's house, he is worthy of greater honor than Moses.

5–6a. Moses was faithful as a servant in all God's house, testifying to what would be said in the future. But Christ is faithful as a son over God's house.

a. The author repeats what he already said in Hebrews 3:2. There he

---

3. See, for example, the RSV and *Moffatt*.

compares Moses and Jesus; here he contrasts the two. He literally quotes the Septuagint version of Numbers 12:7, although the word order varies.

b. Moses is called a servant; Christ, a son. The contrast is heightened by the use of two different prepositions: Moses was a servant *in* God's house, whereas Christ is a son *over* God's house.

c. The author chooses the term *servant* to describe Moses. Note that he does not call Moses a slave or an attendant. This word (*servant*) occurs frequently in the Old Testament, but only once in the original Greek of the New Testament (Heb. 3:5). It means that a person is in service to someone who is superior. Also, it connotes one who wishes to serve, in contrast to a slave who must serve.

d. Moses proved faithful in the function God had given him and served honorably with distinction (Josh. 1:1–4). Christ also is faithful, although he occupies a different position. He is the son to whom God has given authority over the house; that is, the household of God (Heb. 10:21).

e. Moses functioned as a prophet and was a prototype of Jesus, the great prophet (Deut. 18:15, 18). He testified to what would be said in the future, specifically the gospel that Jesus proclaimed as the fullness of God's revelation (Heb. 1:2).[4]

6b. And we are his house, if we hold on to our courage and the hope of which we boast.

The metaphor that describes the people of God as a house or a building occurs rather frequently in the New Testament (I Cor. 3:16; 6:19; II Cor. 6:16; I Peter 2:5). We are the house of God, says the author of Hebrews. This means that now the believers in Jesus Christ, not the Jews, constitute the household of God (Eph. 2:19–22; I Tim. 3:15). Only Christians acknowledge Christ Jesus as the chief cornerstone. For only in him "the whole body, supported and held together by its ligaments and sinews, grows as God causes it to grow" (Col. 2:19).

There are two limitations.

a. "If we hold on to our courage." We can no longer be part of the house unless we have courage. For the Hebrew Christians the temptation to return to Judaism was not at all imaginary. They were exhorted to hold on to their faith in Christ against fierce opposition from their Jewish countrymen. But Gentile Christians, too, must be vigilant in the face of persecution (I Thess. 2:14). The word *courage* is significant for the Christian because it relates to his boldness, openness, and frankness in preaching and teaching the gospel.

b. "And the hope of which we boast."[5] If the readers of this epistle do not

---

4. Numerous commentators, including John Calvin, Franz Delitzsch, B. F. Westcott, Hugh Montefiore, and Hughes, interpret the clause to refer to the message "which was first announced by the Lord" (Heb. 2:3).

5. On the basis of a number of influential manuscripts (including Codices Sinaiticus, Alexandrinus, Ephraemi, and Bezae) the KJV, NKJV, RV, ASV, NASB, and *Phillips* add the phrase *firm* [or: steadfast] *unto the end.* Note also that the phrase occurs in Heb. 3:14, where in the original it is grammatically correct; this is not the case in Heb. 3:6.

hold on to the hope of which they boast, then they are no longer part of the household of God. Later in the epistle the writer explains what he means by hope. He speaks of the unchangeable nature of God's purpose and the impossibility that God would lie. Says the author, "We who have fled to take hold of the hope offered to us may be greatly encouraged. We have this hope as an anchor for the soul, firm and secure" (Heb. 6:18–19).

As God is true to his purpose and being, so the Christian must be a true reflection of his Creator and Redeemer. If he fails, he ceases to be part of God's house. Therefore, throughout the epistle, but especially in Hebrews 10:23, the author exhorts his readers to be true to their calling: "Let us hold unswervingly to the hope we profess, for he who promised is faithful."

Doctrinal Considerations in 3:1–6

In the first verse of Hebrews 3, two titles are given to the recipients of the epistle and two to Jesus. Jesus has called the recipients brothers and they confess his name, just as he is not ashamed to declare their names.

The structure of Hebrews 3:1 can be represented in a diagram:[6]

BROTHERS
          holy

                    and sharers in the
                    heavenly calling

                    fix your thoughts on

JESUS
          the
          apostle and
          high priest whom

WE
          confess

Verses 2–6a of Hebrews 3 display a remarkable parallelism in which the symmetry is lucid and logical. See the following outline.

3:2	Jesus	faithful	Moses	house
3:3	Jesus	greater honor	Moses	
			builder	house
3:4	God		builder	
3:5	Moses	faithful	servant	house
3:6a	Christ	faithful	son	house

Greek Words, Phrases, and Constructions in 3:1–6

Verse 1

κατανοήσατε—the aorist active imperative, second person plural of the compound intensive verb (from κατά [down] and νοέω [I put my mind to]) conveys

---

6. Consult Pierre Auffret's interesting "Essai sur la structure littéraire et l'interprétation d'Hébreux 3, 1–6," *NTS* 26 (1980): 380–96.

the message of thoroughly and carefully noticing someone or something; in this case, Jesus. See Hebrews 10:24.

Verse 2

τῷ ποιήσαντι—a literal translation of this aorist active participle in the dative singular is "to the one who made" him and could refer to the humanity of Jesus. It is better to translate the participle as "to the one who appointed" him. Then it relates to the office of Christ as apostle and high priest.

Verse 5

θεράπων—the word belongs to the family of the verb θεραπεύω (I serve, venerate, care for, cure). The Septuagint uses the noun as a translation of 'ebed (attendant, servant); the noun θεράπων denotes willing service, whereas δοῦλος or παῖς indicates slavish submission.

Verse 6

παρρησίαν—translated "boldness, frankness, openness, confidence," the noun is a combination of πᾶν (all) and ῥῆσις (speech, word), from ἐρῶ (I speak). It conveys the meaning, therefore, of having the freedom to speak to everyone.[7]

---

7 So, as the Holy Spirit says:

"Today, if you hear his voice,
8   do not harden your hearts
  as you did in the rebellion,
    during the time of testing in the desert,
9 where your fathers tested and tried me
  and for forty years saw what I did.
10 That is why I was angry with that generation,
  and I said, 'Their hearts are always going astray,
  and they have not known my ways.'
11 So I declared on oath in my anger,
  'They shall never enter my rest.' "

12 See to it, brothers, that none of you has a sinful, unbelieving heart that turns away from the living God. 13 But encourage one another daily, as long as it is called Today, so that none of you may be hardened by sin's deceitfulness. 14 We have come to share in Christ if we hold firmly till the end the confidence we had at first. 15 As has just been said:

"Today, if you hear his voice,
  do not harden your hearts
  as you did in the rebellion."

16 Who were they who heard and rebelled? Were they not all those Moses led out of Egypt? 17 And with whom was he angry for forty years? Was it not with those who sinned, whose bodies fell in the desert? 18 And to whom did God swear that they would never enter his rest if not to those who disobeyed? 19 So we see that they were not able to enter, because of their unbelief.

---

7. Hans-Christoph Hahn, *NIDNTT,* vol. 2, p. 734.

B. A Warning Against Unbelief
3:7–19

One of the stylistic devices that the author uses to introduce a quotation of the Old Testament is the formula *God says* or *the Holy Spirit says*. The writer refers to the Old Testament writer as only a mouthpiece of God (see, for example, Heb. 4:7). That is, God is the primary author of Scripture, and man is the secondary author through whom God speaks.[8] Scripture, for the author of Hebrews, is God's Word, and that Word is divine. He indeed has a high view of Scripture.

Many times in his epistle the author quotes a passage from the Old Testament without a smooth transition in the context. The author first quotes Scripture, subsequently explains it by applying the words to the readers of his epistle, and afterward at times supports his application with examples taken from biblical history.

Consider, then, the third chapter of Hebrews. In the first six verses the author, in drawing a comparison between Jesus and Moses, declares that Jesus is worthy of greater honor than Moses. Then, without a transition, the writer quotes Psalm 95:7–11. He explains and applies the psalm citation in verses 12–15. And to buttress his application, he provides historical examples (vv. 16–19).

1. Scripture
3:7–11

In the temple ritual and in the synagogue worship services, the use of Psalm 95 was well established. Both Psalms 95 and 96 were known as the psalms of invitation to worship. We may assume that these psalms were a significant part of the early Christian liturgies as well.[9]

a. **7–9. So, as the Holy Spirit says:**
> **"Today, if you hear his voice,**
> > **do not harden your hearts**
> > **as you did in the rebellion,**
> > > **during the time of testing in the desert,**
> > **where your fathers tested and tried me**
> > **and for forty years saw what I did.**

David, whose name is mentioned later in Hebrews 4:7, does not speak. But the Holy Spirit speaks, addressing both the people of God in Old Testament times and the readers of the Epistle to the Hebrews. And it is because of the Holy Spirit, as the author of Hebrews teaches, that Scripture is divinely

---

8. The author of Hebrews introduces God as speaker in 1:5 (Ps. 2:7); 1:7 (Ps. 104:4); 1:13 (Ps. 110:1); 5:5 (Ps. 2:7). Christ is the speaker in 2:12 (Ps. 22:22); 2:13 (Isa. 8:17); 10:5–7 (Ps. 40:6–8). And the Holy Spirit is the speaker in 3:7–11 (Ps. 95:7–11); 10:15–17 (Jer. 31:33–34).

9. Ernst Werner, *The Sacred Bridge* (London: D. Dobson, 1959), pp. 131, 145, 157. Also see Ismar Elbogen, *Der Jüdische Gottesdienst* (Frankfurt: Kaufmann, 1931), pp. 82, 108, 113.

inspired and addresses people throughout the centuries (see I Tim. 3:16; II Peter 1:20–21).[10] The Holy Spirit speaks to man by means of the inspired Word of God.

Today. God's Word is "living and active[,] sharper than any double-edged sword" (Heb. 4:12). At no point does Scripture become outdated and irrelevant. God spoke to the people of Israel in the desert; David composed Psalm 95, through which God addressed the Israelites; the author of Hebrews quotes a number of verses from that psalm and says that the Holy Spirit speaks to those reading his epistle. God's Word still speaks to us today.

If you hear his voice, do not harden your hearts. The reference is to the original hearers and singers of Psalm 95, and is expressed in the form of a wish in the original Hebrew but in the Greek is given as a conditional sentence. The sentence means: If you should hear God's voice, listen to what he has to say to you. Do not be like your forefathers who turned a deaf ear to the voice of God. Therefore, God is saying to you, "Do not harden your hearts. That is, don't ever ignore my voice, for that spells trouble." James in his epistle puts it succinctly: "You adulterous people, don't you know that friendship with the world is hatred toward God? Anyone who chooses to be a friend of the world becomes an enemy of God" (4:4).

The phrase *harden not your hearts* is Semitic in origin, but no one has difficulty understanding its meaning. In our culture we use the concept *deaf* and say that someone, by ignoring the speaker, deliberately refuses to hear. Nevertheless, by doing this the person takes full responsibility for his willful neglect and refusal to hear.

As you did in the rebellion, during the time of testing in the desert. God speaks to his people Israel, and he calls to mind what happened in the desert during the forty-year journey. He even refers to place names: Meribah and Massah (Ps. 95:8). In the Septuagint, these two names are translated *rebellion* and *testing* respectively. The history lesson, however, is to the point. After the people of Israel (at the beginning of their journey) had left the Desert of Sin near Rephidim, they lacked water. When they quarreled with Moses, God told him to strike a rock. He did, and water gushed forth. Moses called the place Massah, which means testing, and Meribah, which is the word for quarreling (see Exod. 17:7). Near the completion of their forty-year journey, the people of Israel quarreled again because of thirst. This time Moses lost his temper, struck the rock twice instead of speaking to it as God had said, and forfeited his place as leader of the Israelites. Consequently he was not allowed to enter the Promised Land. Moses called the place Meribah (Num. 20:13).

Where your fathers tested and tried me and for forty years saw what I did. From the first year through the fortieth year, the people of Israel tried the patience of God. The history of the Israelites' forty years in the wilderness is replete with examples of the unbelief and faithlessness of young

---

10. SB, vol. 3, p. 684.

and old.[11] Yet amidst the rebelliousness of the people of Israel, God showed his mighty acts: a pillar of fire by night to shield them from the desert cold, a cloud by day to protect them from the sun's burning rays, manna to satisfy their hunger, and water out of the rock to quench their thirst; furthermore, their clothes and shoes did not wear out (Exod. 13:21; 16:4–5; 17:6; Deut. 29:5). The Lord God of Israel was their rock and shield for forty years.[12]

> b. **10. That is why I was angry with that generation,**
>   **and I said, "Their hearts are always going astray,**
>   **and they have not known my ways."**
>   **11. So I declared on oath in my anger,**
>   **"They shall never enter my rest."**

God's patience was taxed to the limit by those rebellious people. His anger flared. God was incensed with that generation.[13] Twice God addressed the obstinate Israelites and spoke to them directly.

Their hearts are always going astray, and they have not known my ways. The exact words spoken by God are found in Numbers 14 and Deuteronomy 1, where Moses records the historical narrative of Israel's rebellion. When the people refused to enter the Promised Land, wanted to return to Egypt, and chose another leader, God said to Moses: "How long will these people treat me with contempt? How long will they refuse to believe in me, in spite of the miraculous signs I have performed among them?" (Num. 14:11).

The Israelites did not rebel against God once: after the return of the spies, they put God to the test ten times (Num. 14:22) and refused to listen to his voice. Their hearts were filled with unbelief, and their eyes were blind to the miracles God performed.

They shall never enter my rest. Because the people of Israel treated God with contempt, God solemnly swore: "Not a man of this evil generation shall

---

11. Israel's history was recounted often by psalmists. For example, see Ps. 78:40–42, where the psalmist speaks of Israel's rebellion in the wilderness and of putting God to the test because the Israelites did not remember God's power. And the prophet Amos asks, "Did you bring me sacrifices and offerings forty years in the desert, O house of Israel?" (Amos 5:25; Acts 7:42).

12. A number of writers see in the words *forty years* an allusion to Jerusalem and the destruction of the temple in A.D. 70, for that event marked the end of a forty-year period of rebellion against Jesus by the obstinate Jews of "this generation." Among those who hold this view are F. F. Bruce, Delitzsch, Hughes, Thomas Hewitt, Westcott, and Theodor Zahn. However, there is no explicit reference in the epistle to the temple and its destruction. Writes Hugh Montefiore, "Our author is throughout his Epistle strangely uninterested in contemporary references" (*The Epistle to the Hebrews* [New York and Evanston: Harper and Row, 1964], p. 76). Therefore I do not think, on the basis of the reading *this generation* instead of *that generation*, that we have the assurance that the author in this text wished to indicate when he wrote the Epistle to the Hebrews.

13. Although the Hebrew text lacks the demonstrative pronoun before the noun *generation* in Ps. 95:10, the Septuagint reads "that generation." In the New Testament the textual evidence (the papyri manuscripts and leading codices) is very strong for the reading *this generation*. Among the translations the RV, ASV, NASB, and *Phillips* read "this generation"; the others (KJV, NKJV, NEB, NAB, JB, GNB, MLB, NIV, RSV, and *Moffatt*) have "that generation" or a variant that is similar in meaning.

see the good land I swore to give your forefathers" (Deut. 1:35; see also Num. 14:23). God took the promise of rest away from the unbelieving Israelites and told them they would die in the desert. Their children of twenty years and younger would be allowed to enter the land God had promised to the forefathers.

The land the Israelites were to possess is called a rest, for there they would have a permanent and safe dwelling (Deut. 12:9). The land of Israel would be given to those who had not spurned God. In his anger God swore that all the others would not see the land but would die in the desert. God was saying that he would cease being God—as it were—before he would let those rebellious Israelites enter the land of Canaan.

In the context of the Israelites' possession of the land, the concept *rest* was fulfilled only in a limited sense. The way of life for the wandering nomad had ended and the career of the valiant soldier ceased when the land was conquered. However, the word *rest* has a much deeper meaning, which the author subsequently explains in Hebrews 4.

2. Application
3:12–15

The quotation from the psalm is now applied to the recipients of the Epistle to the Hebrews, and its meaning is especially significant for the people who are in danger of turning away from God. The psalm citation serves as an introduction to a stirring appeal not to fall away from the living God. In a sense, Hebrews 3:12 may be called the summary of the pastoral exhortations in the epistle.

12. See to it, brothers, that none of you has a sinful, unbelieving heart that turns away from the living God.

The connection between Hebrews 3:6b and 3:12 is quite natural if we read the lengthy quotation from Psalm 95 as a parenthetical comment. This passage is an illustrative, historical reminder of the obstinate Israelites who died in the desert and were denied entrance to the land God had promised them.[14] The readers are exhorted to hold on to their courage and hope as members of the household of God. They cannot turn their backs on Christ in unbelief, for turning away from Christ is falling away from God.

For Christians, therefore, the experience of the rebellious Israelites must serve as a warning that should not be taken lightly. Christians must thoroughly examine themselves and one another to see whether anyone has a sinful, unbelieving heart.

The author of Hebrews knows from Scripture that a falling away from God finds its origin, development, and impetus in unbelief. Unbelief—characterized by mistrust and unreliability—first comes to expression in disobedience, which in turn results in apostasy. The signs of apostasy are hardening

---

14. The controversy continues: should the first word of Heb. 3:7, *so*, be taken with the command *do not harden your hearts* (Heb. 3:8) or with Heb. 3:12?

of the heart and an inability to repent (Heb. 3:13; 4:1; 6:6; 10:25–27; 12:15). The following series of contrasts can be made:

unbelief—faith
disobedience—hearing obediently
neglect—steadfastness
apostasy—entrance to life
hardening—salvation

The heart of someone who turns away from God is described as sinful, which means evil or wicked. God does not take the sin of unbelief lightly, for he knows that its origin lies in man's evil heart. "The heart is deceitful above all things and beyond cure. Who can understand it?" (Jer. 17:9). Furthermore, the author of Hebrews indicates that it is possible to find persons with sinful, unbelieving hearts in the fellowship of the Christian church.

Whoever turns from the living God
must fall;
It's he who shares his guilt, his lot
with all:
Family, kin, nation, state,
small and great.

Whoever forsakes God is forsaken;
Whoever rejects God is rejected.
Frequent voices daily claim:
Man who's come of age will settle
down
But they who say so without God
drown.
—Nicholaas Beets

13. But encourage one another daily, as long as it is called Today, so that none of you may be hardened by sin's deceitfulness.

Other portions of Scripture use various metaphors to describe the church. We read that the house of God consists of living stones (I Peter 2:5), not of individual bricks cemented together by mortar. The household to which the believers belong is like a body that is made up of many parts; all the many parts form one body (I Cor. 12:12). Furthermore, all the parts should have equal concern for each other.

These examples provide the background for the exhortation in verse 13. We also are urged to "encourage one another and build each other up" (I Thess. 5:11) so that no member of the church will fall away. If the church were faithful to Jesus individually and collectively, the danger of apostasy would recede to the perimeter of the church. To put it figuratively, we as individual believers, united by faith, have the obligation to expel the forces of unbelief from the sacred precincts of the church, the body of Christ. What

94

salvation, what joy in heaven over one sinner who repents, what victory over Satan if we daily encourage one another and uphold each other in the faith!

> All one body we,
> One in hope and doctrine,
> One in charity.
> —Sabine Baring-Gould

In addition, all of the members of the church are told to exhort one another daily. This in itself is a call to faithfulness. And all members ought to teach and admonish one another with all wisdom (Col. 3:16; see also Acts 14:22; Heb. 10:25).

The author of Hebrews links the exhortation to the lengthy quote from Psalm 95 with the single word *Today*. He calls to mind the experience of the nation Israel in the wilderness; he intimates that the present is a period of grace that God extends until death terminates man's earthly life. And the termination of life may come rather suddenly for some people.

Moreover, the moment will come when God will cease to warn sinful man. When that moment arrives, the day of grace has changed into the day of judgment. Therefore, while there is still time, we are obligated to encourage one another daily, so that no one falls into the deceitful trap of sin.

Finally, the author notes that Satan sends sin as a deceptive agent, singling out individuals here and there, seeking to lead believers astray (Matt. 13:22; Mark 4:19; Rom. 7:11; II Cor. 11:3; Eph. 5:6; Col. 2:8; II Thess. 2:3, 10; II Peter 2:13). Sin enters deceptively by enticing the believer to exchange the truth of God for a lie. Sin presents itself as something attractive and desirable. Because of its appearance—"Satan himself masquerades as an angel of light" (II Cor. 11:14)—sin is an extremely dangerous power confronting the believer. It always attacks the individual, much as wolves stalk a single sheep.

The author of Hebrews is fully aware of sin's deceptive power directed toward individuals. For this reason he stresses the need to pay attention to every person in the church; repeatedly he says "none of you"—that is, not a single one of you (Heb. 3:12–13; 4:1).

Sin is regarded as an agent that hardens man's heart. Note that the verb *to harden* is presented in the passive voice: "so that none of you may be hardened by sin's deceitfulness." Hardening is demonstrated by a refusal to hear the voice of God and a determined desire to act contrary to everything classified as faith and faithfulness. As a sly, deceptive agent of Satan, sin enters the heart of man and there causes the growth and development of unbelief, which becomes evident in hardening of the spiritual arteries.

14. We have come to share in Christ if we hold firmly till the end the confidence we had at first. 15. As has just been said:
    "Today, if you hear his voice,

> do not harden your hearts
> as you did in the rebellion."[15]

The parallel between Hebrews 3:6 and Hebrews 3:14 is striking. The imagery in verse 6 is of the house of God over which Christ has been placed as son and of which we are part. In verse 14 the same relationship is described as a sharing in Christ.[16] And the courage and hope that we should "hold on to" (v. 6) are identified as "the confidence we had at first" (v. 14).

Only those believers who unwaveringly continue to profess their faith in Jesus are saved. Only faith keeps the believers in a living relationship with Jesus Christ. As the writer says in Hebrews 11:6, "Without faith it is impossible to please God." Faith is the basic substance of our sharing in Christ. "Faith is being sure of what we hope for and certain of what we do not see" (Heb. 11:1). The phrase *being sure* is equivalent to "confidence" (Heb. 3:14); this confidence is the basis upon which our faith rests.

What does the author mean when he says, "if we hold firmly till the end the confidence *we had at first*" (italics added)? John Albert Bengel aptly says, "A Christian, so long as he is not *made perfect,* considers himself as a *beginner.*"[17] This confidence is the continual clinging to Christ in faith. As long as our faith in Christ is foundational, we are safe and secure as members of God's household.

To remind us once more of the daily necessity to listen attentively and obediently to the voice of God, the author quotes the now-familiar statement from Psalm 95, "Today, if you hear his voice, do not harden your hearts as you did in the rebellion." Constantly God addresses us by means of his Word, and he expects us who live by faith to give him our undivided attention.

3. Summation
3:16–19

In a concluding paragraph, the author asks a number of rhetorical questions relating to the Israelites who perished in the desert because of unbelief. In a series of self-explanatory questions, the writer makes it clear that unbelief ends in death.

16. Who were they who heard and rebelled? Were they not all those Moses led out of Egypt?

In this first question the author directs attention to the message of the lengthy quotation from Psalm 95, and by means of the second question he provides the answer to the first question. These people had seen the miracles God performed; they had experienced the goodness of God. Day by day

---

15. Punctuation and paragraph division play a role in Greek texts and English translations. Thus, the Nes-Al text places Heb. 3:14 between dashes to indicate a parenthetical thought. The NKJV, MLB, GNB, and NIV end the paragraph with Heb. 3:15. The NASB, RSV, *Moffatt,* ASV, KJV, JB, NAB, and RV end the paragraph with Heb. 3:19. The NEB, Martin Luther, Zahn, R. C. H. Lenski, Delitzsch, Spicq, and Bruce begin a new paragraph with Heb. 3:15.

16. The common translation is "share in Christ." Other versions translate the Greek as "Christ's partners" (NEB) or "partners of Christ" (NAB), or "co-heirs with Christ" (JB).

17. John Albert Bengel, *Gnomon of the New Testament,* ed. Andrew R. Fausset, 7th ed., 5 vols. (Edinburgh: Clark, 1877), vol. 4, p. 376. His italics.

they ate manna, and they could see the presence of God in the pillar of fire by night and in the cloud by day.

By implication the author conveys the message already stated in Hebrews 2:2: "For if the message spoken by angels was binding, and every violation and disobedience received its just punishment, how shall we escape if we ignore such a great salvation?"

17. And with whom was he angry for forty years? Was it not with those who sinned, whose bodies fell in the desert?

Would the behavior of the Israelites have improved in the course of forty years? The answer to this question is given in Exodus and Numbers: Exodus 17 records the first rebellion at the beginning of the forty-year period and Numbers 25 records the grievous sin of immorality at the end of that period. The Israelites had not changed: they remained rebellious and obstinate. The only exceptions, of course, were Joshua and Caleb, who demonstrated their faith and were privileged to conquer and possess the land.

18. And to whom did God swear that they would never enter his rest if not to those who disobeyed?

When the writer asks, "Was it not with those who sinned?" (v. 17), he parallels this question with the clause "if not to those who disobeyed" (v. 18). The verbs *sinned* and *disobeyed* are synonyms: the first verb represents the action followed by just punishment; the second verb reveals the root of the evil. Disobedience is a refusal to hear the voice of God and an obstinate refusal to act in response to that voice. Disobedience is not merely a lack of obedience; rather it is a refusal to obey.

19. So we see that they were not able to enter, because of their unbelief.

The author states, in conclusion, that the rebellious Israelites, in an example that needs no imitation, had to perish in the desert because of unbelief, a sin of openly defying God, refusing to believe, and exhibiting disobedience.

Unbelief is the root of the sin of provoking God. Unbelief robs God of his glory and robs the unbeliever of the privilege of God's blessings. Because of unbelief, rebellious man is denied entrance into the rest that God provides for the members of his household.

Practical Considerations in 3:7–19

Our salvation is of the highest importance and may never be taken lightly. We must heed the admonitions that the author of Hebrews gives us in the form of illustrations from Israel's past (Exod. 17:7; Num. 20:13; Deut. 33:8; Ps. 106:32).

According to Numbers 1, the census of the Israelites took place in the second year after the people came out of Egypt, and the total number of men twenty years and older who were able to serve in Israel's army was 603,550 (Num. 1:46). Double this number (this assumes an equal number of women who were twenty years or older) and divide the total by the number of days the Israelites spent in the wilderness during those thirty-eight years. The result is nearly ninety deaths per day in consequence of God's curse (Num. 14:23; Deut. 1:34–35). A daily reminder of God's anger!

All sins are deviations from the law that God has given his people. The Israelites deliberately chose to follow their own desires and wishes; they demonstrated their devious nature in action and word, in mind and heart. Their attitude stemmed from an evil heart.

Believers have a corporate and an individual responsibility to care for the spiritual well-being of their fellow men. They must consider this responsibility a holy obligation and exhibit utter faithfulness, even if the fruit of their fidelity is not always evident.

We are sharers in Christ when we have accepted the gospel in faith and obedience and show in our lives that what we believe in our hearts we confess with our mouths (Rom. 10:10). Those who consistently fail to confess never shared in Christ and consequently fail to know Christ as their Savior.

Greek Words, Phrases, and Constructions in 3:7–19

Verse 7

τὸ πνεῦμα τὸ ἅγιον—the use of the definite articles before the noun and the adjective occurs in Hebrews 9:8 and 10:15; but also see Hebrews 2:4 and 6:4, where the definite articles are lacking. And see Hebrews 9:14 and 10:29.

ἀκούσητε—the aorist active subjunctive, second person plural of ἀκούω (I hear) indicates the probability that the audience may hear. Also note that the verb is followed by the genitive case φωνῆς instead of the accusative. The genitive calls attention to the sound of the voice and does not necessarily imply understanding or listening obediently to what is said.

Verse 8

σκληρύνητε—the negative prohibition in the aorist subjunctive conveys the meaning that the recipients of the letter had not yet hardened their hearts, but that the possibility was not imaginary.

Verse 12

ἔσται—after the negative μήποτε we would expect the subjunctive. The author uses the future indicative ἔσται in order to express the urgency of listening to his exhortation and the distinct possibility of apostasy.

θεοῦ ζῶντος—definite articles are lacking to focus attention on the absolute power of God to create, uphold, and govern the world. (See II Cor. 3:3; 6:16; I Tim. 4:10; Heb. 9:14; 10:31; 12:22; I Peter 1:23; Rev. 7:2.)

Verse 13

τὸ σήμερον—note the definite article in the neuter singular. The use of τὸ (instead of the usual phrase ἡ σήμερον ἡμέρα) tells the reader that the quotation of Psalm 95 is intended.

Verse 14

ὑπόστασις—in the New Testament ὑπόστασις occurs five times (II Cor. 9:4; 11:17; Heb. 1:3; 3:14; 11:1). In Hebrews the word is theologically important and is translated "being" (1:3), "confidence" (3:14), and "being sure" (11:1).

Verse 18

εἰσελεύσεσθαι—the future middle infinitive is used because of the quotation (Heb. 3:11). The future is the equivalent of an aorist in the sense of a single occurrence.

Summary of Chapter 3

In the first two chapters of the epistle, the author of Hebrews compared Jesus and the angels. In chapter 3 he compares Jesus and Moses. The Jews revered Moses because of his close relationship with God. Moses' career was characterized by faithfulness—no one disputes that fact. However, with a fitting illustration of servant (Moses *in* God's house) and Son (Jesus *over* God's house), the writer of Hebrews clearly demonstrates the superiority of Jesus.

Psalm 95:7–10 is a unique citation, filled with disheartening information about Israel's rebellion and apostasy in the wilderness. The author of Hebrews warns his readers not to fall into the trap of unbelief which leads to a falling away from the living God. The writer stresses the corporate responsibility of the Christian community in warning the individual believer not to turn away from God but to continue to be strong in the faith. The author applies the words of Psalm 95:7–10 directly to his hearers; for him the message is a matter of eternal life or eternal death. In a sense, Hebrews 3:12 may be called one of the nerve centers of the epistle.

4

Jesus' Superiority to Moses, *part 2*

4:1–13

Outline

4 1 Therefore, since the promise of entering his rest still stands, let us be careful that none of you be found to have fallen short of it. 2 For we also have had the gospel preached to us, just as they did; but the message they heard was of no value to them, because those who heard did not combine it with faith. 3 Now we who have believed enter that rest, just as God has said,

"So I declared on oath in my anger,
    'They shall never enter my rest.' "

And yet his work has been finished since the creation of the world. 4 For somewhere he has spoken about the seventh day in these words: "And on the seventh day God rested from all his work." 5 And again in the passage above he says, "They shall never enter my rest."

6 It still remains that some will enter that rest, and those who formerly had the gospel preached to them did not go in, because of their disobedience. 7 Therefore God again set a certain day, calling it Today, when a long time later he spoke through David, as was said before:

"Today, if you hear his voice,
    do not harden your hearts."

8 For if Joshua had given them rest, God would not have spoken later about another day. 9 There remains, then, a Sabbath-rest for the people of God; 10 for anyone who enters God's rest also rests from his own work, just as God did from his. 11 Let us, therefore, make every effort to enter that rest, so that no one will fall by following their example of disobedience.

12 The word of God is living and active. Sharper than any double-edged sword, it penetrates even to dividing soul and spirit, joints and marrow; it judges the thoughts and attitudes of the heart. 13 Nothing in all creation is hidden from God's sight. Everything is uncovered and laid bare before the eyes of him to whom we must give account.

C. An Invitation to Enter God's Rest
4:1–13

1. God's Rest
4:1–5

In the third chapter of his epistle, the writer of Hebrews quotes at length from Psalm 95 and speaks of the unbelievers who were cursed by God and died in the desert. Although the author speaks of the unbelievers in chapter 3, he addresses the believers in chapter 4. The admonition of 3:12–14 is now resumed and is substantially enlarged in 4:1–11. The question that is raised is this: Is the promise of entering God's rest, given to the Israelites but forfeited because of unbelief, still valid in our time? The answer is a resounding yes. The message of entering the rest that God promises is the same and still calls for acceptance in faith. The assurance is that "we who have believed enter that rest" (Heb. 4:3).

1. Therefore, since the promise of entering his rest still stands, let us be careful that none of you be found to have fallen short of it.

The first word *therefore* is rather significant because it looks backward to the quotation and the interpretation of Psalm 95, and points forward to the believers who read the Epistle to the Hebrews. The message of 4:1 can be summarized in three words: fear, promise, failure.

a. *Fear.* The author is a pastor who, filled with concern, strives for the spiritual well-being of his people. He does not want to see a single member of the church fall into the same sin (i.e., unbelief) that was displayed by the Israelites who died in the desert. The author is a shepherd, so to speak, who watches over every sheep in the flock.

But the writer is not the only one in the church to care for the members of the congregation. He exhorts the recipients of his epistle to be equally concerned. Thus he writes, "Let us be careful." He shares his pastoral concerns with all the members—all are responsible for the welfare of the church. To be concerned about one's own salvation is commendable; to pray for one's fellow man is praiseworthy; but to strive for the salvation of everyone within the confines of the church is exemplary. We ought to take careful note of members who may be drifting from the truth in doctrine or conduct and then pray with them and for them. We are constantly looking for spiritual stragglers. Says Philip Edgcumbe Hughes in his commentary on this point, "There is no attitude more dangerous for the church than that of unconcern and complacency."[1]

Most translations have the reading *let us fear* or some variation, denoting something that causes concern and anxiety in a person's heart (Acts 23:10; 27:17, 29; II Cor. 11:3; 12:20; Gal. 4:11).

b. *Promise.* God's promises remain the same for all times and for every generation because God is true to his Word (Deut. 3:18–20; Josh. 1:12–18; 21:45; 23:14; I Kings 8:56; Ps. 89:1; I Cor. 1:9; Heb. 6:18). On the basis of this scriptural truth, I prefer the translation "since the promise of entering his rest still stands." We have the assurance that God's promise is still valid today and did not come to an end with the Israelites in the desert. And because of the certainty that the promise of God still stands, we must have special care for and interest in the spiritual growth and development of fellow believers.

Some translations describe the duration of the promise of entering God's rest: "while the promise of entering his rest remains." Others express the concessive idea, namely, "although there is still left a promise to enter into

---

1. Philip Edgcumbe Hughes, *Commentary on the Epistle to the Hebrews* (Grand Rapids: Eerdmans, 1977), p. 155.

his rest."[2] These translations are to the point and accurate—they stress the continuing validity of God's promise to his people. This promise is in a specific sense still incomplete and open.[3] In other words, the promise will lose its significance only at the end of time when in fact the last of the believers has entered God's rest.

c. *Failure.* For the Israelites on their way to the land of Canaan, for David who composed Psalm 95, for the writer of Hebrews and his readers, and for us today the promise of God is firm and spans the centuries. This does not mean, however, that God is obligated to fulfill his promise when faith is lacking. When man fails God by not believing in his Word, God turns the promise into a threat and a curse as he did during Israel's journey in the wilderness.

What then does the writer of Hebrews imply when he tells his readers that they have the promise of entering God's rest? The answer must be that the idea of rest has taken on a much broader meaning, because when the word *rest* was first used it referred to entering Canaan. The concept included rest from harassment by Israel's enemies in neighboring countries; spiritually it related to a blessed life spent in harmony with the law of God. When David spoke of rest, he lived safely in his palace at Jerusalem. For the recipients of the epistle, the term *rest* had spiritual significance.

In the congregation that originally received the epistle, the possibility that someone had fallen short of appropriating God's promise seems to have been real. The expression *to have fallen short* may have been borrowed from the sports arena; it conveys the meaning of being left behind in the race and thus failing to reach the goal.[4] When someone does not reach the goal, he cannot give even the appearance of having arrived. In the eyes of the spectators in the arena, the contestant has failed. He cannot receive a prize and in many cases even forfeits sympathy.

This type of failure to claim the promise of God's rest may not be found in the church. The writer is direct in his appeal "that *none of you* be found to have fallen short" (italics added; see also 3:12; 4:11). The entire congregation ought to be vigilant about possible lack of interest in spiritual matters. No one may let his guard down. No one may be lost. Responsibility for one another's spiritual interest is the obligation of every believer.

2. For we also have had the gospel preached to us, just as they did; but the message they heard was of no value to them, because those who heard did not combine it with faith.

---

2. R. C. H. Lenski, *The Interpretation of the Epistle to the Hebrews and of the Epistle of James* (Columbus: Wartburg, 1946), p. 125.

3. Bauer, p. 413, translates the phrase "a promise that is still open."

4. Joseph H. Thayer, *A Greek-English Lexicon of the New Testament* (New York, Cincinnati, and Chicago: American Book Company, 1889), p. 646, says the expression means "to fall short of the end." William L. Lane (*NIDNTT*, vol. 3, p. 954) speaks of a "broad range of nuances" for the sixteen times that the word occurs in the New Testament. The primary meaning is to arrive too late for an appointed meeting or event. The secondary nuance, obviously a consequence of the first, is that of failure and of lacking something.

The conjunction *for* links the concept of the promise, given to the Israelites but still valid today (v. 1), with that of the gospel preached to the nation Israel in the desert and to us.

Highlights in verse 2 are the following points.

a. The Word of God, although a continuous revelation from the first book in the Bible to the last, is the same. It is good news for the Israelite and for the Christian.

b. The clause "we also have had the gospel preached to us" receives a certain degree of emphasis. The writer does not say, "We have received the gospel." Instead, he states that the Word has been preached to us for a considerable time so that we are fully evangelized.

c. The Israelites traveling from Egypt to Canaan also had the Word preached to them over an extended period.

d. However, the gospel news (I Thess. 2:13) that the desert travelers heard did not do them any good, because they failed to pay attention.

e. Those who heard the Word *did not combine it with faith* (Rom. 10:16–17). And that was their downfall.

The last clause in 4:2, depending on the wording in a number of ancient manuscripts, varies in translation. There are two usual ways of translating the clause. One of these is, "because it [the Word] was not united by faith in those who heard."[5] This translation is by far the more prevalent, frankly because it fits the context and is readily understood. The manuscript evidence, however, favors the second translation, "because they did not share the faith of those who listened."[6] The implication is that among the Israelites in the desert were two people who obeyed the Word of God: Joshua and Caleb. It is rather strange that the writer is not more explicit; he leaves the reader to fill in the historical details and to draw the necessary conclusions.

Differences exist and the difficulties in the passage are undeniable, but in both translations the emphasis is on the faith that was not shared. During the entire period in which the Israelites had the Good News preached to them, they refused to accept it in faith. Their refusal was not a momentary reaction but a continuous rejection of God's written and spoken Word.

God fulfills his promises only in those who accept his Word in faith and trust, whether that happens to be Joshua, Caleb, or "the soul that on Jesus has leaned for repose." No one among the Israelites could complete the desert journey and enter the Land of Promise except the one who demonstrated true faith in God. And no one shall enter God's eternal rest unless his faith is anchored in Jesus, the Son of God.

3. Now we who have believed enter that rest, just as God has said,
"So I declared on oath in my anger,
'They shall never enter my rest.' "
And yet his work has been finished since the creation of the world.

---

5. Representative translations are KJV, NKJV, ASV, NASB, MLB, and RSV.

6. See, for example, RV, NEB, JB, NAB, and GNB.

After comparing the Israelites who wandered in the desert and the recipients of his epistle, the writer of Hebrews confidently asserts, "Now we who have believed enter that rest." He does not use the future tense ("we will enter"). He says, "We who have believed enter," and thus affirms that God's promise has become reality according to his divine plan and purpose.[7] At the moment—in principle but not yet in full realization—we are entering that rest. As long as we keep our eyes fixed on "Jesus, the author and perfecter of our faith" (Heb. 12:2), we enjoy the rest God has promised, and eventually we shall be with him eternally.

This point raises the following questions.

a. Who enters that rest? The author is quite specific. We; that is, those of us who have believed and have demonstrated our faith in Christ by professing his name (Acts 4:32; 16:31; Rom. 10:9; I Thess. 2:13). And we enter because God's promise still stands.

As God's promise does not lose its validity, so God's threat remains true for everyone who does not accept God's Word in faith. God's Word prevails because he has spoken:

> "So I declared on oath in my anger,
> 'They shall never enter my rest.' "

These words not only apply to Israel's experience in the wilderness, but also remind readers of the epistle that God's promise and threat are equally valid today.

b. What is God's rest? The writer of Hebrews has expected this question, it seems. The next sentence, "And yet his work has been finished since the creation of the world," indicates that.[8] The author explains the word *rest* in his own inimitable way by quoting an expression from Genesis 2:2, which he cites in 4:4. This expression (the words *his work*), along with the rest of the sentence, anticipates the reference to the Genesis account. (It is significant that the writer of Hebrews constantly quotes from the Old Testament Scriptures.[9] He never appeals to the words of Jesus or the teachings of the apostles, although he was acquainted with the gospel [Heb. 4:2]. For him and for the recipients of his epistle, the writings of the Old Testament were authoritative.)

After the world was created, the author tells us, God initiated a new period—a period of rest. God rested from his work of creation at the conclusion of the sixth day. Whereas for the six days of creation the concluding words are "there was evening, and there was morning," for the seventh day

---

7. Ceslaus Spicq, *L'Épître aux Hébreux,* 3d ed., 2 vols. (Paris: Gabalda, 1953), vol. 2, pp. 81–82.

8. Numerous texts and translations combine the sentence with the preceding quote and divide the two only by a comma (see Nes-Al; BF; and KJV, RV, ASV, and RSV as examples). Other translators are of the opinion that the sentence should stand separately, serving as a bridge between the quote from Ps. 95 and the one from Gen. 2:2.

9. F. W. Grosheide, *De Brief aan de Hebreeën en de Brief van Jakobus* (Kampen: Kok, 1955), p. 113.

these demarcations of time are lacking. With the seventh day, then, the period of God's rest began.

4. For somewhere he has spoken about the seventh day in these words: "And on the seventh day God rested from all his work." 5. And again in the passage above he says, "They shall never enter my rest."

Once before, in 2:6, the author has expressed himself rather vaguely about a Scripture passage. He does this deliberately to focus attention not on the precise location of the reference, but on the words themselves. Every reader knows that a reference to the seventh day comes from the creation account in Genesis. The quoted words, however, are more important: "And on the seventh day God rested from all his work."

The term *rest* merits attention, especially if we think of Jesus' words when the Jews persecuted him for healing an invalid on the Sabbath: "My Father is always at his work to this very day, and I, too, am working" (John 5:17). Rest for God does not mean idleness; rather it is a cessation from the work of creation. God continues to enjoy this rest now that the work of his creation is completed.

On the combined strength of the two Old Testament passages—one from Psalm 95 and one from Genesis 2:2—the author concludes that only those persons who believe enter God's rest. This rest, to be sure, has become a reality for the believer. Unbelievers have no access to the rest God provides, for by spurning God's Word they have forfeited the privilege of entering his rest.

Note the author's repeated reference to the solemn oath God swore: "They shall never enter my rest" (Heb. 3:11, 18 [with minor variations]; 4:3, 5). This recurring warning ought not be taken lightly by the reader. And no one can ever say, "It will never happen to me." If the Israelites, entering the land of Canaan, had listened to words spoken by Moses (Deut. 28:1–14) and obeyed the commands of God, they would have been the recipients of all the blessings God had promised. They would have been honored above all the nations of the earth, and they would have enjoyed rest by living in God's favor and grace. For them, life in Canaan would have been living in the presence of God. But one generation after the death of Joshua and the elders who outlived him, the people turned their backs on the God of their fathers (Josh. 2:10), and the promise of God turned into a threat and a curse. It is for this reason, vividly documented by historical fact, that the author of Hebrews repeats the verse *they shall never enter my rest*.

Practical Considerations in 4:1–5

The exhortations in 4:1–3 are in effect an application of the lesson learned from history. As in chapter 3 the unbelieving Israelites were mentioned, so in chapter 4 the believers are addressed. The call to faithfulness and mutual care is earnest and sincere.

The gospel is proclaimed to believers and unbelievers, so that no one can claim the excuse of not having heard the promise of God. Man's failure to listen to God's

Word does not terminate the promises: for the unbeliever these become threats; for the believer they remain promises which in due time are fulfilled.

Believers, because of firm faith, enter God's rest, which is a spiritual state of being in the presence of God. The Genevan Reformer John Calvin had a motto, *Coram Deo* (in the presence of God). The believer by faith lives in harmony with his God. As Calvin puts it: "The highest happiness of man is to be united to his God."[10]

Greek Words, Phrases, and Constructions in 4:1-5

Verse 1

φοβηθῶμεν—the author includes himself in the exhortation and thus identifies himself with the readers. The aorist subjunctive expresses the exhortation to watch over one another's spiritual welfare. The author tells the reader to do so without delay.

ἐπαγγελίας—in the epistle this noun occurs fourteen times and the verb an additional four times. There seems to be word play involved in the Greek when the author speaks of promise (ἐπαγγελία) and preaching the gospel (εὐαγγελίζομαι). The latter verb appears only two times in Hebrews (4:2, 6). The noun ἐπαγγελία is in the genitive absolute construction with a causal connotation.

Verse 2

εὐηγγελισμένοι—together with the verb ἐσμεν, the perfect passive participle forms a periphrastic construction that expresses the idea of a continuous activity that began in the past and lasts into the present. Note that the personal pronoun ἡμεῖς is not used, in order to place emphasis on the verb instead.

ὁ λόγος τῆς ἀκοῆς—the genitive is qualitative in nature (see also Rom. 10:17; I Thess. 2:13) and is related to the aorist active, dative plural participle ἀκούσασιν.

Verse 3

οἱ πιστεύσαντες—the aorist active participle and the preceding definite article modify the main verb εἰσερχόμεθα. The aorist is ingressive.

γενηθέντων—the aorist passive (deponent) participle in the genitive and the words τῶν ἔργων form a genitive absolute construction.

2. God's Day
4:6-11

The emphatic threat "they shall never enter my rest" does not rule out God's honoring his promise to those who believe. Some enter God's rest.

6. It still remains that some will enter that rest, and those who formerly had the gospel preached to them did not go in, because of their disobedience. 7. Therefore God again set a certain day, calling it Today, when a long time later he spoke through David, as was said before:

"Today, if you hear his voice,
do not harden your hearts."

Note these observations.

---

10. John Calvin, *Epistle to the Hebrews* (Grand Rapids: Eerdmans, 1949), p. 96.

a. *Unalterable fact.* From biblical history the reader knows that Joshua and Caleb entered the land of Canaan. They put their trust in God, who kept his Word. They were privileged to enter the Land of Promise, because God does not break his Word. This fact remains throughout the ages and is unchangeable.

Thus the reader of these verses is exhorted to enter God's rest, because God is true to his Word and does fulfill his promise. A careful reading of the first part of 4:6 shows that the thought expressed is somewhat incomplete. That is, the introductory clause, "it still remains that some will enter that rest," needs a concluding remark, perhaps in the form of an exhortation. And this exhortation is given in 4:11, "Let us, therefore, make every effort to enter that rest."[11] If we accept God's Word in faith and do his will obediently, the promise of rest will be fulfilled for us, too. That fact is unquestionable.

b. *Just reward.* Some enter God's rest; others are denied entrance. This is not a matter of injustice nor of favoring one party over another. Rather, the author of Hebrews perceives that the distinction is just. Says he, "Those who formerly had the gospel preached to them did not go in, because of their disobedience." Those people who heard the voice of God from Sinai and who were given the law of Moses refused to accept the promise. They were without excuse, for although they heard the gospel, they chose to disobey. They received their due when entrance into Canaan was denied. Their unbelief turned into disobedience; heart and hand were willfully opposed to God and his Word.

c. *Repeated promise.* God remains in control; he rules and overrules. His promise, which the Israelites ignored and which was consequently nullified, God repeats. "Therefore God again set a certain day, calling it Today."

The word *Today* emphasizes the characteristics of relevance, timeliness, and newness. The text indicates that God set a certain day and mentions that "a long time later he spoke through David." God spanned the centuries from desert life to Davidic rule, from Moses recording Israel's history in the Pentateuch to David composing his songs for the Psalter.[12] He makes his promise available *today,* which is the time for embracing the gracious offer of salvation. God appeals to readers:

> Today, if you hear [my] voice,
> do not harden your hearts.

d. *Timeless validity.* Why is the promise of God always valid? In at least three different verses of chapter 4 the author gives the answer: God has

---

11. John Brown, in *The Epistle to the Hebrews* (Edinburgh: Banner of Truth Trust, 1961), p. 207, labels Heb. 4:6b–10 parenthetical and maintains that the writer chooses this structure "to establish the principle on which this exhortation proceeds."
12. The Hebrew Bible does not have a superscription for Ps. 95. The Septuagint ascribes the psalm to David. The author of Hebrews quotes exclusively from the Septuagint; this translation was, for him and his readers, Scripture. Thus he considered David the composer.

spoken (vv. 3, 4, 7). The simple phrase *as God has said,* which in the original Greek is in the perfect tense, signifies that what God says has permanent validity (see also Heb. 1:13; 10:9; 13:5). No matter how many centuries elapse, God's Word spans the ages; his message is just as clear, firm, and sure today as it was when first uttered. God's Word is divinely inspired and, as Paul says, "useful for teaching, rebuking, correcting and training in right- eousness" (II Tim. 3:16).

8. For if Joshua had given them rest, God would not have spoken later about another day.

The writer clearly appeals to biblical history, specifically to the books of Deuteronomy and Joshua. God promised rest to the wandering Israelites when Moses declared, "But you will cross the Jordan and settle in the land the LORD your God is giving you as an inheritance, and he will give you rest from all your enemies around you so that you will live in safety" (Deut. 12:10; also see Deut. 3:20; 5:33).

This promise was fulfilled literally when Joshua addressed the people of the tribes of Reuben and Gad and the half-tribe of Manasseh: "Now that the LORD your God has given your brothers rest as he promised, return to your homes in the land that Moses the servant of the LORD gave you on the other side of the Jordan" (Josh. 22:4; see also Josh. 1:13, 15; 21:44; 23:1).

The writer demonstrates once again that he knows the Old Testament Scriptures thoroughly, and as an expert theologian he formulates the con- ditional sentence: "For if Joshua had given them rest—and we know that God fulfilled this promise—God would not have spoken later about another day, as he does in Psalm 95." In other words, the rest of which God speaks is a spiritual rest and has much greater significance than living safely in Canaan.

The rest that God intended for his people transcends the temporal and attains the eternal. It is a spiritual rest that is effected by the gospel, whether proclaimed in Old Testament or New Testament days. It is a rest from sin and evil. As Zacharias Ursinus, with the help of Caspar Olevianus, aptly expressed it:

> that every day of my life
> I rest from my evil ways,
> let the Lord work in me through his Spirit,
> and so begin already in this life
> the eternal Sabbath.[13]

9. There remains, then, a Sabbath-rest for the people of God; 10. for anyone who enters God's rest also rests from his own work, just as God did from his.

From Psalm 95 the author has shown that the rest that the Israelites en- joyed in Canaan was not the rest God intended for his people. The intended

---

13. Heidelberg Catechism, answer 103.

HEBREWS

rest is a Sabbath-rest, which, of course, is a direct reference to the creation
account (Gen. 2:2; see also Exod. 20:11; 31:17) of God's rest on the seventh
day.[14]

For the believer the Sabbath is not merely a day of rest in the sense that
it is a cessation of work. Rather it is a spiritual rest—a cessation of sinning.
It entails an awareness of being in the sacred presence of God with his people
in worship and praise. John Newton captured a glimpse of what Sabbath-
rest is to be when he wrote:

> Safely through another week
> God has brought us on our way;
> Let us now a blessing seek,
> Waiting in His courts today;
> Day of all the week the best,
> Emblem of eternal rest.

The day of rest is indeed an *emblem* of eternal rest! During our life span on
earth, we celebrate the Sabbath and realize only partially what Sabbath-rest
entails. In the life to come, we shall fully experience God's rest, for then we
will have entered a rest that is eternal. " 'Blessed are the dead who die in
the Lord from now on.' 'Yes,' says the Spirit, 'they will rest from their labor,
for their deeds will follow them' " (Rev. 14:13).

Who then enters that rest? Only those who die in the Lord? The answer
is: All those who in faith experience happiness in the Lord because they are
one with him. Jesus prays for those who believe in him, "that all of them
may be one, Father, just as you are in me and I am in you" (John 17:21). In
God we have perfect peace and rest.

> My heart, Lord, does not rest
> Until it rests in Thee.
> —Augustine

However, the text indicates that whoever enters God's rest does so only
once. He enters that rest fully when his labors are ended. He then enjoys
uninterrupted heavenly rest from which death, mourning, crying, and pain
have been removed; at that time God's dwelling will be with men; he will
live with them and be their God, for they are his people (Rev. 21:4).

**11. Let us, therefore, make every effort to enter that rest, so that no
one will fall by following their example of disobedience.**

Hebrews 4:6 serves as an introduction to 4:11. With the introductory
clause, verse 11 reads: "Since therefore it remains for some to enter, let us,
then, make every effort to enter that rest." The intervening verses must be
understood as a parenthetical thought.

a. "Let us, therefore, make every effort to enter that rest." From now on,

---

14. H. W. Attridge, in defining God's rest, speaks of type and antitype—rest in Canaan is
the antitype of God's rest upon completing the week of creation. Refer to "Let us strive to
enter that rest: The logic of Hebrews 4:1–11," *HTR* 73 (1980): 279–88.

says the author, let us exert ourselves to enter God's rest. Let us not take that rest for granted but earnestly strive to live in harmony with God, to do his will, and to obey his law. Paul in his Epistle to the Philippians puts the same thought in different words: "Continue to work out your salvation with fear and trembling" (2:12). This eagerness ought to be the hallmark of every believer and the password of the church. We are not to be fanatical, but are to demonstrate inner assurance in obedience to God's Word. The writer of Hebrews does not cease to warn and to exhort his readers. He is utterly serious when he says, "In your struggle against sin, you have not yet resisted to the point of shedding your blood" (Heb. 12:4).

b. "So that no one will fall." The key word in this clause is the term *fall,* which of course is a direct reminder of the desert journey of the Israelites as it is recorded in the Pentateuch and in Psalm 95. These people sinned, and as a consequence of God's curse, their bodies fell in the desert. The word *fall* must be taken in a broader sense than referring only to physical death; it includes falling away spiritually and thus being completely ruined. Those who fall have lost their salvation and deserve eternal destruction.

As a pastor watching over his flock, the writer of Hebrews admonishes his readers to take care of one another spiritually. He stresses the responsibility of each believer toward the individual members of the church. No one in the Christian community should be neglected and thus, left to himself, be allowed to fall (see Heb. 3:12; 4:1).

c. "By following their example of disobedience." The disobedient Israelites who perished in the desert became an example to their descendants. They became the object lesson of how not to live in the presence of God. Fathers would teach their children (Ps. 78:5–8) what the consequences of disobedience were for the rebellious Israelites on the way to the land of Canaan. And they would warn them not to follow this example.

Implicitly the author of Hebrews is saying to his readers: If any of you falls by following the example of the Israelites in the wilderness, he himself will be an example to his contemporaries, and everyone will take his failure as a warning not to make the same mistake. Rather, the reader must do everything in his power to walk the pathway of obedience and to exhort his brother and sister in the Lord to do likewise.

Unbelief leads to willful disobedience, which results in an inability to come to repentance. And what is the conclusion? The answer is forthright and to the point: eternal condemnation. Therefore, says the writer, let us make every effort to enter God's rest.

Doctrinal Considerations in 4:6–11

If Joshua, leading the Israelites into the land of Canaan, had given them rest, the psalmist would not have had to repeat the promise of rest (Ps. 95:11). The rest promised in Psalm 95 and explained in 4:10 is a copy of God's rest; this rest is attained by the believer in personal repentance and an ardent dedication to obey God. When the believer rests from his evil works, he enters the Sabbath-rest granted to the people of God.

God commands us to remember the Sabbath day by keeping it holy and, referring to the creation week and his rest on the seventh day, instructs us to follow his example (Exod. 20:8–11; also see Deut. 5:12–15). The noun *rest* does not convey the thought of idleness but rather of peace. "It stands for consummation of a work accomplished and the joy and satisfaction attendant upon this. Such was its prototype in God."[15]

One of the motifs in the Epistle to the Hebrews is the author's recurring use of statements that describe a condition contrary to fact (see Heb. 4:8; 7:11; 8:7). The writer employs a conditional sentence in each instance and shows that in the Old Testament era rest (Heb. 4:8) and covenant (Heb. 8:7) were incomplete. Perfection, he writes, could not be attained (Heb. 7:11). But Christ brought fulfillment to promise and prophecy when he delivered the fullness of God's revelation.

The name *Joshua* (Heb. 4:8) is equivalent to the name *Jesus* in the Greek New Testament. Joshua, the son of Nun, led the Israelites across the river Jordan into the Land of Promise where they enjoyed rest and peace from wandering and warfare. Jesus leads his people into the presence of God and grants them the eternal Sabbath-rest.

Greek Words, Phrases, and Constructions in 4:6–11

Verse 6

ἀπολείπεται—the compound verb has a directive connotation: "to leave behind." In 4:6 and 9 it has the meaning *to remain*. The present tense expresses lasting validity.

εὐαγγελισθέντες—the aorist passive participle (compare Heb. 4:2) is preceded by the definite article οἱ to indicate a definite group. Between the article and the participle stands the adverb πρότερον (formerly) for emphasis.

ἀπείθειαν—in Hebrews 3:12 and 19 the noun ἀπιστία occurs; in Hebrews 4:6 and 11 the noun ἀπείθεια. The former (unbelief) leads to the latter (disobedience). Disobedience comes to expression in obstinate opposition to God's will.

Verse 7

ὁρίζει—from the noun ὅρος (boundary) the verb ὁρίζω (I mark, define) is derived. The English derivative is the word *horizon*.

προείρηται—a few manuscripts have the perfect active προείρηκεν (he has said before).

Verse 8

εἰ—this conditional clause is contrary to fact. If Joshua had given the Israelites rest—but he did not provide permanent rest—God would not have spoken later about another day as he did in Psalm 95.

---

15. Geerhardus Vos, *Biblical Theology* (Grand Rapids: Eerdmans, 1954), p. 156.

ἐλάλει—in this statement that is contrary to fact, the use of the imperfect tense is eloquent testimony that God's promise is valid for all generations and that God repeats his offer of eternal rest. For the use of the verb λαλέω, see 1:1, 2.

Verse 9

σαββατισμός—the verb σαββατίζω (I keep the Sabbath) is the basis of the noun σαββατισμός, which occurs only once in the New Testament. The ending -μός signifies the progressive act of keeping the Sabbath.

τῷ λαῷ—modified by the genitive τοῦ θεοῦ (the people *of God*), the noun refers to the believers in the Christian community; that is, the people God has elected for himself (Acts 15:14; 18:10; Rom. 9:25; I Peter 2:10; and see Hos. 1:6, 9; 2:23).

Verse 10

ὁ εἰσελθών—the participle in the aorist indicates that entrance into God's rest happens once.

ὥσπερ—in 4:10 and the immediate broader context, the Greek word order is highly significant. Note that the first word and the last word in the sentence receive the emphasis. Also, the author frequently arranges words in the original Greek (see, for instance, the adjective ἄλλης, which modifies the noun ἡμέρας in Heb. 4:8) in such a way as to accentuate them, much the same as we italicize words for emphasis. Last, the enclitic particle περ adds force to the word ὡς. It means "thoroughly," "indeed," "in fact."

Verse 11

σπουδάσωμεν—this is one of the twelve hortatory subjunctives the author employs in Hebrews. Ten of these are in the present tense; the other two (Heb. 4:1, 11), in the aorist tense.

---

3. God's Word[16]
4:12–13

In the last section of the author's discussion about the rest of God that is reserved for the believers, the focus is on the power of God's Word (v. 12) and on man's inability to hide from that Word (v. 13). Because of the rather striking word order and word choice in these verses, the assumption is that the writer has borrowed a line or two from a poem, circulating in the early church, about the Word of God. This is a possibility. The effect of these two verses, however, is to give the discussion about Sabbath-rest a fitting conclusion by appealing to the nature and authority of the Word of God.

12a. The word of God is living and active.

The writer reminds the reader that God's Word cannot be taken lightly; for if the reader does not wish to listen, he faces no one less than God himself (see Heb. 10:31; 12:29). The Bible is not a collection of religious

---

16. Paragraph division differs in Greek texts and translations. Heb. 4:11–13 is taken as a complete paragraph in Merk, Nes-Al, rsv, mlb, nkjv, and *Moffatt*. On the other hand, the United Bible Society (3d ed.), gnb, nab, neb, jb, and niv put 4:11 with the preceding paragraph and place 4:12–13 separately.

writings from the ancient past, but a book that speaks to all people everywhere in nearly all the languages of the world. The Bible demands a response, because God does not tolerate indifference and disobedience.

In their interpretation of verse 12a, some scholars assert that the phrase *Word of God* is a reference to Jesus.[17] This view is difficult to maintain, even though such a reference exists in Revelation 19:13 (where the rider on the white horse is called the Word of God). The phrase *Word of God* occurs at least thirty-nine times in the New Testament and almost exclusively is the designation for the spoken or written Word of God rather than the Son of God. In the introductory verses of the Epistle to the Hebrews, the writer clearly states that *God* spoke to the forefathers in the past, and in the present he spoke to us in his Son (Heb. 1:1–2). In Hebrews Jesus is called the Son of God, but never the Word of God.[18]

In the original Greek, the participle *living* stands first in the sentence and therefore receives all the emphasis. This participle describes the first characteristic of God's spoken and written Word: that Word is alive! For example, Stephen, reciting Israel's history in the desert, says that Moses at Mount Sinai "received living words" (Acts 7:38), and Peter tells the recipients of his first epistle that they "have been born again . . . through the living and enduring word of God" (I Peter 1:23).

A second characteristic is that the Word of God is active. That is, it is effective and powerful. (The original Greek uses a word from which we have derived the term *energy*.) God's Word, then, is energizing in its effect. No one can escape that living and active Word. Just as God's spoken Word brought forth his beautiful creation, so his Word recreates man dead in transgressions and sins (Eph. 2:1–5). As in the wilderness some Israelites refused to listen to God's Word while others showed obedience, so today we see that "the message of the cross is foolishness to those who are perishing, but to us who are being saved it is the power of God" (I Cor. 1:18).

The Bible is not a dead letter, comparable to a law that is no longer enforced. Those people who choose to ignore the message of Scripture will experience not merely the power of God's Word but its keen edge as well.

12b. Sharper than any double-edged sword.

In the ancient world, the double-edged sword was the sharpest weapon available in any arsenal. And in verse 12b, the author of Hebrews likens the Word of God to this weapon. (In a similar passage [Rev. 1:16] we read about the "sharp double-edged sword" coming out of the mouth of Jesus as John

17. Among recent defenders of this view is James Swetnam in "Jesus as *Logos* in Hebrews 4:12, 13," *Bib* 62 (2, 1981): 214–24. The view, although prevalent in the early church and in the Middle Ages, is rejected by modern commentators. Bertold Klappert (in *NIDNTT*, vol. 3, p. 1113) writes, "This word of God, which had its beginning in the words of Jesus (Heb. 2:3) is decisively grounded in the exaltation of Jesus to the right hand of God (Heb. 1:5ff.) and in his installation as eschatological high priest (Heb. 7:1ff.)."

18. Says Henry Alford, *Alford's Greek Testament: An Exegetical and Critical Commentary,* 4 vols. (Grand Rapids: Guardian, 1976), vol. 4, pt. 1, p. 83, "Every where He is the Son of God, not His Word." See also Hugh Montefiore, *The Epistle to the Hebrews* (New York and Evanston: Harper and Row, 1964), p. 87.

saw him on the island of Patmos. Whether this means that the tongue resembles a dagger is an open question.) The symbolism conveys the message that God's judgment is stern, righteous, and awful. God has the ultimate power over his creatures; those who refuse to listen to his Word face judgment and death, while those who obey enter God's rest and have life eternal. Let no one take the spoken and written Word for granted; let no one ignore it; let no one willfully oppose it. That Word cuts and divides, much as the scalpel of a surgeon uncovers the most delicate nerves of the human body.

However, the Word of God also provides protection. Paul in his Epistle to the Ephesians equates the Word with the sword of the Spirit—that is, part of the Christian's spiritual armor (6:17).

12c. It penetrates even to dividing soul and spirit, joints and marrow; it judges the thoughts and attitudes of the heart.

I do not think that the writer of Hebrews is teaching the doctrine that man consists of body, soul, and spirit (I Thess. 5:23). Of course, we can make a distinction between soul and spirit by saying that the soul relates to man's physical existence; and the spirit, to God.[19] But the author does not make distinctions in this verse. He speaks in terms of that which is not done and in a sense cannot be done.

Who is able to divide soul and spirit or joints and marrow? And what judge can know the thoughts and attitudes of the heart? The author uses symbolism to say that what man ordinarily does not divide, God's Word separates thoroughly. Nothing remains untouched by Scripture, for it addresses every aspect of man's life. The Word continues to divide the spiritual existence of man and even his physical being. All the recesses of body and soul—including the thoughts and attitudes—face the sharp edge of God's dividing sword. Whereas man's thoughts remain hidden from his neighbor's probing eye, God's Word uncovers them.

God's Word is called a discerner of man's thoughts and intentions. In the Psalter David says:

> O Lord, you have searched me
> and you know me.
> You know when I sit and when I rise;
> you perceive my thoughts from afar.
> You discern my going out and my lying down;
> you are familiar with all my ways. [Ps. 139:1–3]

And Jesus utters these words:

> As for the person who hears my words but does not keep them, I do not judge him. For I did not come to judge the world, but to save it. There is a judge for the one who rejects me and does not accept my words; that very word which I spoke will condemn him at the last day. [John 12:47–48]

---

19. For a complete discussion on trichotomy, see William Hendriksen, *I–II Thessalonians,* New Testament Commentary series (Grand Rapids: Baker, 1955), pp. 146–50.

The Lord with his Word exposes the motives hidden in a man's heart. In his epistle the author stresses the act of God's speaking to man. For instance, the introductory verses (Heb. 1:1–2) illustrate this fact clearly. And repeatedly, when quoting the Old Testament Scriptures, the writer uses this formula: God, Jesus, or the Holy Spirit says (consult the many quotations, for example, in the first four chapters). The Word is not a written document of past centuries. It is alive and current; it is powerful and effective; and it is undivided and unchanged. Written in times and cultures from which we are far removed, the Word of God nevertheless touches man today. God addresses man in the totality of his existence, and man is unable to escape the impact of God's Word.

13. Nothing in all creation is hidden from God's sight. Everything is uncovered and laid bare before the eyes of him to whom we must give account.

The emphasis in 4:12–13 shifts from the Word of God to God himself. If God's Word uncovers everything, then it follows that God himself is fully aware of all things. It is therefore impossible for man to hide his sinful motives in the dark corners of his heart. God knows. He sees everything; even darkness is as light to him (Ps. 139:12).

Moreover, the past, the present, and the future are all alike to God. While we are bound to time and place, God dwells in eternity and transcends all that he has made in his great creation. He created the magnificent constellations in outer space and hung the stars in place. He also created the tiny spider that busily weaves its web. If then his eye is on the sparrow, does he not know the hidden motives of man? Before we open our mouths to speak, God already knows. If we remain silent, he discerns.

No creature is hidden from God's sight, because with God everything is light—there is no darkness. Man, the pinnacle of God's creation, is invited to walk in that light, so that he may see clearly. Consider these verses:

> Your word is a lamp to my feet and a light for my path. [Ps. 119:105]

> I am the light of the world. Whoever follows me will never walk in darkness, but will have the light of life. [John 8:12]

The unbeliever seeks to hide from God but is unable to do so (Jer. 23:24). Secret sins man can hide from his fellow man, but before God sinful man is "uncovered and laid bare." This latter expression, in the original Greek, refers to the neck. The precise meaning of the word, however, is not clear. Perhaps it indicates that a sinner will have his head pushed up and back so that his face and neck will be exposed to view.[20] Whatever the interpretation may have been, the expression itself is sufficiently clear in context. It is synonymous with the word *uncovered* and indicates that God's all-seeing eye rests upon everything.

---

20. Franz Delitzsch, *Commentary on the Epistle to the Hebrews*, 2 vols. (Edinburgh: Clark, 1877), vol. 1, p. 216.

The clause "to whom we must give account" is rather interesting. The books must be audited, and all the bills, payments, and receipts handed over to be checked. Man must give an account of himself before God, the auditor. The books of man's conscience are open before God's eyes. Nothing escapes him.

In the last day sinners may call to the mountains and the rocks, "Fall on us and hide us from the face of him who sits on the throne and from the wrath of the Lamb!" (Rev. 6:16). In the final judgment, everyone must give an account of himself. Only those who are in Christ Jesus will hear the liberating word *acquitted*.

Doctrinal Considerations in 4:12-13

In a sense, 4:12 is a summary statement of earlier references to the spoken and written Word of God. Whether spoken or written, God's Word is a unity. The same voice speaks with clarity and authority to every generation. It addressed the Israelites in the desert, the citizens of Israel in David's day, and the recipients of the Epistle to the Hebrews in the first century. That voice still speaks today.

The Word of God is living and powerful in the hearts and lives of the believers. Unbelievers, however, brazenly reject the very Word that addresses them. They echo the words of William Ernest Henley:

> It matters not how strait the gate,
> How charged with punishments the scroll,
> I am the master of my fate;
> I am the captain of my soul.

Paul writes to the Corinthians that his preaching is to the one the smell of death, to the other the fragrance of life (II Cor. 2:16). And Calvin observes that God "never promises to us salvation in Christ, without pronouncing, on the other hand, vengeance on unbelievers, who by rejecting Christ bring death on themselves."[21]

The expression *double-edged sword* ought not be taken literally and thus interpreted to mean that one edge is directed toward believers and the other toward unbelievers. The writer uses symbolism to imply that the Word of God does indeed "cut to the heart" (Acts 2:37).

God's knowledge is all-comprehensive, including self-knowledge and complete understanding of all events, past, present, and future.[22] Scripture repeatedly refers to God's omniscience (see Deut. 2:7; I Sam. 16:7; I Chron. 28:9, 12; Job 23:10; 24:23; 31:4; 37:16; Ps. 1:6; 33:13; 37:18; 119:168; 139:1–4).

Hebrews 4:12 teaches that God's Word "judges the thoughts and attitudes of the heart." Here, as elsewhere in the epistle, there is no reference to Christ as the judge. Quoting Deuteronomy 32:36 ("The Lord will judge his people" [Heb. 10:30]), the writer concludes, "It is a dreadful thing to fall into the hands of the living God" (Heb. 10:31).

---

21. Calvin, *Hebrews*, pp. 102–3.
22. Louis Berkhof, *Systematic Theology* (Grand Rapids: Eerdmans, 1953), p. 67.

Greek Words, Phrases, and Constructions in 4:12–13

Verse 12

ζῶν—the use of the present active participle teaches that the Word of God does not merely exist; it must be understood as "having in itself energies of action"[23] (see I Peter 1:23).

ἐνεργής—a variant reading in Codex Vaticanus reads ἐναργής (clear, evident). As an adjective from the verb ἐνεργέω (I am effective), ἐνεργής means "effective, powerful."

τομώτερος—this adjective in the comparative occurs once in the New Testament; it is derived from τομός (sharp), which in turn is from the verb τέμνω (I cut).

δίστομος—the compound adjective *double-edged* (δίς [twice] and στόμα [mouth]) appears in the Septuagint in Judges 3:16 and Proverbs 5:4; and in the New Testament in Hebrews 4:12 and Revelation 1:16; 2:12; 19:15 (variant reading).

διϊκνούμενος—this present middle participle from the deponent verb διϊκνέομαι (I penetrate) occurs once in the New Testament, but see Exodus 26:28 in the Septuagint. The form is a compound of the preposition διά (through) and the verb ἵκω or ἱκνέομαι (I come, reach, arrive at).

μερισμοῦ—from the verb μερίζω (I divide), the noun—because of the ending -μός—shows progressive action. In Thayer's *Lexicon*, preference is given to translating the word passively: "*even to the division*, etc., i.e. to that most hidden spot, the dividing line between soul and spirit, where the one passes into the other."[24]

Verse 13

τετραχηλισμένα—as a perfect passive participle of τραχηλίζω (I seize the neck; I expose by bending back), the word has been interpreted in numerous ways. The basic meaning is "to expose." Because the verb occurs only once in the New Testament, the exact meaning cannot be ascertained.

ὁ λόγος—the noun λόγος appears at the beginning of 4:12 and at the end of 4:13. The latter evidently is in the form of an idiom, "we must give an account," while the former refers to the Word of God.

Summary of Chapter 4

The focus in chapter 4 is not so much on the unbelieving Israelites who refused to obey God as it is on the believers who in faith enter God's promised rest. The unbelieving desert travelers failed to listen to God's voice and perished on the way to the land God had promised. The Christian who lives by faith enters into God's rest, the Sabbath-rest for the people of God. And this entrance into rest can be accomplished only by listening obediently to the gospel.

The first thirteen verses of this chapter form an introduction to the author's discussion about the high priesthood of Jesus the Son of God. Already in 2:17–18 the author introduced this subject, which in succeeding chapters he fully develops and explains.

23. B. F. Westcott, *Commentary on the Epistle to the Hebrews* (Grand Rapids: Eerdmans, 1950), p. 102.
24. Thayer, *Lexicon*, p. 400. His italics.

5

Jesus' High Priesthood

4:14–5:10

Outline

4   14 Therefore, since we have a great high priest who has gone through the heavens, Jesus the Son of God, let us hold firmly to the faith we profess. 15 For we do not have a high priest who is unable to sympathize with our weaknesses, but we have one who has been tempted in every way, just as we are—yet was without sin. 16 Let us then approach the throne of grace with confidence, so that we may receive mercy and find grace to help us in our time of need.

A. Encouragement for the Readers
4:14–16

In his series of illustrations establishing the excellence of Jesus, the writer now contrasts Jesus with Aaron, the high priest. In Hebrews 2:17 and 3:1, the author introduced Jesus as high priest. With occasional digressions,[1] the author writes extensively about the office and work of the high priest (see Heb. 5:5, 10; 6:20; 7:26; 8:1; 9:11; 10:21).

14. Therefore, since we have a great high priest who has gone through the heavens, Jesus the Son of God, let us hold firmly to the faith we profess.

Note the following points:

a. Because of his sonship, Jesus already is great.
b. Thus, being high priest does not make Jesus great.
c. Jesus excels because he is divine.
d. Only Jesus has gone through the heavens.
e. The difference, therefore, between Jesus and Aaron is immeasurable.

The adverb *therefore* ought not be understood to refer to the immediately preceding context but to Hebrews 2:17, where the subject of Christ's priesthood is first introduced.[2] The author, who briefly referred to the "high priest

---

1. The chapter division is somewhat infelicitous at this juncture. Martin Luther in his Bible translation boldly begins chapter 5 at Heb. 4:14. Most commentators believe that the concluding verses of chapter 4 should be interpreted with the following chapter on the high priesthood of Christ.
2. Franz Delitzsch prefers to connect the word *therefore* with the exhortation: "Let us therefore, having a great high priest who hath passed through the heavens, Jesus the Son of God, hold fast by our confession" (*Commentary on the Epistle to the Hebrews,* 2 vols. [Edinburgh: Clark, 1877], vol. 1, p. 217). However, the adverb *therefore* in the Greek has a variety of meanings, which should be determined on the basis of context, "and at times it may be left untranslated." (See Bauer, p. 592.) Indeed, a number of translations delete the adverb.

whom we confess" in Hebrews 3:1, now is ready to explain the significance of Jesus' priesthood.

Since we have a great high priest. The emphasis falls on the term *great,* which also occurs in Hebrews 10:21 ("since we have a great priest over the house of God") and Hebrews 13:20 (where Jesus is called "that great Shepherd of the sheep"). The adjective *great* indicates that Jesus is superior to earthly high priests and shepherds.[3] He is the *great* high priest, not the one who entered the Most Holy Place once a year and sprinkled blood to atone first for his own sins and then for those of the people. Jesus, as the great high priest, excels earthly high priests.

Who has gone through the heavens. The Jewish high priest entered the inner sanctuary of the temple once a year and stood momentarily in the very presence of God. Jesus, by contrast, has entered the heavens and is always in the presence of God (Heb. 9:24). He has been raised from the dead, has ascended to heaven, and sits at the right hand of God the Father. He has gone through and is "exalted above the heavens" (Heb. 7:26). He is majestic in power and glory because he is the Son of God, human and divine.

Let us hold firmly to the faith we profess. The author of Hebrews uses the earthly name of Jesus to focus attention on his ministry, suffering, death, resurrection, and ascension. Jesus could not be in heaven as the great high priest without having performed his priestly work on earth.

Once more the writer of Hebrews intersperses his teaching with exhortation. This exhortation can be connected logically with the first part of the verse ("since we have a great high priest who has gone through the heavens"). Characteristically, the author includes himself in the exhortation when he writes, "Let us hold firmly to the faith we profess" (see also Heb. 3:1; 10:23).

What then is this faith we profess? Is it a formulated confession of faith? Perhaps. But as Philip Edgcumbe Hughes writes, faith "is the belief that is both inwardly entertained by the heart and outwardly professed before men."[4] This is, of course, a paraphrase of Romans 10:10, "For it is with your heart that you believe and are justified, and it is with your mouth that you confess and are saved." This faith we must continue to profess with heart and mouth, joyfully, openly, so that our fellow man, too, may hear about Jesus the Son of God.

15. For we do not have a high priest who is unable to sympathize with our weaknesses, but we have one who has been tempted in every way, just as we are—yet was without sin.

The recipients of the epistle might have raised an objection to the author's teaching: Because Jesus is the Son of God and is exalted in heaven, far

---

3. C. P. Sherman ("A Great High Priest," *ExpT* 34 [1922]: 235) demonstrates from the Hebrew that two terms were used: "the great priest" and "the chief priest." Ceslaus Spicq, in *L'Épître aux Hébreux,* 3d ed., 2 vols. (Paris: Gabalda, 1953), vol. 2, p. 92, notes that in the time between the accession of Herod the Great and the destruction of the temple there were no fewer than twenty-six high priests.

4. Philip Edgcumbe Hughes, *Commentary on the Epistle to the Hebrews* (Grand Rapids: Eerdmans, 1977), p. 171.

removed from man's daily toils and struggles, his priesthood is of little consequence. The author, however, anticipates objections and in Hebrews 4:15 counters them. Not so, he says, for when I introduced the teaching I stated that we, the brothers of Jesus, have a high priest who is merciful and faithful. And "because he himself suffered when he was tempted, he is able to help those who are being tempted" (Heb. 2:18).

The writer makes his point by stating this truth negatively and positively.

a. *Negatively.* The double negative—we do not have a high priest who is unable to sympathize—expresses a positive idea: yes, we have a highly exalted high priest who can descend to our level.

The original recipients of Hebrews knew that the teaching about Jesus' high priesthood was articulated for the first time in this epistle. Perhaps they had to endure hardship, persecution, and isolation from the Jews if they professed the high priesthood of Jesus. They may have wondered: Would the exalted high priest understand their weaknesses if they failed to profess him publicly? Would he understand their situation? Yes, the author assured them, the heavenly high priest is able to sympathize. If we confess his name publicly, he suffers with us when others reproach, scorn, and insult us.

b. *Positively.* Jesus is not only fully divine; he is also fully human and thus understands our weaknesses and our temptations. Furthermore, Jesus himself experienced weaknesses and temptations. At the onset of his ministry, he was tempted by Satan; he coped with thirst, weariness, desertion, and disappointments throughout his earthly ministry.

Jesus, fully acquainted with human nature, is "touched with the feeling of our weaknesses," as B. F. Westcott puts it.[5] He has been tempted—in extent and range—in every way. Nothing in human experience is foreign to him, for he himself has endured it. And he has been tempted just as intensely as we are. The author adds the qualifying phrase *yet was without sin.*

When he was in the wilderness, Jesus experienced hunger, and the devil tempted him by asking him to make bread out of stones (Matt. 4:2–3). While hanging on the cross, he was mocked by chief priests, teachers of the law, and elders, who said, "Let him come down now from the cross . . . for he said, 'I am the Son of God' " (Matt. 27:42, 43). He endured the full range of temptations, although, as the writer notes, without sinning. Sin is the only human experience in which Christ has no part.

The temptations we endure are given to us in accordance with what we are able to bear. God's watchful eye is always upon us, so that we do not succumb. Says Paul:

> No temptation has seized you except what is common to man. And God
> is faithful; he will not let you be tempted beyond what you can bear.

---

5. B. F. Westcott, *Commentary on the Epistle to the Hebrews* (Grand Rapids: Eerdmans, 1950), p. 107. And John Calvin classifies as infirmities the physical as well as the spiritual: "fear, sorrow, the dread of death and similar things." See Calvin's *Epistle to the Hebrews* (Grand Rapids: Eerdmans, 1949), p. 108.

> But when you are tempted, he will also provide a way out so that you
> can stand up under it. [I Cor. 10:13]

We, however, will never be able to fathom the depth of the temptations
Jesus endured. Yet he withstood the depth, as well as the force, of these
temptations. He overcame them as the sinless One.

Is Jesus (the sinless One) able to sympathize with us (weakened by sin) in
our temptations? Because of his sinless nature, says John Albert Bengel, "the
mind of the Savior much more acutely perceived the forms of temptation
than we who are weak," not only during his earthly ministry but also during
his service as the exalted high priest.[6] He anticipates temptations we are
going to face, sympathizes fully with us, and "is able to help [us] who are
being tempted" (Heb. 2:18).

**16. Let us then approach the throne of grace with confidence, so that
we may receive mercy and find grace to help us in our time of need.**

What encouraging words! The writer throughout his epistle exhorts the
readers numerous times, but in this particular verse he has a special word
for us. This time he does not exhort believers to rectify their way of life; he
commends us for coming in prayer to God and urges us to do so confidently.

a. "Let us then approach the throne of grace with confidence." The invitation to approach the throne of grace implies that the readers are already
doing this. The author also uses the same verb in Hebrews 10:22 ("let us
draw near to God with a sincere heart in full assurance of faith"). He later
repeats the same invitation in slightly different wording (see Heb. 7:25;
10:1; 11:6; 12:18, 22).

The verb *approach* may have a religious connotation, because it often referred to the priests who in their cultic service approached God with sacrifices (Lev. 9:7; 21:17, 21; 22:3; Num. 18:3).[7] In Hebrews 4:16 the writer
urges us to come near to the throne of grace in prayer, for the only sacrifice
a believer can bring is a broken and a contrite heart (Ps. 51:17). The great
high priest has brought the supreme sacrifice in offering himself on the
cross on behalf of his people. The merciful and faithful high priest invites
the weak and tempted sinner to come to the throne of grace.

What is meant by the phrase *throne of grace*? This is an explicit reference
to the kingship of the Son of God (Heb. 1:2–4). Jesus sits at the right hand
of God and has been given full authority in heaven and on earth (Matt.
28:18). But the word *grace* implies that the reference is also to the priesthood
of Christ. The sinner who comes to the throne of grace in repentance and
faith indeed finds the forgiving grace of Jesus.

---

6. John Albert Bengel, *Gnomon of the New Testament,* ed. Andrew R. Fausset, 7th ed., 5 vols.
(Edinburgh: Clark, 1877), vol. 4, p. 384.

7. Spicq, *Hébreux,* vol. 2, p. 94. James Moffatt asserts that the verb applies to a court or to
authority. See his *Epistle to the Hebrews,* International Critical Commentary series (Edinburgh:
Clark, 1963), p. 60.

Moreover, we are exhorted to come to the throne with confidence; that is, we may come boldly (Heb. 3:6; 10:19, 35), not rashly or in fear of judgment, but "in full confidence, openness to God and in the hope of the fullness of the glory of God."[8] Jesus invites his people to approach freely, without hesitation. He holds out the golden scepter, as it were, and says, "Come!"

b. "So that we may receive mercy and find grace." Although the terms *mercy* and *grace* are often interpreted as being synonyms, their difference ought to be noted. Westcott makes the distinction succinctly:

> Man needs mercy for past failure, and grace for present and future work. There is also a difference as to the mode of attainment in each case. Mercy is to be "taken" as it is extended to man in his weakness; grace is to be "sought" by man according to his necessity.[9]

The mercy of God is directed to sinners in misery or distress; they receive God's compassion when they approach him. And whereas God's mercy extends to all his creatures (Ps. 145:9), his grace, as the writer of Hebrews indicates in Hebrews 4:16, extends to all who approach the throne of God. Mercy is characterized as God's tender compassion; grace, as his goodness and love.[10]

c. "To help us in our time of need." Help is given at the right moment in the hour of need. The author is not saying that the help is constant, but rather that it alleviates the need of the moment. That need may be material, physical, or spiritual. When we call on the name of the Lord in faith and approach the throne of God, he will hear and answer. He stands ready to help (see Heb. 2:18).

This aid, in the form of grace, comes when temptation seems to sway us. God provides the means to find a way out of our temptations. God is faithful (I Cor. 10:13).

Doctrinal Considerations in 4:14–16

When the writer states that Jesus "has gone through the heavens" (v. 14), he implies that Jesus has entered the presence of God the Father. The Aaronic high priest, by entering the Most Holy Place once a year, stood in the presence of God. Because Jesus appears before God the Father in heaven, he transcends the Aaronic high priest. Therefore, the author of Hebrews calls him the "*great* high priest" (italics added).

The use of the plural noun *heavens* in the original Greek is rather common in

---

8. Hans-Christoph Hahn, *NIDNTT*, vol. 2, p. 736. This sense of assurance, writes Heinrich Schlier, "works itself out in the confidence and openness which [causes one] not [to] be ashamed when [he] stands before the Judge" (*TDNT*, vol. 5, p. 884).
9. Westcott, *Hebrews*, p. 109. Also see Otto Michel, *Der Brief an die Hebräer*, 10th ed. (Göttingen: Vandenhoeck and Ruprecht, 1957), p. 124.
10. Louis Berkhof, *Systematic Theology* (Grand Rapids: Eerdmans, 1953), pp. 71–72.

the Epistle to the Hebrews (Heb. 1:10 [Ps. 102:25]; 4:14; 7:26; 9:23; 12:23, 25). It is possible that the plural, which is also common in the Septuagint and in the New Testament (especially in Matthew's Gospel), conveys in the Epistle to the Hebrews the idea of completeness. However, the author uses the word *heaven* in the singular, too (Heb. 9:24; 11:12; 12:26 [Hag. 2:6]).

In rabbinic writings and in apocryphal literature, the conception of a multilayered heaven is somewhat common. In fact, Paul even speaks of knowing a man "caught up to the third heaven" and "to paradise" (II Cor. 12:2, 4). It seems that Paradise is located in either the third or the seventh heaven. Speculations about the heavenly Jerusalem, the location of God's throne, and the heavenly altar are numerous.

Because of the scarcity of information on this point in the Epistle to the Hebrews, we do well to refrain from speculation. In 4:14, it is implied that God's dwelling place is not in heaven; that is, "not within his creation to which heaven belongs, but above the heavens."[11] Jesus has transcended the heavens, has come to the throne of God, and has taken his place at God's right hand as the great high priest.

If Jesus endured temptations during his earthly ministry as the Son of God, how do we understand the author's teaching that he "has been tempted in every way, *just as we are*" (v. 15; italics added)? Herman N. Ridderbos, commenting on Jesus' temptation in the desert, raises this question in a slightly different form: Could Jesus fall into sin or was the temptation imaginary? Although Jesus as God's Son surpassed Satan and therefore could not fall, Jesus was not necessarily immune to temptation.[12] We admit that for us it is difficult to understand how the Son of God, who could not sin, was tempted just as we are. From our limited perspective, we are unable to explain the difficulty inherent in the biblical teaching about Jesus' sinlessness and temptation.

Greek Words, Phrases, and Constructions in 4:14–16

Verse 14

ἔχοντες—in the context of the verse, the present active participle may express cause.

διεληλυθότα—the perfect active participle, accusative singular masculine, derives from διά (through) and ἔρχομαι (I go). It denotes completed action in the past with lasting results for the present.

κρατῶμεν—a hortatory subjunctive, as a present active from κρατέω (I hold firmly, I keep faithfully; see Rev. 2:25; 3:11).

---

11. Hans Bietenhard, *NIDNTT,* vol. 2, p. 195.
12. Herman N. Ridderbos, *Mattheüs,* Korte Verklaring, 2 vols. (Kampen: Kok, 1952), vol. 1, p. 68. Geerhardus Vos, in *The Teaching of the Epistle to the Hebrews* (Grand Rapids: Eerdmans, 1956), p. 103, asserts that for Christ "there was as much real *appeal* to sin . . . as there is with us, but in His case there was no *issue* of sin." R. Williams argues that Jesus had to have actual participation in the experience of sinning in order to share fully in the human weaknesses of man. Next, Jesus had to subject himself to the process of learning obedience and thus achieve sinlessness when he offered himself on the cross. See Williams's article in *ExpT* 86 (1974): 4–8. Of course, this reasoning controverts Scripture's unequivocal teaching about Jesus' sinlessness (Isa. 53:9; John 8:46; II Cor. 5:21; Heb. 4:15; 7:26; I Peter 1:19; 2:22).

Verse 15

συμπαθῆσαι—in the New Testament the verb appears only twice: in Hebrews 4:15, referring to Jesus, and in Hebrews 10:34, referring to the recipients of the epistle. In extrabiblical literature it occurs numerous times. The aorist tense is constative; that is, the action of the verb does not refer to duration but rather to entirety.

πεπειρασμένον—the perfect passive participle, instead of the aorist passive πειρασθείς (see Heb. 2:18), indicates continued action in the past until its culmination—Jesus' death.

χωρὶς ἁμαρτίας—the last two words in this sentence emphasize the contrast between man, who is tainted by sin, and Jesus, who is sinless. The adverb χωρίς, serving as a preposition, controls the genitive singular ἁμαρτίας.

Verse 16

προσερχώμεθα—we are exhorted, with the hortatory subjunctive, to approach the throne of grace. The present tense suggests that we in fact are doing so.

λάβωμεν. . .εὕρωμεν—the verse shows chiasmus with two verbs and two nouns. The noun *mercy* follows the verb *to receive,* and the noun *grace* precedes the verb *to find.* Both verbs are in the aorist tense.

---

5 1 Every high priest is selected from among men and is appointed to represent them in matters related to God, to offer gifts and sacrifices for sins. 2 He is able to deal gently with those who are ignorant and are going astray, since he himself is subject to weakness. 3 This is why he has to offer sacrifices for his own sins, as well as for the sins of the people.

B. Enablement of the High Priest
5:1–3

After encouraging his readers, the author continues his teaching ministry by defining the qualifications for the one who serves as high priest. The obvious reference is to the institution of the Aaronic priesthood (Heb. 5:4); the high priest's appointment, duties, and obligations were divinely stipulated and were to be meticulously observed.

1. Every high priest is selected from among men and is appointed to represent them in matters related to God, to offer gifts and sacrifices for sins.

Three points require our attention.

a. A high priest is selected. The writer constructs a beautifully balanced sentence in which he describes the selection, appointment, and duty of a high priest. According to the law of Moses (Exod. 28–29, Lev. 8–10, and Num. 16–18), only Aaron and his sons were permitted to serve at the altar. "The priesthood was therefore a fraternity fenced round with irremovable barriers, for they had been fixed forever by natural descent."[13] From what

---

13. Emil Schürer, *A History of the Jewish People in the Time of Jesus Christ,* 5 vols. (Edinburgh: Clark, 1885), vol. 1, div. 2, p. 209.

we are able to learn about the selection process, a high priest was chosen from the members of relatively few influential priestly families. He did not serve actively as high priest for any length of time, as is evident from the Gospels and the Acts (John 18:13; Acts 4:6). The author of Hebrews, however, is not interested in historical details. Rather, he identifies the principle: the high priest is selected from among men. He writes in terms of biblical regulations and not historical aberrations.

b. A high priest is appointed. Note the passive voice of the verb that is used to describe the process of selection and appointment. The writer wishes to indicate that the high priest does not appoint himself, but by implication is appointed by God. The high-priestly office, therefore, is based on a divine calling (Heb. 5:4), especially in view of the high priest's work. That is, a sinful high priest is appointed to represent sinful people in matters related to God.

c. A high priest is to offer sacrifices. In the original Greek, the phrase *matters related to God* is used in Hebrews 2:17, where the author specifies that this includes the high priest's work of "mak[ing] atonement for the sins of the people." This work consists of representing men before God when the people come with gifts and sacrifices. They bring these gifts and sacrifices to the high priest so that he can offer them to God for the sins of the people.

The author of Hebrews explains this concept in a subsequent verse. The phrase *gifts and sacrifices* occurs again in Hebrews 8:3 and is abridged in the next verse where only the term *gifts* appears. In using this condensation, the author seems to imply that the two terms are synonyms, for every gift to God offered for sin is essentially a sacrifice. These gifts, then, the high priest presents to God to remove sin, to bring about reconciliation, and to gain access into God's grace (Rom. 5:2). The high priest is the intermediary between God and his people.

2. He is able to deal gently with those who are ignorant and are going astray, since he himself is subject to weakness.

The high priest, representing man before God, may never lose patience with the one he represents, in spite of that man's sins and shortcomings. As intercessor, the high priest must exercise moderation in expressing anger or sorrow concerning errors and faults of his fellow man. The high priest in the Old Testament era was a type of mediator whose fulfillment came in Jesus Christ.

However, not every sin can be brought to the high priest for remission. The writer of Hebrews is specific, for he says that the high priest deals gently with those who are ignorant and who go astray. Nothing is said about sin committed purposely to grieve God. By implication, the high priest must know the difference between sins perpetrated to vex God (Ps. 95:7–11) and sins committed because of weakness. Sins of ignorance usually result from a lack of paying attention to God's commandments, whereas intentional sins stem from a rebellious heart and mind fully acquainted with the law of God (Num. 15:22–31; also see Lev. 4, 5, and 22:14).

The high priest ought to deal gently with the people but should neither overlook or condone sin nor rank himself above the people. He himself daily confronted temptation and, because of his own human weakness, committed sin. Because the high priest had to cope with his own sinful nature, he was an equal of the people who sought his intercession for the sins they committed in weakness. Moreover, because of his ability to identify with his fellow man, he could deal gently with them in leading them to God.

The writer of Hebrews portrays the weakness, which the high priest shares with the people he helps, as something that clings to him as a garment covers his body. The realization of his own weakness and yielding to temptation causes the high priest to be moderate in expressing anger or grief.

3. This is why he has to offer sacrifices for his own sins, as well as for the sins of the people.

Verse 3 is an explanatory note in which the writer emphasizes what he already has stated in the preceding verse, where he pointed to the weakness of the high priest. Now, making an obvious reference to Leviticus 9:7 and 16:6, 15–16, he says that Aaron is told to sacrifice a sin offering and a burnt offering for himself and for the people. The writer of Hebrews indicates the obligation that the high priest has to offer a sacrifice for himself and the people he represents.

We should remember that, although the author is drawing a parallel between the Levitical high priest and Jesus the great high priest, not everything in the comparison is equal. The most significant difference is that Jesus "does not need to offer sacrifices day after day, first for his own sins, and then for the sins of the people. He sacrificed for their sins once for all when he offered himself" (Heb. 7:27).

For the moment, however, the author speaks of high priests in the Old Testament era. He alludes to the ritual of the annual entrance of the high priest into the Most Holy Place on the Day of Atonement; that is, on the tenth day of the seventh month, Tishri (approximately equivalent to October). According to Leviticus 16, Aaron had to

1. offer a bull for his own sin offering to atone for his own sin and the sin of his household,
2. enter the Most Holy Place with incense,
3. sprinkle the blood of the bull on the atonement cover of the ark,
4. cast lots over two live goats brought by the people,
5. kill one of the goats for a sin offering for the nation, and sprinkle its blood inside the Most Holy Place,
6. place his hands on the head of the live goat and confess the sins of the people, and
7. send the live goat away into the wilderness.[14]

---

14. Charles L. Feinberg, "Day of Atonement," *ZPEB*, vol. 1, p. 414.

The high priest made intercession for his people by praying that God might forgive the sins he himself and they had committed:

> O God, I have committed iniquity,
> transgressed, and sinned before thee,
> I and my house.
> O God, forgive the iniquities and
> transgressions and sins which
> I have committed and transgressed
> and sinned before thee,
> I and my house.[15]

Greek Words, Phrases, and Constructions in 5:1–3

Verse 1

λαμβανόμενος—the present passive participle indicates continuity. The term of office for the high priest was relatively short, and upon termination a successor had to be appointed. The passive voice shows that a man could not appoint himself to this office.

καθίσταται—the form is a present passive indicative, third person singular, from καθίστημι and καθιστάνω (I appoint, put in charge, ordain; see Heb. 7:28; 8:3). The verb should not be interpreted as a middle, for the words τὰ . . . θεόν do not lend themselves as a direct object.

Verse 2

μετριοπαθεῖν—although the verb is related to συμπαθέω (Heb. 4:15), it ought not be considered a synonym.[16] In the New Testament it occurs only once. In the writings of Philo, Plutarch, and Josephus the word means "to restrain or moderate one's anger."

τοῖς ἀγνοοῦσιν καὶ πλανωμένοις—the use of only one definite article indicates that the two participles ἀγνοοῦσιν (present active) and πλανωμένοις (present passive) describe one group of people. The active voice refers to the mental and spiritual condition of the readers; the passive voice implies an agent.

περίκειται—this compound verb is the present passive of περί (around) and κεῖμαι (I lie). The word appears in Mark 9:42, Luke 17:2, and Acts 28:20, as well as Hebrews 5:2 and 12:1.

Verse 3

ὀφείλει—the verb, in the present active, expresses obligation or necessity. Someone may be obligated, because of legal, conventional, or divine necessity, to act or to be the object of action (e.g., receive punishment). In the context of this verse it means the high priest, because of his office, ought to present sacrifices for himself and for the people.

---

15. *Mishna*, Moed Yoma 3.8, ed. H. Danby (London: Oxford University Press, 1967), p. 165.
16. Wilhelm Michaelis, *TDNT*, vol. 5, p. 938.

4 No one takes this honor upon himself; he must be called by God, just as Aaron was. 5 So Christ also did not take upon himself the glory of becoming a high priest. But God said to him,

"You are my Son;
    today I have become your Father."
6 And he says in another place,
    "You are a priest forever,
        in the order of Melchizedek."
7 During the days of Jesus' life on earth, he offered up prayers and petitions with loud cries and tears to the one who could save him from death, and he was heard because of his reverent submission. 8 Although he was a son, he learned obedience from what he suffered 9 and, once made perfect, he became the source of eternal salvation for all who obey him 10 and was designated by God to be high priest in the order of Melchizedek.

C. Fulfillment of the High-priestly Office
5:4–10

Scholars debate whether Hebrews 5:4 ought to be bracketed with the preceding or the following verse. Does the paragraph end with verse 4, or does a new one begin with that verse? Verses 4 and 5 form a unit for the simple reason that they show parallelism—just as Aaron was, so Christ was also. Therefore, it may be preferable to begin a new paragraph with verse 4.

4. No one takes this honor upon himself; he must be called by God, just as Aaron was. 5. So Christ also did not take upon himself the glory of becoming a high priest. But God said to him,

"You are my Son;
    today I have become your Father."
6. And he says in another place,
    "You are a priest forever,
        in the order of Melchizedek."

In these verses the author of Hebrews focuses on the priesthood of Christ by highlighting the following points.

a. The honor of the office. The office of high priest is an honor that God conferred upon the person who assumed the duties of the office. The high priest, from the time of Aaron to the destruction of the temple in A.D. 70, enjoyed proper recognition from the Hebrew community. Without a doubt, next to the civil leader the high priest held the highest office in the land.

The author, however, stresses that no one takes the honor upon himself for self-gratification. No one fills the office of the high priest merely for the sake of entering into the presence of God on the Day of Atonement, of receiving the respect of the Israelite community, or of wearing the beautiful high-priestly robe and turban (Lev. 8:7–9). The honor associated with the office derives from fulfilling the duties assigned to the high priest. He is to serve God on behalf of the people. He is their representative. He fulfills the mediatorial role of pleading for the remission of sin.

b. The calling by God. Moreover, a high priest must be called by God to this honorable office. Of course, this does not mean that there were no exceptions in Israel's history.[17] But the author of Hebrews is not interested in aberrations; he mentions the name of Aaron to call to mind that God inaugurated the high priesthood in Aaron.

In contemporary terms, this means that no one but he who has been called by God ought to assume the office of minister of the gospel. A seminary president once addressed an incoming class of students and, after words of welcome, said to these aspiring theologians: "Unless the Lord has called you to study for the ministry, we don't want you here."

Anyone inducted into sacred office must be called by God. If this is not the case, he is an affront to God and a provocation to his people. That is, he elevates himself above the people he wants to represent; exhibits a haughty instead of a humble spirit; and, because his concept of holiness is deficient, has a perverted perception of God.

c. Similarity with a difference. The parallelism between Aaron and Christ is expressed in terms of the office they fill. Note, for example, that the author does not use the name *Jesus* but uses *Christ,* the name that describes the office and duty of the Son of God. As Aaron was called and appointed by God (Exod. 28; Num. 16–17) to serve as high priest, so "Christ also did not take upon himself the glory of becoming a high priest." Note that the term *honor* in Hebrews 5:4 is a synonym of the word *glory.*

Yet the difference between Aaron and Christ is profound, because God (as this verse implies) has crowned Christ with glory and honor as high priest. Jesus did not presumptuously appropriate the office of high priest.

d. The Son of God. The author of Hebrews seems to anticipate that someone may raise the objection that Jesus and Aaron, apart from a few similarities pertaining to the office of high priest, have very little in common. That is true, says the writer; and once more he quotes Psalm 2:7, where God says to the Son:

> You are my Son;
> today I have become your Father.

The first time the author uses the quotation to compare the Son with angels (Heb. 1:5). Now the psalm citation indirectly contrasts Christ and Aaron. Jesus is the Son of God, and yet he is called and appointed by God to serve as high priest.

---

17. The history of the high priesthood in Israel from the time of Aaron to the destruction of Jerusalem in A.D. 70 has been recorded, although in summary form, by Josephus in *Antiquities of the Jews* 20.10 (LCL). Numerous men, from the second century before Christ to the cessation of the priesthood, were neither of Aaronic descent nor appointed by God. See especially Schürer, *History of the Jewish People,* vol. 1, div. 2, pp. 195–202. F. F. Bruce, in *The Epistle to the Hebrews,* New International Commentary on the New Testament series (Grand Rapids: Eerdmans, 1964), p. 92, n. 19, lists names and terms of office of persons who were appointed high priest by civil rulers.

In Hebrews 4:14, the writer combines the two concepts of sonship and high priesthood. Says Geerhardus Vos, "He gives exceptionally high value to the high priesthood of Christ, and derives its eminence from the Sonship."[18]

Now it is true that Psalm 2 stresses the royal status of the Son, who received the nations as his inheritance and who rules them with an iron scepter. How then, someone objects, can the Christ be high priest as well? The author expects the question and, as he has done before, uses the Old Testament to give an answer and prove his point.

e. The priest of God. The idea of a king-priest appears in the Old Testament at various places. The first reference we note is Genesis 14:18, where Melchizedek is introduced as king of Salem and priest of God Most High. Next, in Psalm 110:1 David speaks of royalty: "Sit at my right hand until I make your enemies a footstool for your feet." In Psalm 110:4 the reference is to priesthood: "You are a priest forever, in the order of Melchizedek." Finally, Zechariah, who symbolically refers to the Branch (i.e., the Messiah), writes what the Lord Almighty says:

> It is he who will build the temple of the LORD, and he will be clothed with majesty and will sit and rule on his throne. And he will be a priest on his throne. And there will be harmony between the two. [6:13]

The writer of Hebrews was thoroughly familiar with the teaching of the Old Testament. In order to be precise as to the type of priesthood Jesus assumed, he quotes Psalm 110:4, "You are a priest forever, in the order of Melchizedek." We should note that just as God addresses the Son in Psalm 2:7, so he speaks to him in Psalm 110:1 and 4. Thus God announces the kingship and the priesthood of his Son. "The Epistle to the Hebrews stands alone among the New Testament books in calling Christ priest."[19] The cause for this neglect may perhaps be found in the history of the Jewish people. Throughout the ages the Jews had expected a king from David's house. This king would deliver them from foreign oppression. And this king, because David's line was from the tribe of Judah, could not be a priest; priests were descendants of Aaron in the tribe of Levi. Therefore, Jesus was known as *king*. At his birth the wise men called him "king of the Jews" (Matt. 2:2), and this appellation was commonplace during the trial and crucifixion of Jesus. He was not known as *priest*.

Already in the first chapter of Hebrews, the author quoted Psalm 110:1 as irrefutable evidence of Christ's kingship. Now in chapter 5 he cites Psalm 110:4 to describe the unique function and purpose of Christ's priesthood. He makes it clear, although he explains the details in chapter 7, that Jesus' priesthood differs from that of Aaron. Jesus is "a priest forever, in the order of Melchizedek."

---

18. Vos, *Teaching*, p. 77.

19. Ibid., p. 91. The term *priest* occurs 31 times in the New Testament, 14 of which appear in Hebrews. The word *high priest* is featured 123 times in the Gospels, Acts, and Hebrews. The expression does not occur in the Epistles and Revelation. In Hebrews it is used 18 times. In short, it is the writer of the Epistle to the Hebrews who develops the doctrine of the priesthood of Christ.

7. During the days of Jesus' life on earth, he offered up prayers and petitions with loud cries and tears to the one who could save him from death, and he was heard because of his reverent submission.

The writer of Hebrews wants to prove that Jesus did not become a priest after his ascension, but that already during his life on earth the Lord offered up prayers and petitions. The reference to Jesus' earthly life seems to be related to his suffering at Gethsemane. In one sentence the literary artist portrays Jesus in spiritual agony.

a. *Setting.* Although the author has mentioned the name *Jesus* in preceding chapters (Heb. 2:9; 3:1; 4:14), in the present passage he clearly has the Gospel account in mind. He does not quote any specific words of Jesus, but the references are to the experience at Gethsemane (Matt. 26:36–46; Mark 14:32–42; Luke 22:39–46) and to the so-called little Gethsemane incident (John 12:27).

Admittedly, the Gospel writers do not tell us whether Jesus in Gethsemane prayed with loud cries and tears. However, we may infer from the words of Jesus that his agony was intense. Matthew and Mark report that Jesus said, "My soul is overwhelmed with sorrow to the point of death" (Matt. 26:38; Mark 14:34), and Luke writes that Jesus' agony was so acute that "his sweat was like drops of blood falling to the ground" (Luke 22:44).

b. *Function.* At first the phrase *offered up prayers and petitions* seems to be somewhat liturgical. However, the expression, describing Jesus' mediatorial work in the Garden of Gethsemane, must be understood to connote sacrificial activity—Jesus with prayer and petition functioned as priest. On behalf of sinners, whose sin he had taken upon himself, he prayed to God.

The prayers and petitions Jesus uttered cannot accurately be called offerings and have little resemblance to the work of the priest at the altar. But if we consider the function of Jesus' earthly life, especially the last days of his life, we see him offering himself as the sacrificial Lamb of God to atone for the sins of his people. In the Garden of Gethsemane, Jesus prayed, "My Father, if it is possible, may this cup be taken from me. Yet not as I will, but as you will" (Matt. 26:39) and "My Father, if it is not possible for this cup to be taken away unless I drink it, may your will be done" (Matt. 26:42). These prayers and petitions are far removed from liturgical worship. They reveal the depth of Jesus' spiritual and even physical agony expressed by the "drops of blood falling to the ground."

Jesus as the sin-bearer faced the wrath of God against sin. "God made him who had no sin to be sin for us" (II Cor. 5:21). And because of our sins, Christ stood before God as the most wicked of all transgressors. He stood alone as our substitute. The words of Ben H. Price capture this thought poetically:

> It was alone the Savior prayed
> In dark Gethsemane;
> Alone He drained the bitter cup
> And suffered there for me.

> Alone, alone, He bore it all alone;
> He gave Himself to save His own,
> He suffered, bled and died alone, alone.

c. *Manner.* That the evangelists do not record that Jesus uttered his prayers and petitions "with loud cries and tears" does not imply that Jesus' prayers to God were quiet. In fact, his words from the cross were uttered in a loud voice (Matt. 27:46, 50; Mark 15:34, 37; Luke 23:46). Jesus saw the cup of God's wrath handed to him; he felt the curse of God (Gal. 3:13); and he realized that God's judgment was pronounced upon him. He faced death, which for him was not only physical death. If Jesus had died a martyr's death on a cross outside Jerusalem, it would hardly be noteworthy, because numerous people have met equally violent deaths.

However, Jesus died the so-called second death (Rev. 2:11; 20:6, 14; 21:8). What Jesus experienced in the Garden of Gethsemane and on the cross was eternal death. His cry, "My God, my God, why have you forsaken me?" reflected complete separation from God. And that is death unimaginable. We cannot fathom the depth of Jesus' agony when he experienced eternal death. We can only describe it, as the author of Hebrews does. We conclude by saying that Jesus in his separation from God experienced hell itself.

d. *Addressee.* Throughout his earthly ministry Jesus spent much time in prayer, calling God his Father. The intimate relation between Father and Son is especially evident in the high-priestly prayer recorded in John 17. Jesus' prayers uttered in Gethsemane and from the cross also were directed to the Father (Matt. 26:39, 42; Mark 14:36; Luke 22:42; 23:34, 46).

Jesus addressed his prayers "to the one who could save him from death." Many questions can be raised at this point. We could ask why Jesus prayed for deliverance from death when he knew that he was sent to give his life "as a ransom for all men" (I Tim. 2:6). Jesus himself, as the Second Person of the Trinity, had agreed to the decree to redeem mankind by sending the Son of God to earth. His prayer, therefore, did not arise out of ignorance. From one point of view, Jesus knew that the Father had commissioned him to redeem the world through the Son's sacrificial death. From another point of view, Jesus saw the horrors of enduring the indescribable agonies of being forsaken by God and experiencing eternal death.

Jesus fully submitted to the Father's will to enter death in order to remove the curse, fulfill the sentence pronounced against him, and redeem his people. Because of Christ's atoning work and victory over death and the grave, we shall never know the weight of sin, the severity of the curse, the penalty of judgment, or the meaning of eternal death and hell. We have been acquitted and set free because of Jesus, our high priest.

In Gethsemane Jesus prayed that the will of God might be accomplished in respect to the bitter cup of death Christ had to drink. Although this will was done, God did not leave his Son, for "God raised him from the dead, freeing him from the agony of death, because it was impossible for death to keep its hold on him" (Acts 2:24).

e. *Answer.* The prayers and petitions of Jesus were heard. In Luke 22:43 we read, "An angel from heaven appeared to him and strengthened him." This verse follows immediately the account of Jesus' prayer for the removal of the cup. The fact, however, is that the cup of agony was not removed. After Jesus prayed more earnestly, presumably the same prayer, "his sweat was like drops of blood falling to the ground" (Luke 22:44). The question must be raised whether the appearance of the angel constituted support for Jesus or a prolonging of his agony.[20]

How did God answer Jesus' prayer for deliverance from death? The author of Hebrews does not answer this question directly; instead he writes, Jesus "was heard because of his reverent submission." And here is the answer. Jesus accompanied his prayer with the request that the will of God might prevail. Thus, he reverently submitted to the Father's will. He experienced death, but God raised Jesus from the dead (Gal. 1:1).

Translations disagree about the correct rendering of the last clause of Hebrews 5:7. Some give the reading *because of his godly fear.* Others say, "because of his reverent submission."[21] The author of Hebrews uses the same Greek word in Hebrews 12:28, where the translation is "reverence." Moreover, the term occurs only in the Epistle to the Hebrews and nowhere else in the New Testament. On the basis of consistent use in Hebrews, we do well, perhaps, to understand the word to mean "reverent submission." Westcott comments that the expression "marks that careful and watchful reverence which pays regard to every circumstance in that with which it has to deal."[22] Jesus' life was marked by true submission to his Father's will, for even in Gethsemane he prayed that God's will might be done.

8. Although he was a son, he learned obedience from what he suffered 9. and, once made perfect, he became the source of eternal salvation for all who obey him 10. and was designated by God to be high priest in the order of Melchizedek.

Verses 8–10 are closely connected with the preceding verse. Indeed, in the original Greek the main verb in verses 7 and 8 is "he learned." That is where the emphasis falls in this passage. Therefore, numerous translations end verse 7 not with a period, but with a comma. This is correct, for the two verses are closely related and form a unit. Incidentally, the stress on the main verb, "he learned," gives added support to the reading *because of his reverent submission.*

Consider these questions.

a. Would Jesus have to learn obedience? The author introduces this subject by mentioning the divinity of Jesus first and stating this fact concessively:

---

20. Klaas Schilder shows that *after* the arrival of the angel Jesus began to sweat drops of blood. The coming of the angel caused intensified anguish. Refer to *Christ in His Sufferings* (reprint; Minneapolis: Klock and Klock, 1978), p. 358.
21. The earliest translations in Latin that show the difference are the Old Latin, which reads *a metu* (from fear), and the Vulgate, which has *pro sua reverentia* (because of his reverence).
22. Westcott, *Hebrews,* p. 127.

"although Jesus was the Son of God." He does not say that because Jesus was divine he had to learn obedience. Jesus did not have to learn anything concerning obedience, for his will was the same as God's will. However, in his humanity Jesus had to show full obedience; he had to become "obedient to death—even death on a cross!" (Phil. 2:8). As one version has it: "son though he was, he learned obedience in the school of suffering."[23]

b. What was the obedience Jesus had to learn? Translations, for reasons of style and diction, speak of obedience. In the original Greek, however, a definite article precedes the noun so that it reads "*the* obedience"; that is, the well-known obedience expected from the Lord.

When we interpret this verse we are not to think in terms of contrasts. It is true that sinful man needs to correct his ways by listening to God's Word and turning from disobedience to obedience. But Christ, the sinless One, did not learn by unlearning. Rather, through his active and passive obedience, Christ provides eternal life for the sinner and a discharge of man's debt of sin. Says Paul in Romans 5:19, "For just as through the disobedience of the one man the many were made sinners, so also through the obedience of the one man the many will be made righteous."

c. How was Jesus made perfect? The question is legitimate, for Jesus, as the Son of God, is perfect from eternity. But in his humanity, "Jesus grew in wisdom and stature, and in favor with God and men" (Luke 2:52). We see his development in the school of obedience. As the burden becomes more taxing for Jesus, so his willingness to assume the task his Father has given him increases.

In the Garden of Gethsemane and on Calvary's cross, he endured the ultimate tests. Jesus was made perfect through suffering. His perfection "became the source of eternal salvation for all who obey him." The author of Hebrews in effect repeats the thought he expressed in Hebrews 2:10— Jesus, made perfect through suffering, leads many sons to glory. Perfection, therefore, must be seen as a completion of the task Jesus had to perform.

d. What does the writer mean by "the source of eternal salvation"? The writer of Hebrews calls Jesus the "author" of salvation (Heb. 2:10) and the "source" of salvation. These two expressions are synonymous. Jesus is the captain, the chief, the originator, and the cause.

When the author uses the word *source,* he does not open a discussion on the primary cause of salvation; God the Father commissioned his Son to effectuate salvation. Instead the writer uses the term *source* in the context of his discussion about the high priesthood of Christ. By accomplishing his redemptive work, especially in Gethsemane and at Golgotha, Jesus is the source of eternal salvation (Isa. 45:17). Only those people who obey him will share in the salvation Jesus provides. F. F. Bruce describes the concept of

---

23. See the NEB for this translation. Kenneth Taylor paraphrases this verse: "And even though Jesus was God's Son, he had to learn from experience what it was like to obey, when obeying meant suffering" (LB).

139

obedience adequately when he writes, "The salvation which Jesus has procured, is granted 'unto all them that obey him!' There is something appropriate in the fact that the salvation which was procured by the obedience of the Redeemer should be made available to the obedience of the redeemed."[24]

e. How does the author of Hebrews conclude his discussion about the priesthood of Christ? He states that God designated Jesus to be high priest in the order of Melchizedek. That is significant, because this section about the high priesthood of Christ, beginning with Hebrews 4:14, is presented in terms of Aaron's priesthood. The section continues and concludes with a clear reference to the priesthood of Melchizedek.

Note the following observations.

Not the writer of Hebrews but God designates Christ as high priest in the order of Melchizedek (Ps. 110:4). The writer of Hebrews searches the Old Testament and shows that God addresses his Son as high priest.

The topic of the high priesthood of Christ is important to the author of Hebrews. He introduces the subject in Hebrews 2:17; after a discussion about Israel's disobedience in the desert and the meaning of rest the author returns to the subject in Hebrews 4:14–5:10; and the theme eventually is fully treated in Hebrews 7.

We also note that Jesus fulfilled the priestly duties of Aaron when he, in his submission and suffering, brought the task God had given him to completion. Thus Jesus became "the source of salvation for all who obey him." This could never be said of Aaron or any of the high priests who succeeded him.

The subject of Christ's high priesthood in the order of Melchizedek is deep. In fact, the writer of Hebrews calls it "hard to explain" (Heb. 5:11), although after a pastoral word to his readers he does explain it fully.

Doctrinal Considerations in 5:4–10

In chapter 1 the author introduces the Son as king when he quotes Psalm 110:1 in Hebrews 1:13. But the subject of Jesus' kingship does not need to be explored; the priesthood of Jesus needs attention because the author of Hebrews portrays Jesus as mediator. That role of mediator was given not to a king, but to the priest. In other words, the author explains the priestly office of Christ by quoting directly from the Old Testament.

Among the writers of the New Testament, only the author of Hebrews, an expert student of the Scriptures, teaches the doctrine of Christ's priesthood. Paul, for example, touches on the intercessory work of Jesus (Rom. 8:34) and the concept of mediator (I Tim. 2:5–6). Nowhere in his epistles does he discuss the teaching of Jesus' priesthood. That has been done by the writer of Hebrews.[25]

---

24. Bruce, *Hebrews*, p. 105.
25. Peter calls believers a "holy priesthood" (I Peter 2:5), and John refers to them as "a kingdom and priests" (Rev. 1:6). But neither John nor Peter speaks of the priesthood of Christ. See also John 17:19; Rom. 5:2; I Peter 3:18; and I John 2:1.

Did God appoint Jesus to serve as the Aaronic high priest or to function as a priest in the order of Melchizedek? The Scriptures teach that Christ was appointed in the order of Melchizedek and that he could not serve as priest in the order of Aaron because he belonged to the tribe of Judah and not to the tribe of Levi (Heb. 7:14–17). And yet through his sacrificial death Jesus fulfilled the responsibilities of the Levitical priesthood.

The duties of the Aaronic high priest were to become thoroughly familiar with man's spiritual weakness, to represent him before God, and to offer sacrifices and gifts to God on his behalf. The high priest on the Day of Atonement shed the blood of a sacrificial animal for himself and for the people. Jesus offered himself as "for all time one sacrifice for sins" (Heb. 10:12). Later he sat down as priest and king at the right hand of God.

In Hebrews 5:7–8 the author stresses two conditions that Jesus as high priest has to fulfill: he must bring an offering, and he must learn obedience. The author of Hebrews deliberately repeats the theme about the priesthood of Christ in Hebrews 2:11–18; 5:5–10; and 7:23–28.

Greek Words, Phrases, and Constructions in 5:4–10

Verse 4

καλούμενος—this present passive participle, from καλέω (to call), is followed by the agent *by God*. It constitutes a call to an office; its parallel is in Hebrews 5:10 ("was designated by God to be high priest").

καθώσπερ—the combination of καθώς (just as) and οὕτως (so; see Heb. 5:3) shows contrast and comparison. The two adverbs indicate a link between verses 4 and 5. Note the stress particle περ, which has been added to καθώς as an enclitic.

Verse 5

οὕτως—this adverb finds its antecedent in the preceding καθώσπερ.

γεγέννηκα—the perfect active indicative of γεννάω (to beget). See Hebrews 1:5.

Verse 7

τε καί—two nouns or concepts of similar import are often combined by the adjunct τε with καί. The nouns *prayers* and *petitions* therefore are synonyms.

ἱκετηρία—the substantivized adjective in the feminine used to be followed by either the noun ἐλαία (olive tree, olive branch) or the noun ῥάβδος (rod, staff, stick). Around this branch or rod wool was wound, and then it was used by a suppliant.

σῴζειν—the present active infinitive (to save) must be seen in relation to the noun σωτηρία (salvation; Heb. 5:9). Also, the present tense testifies to God's constant power to save his Son from death.

ἀπὸ τῆς εὐλαβείας—the preposition ἀπό is causal. The noun εὐλαβείας, preceded by the definite article, can mean either reverential fear toward God (see Heb. 12:28, where the word is translated "reverence") or piety. Still others prefer the translation *fear*; that is, horror.

Verse 8

υἱός—the definite article has been omitted deliberately to express the absolute relationship of Father and Son. That is, there is only one Son.

ἔμαθεν. . .ἔπαθεν—it is obvious that the author has a play on words in mind. The first verb is the aorist active from μανθάνω (I learn) and the second is the aorist active of πάσχω (I endure).

Verse 9

τελειωθείς—the author of Hebrews used the verb τελειόω (to complete, finish, perfect) at least three times of Jesus (2:10; 5:9; 7:28). Here the aorist passive participle is given, which refers to Jesus' sacrificial work in Gethsemane and on the cross.

ὑπακούουσιν—note the use of the present tense of the active participle. Not only does the verb have the meaning of obeying, but also in the broader context it conveys the idea of believing in Christ.

Verse 10

προσαγορευθείς—the verb in the aorist passive participle form occurs only once in the New Testament. However, it appears frequently in extracanonical literature and means "to call, name, designate."

Summary of Chapter 5

In the religious life of the Jew, no man received greater esteem than the high priest. Under his supervision were the priests who were commissioned to take charge of routine tasks. The high priest, man's representative before God, entered the Most Holy Place once a year on the Day of Atonement and sprinkled blood for the remission of sin. Aaron was the first high priest to enter into the presence of God behind the curtain in the ancient tabernacle.

However, Jesus is superior to Aaron because Jesus "has gone through the heavens." That is, he entered into the very presence of God, whereas the high priests were accustomed merely to entering the symbolical presence in the tabernacle or temple once a year. In his glorified human nature, Jesus has entered the presence of God. Fully acquainted with human weaknesses and temptations, he intercedes in our behalf when we approach the throne of God in prayer.

The author of Hebrews depicts Jesus in his role of high priest, fulfilling the responsibilities of the high priesthood of Aaron and assuming the priesthood in the order of Melchizedek.[26] As a priest in the order of Melchizedek,

---

26. F. W. Grosheide, *De Brief aan de Hebreeën en de Brief van Jakobus* (Kampen: Kok, 1955), p. 132. The question is raised whether Jesus could be both sacrifice and priest at the same time. In his dying he presents himself as a sacrifice to God. But note that Jesus did not commit suicide; rather his life was taken. Thus he became a sacrifice for sin.

Jesus offered himself as a sacrifice for sin. This fulfilled the requirements of the Old Testament sacrificial system.

God appointed Jesus as high priest not when Jesus entered heaven, but prior to his coming to earth. According to Psalm 110:4 ("You are a priest *forever,* in the order of Melchizedek"; italics added), Jesus' priesthood is eternal. He was already priest before he began his earthly life.

6

Exhortations

5:11–6:20

Outline

5 11 We have much to say about this, but it is hard to explain because you are slow to learn. 12 In fact, though by this time you ought to be teachers, you need someone to teach you the elementary truths of God's word all over again. You need milk, not solid food! 13 Anyone who lives on milk, being still an infant, is not acquainted with the teaching about righteousness. 14 But solid food is for the mature, who by constant use have trained themselves to distinguish good from evil.

6 1 Therefore let us leave the elementary teachings about Christ and go on to maturity, not laying again the foundation of repentance from acts that lead to death, and of faith in God, 2 instruction about baptisms, the laying on of hands, the resurrection of the dead, and eternal judgment. 3 And God permitting, we will do so.

4 It is impossible for those who have once been enlightened, who have tasted the heavenly gift, who have shared in the Holy Spirit, 5 who have tasted the goodness of the word of God and the powers of the coming age, 6 if they fall away, to be brought back to repentance, because to their loss they are crucifying the Son of God all over again and subjecting him to public disgrace.

7 Land that drinks in the rain often falling on it and that produces a crop useful to those for whom it is farmed receives the blessing of God. 8 But land that produces thorns and thistles is worthless and is in danger of being cursed. In the end it will be burned.

9 Even though we speak like this, dear friends, we are confident of better things in your case—things that accompany salvation. 10 God is not unjust; he will not forget your work and the love you have shown him as you have helped his people and continue to help them. 11 We want each of you to show this same diligence to the very end, in order to make your hope sure. 12 We do not want you to become lazy, but to imitate those who through faith and patience inherit what has been promised.

A. Do Not Fall Away
5:11–6:12

1. Slow Learners
5:11–14

A teacher knows that not every student is quick to learn, is perceptive, and is blessed with a retentive memory. Numerous times the teacher has to repeat his lessons and exercise patience with students who by nature are slow learners. The writer of Hebrews interrupts his explanation of Christ's priesthood in order to admonish his readers to be better students of the Word.

11. We have much to say about this, but it is hard to explain because you are slow to learn. 12a. In fact, though by this time you ought to be

147

teachers, you need someone to teach you the elementary truths of God's word all over again.

An experienced teacher senses when the students are no longer absorbing the lesson material. He knows that students do not always advance in their learning skills and that sometimes a word of rebuke or correction is very much in place. The words of the author of Hebrews are sharp and pointed. Something has gone drastically wrong in the learning process. By all standards the readers should have graduated, but they have failed their examinations because of a lack of interest, diligence, and adequate preparation.

The author had planned to continue his teaching on the high priesthood of Jesus in the order of Melchizedek.[1] However, the material is too advanced for his readers, his theology is too deep, and his students are too lazy. The subject matter, says the writer, is difficult to explain, not because of the writer's lack of skill, but because of the readers' inability to comprehend. The writer becomes rather personal and says, "You are slow to learn." The author, then, is forced to divert his attention from the topic of the priesthood.

How many years are needed in preparation for teaching the Christian faith? The author does not specify the number of years, but he points out that by the time of his writing the readers should have been teachers. The time allotted to learn the teachings of the faith has been ample; his readers are under obligation to pay dividends—they ought to be able to teach others the teachings of God's Word. But they are unable to do so.

The Christian church must grow in order to exist. Those who have heard the gospel and have accepted it in faith are required to share their knowledge with others who need instruction. When the writer of Hebrews says, "By this time you ought to be teachers," he is not speaking about professionally qualified educators. Rather, he addresses himself to the believer who has heard Bible stories and has been taught the doctrine of salvation, but nevertheless fails to put his ability to work in leading others to a knowledge of salvation in Christ. What a disappointment when a Christian who is given the opportunity to witness for Christ and teach the gospel declines because he feels inadequate! The author of Hebrews speaks to this situation.

You need someone to teach you the elementary truths of God's word all over again. What an admonition! What a rebuke! Writers of catechisms in the time of the Reformation incorporated three Christian documents into their teachings: the Apostles' Creed, the Ten Commandments, and the Lord's Prayer. These they considered the ABC's of the Christian faith. If a believer knew how to explain the basic doctrines of these three elements of Christian belief, he was expected to testify for Christ and teach others.

Although we do not know exactly what the writer of Hebrews means by "elementary truths of God's word," we do not go amiss if we say: the basic

---

1. The word *this* in verse 11 is rather general and may be interpreted as "this subject" (JB) or "this matter" (GNB).

teachings of the Bible.[2] Of course, he enumerates the elementary teachings of Christ in Hebrews 6:1–2. The author states that if his readers do not know even the elementary truths, someone has to teach them anew.

12b. You need milk, not solid food! 13. Anyone who lives on milk, being still an infant, is not acquainted with the teaching about righteousness. 14. But solid food is for the mature, who by constant use have trained themselves to distinguish good from evil.

The rebuke of the author is comparable to Paul's stern remarks to the believers in Corinth: "Brothers, I could not address you as spiritual but as worldly—mere infants in Christ. I gave you milk, not solid food, for you were not yet ready for it. Indeed, you are still not ready" (I Cor. 3:1–2). Milk is given to the very young, and when they are older they receive solid food. The babes in the faith cannot digest the solid food of God's Word; they need spiritual milk instead.[3]

If there is anything a child dislikes, it is to be called a baby. That is too degrading and goes against his innate desire: to grow up! He wants to become independent. He looks ahead and compares himself constantly with those children who are older and more mature.

The author of Hebrews calls the reader of his epistle "an infant." To him it is incredible that adults in the faith are still nurtured on spiritual milk, not solid food. He uses the word *infant* to put his readers to shame.[4] As a pastor, he is not afraid to rebuke them, to admonish them, and to direct them to a higher level of development. They must realize that growth demands solid food. They will never advance on a diet of milk.

Anyone who lives on milk . . . is not acquainted with the teaching about righteousness. The writer keeps on rebuking his readers. Drawing a logical inference from the illustration of babies who exist on milk alone, the author indicates that just as infants do not know the difference between right and wrong, so the recipients of his letter are unacquainted with "the teaching about righteousness." A mere infant is unaccustomed to making decisions about correct conduct because he needs to be taught on a daily basis (I Cor. 14:20; Eph. 4:14). Of course, we must understand that the writer is using a metaphor in order to make this point.

I do not think that the phrase *teaching about righteousness* within the context of figurative language was meant to convey theological truth.[5] Elsewhere in the New Testament (for example, I Cor. 1:30), the word *righteousness* is

2. See Acts 7:38; Rom. 3:2; I Peter 4:11; these verses relate to the Old Testament. The expression in Heb. 5:12 is broader in scope.

3. Hans Kropatschek, *NIDNTT*, vol. 2, p. 269.

4. The jb uses the word *baby*, and the kjv, nkjv, and *Moffatt* have "babe."

5. Philip Edgcumbe Hughes, Ceslaus Spicq, and B. F. Westcott interpret the phrase theologically. In an explanatory footnote, the jb points out, " 'The doctrine of righteousness' like 'God's oracles' can mean either the O.T., cf. 2 Tm. 3:16, or the whole body of doctrine. Here it seems to mean all that Christ taught about the righteousness of God as applied to mankind, Rm. 3:21–26, and especially about his own priesthood of mediation, prefigured by Melchizedek, the 'king of righteousness', 7:2."

understood implicitly or explicitly as God's righteousness—a concept that is commonly stressed in Paul's letters.[6] We, however, ought to look at the phrase in question not from a theological perspective but from a contextual point of view.[7]

The contrast between infants and adults is shown in verse 14: "But solid food is for the mature, who by constant use have trained themselves to distinguish good from evil." Adults need solid food, not a diet of milk, for nourishment. The writer calls adults mature people—those who are constantly making decisions concerning ethical conduct. Their mental and spiritual training is perpetually put to use when they distinguish between good and evil. These people from childhood to maturity have trained and continue to train their spiritual and moral senses. Adults are repeatedly confronted with moral decisions that need to be made. And because of their experience, adults are able to make wise choices in distinguishing between good and evil.

Adults gain experiential knowledge that is still absent in children. As children mature they, too, will acquire the moral sense of discriminating between good and evil; and for them, too, this skill of differentiating will become second nature.

The author uses the metaphor of milk for infants and solid food for adults to spur his readers to spiritual and intellectual activity. He wants to have them understand the biblical implications of Jesus' high priesthood.

Practical Considerations in 5:11–14

We should guard against being critical of the original recipients of the epistle, for we ourselves show the same characteristics. We who have heard the gospel proclaimed for numerous years—many of us since childhood—often do not demonstrate spiritual discernment. Although we have God's revelation in the Old and New Testaments, we remain slow learners.

Surveys conducted by local pastors or by Christian agencies invariably reveal that church members do not know the basic principles of Scripture or, if they do know, they are unable to apply these basic teachings.

The ABC's of the Christian faith are readily mastered by any sincere believer who, in turn, should be capable of imparting this elementary knowledge to people unacquainted with the gospel. On this elementary level the Christian church fails to communicate effectively and thus stymies growth and development.

Yet the corporate responsibility of the church is to formulate the teachings of the Christian faith. The doctrines of God, man, Christ, salvation, the church, and the end of the age belong to the entire church and not merely to a few gifted theolo-

---

6. Horst Seebass, in a study on the word *righteousness*, concludes: "Hebrews shows scarcely any Pauline influence." Refer to *NIDNTT*, vol. 3, p. 365.

7. The various interpretations of the phrase "not acquainted with the teaching about righteousness" range from "the righteousness of God revealed in Christ" to "[lacking] experience of moral truth." Consult, for further details, Hugh Montefiore, *The Epistle to the Hebrews* (New York and Evanston: Harper and Row, 1964), p. 103.

gians who have been instrumental in drafting the precise wording of these doctrines. The church as a body of believers is the responsible agent in formulating,
adopting, teaching, and defending these doctrines of the faith. Therefore, the
individual Christian is exhorted to progress beyond the level of "the elementary
truths of God's word."

Greek Words, Phrases, and Constructions in 5:11–14

Verse 11

νωθροί—the adjective in the nominative masculine plural, translated "lazy" or
"slow to learn," occurs twice in the epistle (5:11; 6:12). It also appears in the
Septuagint (Prov. 22:29; Sir. 4:29; 11:12) and in I Clement 34:1, where it refers to
a "lazy and careless workman."

γεγόνατε—the use of the perfect tense of γίνομαι (I become) indicates a state
that the recipients had acquired in the course of time.

ταῖς ἀκοαῖς—the plural of ἀκοή (the act of hearing) refers specifically to the
ears. The dative is a dative of respect.

Verse 12

καὶ γάρ—the combination of καί and γάρ is rather emphatic and is equivalent
to "in fact" or "yes, indeed."

τὰ στοιχεῖα—the noun is used four times by Paul (Gal. 4:3, 9; Col. 2:8, 20), twice
by Peter (II Peter 3:10, 12), and once in Hebrews. It is derived from στοῖχος (row,
rank, line, course). In Hebrews the noun signifies basic lines or principles of elementary doctrines.

ἡ ἀρχή τῶν λογίων—the presence of the definite article before ἀρχή (beginning)
points to that which is basic. In translation the noun ἀρχή serves adjectivally with
λογίων, and is translated "elementary truths."

Verse 14

ἕξις—a noun derived from the verb ἔχω (I have [future, ἕξω]) and given the
meaning of exercise, practice, or skill. The -σις ending of the noun indicates process
or constant activity. In the New Testament this noun occurs only once; in other
literature, half a dozen times.

τὰ αἰσθητήρια—a noun in the neuter plural (translated "senses") that is derived
from αἰσθάνομαι (I perceive). The noun is rendered "themselves" (NIV); "faculties"
(RSV); or "perceptions" (NEB).

γεγυμνασμένα—the perfect middle participle of γυμνάζω (I exercise, train). The
perfect tense shows continuity from the past into the present, and the middle
indicates an agent acting upon oneself.

διάκρισις—derived from the verb διακρίνω (I differentiate, discriminate), the
noun with the -σις ending reveals a process or an activity in respect to distinguishing
"good from evil."

2. Elementary Teachings
6:1–3

A cursory reading of this passage indicates that the author seems to have had second thoughts. In 5:12–14 he states that his readers cannot digest solid food and must live on milk. In 6:1–3 he tells them "to go on to maturity" and proceeds to prepare them to receive deeper spiritual truths. But upon closer examination we see at work an expert psychologist who rouses his audience by inducing shame. The effect of his remarks about their spiritual eating habits is expected to be positive. His readers want to reach maturity, and the author prudently places himself at their level and, in effect, says that he is one with them in striving for maturity.

1. Therefore let us leave the elementary teachings about Christ and go on to maturity, not laying again the foundation of repentance from acts that lead to death, and of faith in God, 2. instruction about baptisms, the laying on of hands, the resurrection of the dead, and eternal judgment.

Instead of teaching the elementary truths of God's Word once more (see 5:12), the author urges his readers to go beyond these truths. They are not ignorant of the basic teachings of Christian doctrine; they need to be stimulated to progress in their understanding of the faith. They ought to review the *elementary* teachings *about Christ,* so that they are ready to receive further instruction.[8]

The introductory word *therefore* is retrospective.[9] In the preceding verses, the writer contrasts the spiritually weak believer with the mature Christian. And the model he holds before his readers is that of the believer who strives for maturity. He exhorts them to go on to perfection after having left the elementary teachings behind. Actually the author is saying, "Let us . . . go forward to adult understanding" (*Phillips*), and together we are able to do this. The verb ("let us go on") that the author employs is a key word because it conveys the idea of actively exerting oneself to make progress. He includes himself and places himself on his readers' level even though he, as the teacher, really occupies a higher position than the recipients of his letter. This implies that the writer has not yet achieved maturity in spiritual matters. Therefore, the author does not explain the "elementary teachings about Christ" but merely outlines them.

A. Foundation of
1. repentance
2. faith in God

---

8. J. C. Adams, "Exegesis of Hebrews vi.1f.," *NTS* 13 (1967): 378–85.

9. John Brown, in *An Exposition of Hebrews* (Edinburgh: Banner of Truth Trust, 1961), p. 274, suggests that the word *therefore* is not retrospective but prospective. That is, according to Brown, the author regards the recipients who are spiritually immature (5:11–14) as the same people who are depicted in 6:4–6. However, the author uses the adverb *therefore* (διό) in the Greek nine times (3:7, 10; 6:1; 10:5; 11:12, 16; 12:12, 28; 13:12) and seems to give the adverb the meaning *consequently*.

B. Instruction about
1. baptisms
2. laying on of hands
3. resurrection of the dead
4. eternal judgment[10]

a. "Not laying again the foundation." Does the author refer to a standard of instruction in the church of the first century? Perhaps. F. F. Bruce points out that the items listed among the elementary teachings are as much Jewish as they are Christian.[11] We assume that these doctrines were given much more prominence in the Christian church than in the Jewish synagogue. These truths also may have been used as a catechism that new converts were required to learn before they were fully accepted.

Because the readers know that to be members in the church they must have a foundation of repentance and faith, the writer states that it is not necessary to lay that foundation anew. He is spelling out for his audience the difference between the basic doctrines (which he calls a foundation) and the deeper truths of Scripture (which believers ought to study in order to progress in their spiritual lives). He concludes that because of their membership believers already have laid the foundation.[12]

b. "The foundation of repentance from acts that lead to death." The first component of the Christian's spiritual foundation is repentance (Acts 2:38; 3:19). This means turning away from something that is detrimental to one's being. Basically repentance constitutes a negative action, in this case a change of mind that results in no longer performing "acts that lead to death." Repentance, then, is an activity that involves the mind and thinking of a person—a complete turnabout in the life of the believer. No longer does he show an interest in activities that lead to his destruction. He now shuns the effects of sin that bring about death (Rom. 5:12, 21; 6:23; 7:11). Consequently, it would not be necessary for the author to ask his readers to lay the foundation of repentance again.

c. "And of faith in God." Laying a foundation of faith in God was a positive action that believers had taken when they accepted Christ in faith. They turned from their "acts that lead to death" to life in Christ through faith. We would expect the author to write "faith in Christ" instead of "faith in

---

10. Another categorization is threefold: repentance and faith; baptisms and laying on of hands; and resurrection and judgment. However, I understand the word *instruction* as an accusative in the Greek; that is, in apposition to the term *foundation*. The manuscript evidence for the accusative form is weighty. Bruce M. Metzger's explanation in *A Textual Commentary on the Greek New Testament* (London and New York: United Bible Societies, 1975), p. 666—that copyists had changed the word *teaching* from a genitive to an accusative for stylistic reasons—does not seem very satisfactory.

11. F. F. Bruce, *The Epistle to the Hebrews*, New International Commentary on the New Testament series (Grand Rapids: Eerdmans, 1964), pp. 112–13.

12. Consult the article by Jürgen Blunck in *NIDNTT*, vol. 1, pp. 660–62.

God," for Jewish converts to Christianity did not need to be instructed in the doctrine of faith in Israel's God. The difficulty disappears, however, when we realize that throughout his epistle the author speaks of God as revealed in Christ (3:1–6; also see Acts 20:21; I Thess. 1:9–10). Indirectly, the author reminds the reader of Jesus' word, proclaimed at the beginning of this ministry: "The time has come. . . . The kingdom of God is near. Repent and believe the good news" (Mark 1:15). This twofold message from the lips of Jesus is repeated by the apostles. For example, Peter on the day of Pentecost called the people to repentance, and as a result three thousand believers were added to the church (Acts 2:38, 41).[13]

Of course, faith is a prominent theme in Hebrews. Chapter 11 with its brief definition of faith and list of the heroes of faith is eloquent testimony to the author's interest in this theme. For the writer, faith constitutes complete trust as demonstrated by Joshua, who because of his faith entered the land God had promised (4:8). Everyone who puts faith in the gospel, says the author of Hebrews, enters God's rest (4:2–3).[14]

d. "Instruction about baptisms." Next to the foundation of repentance and faith comes the instruction about baptisms, laying on of hands, resurrection of the dead, and eternal judgment. The first phase in the believer's instruction is the teaching concerning baptisms. Interestingly enough, the writer uses not the common Greek word *baptisma* (baptism), but rather the term *baptismos* (washing; Mark 7:4; Heb. 9:10).[15] Furthermore, the word is in the plural.

What is the writer saying? Use of the plural provides sufficient reason to assume that he calls attention to washings other than Christian baptism. What these washings are has been debated at length by numerous scholars. I mention only a few interpretations:

1. purification ceremonies (Qumran)
2. triple immersion in the name of the Trinity
3. multiplicity of baptismal candidates
4. baptisms of water, blood, fire, and the Holy Spirit
5. Levitical washings and Christian baptism[16]

The New Testament does refer to the baptism of John the Baptist (Matt. 3:7; Mark 11:30; Luke 7:29; John 3:23; 4:1; Acts 1:22; 10:37; 18:25) that was still practiced more than twenty-five years after his death (Acts 19:3). Also there is the Jewish rite of baptism for proselytes.

---

13. John Calvin, *Epistle to the Hebrews* (Grand Rapids: Eerdmans, 1949), p. 132.

14. Donald Guthrie, *New Testament Theology* (Downers Grove, Ill.: Inter-Varsity, 1981), p. 597.

15. In the Greek text also see the variant reading in Col. 2:12 and the TR reading of Mark 7:8.

16. Philip Edgcumbe Hughes provides an interesting and almost complete list of possible interpretations. See his *Commentary on the Epistle to the Hebrews* (Grand Rapids: Eerdmans, 1977), pp. 199–202.

The word *baptismos* (which signifies "the act alone," whereas *baptisma* is "the act with the result") is a Jewish-Christian term.[17] The expression in the plural probably expresses a "contrast between Christian baptism and all other religious washings . . . known to the readers."[18]

Finally, the four Gospels and Acts mention the baptism with the Holy Spirit (Matt. 3:11 and parallels; Acts 1:5; 11:16). Although this particular form of baptism is different from the washing that the word *baptismos* describes, it has significance for the next phase of instruction, the imposition of hands.

e. "The laying on of hands." In Acts the imposition of hands results in the outpouring of the Holy Spirit. For example, Peter and John visited the believers in Samaria and placed their hands on the Samaritans, who as a consequence received the Holy Spirit (Acts 8:17). Ananias put his hands on Saul (Paul), who received both his sight and the Holy Spirit (Acts 9:17). In Ephesus, Paul laid his hands on some disciples of John the Baptist who were recipients of the Holy Spirit (Acts 19:6).

Other passages show that the practice of laying hands on someone relates to the ceremony of ordination to service: ministering to the needs of the poor (Acts 6:6); proclaiming the gospel (Acts 13:3); or pastoring the church (I Tim. 4:14; II Tim. 1:6).

Apart from the instances that mention the imposition of hands in connection with healing (Matt. 9:18; Mark 5:23; 6:5; 7:32; 8:23; Luke 13:13; Acts 28:8) and with Jesus blessing the children (Matt. 19:13, 15; Mark 10:16), the New Testament is silent.

What did the practice of laying hands on a believer mean to the first recipients of the Epistle to the Hebrews? John Calvin declares that baptized children, after a period of instruction in the faith, received another rite—that of laying on of hands. This rite was intended as confirmation of their baptism and originated in the time of apostles.[19] This may very well be the explanation of the practice, although substantiating evidence is scarce.

f. "The resurrection of the dead." The next phase in the believer's instruction is his knowledge concerning the resurrection of the dead. Already in Old Testament times the doctrine of the resurrection was known (Ps. 16:10; Isa. 26:19; Ezek. 37:10; Dan. 12:2). In the days of Jesus and the apostles, the general public knew the teaching about the resurrection from the dead (John 11:24), and the Pharisees separated themselves from the Sadducees because the two groups disagreed about this doctrine (Acts 23:6–7).

Jesus taught the doctrine of resurrection by claiming it for himself: "I am the resurrection and the life" (John 11:25); the apostles made this teaching the foundation of their gospel proclamation (Acts 1:22; 2:32; 4:10; 5:30;

---

17. Albrecht Oepke, *TNDT,* vol. 1, p. 545.
18. G. R. Beasley-Murray, *NIDNTT,* vol. 1, p. 149.
19. Calvin, *Hebrews,* p. 134.

10:40; 13:37; 17:31–32; 26:23). The author of Hebrews also refers to this doctrine directly (11:35) and indirectly (2:14–15).

g. "And eternal judgment." The two doctrines of the resurrection and of eternal judgment are logically related, but I do not think that we should explain the first as the resurrection of the righteous and the second as the judgment on the wicked. The author does not provide sufficient information, and therefore we do well to understand the words as general references to these teachings.

Hebrews 6:2 is the only text in the New Testament that gives the reading *eternal judgment*. The passage that is somewhat similar is Acts 24:25, which says, "Paul discoursed on righteousness, self-control and the judgment to come." That Jesus returns "to judge the living and the dead" is a basic teaching eventually formulated in the three ecumenical creeds: the Apostles', the Nicene, and the Athanasian.

3. And God permitting, we will do so.

The text because of its brevity fails to communicate clearly what the author intends to say. Thus it has been explained in various ways.

a. The writer plans to visit the readers after the release of Timothy (13:23); then, arriving with Timothy, he will instruct them in the elementary truths about Christ. The objection to this interpretation is indirectly supplied by the author himself, who wants his readers to advance to maturity. Why would he teach them elementary articles of faith after teaching them doctrines that are "hard to explain" (5:11)?

b. The pronoun *we* is used editorially—the author refers to himself as he does in 5:11. However, the main verb in the preceding verses is in the first person plural ("let us . . . go on to maturity"; 6:1), and the writer counts himself an equal of the recipients of his epistle. Using the editorial *we* in 6:3, therefore, would break the flow of thought.

c. The main verb *let us . . . go on* receives the emphasis in 6:1. The author, after stating the exhortation, simply and positively indicates that he and his readers will fulfill the exhortation. He adds the clause *and God permitting*. That is, although the writer of Hebrews takes his task of teaching and pastoring seriously, God has to open the hearts of the people who receive instruction in the truths of God's Word. In fact, this clause may be understood as an introduction to 6:4–6, where the author teaches that for some people repentance has become an impossibility.

Greek Words, Phrases, and Constructions in 6:1–3

Verse 1

ἀφέντες—the second aorist active participle in the nominative plural from the verb ἀφίημι (I give up). Because of its close relationship to the main verb φερώμεθα, the participle may be understood to connote exhortation (let us leave).

τελειότης—this noun occurs twice in the New Testament—Hebrews 6:1 and Colossians 3:14—and means "perfection, maturity." It is derived from the verb τελειόω (I bring to an end) that appears nine times in Hebrews, more than in any other New Testament book. The noun τελειότης in context is the opposite of νήπιος (5:13).

φερώμεθα—the present middle subjunctive, first person plural of the verb φέρω (I carry). The subjunctive is hortatory; the present tense indicates that the author and readers of Hebrews are indeed going to do this; and the middle shows a reflexive action. Interpreting the verb in the passive voice (let us be carried [by God]) seems to diminish emphasis on human responsibility.

Verse 2

ἐπίθεσις—a noun derived from ἐπιτίθημι (I put or lay upon). The -σις ending points to the activity or the ceremony of the imposition of hands.

ἀνάστασις—this noun has its roots in the verb ἀνίστημι (I rise up). Especially in Acts and in the Epistles, the noun is followed by the noun νεκρῶν, with variations.

Verse 3

ποιήσομεν—this verb from ποιέω (I do) is in the first person plural, future active indicative. The textual variant is ποιήσωμεν—the first person plural, first aorist active subjunctive. Manuscript evidence favors the reading of the future indicative. And this reading is more appropriate in the context than the exhortation *let us do so*.[20]

ἐπιτρέπῃ—the form is the third person singular, present active subjunctive of ἐπιτρέπω (I allow, permit). Although the context and even the verb tense differ, a similar construction occurs in I Corinthians 16:7.

3. No Repentance
6:4–6

In chapters 3 and 4 the author of Hebrews discussed the sin of unbelief that resulted in apostasy. Now in one lengthy sentence (6:4–6) he develops that teaching in greater detail. The emphasis in this sentence falls on the main verb *to be brought back to repentance* (v. 6), which is introduced negatively by the phrase *it is impossible*.

4. It is impossible for those who have once been enlightened, who have tasted the heavenly gift, who have shared in the Holy Spirit, 5. who have tasted the goodness of the word of God and the powers of the coming age, 6. if they fall away, to be brought back to repentance, because to their loss they are crucifying the Son of God all over again and subjecting him to public disgrace.

Throughout the epistle the writer has admonished his readers to accept the Word of God in faith and not to fall into the sin of unbelief that results

---

20. Metzger, *Textual Commentary,* p. 666. However, Zane C. Hodges and Arthur L. Farstad have chosen the aorist subjunctive reading. See *The Greek New Testament According to the Majority Text* (Nashville and New York: Thomas Nelson, 1982), p. 656.

in eternal judgment (2:1–3; 3:12–14; 4:1, 6, 11; 10:25, 27, 31; 12:16–17, 25, 29). In 6:4–6 he does not address the recipients of his letter, but instead he states a truth that emerges from an earlier reference to the Israelites' perishing in the desert because of their unbelief. This truth also applies to the Hebrews, even though the author omits the personal reference in 6:4–6.

Before we discuss the details of the passage, we need to look at the major points that divide the text. We ask three questions.

a. Who are the people mentioned in 6:4–6? They are those characterized by four participles that in the original Greek display poetic rhythm: enlightened, tasted, shared, tasted. There is no particular connection among these participles, although some commentators like to see a sequence of baptism, Lord's Supper, ordination, and perhaps even proclamation in this verse.

Those who have once been enlightened. From the second century to the present, writers have associated the verb *enlightened* with baptism.[21] Added weight is given to this interpretation by the restrictive word *once*. And in the broader context of the passage, the term *baptisms* does appear in 6:2. We can point out many similarities between baptism and enlightenment. For example, the early Christian practice of scheduling baptisms at daybreak utilizes the symbolism of the receding night of sin and the rising sun that illumines the baptismal candidate, who enters a new life.

But the verb *enlightened* also has other meanings. The author uses the word again in 10:32, where the expression seems to be synonymous with "knowledge of the truth" (Heb. 10:26). Besides the two occurrences in Hebrews, the verb appears nine times in the New Testament and has a broader meaning than a reference to baptism (Luke 11:36; John 1:9; I Cor. 4:5; Eph. 1:18; 3:9; II Tim. 1:10; Rev. 18:1; 21:23; 22:5).

Who have tasted the heavenly gift. Suppose that someone has attended the worship services of the church, has made profession of faith, has been baptized, and has taken part in the active life of the church; he has tasted the broken bread and taken the cup offered to him at the celebration of the Lord's Supper. Then this new convert has indeed tasted the heavenly gift.

To limit the interpretation of this phrase ("tasted the heavenly gift") however, is decidedly narrow.[22] The New Testament itself provides a broader explanation. Jesus identifies himself as the "gift of God" when he talks to the Samaritan woman at the well (John 4:10). Peter designates the Holy Spirit the gift of God (Acts 2:38; 8:20; 10:45; 11:17). And in his epistles, Paul mentions "the gift of grace" and "the gift of righteousness." He associates these gifts with Jesus Christ (Rom. 5:15, 17; II Cor. 9:15; Eph. 3:7; 4:7).

---

21. The first to identify enlightenment with baptism was Justin Martyr, *First Apology* 61.12–13; 65.1. In place of the verb *enlightened,* the Syriac Peshitta has "who have once descended to the baptismal pool."

22. B. F. Westcott, *Commentary on the Epistle to the Hebrews* (Grand Rapids: Eerdmans, 1950), p. 148, states: "Any special interpretation, such as the Eucharist or more generally forgiveness, peace and the like, falls short of the general idea which is required here."

Who have shared in the Holy Spirit. The original Greek indicates the close connection between the preceding clause and this one. In the general context of 6:4, we may see a link between the phrase *the laying on of hands* (Heb. 6:2) and the sharing in the Holy Spirit, especially if we understand the heavenly gift to be the Holy Spirit.[23]

Sharing in the Holy Spirit implies that this is done in fellowship with other believers. And the Spirit of God manifests himself in various spiritual gifts given to the members of the church (I Cor. 12:7–11).

Who have tasted the goodness of the word of God. The writer of Hebrews does not specify the extent of the Word, only that the Word is good. When God speaks, man receives a good gift. Once more the writer of Hebrews uses the verb *to taste* to indicate the enjoyment of receiving this gift. This enjoyment consists in hearing the Scriptures proclaimed and in obtaining spiritual nourishment from that Word.

And the powers of the coming age. The continuation of tasting the Word of God is experiencing the powers of the age to come. First, note that the author uses the plural form *powers*. That is, they are part of the "signs, wonders and various miracles" that he has mentioned earlier (2:4). These powers belong to the coming age, but already in this age they are evident. The writer does not say what these powers are, although we note that they are directed toward the advancement of the church throughout the world.

The phrase *the coming age* (with slight variations) occurs only six times in the New Testament: three times in the Gospels (Matt. 12:32; Mark 10:30; Luke 18:30) and three times in the Epistles (Eph. 1:21; 2:7; Heb. 6:5). Because the New Testament writers use this phrase rather infrequently, we ought to exercise prudence in interpreting it. In principle we are able to experience in the present age the powers that belong to the future age.[24] When the coming age dawns, we shall fully realize the supernatural powers we now are allowed to observe.

The author of Hebrews has described a number of experiences some persons have had. In a sense he is deliberatively vague, for he merely lists phenomena but does not clarify who experiences them. He continues, however, and relates what happens to these people.

b. What happens to the people mentioned in 6:4–6? The author adds a participle that many translators preface with the conditional particle *if*.[25]

If they fall away. I am not sure that the author intends to say that the Hebrews will never be apostate. In the preceding chapters he spoke of apostasy and illustrated this by quoting from Psalm 95. The Israelites who in the desert fell away had put blood on the doorpost in Egypt and eaten the

---

23. Bruce, *Hebrews*, p. 121.

24. Hermann Sasse, *TDNT*, vol. 1, p. 206. Also consult George E. Ladd, *A Theology of the New Testament* (Grand Rapids: Eerdmans, 1974), p. 576.

25. The KJV, NKJV, RSV, and NIV have the conditional "if"; the RV, ASV, NASB, *Moffatt*, GNB, and NAB have "and then . . ."; JB has "and yet in spite of this"; and the NEB reads "and after all this."

Passover lamb; they had left Egypt, consecrated their first-born males to the Lord, and crossed the Red Sea; they could see the pillar of cloud by day and the pillar of fire by night; they had tasted the waters of Marah and Elim and daily ate the manna God provided; they had heard the voice of God from Mount Sinai when God gave them the Ten Commandments (see Exod. 12-20). Yet these same Israelites hardened their hearts in unbelief, and because of their disobedience they fell away from the living God (Heb. 3:12, 18; 4:6, 11). The author of the Epistle to the Hebrews teaches that apostasy that rises from unbelief results in a hardening of the heart and an inability to repent (3:13; 4:2; 6:6; 10:26; 12:15).

On the other hand, the writer speaks encouraging words to the recipients of his epistle. In the extended context he writes: "Even though we speak like this, dear friends, we are confident of better things in your case—things that accompany salvation" (6:9).

What does the passage (6:4-6) mean for the original readers of Hebrews? Does the author merely sound a warning or does he think that the Israelites' example would be imitated by the people he addresses in his letter? The constant, repetitive, and heartfelt warnings of the author prove conclusively that apostasy can occur (3:12-13; 4:1, 11; 12:15). Repeatedly he places before the readers the responsibility of guarding the spiritual well-being of each other, "so that no one will fall by following their [the Israelites'] example of disobedience" (4:11).

A distinction must be made at this point. The author speaks about falling away, not about falling into sin. For example, Judas fell away from Jesus and never returned to him; Peter fell into sin but soon afterward saw the resurrected Jesus. The two concepts (apostasy and backsliding) may never be confused. In 6:6, the author refers to apostasy; he has in mind the person who deliberately and completely abandons the Christian faith.[26]

Apostasy does not take place suddenly and unexpectedly. Rather it is part of a gradual process, a decline that leads from unbelief to disobedience to apostasy. And when the falling away from the faith happens, it leads to hardening of the heart and the impossibility of repentance.[27] The author, using the example of the Israelites, has shown the process that results in apostasy (3:18; 4:6, 11).

If the Israelites in the days of Moses deliberately disobeyed the law of God and "received its just punishment" (2:2; and see 10:28), "how much more severely do you think a man deserves to be punished who has trampled the Son of God under foot" (10:29)?

Where do the recipients of the epistle fit into this process? The author chides them for being slow to learn (5:11), lazy (6:12), and feeble (12:12).

---

26. Falling away "must consist in a *total renunciation* [italics his] of all the constituent principles and doctrines of Christianity," writes John Owen in *An Exposition of Hebrews,* 7 vols. in 4 (Evansville, Ind.: Sovereign Grace, 1960), vol. 5, p. 86.

27. F. W. Grosheide, *De Brief aan de Hebreeën en de Brief van Jakobus* (Kampen: Kok, 1955), p. 44.

Constantly he exhorts them to strengthen their faith (4:2; 10:22–23; 12:2). If their faith continues to weaken, they will fall prey to unbelief that leads to disobedience and apostasy.

It is impossible . . . to be brought back to repentance. We notice at least two items in this passage that are purposely vague. First, in the preceding verses (5:11–6:3) and the following verses (6:9–12), the writer uses the first and second person plural pronouns *we* and *you*, but in verses 6:4–6 the third person plural pronouns *those* and *they* occur. Second, the subject of the verb *to be brought back* is missing. The writer does not reveal the identity of the implied agent. Is he saying that God does not permit (6:3) a second repentance? Or does he mean that a person who has fallen away from the living God cannot be restored to repentance because of the sinner's hardened heart? Although the writer does not provide the answer, we assume that both questions could receive an affirmative response.

The use of the pronoun *we* in the broader context of 6:4–6 demonstrates that God never fails the believer who in faith trusts in him. God makes "the unchanging nature of his purpose very clear to the heirs of what was promised" (6:17), and he does so by swearing an oath. And the heirs of the promise are the author and readers of the Epistle to the Hebrews.

Is the Christian church unable to bring a hardened sinner back to the grace of God?[28] Again the writer does not provide an answer in the context of the passage. In another connection, however, he repeats the general sentiment of 6:4–6 and writes: "If we deliberately keep on sinning after we have received the knowledge of the truth, no sacrifice for sins is left" (10:26). The author does not say anything about restoring a hardened sinner; what he refers to is the impossibility of removing sin because the person sins deliberately. The word *deliberately* received all the emphasis in the original Greek because it stands first in the sentence. If a person who is familiar with "the elementary teaching about Christ" sins deliberately, restoration by way of repentance is an impossibility.

c. Why is this so? The writer of the epistle gives two reasons: "to their loss they are crucifying the Son of God all over again" and they are "subjecting him to public disgrace."

Of course the author obviously is using a metaphor; those who have fallen away do not literally crucify the Son of God and put him to open shame. Note that the writer uses not the personal name *Jesus* or the official name *Christ*, but rather the appellation *Son of God* to express on the one hand the divine exaltation of the Son and on the other hand the utter depravity of the sinner who has turned away from, as well as against, the Son of God.

The one who has fallen away declares that Jesus ought to be eliminated. As the Jews wanted Jesus removed from this earth and thus lifted him up

---

28. Verlyn D. Verbrugge, in "Towards a New Interpretation of Hebrews 6:4–6," *CTJ* 15 (1980): 70, interprets the passage to refer to the congregation the author addresses. Thus he inserts the word *us* in verse 6: "It is impossible for us to restore to repentance those who have fallen away."

from the ground on a cross, so the apostate denies Jesus a place, banishes him from this earth, and metaphorically crucifies the Son of God again. Thus he treats Jesus with continuous contempt and derision and knowingly commits the sin for which, says the author of the epistle, there is no repentance (6:6) and no sacrifice (10:26). The sinner can expect God's judgment that will come to him as a "raging fire that will consume the enemies of God" (10:27).

Doctrinal Considerations in 6:4–6

The connection between verses 3 and 4 should not be overlooked. The words *God permitting* must be seen in relation to the phrase *it is impossible*. Of course, Jesus said in regard to salvation that "with God all things are possible" (Matt. 19:26; Mark 10:27; Luke 18:27). The context here, however, differs. God changes the heart of sinful man to make him receptive to the gospel. But God does not permit willful sin to go unpunished. Thus it is impossible to bring such a person to repentance.

The Old Testament, at various places, speaks about the consequences of sinning willfully against God. For example, in Numbers 15:30–31, God says, "Anyone who sins defiantly, whether native-born or alien, blasphemes the LORD, and that person must be cut off from his people. Because he has despised the LORD's word and broken his commands, that person must surely be cut off; his guilt remains on him."

Acquainted with the teachings of the Old Testament on this subject, the writer of Hebrews compares the man who sinned by rejecting the law of Moses with someone "who has trampled the Son of God under foot" and "has insulted the Spirit of grace" (10:29). He poses a rhetorical question: Will not the person who has offended the Son of God and the Holy Spirit receive more severe punishment than the one who rejected the law of Moses?[29] The answer is: Of course.

God does not permit anyone to despise willfully his Son, his Word, and his Spirit. Deliberately sinning against God in full awareness and knowledge of God's divine revelation constitutes sin against the Holy Spirit (Matt. 12:32; Mark 3:29; Luke 12:10).[30] This sin God does not forgive.

Theological questions about the genuineness of repentance and faith of people who fall away from Christ remain unanswered. The writer refuses to judge people; instead he warns them not to fall into the same error that the Israelites in the desert committed. He encourages his readers to grow spiritually and continue to obey God's Word.

We face a mystery when we see God leading the chosen nation of Israel out of Egypt and then destroying the people who were twenty years old and more in the desert (Num. 14:29); when we see Jesus spending a night in prayer before he appointed Judas as one of his disciples (Luke 6:12, 16) and later declaring that Judas was "doomed to destruction" (John 17:12); and when we see Paul accepting

---

29. Ladd, *Theology of the New Testament*, p. 586.
30. "No apostasy could be more final than this," writes Guthrie, *New Testament Theology*, p. 596.

Demas as a fellow evangelist who years later deserted Paul because Demas "loved this world" (II Tim. 4:10).

The writer of Hebrews observes that disobedient Israelites died in the desert because of unbelief. By analogy, the possibility that individuals who have professed the name of Christ will fall away is real (Matt. 7:21–23). Is it possible for true believers to turn away from Christ? Constantly the author exhorts the recipients of his epistle to remain faithful, for God is faithful. God does not break his good promises to his people. "God is not unjust" (6:10). Therefore, says the writer, "imitate those who through faith and patience inherit what has been promised" (6:12).

Greek Words, Phrases, and Constructions in 6:4–6

Verse 4

ἀδύνατον—this adjective in the neuter singular appears four times in Hebrews (6:4, 18; 10:4; 11:6). As the first word in a lengthy sentence, it receives great emphasis. Note that ἀδύνατον is far removed from its complement ἀνακαινίζειν in 6:6.

ἅπαξ—the word occurs fourteen times in the New Testament, eight of which are in Hebrews. Its placement in 6:4 is significant: between the definite article (those) and the participle (have been enlightened). The word is contrasted with πάλιν (6:6).

φωτισθέντας—it is noteworthy that the first five participles, excluding μέλλοντος (6:5) in 6:4–6 are in the aorist tense and that the last two participles (6:6) are in the present tense. φωτισθέντας is used twice in Hebrews (6:4; 10:32).

γευσαμένους—closely connected to the preceding participial phrase with the adjunct τε is the clause "who have tasted the heavenly gift." The aorist middle participle from the verb γεύομαι (I taste) governs the noun *gift* in the genitive case. In 6:5 the same participle takes the accusative case of the noun *word*. To maintain that the use of the genitive is partitive and that of the accusative holistic in these two instances is not without difficulty. For example, the accusative case is also used in John 2:9 for "the water that had been turned into wine." A holistic interpretation in that verse is impossible.[31] Therefore, I suggest that the variation in Hebrews 6:4, 5 is stylistic.

γενηθέντας—the aorist passive participle is deponent and is therefore translated in the active voice.

Verse 5

ῥῆμα—the word is described as καλόν (good). Generally the translation *goodness of the word* is given to indicate that "the gospel and its promises [are] full of consolation."[32] See the Septuagint reading of Joshua 21:45; 23:15; Zechariah 1:13.

Verse 6

παραπεσόντας—this compound in the aorist active participial form occurs once in the New Testament; it appears in the Septuagint reading of Ezekiel 14:13; 15:8. It is synonymous with the verb ἀποστῆναι (to fall away) in Hebrews 3:12.

---

31. Grosheide, *Hebreeën*, pp. 144–45.
32. Joseph H. Thayer, *A Greek-English Lexicon of the New Testament* (New York, Cincinnati, and Chicago: American Book Company, 1889), p. 332.

ἀνακαινίζειν—not the aorist tense but the present tense is used in this active infinitive to express the progressive idea of the verb. It is introduced by the adjective ἀδύνατον (6:4) and signifies the impossibility of renewing the fallen sinner. The verb occurs in early Christian literature "in connection with regeneration and baptism."[33]

ἀνασταυροῦντας—this active participle, as well as the one that follows, is in the present tense. The tense of the participles reflects the reason why repentance is impossible. Consequently the translation of the participles expresses cause. The prefix ἀνά signifies "again."

παραδειγματίζοντας—the word is a compound from the preposition παρά (beside) and δείκνυμι (I show). It can have a favorable connotation in the sense of "to set forth as an example" and a negative connotation of "to subject to public disgrace." Like the preceding participle, the word appears only once in the New Testament (with the exception of the variant reading in Matthew 1:19).

---

4. Blessings of God
6:7-12

7. Land that drinks in the rain often falling on it and that produces a crop useful to those for whom it is farmed receives the blessing of God. 8. But land that produces thorns and thistles is worthless and is in danger of being cursed. In the end it will be burned.

In the agrarian society of the first century, people lived much closer to the land than many of us in our day. When the writer of Hebrews depicts the rainfall, the crops, the thorns, and the thistles, his readers readily understand the significance of the author's illustration. We are more analytical and like to see the comparison presented schematically.

Land
that drinks in the rain
often falling on it
and

that *produces a crop* *useful* to those for whom it is farmed *receives the blessing* of God.	that *produces thorns and thistles* is *worthless* and in danger of *being cursed.* In the end it will be burned.

Note the following observations.

a. The rain keeps falling on the land as a continual blessing from God; the land drinks in the rain.

b. One part of the land is being cultivated, and as a result of this diligent labor it keeps on producing the fruit of the field to nourish the people; in full view of everyone God is blessing the land, the laborers, and the persons receiving the crops.

---

33. Johannes Behm, *TDNT,* vol. 3, p. 451.

c. Although the rain keeps falling on the other part of the land, too, no one tills the field, sows seed, and plants seedlings. The owner of the field does not seem to show interest in his land, and therefore thorns and thistles have taken the place of fruit-bearing crops. The useless land eventually will be cleared of these thorns and thistles by burning them.

d. The contrast between productive land and worthless land is expressed in a few places in the Old Testament (Gen. 1:11–12; 3:17–18; Isa. 5:1, 6).

e. Verses 7–8 serve to illustrate the teaching of verses 4–6. When we look at the illustration, we can see the broad lines of the picture; however, the details are somewhat obscure and cannot be distinguished. The lines are these: God's blessings, in the form of rain, keep falling on the land. The structure of the land, together with the diligent labor of the workers, brings forth a crop; but in the absence of laborers working the field, the rain nourishes only thorns and thistles that grow in abundance. By analogy, believers and those who have fallen into unbelief receive continual blessings. If the heart of man is evil, all the blessings of God do not make him prosper spiritually. Instead, God's blessings, when they are rejected by an unbelieving heart, eventually are turned into a curse. And the unbeliever stands condemned.

f. The purpose of the author's illustration is to warn the recipients of his letter that merely observing, tasting, and experiencing the blessings of God cannot save a person unless genuine spiritual rebirth has taken place. When rebirth is evident and God's blessings are received with thanksgiving, spiritual life develops and brings forth fruit. The words of Jesus ("by their fruit you will recognize them" [Matt. 7:20]) tell the story. Not the rain alone, but the rain and the labor expended in tilling the land, determine the crop that the land produces.

9. Even though we speak like this, dear friends, we are confident of better things in your case—things that accompany salvation. 10. God is not unjust; he will not forget your work and the love you have shown him as you have helped his people and continue to help them.

The pastor-teacher speaks words of tender love to his people. He addresses them as dear friends and by this term conveys his pastoral love to them. The writer wants to relate that in his opinion the readers are heirs of the promise of salvation. The recipients of his epistle ought not think that they are the apostates described in the preceding passage. All that the author wants to do in these verses is to warn them to avoid unbelief. Now he encourages his readers by assuring them that they are to receive better things that pertain to their salvation.

Speaking in the plural (the first person *we*), the author says "we are confident." Presumably he employs the word *we* editorially, as he has done at other places (for example, 5:11).[34] He instills assurance in the hearts and

---

34. R. C. H. Lenski, in *The Interpretation of the Epistle to the Hebrews and of the Epistle of James* (Columbus: Wartburg, 1946), pp. 189–90, thinks that the pronoun *we* refers to persons who were with the author when he wrote his epistle.

minds of the readers, and as a faithful pastor he ministers to the needs of his people. He does not drive them to despair. He looks at the positive marks the readers display in their labor of love. Therefore, he writes that he is absolutely positive about their glorious future, for they will receive "things that accompany salvation." What these better things are the author does not say. The context seems to indicate that he contrasts the miserable destiny of the apostate and the glorious inheritance of the believer. Believers are sure of better things to come—things closely associated with salvation.

Someone could raise the question of fairness concerning man's destiny. God is just, counters the writer. He knows exactly what he is doing because he has your spiritual well-being in mind always. He remembers your labor performed in his service as you, out of loving concern, helped others in need.

Scripture teaches that God will forgive wickedness and will no longer remember the sins (Jer. 31:34) of those people who know the Lord and who have his law written on their hearts. Sin God forgets, but deeds of kindness done in the interest of his people he remembers. These deeds may be forgotten by those who perform them, whether these consist of feeding the hungry, welcoming strangers, clothing the poor, or visiting the sick and the prisoner. Jesus' word is to the point: "I tell you the truth, whatever you did for one of the least of these brothers of mine, you did for me" (Matt. 25:40). The labors of love ultimately are performed for Jesus, and deeds of kindness God does not forget.

One of the characteristics of the writer is that he introduces a subject at one point and returns to it later at another place where he provides additional information. In 6:10 he merely states that his readers have done works of love. In 10:32–34 he reminds them of having endured suffering when they helped those who were persecuted, of sympathizing with those in prison, and of rejoicing when their property was confiscated.

The readers demonstrated their love for their neighbors when troubles and hardship were evident, and they continued to show unselfish love. This love is the fruit of a regenerated heart that is always ready to serve God's people. Their lives exemplify the field that brings forth a crop useful for God's people, in marked contrast to the author's picture of a field overgrown with thorns and thistles.

God is just. He does not forget to bless that which is good and to punish that which is evil. On those who have fallen away and have hardened their hearts, he brings judgment; on those who reflect God's virtues, he showers his blessings. And what are these blessings? In this earthly life the believer receives strength to withstand temptation and trials so that his faith continues to grow and develop; in the life of the coming age these blessings consist of being with Jesus eternally and fully appropriating the reality of salvation.

11. We want each of you to show this same diligence to the very end, in order to make your hope sure. 12. We do not want you to become

lazy, but to imitate those who through faith and patience inherit what has been promised.

As a true pastor the writer is concerned about the spiritual life of the individual church member. Throughout his epistle he has taken an interest in the individual (3:12; 4:1, 11) and has stressed the corporate responsibility of the church. He is not satisfied that many believers are developing spiritually; he wants everyone to make progress. Thus he proves to be an imitator of Jesus, who does not wish to see any of his people wander. In short, he is the shepherd tending the spiritual flock.

Once again the author employs the plural pronoun *we* editorially. What he desires ("we want") is that everyone individually show the same diligence in ministering in love to the needs of God's people. He fears that some members of the church are deficient in the virtue of hope. This deficiency will be detrimental to the spiritual development of the believer.

In Hebrews 6:10–12 the writer features three well-known virtues: love, hope, and faith. Mentioned frequently in the New Testament, these three virtues are integrally related to one another.[35] To use an illustration, the Christian's spiritual growth is supported by the tripod of faith, hope, and love. When one of the legs of this tripod bends, the other two legs will fall, and spiritual development ceases.

The apostles constantly urge the believers to grow spiritually. For example, Peter, in his second epistle, encourages his readers to "grow in the grace and knowledge of our Lord and Savior Jesus Christ" (3:18) and to "be all the more eager to make your calling and election sure" (1:10). When the writer of Hebrews exhorts his readers about making their hope sure, he puts into service the word *diligence,* which "expresses something of the greatness of the Christian's responsibility for the development of his life."[36] Believers must show this diligence "to the very end," says the writer. Many desire to have full assurance but fail to put forth any effort toward diligence.

Admonishing the recipients of his letter not to become lazy, the writer resorts to sound psychology. Earlier he indicated that they had not progressed beyond "the elementary truths of God's word" (5:12) and were still infants in the faith. In 6:12 he does not say that they have been lazy; rather, he exhorts them and says, "We do not want you to become lazy." He speaks words of encouragement. He is positive in his evaluation; he exhorts them to imitate those who are inheriting the promises through faith and patience; he directs their attention to the saints who have appropriated God's promises. Claiming these promises always calls for faith and patience.

Although the writer does not specify in 6:12 who the inheritors are, the

---

35. Paul mentions the triad in Rom. 5:1–5; I Cor. 13:13; Gal. 5:5–6; Col. 1:4–5; I Thess. 1:3; 5:8. Peter cites these qualities in I Peter 1:21–22. And the writer of Hebrews refers to them in 6:10–12 and 10:22–25.

36. Wolfgang Bauder, *NIDNTT,* vol. 3, p. 1169.

context reveals that he is thinking of Old Testament saints—Abraham (6:13) and the heroes of faith (chap. 11)—and saints of his own day.

Believers are inheritors of God's promises. The word *inherit* calls attention to the dividing of a legacy; an inheritor is entitled to possess part of that legacy. The legacy in this case consists of God's promises given to all believers. The author of Hebrews tells the readers to imitate the saints in their faithful trust, perseverance, and zeal. He introduces the subject of faith, hope, and love in 6:10–12; and true to form he elaborates on and fully discusses the topic in 10:22–24, 35–39; and 11.

Doctrinal Considerations in 6:7–12

The Christian is familiar with the themes of faith and love, but the theme of hope does not receive the attention the other two topics do. In our day of instant success, hope may seem outmoded. But in the days of Jesus and the apostles, this concept was relevant. Except for Mark, James, II Peter, Jude, and Revelation, the motif of hope appears in all the books of the New Testament. Paul stresses the concept more than any other New Testament writer.[37] Hope teaches endurance and an eager anticipation of that which will become reality. God promises eternal life to everyone who believes in his Son, and the believer expects the promise of eternal life to be fulfilled. Thus hope arises from and supports faith. "There can be no hope without faith in Christ, for hope is rooted in him alone. Faith without hope would, by itself, be empty and futile."[38]

To make his teaching graphic, interesting, and practical, the author applies illustrations taken from the world in which his readers lived. His illustration from agrarian life is apt and speaks to the recipients of his letter because they are able to relate to his teaching.

Greek Words, Phrases, and Constructions in 6:7–12

Verse 7

γῆ—this noun in the nominative singular lacks the definite article, yet it is qualified by participles and adjectives. It is the subject of the verb μεταλαμβάνει (it shares) and is the unifying factor in both verses 7 and 8.

εὔθετον—a two-ending adjective in the accusative singular; it modifies the noun βοτάνην (crop). The adjective is a compound derived from εὖ (well) and θετός (placed; an adjective from the verb τίθημι [I place]). The word contrasts with ἀδόκιμος (worthless) in the next verse. Note also that εὐλογίας (blessing) is contrasted with κατάρας (curse).

---

37. The noun *hope* occurs forty-eight times in the New Testament, thirty-one of which are in Paul's epistles and five in Hebrews. The verb *hope* appears thirty-one times, nineteen times in Paul's letters and once in Hebrews.

38. Ernst Hoffmann, *NIDNTT,* vol. 2, p. 242.

Verse 8

ἀδόκιμος—this two-ending adjective is derived from the privative ἀ (not) and δόκιμος (accepted; from the verb δέχομαι [I accept]). Some translations give the reading *rejected*; however, because this is not a moral issue, it is better to translate the word as "worthless."

κατάρας—a noun in the genitive singular. It is genitive because of the adverbial preposition ἐγγύς (near). The noun is composed of κατά (down) and ἀρά (curse).

Verse 9

πεπείσμεθα—the use of the perfect passive (from πείθω, I persuade) instead of the perfect active πεποίθαμεν (we trust) is significant because it expresses the passive idea. The writer indicates that he has gained confidence in his readers on the basis of a lengthy investigation.[39]

ἐχόμενα—a participial form (present middle neuter plural accusative) from the verb ἔχω (I have, hold).[40] In the middle the meaning is to hold oneself to something. The participle, then, signifies closeness, accompaniment, or associations; it controls the genitive case of the word σωτηρίας (salvation).

Verse 10

ἐπιλαθέσθαι—the aorist middle from ἐπιλανθάνομαι (I forget) is followed by the genitive case of ἔργον (work); verbs of remembering and forgetting govern the genitive. The aorist is constative.

ἧς—the genitive case of the relative pronoun in the feminine gender is attracted to the antecedent ἀγάπης on which it depends.

διακονήσαντες—the aorist tense of this active participle relates to a past event. The present tense of διακονοῦντες refers to the deeds of love performed in the time when the author wrote his epistle.

Verse 11

πληροφορίαν—this noun occurs twice in Hebrews (6:11; 10:22), and twice in Paul's epistles (Col. 2:2; I Thess. 1:5). It is derived from the verb πληροφορέω (I fulfill, convince fully) and means "full assurance."

---

13 When God made his promise to Abraham, since there was no one greater for him to swear by, he swore by himself,   14 saying, "I will surely bless you and give you many descendants."   15 And so after waiting patiently, Abraham received what was promised.

16 Men swear by someone greater than themselves, and the oath confirms what is said and puts an end to all argument.   17 Because God wanted to make the unchanging nature of his purpose very clear to the heirs of what was promised, he confirmed it with an oath.   18 God did this so that, by two unchangeable things in which it is impossible for God to lie, we who have fled to take hold of the hope offered to us may be greatly encouraged.   19 We have this hope as an anchor for the soul, firm and secure. It enters the inner sanctuary behind the

---

39. Grosheide, *Hebreeën*, p. 148.
40. A. T. Robertson, in *A Grammar of the Greek New Testament in the Light of Historical Research* (Nashville: Broadman, 1934), p. 485, points out that many verbs in the passive voice "retain the accusative of the thing."

curtain, 20 where Jesus, who went before us, has entered on our behalf. He has become a high priest forever, in the order of Melchizedek.

B. Hold on to God's Promise
6:13–20

1. The Promise to Abraham
6:13–15

If there is anyone in Old Testament times who exemplifies the concept *hope,* it is Abraham. "Against all hope, Abraham in hope believed and so became the father of many nations" (Rom. 4:18). Exhorting his readers to have the full assurance of hope, the author illustrates his admonition by calling attention to Abraham. The patriarch known as the father of believers demonstrates that faith and hope are interrelated. Faith gives birth to hope, and hope in turn strengthens faith.

13. When God made his promise to Abraham, since there was no one greater for him to swear by, he swore by himself, 14. saying, "I will surely bless you and give you many descendants."

Illustrations can be more effective at times than plain teaching. Earlier in chapter 6, the author illustrated the hardness of the unbeliever's heart by using the example of worthless land that was about to be cursed and burned (vv. 7–8). Once more he resorts to an illustration. What better example can he hold before the Hebrews than the life of faith and hope that Abraham lived?

Abraham was seventy-five years old when he received the promise: God would make him into a great nation in the land he would show Abraham (Gen. 12:1–9). God appeared to him at Shechem and promised to give the land to Abraham's offspring (Gen. 12:6–7). God repeated this promise after Abraham and Lot separated (Gen. 13:14–17).

Some years later, Abraham wanted to make Eliezer of Damascus his heir, because God still had not given Abraham a son. God told Abraham that his descendants would be as numerous as the stars in the sky (Gen. 15:5). When Abraham was eighty-six years old, Ishmael was born (Gen. 16:16); but God told him that Isaac, not Ishmael, was the fulfillment of the covenant promise (Gen. 17:21; 21:12). Isaac was born when Abraham was a hundred years old (Gen. 21:5).

Abraham put his hope in God and trusted that God would keep his promise to make Abraham into a great nation. He waited twenty-five years for God to fulfill that promise. Sixty years after the birth of Isaac, Jacob and Esau were born (Gen. 25:26). When these children were 15 years old, Abraham died at the age of 175 (Gen. 25:7). At the time of his death, Abraham had one son of the covenant (Isaac) and one grandson of the covenant (Jacob).

God tested Abraham's faith on a mountain in the region of Moriah by telling him to sacrifice his son Isaac. God rewarded that faith by reiterating, on oath, the promise that Abraham had received: "I will surely bless you and make your descendants as numerous as the stars in the sky and as the sand on the seashore" (Gen. 22:17). God gave Abraham this sworn promise not because he was God's friend (James 2:23), but because Abraham "was singled out as a pattern and example for all believers."[41] As the author of the Epistle to the Hebrews asserts at the conclusion of chapter 11, Abraham was commended for his faith, yet he did not receive "what had been promised" (v. 39). That is, Abraham and all the other heroes of faith lived by faith and hoped for the coming of Christ. But they were not given the privilege of seeing the fulfillment of this promise. The recipients of the epistle, however, no longer lived with the promise. For them Christ fulfilled it.

God spoke to Abraham in human terms when he addressed the father of believers: "I swear by myself, declares the LORD, . . . I will surely bless you" (Gen. 22:16, 17). God did not have to swear to guarantee the trustworthiness of his Word; his Word is true, and God will keep his promise. But God adapted himself to the ways of man and swore by himself (Exod. 32:13; Ps. 95:11; Isa. 54:9).

The writer of Hebrews notes that man always swears by someone greater than himself; however, God has no one to excel him. Therefore, "he swore by himself." The author constantly makes comparisons in his epistle. In this instance, however, he admits that "there was no one greater for [God] to swear by."

God in a sense identified himself with his Word when he swore and gave Abraham the promise. The solemn promise came directly in response to Abraham's faith, but its fulfillment would take centuries. When the fulfilling of a promise takes time, it needs added assurance in order to ward off doubt.

Abraham could see fulfillment of the promise only in Isaac, but that was only the beginning of all that God meant by the promise. Therefore, God swore an oath. The oath assured Abraham that God would keep his Word in spite of the years of waiting that were in store for the recipients of the promise. Abraham indeed would have numerous descendants.

15. And so after waiting patiently, Abraham received what was promised.

Abraham waited for twenty-five years to see the promise of Isaac's birth fulfilled. But he never saw the descendants promised him on oath when God said, "I will surely bless you and give you many descendants." The father of believers saw only a partial fulfillment.[42]

Is there a conflict between 6:15 and 11:39? Hardly. At the end of the author's discussion of the heroes of faith he says, "These were all commended

---

41. Owen, *Hebrews*, vol. 3, p. 223.
42. Ernst Hoffmann, *NIDNTT*, vol. 3, p. 73. The writer of Hebrews "ascribes to the patriarchs an understanding of the promise which looks far beyond all historical foreshadowings and partial fulfillments, to an eternal consummation (11:10–16)."

for their faith, yet none of them received what had been promised" (11:39). When we consider still another passage of Scripture, we gain additional insight. Although the full intent of Jesus' word concerning Abraham is uncertain, Jesus in his controversy with the Jews told them: "Your father Abraham rejoiced at the thought of seeing my day; he saw it and was glad" (John 8:56).[43] Abraham waited patiently for God's specific promise to him (Isaac's birth), saw the next generation when Jacob and Esau were born, and claimed the promise of the coming of the Messiah for himself. Abraham was not only a man of faith, but also a man of hope.

Greek Words, Phrases, and Constructions in 6:13–15

Verse 13

ἐπαγγειλάμενος—the aorist middle participle from ἐπαγγέλλομαι (I promise) appears three times in Hebrews (6:13; 10:23; 11:11). In verb form it occurs once (Heb. 12:26). The aorist tense of the participle may be understood to be contemporaneous with the aorist of the main verb ὤμοσεν (he swore).[44] Because God repeated his promise to Abraham, it is advisable not to be too dogmatic but to understand that the aorist tense of the participle refers to all the incidents relating God's promise to Abraham.

εἶχεν—the imperfect active indicative of ἔχω (I have, hold) combined with the infinitive ὀμόσαι (to swear) has the meaning *was able, could* (see, for example, Matt. 18:25).

Verse 14

εὐλογῶν—this present active participle of εὐλογέω (I bless) together with the future active εὐλογήσω represents a Hebrew infinitive absolute construction that has been carried into the Greek because it is used in the Septuagint. In the Hebrew the combination of participle and verb strengthens the concept expressed; in the Greek the participle is redundant. Also in the sequence πληθύνων πληθυνῶ (multiplying, I will multiply) the emphatic use of the participle is evident. The redundancy is avoided in translation by rendering the participle as "surely": "I will surely bless you and I will surely multiply you."

Verse 15

μακροθυμήσας—the aorist active participle from μακροθυμέω (I have patience), a compound construction from μακρός (long) and θυμός (passion), expresses Abraham's patient expectation. The participle describes Abraham's spiritual disposition.

---

43. Ceslaus Spicq, in *L'Épître aux Hébreux*, 3d ed., 2 vols. (Paris: Gabalda, 1953), vol. 2, p. 160, mentions the possibility of Abraham's receiving some type of revelation about the birth of the Savior. Leon Morris, however, in his *Gospel of John*, New International Commentary on the New Testament series (Grand Rapids: Eerdmans, 1970), p. 472, more cautiously suggests "that Abraham's general attitude to this day was one of exultation, rather than [that Jesus referred] to any one specific occasion in the life of the patriarch."

44. Grosheide, *Hebreeën*, p. 153.

ἐπέτυχεν—the verb ἐπιτυγχάνω (I obtain, attain) occurs four times in the New Testament (Rom. 11:7; Heb. 6:15; 11:33; James 4:2), always in the aorist active tense. It is a compound from ἐπί (on, toward) and τυγχάνω (I obtain, get). The compound is more intensive than the simple verb.

---

2. Heirs of the Promise
6:16–20

After providing the illustration that portrays Abraham as the recipient of the promise, the author of the epistle applies the teaching of the promise to all believers. As God assured Abraham of the veracity of his Word and therefore swore an oath, so also for the believers, called heirs of the promise, God confirms the promise with an oath.

16. Men swear by someone greater than themselves, and the oath confirms what is said and puts an end to all argument.

As the Scriptures reveal, Jewish people resorted quickly to swearing an oath. They might swear by heaven (Matt. 5:34; 23:22; James 5:12), by the earth (Matt. 5:35; James 5:12), by the temple (Matt. 23:16), by Jerusalem (Matt. 5:35), or in the name of the Lord God (Gen. 14:22; Deut. 6:13; 10:20; Judges 21:7; Ruth 1:17; Jer. 12:16).

Most of the oaths were sworn in the name of God or that which was associated with God (heaven, the temple, or Jerusalem). That does not mean that the Jew identified God with the objects used as substitutes, but rather that the Jew of Jesus' day did not take his oaths seriously. Jesus forbade the swearing of an oath (Matt. 5:33–37) because of this sinful practice. He taught that a man's word must be unquestionably true so that, as a consequence, oaths would no longer be necessary.

In a court of law, however, the judge administers an oath in order to uphold the truth. Indeed, "men swear by someone greater than themselves" when they invoke the name of God. They appeal to God because he is the ultimate truth, and thus in case they break the oath they risk divine revenge. In court the truth must be spoken by defendant, plaintiff, and their lawyers.[45] The oath, then, settles the truth in any dispute.

17. Because God wanted to make the unchanging nature of his purpose very clear to the heirs of what was promised, he confirmed it with an oath.

Once again we read an argument that leads from the lesser to the greater. The Epistle to the Hebrews is replete with examples of this type of argument. Man, by appealing to God, establishes the truth in a particular matter. How much more significant, by comparison, is the oath God himself swears to confirm the certainty of fulfilling his promises to those who have received

---

45. The author of Hebrews borrows terminology from Egyptian civil law. Refer to Adolf Deissmann, *Bible Studies* (Winona Lake, Ind.: Alpha Publications, 1979), p. 107.

them. The message that the author of Hebrews conveys is that man can depend on the utter truthfulness of God.

Actually the oath God swears is superfluous, for God himself is truth. Man because of sin confirms the truth of his words by invoking God's name, but God does not need to establish the truth. Jesus' prayer to the Father testifies to this: "Your word is truth" (John 17:17).

Why, then, does God swear an oath? He wants to effectively show the heirs of the promise that they can rely fully on his Word. Accommodating himself to human customs, God swears an oath. He is conscious of man's weak faith. Therefore, to give man added assurance of the complete reliability of God's Word, God provides the extra affirmation.

Reading Genesis 22:16–17, we receive the impression that God gave the promise to Abraham, for he is the one who obtains the blessing. "I will surely bless you," God says to Abraham. But the writer of the Epistle to the Hebrews makes the divine blessing applicable to all believers by calling them heirs of the promise. That means that God's promise to Abraham transcends the centuries and is in Christ as relevant today as it was in Abraham's time (Gal. 3:7, 9, 29). The oath God swore to Abraham was meant for us to strengthen us in our faith.

When the author writes, "God wanted to make the unchanging nature of his purpose very clear," he reminds us that the purpose of God is to make us heirs. Furthermore, according to God's will, this purpose has been determined in eternity (Eph. 1:4–5, 11).[46] God's purpose to save the believers in Jesus Christ is firm, unchanging, and inviolable.

No believer ought to doubt God's will to save him, for God gives him perfect assurance that the nature of God's purpose is unchanging. The believer, who has eternal security because of this unchanging will of God, can sing Fanny J. Crosby's hymn:

> Blessed assurance, Jesus is mine!
> O what a foretaste of glory divine!
> Heir of salvation, purchase of God,
> Born of His Spirit, washed in His blood.

Hebrews 6:17 teaches that God not only made the promise to believers but also is the guarantor of the promise. God makes the promise of salvation, and at the same time he becomes the intermediary who ensures that the promise is fulfilled. The word *intermediary* implies that there are two other parties: the one who gives the promise and the one who receives it. Between these two parties stands God as guarantor.

18. God did this so that, by two unchangeable things in which it is

---

46. Dietrich Müller (*NIDNTT*, vol. 3, p. 1018) writes, "The purpose of divine election far precedes the act of historical election." Gottlob Schrenk explains that "the purpose of his will" encompasses the foreordination and predestination mentioned in Eph. 1:4–5, 11 and in effect "has the final word." *TDNT*, vol. 1, p. 635.

impossible for God to lie, we who have fled to take hold of the hope offered to us may be greatly encouraged.

The available evidence accumulates, as the author notes. God has given his unchangeable promise and he confirmed this promise with an unchangeable oath. Besides noting these "two unchangeable things," the writer declares that God cannot lie. These statements have a built-in redundancy, for God by nature is the personification of truth. "God is not a man, that he should lie, nor a son of man, that he should change his mind" (Num. 23:19; see also I Sam. 15:29; Ps. 33:11; Isa. 46:10–11; Mal. 3:6; James 1:17).

If then God accommodates himself to man's custom of swearing an oath to establish the truth, the implication is that when a Christian refuses to accept this oath-confirmed promise of salvation and turns to sin or another religion, he risks being blasphemous.[47] This person intimates that God's Word cannot be trusted and that God is a perjurer.

But in this verse the writer stresses the positive, for he returns to the use of the first person plural. Says he, "We who have fled to take hold of the hope offered to us may be greatly encouraged." The author directs his lesson on the unchangeableness of God's purpose to us who believe the Word of God, and he writes to encourage us in our flight from sin. The words *we who have fled* are somewhat vague because the writer does not provide specific place names or circumstances. However, the general context indicates that we who believe have escaped the power of willful unbelief and thus we turn to God "to take hold of the hope offered to us." We are the people who "for refuge to Jesus have fled."

As true heirs of the promise, we take hold of the hope that God offers us. We have fled as fugitives and cling to the one who offers new life. The author uses a figure of speech by which a single word conveys an entire concept.[48] That is, we must understand that the word *hope* refers to the one who gives that hope. God himself has provided hope through the promises of his Word. And we whom the author of Hebrews exhorts "to make [our] hope sure" (6:11) are invited to appropriate the hope that God places in full view before us.

Taking hold of hope is not something that we do halfheartedly. On the contrary, we must attain the hope offered to us with the strong encouragement that we receive from God's Word. In short, God holds out to us hope and at the same time strenuously urges us to accept and appropriate it.

19. We have this hope as an anchor for the soul, firm and secure. It enters the inner sanctuary behind the curtain.

The author, true to form, introduces a certain topic rather briefly in order

---

47. Spicq, *Hébreux*, vol. 2, p. 162.

48. The figure is called metonomy. Louis Berkhof, in *Principles of Biblical Interpretation* (Grand Rapids: Baker, 1950), pp. 83–84, explains the figure as "a mental [relation] rather than a physical one." He provides the example of Paul's reference to the Holy Spirit—"Quench not the Spirit" (I Thess. 5:19, KJV)—by which Paul intends to describe "the special manifestations of the Spirit."

to explain it fully in subsequent verses. In a brief exhortation he presents the subject *hope* (6:11); after discussing the absolute dependability of God's promise to the believer, he explains the significance of hope (6:18–19). Hope, says the writer, is like an anchor; it gives stability and security to the soul.

The imagery is vivid and telling. The author paints a picture of a boat, battered by the waves but held in place by an unseen anchor that clings to the bottom of the sea. So man's soul, buffeted by winds and waves of doubt, has a secure anchor of hope firmly fixed in Jesus.[49] This anchor gives stability to man's soul, and that includes "the whole inner life of man with his powers of will, reason, and emotion."[50] We relate to the image of an anchor and express our feelings in the words of Priscilla J. Owens:

> We have an anchor that keeps the soul
> Steadfast and sure while the billows roll;
> Fastened to the Rock which cannot move,
> Grounded firm and deep in the Savior's love.

But the Hebrews of Old Testament times and the Jews of the first century had a dislike for the sea. A reflection of this fact is that the word *anchor* never occurs in the Old Testament; and only four times in the New Testament, three of which appear in the account of Paul's shipwreck (Acts 27:29, 30, 40). Therefore the author rather abruptly switches metaphors and mentions the veil of the Most Holy Place. The recipients of the Epistle to the Hebrews were much more attuned to the worship services of tabernacle and temple; they knew the construction of the sanctuary; and the clause "it enters the inner sanctuary behind the curtain" was meaningful to them.

The author of the epistle has come to the end of his exhortation that began after he had introduced Jesus as "high priest in the order of Melchizedek" (5:10). He returns to the subject of the high priesthood of Christ with a reference to "the inner sanctuary behind the curtain." The words immediately reminded the readers of the Day of Atonement, when the high priest entered into the presence of God (Lev. 16:2, 12). Moreover, the Hebrews knew from the gospel proclaimed to them that at Jesus' death the curtain of the temple was torn from top to bottom, exposing the Most Holy Place to the view of all who were inside the temple. They understood the reference to the inner sanctuary figuratively and associated it with heaven. Already the writer had called attention to this fact when he wrote, "We have a great high priest who has gone through the heavens, Jesus the Son of God" (4:14).

20. Where Jesus, who went before us, has entered on our behalf. He has become a high priest forever, in the order of Melchizedek.

---

49. "The anchor of hope was a fairly common metaphor in the late Greek ethic," writes James Moffatt in his *Epistle to the Hebrews,* International Critical Commentary series (Edinburgh: Clark, 1963), p. 89. Westcott adds that the symbol of the anchor, often with that of a fish, occurred on gravestones. *Hebrews,* p. 163.
50. Günther Harder, *NIDNTT,* vol. 3, p. 684.

Our hope is pinned on Jesus, who has entered the heavenly sanctuary. An anchor lies unseen at the bottom of the sea; our hope lies unseen in the highest heaven. "For in this hope we were saved," writes Paul. "But hope that is seen is no hope at all" (Rom. 8:24). Our anchor of hope has absolute security in that Jesus in human form, now glorified, has entered heaven. And he has entered heaven in his humanity as a guarantee that we, too, shall be with him. This guarantee is indicated by the phrase *who went before us*. (In the Greek the equivalent expression is the word *prodromos*, which means "forerunner.") He goes ahead and we follow. Also note that the name *Jesus* and not *Christ* (5:5) occurs—a distinct reminder of the earthly life of the Lord. Jesus ascended in his glorified human body to heaven and entered the presence of God. As Jesus' human body has come into God's presence, so our bodies will enter heaven.[51] That is our hope.

Jesus "has become a high priest forever." This rather short sentence is filled with meaning.

a. Jesus *has become* a high priest. He did not become high priest when he ascended into heaven. Rather, he took his place at the right hand of God the Father because he accomplished his atoning work on the cross. He indeed was the sacrificial Lamb of God offered for the sin of the world; as the writer of Hebrews puts it, "Christ was sacrificed once to take away the sins of many people" (9:28).

b. Jesus has become *a high priest*. The writer has called Jesus high priest in Hebrews 2:17; 3:1; 4:14–15; and 5:5, 10. He will explain the concept *high priest* in succeeding chapters, but in 6:20 the author stresses that Jesus entered heaven as high priest, as the one who atoned for the sins of God's people. He opened the door to heaven because of his high-priestly work.

c. Jesus has become a high priest *forever*. An Aaronic high priest served in the capacity of high priest for a limited duration. Jesus serves forever. The high priest entered the Most Holy Place once a year. Jesus is in heaven forever. "Because Jesus lives forever, he has a permanent priesthood" (7:24). Constantly he intercedes for us (Rom. 8:34; Heb. 7:25; 9:24).

By his death on the cross, Jesus fulfilled the responsibilities of the Aaronic priesthood. But as a high priest he had to belong to a different order. The writer of Hebrews showed that according to Psalm 110:4 God designated Jesus as high priest forever in the order of Melchizedek (5:6, 10). The writer will explain this topic in the next few chapters.

Doctrinal Considerations in 6:13–20

Joshua told the elders, leaders, judges, and officials of Israel that God had fulfilled all the promises given to them (Josh. 23:14). Every promise God has fulfilled. Not only Joshua but also every believer can testify that God keeps his Word. The

---

51. George E. Rice, "The Chiastic Structure of the Central Section of the Epistle to the Hebrews," *Andrews University Seminary Studies* 19 (1981): 243.

promises made to our spiritual forefathers are repeated and given to us in our generation. To Abraham God said, "I will establish my covenant as an everlasting covenant between me and you and your descendants after you for the generations to come, to be your God and the God of your descendants after you" (Gen. 17:7). Throughout Scripture we read the promise *I will be your God*. Because of the redeeming work of Christ, believers are in that covenant God made with Abraham and are Abraham's spiritual offspring (Gal. 3:16).

God's Word is sure. God does not lie, as Paul explicitly states (Titus 1:2). In the Epistle to the Hebrews God's promise is reinforced—as if it needed support—by an oath sworn by God himself. The point is that God's Word is absolutely reliable. After exhorting the recipients to make their hope sure (6:11) and by encouraging them to have their hope anchored in Jesus, the writer continues his exposition about the high priesthood of Christ. This doctrine is basic to the Epistle to the Hebrews.

Greek Words, Phrases, and Constructions in 6:16–20

Verse 16

μείζονος—the comparative adjective from μέγας (great) is in the genitive singular case because the verb ὀμνύω (I swear) is followed by the preposition κατά, which demands the genitive. The gender of the comparative is either masculine or neuter; the masculine means "someone," and the neuter "something." Although it is possible to use the translation *something*, we do well to translate the adjective as "someone."

ἀντιλογία—this noun derived from ἀντί (against) and λέγω (I speak) occurs four times in the New Testament (Heb. 6:16; 7:7; 12:3; Jude 11).

Verse 17

ἐν ᾧ—although the nearest antecedent is the preceding noun ὅρκος (oath), this relative pronoun is dependent on the content of 6:16. Some translators give the prepositional phrase the meaning *and so, thus*, or *wherein*; others leave it untranslated.

βουλόμενος and βουλή—the choice of the present middle participle, nominative singular of βούλομαι (I want) together with the noun βουλή (decision, purpose) is deliberate; these two are coupled together for reinforcement. The present participle denotes God's desire to make known the decision that he had made beforehand.

τὸ ἀμετάθετον—this substantivized verbal adjective is a compound consisting of ἀ (un-, not), μετα (after), and τίθημι (I place, put). The verb μετατίθημι (I change, transfer) occurs in Hebrews 7:12; 11:5. The verbal adjective implies a passive idea with overtones of necessity: that which cannot be changed. In the New Testament, the word is used only by the author of Hebrews in 6:17, 18.

ἐμεσίτευσεν—the aorist active indicative of μεσιτεύω (I mediate) occurs once in the New Testament. It relates to the adjective μέσος (middle) and the noun μεσίτης (mediator).

Verse 18

πραγμάτων—this noun appears eleven times in the New Testament, three of which are in Hebrews (6:18; 10:1; 11:1). Derived from πράσσω (I practice), the noun in 6:18 means "facts." The two facts are the promise and the oath. The preposition διά (through, by means of) requires the genitive case.

τὸν θεόν—a few major Greek manuscripts (for example, Codex Vaticanus and Codex Bezae) omit the definite article to express the meaning *for one who is God.* However, the rest of the manuscripts, including a papyrus document, have the definite article.

καταφυγόντες—the second aorist active participle of the verb καταφεύγω (I flee for refuge) has a perfective connotation;[52] that is, "to escape completely."

κρατῆσαι—the first aorist infinitive of κρατέω (I hold faithfully) is constative; that is, comprehensive. The infinitive is closely linked to the preceding participle καταφυγόντες.

Verse 19

ἀσφαλῆ τε καὶ βεβαίαν—these two descriptive adjectives modify the noun ἄγκυραν. The presence of the particle τε with καί conveys the meaning *not only . . . but also.* ἀσφαλῆ is an adjective derived from ἀ (un-, not) and σφάλλω (I cause to fall, fail). The adjective βεβαίαν is featured five times in Hebrews (2:2; 3:6, 14; 6:19; 9:17) out of a total of nine times in the New Testament (Rom. 4:16; II Cor. 1:6; II Peter 1:10, 19).

τὸ ἐσώτερον—the comparative adjective of the adverb ἔσω (within) may be translated "the inner part" of the sanctuary. Some scholars interpret the adjective as a preposition that controls the genitive case of καταπετάσματος. We do well to translate the phrase as "the inner sanctuary behind the curtain."

Verse 20

πρόδρομος—this noun appears once in the New Testament. Its roots are in πρό (before) and τρέχω, ἔδραμον (I run, ran), and it refers to Jesus, who has entered heaven to prepare a place for those who believe in him (John 14:3).

γενόμενος—in Hebrews 2:17 the author gives the aorist subjunctive form γένηται ("that [Jesus] might become"); in 6:20 γενόμενος is the aorist middle participle, translated "he has become." The aorist is culminative. Jesus' mission on earth has been culminated, yet his activities as interceding high priest continue.

Summary of Chapter 6

The chapter which begins at 5:11 and ends at 6:20 is a lengthy pastoral exhortation. It is an interlude. Before the author explains the doctrine of the high priesthood of Christ in the order of Melchizedek, he exhorts his readers to faithfulness. First, he admonishes them because of their dullness in learning the basic doctrines of God's Word. Next, he delineates what these elementary teachings are: repentance, faith, baptism, ordination, resurrection, and judgment. He exhorts the recipients of his letter to advance in their understanding of these teachings.

Throughout the epistle the author warns the Christians against the sin of

---

52. Robertson, *Grammar,* p. 827.

unbelief (3:12; 4:1, 11; 10:26, 29; 12:15, 28–29). He describes the rebellious Israelites who perished in the desert because of this sin (3:16–19). In 6:4–6 the author pursues that same theme by referring to those persons who have hardened their hearts after receiving a knowledge of the truth. These people continue to crucify Jesus and to despise him. They do so in open rebellion. For such persons, says the author, there is no possibility of being brought back to repentance. They are lost forever.

This observation serves as a warning to the readers not to fall into the sin of unbelief, but to demonstrate their diligence in exhibiting the qualities of faith, hope, and love. The author singles out the virtue of hope and encourages them to make hope a priority in their spiritual lives. He commends them for their loving care shown to people in need and assures them that they are the recipients of the blessings of salvation. He exhorts them to cultivate hope. He points to Jesus, the forerunner who has entered heaven as high priest and who by his presence in heaven guarantees them entrance.

Hope is anchored in the finished work of Christ, who atoned for the sins of his people.

7

Jesus: High Priest like Melchizedek

7:1–28

Outline

7 1 This Melchizedek was king of Salem and priest of God Most High. He met Abraham returning from the defeat of the kings and blessed him, 2 and Abraham gave him a tenth of everything. First, his name means "king of righteousness"; then also, "king of Salem" means "king of peace." 3 Without father or mother, without genealogy, without beginning of days or end of life, like the Son of God he remains a priest forever.

4 Just think how great he was: Even the patriarch Abraham gave him a tenth of the plunder! 5 Now the law requires the descendants of Levi who become priests to collect a tenth from the people—that is, their brothers—even though their brothers are descended from Abraham. 6 This man, however, did not trace his descent from Levi, yet he collected a tenth from Abraham and blessed him who had the promises. 7 And without doubt the lesser person is blessed by the greater. 8 In the one case, the tenth is collected by men who die; but in the other case, by him who is declared to be living. 9 One might even say that Levi, who collects the tenth, paid the tenth through Abraham, 10 because when Melchizedek met Abraham, Levi was still in the body of his ancestor.

A. Melchizedek, King and Priest
7:1–10

1. The History of Melchizedek
7:1–3

After an interlude of exhortations and admonitions, the author returns to the topic of Christ's priesthood that was introduced in 2:17; 3:1; 4:14; and especially 5:6, 10. In chapter 7, he begins to explain the significance of the quotation from Psalm 110:4 ("You are a priest forever, in the order of Melchizedek," 5:6; see also 6:20). The heart of the doctrinal section of the Epistle to the Hebrews lies in the discussion of the high priesthood of Christ recorded in chapter 7. All of the preceding material in this chapter is introductory.[1]

1. This Melchizedek was king of Salem and priest of God Most High. He met Abraham returning from the defeat of the kings and blessed him, 2. and Abraham gave him a tenth of everything. First, his name means "king of righteousness"; then also, "king of Salem" means "king of peace."

---

1. Simon J. Kistemaker, *The Psalm Citations in the Epistle to the Hebrews* (Amsterdam: Van Soest, 1961), p. 98.

Melchizedek is not familiar to us, for his name occurs only twice in the Old Testament (Gen. 14:18; Ps. 110:4). Although the historical account in Genesis 14 provides more information than Psalm 110, the details nevertheless are not elaborate.

First, the name *Melchizedek* has the same ending as that of Adoni-Zedek, the king of Jerusalem who is mentioned in Joshua 10:1, 3. The first part of the name (*Melchi*) means "my king" and the second part (*zedek*) means "righteous"—that is, "my king is righteous." The author of Hebrews interprets the name as "king of righteousness" (7:2).

Melchizedek was king of Salem at the time Abraham defeated the forces of Kedorlaomer. Upon Abraham's return from the northern part of Canaan, Melchizedek met him and offered him bread and wine. We are told that Melchizedek was a priest of God Most High, that he blessed Abraham, and that he received a tenth of the spoils Abraham had gathered (Gen. 14:18–20).

Both the Genesis account and the Epistle to the Hebrews portray Melchizedek as a historical figure who was a contemporary of Abraham.[2] Melchizedek was king of Salem, a city generally identified with Jerusalem (Ps. 76:2),[3] and he was priest of God Most High. In the Gentile world of Abraham's day, traces of true worship of God the "Creator of heaven and earth" remained (Gen. 14:19). Melchizedek served Abraham's God and "had carried on the tradition from the time of Paradise when mankind recognized only one true God."[4]

Abraham gave Melchizedek a tenth of the spoils. Although Genesis 14:20 ("Then Abram gave him a tenth of everything") is very brief, the author of Hebrews reasons from the silence of Scripture and constructs his argument on the significance of the king-priest Melchizedek. The Genesis account teaches that Abraham had sworn an oath to God that he would not keep any of the spoils for himself (Gen. 14:22–23). Abraham recognized Melchizedek as God's representative and therefore by giving Melchizedek a tenth he brought the tithe to God.

Melchizedek as king-priest was God's representative, for he was king of righteousness as his name implies. He was a king who established and promoted righteousness in his kingdom. Also, he was king of Salem, and the

---

2. Jewish writers, the Dead Sea Scrolls, and early Christian authors interpret Melchizedek's person in various ways, from an angel (i.e., an eschatological deliverer) to a historical figure. See "Excursus I: The Significance of Melchizedek," in Philip Edgcumbe Hughes's *Commentary on the Epistle to the Hebrews* (Grand Rapids: Eerdmans, 1977), pp. 237–45. For a detailed bibliography see Bruce A. Demarest's "Melchizedek, Salem," in *NIDNTT*, vol. 2, pp. 590–93. Also see his *History of Interpretation of Hebrews 7:1–10 from the Reformation to the Present* (Tübingen: Mohr Siebeck, 1976).

3. The name *Salem* is identified by some writers with Salim near Aenon (John 3:23), where John the Baptist stayed. However, Josephus associated Salem with the city of Jerusalem (see his *Jewish Wars* 6.438 and his *Antiquities of the Jews* 1.180, LCL).

4. Gerhard Charles Aalders, *Bible Student's Commentary: Genesis*, 2 vols. (Grand Rapids: Zondervan, 1981), vol. 1, p. 289.

word *Salem* means "peace." Of course, the two characteristics, righteousness and peace, are messianic (see Isa. 9:6–7). They describe Jesus, who according to Psalm 110:1 and 4 fills the roles of priest and king.

3. Without father or mother, without genealogy, without beginning of days or end of life, like the Son of God he remains a priest forever.

We ought not take this verse literally, for the author, reasoning from silence (Gen. 14:18–20), is comparing Melchizedek with the priests who descended from Aaron. The writer expected a priest to establish and prove his priestly descent. During the time of Ezra and Nehemiah, the priests determined on the basis of the law of Moses that only the descendants of Aaron were to serve as priests in the sacrificial system (Exod. 28 and 29; Lev. 8, 9, and 10; Num. 16, 17, and 18; Ezra 2:61–63; Neh. 7:63–65).

We can understand that belonging to this close-knit community of priests was a unique privilege; a priest presented sacrifices from the people to God and served as an intermediary between man and God. "Thus a priest is one who brings men near to God, who leads them into the presence of God."[5] A prerequisite for holding the office of priest, therefore, was a proven genealogy. Tnis genealogy was of the greatest importance. For example, the Jewish historian Josephus assures his readers that he was born into a priestly family, that he can prove his descent, and that he nas found his genealogy recorded in "public registers."[6]

Melchizedek, by contrast, does not have a genealogy; the names of his father and mother are lacking. Yet this man is priest of God Most High. Melchizedek's age is not mentioned either. Yet for all the other persons prominent in the history of salvation genealogical information is supplied (for example, Adam lived 930 years [Gen. 5:5]; Noah, 950 years [Gen. 9:29]; and Abraham, 175 years [Gen. 25:7]). Melchizedek, therefore, is unique. He does not fit into the genealogies recorded in Genesis. He seems to belong to a different class.

What the author of Hebrews has written about Melchizedek applies directly to the Son of God. In comparing Melchizedek with Jesus, the author uses the word *like* (7:3, 15) because he sees a similarity. He does not say that these two are identical; he only compares and discerns resemblance. Melchizedek was a historical figure, in the writer's opinion; but because genealogical references that would classify him as a member of the Levitical priesthood are not available, he states that Melchizedek "remains a priest forever."

---

5. Geerhardus Vos, *The Teaching of the Epistle to the Hebrews* (Grand Rapids: Eerdmans, 1956), p. 94.

6. Josephus, *Life* 1.6 (LCL). Emil Schürer, in *A History of the Jewish People in the Time of Jesus Christ*, 5 vols. (Edinburgh: Clark, 1885), vol. 1, div. 2, p. 210, writes: *"The primary requisite in a priest was evidence of his pedigree."* Italics his.

Greek Words, Phrases, and Constructions in 7:1–3

Verse 1

τοῦ ὑψίστου—this form is an adjective in the superlative, but is understood to indicate rank: in the highest degree. The adjective serves the purpose of describing the only true God whom both Abraham and Melchizedek worship (Gen. 14:19–20, 22). It occurs thirteen times in the New Testament, nine times in the Gospel of Luke and Acts, and once in Hebrews (7:1).

κοπῆς—although the word occurs once in the New Testament, from its usage in the Septuagint (Gen. 14:17; Deut. 28:25; Josh. 10:20; Jth. 15:7) the meaning is clear. Derived from the verb κόπτω (I cut), it refers to a slaughter, or figuratively to a defeat.

Verse 3

ἀπάτωρ ἀμήτωρ—these two nouns appear only in Hebrews 7:3, in classical Greek literature, and in Philo. The nouns refer to orphans, foundlings, illegitimate children, and disowned sons or to gods who came into being without father or mother. Philo uses these words in his allegorical interpretation on the origin of the high priest.[7] In Hebrews 7:3, we note the additional word ἀγενεαλόγητος (without genealogy) used climactically by the author of Hebrews to show that in the early chapters of Genesis, where genealogies are frequent, a priestly genealogy for Melchizedek is missing. The three Greek words, therefore, must be understood in the historical setting of Genesis.

ἀφωμοιωμένος—the perfect passive participle of the verb ἀφομοιόω (I make similar) expresses duration; the compound form makes the participle emphatic. Note that Melchizedek is compared with the Son of God, not the Son of God with Melchizedek.[8] That is, the focus is on the eternal Son of God. Also note that the author of Hebrews writes not "Jesus" or "Christ" but "Son of God." The appellation stresses his eternal rather than temporal existence.

διηνεκές—this neuter adjective is derived from the verb διαφέρω (I carry through) in its aorist form διήνεγκα; it means "continuous, uninterrupted." Only the writer of Hebrews employs the word (7:3; 10:1, 12, 14).

---

2. The Significance of Melchizedek
7:4–10

In chapter 7 the writer of Hebrews presents an exegesis of Psalm 110:4 ("You are a priest forever, in the order of Melchizedek"), which is quoted in 5:6 and referred to in 5:10 and 6:20. Stating the quotation in summary form, the author explains it in reverse order. He begins with the name *Melchizedek* and places it in a historical context (7:1–3); in the next section he discusses the words *priest* (7:4–10) and *priestly order* (7:11–12); he devotes

---

7. Gottlob Schrenk, *TDNT,* vol. 5, pp. 1019–21. Also see Otfried Hofius, "Father," *NIDNTT,* vol. 1, p. 616.

8. John Albert Bengel, *Gnomon of the New Testament,* edited by Andrew R. Fausset, 7th ed., 5 vols. (Edinburgh: Clark, 1877), vol. 4, p. 403.

two verses to the personal pronoun *you* (7:13–14); and he elaborates on the expression *forever* in the next ten verses (7:15–25).[9]

4. Just think how great he was: Even the patriarch Abraham gave him a tenth of the plunder! 5. Now the law requires the descendants of Levi who become priests to collect a tenth from the people—that is, their brothers—even though their brothers are descended from Abraham.

Having placed Melchizedek in historical perspective, the author wants the readers to pay particular attention to the greatness of this priest who received tithes from and blessed Abraham. In the minds of his Hebrew audience Abraham was considered a great man; he was called the friend of God (II Chron. 20:7; Isa. 41:8; James 2:23) and the father of the nation Israel, the patriarch (Isa. 51:2). The writer stresses the word *patriarch* to underscore the greatness of Abraham.

However, someone greater than Abraham appeared at the time when Abraham returned victoriously from defeating four kings in northern Canaan and from setting five kings free. Abraham had reached a pinnacle in his leadership career in the southern part of Canaan. But upon his return, Abraham paid tribute to Melchizedek by giving him a tenth of the plunder. Literally the text reads: "Abraham gave him a tenth of the top of the heap." Abraham gave him the best!

Even though customs and cultures differ with respect to tithing, we have no difficulty understanding that the one who receives the tithe (Melchizedek) is greater than the one who gives the tithe (Abraham). The readers of the Epistle to the Hebrews had to acknowledge the superiority of Melchizedek.[10] They were acquainted with the command on tithing specified in the law of Moses (Lev. 27:30–33; Num. 18:21, 24, 26–29; also see Deut. 12:17–19; 14:22–29; 26:12–15).

Perhaps we may parallel the tithing of the ancients and our paying taxes. All of us are familiar with taxes, although the tax laws vary from time to time and from area to area. Similarly the rules on tithing recorded in the Old Testament vary and may reflect changing circumstances in the development of the Israelite nation.[11] However, the writer of Hebrews is not interested in stressing differences in tithing; his intention is to stress the receiving of the tithe.

"The law requires," says the writer, that the priests gather the tithe. He mentions the name of Levi, not that of Aaron, in order to show that the work of collecting the tithe belonged to the entire tribe of Levi—the Levites

---

9. Kistemaker, *Psalm Citations*, p. 118.

10. Jewish writers identified Melchizedek with Shem the son of Noah, who may have been a contemporary of Abraham (Gen. 11:11). If Shem were living at the time of Abraham, he would be more venerable than the patriarch. Consult Nedarim 32b, Nashim, and Sanhedrin 108b, Nezikin, *Talmud*, vol. 3.

11. Gerald F. Hawthorne, "Tithe," *NIDNTT*, vol. 3, p. 852.

and the priests.[12] According to the law, the Levites were to gather the tithe and they in turn would give a tenth to the priests (Num. 18:28).

We make three observations.

a. In 7:4–10, the author of the epistle employs names representatively: Abraham is called the patriarch—the head of a nation and the father of believers; Levi, whose descendants become priests, is the tribal head.

b. Levi stands closer genealogically to Abraham than to Aaron, so the author is able to refer to the rest of the Israelites as "their brothers [who] are descended from Abraham."

c. Because of the writer's exegetical method of explaining the quotation from Psalm 110:4, the word *priest* assumes added importance in the present context. This particular term has great significance in the author's discourse on the priesthood of Christ.

In verses 4 and 5 the author presents a series of contrasts: the priests as descendants of Levi are more respected than the rest of the people; father Abraham is greater than his descendants; Melchizedek, because he received the tithe, is superior to the patriarch Abraham.

6. This man, however, did not trace his descent from Levi, yet he collected a tenth from Abraham and blessed him who had the promises. 7. And without doubt the lesser person is blessed by the greater.

Already before Abraham met Melchizedek, God had given the patriarch the promises (Gen. 12:2–3; 13:14–17) and had blessed him. Abraham became the great-grandfather of Levi, whose descendants became priests in Israel.

Melchizedek, by contrast, had no genealogy and had not received the promises. He stood alone in all his grandeur as king of Salem and priest of God Most High. Abraham, fully aware of Melchizedek's stature, offered him tithes and in return received blessing when Melchizedek said:

> Blessed be Abram by God Most High,
>   Creator of heaven and earth.
> And blessed be God Most High,
>   who delivered your enemies into your hand. [Gen. 14:19–20]

This priest of God Most High did not exact tithes from Abraham as Levitical priests imposed a tithe on their fellow Israelites in later years. Of his own accord Abraham gave Melchizedek a tenth of the spoils, because he recognized him as God's representative. And this representative imparted a divine blessing on Abraham.

Simple logic tells us, says the writer, that "the lesser person is blessed by the greater." This fact is evident in three instances: the blessing that Isaac pronounced on Jacob, that Jacob gave his sons, and that Moses bestowed upon the Israelites (Gen. 27:27–29; 48:15–16; 49; Deut. 33). Sons do not

---

12. F. W. Grosheide, *De Brief aan de Hebreeën en de Brief van Jakobus* (Kampen: Kok, 1955), p. 166.

bless their fathers, but dying fathers pronounce blessings on their sons. In the case of Melchizedek blessing Abraham, we see that the king-priest delivers the blessing of God Most High to the patriarch. Abraham had given Melchizedek a tithe of the plunder because Abraham saw he was God's representative.[13] In return this representative invoked God's blessing upon Abraham. Melchizedek functioned as God's mouthpiece and, therefore, was greater than Abraham. He acted in the capacity of priest, and that made him superior to Abraham.

8. In the one case, the tenth is collected by men who die; but in the other case, by him who is declared to be living. 9. One might even say that Levi, who collects the tenth, paid the tenth through Abraham, 10. because when Melchizedek met Abraham, Levi was still in the body of his ancestor.

In our age and culture we are somewhat puzzled when we read 7:8–10. If the author of Hebrews presents an explanation of Genesis 14:18–20, and if on the basis of the silence of Scripture he reads matters pertaining to Melchizedek, Abraham, and Levi into the text, we have difficulty understanding him.

The author, however, is a trained theologian who applies logic in a manner differing from ours. He reasons like a rabbi of the first century. He uses a methodology in explaining the Scriptures that is strictly rabbinical. He is a typical Jewish-Christian author who, filled with the Holy Spirit, writes the inspired Word of God.

Two points stand out in the author's presentation.

a. The permanent priesthood of Melchizedek. The exact wording is that Melchizedek "is declared to be living." Does this mean that Melchizedek never died? If he were a supernatural being, he would be the Son of God. But the writer says that Melchizedek was "like the Son of God" (7:3). Although Scripture is silent about the death of Melchizedek, we nonetheless conclude that he died. Yet in the two places (Gen. 14:18–20; Ps. 110:4) in which his name is mentioned Melchizedek (in relation to his priesthood) is described as "living." This means that the priesthood of Melchizedek is permanent.

b. By contrast, there was a succession of Levitical priests. A priest might assume his priestly duties "as soon as the first signs of manhood made their appearance," but according to rabbinical tradition "he was not actually installed till he was twenty years of age."[14] The period of service for a priest might cover twenty to thirty years, but the end would come. The writer of

---

13. John Calvin, *Epistle to the Hebrews* (Grand Rapids: Eerdmans, 1949), p. 161. Also see Hans-Georg Link's article "Blessing" in *NIDNTT*, vol. 1, pp. 206–15.

14. Schürer, *History of the Jewish People*, vol. 1, div. 2, p. 215. Note also that the following passages imply that a priest was installed at age thirty and served until he reached the age of fifty: Num. 4:3, 23, 30, 35, 39, 43, 47; also see I Chron. 23:3. Num. 8:23–26 speaks of Levites twenty-five years of age. And I Chron. 23:24, 27; II Chron. 31:17; and Ezra 3:8 mention the twenty-year-old priest.

the epistle describes the priests as "men who die." Their term of office is limited.

"One might even say" is an expression that occurs only once in the New Testament. What is being said is rather unusual, because Levi, the great-grandchild of Abraham, is said to have paid Melchizedek a tithe. The use of the name *Levi* must be understood figuratively, for Levi himself did not collect tithes—his descendants did. Also Abraham, who paid the tenth to Melchizedek, functions as a representative; he represents the tribe of Levi that was appointed to collect the tenth.

From our perspective, the author's reasoning may be somewhat difficult to accept. And yet the Bible is replete with examples of representatives whose actions affected the lives of their descendants. For example, Joshua made a peace treaty with the Gibeonites that bound the Israelites for centuries (Josh. 9:15). In the same way, Abraham represented the Levitical priesthood, which was entrusted with the task of gathering the tithes of the people, and in this capacity Abraham offered the tithe to Melchizedek. The Levitical priesthood paid homage to the priesthood of Melchizedek.

Consider also the time when Melchizedek met Abraham. The meeting took place years before the birth of Isaac and more than a century before Levi was born. Abraham, then, represented Levi and his descendants. The author of Hebrews modestly writes, "Because when Melchizedek met Abraham, Levi was still in the body of his ancestor." The point is that Melchizedek's priesthood is to be preferred to that of Levi.

Doctrinal Considerations in 7:1-10

In this section (7:1-10) the author stresses the principle of life with reference to Melchizedek and to Levi. Melchizedek is portrayed as a person "without beginning of days or end of life" (7:3) and as one "who is declared to be living" (7:8). Because of his likeness to the Son of God and because he thus is a type of Christ, Melchizedek lives on scripturally although not historically. The author of Hebrews bases his theological observations on the scriptural references to Melchizedek.

The principle of life the author applies to Levi as well, but in a different way. The descendants of Levi entrusted with the task of collecting the tithe are subject to death; they are "men who die" (7:8). But Levi, as the tribal head, existed "in the body of his ancestor" (7:10) at the time Melchizedek met Abraham.

In Hebrews 7:1-10 the writer purposely avoids speaking about Christ. He places the greatness of Melchizedek in historical perspective in order to compare Christ with the king-priest in succeeding verses. The superiority of the Son of God, however, the author demonstrates by saying that Melchizedek is "like the Son of God" (7:3).

The focus, then, is on the greatness of Melchizedek, who surpassed the patriarch Abraham. To underscore the position of Abraham the author notes that the patriarch "had the promises" (7:6). Abraham represents the line of believers. For example, Abraham is listed first in the genealogy of Jesus recorded in Matthew 1. Abraham is the father of believers. Yet Melchizedek, says the writer of Hebrews, transcends him because Melchizedek received Abraham's tithe.

Paying the tithe to the priest of God Most High was Abraham's acknowledgment that God himself had given him the victory in the conflict and the plunder of the battlefield (Gen. 14). Thus he paid the tithe to God's representative.

The principle of tithing God instituted by law (for example, Num. 18:21) and enjoined the Israelites to comply. The tithe represents a tenth part of that which God gives the tither. In Old Testament times, the tithe sustained the priest, the Levite, and the services at the sanctuary. In the New Testament, Jesus teaches that "the worker deserves his wages" (Luke 10:7); Paul repeats this rule both indirectly and directly when he writes concerning the financial support of those who proclaim the gospel (I Cor. 9:14; I Tim. 5:17–18).[15] The New Testament, however, lacks specific injunctions about tithing.

Greek Words, Phrases, and Constructions in 7:4–10

Verse 4

θεωρεῖτε—this verb can be either the present indicative or the present imperative. In view of the verb's position in the sentence—it stands first and thus receives emphasis—the present imperative is preferred. The verb θεωρέω conveys the meaning of looking intently at someone or something for the purpose of intellectual study.

ἀκροθινίων—the genitive neuter plural is a compound from ἄκρος (the highest) and θίς, θινός (heap). For example, the flour at the top of the heap was considered the best part. The noun ἀκροθίνια means "first fruits."

πατριάρχης—this is a compound noun derived from πατριά (nation) and ἄρχω (I rule). The word appears four times in the New Testament and describes David (Acts 2:29), the twelve sons of Jacob (Acts 7:8, 9), and Abraham (Heb. 7:4). The author of Hebrews places the noun, preceded by the definite article, at the end of 7:4 for emphasis.

Verse 5

τὴν ἱερατείαν—this noun, translated "priestly office," occurs twice in the New Testament, here and in Luke 1:9. (Its synonym ἱερωσύνη appears four times in Hebrews [7:11, 12, 14 (variant reading), 24]). The word "expresses the actual service of the priest and not the office of priesthood."[16]

λαόν—in the Epistle to the Hebrews this noun generally refers to the church (see 2:17; 4:9; 10:30; 11:25; 13:12) and is qualified by the phrase *of God*. In 7:5, the author explains the word *people* by adding the note *that is, their brothers*.

Verse 6

δεδεκάτωκεν—the perfect active indicative from the verb δεκατόω (I collect tithes) reflects the permanence of the action—the lasting effect of the tribute to Melchizedek. The tense of this verb stresses the significance of the deed.

---

15. John Owen, *An Exposition of Hebrews*, 7 vols. in 4 (Evansville, Ind.: Sovereign Grace, 1960), vol. 3, p. 354.

16. B. F. Westcott, *Commentary on the Epistle to the Hebrews* (Grand Rapids: Eerdmans, 1950), p. 176.

εὐλόγηκεν—the perfect active indicative from the verb εὐλογέω (I bless) is translated as a simple past tense *he blessed*. The perfect tense, however, expresses the permanence of Melchizedek's blessing. Hebrews 7 features numerous verbs in the perfect tense (see vv. 6, 9, 11, 16, 20, 23, 26, 28).

Verse 8

ὧδε μὲν . . . ἐκεῖ δέ—unfortunately this precise balance in grammatical structure with *here* and *there* has been omitted for stylistic reasons in numerous translations.

ἀποθνῄσκοντες—the present tense of this active participle from the verb ἀποθνῄσκω (I die) has been chosen and placed deliberately before the noun ἄνθρωποι (men). The word order in the Greek is unique. Literally translated, 7:8 reads: "And here on the one hand tithes dying men receive, there on the other hand it is declared that he lives."

---

11 If perfection could have been attained through the Levitical priesthood (for on the basis of it the law was given to the people), why was there still need for another priest to come— one in the order of Melchizedek, not in the order of Aaron?　12 For when there is a change of the priesthood, there must also be a change of the law.　13 He of whom these things are said belonged to a different tribe, and no one from that tribe has ever served at the altar.　14 For it is clear that our Lord descended from Judah, and in regard to that tribe Moses said nothing about priests.　15 And what we have said is even more clear if another priest like Melchizedek appears,　16 one who has become a priest not on the basis of a regulation as to his ancestry but on the basis of the power of an indestructible life.　17 For it is declared:

"You are a priest forever,
in the order of Melchizedek."

18 The former regulation is set aside because it was weak and useless　19 (for the law made nothing perfect), and a better hope is introduced, by which we draw near to God.

B. Melchizedek's Superior Priesthood
7:11–19

1. Imperfection of the Levitical Priesthood
7:11–12

One of the recurring motifs in the Epistle to the Hebrews is that of God introducing a new order and thereby bringing the old order to an end. In 4:8 Joshua's concept of rest is completely overshadowed by God's rest. In 8:13 the first covenant is declared obsolete because the new covenant has taken its place. And in 7:11–12 the Levitical priesthood (which was established by divine law) has been superseded by the priesthood of Melchizedek; this necessitates a change in that law.

11. If perfection could have been attained through the Levitical priesthood (for on the basis of it the law was given to the people), why was there still need for another priest to come—one in the order of Melchizedek, not in the order of Aaron?

The old order changeth,
yielding place to new.

Thus wrote Alfred Tennyson about the death of King Arthur. These two lines, although from a different setting, capture the thought of Hebrews 7:11. The termination of the Levitical priesthood did not take place when Jesus died on the cross. The Aaronic order came to an end with the destruction of the temple in A.D. 70. The new order, however, was inaugurated with Jesus' death and existed simultaneously with the Levitical priesthood until Jerusalem was destroyed.

The Aaronic priesthood that had served the nation Israel since the exodus proved to be a failure in procuring salvation for God's people. That is, says the writer of the epistle, because "the blood of goats and bulls and the ashes of a heifer sprinkled on those who are ceremonially unclean sanctify" the people and cleanse them only on the outside (9:13). The priests could not cleanse the soul from sin. Inwardly the burden of guilt and the stain of sin remained. Only the blood of Christ, says the author, will "cleanse our consciences from acts that lead to death, so that we may serve the living God" (9:14).

The Levitical priesthood was established centuries after that of Melchizedek (Gen. 14:18–20). God had not forgotten the priestly order of Melchizedek, for through David he spoke of this order again in Psalm 110:4.

No one therefore could ever say that the order of Melchizedek was replaced by the Levitical priesthood. The fact that God himself in David's psalm declares that his Son (see Ps. 110:1 and Matt. 22:41–45) is priest forever in the order of Melchizedek is irrefutable evidence of the superiority of this priesthood (Ps. 110:4). By implication, contends the author, the Levitical priesthood did not attain perfection. It was meant to be provisional, for it was superseded by an entirely different order—that of Melchizedek.

Even though the author of Hebrews bases his argument on Scripture and puts it to his readers in the form of a question, the matter itself was a sensitive one for the Jewish religious structure of his day. Under the administration of the Levitical priesthood the law was given to the people. The law was then inseparably linked to the religious hierarchy of Israel. Anyone who dared to change the Aaronic priesthood was accused of tampering with the law of Moses. And anyone who was accused of speaking contrary to the law could be killed. In fact, Stephen was put to death because, so his accusers said, he spoke against the law (Acts 6:13). Paul was beaten by an angry mob that shouted, "This is the man who teaches all men everywhere against our people and our law and this place" (i.e., the temple; Acts 21:28).

God, however, did not give the people his law in order to displace the Aaronic priesthood; the priesthood itself was linked to the law. Without the priesthood there was no law! That is basic. The priests taught God's law and his promises. These men with all their imperfections were the mainstay of Israel's faith, for the very words of God were entrusted to them (Rom. 3:2).

12. For when there is a change of the priesthood, there must also be a change of the law.

In this sentence the first word *for* is significant because it tells us how the change will take place. In the preceding verse we are told that the Aaronic priesthood was unable to reach perfection. In 7:12 we learn that a change in the law must accompany the change in the priesthood.

We ought to look at the verse, however, through the eyes of a person of Jewish descent in the first century of the Christian era. The law of God was valid eternally and could not be terminated. The apocryphal literature of that era, as well as the rabbinical books of somewhat later date, speak of the lasting validity of the law.[17] Jesus, in a certain sense, reflected that sentiment when he said: "I tell you the truth, until heaven and earth disappear, not the smallest letter, not the least stroke of a pen, will by any means disappear from the Law until everything is accomplished" (Matt. 5:18). But Jesus fulfilled the law (Matt. 5:17), not to set it aside but to effect a change.

If then a change of the law had to occur, God himself would have to accomplish the change. And this is exactly what God did when, centuries after the law was given, he said through David, "The LORD has sworn and will not change his mind: 'You are a priest forever, in the order of Melchizedek' " (Ps. 110:4). God changed the law by appointing his Son high priest in another order and confirming the change with an oath (Heb. 7:28). With the coming of Christ the priestly order was transformed and transferred.[18] With his once-for-all sacrifice, Christ fulfilled the law and made the Levitical priesthood obsolete.

2. Inappropriate Service for Judah's Descendant
7:13–14

No one could ever object to Jesus' high priesthood in the order of Melchizedek by saying that the Levitical order had superseded the priesthood of Melchizedek. Psalm 110:4 is ample proof that God himself centuries later appointed his Son, by oath, in the priestly order of Melchizedek.

13. He of whom these things are said belonged to a different tribe, and no one from that tribe has ever served at the altar.   14. For it is clear that our Lord descended from Judah, and in regard to that tribe Moses said nothing about priests.

The Hebrews would have no difficulty accepting the messianic teaching of Psalm 110, with its distinct reference to the royal office of the Messiah. Also the Scriptures clearly taught them that the Christ was to come from David's family (II Sam. 7:12; Ps. 89:3–4; Jer. 23:5) and from the town of Bethlehem (Mic. 5:2; Matt. 2:6; and see John 7:42). And when the Gospels in written form began to circulate, the genealogies of Jesus recorded in Matthew 1:1–17 and Luke 3:23–38 showed his royal descent from the line of David.

To make Jesus, who belongs to the tribe of Judah, serve at the altar is contrary to the law. Remember that Uzziah king of Judah "entered the temple of the LORD to burn incense on the altar of incense" and was stricken

---

17. SB, vol. 1, pp. 244–46.
18. Ceslaus Spicq, *L'Épître aux Hébreux*, 3d ed., 2 vols. (Paris: Gabalda, 1953), vol. 2, p. 190.

with leprosy (II Chron. 26:16–21).[19] God had appointed the descendants of Levi to minister first at the tabernacle and later at the temple (Num. 1:50–53; 3:10, 38; 4:15, 19–20). Anyone from another tribe who approached the sanctuary would be put to death.

Psalm 110:4, in the context of the Epistle to the Hebrews, teaches two points. First, God overruled the law concerning the Levitical priesthood, because he as the maker of the law had the authority to change it. Second, belonging to the priestly order of Melchizedek is entirely different from being a descendant of any of the tribes of Israel.

Jesus descended from the tribe of Judah (Ps. 132:11; Isa. 11:1, 10; Luke 1:32; Rom. 1:3; Rev. 5:5). But his descent could attest only to his royalty. Moses said nothing about priests from the tribe of Judah, and therefore Jesus would trangress the Mosaic law if he assumed the priestly functions given to the descendants of Aaron.[20]

As a descendant of David, Jesus established not an earthly kingdom, but a spiritual kingdom. Similarly, Jesus did not inaugurate another priestly order to replace the Aaronic priesthood here on earth. Jesus is the "great high priest who has gone through the heavens" (Heb. 4:14). His priesthood is spiritual, heavenly, eternal.

3. Indestructible Life
7:15–19

Jesus' priesthood finds its origin not in the Levitical order but in the order of Melchizedek. The writer of the Epistle to the Hebrews purposely states that Jesus was confirmed as priest not by proving his descent from Levi but by demonstrating the indestructibility of his life.

15. And what we have said is even more clear if another priest like Melchizedek appears,   16. one who has become a priest not on the basis of a regulation as to his ancestry but on the basis of the power of an indestructible life.   17. For it is declared:
> **"You are a priest forever,**
> **in the order of Melchizedek."**

We who live in a different era and in another culture are unable to fathom the turmoil that must have taken place when Jew and Christian realized the Levitical priesthood had definitely ended in A.D. 70. After Jesus' ascension, Christians continued to attend the prayer services and festivals at the temple in Jerusalem (Acts 3:1; 20:16; 21:26). The end of an era, however, had come

---

19. Both David and Solomon, belonging to the tribe of Judah, offered sacrifices on several occasions (see II Sam. 6:13, 17–18; 24:25; I Kings 3:4; 8:62–64). But the sacrifices apparently were performed by the priests at the request of David or Solomon.

20. In an interesting study Philip Edgcumbe Hughes traces the descent of the Messiah from Levi and Judah from the teaching of the Dead Sea Sect; *The Testaments of the Twelve Patriarchs*; and the writings of Irenaeus, Origen, and Cyprian. See his *Hebrews*, pp. 260–63. Also consult R. H. Charles, *The Apocrypha and Pseudepigrapha of the Old Testament in English*, 2 vols. (Oxford: Clarendon, 1913), vol. 2, pp. 282–367. And see M. deJonge's article "Christian Influence in the Testaments of the Twelve Patriarchs" in *Studies on the Testaments of the Twelve Patriarchs*, ed. M. deJonge (Leiden: Brill, 1975), p. 222.

because Jesus by his death on the cross had fulfilled the law. Jesus had become the great high priest, but not in the Aaronic order; he appeared as a priest like Melchizedek.

The Christian community had to realize the significance of Jesus' sacrifice in relation to the Levitical priestly order. When the author told the Hebrews that he had much to say about Jesus' priesthood in the order of Melchizedek, he mentioned that his teaching was *hard* to explain (5:11). The time had come for believers of Jewish descent to understand the implications of Jesus' sacrifice on the cross: by his once-for-all sacrifice, Jesus had fulfilled the demands of the law and thus ended the need for sacrifices. The Levitical priesthood then was obsolete. Because the author's contemporaries were conditioned to think of the priesthood only in terms of the Levitical order, his emphasis on the priesthood of Christ was indeed "hard to explain" and no doubt hard to accept.

The Aaronic priestly order terminated because of Christ's sacrificial death; the priesthood of Christ, however, continues. We should note that the writer calls Jesus a "priest like Melchizedek"; he uses the term *priest,* not *high priest.* Concludes Geerhardus Vos: "Where a comparison with Aaron is expressed or implied, Christ is called *High Priest* (2:17; 4:14; 5:1; 7:26, 28; 8:13; 9:11–12). When the comparison is between Christ and the Levitical order, He is called priest."[21]

Christ's priesthood is different for two reasons.

a. Jesus did not have to base his priesthood on a genealogy that proved his descent from Aaron. He was like Melchizedek in that no ancestry is mentioned.

b. A priest in the Levitical order served on a temporary basis because he eventually died. By contrast, Jesus is a priest forever. That is, as an only priest—no other priests are serving with him—he lays claim to "the power of an indestructible life." A Levitical priest served because an external law gave him the privilege of service; Jesus serves because of an inward power that characterizes an endless life.[22]

The expression *indestructible life* is unique in the New Testament. Although Jesus offered himself as a sacrifice on the cross, his life did not end. He conquered death and lives forever, presently seated at God's right hand in heaven (Heb. 1:3). Through his unique sacrifice he fulfilled the responsibilities of the Aaronic priesthood, and through his endless life he assumes the priesthood in the order of Melchizedek.

Lest someone object to the priesthood of Christ, the writer once again quotes Psalm 110:4 and introduces the psalm citation with the words *for it is declared.* The implied agent is God himself. God has appointed Jesus high priest forever, in the order of Melchizedek. The author purposely repeats himself, for he has quoted and alluded to Psalm 110:4 a number of times

---

21. Vos, *Teaching*, p. 94.

22. "The 'law' is an outward restraint: the 'power' is an inward force," observes Westcott in *Hebrews*, p. 184.

(5:6, 10; 6:20; 7:11; also see 7:21, where he stresses the permanence of
Jesus' priestly office by referring to the oath God swore).

**18. The former regulation is set aside because it was weak and use-
less 19. (for the law made nothing perfect), and a better hope is introduced, by which we draw near to God.**

This rather lengthy sentence falls into three parts that show balance and
contrast. The first part has an explanatory clause that is placed within
parentheses.

> a.   the former regulation—a better hope
> b.   is set aside—is introduced
> c.   because—by which
>   it was weak and useless—we draw near
>   (for the law made
>   nothing perfect)

a. The first part of the contrast consists of the adjective *former* and the
noun *regulation*. The word *former* actually means "introductory" or "that
which precedes." The implication is that the introductory regulation is temporary and will be succeeded by that which is permanent. The author of
Hebrews continues to explain the significance of a tentative regulation that
must yield to something that is abiding. The regulation was intended for the
members of the priesthood; the hope (anchored in Jesus Christ, 6:19–20)
is for every believer.

In the second part of this sentence, the adjective *better* emphasizes the
quality of the hope. Although hope was present during the era of the Levitical priesthood, after the sacrifice of Christ hope has taken on a new di-
mension.[23] The author speaks of better hope in the sense of a true, living,
new, and perfect hope. It is the hope that the believer has in Jesus Christ
through his gospel. And that good news for the believer—forgiveness of
sins, eternal life, and entrance to heaven—constitutes the better hope that
surpasses "the former regulation."

b. The second part of the contrast concerns the action of both regulation
and hope: the one is set aside, the other is introduced. For the writer to state
categorically that the divine command about the Levitical priesthood was
discarded and to add that "the law made nothing perfect" called for courage.
A believer trained in Old Testament law considered the command about the
priesthood in particular and the law in general sacrosanct.

But the author is able to write these words in full confidence. He indicates
that the "former regulation" was introductory to something much better. In
fact, the "better hope" has arrived and the time has come to put the substitute
away. In his providence God instituted the Levitical priesthood. The priests
offered animal sacrifices so the people might obtain remission of sin. These

---

23. The adjective *better* occurs eighteen times in the original Greek of the New Testament
(twelve of which occur in the Epistle to the Hebrews—1:4, 6:9; 7:7, 19, 22; 8:6; 9:23; 10:34;
11:16, 35, 40; 12:24).

sacrifices by themselves could not cleanse the consciences of the believers (9:14) and were inadequate to atone for sin; they pointed to Christ. After Jesus as the Lamb of God brought the supreme sacrifice that "takes away the sin of the world" (John 1:29), the need for animal sacrifices offered by the priests was eliminated.

"A better hope is introduced." The author does not say to whom or to what we are introduced, but the context reveals that we are brought into the presence of Jesus our high priest. The believer no longer needs to approach God through the services of a mortal priest. He can go directly to Jesus Christ, for through him he has direct access to the throne of grace (4:14–16). His hope, then, is centered in Jesus Christ, his Savior and Lord.

c. The third element in the contrast gives the cause and the means. The Levitical priesthood was discarded *because* the regulation "was weak and useless"; and *by* a better hope we have access to God.

We nowhere read that the Levitical priesthood and the accompanying regulation were of no value. They had their rightful place in the era prior to the coming of Christ. However, the command with its bearing on the priesthood was "weak and useless." It was incapable of removing the curse God had pronounced upon the human race; it could not effect eternal salvation for the believer. David testified to the inadequacy of animal sacrifices when he confessed his sin to God: "You do not delight in sacrifice, or I would bring it; you do not take pleasure in burnt offerings" (Ps. 51:16). The command was external and pertained to the duties performed by the priests; it was unable, however, to lead the believer into the presence of God.

What the law could not do, for it made nothing perfect (Rom. 8:3), Jesus did by his perfect sacrifice on the cross: he opened the way to God. In the capacity of high priest Jesus, by entering the Most Holy Place, reconciled God and man. Therefore the believer has full communion with God.

Doctrinal Considerations in 7:11–19

In the desert of Sinai God delivered the Ten Commandments to the Israelites to make them into "a kingdom of priests and a holy nation" (Exod. 19:6; also see I Peter 2:9). Although the people affirmed the objective to live obediently before God ("We will do everything the LORD has said," Exod. 19:8; 24:3), they never attained perfection. The Israelites were sinners whose transgression had to be removed.

"Israel, in its sinful life, could not exist before God; it needed atonement provided by another life. Yet the lives of the sacrificial animals could not accomplish this atonement."[24] Also the priesthood, instituted to lead the Israelites in a life of consecration and perfection, failed. That God later declared on oath the inauguration of a priest in the order of Melchizedek (Ps. 110:4) proved the weakness of the Aaronic priesthood.

---

24. S. G. DeGraaf, *Promise and Deliverance,* trans. H. Evan Runner and Elisabeth Wichers Runner, 3 vols. (Saint Catharines: Paideia, 1977), vol. 1, p. 301.

God himself imposed his law on the Israelites. As lawgiver he stood above the commandments and ordinances he had enacted. Thus at the proper time he could supplant a particular law—the one pertaining to the Levitical priesthood—and institute a new order. The priesthood in the order of Melchizedek differed radically from that of Aaron. It was not based on law, although it was confirmed by oath (Ps. 110:4). Rather it is a *spiritual* priesthood, fulfilled in Jesus Christ and settled in heaven (Heb. 4:14; 6:20; 7:26; 8:1; 9:11; 10:21).

Jesus' priesthood is distinct from the priestly order of Levi's descendants. His priesthood coincides with his kingship (Ps. 110:1–2) and therefore is *royal*. Jesus is king and priest at the same time. Aaron and his heirs could be only priests.

The brevity of life of the priests in the order of Aaron testified to the passing character of the Levitical office. The priestly genealogies were silent witnesses to the transitory nature of the priesthood. By contrast, the priesthood of Jesus is eternal.[25]

Greek Words, Phrases, and Constructions in 7:11–19

Verse 11

τελείωσις—the ending -σις reveals a process of the act of reaching perfection. The noun stems from the verb τελειόω (I accomplish, make perfect).

ὁ λαός—the definite article with the noun conveys the idea that the law was given, via the priesthood, to *all* the people of God.

νενομοθέτηται—the perfect passive, third person singular, of the verb νομοθετέω (I enact laws) marks the time when the law was given and expresses the lasting significance of the event.

ἕτερον—of the five times the author uses this adjective, three refer to Jesus' priesthood (7:11, 13, 15). The author stresses the dissimilarity of Christ's priestly office and the Levitical priesthood.

Verse 12

νόμου—a change in the priesthood necessitated a change in the law. Jesus became high priest not in the Levitical order (on the basis of law), but in the τάξις (order) of Melchizedek.

μετάθεσις—together with the present passive participle μετατιθεμένης (genitive absolute) this noun with its ending -σις denotes a process of change.

Verse 13

μετέσχηκεν—the perfect active, third person singular of the verb μετέχω (I partake) directs attention to a point in time in which Jesus became a descendant of Judah. The perfect signifies continuous validity; the active voice shows that Jesus voluntarily became man.

προσέσχηκεν—the author has a penchant for choosing cognate expressions. This verb, from προσέχω (I apply myself to), demands a supplied ἑαυτόν (himself) and a dative for the object (altar).

---

25. Westcott, *Hebrews*, p. 183.

Verse 14

πρόδηλον—this adjective from πρό (openly) and δῆλος (evident) is closely related to κατάδηλος (thoroughly evident) in verse 15.

ἀνατέταλκεν—the perfect active, third person singular, of ἀνατέλλω (I rise, descend from) is related to ἀνατολή in Luke 1:78, where the reference to the rising of the sun is a metaphor of the Messiah's coming.

Verse 16

ἐντολῆς σαρκίνης—the adjective σαρκίνης modifying the noun *commandment* points to the lineage that a priest had to prove before he could assume office.

γέγονεν—from the verb γίνομαι (I become), the perfect active demonstrates the endless duration of Christ's priesthood.

Verse 18

ἀθέτησις—this noun appears also in 9:26. It derives from the privative ἀ (not) and the verb τίθημι (I place). With the ending -σις it denotes a process of annulling a commandment. Also, it is a juridical term.

Verse 19

ἐπεισαγωγή—this compound noun consists of ἐπί (toward), εἰς (into), and ἀγωγή (leading). It means "an introduction." The word occurs only in this verse in the entire New Testament.

---

20 And it was not without an oath! Others became priests without any oath, 21 but he became a priest with an oath when God said to him:
"The Lord has sworn
and will not change his mind:
'You are a priest forever.' "
22 Because of this oath, Jesus has become the guarantee of a better covenant.

23 Now there have been many of those priests, since death prevented them from continuing in office; 24 but because Jesus lives forever, he has a permanent priesthood. 25 Therefore he is able to save completely those who come to God through him, because he always lives to intercede for them.

26 Such a high priest meets our need—one who is holy, blameless, pure, set apart from sinners, exalted above the heavens. 27 Unlike the other high priests, he does not need to offer sacrifices day after day, first for his own sins, and then for the sins of the people. He sacrificed for their sins once for all when he offered himself. 28 For the law appoints as high priests men who are weak; but the oath, which came after the law, appointed the Son, who has been made perfect forever.

C. Christ's Superior Priesthood
7:20–28

1. By Oath
7:20–22

The Aaronic priesthood was instituted by divine law; Christ's priesthood, by divine oath. A law can be annulled; an oath lasts forever.

True to form, the author first introduces a new concept with a simple word or phrase, then returns to it later to give a complete explanation. In 7:22 he mentions the word *covenant*; in the next two chapters he explains the doctrine of the covenant to the fullest extent.

20. And it was not without an oath! Others become priests without any oath, 21. but he became priest with an oath when God said to him:
"The Lord has sworn
and will not change his mind:
'You are a priest forever.' "
22. Because of this oath, Jesus has become the guarantee of a better covenant.

The first word *and* is significant. It provides additional proof of the superiority of Christ's priesthood. The proof comes from the first part of Psalm 110:4. The author of the epistle quotes and alludes to this psalm citation a number of times (5:6, 10; 6:20; 7:11, 17) to call attention to the priesthood of Christ in the order of Melchizedek.

How did Christ become a priest? Psalm 110:4 unequivocally states that God swore an oath when he appointed Christ. This is unique. God told Moses to consecrate Aaron and his sons to the priesthood and stipulated, "The priesthood is theirs by a lasting ordinance" (Exod. 29:9). But God did not swear an oath; he only administered an ordinance. No law was enacted when God appointed Christ to the priesthood of Melchizedek. Instead God swore an oath.

By human standards Christ, not God, should have sworn the oath of office. For example, when a government official is about to assume his task, he is sworn in. The appointee declares on oath that he will execute his duties to the best of his ability in accordance with the laws of the land.

In this instance, however, God purposely takes the initiative and swears an oath. He confirms his promise to Abraham by swearing an oath to guarantee that his purpose does not change (Gen. 22:16; Heb. 6:13). A second time, when God installs his Son as priest in Melchizedek's order, he swears an oath to vouch for the unalterable nature of the appointment. When God's people confess sin, God changes his mind (see for example Exod. 32:14). But when God swears an oath, his purpose is unchangeable. Because he swore an oath when he instituted Christ's priesthood, that priesthood is eternal.

What is the purpose of confirming Christ's priesthood with an oath? "Because of this oath," says the writer, "Jesus has become the guarantee of a better covenant." Two concepts the author introduces. One is embodied in the word *guarantee* (which appears once in the entire New Testament) and the other in the word *covenant* (an expression that recurs seventeen times in the epistle).

Even though the term *guarantee* is unique, its synonym *mediate* is not (Gal. 3:19–20; I Tim. 2:5; Heb. 8:6; 9:15; 12:24). These two words in the epistle are interchangeable, and the writer uses them to stress God's absolute reliability in fulfilling the covenant he has made with his people. God has appointed his Son not merely to be the guarantor who represents man to God. In addition, Jesus is the believer's guarantee that all God's promises will be fulfilled. That is, no promise God has made to us can ever be broken, for Jesus gives the assurance that his perfection will be our perfection,[26] our bodies "will be like his glorious body" (Phil. 3:21), and his ascension guarantees our entrance into heaven (John 14:3).

Note that the author uses the name *Jesus* purposely. This name summarizes the work of our Savior—he saves "his people from their sins" (Matt. 1:21). The writer places the name last in the sentence (in the Greek) to give it full emphasis.

The second concept that the author introduces is contained in the noun *covenant*, qualified by the adjective *better*. In context the adjective actually means "eternal." The covenant God makes with his people is an agreement that has two parties, promises, and a condition. The parties are God and his people. The promises are: "I will put my laws in their minds and write them on their hearts," says God, "I will be their God, and they will be my people" (Jer. 31:33; Heb. 8:10). And the condition is faith.

Why is this covenant called "better"? In the old covenant that God made with the Israelites at Mount Sinai, Moses acted as mediator between God and his people. But Moses could never guarantee the covenant. In the new covenant Jesus is both mediator and guarantor because of his atoning work. Jesus guarantees the fullness of God's covenant with us.

> To Thee, O Lord, alone is due
> All glory and renown;
> Aught to ourselves we dare not take,
> Or rob Thee of Thy crown.
> Thou wast Thyself our Surety
> In God's redemption plan
> In Thee His grace was given us,
> Long ere the world began.
> —Augustus M. Toplady
> (Revision by Dewey Westra)

2. For Eternity
7:23–25

In this passage, the author states an additional reason that Jesus' priesthood differs from that of Aaron: the Levitical priesthood attests to its transitoriness by the deaths of those who held the priestly office; Jesus, who is eternal, fills an everlasting office as intercessor for "those who come to God."

23. Now there have been many of those priests, since death prevented them from continuing in office;   24. but because Jesus lives forever, he

26. Oswald Becker, *NIDNTT*, vol. 1, p. 372. Also see Herbert Preisker, *TDNT*, vol. 2, p. 329.

has a permanent priesthood. **25. Therefore he is able to save completely those who come to God through him, because he always lives to
intercede for them.**

These verses form one lengthy sentence in the Greek text. They convey
three basic ideas that can be described in the terms *problem* (v. 23), *person*
(v. 24), and *purpose* (v. 25).

a. The problem relates to the length of the priest's term in office. By law,
the Aaronic priesthood would "continue for all generations to come" (Exod.
40:15), but in reality the priestly office was temporal. Every priest was subject
to death, and therefore a seemingly endless succession of priests emerged.
Death determined the extent of the high priest's service, for death is no
respecter of persons. The high priest was powerless in the face of death.

A somewhat literal translation of the first part of this verse reads, "and
they that have become priests are many."[27] The list of names of high priests
who served for long or short periods of time is extensive,[28] but the concluding comment for every one of them is this: "and he died."

b. Next, the author contrasts the Levitical priesthood with the person of
Jesus. What a contrast when we look at Jesus! The priests were many; Jesus
is the only priest. Their term of office was limited by death; "Jesus lives
forever." The Aaronic high priest was overcome by death; Jesus conquered
death.

The writer of Hebrews has chosen the name *Jesus* to illuminate the earthly
life of our Lord. This name describes his birth, ministry, suffering, death,
resurrection, and ascension. However, Jesus is no longer a citizen of this
earth; his residence is in heaven, where he abides forever. Because of his
eternity, Jesus' high priesthood is unchangeable. That is, no one can terminate his priestly office. Death is conquered. And God has sworn an oath
that his Son will serve as priest forever in the order of Melchizedek. No one
can take Jesus' place, for he is the one and only high priest.

c. What purpose does Jesus' permanent priesthood serve? In fact, it serves
many purposes. First, "he is able to save completely those who come to God
through him." Jesus is a Savior who does his work completely, fully, and to
perfection.[29] He sets man free from the curse of sin and accomplishes restoration between God and man; through Jesus man is united with his God
(John 17:21).

Second, Jesus as eternal high priest lives not for himself, but for the people
who look to him for help (2:17–18; 4:14–16). He is their Mediator, truly
God and truly man. Without ceasing he pleads for us; standing between

---

27. The context of 7:23 calls for a translation in the past tense. This is exactly what most
translators have used. The exception is the NEB: "Those other priests are appointed in numerous succession, because they are prevented by death from continuing in office."

28. See Josephus, *Antiquities* 20.10 (LCL).

29. Numerous translators understand the first clause of 7:25 to refer to time rather than to
extent or degree. Thus GNB, NASB, NAB, RSV, and *Moffatt* have the reading "he is able to save
forever" (with individual variations; italics added).

God and man, he constantly intercedes for those who come to God in prayer (Rom. 8:34; Heb. 9:24). God grants us everything we need for the furtherance of his name, his kingdom, and his will. He answers our prayers for daily sustenance, remission of sin, and protection from the evil one.

Third, Jesus taught: "No one comes to the Father except through me" (John 14:6). The writer of Hebrews repeats this very thought and reminds his readers that prayers to God must be offered in the name of Jesus.

Fourth, knowing that Jesus is always praying for us in heaven, we long to be with him. We have the assurance that as he lives eternally before God so shall we live forever with him. Presently we come to God in prayer, but at the end of our earthly stay he will take us home to be with him eternally.

Doctrinal Considerations in 7:20–25

When God swears an oath he establishes the absolute dependability and trustworthiness of his word. His oath is somewhat different from that of man. Man swears by God to testify of his innocence, to declare his intention to keep a vow, and to speak the truth before a court of law. God swears by himself—because there is no one greater by whom he can swear—to give further substance to his promise (with Abraham, Gen. 22:16), to his covenant (with Israel's forefathers, Deut. 4:31), and to his confirmation of his Son's priesthood (Ps. 110:4). When God adds an oath to what he has said, his word is unalterable.

Christ's priesthood is unchangeable because it is not bound to a law. The Levitical priesthood instituted by law was open to transgression and violation. Christ's priesthood in the order of Melchizedek was confirmed by oath and therefore is inviolable.[30]

When the author of the Epistle to the Hebrews mentions the concept *salvation,* he always links it directly to the atoning work of Jesus. Thus the salvation Christ offers the believers is eternal (5:9); it is described as great (2:3); and its author has been made "perfect through suffering" (2:10).

Greek Words, Phrases, and Constructions in 7:20–25

Verse 20

ὁρκωμοσίας—this combination of ὅρκος (oath) and ὄμνυμι (I swear) occurs four times in the New Testament (Heb. 7:20 [twice], 21, 28). In Hebrews 6:16 the author writes the noun and the verb separately (see Luke 1:73; Acts 2:30; James 5:12). The preposition (adverb) χωρίς governs the genitive case.

οἱ μέν—this construction balanced by ὁ δέ in the next verse expresses contrast: priests over against Jesus. The author employs this device three times (7:18–19; 7:20–21; and 7:23–24).

εἰσὶν . . . γεγονότες—the perfect middle participle of γίνομαι (I become) combined with a form of the verb *to be*, εἰσὶν (present active), constitutes a periphrastic construction. See also 7:23.

---

30. Walther Günther, *NIDNTT,* vol. 3, p. 585.

Verse 22

διαθήκης—this noun derived from the verb διατίθημι (I decree) appears seventeen times in Hebrews out of a total of thirty-three times in the New Testament. The author of Hebrews develops the doctrine of the covenant chiefly in chapters 8 and 9.

ἔγγυος—only in this verse does ἔγγυος occur in the New Testament. See also the Septuagint, where it appears three times (Sir. 29:15, 16; II Macc. 10:28). It conveys the idea of guarantor and is a synonym of μεσίτης (mediator).

Verse 23

διά—this preposition followed by the neuter article τό and the present passive infinitive κωλύεσθαι (to be hindered) expresses the reason that the number of priests increased: they were prevented from continual service by death (θανάτῳ).

παραμένειν—the complementary infinitive, present active, of παραμένω (I continue in office). This compound verb referring to priests on earth is set in opposition to the simple present active verb μένειν (to remain) referring to Jesus (v. 24).

Verse 24

ἀπαράβατον—as a verbal adjective the word expresses a passive idea: "it cannot be transgressed." This compound finds its origin in ἀ (not), παρά (beyond), and βαίνω (I go, walk, step).

Verse 25

ζῶν—the present active participle from ζάω (I live) may denote cause: because he lives.

ἐντυγχάνειν—Jesus lives for the purpose of making intercession. The word occurs only five times in the New Testament (Acts 25:24; Rom. 8:27, 34; 11:2; Heb. 7:25) but frequently in other sources. The basic meaning of the verb is "to approach someone with a petition." In this verse the present active infinitive is introduced by εἰς τό.

---

3. In Sacrifice
7:26–27

After explaining the quotation from Psalm 110:4, the author of Hebrews presents a comprehensive summary. He gives a full description of our only high priest Jesus Christ and compares his perfect sacrifice with the daily sacrifices offered by the Levitical priests. Jesus' death on the cross was a once-for-all event.

26. Such a high priest meets our need—one who is holy, blameless, pure, set apart from sinners, exalted above the heavens.

The writer has arrived at a peak in his discussion of Christ's priesthood. He looks back at the magnificence of Jesus' position and describes his greatness in the one word *such.* He stands in awe of the magnitude of the work of salvation performed by our heavenly high priest. And he looks forward.

The author diverts his attention to the needs of the believers on earth and includes himself in the expression *our need*. He realizes that Jesus is not a distant high priest, enthroned in heaven, far removed from the daily needs of his people. Jesus is eminently suited to be our high priest.

Why is Jesus qualified to meet our needs? He is sinless. With respect to his character, he is holy, blameless, and pure. And regarding his status, he is separated from sinners and exalted above the heavens.

The author lists five characteristics.

a. *Holy.* Jesus is holy. That means he is like God and in every aspect without sin.[31] He is incomparably pure and as God's high priest he fulfills the will of God flawlessly. His chief desire is to glorify God's name and to extend God's rule.

b. *Blameless.* The adjective *holy* concerns the inner disposition of Jesus; the word *blameless* relates to his external life. Note the implied contrast between Jesus, who is blameless, and the Aaronic high priests, tainted by sins, who were blameworthy. Aaron had to bring a "sin offering to make atonement for himself and his household" (Lev. 16:11) before he could function as a high priest for the people of Israel. Jesus, however, is completely sinless and therefore free from guilt and blame.

c. *Pure.* The environment of sin has a way of touching everyone entering that environment. Sin defiles the person it touches. Although Jesus lived on earth and ministered to sinful people, he himself remained undefiled. He may be compared with a physician who works among the sick at the time of an epidemic, but who is immune. Jesus is unstained by sin.

d. *Set apart.* The reason that Jesus remains untouched by sin lies in the act of separation. Jesus has been separated from sinners by God. Although he fully shares our humanity, he does not participate in our sin. He is therefore different. Although he was called a friend of sinners (Matt. 11:19), he himself remained without sin. I think that interpreting the phrase *set apart from sinners* to refer only to the ascension of Jesus is one-sided.[32] As our heavenly high priest Jesus sympathizes with us in our weaknesses, because he has been tempted just as we are tempted. He knows our problems, because he is one of us—except that he is sinless (2:14; 4:14–15).

e. *Exalted.* Already in Hebrews 1:3, the author referred to Jesus' exaltation by depicting him seated "at the right hand of the Majesty in heaven." In 7:26 the writer describes the position of Christ in comparable terms. He says that Jesus has been "raised to greater heights than the heavens."[33] Paul also speaks of Christ's exaltation: "He who descended is the very one who

---

31. Horst Seebass, *NIDNTT,* vol. 2, p. 238. Also see Friedrich Hauck, *TDNT,* vol. 5, p. 492.

32. For example, Bengel in his *Gnomon,* vol. 4, p. 409, explains the phrase in one short sentence: "He was separated when he left the world." From the Babylonian Talmud we learn that the high priest would separate himself from his house for seven days before the Day of Atonement and take up residence in one of the rooms of the temple. See Yoma 1:1, Seder Moed, *Talmud,* vol. 3. And see SB, vol. 3, p. 696.

33. Bauer, p. 850.

ascended higher than all the heavens" (Eph. 4:10). The meaning is clear: Jesus occupies the highest position imaginable.

27. Unlike the other high priests, he does not need to offer sacrifices day after day, first for his own sins, and then for the sins of the people. He sacrificed for their sins once for all when he offered himself.

Sometimes we have to make a trite remark to convey a fundamental truth. Thus we say that verse 27 follows verse 26 in order to point out that 7:26 is introductory to the next verse. This simple fact is frequently overlooked, and explanations of 7:27a are varied.

For example, one explanation is that the phrase *day after day* means "year after year." That is, once a year on the Day of Atonement the high priest enters the Most Holy Place. Therefore the phrase refers to the annual sacrifices on that particular day. However, the writer is fully acquainted with the Mosaic stipulations, for he indirectly mentions the Day of Atonement in 9:7, 25 and 10:1, 3. Why would he write "day after day" when in fact he meant once a year?

Another explanation relates the phrase *day after day* to the daily grain offering and burnt sacrifice offered by Aaron and his sons (Lev. 6:14–16; Exod. 29:38–42; Num. 28:3–8). Although the explanation has merit, difficulties surround this interpretation.[34]

A third possibility is to interpret the phrase as a reference to the daily offerings in general and to the Day of Atonement in particular.[35] This explanation is all-inclusive and, in a sense, moves from the lesser sacrifices to the greater sacrifice on the Day of Atonement.

The contrast in 7:27 is between Jesus and the Aaronic high priest, and because of the introductory verse (26) the emphasis falls on the negative: Jesus "does not need to offer sacrifices day after day." Our heavenly high priest is completely different; he is sinless, blameless, spotless. He has no need to offer a sacrifice for himself either on a daily or an annual basis. He is set apart from sinners. He is holy.

High priests appointed to represent sinful people were themselves defiled by sin. Coming before God, they were fully conscious of their own sins which in effect nullified their efforts to serve God. To become efficient, they had to offer animal sacrifices that removed their own sins. Then they brought sacrifices to God for the sins of the people. God told them that the blood of an animal atoned for sin. They had to admit that the constant repetition of these offerings was a clear indication that these sacrifices could not cope with the enormity of sin. The Aaronic priesthood displayed the marks of temporality and basic ineffectiveness. It had to be replaced by a priest who is eternal and by an offering that is effective.

---

34. The writers of SB, vol. 3, p. 698, point out that the order of presenting the offerings was first for the sins of the high priest and then for the sins of the people of Israel (Lev. 16:6–19; Heb. 7:27). According to the practice that prevailed in later years, the burnt offering for the sins of the people came first and the grain offering for the high priest last.
35. Hughes, *Hebrews*, p. 277.

Jesus, the Savior of his people, "sacrificed for their sins once for all when he offered himself." He offered himself because God asked him to make this supreme sacrifice and thus atone for the sins of his people. God told the Israelites to sacrifice animals as substitutes; he gave his Son as *the* substitute. God forbade the people of Israel the practice of offering human beings to idols (Lev. 18:21; 20:2–5; II Kings 17:17, 19; Ezek. 20:31); he himself offered his only Son (John 3:16).

Jesus voluntarily died on the cross and by his death presented himself as the once-for-all sacrifice. The expression *once for all* reveals that the Levitical system has come to an end. The author of Hebrews introduces this thought and explains the details in a subsequent chapter.

4. To Perfection
7:28

The time has come for a concluding statement. The writer summarizes his teaching on the eternal priesthood of Jesus before he begins a new topic: the covenant.

28. For the law appoints as high priests men who are weak; but the oath, which came after the law, appointed the Son, who has been made perfect forever.

The Epistle to the Hebrews is an epistle of contrasts. And this verse is no exception. Note the structure:

For—but
the law appoints—the oath appointed
as high priests men—the Son
who are weak—who has been made perfect forever

The law given by God to Moses has been compared with the oath God swore centuries later. In both instances—the giving of the law and the swearing of the oath—God appoints. First he appoints a high priest; then he appoints the Son. The institution of the priesthood took place in the early part of the forty-year period in the wilderness. The oath was given in a subsequent century (Ps. 110:4).

The law appoints "as high priests men who are weak." The term *weak* does not refer to physical ailments, for Jesus shared our weaknesses when he was on earth (4:15). Rather, it relates to our sinful condition and is therefore synonymous with sin. God appoints high priests who are weak because of their sinful state. He knew that these men would succumb to sin and reveal their moral weakness.

The writer has chosen the term *weak* perhaps purposely to make a distinction between sin committed in weakness and sin perpetuated deliberately. A high priest who sinned intentionally could not remain in office. For premeditated and willful sin, God does not provide atonement (Heb. 9:7).

God placed sinful high priests in office by law; he appointed his Son as high priest by oath. The superiority of the Son to the Aaronic high priests the writer of Hebrews succinctly demonstrates, for the swearing of the oath was of greater importance than the giving of the law. A law can be repealed; an oath stays forever. The Son is not subject to weakness or change, because he "has been made perfect forever."

The expression *Son* reminds us of chapter 1, where the author teaches the Son's superiority to creation, including the angels (1:2, 3, 5, 8; also see 3:6; 4:14; 7:3). The Son is eternal; high priests are mortal and therefore temporal. The Son is sinless and consequently perfect; high priests are sinners and in need of redemption. The Son because of his suffering on the cross has been made perfect (2:10). Because of this perfection "he is able to save completely those who come to God through him" (7:25).

Doctrinal Considerations in 7:26–28

Jesus our high priest is holy. This adjective *holy* in the original Greek appears only eight times in the New Testament (Acts 2:27; 13:34–35; I Tim. 2:8; Titus 1:8; Heb. 7:26; Rev. 15:4; 16:5); five are quotations from and allusions to the Old Testament. The word is unique, and for this reason the author of Hebrews uses it to portray the holiness of Jesus. When it is applied to men—for example, in Titus 1:8 Paul writes that among other requirements an elder must be holy—the term implies a participation in Jesus' holiness.[36]

Jesus has taken a place that is higher than the heavens. Before coming to earth, Christ was in heaven. But after his atoning work was completed and he ascended to heaven, he was "exalted above the heavens." The idea expressed by the author is set forth in a comparative way: Christ is not in heaven but in a place that is even higher than the heavens.

The author of Hebrews teaches that Jesus is priest and at the same time became sacrifice. Christ in his once-for-all offering of himself on the cross fulfilled the responsibility of the priesthood of Aaron (9:25–26). By his death he put an end to the offerings for the sins of the people (7:27; 9:12; 10:10, 18). By oath appointed, Jesus serves as high priest forever in the order of Melchizedek.

The Aaronic high priest could never present a genuine sacrifice as requested by God. A genuine sacrifice could be brought only by Jesus, who had the power to defeat death (2:15; 9:27–28) and the ability to show perfect obedience (5:8–10).

Greek Words, Phrases, and Constructions in 7:26–28

Verse 26

ὅσιος—this adjective, related to the noun ὁσιότης (devoutness) and the adverb ὁσίως (in a holy manner), conveys the idea of partaking of God's holiness.

ἀμίαντος—derived from the privative ἀ (not) and the verb μιαίνω (I stain; defile), this verbal adjective has a passive connotation in the sense of "he cannot be defiled." The word denotes moral purity, especially with reference to the high priest (see

---

36. Westcott understands the concept *holy* as "a particular moral position." See his *Hebrews*, p. 194.

also Heb. 13:4, where the word is used in the context of marriage). Undefiled, according to John Albert Bengel, means to derive "*no stain* from other *men*."[37]

κεχωρισμένος . . . γενόμενος—the first participle is the perfect passive from χωρίζω (I separate); the second is the aorist middle from γίνομαι (I become). The perfect tense denotes the lasting state which delineates a difference between Christ and man. The use of the aorist tense implies that there was a time in which Jesus was not exalted above the heavens.

Verse 27

ἀναφέρειν—the present active infinitive is a compound of ἀνά (up; again) and φέρω (I bring). The verb is paralleled by προσφέρω (I offer), which occurs nineteen times in Hebrews; ἀναφέρω appears four times. In 9:28 both verbs are used. Westcott makes the following distinction: "From these usages [in the Septuagint] it appears that in ἀναφέρειν (*to offer up*) we have mainly the notion of an offering made to God and placed upon His altar, in προσφέρειν (*to offer*) that of an offering brought to God. In the former the thought of the destination of the offering prevails: in the latter that of the offerer in his relation to God."[38]

Verse 28

τῆς μετὰ τὸν νόμον—the definite article τῆς specifies the oath God swore: after the law was given. The author of Hebrews places the word of the oathswearing (ὁ λόγος) over against the law (ὁ νόμος). God gave the Israelites his law in the days of Moses; he swore an oath in the time of David (Ps. 110:4).

τετελειωμένον—this perfect passive participle from the verb τελειόω (I complete) communicates the idea of permanence. The passive voice intimates that God is the agent. The Son has been made "perfect through suffering" (2:10). The writer of Hebrews purposely uses the term υἱόν (son) without the definite article to express the absolute significance of Jesus' sonship. Only Jesus is the Son of God, "made perfect forever."

Summary of Chapter 7

Melchizedek, mentioned only twice in the entire Old Testament (Gen. 14:18; Ps. 110:4), is the focus of attention in the first part of Hebrews 7. The author of the epistle demonstrates his theological skills as he explains the priesthood of Christ in the order of Melchizedek.

From a modern point of view the writer's arguments appear to be somewhat labored. He seems to be reading more into the Old Testament passages that mention Melchizedek than the passages actually say. But the original readers were Hebrews. They believed that the divinely instituted Levitical priesthood was inviolable. They knew that the priesthood of Aaron had to be perpetual, because God himself had ordained the priesthood by law.

The author of Hebrews counters the objections of readers of the Old

---

37. Bengel, *Gnomon*, vol. 4, p. 409. Italics his.
38. Westcott, *Hebrews*, p. 197. Also consult Konrad Weiss, *TNDT*, vol. 9, pp. 61, 66.

Testament Scriptures by discussing the differences between the Aaronic priesthood and the superior order of Melchizedek. These differences consist of the absence of a genealogy for Melchizedek; the homage and tithe Abraham paid Melchizedek; and the confirmation of Melchizedek's priesthood by divine oath centuries after the Levitical priesthood was established by law.

The evidence that shows God's design in terminating the temporal priesthood of Aaron and inaugurating the eternal priesthood of Melchizedek is irrefutable. Jesus, to whom the author indirectly referred and who at last is mentioned by name, has become high priest in Melchizedek's order and is a "guarantee of a better covenant" (7:22).

Already in earlier passages the author describes the characteristics of the high priest (2:17–18; 4:14–15; 5:1–5). In 7:26–28 the writer centers his explanation of the heavenly high priest on holiness, sinlessness, sacrifice, and perfection. The theme of Jesus' perfection, introduced in 2:10 and implied in 7:11, culminates in the words: "the Son . . . has been made perfect forever."

8

Jesus: High Priest and Sacrifice, *part 1*

8:1–13

Outline

8 1 The point of what we are saying is this: We do have such a high priest, who sat down at the right hand of the throne of the Majesty in heaven,   2 and who serves in the sanctuary, the true tabernacle set up by the Lord, not by man.

A. The Heavenly Sanctuary
8:1–2

The claims to Jesus' priesthood the author expounded in chapter 7. In Hebrews 8, he explains the task of the high priest, Jesus Christ, and alludes to Psalm 110:1.

1. The point of what we are saying is this: We do have such a high priest, who sat down at the right hand of the throne of the Majesty in heaven,   2. and who serves in the sanctuary, the true tabernacle set up by the Lord, not by man.

The preceding chapter delineates the surpassing excellence of Christ's priesthood in the order of Melchizedek. The author of Hebrews provides the readers with a lucid exposition of Psalm 110:4. However, he does not want them to lose sight of the first verse of that psalm. That verse portrays Jesus as king. Jesus, therefore, is the king-priest, as Psalm 110 clearly teaches. Although the writer has stressed the importance of Jesus' priesthood in the Melchizedekian order, he desires his readers to recognize Jesus' kingship, too. Hence, he writes the introductory clause, "the point of what we are saying is this," and asserts that our high priest sat down at the right hand of God and serves in the true tabernacle.[1]

In the introduction of the Epistle to the Hebrews the author implicitly mentions the priesthood and the kingship of the Son (1:3; also see 1:13). After completing his priestly duties, Jesus "sat down at the right hand of the Majesty in heaven." In Hebrews 10:12 and 12:2 the writer returns to this same theme: Jesus is priest and king.

In typical Hebraic form, the writer's choice of the phrase *of the Majesty in*

---

1. Most translations use the word *point* (with variations) in Heb. 8:1. Thus RV and ASV have "chief point"; the NAB, NASB, NEB, NKJV, MLB, and R. C. H. Lenski have "main point"; JB has "great point"; GNB, "whole point"; and NIV, *Moffatt,* and RSV simply "point." However, the KJV features the term *the sum*; and *Phillips,* "to sum up."

heaven is a substitute for the word *God.* Jesus sat down in the place of honor: at the right hand of God.

The verb *to sit down* is significant. "Sitting was often a mark of honour or authority in the ancient world: a king sat to receive his subjects, a court to give judgment, and a teacher to teach."[2] The Book of Revelation in particular describes God, who sits on the throne (4:2, 10; 5:1, 7, 13; 6:16; 7:10, 15; 19:4; 21:5), and Jesus, who shares that throne (1:4–5; 3:21; 7:15–17; 12:5).

The throne of God and the sanctuary (the true tabernacle) bring king and high priest together into one place. This is not at all surprising if we think of the tabernacle in the desert, where God placed his throne in the Most Holy Place (Lev. 16:2). God took up residence behind the veil in the Tent of Meeting. In Revelation 16:17, temple and throne are mentioned together: ". . . out of the temple came a loud voice from the throne, saying, 'It is done!' " Justice and mercy flow forth from the throne and the sanctuary, from the king and the high priest.

By his sacrificial death, Jesus finished his atoning work on earth. Upon his ascension, he entered the presence of God (the sanctuary) and sat down at God's right hand. Says the writer of Hebrews, Jesus "serves in the sanctuary, the true tabernacle set up by the Lord, not by man."

Three matters come to mind when we consider Hebrews 8:2.

a. Jesus is serving in the sanctuary. His ministry in the heavenly sanctuary is superior to the priestly service on earth (8:5–6) because he is the only high priest who has ascended to heaven. God did not need to descend to earth to accept a sacrifice offered by priests. God had appointed the heavenly high priest by oath to serve eternally in God's sanctuary. Jesus brought his once-for-all offering and, entering the true sanctuary, began his priestly ministry in the presence of God.[3]

b. Jesus serves in the sanctuary that is the true tabernacle. The writer of Hebrews does not leave the reader in doubt regarding the identity of tabernacle and sanctuary and their place. In the next chapter he explains the term *tabernacle*: Christ "went through the greater and more perfect tabernacle that is not man-made, that is to say, not a part of this creation" (9:11). And he adds: "For Christ did not enter a man-made sanctuary that was only a copy of the true one; he entered heaven itself, now to appear for us in God's presence" (9:24).[4] Tabernacle and sanctuary are the same.

c. Jesus serves as high priest in the true tabernacle. This true tabernacle

---

2. Richard Thomas France, *NIDNTT,* vol. 3, p. 588. Also see Carl Schneider, *TDNT,* vol. 3, p. 442.

3. Leopold Sabourin, "Liturge du sanctuaire et de la tente véritable (Héb. VIII 2)," *NTS* 18 (1971): 87–90.

4. For a systematic presentation of the various interpretations of the expression *the true tabernacle,* see Philip Edgcumbe Hughes, *Commentary on the Epistle to the Hebrews* (Grand Rapids: Eerdmans, 1977), pp. 283–90. See also the same material published under the title "The Blood of Jesus and His Heavenly Priesthood in Hebrews. Part III: The Meaning of 'The True Tent' and 'The Greater and More Perfect Tent,' " *BS* 130 (1973): 305–14.

has been set up by the Lord, as the writer reminds us. What he means is that God gave Moses a copy of the tabernacle which the Lord God showed him (Exod. 25:9, 40). The copy was on earth; the true tabernacle is in heaven. Does Scripture mention a tabernacle in heaven? Yes, Isaiah says that he saw "the Lord seated on a throne, high and exalted, and the train of his robe filled the temple" (Isa. 6:1; see also Mic. 1:2). That sanctuary has not been erected by man, but by God. God would never have set it up if he had not appointed Christ to serve in that tabernacle. After his atoning work was accomplished, Jesus entered God's sanctuary and there represents the interests of all his people. From God's tabernacle flow blessings that surpass any blessings from the Levitical sacrificial system.

---

3 Every high priest is appointed to offer both gifts and sacrifices, and so it was necessary for this one also to have something to offer. 4 If he were on earth, he would not be a priest, for there are already men who offer the gifts prescribed by the law. 5 They serve at a sanctuary that is a copy and shadow of what is in heaven. This is why Moses was warned when he was about to build the tabernacle: "See to it that you make everything according to the pattern shown you on the mountain." 6 But the ministry Jesus has received is as superior to theirs as the covenant of which he is mediator is superior to the old one, and it is founded on better promises.

B. Jesus the Mediator
8:3–6

3. Every high priest is appointed to offer both gifts and sacrifices, and so it was necessary for this one also to have something to offer. 4. If he were on earth, he would not be a priest, for there are already men who offer the gifts prescribed by the law.

An effective teacher repeats his lesson often in the same words. The writer of Hebrews is no exception, for 8:3 is a virtual repetition of 5:1. Besides, the author continues his descriptive method of teaching by presenting contrast. Note the contrast in 8:3.

1. High Priest
8:3

for—and so
every high priest—for this one also
is appointed—it was necessary
to offer—to have to offer
both gifts and sacrifices—something

The New International Version omits the first word *for* that has its counterpart in *and so*. Although the term *high priest* is qualified by the adjective *every*, the text conveys the implication that there had been a long succession of high priests. Over against the numerous high priests stands Jesus. The author of Hebrews does not refer to him by name; he says "this one" in order to remind the reader of the priest-king serving in the heavenly sanctuary.

The contrast between the continual offerings of the high priest in the form of "both gifts and sacrifices" and the single offering, simply mentioned as "something," is significant. What this "something" consists of the author does not specify in 8:3, but in 9:14 he elaborates. Also, in the original Greek the two verbs *to offer* delineate the difference, in that the first one, pertaining to every high priest, indicates continuous occurrence. The second *to offer* verb, used with reference to Jesus, shows a single event.

2. Service
8:4–6

In 8:4 the author continues his use of contrasts with a conditional sentence that is contrary to fact. That is, the two parts of the sentence demand counterparts which are implied.

"If he were on earth"—but he is in heaven
"he would not be a priest"—but he is our priest

The sanctuary in which Christ serves as high priest is in heaven, not on earth. During his ministry on earth he could not be priest at all because he belonged to the tribe of Judah, rather than the tribe of Levi. However, the writer of the epistle does not state or imply that Christ could not bring his once-for-all offering on Calvary's cross.[5] He only notes that those who are part of the Levitical priesthood offer gifts that are "prescribed by the law." Jesus did not belong to the priestly clan of Levi and therefore could not serve at the altar. Instead, he serves in the true tabernacle, in the presence of God.

5. They serve at a sanctuary that is a copy and shadow of what is in heaven. This is why Moses was warned when he was about to build the tabernacle: "See to it that you make everything according to the pattern shown you on the mountain."

The contrast continues. This verse explains the service, the building, and the pattern of the tabernacle on earth; the next verse portrays Jesus as the mediator of a better covenant. Hebrews 8:5 describes the construction of the earthly sanctuary. Three main points stand out.

a. "Copy and shadow." Jesus entered the heavenly sanctuary in God's presence, but the priests served God in the tabernacle that the Israelites constructed in the time of Moses.[6]

The two words *copy* and *shadow,* although different in meaning, complement each other; one provides what the other lacks. The term *copy* denotes substance, and the noun *shadow* may be understood as a "reflection . . . of

---

5. Geerhardus Vos, *The Teaching of the Epistle to the Hebrews* (Grand Rapids: Eerdmans, 1956), p. 113.
6. Throughout his epistle the writer directs the reader's attention to the period that the nation Israel spent in the desert. The temple he never mentions; rather, the tabernacle is for him the place of worship (Heb. 8:2, 5; 9:2, 3, 6, 8, 11, 21; 13:10).

the heavenly original."[7] We receive the mental picture of the heavenly original casting a shadow on the earth. But this shadow has form and substance.

The writer of Hebrews intends to say that the priests who served in the sanctuary had to realize the limitations: the tabernacle structure was but a copy and the sacrifices were only a shadow. In the following chapter, where he elucidates the significance of sacrifices, the author explains the meaning of 8:5. Says he: "It was necessary, then, for the copies of the heavenly things to be purified with these sacrifices, but the heavenly things themselves with better sacrifices than these. For Christ did not enter a man-made sanctuary that was only a copy of the true one; he entered heaven itself, now to appear for us in God's presence" (9:23–24; also see 10:1).

b. "Build the tabernacle." If Moses built a tabernacle according to a copy of a heavenly original, what then is the appearance and the function of the heavenly sanctuary? Speculation about a heavenly sanctuary originated with, and at the same time fascinated, Jewish teachers in the time of the apostles and afterward.[8] They speculated on what Moses was permitted to observe when God instructed him. Did Moses see more than what is recorded in Exodus 33:18–23 (when God showed him the glory of the Lord)?[9]

No tabernacle of the same proportions as Moses built exists in heaven. Scripture fails to give any dimensions of the celestial tabernacle. Nor do we have the liberty to say that the heavenly tabernacle exists only in the mind of God. Avoiding either extreme, we ought to take note of the following Scripture passages where God instructed Moses to build the tabernacle:

1. "See that you make them according to the pattern shown you on the mountain" (Exod. 25:40).
2. "Set up the tabernacle according to the plan shown you on the mountain" (Exod. 26:30).
3. "Make the altar hollow, out of boards. It is to be made just as you were shown on the mountain" (Exod. 27:8).
4. "The lampstand was made exactly like the pattern the LORD had shown Moses" (Num. 8:4).[10]

Because the Bible is a book about man's redemption and not a revelation about heaven, we ought to let the Scripture speak. Where the Scriptures are

---

7. Heinrich Schlier, *TDNT,* vol. 2, p. 33. Also see Ralph P. Martin, *NIDNTT,* vol. 2, p. 291.

8. For instance, see the writings of Philo, *Life of Moses* 2.76; *Allegorical Interpretation* 3.102. And the *Talmud,* Kodashim, vol. 1, relates a saying from Rabbi Jose ben Judah: "An ark of fire and a table of fire and a candlestick of fire came down from heaven; and these Moses saw and reproduced, as it is written, 'And see that thou make them after their pattern, which is being shown thee in the mount' " (Menachoth 29a). Also see SB, vol. 3, pp. 702–4.

9. John Owen, in his *Exposition of Hebrews,* 7 vols. in 4 (Evansville, Ind.: Sovereign Grace, 1960), vol. 6, pp. 44–45, remarks: "Whether this representation were made to Moses by the way of internal vision, as the temple was represented unto Ezekiel, or whether there were an ethereal fabric proposed unto his bodily senses, is hard to determine."

10. The construction of the temple of Solomon followed a plan David gave Solomon in writing. " 'All this,' David said, 'I have in writing from the hand of the LORD upon me, and he gave me understanding in all the details of the plan' " (I Chron. 28:19; also see v. 12).

silent, we must be reticent. All we know is that Christ entered the heavenly sanctuary that is not manmade (Heb. 9:24). Its earthly counterpart was the ancient tabernacle that Moses erected according to the pattern God showed him.

c. "The pattern." Moses received from God the blueprints for the construction of the tabernacle and was repeatedly told to follow the instructions carefully (Exod. 25:40; also see Acts 7:44).

What precisely did Moses see when God gave him the pattern? To put it differently: Did Moses receive only the pattern, or did he see the original? If he were given the blueprint of the tabernacle, then he received, in effect, a plan from which he had to build a model—the tabernacle in the desert.[11]

We do not know what Moses saw when God gave him the pattern for the earthly tabernacle. Scripture tells us that our high priest Jesus Christ has gone "through the greater and more perfect tabernacle that is not manmade, that is to say, not a part of this creation" (Heb. 9:11). This information is a source of comfort for us because we know that as our heavenly high priest, Jesus intercedes for us. He is our mediator.

6. But the ministry Jesus has received is as superior to theirs as the covenant of which he is mediator is superior to the old one, and it is founded on better promises.

This verse is actually a continuation of 8:4, with the pronoun *he* (i.e., Jesus) as the subject of the sentence. Although the author of Hebrews contrasts Jesus with the Levitical priests, in 8:6 the primary emphasis is upon the difference in covenants rather than the difference in ministry. The author somewhat abruptly introduces the concept of covenant that he mentioned in 7:22. He is ready now to explain the implications of the new covenant that is superior to the old covenant. And he shows that the Christ is the mediator of this new covenant.

Twice in this verse the word *superior* occurs: the ministry Jesus has obtained is superior to that of the priests, and the new covenant is superior to the old one.

What is the ministry Christ has received?[12] The word *ministry* relates to the work in the tabernacle or sanctuary. If Jesus had merely fulfilled the responsibilities of the Aaronic priesthood with his personal sacrifice, his work would be incomplete. Jesus fulfilled the obligations of the Levitical priesthood and ushered in the era of the high priest in the order of Melchizedek. The old system has yielded its place to the new, and in that new covenant Jesus has become the mediator.

In Old Testament times, high priests served as mediators between God

---

11. F. W. Grosheide, *De Brief aan de Hebreeën en de Brief van Jakobus* (Kampen: Kok, 1955), p. 189. See also Leonhard Goppelt, *TDNT*, vol. 9, p. 258.

12. The term *ministry* belongs to a word group that includes, in the original Greek, the verb *to serve* (10:11), the noun *ministry* (8:6; 9:21), the noun *servant* (1:7; 8:2), and the adjective *serving* (1:14).

and man. They were mediators on the basis of the old covenant God had made with his people, but this covenant has become obsolete (8:13) because the new one has taken its place. In succeeding verses the author explains why the new covenant is superior to the old one.

However, the author gives a preliminary reason as to why the new covenant is better than the old. Says he, "It is founded on better promises." By implication, the promises given by God to his people in earlier days were inadequate. The promises of the old covenant went together with the law of Moses; new covenant promises include God's law put in the minds and written on the hearts of his people, the teaching of knowledge of the Lord, and the forgiving of sin (8:10–12).

Doctrinal Considerations in 8:1–6

When Jesus told the disciples in the upper room on the eve of his death, "And if I go and prepare a place for you, I will come back and take you to be with me that you also may be where I am" (John 14:3), his promise included sitting with Christ on his throne (Rev. 3:21). Christ "has made us to be a kingdom and priests to serve his God and Father" (Rev. 1:6). Believers are kings and priests with Christ. What a glorious promise!

Christ's divine kingship differs from that of earthly kings. His kingship is one of service: he intercedes for his people; that is, he presents the prayers and praises of his people before the throne of God.[13] He guarantees a place for his people in his Father's house. Christ is the king-priest who rules and serves his people.

The Levitical priests served God in the sanctuary erected by man. Incidentally, the writer of the epistle consistently quotes from and alludes to passages of the Old Testament that mention the tabernacle. Never does he mention the temple in Jerusalem. Even in Hebrews 13, where he continually exhorts the readers and addresses his contemporaries, he refers to the tabernacle (13:10), the high priest who takes animal blood into the Most Holy Place ("but the bodies are burned outside the camp" [13:11]), and to Jesus, who "suffered outside the city gate" (13:12). The context for the author's teaching is the experience of the Israelites in the wilderness. That means the writer refers to the beginning of the nation Israel when God made a covenant with the Israelites at Mount Sinai, gave his people the law, and instituted the Levitical priesthood.

Jesus, having fulfilled the responsibilities of the Aaronic priesthood, serves God eternally in "the true tabernacle" as high priest in the order of Melchizedek. Thus his priesthood is superior to that of the sons of Levi. Jesus by his sacrificial death fulfilled the demands of the Old Testament law and therefore made the old covenant obsolete. The new covenant, sealed with the blood of Christ, is superior to the old one (Matt. 26:28; Mark 14:24; Luke 22:20; I Cor. 11:25).

---

13. B. F. Westcott, *Commentary on the Epistle to the Hebrews* (Grand Rapids: Eerdmans, 1950), p. 229.

Greek Words, Phrases, and Constructions in 8:1–6

Verse 1

κεφάλαιον—this neuter substantivized adjective, without the definite article, means "the main point" or "the summary." The first meaning is preferred.

ἐπὶ τοῖς λεγομένοις—the preposition ἐπί followed by the dative case may be translated "about"[14] or "in addition to."[15] The definite article τοῖς and the present passive participle λεγομένοις are in the neuter dative plural case. The author uses the present tense to stress the significance of his discussion—"the things that are being said."

Verse 2

τῶν ἁγίων—the neuter genitive plural adjective with the definite article is substantivized and refers to the sanctuary. The author does not distinguish between tabernacle and Most Holy Place (but see 9:3).

λειτουργός—the difference between the two word groups represented by the verbs λειτουργέω (I serve in a public office or religious ministry) and λατρεύω (I serve) is not very pronounced in the Epistle to the Hebrews, because both word groups relate to the worship of God.[16]

Verse 3

δῶρά τε καὶ θυσίας—the phrase is a repetition of Hebrews 5:1.

προσενέγκῃ—the aorist tense signifies single occurrence. The verb is the aorist subjunctive active of προσφέρω (I offer). The use of the subjunctive is futuristic.[17]

Verse 5

κεχρημάτισται—the perfect passive indicative of the verb χρηματίζω (I admonish, instruct) denotes instruction given by God to man in the form of revelation. This divine revelation often was conveyed as a warning. The perfect tense implies lasting validity.

ὅρα ποιήσεις—the present active imperative ὅρα and the future active indicative are placed next to each other without the use of καί. The words, as a quotation, are from Exodus 25:40, with minor variation.

Verse 6

τέτυχεν—the verb τυγχάνω means "I hit the mark" and, more generally, "I attain." The use of the perfect indicates duration.

---

14. A. T. Robertson, *A Grammar of the Greek New Testament in the Light of Historical Research* (Nashville: Broadman, 1934), p. 605.

15. Bauer, p. 287. Also see Harvey E. Dana and Julius R. Mantey, *A Manual Grammar of the Greek New Testament* (New York: Macmillan, 1957), p. 107.

16. R. C. Trench, *Synonyms of the Greek New Testament* (Grand Rapids: Eerdmans, 1953), p. 126. See also Klaus Hess, *NIDNTT*, vol. 3, pp. 549–53; and Hermann Strathmann, *TDNT*, vol. 4, pp. 58–65 and 215–22.

17. Robertson, *Grammar*, p. 928.

ὅσῳ—this relative adjective lacks the corresponding adjective τοσούτῳ. Compare
Hebrews 1:4.

ἥτις—the indefinite relative pronoun takes the place of the simple relative pronoun. It denotes cause and thus gives the reason why the new covenant is superior
to the old one.

νενομοθέτηται—see Hebrews 7:11.

---

7 For if there had been nothing wrong with that first covenant, no place would have been
sought for another. 8 But God found fault with the people and said:
"The time is coming, declares the Lord,
    when I will make a new covenant
with the house of Israel
    and with the house of Judah.
9 It will not be like the covenant I made with
    their forefathers
when I took them by the hand
    to lead them out of Egypt,
because they did not remain faithful to my covenant,
and I turned away from them,

                                                    declares the Lord.

10 This is the covenant I will make with the
        house of Israel
    after that time, declares the Lord.
I will put my laws in their minds
    and write them on their hearts.
I will be their God,
    and they will be my people.
11 No longer will a man teach his neighbor,
    or a man his brother, saying, 'Know the Lord,'
because they will all know me,
    from the least of them to the greatest.
12 For I will forgive their wickedness
    and will remember their sins no more."
13 By calling this covenant "new," he has made the first one obsolete; and what is obsolete
and aging will soon disappear.

C. God's New Covenant
8:7–13

One of the author's characteristics is to quote lengthy passages from the
Old Testament (for example, in 2:6–8 [Ps. 8:4–6]; 3:7–11 [Ps. 95:7–11];
and 10:5–7 [Ps. 40:6–8]). Usually he explains and applies these passages in
the succeeding context. However, when he quotes Jeremiah 31:31–34 in
8:8–12, he refrains from giving an explanation in the following chapter—
instead, he quotes the passage again, in 10:16–17. The author puts the
quotation in the present context to prove his point that God has revealed
the replacement of the old covenant by the new.

7. For if there had been nothing wrong with that first covenant, no

place would have been sought for another. 8a. But God found fault with the people and said . . .

Unfulfilled conditional sentences appear repeatedly in the Epistle to the Hebrews (see among others 4:8, 7:11, and 8:4). Also in 8:7 the sentence is conditional. The argument demands an implied response: "if there had been nothing wrong with that first covenant" (but there was, for it was inadequate), then "no place would have been sought for another" (but God indeed confirmed the new covenant in Jeremiah 31:31–34).

For the author of the epistle, the Old Testament had not lost its validity when New Testament revelation overshadowed it. Not at all. For him, the Old Testament remained the living Word of God (1:1). But the coming of Christ and his ministry brought fulfillment to promise and prophecy. Therefore the writer explains the passage from Jeremiah 31 in the light of Jesus' coming. When Christ came into the world, he abolished the old and established the new. The author employs the terms *first* and *second* ("another" in the NIV).[18]

Speaking through David, in Psalm 110:4 God revealed the superiority of Melchizedek's priesthood; this superiority is also revealed through Jeremiah's prophecy. In this prophecy God also revealed the superiority of a new covenant. God himself instructed his people in the Old Testament Scriptures, but these truths remained hidden until the author of Hebrews employed them in his teachings.

Did God make a mistake when he established a covenant that had to be replaced in later years? No, God's word is true and without error. The fault in the first covenant did not lie with God but with the people who were God's covenant partners. They did not keep the conditions stipulated in the covenant, and therefore "God found fault with the people."[19] However, if the people were to blame for not keeping the covenant stipulations, the covenant itself could still be faultless. But in quoting Jeremiah 31:31–34, the author of the epistle shows the weakness of the first covenant: it was not put in the minds or written on the hearts of the people (8:10).[20] Therefore, the old covenant had to be replaced by the new.

8b. "The time is coming, declares the Lord,
 when I will make a new covenant
 with the house of Israel
 and with the house of Judah.
9. It will not be like the covenant
 I made with their forefathers
 when I took them by the hand

---

18. The author has a penchant for the use of the adjective *first*. See 8:7, 13; 9:1, 2, 8, 15, 18; 10:9.

19. "The context does not seem to indicate that the intrinsic nature of the commandments was changed, but rather the mode of reception of the covenant," says Thomas McComiskey in *NIDNTT*, vol. 2, p. 145.

20. John Calvin, *Epistle to the Hebrews* (Grand Rapids: Eerdmans, 1949), p. 187.

to lead them out of Egypt,
because they did not remain faithful to my covenant,
and I turned away from them,

declares the Lord."

A covenant is drawn up when two parties agree on a contract. The contract spells out stipulations that the parties must honor and a condition that, in case either party fails to meet the requirements of the contract, the contract loses its binding force.

In 8:8b–9, a description of the old covenant is given: the two parties are mentioned; the stipulations of the covenant are implied; and the condition is applied.

a. *Two parties*. Twice in the first part of the quotation the prophet Jeremiah uses the phrase *declares the Lord*. The Lord God of Israel made a covenant with his people when he led them out of Egypt and had them stand at the foot of Mount Sinai to receive his law (Exod. 20:1–17). The first party in the covenant is God. He initiated it; he addressed the people of Israel at the beginning of their nationhood; and he turned away from them when they failed to remain faithful to the Sinaitic covenant.

God declared that he would "make a new covenant with the house of Israel and the house of Judah," but he did not disclose when the new contract would be signed. The reference *the time is coming* is decidedly indefinite. In historical perspective, the prophecy of Jeremiah could not have been directed to Israel's restoration after the exile, because the Old Testament indicates that the old covenant was in force after the exile.[21] The prophecy, therefore, heralds the coming of the Messiah and the establishing of the new covenant in his blood (see Matt. 26:28 and parallels).

The phrases *house of Israel* and *house of Judah* call attention to the reunification of the nation Israel; however, because the ten tribes of Israel failed to return after the exile, the phrases ought to be understood in a more universalistic sense to include both Jews and Gentiles.

b. *Implied stipulations*. The old covenant God made with the people of Israel was God's promise that he would be their king. As king, God demanded obedience from his people. For this reason he gave them the law at Sinai and told them that they would be "a kingdom of priests and a holy nation" (Exod. 19:6).

The Israelites were asked to obey God's law with heart, soul, and strength (Deut. 6:5) and thus to demonstrate their constant love for God. They listened to God's commandments but neglected to obey him. The law remained something external, for it was not written on their hearts. Consequently, they refused to remain faithful to God's covenant.

c. *Applied condition*. God's response to the rebellious Israelites was to turn away from them. The relation between God and his people at first had been

---

21. Gerhard Charles Aalders, *De Profeet Jeremia*, Korte Verklaring, 2 vols. (Kampen: Kok, 1954), vol. 2, p. 88.

intimate. God said, "I took them by the hand to lead them out of Egypt." God wanted his people to walk with him hand in hand, in full assurance and confidence. But when the Israelites decided to walk alone, to disobey God's law, and to ignore his voice calling them to himself, he "turned away from them."[22] That is, God neglected them by leaving them to their own willful ways. Instead of demonstrating tender loving care for his covenant people, God assumed an attitude of unconcern for obstinate covenant breakers. By turning away from them God made it known that the time for a new covenant would come. He remains a covenant God.

10. **"This is the covenant I will make with the**
    house of Israel
    after that time, declares the Lord.
    I will put my laws in their minds
    and write them on their hearts.
    I will be their God,
    and they will be my people.
11. **No longer will a man teach his neighbor,**
    or a man his brother, saying, 'Know the Lord,'
    because they will all know me,
    from the least of them to the greatest.
12. **For I will forgive their wickedness**
    and will remember their sins no more."

The description of the new covenant is positive; the stipulations are not implied but clearly stated in the form of four promises (8:6).

a. *Written law.* For the third time in this lengthy quotation Jeremiah writes "declares the Lord." God himself makes the new covenant with the people who belong to the messianic age. That is, Jew and Gentile as believers make up "the house of Israel." The era of the old covenant, characterized by the exclusiveness of the nation Israel, has made way for a new age in which all nations are included (Matt. 28:19).

Who belongs to the house of Israel? All those people, says God, in whose minds I will put my laws and upon whose hearts I will write them. The expressions *minds* and *hearts* (parallel terms) represent man's inner being. God's people experience the permeating power of God's Word, so that his law becomes a part of their conscience. That conscience is directed to the law of God, much the same as a compass needle invariably points north.

b. *Covenant God.* Throughout Scripture God's recurring message to his people is the promise: "I will be their God, and they will be my people" (see, for example, Exod. 6:7; Lev. 26:12; Jer. 7:23; 11:4; II Cor. 6:16; Rev. 21:3). God wanted to make the Israelite nation his special people; they were his "treasured possession." However, Israel could lose this favored status if the

---

22. The translation of Jer. 31:32b in the Hebrew text ("because they broke my covenant, though I was a husband to them, declares the LORD") differs from the reading in Heb. 8:9b, which is based on the Septuagint.

people refused to keep the law of God. The covenant stipulated that God's people would live a life of obedience.

In New Testament times, too, God addresses the believers in Jesus Christ and gives them the covenant promise: "I will be [your] God, and [you] will be my people." In this new covenant, God is inseparably united with his people because God's law has been inscribed on their hearts. He communicates with his people through his revelation, and they communicate with him through prayer. He encourages them to approach the throne of grace with confidence (Heb. 4:16), and he makes it known that his name has been written on their foreheads (Rev. 14:1; 22:4). He wants to have them address him as Father, for they are his children.

> Ye children of God's covenant,
> Who of His grace have heard,
> Forget not all His wondrous deeds
> And judgments of His word.
> The Lord our God is God alone,
> All lands His judgments know;
> His promise He remembers still,
> While generations go.
> —*Psalter Hymnal*

c. *Universal knowledge.* The next promise flows from the preceding promises. The knowledge of the Lord shall be universal. In the history of Israel, God's revelation came piecemeal "through the prophets at many times and in various ways" (Heb. 1:1), and in one instance the Book of the Law was discovered in the temple of the Lord. While the Book of the Law gathered dust, the people lived in ignorance (II Kings 22; II Chron. 34:14–28). Ignorance of God's revelation was appalling, and God's prophets repeatedly registered their complaints (see Isa. 1:3; Jer. 4:22; Hos. 4:6).

What a difference in New Testament times! Knowledge of the Lord will be universal, covering the earth "as the waters cover the sea" (Isa. 11:9; Hab. 2:14). The need for individual teaching—"a man teach his neighbor, or a man his brother," "from the least of them to the greatest"—will disappear because all people will know the Lord. Filled with the knowledge of the Lord, even novices in the faith are able and equipped to witness for him. All those who have the law of God in their hearts and minds acknowledge God's grace and mercy. They know that their sins have been forgiven and that their record has been wiped clean.

d. *Complete remission.* When God forgives sin, he does so by never remembering man's sin again. That means that when forgiven, man is like Adam and Eve in Paradise: without sin. Man, forgiven by God, is accepted as if he had never sinned at all. God says, "I will remember [his] sins no more." In the new covenant, grace and mercy are freely given to all God's children. God gives these blessings in the name of his Son, who is the mediator of a new covenant. This new covenant established through the death of Jesus on the cross is the believer's guarantee that his sins are forgiven and forgotten.

13. By calling this covenant "new," he has made the first one obsolete; and what is obsolete and aging will soon disappear.

God himself introduced the word *new* when he said, "I will make a new covenant with the house of Israel and with the house of Judah" (8:8). In Christ the new covenant has become reality; consequently, the old covenant has become obsolete. God himself told his people, at first through the prophecy of Jeremiah and then in New Testament times through the writer of Hebrews. The Jew of the first century, therefore, had to realize that the era of the covenant God made with his people at Sinai had ended.

Already in the days of Jeremiah, approximately six hundred years before the birth of Christ, God spoke of a new covenant. By implication, the existing covenant was then already "obsolete and aging."[23]

What then is the difference between the old and the new? For one thing, in the days of the old covenant the sinner repeatedly had to present animal offerings to the Lord God to obtain remission of sin. In the new covenant sinners are forgiven through the one-time sacrifice of Jesus. Their offerings consist of dedicated lives that express gratitude to God and joyfully keep his commands.

The old covenant was rather restrictive; it was made with Israel, God's special people. The new covenant embraces all nations; all those who believe in Jesus Christ are his "treasured possession." Therefore, with the coming of Pentecost, the new covenant made its presence felt. The old covenant had to be put away.

The writer of Hebrews, however, does not specify a time or describe circumstances when the old covenant will disappear. His conclusion to chapter 8 is rather general: "and what is obsolete and aging will soon disappear."

Doctrinal Considerations in 8:7–13

The old covenant was based on the law of God given to the Israelites during the first part of their wilderness journey. Although the law which was basic to the covenant was perfect, it could not make man perfect (Heb. 7:11, 19). Because of the inherent weakness—not in the covenant, as such, but in man—God inaugurated a new covenant. The new came forth out of the old and for a while both covenants existed side by side: the new took over when the old began to disappear (8:13).

The inadequacy of the old covenant was completely overshadowed by the adequacy of Christ. Christ became the mediator of this new covenant that was superior to the old covenant. The writer of Hebrews employs comparative adjectives to indicate the difference between old and new: Christ's *superior* ministry, the *superior* covenant, and the *better* promises (8:6). Jesus is "the guarantee of a *better* covenant" (7:22; italics added).

---

23. Hughes ventures the idea that 8:13 is an oblique reference to the temple services prior to the destruction of Jerusalem. He sees this reference, then, as a silent witness to the time when the epistle was written—before A.D. 70.

Whereas the old covenant was an external manifestation of God's grace, the new covenant involves the individual believer. God made the old covenant with the nation Israel and gave the people his laws written on tablets of stone. He establishes the new covenant with the believer in Christ and writes God's law on the believer's heart. With this law written on his inmost being, the believer has an intimate relationship with God through Christ.

The new covenant has two parties: God and his people. To be precise, the people of God are the true believers who have experienced genuine repentance and who demonstrate saving faith in Christ. God gives his people the promise: "I will be [your] God, and [you] will be my people" (8:10). God assumes that his people will keep the demands of his law written on their hearts, that they will always show their love and obedience to him, and that they will grow in their knowledge of salvation. God will not forget his promise. In fact, "He cannot and may not break His covenant; He has committed Himself to maintaining it with a freely given and precious oath: His name, His honor, His reputation depends on it."[24]

Greek Words, Phrases, and Constructions in 8:7–13

Verse 7

εἰ—this conditional particle, followed by the imperfect indicative ἦν in the protasis and οὐκ ἄν in the apodosis, introduces the contrary-to-fact condition.

τόπος—the word *place* refers to the history of redemption.

Verse 8

μεμφόμενος—together with ἄμεμπτος (blameless) in 8:7, the present middle participle derives from μέμφομαι (I find fault). The participle can take either αὐτούς as direct object or αὐτοῖς. The external manuscript evidence for either reading is about equally divided. The reading αὐτοῖς can also be connected with the verb λέγει (he said to them).

συντελέσω—the future active indicative from συντελέω (I fulfill) differs from the Septuagint text (Jer. 38:31), which reads διαθήσομαι (from διατίθημι, I decree, ordain). In this rather lengthy citation—the longest in the entire New Testament—numerous variations from the Septuagint text appear. Whether these variations originated during the process of copying the text or because of liturgical usage in the church is difficult to determine.[25]

καινήν—the adjective is used with διαθήκη in I Corinthians 11:25 and II Corinthians 3:6, in addition to Hebrews 8:8. The adjective conveys the idea of newness that comes forth out of the old and may even exist alongside the old: the Old Testament and the New Testament.

Verse 9

ἐπιλαβομένου μου τῆς χειρὸς αὐτῶν—the genitive absolute construction consists of the aorist middle participle from ἐπιλαμβάνομαι (I take hold of) and the personal

---

24. Herman Bavinck, *Our Reasonable Faith* (Grand Rapids: Eerdmans, 1956), pp. 274–75.

25. Simon J. Kistemaker, *The Psalm Citations in the Epistle to the Hebrews* (Amsterdam: Van Soest, 1961), pp. 41–42.

pronoun μου from ἐγώ (I). The participle governs the genitive case of τῆς χειρός (the hand); the pronoun αὐτῶν is possessive. The construction of this phrase is somewhat unusual.[26]

ἠμέλησα—the aorist active indicative of ἀμελέω (I neglect, disregard), derived from ἀ (not) and μέλω (I care for). The verb is expressive. See also Matthew 22:5, I Timothy 4:14, and Hebrews 2:3.

Verse 11

γνῶθι τὸν κύριον—the second aorist active imperative of γινώσκω (I know) expresses the concept of learning the commandments of God. The verb is followed by εἰδήσουσιν, the future perfect of οἶδα (I know), understood as a simple future indicative. The contrast between γινώσκω and οἶδα is significant in this verse. The first means acquiring knowledge, the second possessing knowledge.

Verse 13

ἐν τῷ λέγειν—the articular present infinitive with the preposition ἐν is in the dative case. The dative expresses time; that is, "while he is saying."

πεπαλαίωκεν—from the verb παλαιόω (I make old), the perfect active suggests action with lasting result. The active, not the passive, is used to indicate that God has declared the covenant old.

ἀφανισμοῦ—this noun, translated as "disappearance," derives from the verb ἀφανίζω (I make invisible), which is a compound of ἀ (not) and φαίνω (I appear). The genitive case is dependent on the adverb ἐγγύς (near), which is pressed into service as a preposition.

Summary of Chapter 8

In some ways chapter 8 is an extended commentary on 7:22, where the author introduces the concept *covenant*. He explains the word by quoting at length from a prophetic passage in the Book of Jeremiah. Yet he fails to interpret the term *covenant*. He does that in the following chapter (9:15–22). The quotation from Jeremiah 31:31–34, however, serves the purpose of showing the readers that God himself in the days of Jeremiah had already declared the covenant made with Israel to be obsolete.

The author, as a careful teacher of theology, utilizes the Old Testament Scriptures to show that God revealed the appearance of the new covenant centuries before the birth of Christ. Just as God himself appointed Christ as high priest in the order of Melchizedek, so he established a new covenant of which Christ would be the high priest.

The old order of the Levitical priesthood eventually had to come to an end. The sanctuary at which the priests served was "a copy and shadow of what is in heaven." By contrast, the sanctuary at which Jesus serves as high

---

26. Robertson, *Grammar*, p. 514.

priest is the true tabernacle in the presence of God himself. The earthly sanctuary was temporal; the heavenly sanctuary is eternal.

As the heavenly tabernacle is superior to the earthly sanctuary, so the new covenant, of which Jesus is the mediator, is superior to the old covenant. The new covenant is better because of the promises God gives to his people. And Jesus, who is the mediator of this new covenant, guarantees these promises: to know God, to treasure his revelation, and to experience complete forgiveness of sin.

9

Jesus: High Priest and Sacrifice, *part 2*

(9:1–28)

Outline

9 1 Now the first covenant had regulations for worship and also an earthly sanctuary. 2 A tabernacle was set up. In its first room were the lampstand, the table and the consecrated bread; this was called the Holy Place. 3 Behind the second curtain was a room called the Most Holy Place, 4 which had the golden altar of incense and the gold-covered ark of the covenant. This ark contained the gold jar of manna, Aaron's staff that had budded, and the stone tablets of the covenant. 5 Above the ark were the cherubim of the Glory, overshadowing the atonement cover. But we cannot discuss these things in detail now.

6 When everything had been arranged like this, the priests entered regularly into the outer room to carry on their ministry. 7 But only the high priest entered the inner room, and that only once a year, and never without blood, which he offered for himself and for the sins the people had committed in ignorance. 8 The Holy Spirit was showing by this that the way into the Most Holy Place had not yet been disclosed as long as the first tabernacle was still standing. 9 This is an illustration for the present time, indicating that the gifts and sacrifices being offered were not able to clear the conscience of the worshiper. 10 They are only a matter of food and drink and various ceremonial washings—external regulations applying until the time of the new order.

D. The Earthly Sanctuary
9:1–10

1. The First Covenant and the Tabernacle
9:1–5

Every chapter in the Epistle to the Hebrews has its own central message. For example: chapter 5, Christ is superior to Aaron the high priest; chapter 7, Christ is high priest in the order of Melchizedek; and chapter 9, Christ offers himself as a sacrifice once for all.

Although the topic of the covenant has become an integral part of the epistle at this point, the author nevertheless has to link the topic to the continuing discussion of the priesthood of Christ. In chapter 9 the author of Hebrews brings together these two strands and weaves them into a grand design. He portrays the construction of the tabernacle of the desert period, enumerates the various furnishings inside the sanctuary, and mentions the Most High Place with the ark and the cherubim.

1. Now the first covenant had regulations for worship and also an earthly sanctuary.

The writer of Hebrews contrasts the old and new covenants in the last verse of the preceding chapter. Consistently he calls the old covenant the first (8:7, 13; 9:1, 15, 18). Because he has already spoken of the tabernacle Moses was told to build (8:5), he now has to show a connection between covenant and tabernacle.

As a trained theologian the writer has the Old Testament Scriptures at hand. The first covenant was confirmed by the people of Israel just before Moses received the design for the construction of the tabernacle (Exod. 24). The design for the tabernacle and its contents, the regulations for worship, and the construction of the "earthly sanctuary" are recorded in succeeding chapters. Incidentally, the descriptive adjective *earthly* must be understood as the counterpart of the description *greater and more perfect* that is applied to the "tabernacle that is not man-made" (9:11; also see 8:2).

The covenant, says the writer, includes two matters.

a. "Regulations for worship." God did not leave the practice of worship to the invention of the Israelites. With the design for the tabernacle, God also gave Moses the detailed ordinances for divine worship (see, for instance, Exod. 29, 30). In other words, Moses passed on to the Israelites God-ordained regulations for worship.

b. "Earthly sanctuary." Rules for worship and the mandate for the erection of the sanctuary are closely connected in Exodus 25–30. And even in Hebrews 9:1, the phrases *regulations for worship* and *earthly sanctuary* are joined by a connective particle that is translated "and also."

The word *sanctuary* may have been chosen for stylistic reasons. The writer uses the term *tabernacle* in the next verse, but throughout his epistle he refrains from employing the expression *temple*. Some commentators see this choice of words as a clear indication that when the author wrote Hebrews, the Jerusalem temple already had been destroyed. Other commentators say that the choice is a matter of basics: the tabernacle is basic to the temple. Although this comment is commendable, I think that the determinative factor in the writer's choice of words, at least for chapters 8 and 9, is the close link between the confirmation of the covenant (Exod. 24) and the mandate to construct the tabernacle (Exod. 25–27).

2. A tabernacle was set up. In its first room were the lampstand, the table and the consecrated bread; this was called the Holy Place. 3. Behind the second curtain was a room called the Most Holy Place, 4. which had the golden altar of incense and the gold-covered ark of the covenant. This ark contained the gold jar of manna, Aaron's staff that had budded, and the stone tablets of the covenant.

Mainly from passages in Exodus 16, 25, 26, and 30, as well as in Numbers 17, the author gleaned the information for his description of the interior and furniture of the tabernacle. Note that he describes the tabernacle as a structure with two rooms: the first room is called the Holy Place, and the second room is known as the Most Holy Place.

a. *The first room.* In the Holy Place, the larger of the two rooms, were the lampstand, the table, and the consecrated bread. The lampstand, according to Exodus 25:31–39, was a most beautifully crafted piece of furniture. It was made of seventy-five pounds (thirty-four kilograms) of gold, consisting of a base and shaft from which six branches extended—three to one side of the shaft and three to the other. At the top of these six branches and shaft were cups decorated "like almond flowers with buds and blossoms" (Exod. 25:34). The lampstand was placed on the south side of the Holy Place (Exod. 40:24).

The table, made of acacia wood, was about 3¾ feet (about 1.1 meters) long and 2¼ feet (about 0.7 meter) wide. It was covered with pure gold (Exod. 25:23, 24), and the "bread of the Presence" (Exod. 25:30) was placed on it. The table was located on the north side of the Holy Place (Exod. 40:22).

Twelve loaves of bread, representing the twelve tribes of Israel, were placed on this table (Lev. 24:5–9). The bread was known as "the bread of presentation" or "consecrated bread" (see Matt. 12:4; Mark 2:26; Luke 6:4). The author of the epistle mentions table and bread in the same breath to indicate that they belong together.

b. *The second room.* Inside the tabernacle was another curtain that separated the Most Holy Place from the Holy Place. This room contained, according to the writer of Hebrews, "the golden altar of incense and the gold-covered ark of the covenant." Questions about these two items have caused much debate. We shall consider them in sequence.

1. "The golden altar of incense." The altar for burning incense was made of acacia wood and covered with pure gold. It was square, about 1½ feet (about 0.5 meter) in length and width and about 3 feet (about 0.9 meter) high (Exod. 30:1–6). God instructed Moses to "put the altar in front of the curtain that is before the ark of the Testimony" (Exod. 30:6), and this is exactly what Moses did (Exod. 40:26). The writer of the Epistle to the Hebrews, however, states that the altar was with the ark in the Most Holy Place, but this is contrary to the divine instructions Moses received and followed. See the diagram of the tabernacle (Fig. 1).

Obviously, we face a problem that is not easy to solve. Some commentators are rather quick in saying that the author must have made a mistake or was

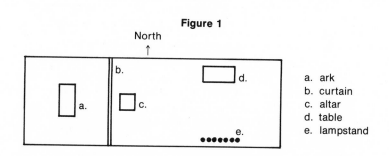

Figure 1

North
↑

a. ark
b. curtain
c. altar
d. table
e. lampstand

unacquainted with the description of the interior of the tabernacle.[1] But that is hardly plausible in view of the detailed knowledge of the Old Testament Scriptures he exhibits in his epistle. Admittedly, the author could have been influenced by the description of Solomon's temple in which the altar "belonged to the inner sanctuary" (I Kings 6:22). However, the author of Hebrews makes no mention of Solomon's temple. In the postexilic temple the altar of incense was located in the Holy Place, not in the Most Holy Place (Luke 1:11). Zechariah was a priest (not a high priest) who "was chosen by lot . . . to go into the temple of the Lord and burn incense" (Luke 1:9). He could serve only in the Holy Place.[2]

Other commentators take the expression *the altar of incense* to mean "censer," that is, a container for burning incense. This interpretation, which was common in the Middle Ages and the time of the Reformation (see the Bible translations of that day), is based on the translation of the Greek word for "altar of incense."[3] In II Chronicles 26:19 and Ezekiel 8:11, the translation is "censer." The interpretation, then, is that the high priest used the container for burning incense once a year and that he left it permanently in the Most Holy Place. Thus the censer was always with the ark in the inner sanctuary. This view does not seem to remove the difficulties we face. The passages in Exodus 30 and 40 speak of an altar, not of a censer. Also, the altar of incense filled an important function in the Holy Place. Every morning and every evening Aaron or one of his male descendants had to burn incense on the altar (Exod. 30:7–8). The altar of incense was much more significant than a censer.

However, on the Day of Atonement the high priest had "to take a censer full of burning coals from the altar before the LORD and two handfuls of finely ground fragrant incense and take them behind the curtain" (Lev. 16:12). On that special day, once a year, the censer became the extension of the altar of incense. The smoke of the incense had to conceal the atonement cover of the ark, so that the high priest would not die (v. 13). The function of the altar could not be obstructed by a curtain separating the Most Holy Place from the Holy Place. Thus, the censer momentarily entered behind the curtain as an extension of the altar of incense.

We should also note that on the Day of Atonement the high priest cleansed

---

1. Hugh Montefiore, *The Epistle to the Hebrews* (New York and Evanston: Harper and Row, 1964), p. 145, writes: "Possibly our author has made a slight slip and placed the altar in the wrong part of the Tent." Myles M. Bourke in "The Epistle to the Hebrews," *The Jerome Biblical Commentary*, vol. 2, *The New Testament and Topical Articles* (Englewood Cliffs, N.J.: Prentice-Hall, 1968), p. 396, states: "It seems that the author has made a mistake here, caused probably by the fact that he was not speaking from personal knowledge of the Temple, which replaced the Mosaic Tabernacle, but was merely repeating, and in this case misinterpreting, the description of the Tabernacle found in Exodus."

2. For comments of Jewish contemporaries see Philo in *The Life of Moses* 2.101 (LCL); Josephus, *Jewish Wars* 5.21 and *Antiquities of the Jews* 3.147, 198 (LCL); and *Talmud*, Yoma 47a; Moed 3. SB, vol. 3, p. 737.

3. The KJV and RV read "golden censer."

the altar of incense by sprinkling animal blood on the horns of the altar (Exod. 30:10). Once a year the altar was "most holy to the LORD" (v. 10) and could be mentioned with the ark of the covenant.

In Hebrews 9 the author stresses the prominence of the Day of Atonement (v. 7). For him, the altar of incense and the ark were the most important objects.

2. "The gold-covered ark of the covenant." A chest made of acacia wood, the ark was 3¾ feet (about 1.1. meters) long, 2¼ feet (about 0.7 meter) wide, and 2¼ feet (about 0.7 meter) high. It was completely covered with pure gold. It was permanently located in the Most Holy Place except when the Lord God told the Israelites to continue their wilderness journey. Then the priests were to carry the ark. Later, except when the ark was in Philistine cities and in the houses of Abinadab (I Sam. 4 and 6) and Obed-Edom (II Sam. 6:10–12), the ark remained in the tabernacle and subsequently the temple.[4]

The ark "contained the gold jar of manna, Aaron's staff that had budded, and the stone tablets of the covenant." These objects came from Israel's history. First, the jar filled with manna was placed "before the LORD to be kept for the generations to come" (Exod. 16:33). The author of Hebrews used the Septuagint translation of the Hebrew text, for that translation has the reading *gold jar*. Only the author conveys the information that the gold jar had a place inside the ark.

The second item was Aaron's staff that "had not only sprouted but had budded, blossomed and produced almonds" (Num. 17:8). This staff was put "in front of the Testimony" (v. 10). The Old Testament provides no information about depositing the staff inside the ark. If the ark indeed contained this rod, it would have had to conform to the size of the ark. When the ark was placed in the temple of Solomon, it contained nothing "except the two stone tablets that Moses had placed in it at Horeb" (I Kings 8:9; II Chron. 5:10). Because of Scripture's silence, we are unable to draw any conclusions on these matters.

The two stone tablets inscribed with the Ten Commandments were to be placed in the ark. And this was exactly what Moses did (Deut. 10:1–5). The author of Hebrews calls the ark and the tablets covenant objects. That is, both the ark and the Ten Commandments testifed to the covenant relationship God had with the Israelites. The ark symbolized God's sacred presence in the midst of his people and gave visual meaning to God's promise, "I will be your God." The two stone tablets were a constant reminder to the people of Israel to keep the law of God, so that in obedience they could be his people.

5a. Above the ark were the cherubim of the Glory, overshadowing the atonement cover.

The writer returns to his description of the lid of the sacred chest. It was

---

4. After the exile, the rebuilt temple seemed to have had nothing at all in the Most Holy Place. Josephus, *Jewish Wars* 1.152–53; *Antiquities* 14.71, 72 (LCL).

made of pure gold and measured 3¾ feet (about 1.1 meters) by 2¼ feet (about 0.7 meter). On top of the cover were two angels, called cherubim, made of hammered gold. These two faced each other, with wings outspread covering the ark, and looked down toward the ark (Exod 25:17–22; 37:6–9).

God placed cherubim at the east side of the Garden of Eden "to guard the way to the tree of life" (Gen. 3:24). The posture of the cherubim on the cover of the ark projects the idea of guarding the way to God. Between the two cherubim God dwells, for from that place Moses heard God speak (Num. 7:89). God is "enthroned between the cherubim" (I Sam. 4:4; II Sam. 6:2; II Kings 19:15; Ps. 80:1; 99:1; Isa. 37:16).

The expression *cherubim of the Glory,* an obvious reference to God's glory, represents a glimpse of the heavenly glory. As Paul puts it in his First Epistle to Timothy: "God ... alone is immortal and ... lives in unapproachable light, whom no one has seen or can see" (6:15–16).

With their outspread wings the cherubim were "overshadowing the place of atonement." Another translation for "atonement cover" is "mercy seat." God appeared "in the cloud over the atonement cover" (Lev. 16:2), and no one, not even the high priest, was permitted to approach God. Who then might come before God? Only on the Day of Atonement might the high priest come sprinkling the blood of a bull seven times on the atonement cover (Lev. 16:14). The lasting ordinance was: "Atonement is to be made once a year for all the sins of the Israelites" (v. 34). God showed mercy once a year.

5b. But we cannot discuss these things in detail now.

The author is vitally interested in showing the insufficiency of gifts and sacrifices brought to God, for they could not "clear the conscience of the worshiper" (9:9). He is eager to discuss the sufficiency of Christ's sacrifice (9:11–14). Therefore, he somewhat abruptly discontinues the consideration of the tabernacle furniture. An extended discussion on this topic would not suit the author's purpose.

Greek Words, Phrases, and Constructions in 9:1–5

Verse 1

εἶχε—the descriptive imperfect active indicative of ἔχω (I have, hold) relates to the entire span of history in which the old covenant functioned.

ἡ πρώτη—the noun must be supplied. The context seems to suggest the word διαθήκη (see 8:13). Some manuscripts have the reading σκηνή (tabernacle).

δικαιώματα—this noun belongs to the family that has the basic root δικ (show, point).[5] The noun translated "regulations" lacks the definite article (see 9:10). The -μα ending of the singular expresses the result of an action; that is, God spoke to the Israelites and laid down divine regulations.

---

5. Bruce M. Metzger, *Lexical Aids for Students of New Testament Greek* (Princeton, N.J.: published by the author, 1969), p. 54.

λατρείας—this noun can be either a genitive singular as an objective genitive (for worship) or an accusative plural (see 9:6, which has the definite article). The genitive singular is preferred.

Verse 2

σκηνή—the position of this noun is unique: without the definite article it stands first in the sentence and thus receives all the emphasis it needs. The noun, however, is defined by the definite article and adjective ἡ πρώτη. The adjective conveys the idea of two rooms in one tabernacle, not two tabernacles.

ἅγια—the accent mark indicates that this substantivized adjective is the neuter plural, not the feminine singular, which is ἁγία. The adjective lacks the definite article (see also 9:24). The writer of Hebrews builds a sequence of τὸ ἅγιον (9:1), ἅγια (9:2), and ἅγια ἁγίων (9:3). Says Norman H. Young, "It is best to take verse 2 as a neuter plural and allow the use of this form for a description of the outer tent (as in verse 2) as exceptional."[6]

Verse 3

μετά—this preposition controls the accusative case of τὸ καταπέτασμα as an accusative of place. For the use of καταπέτασμα, see Hebrews 6:19. This noun is modified by the adjective δεύτερον, which implies a first curtain of less importance than the second.

ἅγια ἁγίων—the definite articles are lacking. See the Septuagint reading of Exodus 26:33; I Kings 6:16; 7:50; 8:6; II Chronicles 4:22; 5:7.

Verse 4

ἔχουσα—as a feminine present participle of ἔχω (I have, hold), it takes θυμιατήριον (altar) and κιβωτόν (ark) as direct objects. The participle does not differentiate and treats both objects alike.

περικεκαλυμμένην—a perfect passive participle derived from the compound περί (around) and καλύπτω (I cover). In 9:4, the author emphasizes the beauty of the Most Holy Place by using the noun *gold* once and the adjective *golden* twice.

Verse 5

αὐτῆς—the antecedent of this pronoun is τὴν κιβωτόν (9:4). It is in the genitive case because of the adverb ὑπεράνω (above) used as a preposition.

κατασκιάζοντα—this present active participle from κατασκιάζω (I overshadow) has a single occurrence in the New Testament. It is an intensive compound with the meaning "covering the lid of the ark completely with shade." And last, the participle is singular, whereas its subject χερουβίν is a transliterated plural.

---

6. Norman H. Young, "The Gospel According to Hebrews 9," *NTS* 27 (1981): 198. James Swetnam, in "Hebrews 9:2," *CBQ* 32 (1970): 205–21, gives the interpretation that "what the author has in mind when he uses the word *hagia* is the elements of the eucharistic bread" (p. 208).

2. The High Priest and the Most Holy Place
9:6–10

The author of Hebrews in 9:6–10 places in sharper focus the contrast alluded to in 9:1. He shows that the "regulations for worship" were external and consequently temporal. And he notes that the high priest entered the Most Holy Place only once a year; priests had no access to the inner sanctuary. As representatives of the people, priests and high priests faced limitations.

6. When everything had been arranged like this, the priests entered regularly into the outer room to carry on their ministry. 7. But only the high priest entered the inner room, and that only once a year, and never without blood, which he offered for himself and for the sins the people had committed in ignorance.

From a description of tabernacle and sanctuary furniture, the author moves to an explanation of the duties of priests and high priest. He notes that "the priests entered regularly into the outer room to carry on their ministry." The Old Testament teaches what these duties were: to burn incense every morning and evening (Exod. 30:7–8), to tend to the lamps of the lampstand "from evening till morning" (Exod. 27:21), and to replace the twelve loaves on the table each Sabbath (Lev. 24:8–9). The New Testament teaches that according to a custom of that day, priests were chosen by lot to enter the temple and burn incense (Luke 1:9).

However, because priests were not allowed to go beyond the Holy Place, they did not have access to God. That privilege was given to the high priest. But even he was restricted in approaching God. First, of all the people in Israel, he alone was appointed to enter the presence of God. Next, he was permitted to come before God only once a year, that is, on the Day of Atonement (the tenth day of the seventh month—about the end of September to the beginning of October [Lev. 23:26; Num. 29:7]). On this particular day, the high priest entered the Most Holy Place. A third restriction was that he might never enter without the sacrificial blood of an animal: the blood of a bull at first and then the blood of a goat (Lev. 16:14–15). The high priest, therefore, went into the inner sanctuary twice. The last stipulation concerned sin. The high priest sprinkled the blood of the bull on and in front of the cover of the ark (called the atonement cover) as a sin offering for himself and his household (Lev. 16:11, 14). He offered this blood to God for the purpose of covering his sin and the sin of his family. After that, he entered the Most Holy Place again, but now with the blood of a goat. This he sprinkled on and before the atonement cover. This offering covered the sins of the people (vv. 15–16).

Whereas the Old Testament teaches that the high priest made "atonement for the Most Holy Place because of the uncleanness and rebellion of the Israelites, *whatever their sins [had] been*" (Lev. 16:16, italics added), the author of Hebrews writes that the high priest offered sacrifices "for the sins the people had *committed in ignorance*" (Heb. 9:7, italics added). The Old Testament makes a clear distinction between sins committed unintentionally (that is, in ignorance) and those sins man commits defiantly. Unintentional sins will be forgiven; intentional sins cannot be forgiven, for the man who commits them "blasphemes the LORD" (Num. 15:22–31, especially v. 30). The writer of Hebrews underscores the consequences of intentional sin (see 3:16–19; 6:4–6; and 10:26–27). He also mentions the duties of the high priest, who "is able to deal gently with those who are ignorant and are going astray" (5:2). The good news is that God forgives sin. Nevertheless, access to God was restricted when the old covenant was in force.

8. The Holy Spirit was showing by this that the way into the Most Holy Place had not yet been disclosed as long as the first tabernacle was still standing.

The author's high view of Scripture is expressed once more. In Hebrews 3:7 he introduced the Holy Spirit as speaker of a psalm citation (see also 10:15). The Spirit speaks and interprets the Word of God. He discloses the meaning of the Word (John 14:26; 15:26) and guides the believer in the truth.[7] The Holy Spirit makes it plain that he is involved in the work of redemption.

We note two things.

a. The way to God's presence was not yet opened during the time of the old covenant. That means the people were not allowed to enter the tabernacle; only the priests went into the outer sanctuary to perform their duties. The priests, however, were forbidden to appear before God in the inner sanctuary; only the high priest, as the representative of the people and the priests, might enter the Most Holy Place once a year. Apart from this single exception, God had effectively separated himself from man. A curtain veiled the way to God.

b. The Holy Spirit indicated that "the way into the Most Holy Place had not . . . been disclosed" until the coming of Jesus. By his death, the Son of God opened the way to God. When Jesus died on Calvary's cross, "the curtain of the temple was torn in two from top to bottom" (Matt. 27:51; Mark 15:38). Although the Most Holy Place was empty at the time of Jesus' death, the tearing of the curtain signified that the separation between God and man had ended.

This separation would not end "as long as the first tabernacle was still standing." The word *first* may mean first in rank. If this is the interpretation of "first," the word refers to the inner sanctuary. But because of the tearing of the curtain, the first room had ceased to exist separately. The first and second rooms became one, and man gained access to God without priestly mediation.

We can also understand the expression *first* to mean the earthly sanctuary made by Moses in the desert. The implied second sanctuary, then, is the heavenly "tabernacle set up by the Lord" (Heb. 8:2; see also 9:11).

---

7. The tense of the participle *showing* in Heb. 9:8 can be translated either in the past tense (NAB, NIV) or in the present tense (JB, GNB, MLB, RSV, NEB, *Phillips*, NASB).

Of the two interpretations, the second seems to be more in line with the author's train of thought. He exhorts the believers to approach God, for "we have confidence to enter the Most Holy Place by the blood of Jesus" (10:19).

9. This is an illustration for the present time, indicating that the gifts and sacrifices being offered were not able to clear the conscience of the worshiper.

Some translations take the words "this is an illustration for the present time" parenthetically.[8] But this is not necessary if we understand the antecedent of the word *this* to be "the first tabernacle." This structure and all that is represented served as an illustration—the original Greek has the word *parable*. What does the illustration prove? It shows that the sacrificial system of the first tabernacle period failed to bring perfection because "the gifts and sacrifices being offered were not able to clear the conscience of the worshiper."

The writer sees the first tabernacle as an illustration of that which is real. The illustration itself, then, is not identical to reality. To make this clear to the reader, the author introduces the word *conscience*. That is a significant word, for man's conscience is the barometer of his moral sensitivity to deeds performed. Before the death of Christ, believers driven by a guilty conscience brought gifts and sacrifices to God. But these offerings, given to the priest who served as intermediary, did not quiet the awakened conscience of the worshiper. Gifts and sacrifices failed to remove guilt that continued to bother the believer's conscience. They could not clear the conscience of the sinner who came to God with offerings. They were unable to make the worshiper whole, perfect, and complete with respect to his conscience.

Therefore, the illustration points to reality. Gifts and sacrifices made the believer outwardly clean, ceremonially, but the blood of Christ removes sin, cleanses the conscience, and makes man whole. That is reality (see Heb. 9:13–14).

10. They are only a matter of food and drink and various ceremonial washings—external regulations applying until the time of the new order.

What do these gifts and sacrifices accomplish? The first thing we must keep in mind is that they were on the same level as divine injunctions that regulated the life of the Old Testament believer. These commandments pertained to the daily practices of eating, drinking, and staying clean outwardly. Next, these regulations were imposed on the believer by God when he spoke through Moses. God gave the Israelites rules concerning clean and unclean foods (Lev. 11; see also Heb. 13:9), grain offerings and drink offerings (Num. 6:15, 17; 28:7–8), and matters of cleanliness (Num. 19:13). These rules and regulations are only external. The writer stresses the word *only* to mean "that and nothing more." We see that the author has returned to the subject of external regulations that he introduced in 9:1.

To return to the question: "What do these external rules accomplish?" We

---

8. See the rsv, neb, and *Moffatt*.

must say they were not unprofitable. God gave them to his people for their own benefit and well-being; also he gave them the assurance that they were his special people who lived in harmony with his laws and rules. But apart from these objectives the external regulations did not advance the believer in his search for the cleansing of his soul. External rules achieve external objectives. A God-fearing Israelite could abstain from unclean food, cleanse himself from defilement, offer acceptable gifts and sacrifices to God; yet he remained within the structure of the old covenant. Keeping the commandments actually became a preventive action on the part of the Israelite; this enabled him to stay within the nation Israel and to continue as a member of God's people. But the external ceremonial rules and regulations were not meant to cleanse the believer's conscience and to renew him spiritually.

In both verses 9 and 10, the author employs the word *time*—"for the present time" and "until the time of the new order." Both verses convey the idea of a limited period: the first use refers to the time in which we see the first tabernacle as an illustration of reality; the second relates to the coming of the messianic age in which the new order prevails.

Practical Considerations in 9:1–10

We know that the Jewish people of Jesus' day were burdened by the numerous manmade laws they had to observe (Matt. 23:3–4). For instance, on one particular Sabbath, Jesus' disciples picked ears of grain, rubbed them in their hands, and ate the kernels of grain (Luke 6:1 and parallels). In the eyes of the Pharisees, the disciples had transgressed the commandment "Remember the Sabbath day by keeping it holy" (Exod. 20:8). They were guilty on two counts: first, they had violated the manmade law "you shall not harvest on the Sabbath" when they picked the ears of grain; and second, they had rubbed the ears of grain in their hands in violation of the manmade law "you shall not thresh on the Sabbath."

Although we may smile at practices current in first-century Palestine, we ought to be careful not to elevate our traditions to the level of law and enforce them rigidly. Especially with traditions relating to worship services, we have a tendency to be unbending. Although many of our traditions have become sacred, we should be careful not to stress external observances of certain practices at the expense of internal attitudes and needs. "The sacrifices of God are a broken spirit; a broken and contrite heart, O God, you will not despise" (Ps. 51:17).

Through the faithful preaching of God's Word, man's conscience must become increasingly sensitive. As a compass needle constantly points north, so our consciences always must turn to Scripture first. Our spiritual forefathers, discussing matters pertaining to life or conduct, used to ask, "What does the Bible say?" That question is still valid today.

Greek Words, Phrases, and Constructions in 9:6–10

Verse 6

κατεσκευασμένων—the perfect passive participle in the genitive absolute construction derives from the intensive compound verb κατασκευάζω (I prepare thoroughly). The perfect tense denotes the resultant state of those things that had been arranged.

διὰ παντός—the noun χρόνου (in the genitive case) should be supplied to make the phrase complete, but it was never used. The expression means "always, continually, regularly."

εἰσίασιν—this present active indicative form is from the compound verb εἰς (into) and εἶμι (I go).

Verse 7

ἅπαξ τοῦ ἐνιαυτοῦ—the genitive of time is introduced by the adverb ἅπαξ (once). This adverb appears fifteen times in the New Testament, eight of which are in Hebrews.

ἀγνοημάτων—apart from three occurrences in the Septuagint, this noun appears only once in the New Testament. The -μα ending indicates the result of an action; the privative ἀ (not) combines with the verb γνοέω (from γινώσκω, I know). The genitive case depends on the preposition ὑπέρ.

Verse 8

δηλοῦντος—the present active participle in the genitive absolute construction from δηλόω (I make known) is followed by the indirect discourse clause with the accusative subject τὴν ὁδόν (the way) and the perfect passive infinitive πεφανερῶσθαι (from φανερόω, I reveal).

τῶν ἁγίων—because the adjective can be either masculine or neuter, it can be interpreted to mean "saints" (masculine) or "holy things" (neuter). The context favors the use of the neuter with the translation *Most Holy Place*. The genitive is objective.

ἐχούσης—with the noun σκηνῆς (tabernacle) it forms the genitive absolute construction.

Verse 9

ἐνεστηκότα—the perfect active participle derives from ἐνίστημι (I am present, have come).

τελειῶσαι—the aorist active infinitive from τελειόω (I complete, perfect) governs the accusative present participle τὸν λατρεύοντα (the worshiper). The aorist is ingressive.

Verse 10

μόνον—an adverb. The meaning is "only that and nothing more." As a first word in the sentence, it is rather emphatic.

διορθώσεως—derived from διά (through) and ὀρθός (straight), this noun in the genitive case conveys the idea of making something thoroughly straight, of bringing about a reformation.

---

11 When Christ came as high priest of the good things that are already here, he went through the greater and more perfect tabernacle that is not man-made, that is to say, not a part of this creation.   12 He did not enter by means of the blood of goats and calves; but he

entered the Most Holy Place once for all by his own blood, having obtained eternal redemption. 13 The blood of goats and bulls and the ashes of a heifer sprinkled on those who are ceremonially unclean sanctify them so that they are outwardly clean. 14 How much more, then, will the blood of Christ, who through the eternal Spirit offered himself unblemished to God, cleanse our consciences from acts that lead to death, so that we may serve the living God!

15 For this reason Christ is the mediator of a new covenant, that those who are called may receive the promised eternal inheritance—now that he has died as a ransom to set them free from the sins committed under the first covenant.

16 In the case of a will, it is necessary to prove the death of the one who made it, 17 because a will is in force only when somebody has died; it never takes effect while the one who made it is living. 18 This is why even the first covenant was not put into effect without blood. 19 When Moses had proclaimed every commandment of the law to all the people, he took the blood of calves, together with water, scarlet wool and branches of hyssop, and sprinkled the scroll and all the people. 20 He said, "This is the blood of the covenant, which God has commanded you to keep." 21 In the same way, he sprinkled with the blood both the tabernacle and everything used in its ceremonies. 22 In fact, the law requires that nearly everything be cleansed with blood, and without the shedding of blood there is no forgiveness.

23 It was necessary, then, for the copies of the heavenly things to be purified with these sacrifices, but the heavenly things themselves with better sacrifices than these. 24 For Christ did not enter a man-made sanctuary that was only a copy of the true one; he entered heaven itself, now to appear for us in God's presence. 25 Nor did he enter heaven to offer himself again and again, the way the high priest enters the Most Holy Place every year with blood that is not his own. 26 Then Christ would have had to suffer many times since the creation of the world. But now he has appeared once for all at the end of the ages to do away with sin by the sacrifice of himself. 27 Just as man is destined to die once, and after that to face judgment, 28 so Christ was sacrificed once to take away the sins of many people; and he will appear a second time, not to bear sin, but to bring salvation to those who are waiting for him.

E. Jesus' Sacrificial Blood
9:11–28

1. Christ's Blood Cleanses Our Consciences
9:11–14

Repetition is the mother of learning. This is a basic rule that the author of Hebrews applies consistently. He introduced the theme of the high priest's entering the Most Holy Place in 9:7; he expands it in 9:11–12; and he summarizes it in 9:25.[9] Christ offered his own blood to obtain redemption for his people.

11. When Christ came as high priest of the good things that are already here, he went through the greater and more perfect tabernacle that is not man-made, that is to say, not a part of this creation. 12. He did not enter by means of the blood of goats and calves; but he entered the Most Holy Place once for all by his own blood, having obtained eternal redemption.

---

9. Young, "The Gospel According to Hebrews 9," p. 199.

These two verses form one beautifully constructed, balanced sentence.[10] The basic thought is that Christ went through the tabernacle (v. 11) and entered the Most Holy Place (v. 12). Commentators have been puzzled by the identity of the tabernacle: what does the author of Hebrews mean by the phrase *greater and more perfect tabernacle?*

Let us note the following points as we seek an answer.

a. *Arrival.* The author returns to his theme that Jesus is high priest (2:17; 3:1; 4:14; 5:5, 10; 6:20; 7:26–28; 8:1–2). He purposely introduces Jesus as Christ (not as Jesus or Son) to show that he is the Messiah, the One whom Israel expected to come. And he states that Christ's arrival has indeed occurred, for Christ has appeared as high priest.

The text can be translated in two ways. Some translations read, "Christ came as high priest of the good things that are already here." Other translations have the reading "of the good things to come." The one translation relates to the present; the other, to the future.

How do we resolve the difficulty? That is, which of the two translations is to be preferred? The reading *good things to come* is similar to the wording of Hebrews 10:1. Possibly a scribe copying 9:11 may have been influenced by the reading of 10:1. The more difficult reading is the one that lacks an immediate parallel and therefore is preferred—in this case "the good things that are already here."

What are these good things that Christ has provided? The author of Hebrews does not say. But we assume that he intimates the close fellowship that God has with his people, the knowledge of God and his law in the hearts and minds of his people, and the remission of sin that God has given his people (8:10–12). The blessings Christ has brought since his coming are innumerable; for this reason the author speaks in general terms and writes "the good things that are already here."

b. *Destiny.* Christ "went through the greater and more perfect tabernacle that is not man-made." We ought to note that the writer has chosen the official title *Christ* and not the personal name *Jesus.* He places the emphasis, then, on the official function of Christ as high priest.

Also we note that 9:11 has a parallel in 8:1–2, "We do have such a high priest, who sat down at the right hand of the throne of the Majesty in heaven, and who serves in the sanctuary, the true tabernacle set up by the Lord, not by man." And 9:11 has another parallel in 9:24, "For Christ did not enter a man-made sanctuary that was only a copy of the true one; he entered heaven itself, now to appear for us in God's presence." These passages reveal that "the greater and more perfect tabernacle" is in heaven, that is, in the presence of God. We ought not take the words *went through* literally in the sense that Christ passed through the tabernacle to another place. In 4:14 the author of Hebrews writes that "we have a great high priest who has gone

---

10. In the original Greek, verses 11 and 12 form one lengthy sentence that has been carefully constructed. See the article by Albert Vanhoye, "Par la tente plus grande et plus parfaite . . ." in *Bib* 46 (1965): 1–28. Also see James Swetnam's article, "The Greater and More Perfect Tent. A Contribution to the Discussion of Hebrews 9:11," in *Bib* 47 (1966): 91–106.

through the heavens." He wishes to convey the thought that Jesus has gone into heaven.

The writer expresses himself rather pointedly by saying that the greater and more perfect tabernacle is not manmade, "that is to say, not a part of this creation." In the early centuries of the Christian era, Bible interpreters understood the word *tabernacle* in 9:11 to mean Christ's body, but the author of Hebrews rules this out by his explanatory comment that the tabernacle is "not a part of this creation." Anything belonging to God's creation, even the visible sky, is ruled out by the author's pointed comment. God's dwelling in heaven, where angels surround his throne and the numberless multitudes of saints sing his praises, is uncreated; it does not belong to creation revealed to us by God's Word and work. The tabernacle that Moses built and God filled with his glory (Exod. 40:35) differs from "the greater and more perfect tabernacle" in heaven. The heavenly tabernacle gives the saints free access to God because no veil separates God and man. Christ opened the way to God on the basis of his mediatorial work on earth.

c. *Means.* How did Christ enter heaven? By means of his death on the cross! The writer puts it this way: "He did not enter by means of the blood of goats and calves; but he entered the Most Holy Place once for all by his own blood."

The expression *goats and calves* is a reminder of the Day of Atonement. On that day, once a year, the high priest entered the Most Holy Place with the blood of a bull and of a goat. The high priest had to sprinkle the blood of the bull as an atonement for his own sins and the blood of the goat as an atonement for the sins of the people (Lev. 16:11–17). The implication is that the blood of animals effected forgiveness and reconciliation.

How different with the great high priest Jesus Christ! Christ "entered the Most Holy Place once for all by his own blood, having obtained eternal redemption." He is high priest and sacrifice at the same time. He is the people's representative before God. He sheds his blood in behalf of his people.

Obviously, the writer depicts the atoning work of Christ figuratively. That is, when Jesus died on the cross, he did not enter the Most Holy Place of the temple. And when he cried, "It is finished" (John 19:30), he did not need to take his blood into the heavenly tabernacle.[11] Christ completed his atoning work on Calvary's cross. When he suffered and died on the cross, in a sense he entered the Most Holy Place of the temple. God affirmed this by tearing the curtain of the temple in two from top to bottom (Mark 15:38).

d. *Purpose.* The purpose for Christ's sacrificial death is summarized in the clause *having obtained eternal redemption.* After his figurative entrance into the Most Holy Place of the temple in Jerusalem, he once for all, on the strength of his own sacrificial blood shed on the cross, procured redemption of ever-

---

11. Leon Morris, *The Expositor's Bible Commentary*, vol. 12, *Hebrews* (Grand Rapids: Zondervan, 1981), p. 86.

lasting validity for all his people. Christ obtained this redemption for himself, that is, for the benefit of his people.[12] He bought his people with the price of his blood; he redeemed them with his death. Their redemption became eternally valid when Christ figuratively entered the Most Holy Place. "In bringing many sons to glory," writes the author of Hebrews, "it was fitting that God . . . should make the author of their salvation perfect through suffering" (2:10).

13. The blood of goats and bulls and the ashes of a heifer sprinkled on those who are ceremonially unclean sanctify them so that they are outwardly clean. 14. How much more, then, will the blood of Christ, who through the eternal Spirit offered himself unblemished to God, cleanse our consciences from acts that lead to death, so that we may serve the living God!

These two verses show contrast—characteristic of the Epistle to the Hebrews. The author states a fact that relates to the animal sacrifices of the Old Testament era. God had stipulated by law how sinners might be cleansed and restored to holiness. He had ordained these laws to sanctify those who were ceremonially unclean. But merely observing these laws affected the sinner only externally, not internally. Those who were sprinkled, as the text says, were cleansed with respect to their bodies. Their consciences, however, remained unaffected.

In the preceding verse (v. 12) the writer already mentioned "the blood of goats and calves." The reference, of course, is to the stipulations the high priest had to observe on the Day of Atonement (Lev. 16). In addition, the author now describes the practice of sprinkling the unclean person with water of cleansing (Num. 19). A red heifer in perfect condition and that had never been harnessed had to be slain and burned. As it was being burned, the priest had to throw cedar wood, hyssop, and scarlet wool onto the heifer. The ashes then were gathered and kept for use in the ceremony of sprinkling the water of cleansing.

Anyone who had touched a dead body was considered unclean for seven days. Ashes from the burned heifer were put into a jar; fresh water was poured over them; and with hyssop dipped into the water, an unclean person was sprinkled on the third and seventh days.

Allegorical interpretations of this passage (Num. 19) are numerous. For example, the heifer symbolizes the propagation of life; ashes are an antidote to pollution; the colors of the red heifer and of the scarlet wool portray vitality; cedar wood stands for durability; and hyssop is the emblem of cleansing. However, fanciful elucidations are highly subjective and ultimately of little value. We do well to look at the author's purpose for introducing the matter of "the blood of goats and bulls and the ashes of a heifer."

The author contrasts two incidents: the ceremonial acts performed by the believer to secure cleansing and the shedding of the blood of Christ. The

---

12. Burkhard Gärtner, *NIDNTT*, vol. 3, p. 529.

religious observance of the Day of Atonement, although significant in itself, nevertheless fostered an external perception of the sacrifices. This became especially evident in the act of sprinkling the water of cleansing on the person who was declared unclean because of defilement. A person who had touched a dead body was considered unclean, but water of cleansing sanctified him. The thought that uncleanness was something external and not internal prevailed. Jesus rebuked the Pharisees on one occasion when he said, "Now then, you Pharisees clean the outside of the cup and dish, but inside you are full of greed and wickedness" (Luke 11:39).

The argument that the author develops proceeds from the lesser to the greater. The *lesser* part is the ceremonial act of using the blood of goats and bulls and the ashes of a heifer to sanctify a sinner externally. The *greater* part is that the blood of Christ cleanses the sinner's conscience to make him an obedient servant of God. Unquestionably, sin is an internal matter that issues from the heart of man. The writer of Proverbs calls the heart "the wellspring of life" (4:23). And Jesus describes the heart as the source of evils: "For from within, out of men's hearts, come evil thoughts, sexual immorality, theft, murder, adultery, greed, malice, deceit, lewdness, envy, slander, arrogance and folly" (Mark 7:21–22). The act of cleansing man from sin must begin with his inner being; as the author of Hebrews writes, "our consciences." How are our consciences cleansed? I call attention to the following phrases.

a. "The blood of Christ." Although the blood of animals in a sense served the same function as did the blood of Christ, the contrast introduced by "how much more" is so immense that we cannot speak of a comparison. The blood of Christ is the agent that cleanses the conscience of man, that breaks him from "acts that lead to death," and that makes man willing and ready to serve God. Christ's blood cleanses man from sin. Robert Lowry sang:

> For my cleansing this I see—
> Nothing but the blood of Jesus;
> For my pardon this my plea—
> Nothing but the blood of Jesus.

b. "Through the eternal Spirit." Some translations render the word *spirit* with a capital letter, and others use a lower-case letter. In the original Greek all the letters were written uniformly, so that we cannot determine whether the author of Hebrews meant one or the other.

What can we learn from the theological context of this passage? What do the Scriptures say? Again, we cannot be certain as to the exact intention of the author as we view the rest of Scripture. The four Gospels say nothing about the Holy Spirit's role in the suffering of Christ. On the other hand, when Jesus preached in his hometown synagogue at Nazareth, he read from the prophecy of Isaiah, "The Spirit of the Lord is on me" (Luke 4:18; Isa. 61:1; and see Isa. 42:1). Says Donald Guthrie, "The statement in Hebrews is a logical deduction from the gospel portrait of Jesus."[13] Even though we would have been more certain if the author had written "Holy Spirit" instead of "eternal Spirit," we know that Jesus was indeed led by the Holy Spirit. For example, Luke writes: "Jesus, full of the Holy Spirit, returned from the Jordan and was led by the Spirit in the desert, where for forty days he was tempted by the devil" (Luke 4:1–2).

c. Christ "offered himself unblemished." As high priest, Christ presented himself as a sacrifice. He offered himself to God spontaneously and blame-lessly. But unlike the Aaronic high priest who had to sacrifice an animal to remove his own sin, the sinless Christ offered his body for the sins of his people. He laid down his life for his sheep. As John, describing the death of Jesus on the cross, testifies, Jesus "bowed his head and gave up his spirit" (19:30). Jesus willingly, purposefully, and conscientiously faced death and offered himself to God.

Why did Christ offer himself to God? To "cleanse our consciences from acts that lead to death." In 6:1 the author introduced the phrase "from acts that lead to death." The wording implies the destructive effects of sin in the life of the believer. That is, the blood of Christ effectively cleanses man's conscience by turning him from a life that leads to spiritual death to a life spent in love and obedient service for God. The believer keeps God's com-mandments not because of obligation but out of a sense of gratitude for what Christ in God has done for him. The believer, saved from a life of sin that leads to death, now lives a life of service for his living God.

Doctrinal Considerations in 9:11–14

The biblical doctrine of atonement encounters opposition voiced by those ad-vocates who portray God as a God of love. They contend that God could not have demanded that Christ shed his blood in order to appease an angry God.[14] They object to a "blood theology" because, they say, it runs contrary to the love of God. However, the love of God does not annul his justice. Man is a sinner who because of sin stands condemned before God. Of his own free will, Christ took the place of sinful man and paid the penalty for him. By shedding his own blood, Christ endeavored to obtain eternal redemption, that is, "to bring salvation to those who are waiting for him" (9:28). The writer of Hebrews unequivocally teaches the doc-trine of atonement. Says he, Christ "entered the Most Holy Place once for all by his own blood" (9:12).

In this section and in other parts of his epistle, the author of Hebrews teaches the unique doctrine that Christ became priest and sacrifice. Christ became subject and object at the same time: he served at the altar as priest and was laid on the altar as sacrifice. Christ shed his blood as sacrifice on Calvary's cross and figuratively

---

13. Donald Guthrie, *New Testament Theology* (Downers Grove, Ill.: Inter-Varsity, 1981), p. 568. Also see F. F. Bruce, *The Epistle to the Hebrews,* New International Commentary on the New Testament series (Grand Rapids: Eerdmans, 1964), p. 205.
14. Louis Berkhof, *Systematic Theology* (Grand Rapids: Eerdmans, 1953), p. 382.

as high priest entered the Most Holy Place of the temple. Scripture teaches that the offering of his sacrifice was completed on earth; in the capacity of high priest, Christ entered "the greater and more perfect tabernacle" in heaven, that is, the presence of God.

The writer of Hebrews deletes numerous details from the laws concerning the Day of Atonement and the ceremonial cleansings for persons declared unclean. He purposely omits these details to put in stark relief the contrast between the external observance of religious ceremonies and the inner transformation of a man cleansed by the blood of Christ. That, for him, is the difference between life in the days of the old covenant and that in the era of the new covenant.

Greek Words, Phrases, and Constructions in 9:11–14

Verse 11

παραγενόμενος—this aorist middle (deponent) participle of the verb παραγίνομαι (I arrive, appear) shows that Christ served as high priest before his ascension to heaven. The participle, expressing a temporal connotation, points to the entire ministry of Christ. The preposition παρά (alongside of) strengthens the main verb γίνομαι and gives it direction.

γενομένων—the aorist middle participle from γίνομαι (I am, become) has a variant in a number of leading manuscripts. The variant is μελλόντων—present active participle of μέλλω (I am about to). The first reading, however, seems to have a better geographical representation of manuscripts and is therefore preferred. See also 10:1 for similar wording of the second reading.

χειροποιήτου—a compound adjective consisting of the noun χείρ (hand) and the noun ποιητής (a maker). The adjective occurs six times in the New Testament and generally is used with reference to buildings; that is, temples (Mark 14:58; Acts 7:48; 17:24; Eph. 2:11; Heb. 9:11, 24).

Verse 12

τὰ ἅγια—the substantivized adjective in the neuter plural preceded by the definite article stands for the sanctuary and even the Most Holy Place in tabernacle and temple.

λύτρωσιν—this noun conveys the meaning *ransom, deliverance, redemption* and appears three times in the New Testament (Luke 1:68; 2:38; Heb. 9:12). In the context of Hebrews 9 the word connotes as much ransom as redemption. See also 9:15.

Verse 13

εἰ—the particle introduces a simple fact conditional clause that expresses certainty. The apodosis to this lengthy sentence is given in 9:14.

ῥαντίζουσα—the feminine present active participle from the verb ῥαντίζω (I sprinkle) modifies the noun σποδός (ashes), which is feminine. Perhaps it is best to link the participle only to the noun *ashes* and not to the preceding noun τὸ αἷμα (blood).

253

Verse 14

πόσῳ μᾶλλον—the combination of these two words always introduces a so-called dative of degree of difference. The difference lies in the comparison stated in the two parts of the conditional sentence, beginning with εἰ γάϱ (for if).

αἰωνίου—some manuscripts have the variant reading ἁγίου (holy) that removes the ambiguity created by the reading *eternal*. However, the manuscript evidence lacks the strength to give the reading *holy* authenticity.

καθαϱιεῖ—the future tense from the verb καθαϱίζω (I cleanse) expresses certainty because its fulfillment is expected.

ἡμῶν—to determine whether the reading should be ἡμῶν (our) or ὑμῶν (your) is not easy, because the manuscript evidence is equally divided. Perhaps the author's use of exhortations in the broader context favors the translation *our*.[15] On the whole, although the difference itself is insignificant, the author seems to include himself whenever he addresses the recipients of his epistle.

---

2. Christ's Death and the First Covenant
9:15

Weaving his artistic verbal cloth, the author of Hebrews is ready to bring in the concepts of mediator and covenant. In chapter 8, especially verse 6, he introduced the role of mediator that Jesus has been given. Having explained Christ's death and its effect in chapter 9, he now develops the significance of this mediatorial role in relation to the covenant that God has made with his people.

15. For this reason Christ is the mediator of a new covenant, that those who are called may receive the promised eternal inheritance—now that he has died as a ransom to set them free from the sins committed under the first covenant.

When the author writes "for this reason," he wants us to look at verses 13 and 14 specifically and the preceding context generally. In these two verses, the writer contrasts the sacrifices of the first covenant with the sacrifice of Christ that introduces a new relationship. In verse 15, the author summarizes and says, "Christ is the mediator of a new covenant."

Before we proceed any further, we ought to take note of the institution of the first covenant, recorded in Exodus 24. Moses read the Law of God to the Israelites, who responded, "Everything the LORD has said we will do" (v. 3). Then burnt offerings and fellowship offerings were presented to God, and blood was sprinkled on the altar. Moses then read the Book of the Covenant to the people, who said, "We will do everything the LORD has said; we will obey" (v. 7). Thereupon Moses, sprinkling blood on the people, said, "This is the blood of the covenant that the LORD has made with you in accordance with all these words" (v. 8).

---

15. Bruce M. Metzger, *A Textual Commentary on the Greek New Testament* (London and New York: United Bible Societies, 1975), p. 668.

Here are the characteristics of this covenant:

1. The covenant God made with his people had two parties: God and the Israelites entered into a solemn commitment on the basis of the content of the Book of the Covenant.
2. The covenant was sealed by the death of animals that were offered to God. The blood of those animals was sprinkled on altar and people.
3. The covenant was ratified by the people who promised obedience to God.

Why did this covenant become obsolete? The author quotes a lengthy passage from Jeremiah 31 in chapter 8, and in the first part of the next chapter he explains that the regulations of the first covenant were external (9:1, 10). "The gifts and sacrifices being offered were not able to clear the conscience of the worshiper" (9:9). Sins committed against God, as a violation of the covenant promise, could not be erased from man's conscience by presenting gifts and offerings to God. The blood of animals sacrificed to atone for man's transgressions sanctified him outwardly, but inwardly man struggled with a guilty conscience.[16] The first covenant, then, needed to be replaced.

By his sacrifice on the cross, Christ validated the new covenant that he instituted at the time he celebrated the Passover with his disciples. He said: "This cup is the new covenant in my blood, which is poured out for you" (Luke 22:20; also see the parallel passages in Matt. 26:28; Mark 14:24; and I Cor. 11:25).

Christ has become the mediator of this new covenant (12:24). He stands between God and man. By his death he removes sin and guilt, and thus all "those who are called may receive the promised eternal inheritance." Through the mediatorial work of Christ, they who are effectively called inherit salvation. And that inheritance is eternal.

What is the meaning of "new" in the expression *new covenant*? First, the new comes forth out of the old. That is, the new covenant has the same basis and characteristics as the old covenant. Next, in both covenants, sacrifices were presented to God; but whereas the sacrifices offered to atone for the transgressions of the people in the time of the first covenant could not set the sinner free, the supreme sacrifice of Christ's death redeemed God's people and paid for their sins. Moreover, in the structure of the first covenant, the mediator (i.e., the high priest) was imperfect. In the new covenant Christ is the mediator who guarantees the promise of salvation. God puts his laws in the minds and writes them on the hearts of his redeemed people, so that as a result they know God, experience remission of sin, and enjoy covenantal fellowship with him.

---

16. "The implication is that these transgressions were the reason for the lack of efficacious reception of the heritage connected with the first diatheke." See James Swetnam, "A Suggested Interpretation of Hebrews 9:15–18," in *CBQ* 27 (1965): 380.

Greek Words, Phrases, and Constructions in 9:15

Verse 15

γενομένου—the aorist middle (deponent) participle of the verb γίνομαι (I am, become) in the genitive singular is part of the genitive absolute construction with the noun θανάτου (death). The aorist denotes single occurrence.

ἐπί—as a preposition with the dative it expresses time or occasion and is translated "under." The GNB translation is, "while the first covenant was in effect."

παραβάσεων—this articular noun in the genitive plural of παράβασις (transgression) is used figuratively: it refers to the sinner who committed the transgression.

κεκλημένοι—of all the New Testament epistles, only Hebrews has the perfect passive participle of καλέω (I call). The use of the perfect expresses the all-inclusive extent of the call.

---

3. Christ's Blood Procures Forgiveness
9:16–22

The word *covenant* implies sin. Sin necessitates the making of a new covenant and the shedding of blood. The shedding of blood leads to death and remission of sin.

16. In the case of a will, it is necessary to prove the death of the one who made it, 17. because a will is in force only when somebody has died; it never takes effect while the one who made it is living.

At times a word can have two entirely different meanings that can be distinguished only by the context in which they are used. For example, the word *letter* may mean either "one of the letters of the alphabet" or "an epistle." In English this one word serves two meanings; in other languages two different words express these meanings.

In the original Greek one word (*diathēkē*) serves the purpose of conveying the concepts *covenant* and *will* or *testament*. In 9:15 the context is a religious setting, and the word means "covenant"; the author speaks of the new covenant of which Christ is the mediator and of the first covenant which, by implication, has been superseded. In the next two verses (16 and 17), the writer switches from the religious setting to a legal framework.[17] Now he introduces the concept of a last will. A lawyer draws up a will for a client who apportions his belongings to various people and agencies. But this last will becomes valid only upon the death of the person who made it. While the person is living, the will is nothing but a document, even though a lawyer testifies to its legality. Also this will may be changed and rewritten, but the moment the maker of the will dies, the words in the will are unalterable.

How do verses 16 and 17 relate to 9:15? What is the connection between the word *covenant* and the word *will*? In verse 15 the author teaches that Christ, the mediator of a new covenant, died a sacrificial death to redeem

---

17. Johannes Behm, *TDNT,* vol. 2, p. 131.

those who will receive their promised inheritance. In the following two verses, he states that the death of the maker of a will validates this document. The implication is that the maker of the covenant is God, who has also made a will. Christ, the Son of God, is not the maker of a covenant or a will. Functioning as a mediator and as a guarantor, he sees that the conditions of the covenant are met and that its promises are honored. Christ died to fulfill these conditions. But at the same time, Christ's death validates the last will and testament, so that believers indeed "may receive the promised eternal inheritance" (9:15). Christ is their guarantor.

In a sense, verses 16 and 17 serve as an analogy. But analogies have their limitations, and so does this one. Upon his death, a person leaves his possessions to his heirs; these heirs themselves face death and in time die. Christ, however, died but rose from the dead; the heirs receive an eternal inheritance and live with him forever.[18]

18. This is why even the first covenant was not put into effect without blood. 19. When Moses had proclaimed every commandment of the law to all the people, he took the blood of calves, together with water, scarlet wool and branches of hyssop, and sprinkled the scroll and all the people. 20. He said, "This is the blood of the covenant, which God has commanded you to keep." 21. In the same way, he sprinkled with the blood both the tabernacle and everything used in its ceremonies. 22. In fact, the law requires that nearly everything be cleansed with blood, and without the shedding of blood there is no forgiveness.

Two matters stand out: first, the expression *first covenant* relates to the same phrase in 9:15. Therefore the two intervening verses, given in the form of an analogy, may be placed within parentheses.[19] Second, in verses 18–22 the word *blood* appears six times. Because of this repetition it receives emphasis in this section. We shall examine the term *blood* in the context of each verse in which it occurs.

a. "Not put into effect without blood." The institution of the first covenant is recorded in Exodus 24. Moses read the law of God to the people, presented burnt offerings and fellowship offerings to God, sprinkled the blood of young bulls (sacrificed in these offerings) on the altar and on the people, read the Book of the Covenant to the people, and said, "This is the blood of the covenant that the LORD has made with you in accordance with all these words" (Exod. 24:8). The writer of Hebrews observes that this first covenant was sealed with blood.[20] And he notes the connection between the first and the second covenants: Christ shed his blood and thus sealed this

---

18. R. C. H. Lenski in *The Interpretation of the Epistle to the Hebrews and of the Epistle of James* (Columbus: Wartburg, 1946), p. 307, cautions not to press the analogy too far. Also see Bruce, *Hebrews,* p. 213.

19. Geerhardus Vos, *The Teaching of the Epistle to the Hebrews* (Grand Rapids: Eerdmans, 1956), p. 40.

20. John Murray, *The Covenant of Grace* (London: Tyndale, 1953), p. 27.

new covenant with his blood. His death made the new covenant valid and effective.

b. "The blood of calves." If we compare the biblical account of the institution of the first covenant, recorded in Exodus 24, with the description in Hebrews 9:19, we must conclude that the writer of Hebrews relied on oral tradition, extrabiblical material, or the five books of Moses. Perhaps he gained his material from various passages of these books. The differences are pronounced:

Exodus 24:5–6, 8	*Hebrews 9:19*
Then [Moses] sent young Israelite men, and they offered burnt offerings and sacrificed young bulls as fellowship offerings to the LORD. Moses took half of the blood and put it in bowls, and the other half he sprinkled on the altar…[and] on the people.	[Moses] took the blood of calves [and goats],[21] together with water, scarlet wool and branches of hyssop, and sprinkled the scroll and all the people.

On the Day of Atonement the priests offered a young bull and a goat (Lev. 16:3–28). The author of Hebrews, therefore, could have combined the account of the sacrificial ceremony of the Day of Atonement with that of the institution of the first covenant. Also, he may have gleaned the phrase "scarlet wool and branches of hyssop" from the description of the ceremony of the cleansing of a person with an infectious skin disease (Lev. 14:4, 6). In these verses the expression *scarlet yarn and hyssop* occurs. Then, in the passage that describes the water of cleansing, hyssop, scarlet wool, and water are mentioned (Num. 19:6, 9, 18).

According to the Exodus account, Moses sprinkled the blood of young bulls on the altar and on the people. He read to the people from the Book of the Covenant. We may assume that he sprinkled blood on this book, too. Philip Edgcumbe Hughes surmises that "on the day of solemn ratification of the former covenant, Moses would have sprinkled not only the altar he had built and the people but also the book he had written."[22]

c. "The blood of the covenant." From a New Testament perspective we immediately see a resemblance between the words of Moses cited by the author of Hebrews and the words spoken by Jesus when he instituted the Lord's Supper.

Moses said to the Israelites, "This is the blood of the covenant that the LORD has made with you in accordance with all these words" (Exod. 24:8).

---

21. Most translations include the words *and goats*. The NIV omits them, no doubt on the basis of the principle that "in general the shorter reading is to be preferred." Editions of the Greek New Testament support the inclusion of the disputed words, although they are put in brackets to indicate a measure of uncertainty.

22. Philip Edgcumbe Hughes, *Commentary on the Epistle to the Hebrews* (Grand Rapids: Eerdmans, 1977), p. 376.

The writer of Hebrews has Moses say, "This is the blood of the covenant, which God has commanded you to keep" (Heb. 9:20). The variation of "the LORD has made with you" and "God has commanded you" is one of form, not of content.

We would have expected the author of Hebrews to refer directly to the well-known words spoken by Jesus at the institution of the Lord's Supper and repeated whenever this supper is celebrated. Jesus said, "This is my blood of the covenant, which is poured out for many" (Mark 14:24). The purpose for Christ's shed blood is given more explicitly in Matthew's Gospel: "for the forgiveness of sins" (Matt. 26:28). The connection between the words that Moses spoke when the first covenant was instituted and the words that Jesus uttered when he brought into practice the celebration of the Lord's Supper is plain. Perhaps because of the self-evident link, the writer of Hebrews has left the missing details for the readers of his epistle to supply.

d. "Sprinkled with the blood." Once again we note a difference between the Old Testament account (Exod. 40:9–11) and the words of the author of Hebrews (9:21). When Moses set up the tabernacle, God told him to "take the anointing oil and anoint the tabernacle and everything in it; consecrate it and all its furnishings, and it will be holy" (Exod. 40:9). The writer of Hebrews, however, asserts that Moses "sprinkled with the blood both the tabernacle and everything used in its ceremonies" (9:21). In the account of the ordination of Aaron and his sons, we read that Moses killed a bull and with the blood purified the altar. Already he had consecrated the tabernacle and everything in it, including the altar, with oil; he even anointed Aaron with oil (Lev. 8:10–15). Because of this parallel account in the Book of Leviticus, we can safely assume that the writer with his intimate knowledge of the Old Testament Scriptures relied on the account of Leviticus more than that of Exodus.

Josephus comments on the inaugural ceremonies of the tabernacle and the ordination of Aaron and his sons. He, too, speaks of purifying Aaron and his sons and their garments "as also the tabernacle and its vessels, both with oil that had been previously fumigated . . . and with the blood of bulls and goats."[23] Josephus, like the author of Hebrews, is fully acquainted with the biblical record in Leviticus 8. Yet both writers contend that Moses purified with the sprinkled blood the tabernacle and its vessels. That information is not found in Leviticus; most likely it had come to them by oral tradition.

e. "Cleansed with blood." The writer of Hebrews testifies that his constant emphasis on purification with blood is not his own idea. He bases it on the law of God. Says he, "In fact, the law requires that nearly everything be cleansed with blood" (9:22). That law is recorded in Leviticus 17:11 where God through Moses says to the Israelites: "For the life of a creature is in the blood, and I have given it to you to make atonement for yourselves on the altar; it is the blood that makes atonement for one's life."

---

23. Josephus, *Antiquities* 3.206 (LCL).

Note that the author writes, "The law requires that *nearly* everything be cleansed with blood" (italics added). The term *nearly* leaves room for exceptions, because some items might be cleansed by water or by fire (see Lev. 15:10 and Num. 31:22–24).

f. "Shedding of blood." The second part of Hebrews 9:22 is even more direct: "and without the shedding of blood there is no forgiveness." These two—the pouring out of blood and the forgiveness of sin—go hand in hand. The one does not exist without the other. The first part of the verse implies that exceptions were permitted, for the author says that "nearly everything" needs to be cleansed with blood. But in the second half of the verse, the writer does not allow exceptions. He posits negatives: *without* the shedding of blood there is *no* forgiveness.

The absolute demand for blood to secure remission of sin responds to the terms of the covenant. Transgression of the laws of the covenant that were agreed upon and ratified by the Israelites constitutes a serious offense. This sin can be removed only by death, that is, the substitutionary death of an animal whose blood is shed for the sinner.

The new covenant, instituted by Christ on the eve of his death, is sealed in his blood that has been shed on Calvary's cross for remission of sin. Jesus' words, "This is my blood of the covenant, which is poured out for many for the forgiveness of sins" (Matt. 26:28), are clearly echoed in the second part of Hebrews 9:22.

Doctrinal Considerations in 9:16–22

When God promised Abraham that he would bless him and give him numerous descendants, he confirmed his promise with an oath. The oath that God swore made his promise unalterable (Gen. 22:16–17; Heb. 6:16–17). When God made a covenant with his people, he gave it to them as a last will and testament. To make this will valid for his people, God's Son died. Upon Christ's death, the will became effective, and its wording, unalterable.

God made a covenant with sinful people. He instructed them to sacrifice animals whose shed blood would cleanse them from sin. But because the people of Israel did not remain faithful to the covenant God had made with them, through the prophet Jeremiah he announced that he would make a new covenant with people upon whose minds and hearts his law was written (Jer. 31:31–34; Heb. 8:8–12).

Christ became the mediator of this new covenant, and through his faithfulness, he fulfilled its demands. For the sins of his people he shed not the blood of animals but his own. The writer of Hebrews posits God's demand for restitution of a broken covenant agreement by saying, "Without the shedding of blood there is no forgiveness" (9:22). The counterpart of this statement is the Christian's jubilation, "Because Christ shed his blood, I have been forgiven!"

Greek Words, Phrases, and Constructions in 9:16–22

Verse 16

φέρεσθαι—the present passive infinitive of φέρω (I carry) means "to bring news by announcing it." The translation *to announce* is therefore acceptable: "The death of a testator must be announced" (*Moffatt*).

Verse 17

ἐπὶ νεκροῖς—the Greek is rather descriptive by saying that a will is made valid on the basis of corpses; that is, when death has occurred.

μήποτε—the use of the negative participle μή instead of οὐ is noteworthy, for it shows that the author expects debate on the validity of a will.

Verse 18

ἐγκεκαίνισται—this compound verb in the perfect passive indicative (from ἐγκαινίζω, I renew, initiate) portrays the lasting effect of the first covenant from the day God initiated it in the Sinai desert to the time Christ instituted the new covenant on the eve of his death.

Verse 19

λαληθείσης—the genitive absolute construction governs this aorist passive participle of λαλέω (I speak) and the adjective πάσης (every) and noun ἐντολῆς (commandment). The words ἐντολή and ὁ νόμος (the law) are virtually synonymous in this context. Moses read them to the people from the scroll.

Verse 22

σχεδόν—an adverb derived from the verb ἔχω (I have, hold), that is, "to be held near," and thus "nearly, almost." The word appears three times in the New Testament (Acts 13:44; 19:26; Heb. 9:22).

αἱματεκχυσίας—the author coins a noun from the noun αἷμα (blood) and the verb ἐκχύνω (I pour out). These two words also occur in Jesus' declaration, "This is my *blood* of the covenant, which is *poured out* for many for the forgiveness of sins" (Matt. 26:28, italics added; see also Mark 14:24 and Luke 22:20).

ἄφεσις—this noun includes the concept *sins*. It refers to the forgiveness of sins, and as such it is an echo of Matthew 26:28.

---

4. Christ's Perfect Sacrifice
9:23–28

Characteristic of the author's style is his frequent repetition of a certain theme. For example, in chapter 8 he wrote that as high priest Christ entered the heavenly sanctuary (8:2). He repeats this theme in the next chapter.

Christ came as high priest, he says, and "went through the greater and more perfect tabernacle that is not man-made" (9:11). Once more he returns to this theme in the following verses (9:23–28).

23. It was necessary, then, for the copies of the heavenly things to be purified with these sacrifices, but the heavenly things themselves with better sacrifices than these.

In this text two matters stand out: the copies of heavenly things and the heavenly things themselves. The copies, of course, are the earthly sanctuary and everything pertaining to it; the heavenly sanctuary is in the presence of God. We shall consider these two successively.

a. "Copies of the heavenly things." The author says that the purification of the tabernacle, altar, utensils, and scroll was necessary. The word *necessary* indicates that the law requires that these items be purified. And that is exactly what the author states in the preceding verse (9:22). He concludes that "without the shedding of blood there is no forgiveness." God himself instructed the people of Israel, through Moses, to cleanse themselves from sin by shedding the blood of animals at the altar of the sanctuary. This blood was adequate to allow the high priest to enter the Most Holy Place of the tabernacle, but a better sacrifice was needed before a mediator could appear in God's presence in heaven.

b. "The heavenly things themselves." The tabernacle built by Moses was "a copy and shadow of what is in heaven" (8:5). The heavenly sanctuary is "the greater and more perfect tabernacle that is not man-made" (9:11). Christ entered this sanctuary after he had shed his blood on Calvary's cross.

The author of Hebrews now refers to the blood of Christ as "better sacrifices." The plural term *sacrifices* stands for the singular "blood of Christ." The adjective *better* marks the difference between earthly things and heavenly things; that is, the blood of animals cleansed the tabernacle and everything pertaining to it, so that the high priest might enter the Most Holy Place. The blood of Christ cleanses the heavenly things, so that he might enter heaven in God's presence (9:24).

Was it necessary to cleanse heavenly things? The heavenly sanctuary is not manmade and therefore is untainted by sin. It does not need to be cleansed. Before we are able to answer the question, we must understand the expression *heavenly things* in a spiritual sense. The true sanctuary, says the author of Hebrews, is heaven itself (9:24), and heaven is the place where God and his people dwell together. It is the place where the people of God serve him by offering themselves as living sacrifices. Then why does the author write that the heavenly things had to be cleansed? Heaven became a sanctuary for God's people only when the blood of Christ was shed for them. Christ's blood, then, became the basis for their entrance into heaven.

Without Christ's blood God does not open heaven for us and does not accept our living sacrifices. We stand condemned before God in our sins, and heaven remains closed to us. However, the blood of Christ has made heaven into a sanctuary for us, so that we may live there. At the same time, it remains God's dwelling place.

The blood of Christ provides remission of our sins but also sanctifies our presence in heaven. It makes us more delightful than angels and our service of praise more acceptable than that of the angels. We are God's adopted sons and daughters who are "heirs of God and co-heirs with Christ" (Rom. 8:17).

Moreover, Christ's shed blood gives heaven itself added significance. Not only is heaven the sanctuary for God's people, but it is also the place where its inhabitants testify of Christ's redeeming love, his marvelous grace, and his sanctifying power. To Christ they sing a new song, recorded in Revelation 5:9–10:

> With your blood you purchased men for God
> from every tribe and language and people and nation.
> You have made them to be a kingdom and priests to serve our God.

24. For Christ did not enter a man-made sanctuary that was only a copy of the true one; he entered heaven itself, now to appear for us in God's presence.

Even though God caused the veil in the temple to split from top to bottom at the time of Jesus' death (Matt. 27:51), Jesus himself never entered "a man-made sanctuary." When the author of Hebrews spoke of "better sacrifices" (9:23), he made a comparison between the animal sacrifices and the blood of Christ. Although we readily see that Christ's sacrifice is better, we see that in essence the comparison is inadequate.

Animal sacrifices were temporary measures; the high priests, mortal; and the sanctuary, a manmade copy. By contrast, Christ's once-for-all sacrifice is permanent; our high priest, eternal; and the heavenly sanctuary, the true one.

The writer of the epistle first notes which sanctuary Christ did not enter, namely, a manmade copy of the original. The high priest once a year entered the Most Holy Place of this earthly sanctuary to enter the presence of God on behalf of the people. Second, the author notes that Christ "entered heaven itself" and, by implication, the true sanctuary. He entered heaven as high priest to represent us in the presence of God. Only once a year the Levitical high priest spent a few moments in the Most Holy Place as man's representation before God; however, Christ, always in God's presence, constantly represents us as our attorney-at-law (Rom. 8:34; Heb. 7:25; I John 2:1).

25. Nor did he enter heaven to offer himself again and again, the way the high priest enters the Most Holy Place every year with blood that is not his own. 26a. Then Christ would have had to suffer many times since the creation of the world.

By drawing a parallel with the Levitical high priest, the author of Hebrews underscores the profound differences between Christ's priesthood and the

Levitical priesthood. The writer is questioned, as it were, by a Jewish reader who poses a number of arguments.

a. As high priest Christ could never have entered the Most Holy Place of an earthly sanctuary. He belonged to the tribe of Judah, not to the tribe of Levi.

True, that is why he entered heaven.

b. A Levitical high priest annually offered sacrificial blood before God in the Most Holy Place. If Christ is high priest, he will have to do the same in heaven.[24]

Correct, but Christ offered himself on the cross. He shed his blood at Calvary, not in the heavenly sanctuary.

c. The high priest offered the sacrifices of a bull and a goat on the Day of Atonement, but Christ offered himself only once.

Yes, but apart from those people who were raised from the dead, man cannot die twice.

d. On the Day of Atonement the high priest presented animal blood to God, but Christ offered his own blood.

True; if Christ had offered blood other than his own, he would have been identical to the Levitical high priest. Note that the high priest could not present his own blood as a sacrifice, because he himself was a sinner. Christ, the sinless One, could and did offer his own blood for sinners.

e. Once a year the high priest went in and out of the Most Holy Place, but Christ entered the heavenly sanctuary only once.

Exactly. If Christ had to leave heaven and come to earth to die once more—which is absurd—his atoning work would be worthless. Christ's sacrifice is unique.

The writer of Hebrews sums up the matter in one telling statement: If Christ had to offer himself again and again, he "would have had to suffer many times since the creation of the world." And that, of course, cannot be. Rather, Christ's sacrifice on the cross is so effective that it removes the sins of all the Old Testament believers. His sacrifice is retroactive and goes back to the creation of the world, that is, to the time that Adam fell into sin. Thus, Christ's sacrifice is valid for all believers, whether they lived before or after the coming of Christ. His sacrifice is for all times.

26b. But now he has appeared once for all at the end of the ages to do away with sin by the sacrifice of himself.

After making a statement that obviously could not be true, the author now describes conclusively the reason for Christ's coming into the world: "to do away with sin." The adverb *now* refers not to time but to reality. The writer in effect is saying: "This is how it is."

Why did Christ appear on this earth? In simple terms: to cancel sin. He

---

24. The NIV correctly inserts the phrase *did he enter heaven*. The sentence in the Greek is incomplete and needs to be supplemented with the inserted phrase to achieve balance and to complete the meaning.

removed the debt of sin that was written on the believer's account. Christ's coming brought an end to that debt. And the account now shows the word *paid*.

How did Christ remove sin? He himself became the sacrifice that was required to pay for the sins of the whole world (I John 2:2). As Christ's forerunner, John the Baptist, put it: "Look, the Lamb of God, who takes away the sin of the world!" (John 1:29). Christ had no substitute. He sacrificed himself as a substitute for sinners. By his death he paid the debt "to take away the sins of many people" (9:28).

What is the significance of Christ's appearance? The Levitical high priest year after year entered the inner sanctuary. His entrance into God's presence had only a temporal effect. By contrast, Christ's appearance is a single occurrence—it happened once for all. He entered heaven once, that is, at the time of his ascension. The effect of his single appearance lasts forever.

When did Christ come? The author of Hebrews writes, "at the end of the ages." This does not have to refer to the end of time, because in the same context the writer says that Christ will appear a second time (v. 28). The expression apparently points to the total impact of Christ's coming and the effect of his atoning work. And because of his triumph over sin, we live in the last age.

27. Just as man is destined to die once, and after that to face judgment,   28. so Christ was sacrificed once to take away the sins of many people; and he will appear a second time, not to bear sin, but to bring salvation to those who are waiting for him.

The writer of the epistle has a fondness for the word *once*; he uses it eight times (6:4; 9:7, 26, 27, 28; 10:2; 12:26, 27).

In the contrast expressed in these two verses, the term *once* takes a prominent place: "man is destined to die once" and "Christ was sacrificed once." Because of Adam's sin God pronounced the sentence of death upon the human race (Gen. 3:19). Every person faces death once, with the exception of those people who were raised from the dead. No one can escape death. By becoming human, Christ was placed under the same death sentence. He, too, died once.

By implication, man receives the death penalty because of sin. The author of Hebrews indicates as much by adding the clause "and after that to face judgment." Death and judgment follow each other in logical sequence, for man must appear in court to account for sin. "For God will bring every deed into judgment, including every hidden thing, whether it is good or evil" (Eccl. 12:14).

The exact time of the judgment the writer of the epistle purposely omits. He calls attention not to judgment as such but to Christ who "will appear a second time." His concluding remark is that Christ brings "salvation to those who are waiting for him." And that is most important. The writer does not minimize the significance of the judgment. He introduces the topic here; in the next chapter he applies it.[25] He says that if we "deliberately keep on sinning," then all that is left is "a fearful expectation of judgment and of raging fire that will consume the enemies of God" (10:26, 27).

In the comparison that characterizes verses 27 and 28, the emphasis falls on Christ. The Messiah was sacrificed once; and he will appear again.

At the conclusion of his teaching about the atoning work of Christ, the author writes that Christ was sacrificed. In the context of this chapter, the writer has made it clear that Christ offered himself as a sacrifice for sin. Therefore, the words *was sacrificed* must be understood within the context in which they are used: Christ offered himself for the purpose of removing the sins of many people.

Already Isaiah prophesied about the redemptive work of Christ. In the well-known chapter on the suffering Messiah, Isaiah writes: "My righteous servant will justify many, and he will bear their iniquities. . . . For he bore the sin of many, and made intercession for the transgressors" (53:11–12).

Not only has Christ completed his atoning work as high priest; he has also given us the promise that he will return. The Scriptures are very explicit about the return of Christ; it is a promise that is mentioned again and again. When Christ returns, says the author of Hebrews, he comes not to remove sin. That task he finished when he came the first time. When he comes again, he brings salvation to those who are awaiting him.

The last part of verse 28 expresses a note of joy and happiness: Christ is coming! They who are eagerly expecting his return constantly pray the petition found at the conclusion of the New Testament and uttered in response to Jesus' promise, "Yes, I am coming soon." They pray, "Amen. Come, Lord Jesus" (Rev. 22:20).

Joyfully the believers look forward to the day of Jesus' return, for then the Lord will dwell forever with his people, as he has promised. Upon his return he will bring full restoration to all who eagerly await him. When Christ dwells forever with his people, they experience salvation full and free.

Doctrinal Considerations in 9:23–28

The Epistle to the Hebrews is an epistle that features contrasts; in every chapter and in numerous verses, the author compares Christ with angels, Moses, Aaron, or the Levitical priesthood. In this particular section, he shows the unsurpassable excellence of the high-priestly work of Christ. A high priest was appointed to represent the people before God, but the actual time he spent in God's presence was minimal; it occurred only once a year on the Day of Atonement. Our great high priest entered heaven once and stays forever in the presence of God as our mediator, advocate, intercessor, and guarantor.

Moreover, the high priest had to present animal blood before God in the Most Holy Place. His own blood would have been unworthy because he himself was a

---

25. Guthrie, *New Testament Theology*, p. 863.

sinner. But even animal blood had only a limited effect, for the high priest had to appear before God every year again with additional blood. The writer of Hebrews somewhat later observes, "It is impossible for the blood of bulls and goats to take away sins" (10:4). The sacrifice of Christ's blood, however, has lasting effect. It terminates the ruling power of sin in the mind of man (Rom. 8:2).[26] Christ's blood cleanses the church, so that he is able to present it "without stain or wrinkle or any other blemish . . . holy and blameless" (Eph. 5:27). And the blood of Christ wipes the record clean: a sinner forgiven by God stands before him as if he had never sinned at all.

Last, the Levitical high priest, after performing his duties in the inner sanctuary, reappeared to the people he had represented before God. But when Jesus returns from the heavenly sanctuary, he comes to restore his people by granting them the gift of salvation. When Christ comes again, "he will appear as the perfecter of salvation" for all those who put their trust in him and await his return.[27]

Greek Words, Phrases, and Constructions in 9:23−28

Verse 23

ἀνάγκη—this noun appears four times in Hebrews (7:12, 27; 9:16, 23) and expresses a condition imposed by a law or binding obligation. It is stronger than the verb πρέπει (it is fitting) and similar to δεῖ (it is necessary). The noun stands first in the sentence to receive emphasis.

Verse 24

ἐμφανισθῆναι—the aorist passive infinitive of ἐμφανίζω (I make visible) expresses the culminative idea. Christ's appearance is once for all and has lasting significance.

Verse 26

ἔδει—the use of the imperfect active indicative in this clause is the same as in a conditional sentence that expresses unreality. The first part (*protasis*) of the conditional sentence is lacking. The writer gives only the last part (*apodosis*).[28]

πεφανέρωται—the perfect passive indicative of φανερόω (I reveal, appear) refers to "Christ previously hidden from view in heaven but after his incarnation made visible on earth as a man among men."[29]

---

26. John Owen, *An Exposition of Hebrews*, 7 vols. in 4 (Evansville, Ind.: Sovereign Grace, 1960), vol. 6, p. 403.

27. Johannes Schneider and Colin Brown, *NIDNTT*, vol. 3, p. 215.

28. "When a condition is assumed as unreal and refers to present time, the imperfect tense is used both in the protasis and apodosis in normal constructions. . . . [In] Heb. 9:26 . . . we only have apodosis." A. T. Robertson, *A Grammar of the Greek New Testament in the Light of Historical Research* (Nashville: Broadman, 1934), p. 887.

29. Joseph H. Thayer, *A Greek-English Lexicon of the New Testament* (New York, Cincinnati, and Chicago: American Book Company, 1889), p. 648.

Verse 27

κρίσις—the author has chosen a word that reveals action, that is, the process of judging. By contrast, the noun κρίμα shows the result of this judicial activity; it is the verdict, the sentence of condemnation.

Verse 28

ὁ Χριστός—note the use of the definite article. Although the noun occurs without the article in 9:24, here the emphasis on Christ's designation, the Messiah, is pronounced.

προσενεχθείς . . . ἀνενεγκεῖν—the author has a play on words with two verb forms that find their roots in φέρω (I bear), πρός (toward), and ἀνά (up).

Summary of Chapter 9

To point out the supremacy of Christ's priesthood, the author of Hebrews presents a description of the earthly tabernacle, its contents, and the priestly ministry in and around this sanctuary. The sacrifices, however, were external observances, for they were unable to cleanse the guilty conscience of the sinner.

With the blood of animals man could not obtain redemption, for he remained unclean. How different the sacrifice of Christ! By his one offering, Christ cleansed the sinner's conscience, led him from death to life, and became the mediator of the new covenant.

In this chapter the author presents an exposition on the meaning of the covenant. Because sin affected the stipulations of the first covenant, God told Moses to sacrifice animals and to sprinkle their blood on the tabernacle, its contents, and on the people. "Without the shedding of blood there is no forgiveness."

When Christ came in the official capacity of high priest and mediator of the new covenant, he offered himself once for all and entered the heavenly sanctuary to appear in behalf of the believers in the presence of God. By his death on the cross, Christ removed "the sins of many people."

The chapter ends with the promise that Christ will return, not to remove sin as a high priest, but to bring salvation to those who wait for him in faith. Jesus is coming again.

10

Jesus: High Priest and Sacrifice, *part 3*

(10:1–18)

and More Exhortations

(10:19–39)

Outline

Jesus: High Priest and Sacrifice (continued)

More Exhortations

10 1 The law is only a shadow of the good things that are coming—not the realities themselves. For this reason it can never, by the same sacrifices repeated endlessly year after year, make perfect those who draw near to worship. 2 If it could, would they not have stopped being offered? For the worshipers would have been cleansed once for all, and would no longer have felt guilty for their sins. 3 But those sacrifices are an annual reminder of sins, 4 because it is impossible for the blood of bulls and goats to take away sins.

5 Therefore, when Christ came into the world, he said:
> "Sacrifice and offering you did not desire,
>> but a body you prepared for me;
> 6 with burnt offerings and sin offerings
>> you were not pleased.
> 7 Then I said, 'Here I am—it is written
>> about me in the scroll—
> I have come to do your will, O God.' "

8 First he said, "Sacrifices and offerings, burnt offerings and sin offerings you did not desire, nor were you pleased with them" (although the law required them to be made). 9 Then he said, "Here I am, I have come to do your will." He sets aside the first to establish the second. 10 And by that will, we have been made holy through the sacrifice of the body of Jesus Christ once for all.

11 Day after day every priest stands and performs his religious duties; again and again he offers the same sacrifices, which can never take away sins. 12 But when this priest had offered for all time one sacrifice for sins, he sat down at the right hand of God. 13 Since that time he waits for his enemies to be made his footstool, 14 because by one sacrifice he has made perfect forever those who are being made holy.

15 The Holy Spirit also testifies to us about this. First he says:
> 16 "This is the covenant I will make with them
>> after that time, says the Lord.
> I will put my laws in their hearts,
>> and I will write them on their minds."

17 Then he adds:
> "Their sins and lawless acts
>> I will remember no more."

18 And where these have been forgiven, there is no longer any sacrifice for sin.

Jesus: High Priest and Sacrifice

F. Jesus' Effective Sacrifice
10:1–18

1. Shadows of Reality
10:1–4

The author of Hebrews is about ready to furnish additional proof from Scripture that Jesus had come to set aside the numerous offerings for sin.

God had prepared a body for Jesus, who appeared to do God's will. And by his sacrifice Christ effectively removed sin. The difference between the sacrifices offered during the Levitical era and the one and only sacrifice of Christ is profound.

1. The law is only a shadow of the good things that are coming—not the realities themselves. For this reason it can never, by the same sacrifices repeated endlessly year after year, make perfect those who draw near to worship.

As is characteristic of the epistle, contrast is a predominant feature in this verse. Here the law, presumably the entire Old Testament, is depicted as a shadow of the real things. That is, the author of Hebrews contrasts earthly institutions with heavenly realities. He already introduced this contrast when he mentioned the sanctuary in the desert. He called it "a copy and shadow of what is in heaven" (8:5).

The word *shadow* has numerous connotations. Here are a few familiar ones: the shadow of the umbrella protected them from the hot sun; fleeting shadows dart across the field; this man cannot stand in the shadow of his predecessor; the shadow of the sundial indicates the time of day.

The author of Hebrews employs the term *shadow* in the sense of an indicator of "the good things that are coming." The wording is similar to that of 9:11, "the good things that are already here." The writer fails to explain what he means by the words *good things that are coming*. We assume that he means the blessings of salvation (see Isa. 52:7; Rom. 10:15).

The noun *shadow,* however, stands for the dim representation of the real things; the writer calls them "the realities themselves." What he actually means is this: these realities bask in the heavenly light and cast a shadow (as an indicator) upon practices stipulated by Old Testament law. We know that these practices pertained to the sacrifices offered to God year after year. The law prescribes the ritual, for example, for the sacrifices on the Day of Atonement. But this legislated worship failed to make the worshiper holy. "The law is only a shadow," writes the author.

What then are the realities themselves? Simply put, they are the atoning work of Christ and its consequences. Later the writer says, "Because by one sacrifice [Christ] has made perfect forever those who are being made holy" (10:14). In Christ, then, we inherit the good things to come.

> How vast the benefits divine
> which we in Christ possess!
> We are redeemed from guilt and shame
> and called to holiness.
> —Augustus M. Toplady

The sacrifices of the Levitical system were unable to perfect the worshiper. That observation minimizes not the Old Testament law, which God himself enacted, but the effectiveness of the sacrifices.

2. If it could, would they not have stopped being offered? For the worshipers would have been cleansed once for all, and would no longer have felt guilty for their sins. 3. But those sacrifices are an annual reminder of sins, 4. because it is impossible for the blood of bulls and goats to take away sins.

The author's rhetorical question demands a positive answer: yes, they would have stopped. But among the people of Israel who lived before and after the exile, the art of offering sacrifices to God had become a mechanical deed. It was no longer a matter of a personal relationship with God. A mechanical conception of the act of sacrificing animals to God controlled the mind of the worshipers. The act of shedding blood seemed to them to secure forgiveness of sins.

The Jews should have known, however, that these animal sacrifices were totally inadequate. Animal sacrifices were mere substitutions, nothing more. Although God had instituted these practices so that man would not have to offer his own life, they were only substitutes. The writers of the Old Testament Scriptures voice God's dissatisfaction with the sacrificial system. They write that the significance of a sacrifice to God ought to be found not in the animal that was offered but in the worshiper's heart that was broken and contrite (I Sam. 15:22; Ps. 40:6; 50:8–10; 51:16–17; Isa. 1:10–12; Jer. 7:21–23; Hos. 6:6; Amos 5:21–23).

God takes sin seriously. He is not satisfied with a sacrifice that is presented to him without a broken and a contrite heart. He desires a life of obedience and dedication to doing his will.[1]

Believers in Old Testament times knew that an animal sacrifice would not be able to cleanse them from sin. Every year on the Day of Atonement the high priest would enter the Most Holy Place with blood of a slain animal. But the high priest could never say to the worshipers: "This blood has removed your sins once for all, and therefore this sacrifice has been the last." No, the annual return of the high priest from the inner sanctuary on the Day of Atonement proved that the sacrifices were inadequate and ineffective. The worshipers continued to feel guilty for their sins.

The covenant that God had made with the people of Israel had one serious deficiency: it was unable to take away the consciousness of sin. "The main deficiency in the old covenant was that it could not accomplish forgiveness."[2] The blood of sacrificial animals cannot take away sin. Only the blood of Christ, shed once for all, removes sin and cleanses man's consciousness of guilt. The sacrifice of Christ put an end to the sacrifices stipulated by Old Testament law. "Christ is the end of the law," says Paul (Rom. 10:4). The writer of Hebrews intimates a variant: "Christ is the end of old-covenant sacrifices." By offering himself as sacrifice, Christ marked the end of the

---

1. Simon J. Kistemaker, *The Psalm Citations in the Epistle to the Hebrews* (Amsterdam: Van Soest, 1961), p. 126.
2. Julius Schniewind and Gerhard Friedrich, *TDNT*, vol. 2, p. 284.

Levitical priesthood with its sacrifices and offerings, and terminated the validity of the first covenant.

2. Jesus Christ Set Aside the Shadows to Establish Reality
10:5–10

5. Therefore, when Christ came into the world, he said:
"Sacrifice and offering you did not desire,
    but a body you prepared for me;
6. with burnt offerings and sin offerings
    you were not pleased.
7. Then I said, 'Here I am—it is written about me
    in the scroll—
    I have come to do your will, O God.' "

The contrast between the Levitical sacrificial system and Christ's sacrifice is summarized in the expression *therefore*. "When Christ came into the world" is actually a Semitic way of saying "when Christ was born."[3] Especially in the Gospel of John, the phrase refers to Christ's coming in human form to his people (1:9; 6:14; 12:46; 16:28; 18:37).

The author of Hebrews introduces a psalm quotation that comes from David. However, the author makes the quotation messianic by putting it on the lips of Christ. Note the emphasis the writer places on the fact that Christ speaks: "he said" (10:5), "then I said" (10:7), "first he said" (10:8), and "then he said" (10:9). With this quotation the author bases his teaching on the Scriptures of the Old Testament. In this quotation, Christ says that he offers himself to do the will of God. And that is the essential meaning of true sacrifice.

Before we come to the purpose of the quotation in the context of this chapter, we should note these points.

a. *Parallelism.* The words of Psalm 40:6–8 display typical Hebraic parallels common in the wisdom literature of the Old Testament. The author of Hebrews is fully aware of this literary device, because in his explanation of the quoted words he changes the poetical lines to prose (10:8–9).

In parallel columns, here is the quotation in somewhat abbreviated form:

Sacrifice	—	with burnt offerings
and offering		and sin offerings
you did not desire	—	you were not pleased
but a body you prepared	—	here I am, I have come to
for me		do your will

---

3. German scholars aptly refer to this linguistic similarity. See SB, vol. 2, p. 358; Edward Riggenbach, *Der Brief an die Hebräer* (Leipzig and Erlangen: Deichert, 1922), p. 300; Gustaf Dalman, *The Words of Jesus* (Edinburgh: Clark, 1909), p. 172; and Otto Michel, *Der Brief an die Hebräer*, 10th ed. (Göttingen: Vandenhoeck and Ruprecht, 1957), p. 223.

These three parallel expressions constitute the message Christ brings. The last lines, of course, are completely dissimilar in wording; the meaning about doing the will of God, in the body God prepared for Christ, is clear.

b. *Difference.* The difference in wording between Hebrews 10:5 ("but a body you prepared for me") and Psalm 40:6 ("but my ears you have pierced") appears formidable. It stems from the Greek translation, the Septuagint, which the writer of Hebrews used exclusively in quoting from the Old Testament. For him and for his readers, the Septuagint version was Scripture. We have no knowledge how the difference arose. Attempts to explain this difference by referring to Exodus 21:6 and Deuteronomy 15:17 are not at all convincing. In these passages a law is prescribed concerning a servant who voluntarily decides to stay with his master for life and as a sign of servanthood has his ear lobe pierced. Not the outer ear but the inner ear is important. Therefore, Isaiah 50:5 is more helpful. The prophet writes, "The Sovereign LORD has opened my ears, and I have not been rebellious." The prophet listens obediently to God's voice to do his will. And that is the meaning of the words "but my ears you have pierced."

c. *Meaning.* The two lines "sacrifice and offering" and "with burnt offering and sin offerings" are not merely eloquent poetry but also indicate the totality of Jewish sacrifices. Although God told the people of Israel to offer sacrifices, he took no pleasure in these offerings. Telling are the words of Samuel to Saul recorded in I Samuel 15:22:

> Does the LORD delight in burnt offerings and sacrifices
>   as much as in obeying the voice of the LORD?
> To obey is better than sacrifice,
>   and to heed is better than the fat of rams.

God is not satisfied only with sacrifices. Sacrifices are but substitutes. Instead he wants genuine, devoted service. He delights in perfect obedience to his will.

God prepared a body for Christ, and Christ showed complete submission to his Father's will. The psalmist says that God pierced—that is, opened—the ears. The author of Hebrews adopts the reading "a body you prepared for me."[4] Both readings signify the same thing: ears have been opened so one may hear and obey God's will. Whereas the one word—ears—is more specific, the other—body—is more general. But both convey the same meaning.

Why did the writer of Hebrews quote Psalm 40:6–8? He found in this quotation the best proof to show the reality that puts aside the shadow of the Levitical sacrifices. The sacrifices, only shadows, are not important; obe-

---

4. The writer of Hebrews quotes from the Septuagint because this translation was familiar to him. In his epistle he provides no indication that he was familiar with the Hebrew text. The Septuagint reading, however, presents the basic meaning of the Hebrew original, even though the words differ.

dience to God's will counts. God delights in obedience (Rom. 12:1–2). Moreover, the words "Here I am, I have come to do your will, O God" have been recorded "in the scroll."[5] That is, the psalmist already testifies to scriptural warrant for the coming of Christ in human form. Although no references are provided, we assume that the psalmist had in mind the books of Moses. And last, in this quotation Christ speaks directly in the first person singular—"Here I am . . . I have come to do your will, O God"—about his work of redemption.

8. First he said, "Sacrifices and offerings, burnt offerings and sin offerings you did not desire, nor were you pleased with them" (although the law required them to be made). 9. Then he said, "Here I am, I have come to do your will." He sets aside the first to establish the second. 10. And by that will, we have been made holy through the sacrifice of the body of Jesus Christ once for all.

As he has shown in other places, the author is an expert in understanding the meaning of the Old Testament Scriptures (see, for example, 2:8–9; 3:16–19; 7:2–3). After quoting Psalm 40:6–8, he presents a brief commentary on these verses. He turns the poetry of the psalm citation into prose and comes to the heart of the matter. He divides the quotation into two parts.

First, Christ said, "Sacrifices and offerings, burnt offerings and sin offerings you did not desire, nor were you pleased with them." The first part, then, expresses the thought that God found no pleasure in the offerings his people presented to him. The author immediately adds the concessive statement, "although the law required them to be made."

But let us go back to the beginning of human history recorded in Genesis. God looked with favor on the offering that Abel brought him, but with disfavor on Cain's offering. Why was Abel's offering—"fat portions from some of the firstborn of his flock"—acceptable, and the offering of Cain—"some of the fruits of the soil"—unacceptable (Gen. 4:3–5)? The writer of Hebrews answers by saying, "By faith Abel offered God a better sacrifice than Cain did. By faith he was commended as a righteous man, when God spoke well of his offerings" (11:4).

The author of Hebrews asserts not that God has an aversion to offerings presented to him, but that sacrifices offered without faith and obedience are an abomination (Isa. 1:11–14; Amos 5:21–22). Through Hosea God says to Israel, "For I desire mercy, not sacrifice, and acknowledgment of God rather than burnt offerings" (6:6).

Second, Christ said, "Here I am, I have come to do your will." The term *will* appears four times in the context of this chapter (10:7, 9, 10, 36). It occurs only once more in Hebrews, in the benediction (13:21). The will of

---

5. Representative translations of this phrase are "in the scroll of the book" (JB), "roll of the book" (RSV), "volume of the book" (KJV), and "the book of the Law" (GNB).

God is central in the life of Christ, and the author of Hebrews exhorts his readers to persevere and do the will of God.

God takes no delight in sacrifices. He is pleased with the unfaltering trust and obedience of his children. Christ, the Son of God, came into this world for the purpose of showing submission and learning "obedience from what he suffered and, once made perfect, he became the source of eternal salvation for all who obey him" (Heb. 5:8–9).

The author summarizes the two statements of Christ in one pithy sentence, "He sets aside the first to establish the second." Christ offered himself as a sacrifice for sin on Calvary's cross. By this act he terminated the Levitical sacrificial system—he set it aside. Next he showed his faithfulness to God by doing his will, and thus he established the second. Doing the will of God caused Jesus to pray in the agony he experienced in the Garden of Gethsemane, "Father, if you are willing, take this cup from me; yet not my will, but yours be done" (Luke 22:42). Christ fully submitted to God's will in perfect obedience.

And what is the effect of that will? The author succinctly includes all believers by saying, "And by that will, we have been made holy." Salvation originates not in man, but in God. By his will we are separated from the world and called to holiness. The implication is that we were alienated from God and lived in a world of sin. Because of God's will, this has changed: "we have been made holy." The verb indicates that at a given moment, someone acted in our behalf to sanctify us, and we have become pure. The writer of Hebrews already referred to this act when he wrote of God's will to make the author of salvation perfect through suffering. "Both the one who makes man holy and those who are made holy are of the same family" (2:11). The one who makes men holy is Jesus Christ.

Rather pointedly the author writes, "Through the sacrifice of the body of Jesus Christ once for all." Apart from the last chapter of Hebrews, where the combination *Jesus Christ* appears twice (13:8, 21), the double name occurs only once in the instructional part of the epistle—in the present context. The writer wants to stress that both the human (Jesus) and the divine (Christ) natures were involved in making us holy. Moreover, Jesus Christ performed the act of sanctification in our behalf by sacrificing his body. This is the only place in the epistle where the author mentions the *bodily* sacrifice of Jesus. The purpose for the stress on the "sacrifice of the body of Jesus Christ" is to demonstrate the reality of his physical death. It is also a reflection of the Septuagint wording of the psalm citation, "but a body you prepared for me" (Heb. 10:5).

And last, the sacrifice of Christ's body is the counterpart of the animal sacrifices of the Levitical system. The difference, however, between the bodily sacrifice of Christ and the sacrifices of animals is profound: Christ's sacrifice was *once for all*; animal sacrifices were countless. Next, Christ offered his own body as a sacrifice; the worshiper in the era of the first covenant offered substitutes. Then also, Christ presented his body voluntarily; animals

277

were sacrificed forcibly against their will.[6] Christ's obedience to his Father's will effected our liberation from the power of sin and conformed us to a life dedicated to God's service. Thus we reflect God's holiness and perfection as we respond to Jesus' exhortation, "Be perfect, therefore, as your heavenly Father is perfect" (Matt. 5:48; see also Lev. 11:44–45; 19:2; 20:7; I Peter 1:16).

Doctrinal Considerations in 10:1–10

For readers of Jewish origin who considered the law of God their most precious possession, the author's assertion—"the law is only a shadow of the good things that are coming"—must have been astounding. If the law was their treasured possession, it would be difficult to imagine that far more desirable things were in store for them. The writer of Hebrews calls these things "the realities themselves," and he explains that they consist of Christ and his redemptive work. Writing to Jewish readers in Colosse about religious observances, Paul says almost the same thing. He writes, "These [regulations] are a shadow of the things that were to come; the reality, however, is found in Christ" (Col. 2:17).

By quoting and applying the verses from Psalm 40, the author of Hebrews shows that Christ has come to do God's will. In doing that will, Christ offered his body as a sacrifice, fulfilled the requirements of the Aaronic priesthood, and terminated the Levitical sacrifices. If Christ had fulfilled only the demands of the Aaronic priesthood, however, there would not have been a new covenant. The writer of Hebrews teaches that after Christ had offered himself without blemish to God, he became the mediator of a new covenant. He cleansed the consciences of the members of this covenant, "so that we may serve the living God!" (9:14). This refers to a higher priesthood that is eternal; it is called the priesthood in the order of Melchizedek. Christ fulfilled the requirements of this priesthood in his dedication to do God's will.

When Christ came into the world, "he [set] aside the first to establish the second" (Heb. 10:9). The author of Hebrews uses the terms *first* and *another, new,* or *second* when he discusses the covenant (8:7, 13; 9:1, 15, 18). Explaining the psalm quotation in 10:8–9, the writer first quotes the words about the sacrificial system of the Aaronic priesthood and then cites the words pertaining to Christ's perfect obedience to God's will. These two verses, in effect, describe the two covenants and the two phases of Christ's priesthood. To atone for the sins of his people (2:17), Christ had to sacrifice his body once for all (10:10). He fulfilled the demands of the first covenant and terminated the first phase of his priesthood; that is, the Aaronic priesthood. Christ established the second covenant when he came to do God's will. Then he also established the second phase of his priesthood, the one of Melchizedek. The Aaronic priesthood typifies Christ's passive obedience; the priesthood of Melchizedek, Christ's active obedience.

---

6. James Denney, *The Death of Christ* (London: Tyndale, 1960), pp. 122, 131. Also see F. F. Bruce, *The Epistle to the Hebrews,* New International Commentary on the New Testament series (Grand Rapids: Eerdmans, 1964), p. 234; and Leon Morris, *The Expositor's Bible Commentary,* vol. 12, *Hebrews* (Grand Rapids: Zondervan, 1981), p. 100.

Greek Words, Phrases, and Constructions in 10:1–10

Verse 1

κατ' ἐνιαυτόν—the noun ἐνιαυτός (year) is preceded by the preposition κατά, which gives it a distributive meaning *annually.*

εἰς τὸ διηνεκές—the compound adjective derives from διά (through) and ἠνεκής (from ἤνεγκα, the aorist of φέρω, I carry, bear); it means "carrying through" or "continually." In the New Testament the phrase appears only in Hebrews (7:3; 10:1, 12, 14).

Verse 2

ἐπεὶ οὐκ ἂν ἐπαύσαντο—this is the second part (apodosis) of a second class (contrary-to-fact) conditional sentence.[7] The first part (protasis) is lacking and has been supplied as "otherwise" (JB, RSV), "were matters otherwise" (NAB), and "if it could" (NEB, NIV).

Verse 3

ἀνάμνησις—a noun with a -σις ending to denote a process. It derives from the verb ἀναμιμνήσκω (I remind), occurs four times in the New Testament (Luke 22:19; I Cor. 11:24, 25; Heb. 10:3), and "denotes an unassisted recalling."[8]

Verse 7

ἐν κεφαλίδι βιβλίου —the noun κεφαλίς is a diminutive of the noun κεφαλή (head). It referred to the knob of a rod that held a scroll (βιβλίον); eventually the noun κεφαλίς was used to designate the scroll itself.

γέγραπται—the perfect passive from the verb γράφω (I write) signifies resultant state with lasting effect.

Verse 8

ἀνώτερον—an adverb in the comparative degree from ἄνω (above); thus a higher place in the written column.

αἵτινες—this indefinite relative pronoun has a concessive connotation and may be translated "although."

Verse 9

εἴρηκεν—the perfect active of the deficient verb λέγω (I say) is the main verb of the sentence. The perfect tense indicates completed action with continuing result.

---

7. A. T. Robertson, *A Grammar of the Greek New Testament in the Light of Historical Research* (Nashville: Broadman, 1934), p. 963.
8. Joseph H. Thayer, *A Greek-English Lexicon of the New Testament* (New York, Cincinnati, and Chicago: American Book Company, 1889), p. 40.

Verse 10

ἡγιασμένοι ἐσμέν—the perfect periphrastic construction of the perfect passive participle of ἁγιάζω (I make holy) and the present tense of εἰμί (I am) express action with lasting effect. The participle is descriptive.

---

3. Jesus Offered One Sacrifice
10:11–14

11. Day after day every priest stands and performs his religious duties; again and again he offers the same sacrifices, which can never take away sins. 12. But when this priest had offered for all time one sacrifice for sins, he sat down at the right hand of God.

The quotation from Psalm 40:6–8 included the work of the high priest on the Day of Atonement and the daily duties of every priest. "Sacrifices and offerings, burnt offerings and sin offerings" comprise the entire sacrificial system carried out by the high priest and priests. The author of Hebrews, therefore, highlights the work of the priest and contrasts it with the redemptive accomplishment of Christ. The contrast is complete:

Verse 11	*Verse 12*
Day after day	But[9]
every priest	this priest
stands	sat down
he offers	when [he] had offered
again and again	for all time[10]
the same sacrifices	one sacrifice
which can never	for sins
take away sins	

Day after day the rituals at the sanctuary continued, for when the one priest offered the last sacrifice at the conclusion of a day, the next priest made preparations for the first sacrifice the next morning. Literally rivers of animal blood flowed because of these continual sacrifices; and the succession of the priests, who served by division and were chosen by lot (Luke 1:8–9), seemed to be unending. Innumerable priests had served in times before Jesus' appearance and many served during his ministry. The work of the priest was essentially futile; he had to do the same thing over and over again, and thus his work was never finished. He could never sit down to take

---

9. In the original Greek the two particles *men* and *de* express contrast in verses 11 and 12. They could be translated as "on the one hand" and "on the other hand," but the NIV has omitted a translation for *men* (v. 11) and gives *de* as "but" (v. 12).

10. The phrase *for all time* can be taken with the clause *when he had offered* or with the main verb *sat down*. The majority of translations take the phrase with the clause (NIV, NEB, MLB, RSV, ASV, RV, NKJV, KJV, and *Phillips*); others translate it with the main verb (JB, NAB, *Moffatt*).

a rest from his labors. As the writer of Hebrews puts it, "Every priest *stands*" (italics added). In the sanctuary the furniture included table, lamp, altar of incense, and the ark, but no chair. Furthermore, the sacrifices offered by the Levitical priest were powerless to free man from sin. The words *take away* actually mean to take away sins that completely envelop man and from which only Christ can free him.

By contrast, after offering his one sacrifice for all time Christ *sat down* because he had finished his redemptive task and terminated the Levitical priesthood. His sacrifice effectively removes sin and breaks the power of sin. He entered a period of rest after accomplishing his work, much the same as God rested from his labors upon concluding his work of creation.[11]

Christ entered heaven and took his seat of honor at the right hand of God. He was fully entitled to that place as the priest who has fulfilled his task of removing sin and as the king who has conquered sin and death. What a difference between the priest who performed his religious duties at the sanctuary and Christ, who sat down next to God.

> The priest of the Old Testament stands timid and uneasy in the holy place, anxiously performing his awful service there, and hastening to depart when service is done, as from a place where he has no free access, and can never feel at home; whereas Christ sits down in ever-lasting rest and blessedness at the right hand of Majesty in the holy of holies, His work accomplished, and He awaiting its reward.[12]

13. Since that time he waits for his enemies to be made his footstool, 14. because by one sacrifice he has made perfect forever those who are being made holy.

> The Lord unto His Christ has said,
> Sit Thou at My right hand
> Until I make Thine enemies
> Submit to Thy command.
> *—Psalter Hymnal*

Psalm 110:1 appears frequently in the Epistle to the Hebrews as a direct quotation or an allusion (1:3, 13; 8:1; 10:12; 12:2). Because of Jesus' interpretation and application of this verse in answer to the question of the Pharisees, "What do you think about the Christ? Whose son is he?" (Matt. 22:42 and parallels) and frequent allusions to this quotation in Paul's epistles (Rom. 8:34; I Cor. 15:25; Eph. 1:20; Col. 3:1), I assume that Psalm 110:1 was a basic tenet of faith in the early church. The author of Hebrews employs this verse almost verbatim; he modifies the wording to fit the context of his writing.

---

11. Michel, *Hebräer*, p. 266. Luke's description of "the Son of Man standing at the right hand of God" (Acts 7:56) ought not be forced, because of the symbolism involved.
12. Franz Delitzsch, *Commentary on the Epistle to the Hebrews*, 2 vols. (Edinburgh: Clark, 1877), vol. 2, p. 161.

Since the time of his ascension, Christ has been "waiting for the moment when his enemies will be made his footstool."[13] He waits for the appropriate time, much the same as a farmer waits for the land to yield its produce in harvest season (James 5:7; also see Heb. 11:10). His enemies are all those who oppose Christ's dominion, authority, and power. "The last enemy to be destroyed is death" (I Cor. 15:26). Christ waits for the final destruction of his enemies.

The conquering of Christ's enemies is not as important as the one offering by which he perfected for all times "those who are being made holy." The author of Hebrews teaches the same truth repeatedly. In 2:11 he writes, "Both the one who makes men holy and those who are made holy are of the same family." In 10:10 he refers to the will of God and says, "And by that will, we have been made holy through the sacrifice of the body of Jesus Christ once for all." And last, he speaks of "the blood of the covenant that sanctified" the sinner (10:29).

When does sanctification take place? The use of the present tense of 2:11 and 10:14 seems to indicate that making someone holy is a process, not a once-for-all act. "We have been made holy" (10:10) but are exhorted to "make every effort . . . to be holy" (12:14). We see that sanctification is something received but not yet achieved.[14]

The sacrifice of Christ, unique in itself, brought about holiness for the believer. That is, every believer receives these benefits of Christ's sacrifice on the cross: his sins are forgiven; his conscience is cleansed; he has peace with God, assurance of salvation, and the gift of life eternal. Christ has perfected the believer forever.[15] But even though the author writes that Christ "has made perfect forever those who are being made holy," he shows in other passages the work of perfection is not yet complete in the recipients of his epistle. They are encouraged to resist sin, endure hardship, and submit to discipline (12:4, 7, 9). Perfection, in a sense, is here already and is also not yet here. We have this certainty, however, that we are perfected in Christ, who removed our sin by his sacrifice.

4. Covenant, Law, and Forgiveness
10:15–18

In a few verses the writer of Hebrews brings the teaching part of his epistle to a close. He summarizes the scriptural teachings of Jeremiah 31:33–34, quoted in chapter 8, and draws the conclusion that forgiven sin is forgotten.

---

13. Ernst Hoffmann, *NIDNTT,* vol. 2, p. 245.

14. Donald Guthrie, *New Testament Theology* (Downers Grove, Ill.: Inter-Varsity, 1981), p. 661, asserts, "The N[ew] T[estament] is more concerned with the process of sanctifying or of becoming sanctified than with debating the nature of sanctification."

15. John Owen, *An Exposition of Hebrews,* 7 vols. in 4 (Evansville, Ind.: Sovereign Grace, 1960), vol. 6, p. 493. Owen writes that the purpose of Christ in offering himself was to sanctify the believer first and afterward to perfect him.

15. The Holy Spirit also testifies to us about this. First he says:
16. "This is the covenant I will make with them
after that time, says the Lord.
I will put my laws in their hearts,
and I will write them on their minds."

Once again the author demonstrates his high view of Scripture. He quotes two verses from the prophecy of Jeremiah and ascribes them to the Holy Spirit. In chapter 8, he introduces God as the speaker for this particular passage, but that is nothing new for the author of Hebrews. He introduces either God, Jesus, or the Holy Spirit as speaker. For him the Old Testament Scriptures are divine and are ascribed to the Triune God. God through the Spirit is the author of Scripture (see II Peter 1:19–21).

The writer repeats two verses from the passage quoted from Jeremiah 31:31–34 in chapter 8. The wording is not entirely the same, but the meaning is identical. The first verse (Jer. 31:33) gives the heart of the quotation: God's promise to establish a new covenant with his people. The author has chosen this text to illustrate that with the coming of Christ and the completion of his sacrificial work, the era of the new covenant has commenced. God makes a new covenant with his people, puts his laws in their hearts and writes them on their minds. Believers redeemed by Christ live a life of gratitude by keeping God's commandments. These laws are an integral part of their covenant relationship to God.

17. Then he adds:
"Their sins and lawless acts
I will remember no more."

This second verse (Jer. 31:34) differs considerably from the Old Testament wording. However, we ought not judge the author by modern standards, but we should understand that the author, guided by the Holy Spirit, had the freedom to vary the wording. The meaning remains the same.

These two selected verses from the prophecy of Jeremiah accentuate the accomplishment of Christ's atonement. The Old Testament believers experienced God's forgiving grace, for David writes, "I acknowledged my sin to you . . . and you forgave the guilt of my sin" (Ps. 32:5). And he says elsewhere, "As far as the east is from the west, so far has he removed our transgressions from us" (Ps. 103:12). What is new in the prophecy of Jeremiah, quoted in Hebrews, is that God remembers sins no more in the time of the new covenant. God has forgiven the believer's sins through the one sacrifice of Christ and therefore will never recall them. Sins are forgiven and forgotten.

18. And where these have been forgiven, there is no longer any sacrifice for sin.

For the Christian, because he has never known the ritual of animal sacrifices, the words "there is no longer any sacrifice for sin" are somewhat matter-of-fact. But for the person of Jewish descent in the second half of the first century, these words must have struck with thunderous finality. The age-old Levitical system of presenting sacrifices to God was rendered pointless with the death of Christ. To be sure, the termination took place in A.D. 70 when the Roman army destroyed the sanctuary in Jerusalem.

Christ's sacrifice was final, for it brought an end to all sacrifices for sin. What man was unable to do because of his sin, the curse of death, and his inability to keep the law of God, Christ did. He paid the penalty, removed the curse, and lived a life of perfect obedience. With characteristic brevity B. F. Westcott lists three consequences of sin:

> debt which requires forgiveness,
> bondage which requires redemption,
> alienation which requires reconciliation.[16]

Forgiveness of sins consists of God's pardoning sinners on the basis of Christ's sacrifice and accepting sinners as sons or daughters who have never sinned at all.[17] Set free from the slavery of sin, they have received the gift of life eternal (John 17:3) because they belong to the new covenant of which Christ is the mediator. And the terms of his new covenant call for only one sacrifice offered by Jesus Christ.

Doctrinal Considerations in 10:11–18

In these last few verses, the didactic part of his letter, the writer summarizes his thoughts and concludes that the daily sacrifices are inconsistent with the priesthood of Christ.[18] He reintroduces selected verses from Jeremiah 31:31–34 to stress the significance of the new covenant and the complete remission of sin.

More implicitly than explicitly, the author teaches that all three persons of the Trinity are involved in the work of atonement. At the right hand of God the Father, the Son takes his seat upon completion of his sacrificial work on earth. The Holy Spirit testifies to the establishing of the new covenant that God has made with people whose sins have been forgiven through the bodily sacrifice of Jesus Christ.

Jesus teaches his disciples the Lord's Prayer, to which he adds the comment: "For if you forgive men when they sin against you, your heavenly Father will also forgive you. But if you do not forgive men their sins, your Father will not forgive your sins" (Matt. 6:14–15). The author of Hebrews, guided by the words of Jeremiah's prophecy, teaches that God forgives and forgets man's "sins and lawless acts." The counterpart of this doctrine is that we must not only forgive our fellow man who sins against us. After we have forgiven him we must forget the wrong he has committed. We, too, must live by the principle that forgiven sin is forgotten sin.

---

16. B. F. Westcott, *Commentary on the Epistle to the Hebrews* (Grand Rapids: Eerdmans, 1950), p. 316.

17. R. C. Trench in his *Synonyms of the New Testament* (Grand Rapids: Eerdmans, 1953), p. 119, comments on man's forgiveness: "He, then, that is partaker of the [forgiveness], has his sins forgiven, so that, unless he brings them back upon himself by new and further disobedience (Matt. 18:32, 34; II Peter 1:9; 2:20), they shall not be imputed to him, or mentioned against him any more."

18. John Calvin, *Epistle to the Hebrews* (Grand Rapids: Eerdmans, 1949), p. 230.

Greek Words, Phrases, and Constructions in 10:11–18

Verse 11

ἕστηκεν—the perfect active indicative of the verb ἵστημι (I set, place; stand) has the force of a present tense.

λειτουργῶν—a present participle used circumstantially from the verb λειτουργέω (I perform a religious duty) can best be translated as a finite verb preceded by "and."

αἵτινες—the indefinite relative pronoun is concessive, "although."

περιελεῖν—this compound second aorist infinitive from αἱρέω (I take away, remove) has a perfective idea in the sense of "to take away altogether."[19]

Verse 13

τὸ λοιπόν—the neuter singular used adverbially from λείπω (I leave) has the meaning *the future, from now on.*

τεθῶσιν—because of the temporal conjunction ἕως (until) this verb has been placed in the subjunctive. It is an aorist passive from the verb τίθημι (I place).

Verse 14

τετελείωκεν—the perfect active indicative from τελειόω (I finish, bring to an end) depicts the completed state of the action.

ἁγιαζομένους—this same participle also appears in 2:11. It is a present passive participle with an implied agent.

Verse 18

ὅπου—an adverb of place which lacks the corresponding adverb ἐκεῖ (there) to complete the balance of the sentence.

περί—this preposition is followed by the genitive case of the noun ἁμαρτία (sin) and means "concerning."

---

19 Therefore, brothers, since we have confidence to enter the Most Holy Place by the blood of Jesus, 20 by a new and living way opened for us through the curtain, that is, his body, 21 and since we have a great priest over the house of God, 22 let us draw near to God with a sincere heart in full assurance of faith, having our hearts sprinkled to cleanse us from a guilty conscience and having our bodies washed with pure water. 23 Let us hold unswervingly to the hope we profess, for he who promised is faithful. 24 And let us consider how we may spur one another on toward love and good deeds. 25 Let us not give up meeting together, as some are in the habit of doing, but let us encourage one another—and all the more as you see the Day approaching.

---

19. Robertson, *Grammar*, p. 617.

More Exhortations

A. An Exhortation to Persevere
10:19–25

1. In Full Assurance of Faith
10:19–22

The epistle basically consists of two parts: a dogmatic section (1:1–10:18) and a practical section (10:19–13:25). In the first segment exhorting is the exception; teaching the rule. In the last segment the emphasis is on exhorting and admonishing, with some teaching in chapter 11.

The triad faith, hope, and love stands out clearly in verses 22, 23, and 24. The author discusses the meaning of faith in chapter 11. With numerous admonitions he counsels his readers to hope—that is, to persevere and endure (chap. 12). Love is expressed in helping one another; chapter 13 features many instructions about putting love to work. In a sense, the three verses that include the triad present a brief summary of the next three chapters.

19. Therefore, brothers, since we have confidence to enter the Most Holy Place by the blood of Jesus.

The word *therefore* looks back to the preceding section with its lengthy discussion of the once-for-all sacrifice of Christ and the forgiveness of sin. The author invites the readers to approach God because, he says, "we have confidence to enter the Most Holy Place." These words echo an earlier exhortation, "Let us then approach the throne of grace with confidence" (4:16).

The designation *Most Holy Place* is deliberately chosen. In Old Testament times only the high priest was permitted to enter the inner sanctuary once a year as representative of the people. He entered into God's presence to sprinkle blood on the ark to atone for sin. In New Testament times we have access to God because Jesus shed his blood for our sins and because at his death "the curtain of the temple was torn in two from top to bottom" (Matt. 27:51). We are even encouraged to come into God's presence with confidence.

Note that the author of Hebrews writes, "by the blood of Jesus." He uses the name *Jesus* as a reminder that Jesus saves his people from sin (Matt. 1:21) and that Jesus "is not ashamed to call them brothers" (Heb. 2:11). The writer, too, belongs to the family of Jesus and for that reason addresses his readers as "brothers" (see 3:1, 12; 13:22).

20. By a new and living way opened for us through the curtain, that is, his body.

Translators of the original text of the New Testament are usually guided by a simple rule of thumb: "Translate Greek as it comes." That is, the sequence of the Greek text is carried over more or less into the translation. The translation of Hebrews 10:20 conveys the meaning that the expression *body* clarifies the noun *curtain*. However, other translators and commentators do not follow the above-mentioned rule. Understanding the text differently, they want to interpret it as follows: "By the new, living way which he has opened for us through the curtain, the way of his flesh."[20] In other words, the word *flesh* has become an explanation of "way," not of "curtain." Jesus, then, inaugurated "a new and living way" that consists of his humanity.

To achieve a smooth translation, however, the translators have had to supply the expression *way* in the phrase *the way of his flesh*. The original does not say this. The remark perhaps could be made that if the author of Hebrews had wanted to give an explanation of "a new and living way," he would have done so. Now the evidence appears to favor an explanation for the term *curtain*.[21]

The term *way* is described as "new and living." Unfortunately the translation of "new" is incomplete, for the Greek word actually means "just slaughtered." It is a term relating to religious sacrifices. The adjective *living* signifies that the way Christ has opened up for us is not a road without an exit: a dead-end street. Rather, this road leads us to salvation, into the very presence of God.

Christ has dedicated the way by opening the curtain, "that is, his body." At his death the curtain to the Most Holy Place had to be torn from top to bottom. Likewise the body of Jesus had to be broken, and his blood had to be shed to open for us the way to God. By his sacrifice on the cross, Christ has removed the veil between God and his people.

21. And since we have a great priest over the house of God, 22. let us draw near to God with a sincere heart in full assurance of faith, having our hearts sprinkled to cleanse us from a guilty conscience and having our bodies washed with pure water.

The believer has been given double assurance that he may approach God, first, because he has confidence through the shed blood of Christ and, second, because Jesus is the "great priest over the house of God." Should there be any hesitation at all in the mind of the believer, the writer of Hebrews is saying, let him look to the one and only great priest, Jesus Christ (4:14).

We are exhorted to come to God; in this earthly life we do so in prayer. The great priest takes our prayers and as intercessor presents them for us to God. This priest has been given the responsibility of caring for the church, that is, the house of God (3:6). Christ's priestly task continues even after his atoning work on earth is finished (John 19:30). He has been appointed as the mediator of the new covenant (8:6), and "he is able to save completely those who come to God through him, because he always lives to intercede for them" (7:25).

---

20. NEB. See also Westcott, *Hebrews*, p. 320; Ceslaus Spicq, *L'Épître aux Hébreux*, 3d ed., 2 vols. (Paris: Gabalda, 1953), vol. 2, p. 316: Hugh Montefiore, *The Epistle to the Hebrews* (New York and Evanston: Harper and Row, 1964), p. 173.

21. Numerous short studies on this verse have been published, including those by Joachim Jeremias, "Hebräer 10, 20: tout' estin tes sarkos autou, (Heb. 10, 20): Apposition, Dependent or Explicative?" *NTS* 20 (1974): 100–104; and G. M. M. Pelser, "A Translation Problem. Heb. 10:19–25," *Linguistics and Bible Translating. Neotestamentica* 9 (1974): 53–54.

Believers are absolutely secure because they have a great priest representing them. This great priest never loses sight of those who belong to the house of God, for he and they belong to the same family (2:11).

Even though the author is not explicit, we are exhorted to approach God. In the parallel passage (4:16) he tells us to come to the throne of grace in prayer. The writer now takes this parallel a step further and describes how we are to draw near to God in prayer. Besides having confidence we must come with "a sincere heart in full assurance of faith."

The author stresses that the heart must be sincere if faith is to be genuine. The word *sincere* describes the heart of a person who is honest, genuine, committed, dependable, and without deceit. When the believer's heart is sincere, faith is evident in full assurance. The believer has complete confidence in God, because he fully accepts the truth of the gospel. By contrast, doubt keeps the believer from approaching God. Doubt insults whereas faith exalts.

When the author of Hebrews writes that we draw near to God with "hearts sprinkled to cleanse us from a guilty conscience" and with "bodies washed with pure water," he refers to the internal (hearts) and the external (bodies). The phrase *washed with pure water* reminds us of baptism. But baptism by itself is only an external act objectively experienced. Its counterpart is the sprinkling of our hearts with the blood of Christ (Heb. 9:14). This sprinkling is an internal act that is subjectively appropriated.[22] We are exhorted to approach God with body and soul cleansed from sin.

The heart is the center of our moral life. Says the writer of Hebrews, "Our hearts [are] sprinkled [with the blood of Christ] to cleanse us from a guilty conscience." That blood sets the believer free. He now may freely approach the throne of grace because his conscience is clear. In faith he has claimed for himself forgiveness of sin through Christ. He knows that Christ has removed forever the guilt that hindered him from coming to God.

Baptism was not unknown to the Jew. The law of Moses stipulated that the high priest on the Day of Atonement should bathe himself before putting on his garments to enter the sanctuary (Lev. 16:4; see also Exod. 29:4; Lev. 8:6). And Ezekiel prophesies that God will sprinkle clean water on his people to cleanse them from spiritual impurities (Ezek. 36:25). In his epistle the writer of Hebrews mentions "pure water" used to wash our bodies. That water symbolically cleanses the believer from sin. "Christ loved the church [the house of God] and gave himself up for her to make her holy, cleansing her by the washing with water through the word" (Eph. 5:25–26).

2. By Professing Hope
10:23

23. Let us hold unswervingly to the hope we profess, for he who promised is faithful.

---

22. F. W. Grosheide, *De Brief aan de Hebreeën en de Brief van Jakobus* (Kampen: Kok, 1955), p. 240. Also see Bruce, *Hebrews*, p. 250.

Here is the second exhortation. In the preceding verse the writer tells the readers to draw near to God. Now he exhorts them to "hold unswervingly to the hope we profess." In the preceding passage he introduces the concepts of baptism and remission of sin. Now he speaks of confession of hope as a natural consequence of baptism.

We assume that in the early church a basic confession existed either in the form of "Jesus is Lord" (I Cor. 12:3) or as a trustworthy saying (I Tim. 3:16; II Tim. 2:11–13). Whether the writer of Hebrews has a particular confession in mind is not certain, but he makes it clear that his readers hold to a confession (3:1; 4:14; 10:23; 13:15). The content of this confession is the expectation that Christ will fulfill all the promises he has made and that all those who profess the name of Christ possess these promises. The author states that we profess hope, a virtue he has emphasized throughout his epistle (3:6; 6:11, 19; 7:19; 10:23). Hope relies on faith and looks to the future.

Faith is therefore placed in God alone who is able to fulfill the promises he has made, for God is faithful. We are told to keep on voicing our hope and to do so unfalteringly. God himself unfailingly has honored his promises. In fact, to make his promises unbreakable, God added an oath (Heb. 6:17). "He can as soon cease to exist as cease to be faithful to His promise."[23] The God who saved the believer through the sacrificial death of Christ has promised never to leave "the soul that on Jesus has leaned for repose." And God is faithful, for he promises the believer,

> Never will I leave you;
> never will I forsake you. [Heb. 13:5]

3. Toward Expressing Love
10:24

24. And let us consider how we may spur one another on toward love and good deeds.

This is the third exhortation and the third virtue of the triad faith (v. 22), hope (v. 23), and love (v. 24). Earlier in the epistle the author elaborated on this triad (6:10–12). In harmony with the conclusion of Paul's letter of love (I Cor. 13:13) and other passages where he mentions the triad (Rom. 5:1–5; Gal. 5:5–6; Col. 1:4–5; I Thess. 1:3; 5:8; and see I Peter 1:21–22), the writer of Hebrews shows that love is the greatest because it reaches out to others. Love is communal. For man, love extends to God and one's neighbor. Moreover, "God demonstrates his own love for us in this: While we were still sinners, Christ died for us" (Rom. 5:8).

Carefully consider how we may ardently incite one another to love and to do good works, says the writer. Put your mind to work to find ways to provoke—in the good sense of the word—each other to increase your expres-

---

23. John Brown, *An Exposition of Hebrews* (Edinburgh: Banner of Truth Trust, 1961), p. 464.

sions of love that result in doing noble works.[24] Jesus' summary of the law, that is, the royal law (James 2:8), "Love your neighbor as yourself," often is abbreviated to "Love yourself." But this royal law extends beyond the neighbor to God himself. Deeds done in love for the neighbor honor God the Father. Therefore, keeping and fulfilling the second part of the summary, "Love your neighbor as yourself" (Matt. 22:39), actually constitute keeping and fulfilling the first part of the summary, "Love the Lord your God with all your heart and with all your soul and with all your mind" (Matt. 22:37). And Paul calls the commandment to love one another a "continuing debt" (Rom. 13:8). "Therefore love is the fulfillment of the law," he concludes (v. 10).

4. In Attending the Worship Services
10:25

25. Let us not give up meeting together, as some are in the habit of doing, but let us encourage one another—and all the more as you see the Day approaching.

One of the first indications of a lack of love toward God and the neighbor is for a Christian to stay away from the worship services. He forsakes the communal obligations of attending these meetings and displays the symptoms of selfishness and self-centeredness.

Apparently some members of the Hebrew congregation to whom the epistle originally was addressed showed a disregard for attending the religious services. They did so willfully by deserting the "communion of the saints." From sources dating from the first century of the Christian era, we learn that a lack of interest in the worship services was rather common. The *Didache,* a church manual of religious instruction from the latter part of the first century, gives this exhortation: "But be frequently gathered together seeking the things which are profitable for your souls."[25]

In an earlier chapter the author of Hebrews warns the readers not to follow the example of the disobedient Israelites in the desert, and not to turn away from the living God (3:12). The author exhorts the readers to "encourage one another daily . . . so that none of you may be hardened by sin's deceitfulness" (3:13). He realizes that among some of the members spiritual zeal has declined. Therefore once more he says, "But let us encourage one another" (10:25). Not only the writer of this epistle but also all the members of the church have the communal task of encouraging one another daily. Together we bear the responsibility, for we are the body of Christ.

---

24. Westcott, *Hebrews,* p. 325, expresses his disappointment in our inability to translate the Greek adequately. We translate "good deeds," but the original emphasizes that the deeds themselves are noble.

25. *The Didache (The Apostolic Fathers,* vol. 1), 16.2, p. 333 (LCL). Also see the Epistle of Barnabas (*The Apostolic Fathers,* vol. 1), 4.10, p. 353 (LCL). Even in Jewish sources the same concern is expressed. Rabbi Hillel said, "Separate not thyself from the community" (Aboth 2.4, p. 14, *Talmud*). And Josephus writes in a similar vein; see his *Antiquities of the Jews* 4.203–4 (LCL).

As Christians we must look to the future, that is, to the day when Jesus returns. The closer we come to that day, the more active we should be in spurring one another on in showing love and doing deeds acceptable to God. We would have appreciated more information about "the Day," but the author is as brief as other writers of the New Testament who mention it (see, for example, Matt. 25:13; I Cor. 3:13; I Thess. 5:4). Says Philip Edgcumbe Hughes: "When spoken of in this absolute manner, 'the Day' can mean only the last day, that ultimate eschatological day, which is the day of reckoning and judgment, known as the Day of the Lord."[26]

Practical Considerations in 10:19–25

Of the well-known triad faith, hope, and love, hope seems to be neglected. Writers of the New Testament, however, do not neglect it, for they mention it as many times as faith and love. The Christian in his spiritual life appears to stress the virtues of faith and love, but he says little about hope.

Yet hope guides the believer, for it provides him freedom from the fear of death. He keeps his eyes on Jesus, who has conquered the power of death. He knows that in Jesus he has salvation, righteousness, eternal life, and the assurance of resurrection from the dead. That hope will be realized when Jesus returns.

Christianity is a religion of love that reaches out and brings people together. Sports, performances on the stage or screen, and politics draw large crowds. But Christianity holds people together because it emphasizes participation in worship, praise, and work. Christians need each other to strengthen the wonderful bond of love they share in Jesus Christ.

The author's exhortation to "spur one another on toward love" precedes his remarks about church attendance. When the believer attends the worship service, he expresses his love for Jesus. He realizes that Jesus, the head of the church, is present at the service and desires his presence. To say it somewhat differently, the head of the church cannot function without the body. The believer is part of the body of Christ, which Christ presents "to himself as a radiant church, without stain or wrinkle or any other blemish, but holy and blameless" (Eph. 5:27).

Greek Words, Phrases, and Constructions in 10:19–25

Verse 19

ἔχοντες—this present active participle from ἔχω (I have) denotes cause. It indicates why the believer may draw near to God.

εἴσοδον—from the combination of εἰς (into) and ἡ ὁδός (the way); this noun can mean either the act of entering or entrance. The context favors the first meaning. τῶν ἁγίων is an abbreviated form of τά ἅγια τῶν ἁγίων and refers to the Most Holy Place (see Heb. 9:2, 12).

---

26. Philip Edgcumbe Hughes, *Commentary on the Epistle to the Hebrews* (Grand Rapids: Eerdmans, 1977), p. 416.

Verse 20

πρόσφατον—a compound adjective from πρό (before) and σφάζω (I slay). This term in time signified something new or recent.

σαρκός—this genitive singular noun stands in apposition to the antecedent καταπετάσματος (curtain). To link the genitive σαρκός to the accusative ὁδόν is difficult and grammatically unsound.

Verse 22

προσερχώμεθα—the present middle subjunctive has a variant reading in the form of the present middle indicative. The external evidence (manuscripts) and the internal evidence (context) favor the present subjunctive. This is the first of three hortatory subjunctives; the other two are κατέχωμεν (v. 23) and κατανοῶμεν (v. 24).

ῥεραντισμένοι—together with λελουσμένοι the participle features the perfect tense and the passive voice.[27] The action of the verbs (ῥαντίζω, I sprinkle; and λούω, I wash) occurred in the past but has lasting effect in the present.

Verse 24

ἀλλήλους—this reciprocal pronoun appears only here in the entire epistle. It seems to relate much more to the noun παροξυσμόν (provoking, encouraging) than to the verb κατανοῶμεν (let us consider), even though the verb governs the pronoun as a direct object.

Verse 25

ἐγκαταλείποντες—the present active participle shows that the staying away from the meetings happened. The compound form of the verb indicates a forsaking, that is, an abandoning of the congregation.

ἐπισυναγωγήν—according to Walter Bauer, this noun does not differ from the noun συναγωγή.[28]

ἑαυτῶν—this is the abbreviated *koine* Greek form for ἡμῶν αὐτῶν and is simply translated "our."

---

26 If we deliberately keep on sinning after we have received the knowledge of the truth, no sacrifice for sins is left, 27 but only a fearful expectation of judgment and of raging fire that will consume the enemies of God. 28 Anyone who rejected the law of Moses died without mercy on the testimony of two or three witnesses. 29 How much more severely do you think a man deserves to be punished who has trampled the Son of God under foot, who has treated as an unholy thing the blood of the covenant that sanctified him, and who has insulted the Spirit of grace? 30 For we know him who said, "It is mine to avenge; I will repay," and again, "The Lord will judge his people." 31 It is a dreadful thing to fall into the hands of the living God.

---

27. Robertson, *Grammar,* p. 486, calls them passive verbs with rather remote accusative.
28. Bauer, p. 301.

B. A Warning to Pay Attention
10:26-31

1. To the Knowledge of the Truth
10:26-27

Forsaking the congregation at worship leads to serious consequences. The author warns the believers that the sequel to sinning deliberately is falling "into the hands of the living God" (10:31).

26. If we deliberately keep on sinning after we have received the knowledge of the truth, no sacrifice for sins is left, 27. but only a fearful expectation of judgment and of raging fire that will consume the enemies of God.

The word *deliberately* stands first in the original Greek, and as the opening word of the sentence it receives all the emphasis. The term occurs only twice in the New Testament, here and in I Peter 5:2. It refers to something done intentionally.

In the Old Testament the distinction is made between sins committed unintentionally and sins committed intentionally. The first can be forgiven; the second cannot. Moses writes, "But anyone who sins defiantly, whether native-born or alien, blasphemes the LORD, and that person must be cut off from his people" (Num. 15:30; see also Lev. 4:2, 22, 27; 5:15, 18; Num. 15:24 for unintentional sins).

The author of Hebrews is rather specific. He writes concerning a person who sins intentionally and who keeps on doing this in open rebellion against God and his Word. To reach his readers in a pastoral manner, he even includes himself in the warning not to sin defiantly. He is not talking about a believer who falls into sin unintentionally and finds forgiveness in God's grace and mercy. Rather, he points to the same sin that Jesus calls the sin against the Holy Spirit (Matt. 12:32; Mark 3:29) and that John describes as "a sin that leads to death" (I John 5:16). Although he employs different terms, the writer virtually repeats the same thought he expressed in 3:12 and 6:4–6, where he speaks of falling away from the living God.

Those who turn away from God and "have received the knowledge of the truth" can never say that they sinned in ignorance. The phrase *knowledge of the truth* relates to God's revelation in general and the gospel in particular (see I Tim. 2:4; II Tim. 2:25; 3:7; Titus 1:1). They who at one time received this truth, but now have turned against God and his revelation, are without excuse. Nothing can save them. They know that Christ's sacrifice is the only sacrifice that removes sin. If they deliberately reject Christ and his atoning work, they reject salvation. For them, says the writer, "no sacrifice for sins is left."

What then is left? "Only a fearful expectation of judgment and of raging fire that will consume the enemies of God." A decision against Christ taken deliberately can only result in judgment. And judgment is not merely something that happens at the end of time. Evidence already is being gathered and presented to the jury in preparation for the judgment day. And that is a fearful expectation!

The emphasis falls on the adjective *fearful*. The word occurs three times in the New Testament, all in this epistle (10:27, 31: 12:21). This adjective is translated "fearful," "dreadful," and "terrifying." In all three instances its use pertains to meeting God. The sinner cannot escape God's judgment and, unless he has been forgiven in Christ, faces an angry God on that dreadful day.

Not only the judgment awaits the sinner who will receive the verdict, but also the execution of that verdict. The author vividly portrays the execution as a raging fire that will consume all those who have chosen to be enemies of God. Actually he echoes the words of Isaiah's prophecy, "Let the fire reserved for your enemies consume them" (Isa. 26:11).

2. To God's Judgment
10:28–31

28. Anyone who rejected the law of Moses died without mercy on the testimony of two or three witnesses.

Let no one think that God deals lightly with his enemies and shows them mercy. If anyone deliberately rejected the law of Moses in Old Testament times, that person was put to death without mercy. God instructed the Israelites to banish the sin of apostasy by killing the person who willfully despised God's commandments and turned to idols instead. "Then all Israel will hear and be afraid, and no one among you will do such an evil thing again" (Deut. 13:11; see also vv. 1–10 and 17:2–7). This was a warning to Israel to keep God's law and to serve him wholeheartedly.

Should someone break the commandments, he would not be killed. Only when two or three witnesses verified that he had intentionally despised God and rejected the law of Moses would this offender be put to death. The stipulation that a person be tried on the testimony of two or three witnesses was a rule observed and applied in biblical times (Num. 35:30; Deut. 17:6; 19:15; Matt. 18:16; John 8:17; II Cor. 13:1). Appeal of the sentence would not be granted. The writer of Hebrews summarizes the essence of the verdict in the words *without mercy*. According to God's instructions, the guilty person had to be killed, and the example was to serve as a deterrent.

29. How much more severely do you think a man deserves to be punished who has trampled the Son of God under foot, who has treated as an unholy thing the blood of the covenant that sanctified him, and who has insulted the Spirit of grace?

Once again the author of Hebrews employs the device of contrast. He sets the times of the old covenant over against those of the new covenant. He compares the penalty of physical death with the much more severe sentence of spiritual death. And he differentiates between rejecting the law of Moses and despising the Son of God and the Spirit of God. He asks the reader to reflect on this difference.

The sinner who rebels against God in the times of the new covenant rejects the person of Christ, the work of Christ, and the person of the Holy Spirit. And thus he has committed the unpardonable sin. The writer delineates this sin in three parts.

a. Person of the Son of God. Note that the author again employs the title of Christ, which he used extensively at the beginning of the Epistle to the Hebrews. The title is the highest accorded to Christ. No one can be compared to this Son, for he excels all: angels, Moses, Aaron, and Melchizedek.

What does the sinner do? He tramples under foot this Son of God. To trample something under foot is what we do when we get rid of a bothersome insect.[29] Thus the sinner figuratively takes the exalted Son of God and grinds him into the dirt.

b. Work of the Son of God. The second part is even more significant because it relates to the meaning and purpose of the new covenant. Jesus inaugurated this covenant by his blood to cleanse his people and sanctify them (Matt. 26:28 and parallels).

Jesus shed his precious blood and paid the supreme sacrifice. But this shed blood means nothing to the rebellious sinner. He regards Jesus' blood as the blood of any other human being and Jesus' death as that of any other mortal. He considers Jesus to be a mere man whose death has no significance and whose redemptive work has no value.

The author contrasts the defiant sinner within the Israelite community with the Christian who has abandoned the church; his point is that ignorance cannot be used as an excuse. The sinner knows the Christian faith, for he was sanctified by the blood of the covenant. That is, at one time he professed his faith in Christ, listened to the preaching of the Word of God, and partook of the holy elements when he celebrated the Lord's Supper. But his faith was not an internal fulfillment. In word and deed he now repudiates his relationship to Christ's work. He breaks with his past.

c. Person of the Holy Spirit. The third clause in the description of the unpardonable sin relates to insulting the Spirit of grace (Matt. 12:32; Mark 3:29). The sinner intentionally insults the person of the Holy Spirit. In his conduct, the sinner points out the stark contrast between insults hurled at the Holy Spirit and grace granted by the Holy Spirit. The Spirit is the source of grace (Zech. 12:10). Insulting the third person of the Trinity is the height of sin that cannot be forgiven. Says John Calvin, "To treat him with scorn, by whom we are endowed with so many benefits, is an impiety extremely wicked."[30] God himself confronts the sinner and metes out punishment.

30. For we know him who said, "It is mine to avenge; I will repay,"

---

29. The expression *trample under foot* (or variants) is common in the Old Testament (see, for example, II Kings 9:33; Isa. 26:6; Dan. 8:10; Mic. 7:10; Mal. 4:3). In the New Testament it occurs five times (Matt. 5:13; 7:6; Luke 8:5; 12:1; Heb. 10:29).

30. Calvin, *Hebrews*, p. 248.

and again, "The Lord will judge his people." 31. It is a dreadful thing to fall into the hands of the living God.

Understandably believers are grieved when they hear about and see the conduct of a person who leaves the Christian community by scornfully rejecting the Son of God and insulting the Holy Spirit. They know that vengeance belongs to God, for this is the teaching of his Word.

The author of Hebrews takes the words "It is mine to avenge; I will repay" from the Song of Moses (Deut. 32:35).[31] This song was well known to the readers because they sang it in their worship services. The wording differs somewhat in the original Hebrew and its Greek translation; therefore, scholars have made the suggestion that "the citation in this form may have been stereotyped by apostolic example in the language of the primitive church."[32] The citation occurs in the selfsame wording in Romans 12:19. We may assume that it circulated in the early church as a proverbial saying.

The second quotation comes from both the Song of Moses (Deut. 32:36) and the Book of Psalms (Ps. 135:14). "The Lord will judge his people," writes the author of Hebrews. The intent is to emphasize that judgment is unavoidable. In an earlier setting the writer speaks of the coming judgment (9:27; and see 10:27) and presents it in the form of an accepted truth.

God will judge his people; no one escapes his judgment. Those whose faith is rooted in Jesus Christ find a God of grace and mercy. Their sins have been forgiven because of the Son's sacrifice on the cross. And they will hear the verdict *acquitted*. But they who have spurned the person and work of Christ and have arrogantly despised the Holy Spirit face the infinite wrath of God, the judge of heaven and earth.

When a sinner repents of his sin, approaches the throne of God, and pleads for mercy, God hears and answers. David experienced this when he sinned against God by counting the number of fighting men in Israel and Judah. Said David, "Let us fall into the hands of the LORD, for his mercy is great" (II Sam. 24:14; see also I Chron. 21:13). The sinner who breaks God's law purposely to grieve God has passed the stage of repentance (Heb. 6:4–6). He falls "into the hands of the living God" (also see Heb. 3:12), and that confrontation is indescribable. The writer of Hebrews says it is dreadful.

Practical Considerations in 10:26–31

Preaching sermons on hellfire appears to be something that happened in the past but not today. This type of preaching is considered an oddity of the eighteenth century; it should not be heard from a twentieth-century pulpit.

---

31. The writer of Hebrews usually quotes the Septuagint translation, but not here. The Septuagint has, "In the day of vengeance, I will repay."
32. Delitzsch, *Hebrews*, vol. 2, p. 190. Also see K. J. Thomas, "The Use of the Septuagint in the Epistle to the Hebrews" (Ph.D. diss., University of Manchester, 1959), p. 122. Perhaps the phraseology of the citation prevailed in an oral tradition on which the writers of the Targums and the writers of the New Testament relied.

True. Sermons ought to proclaim the gospel of salvation, the call to repentance, the assurance of pardon, and the message of reconciliation between God and man. Proportionally, Scripture says little about God's burning wrath that consumes his enemies. If Scripture sets the example, we should follow its practice.

Nevertheless, no preacher may fail to warn the people of the dire consequences of turning away from the living God. The recurring theme of the Epistle of Hebrews is one of warning God's people. Note these three texts:

3:12 "See to it, brothers, that none of you has a sinful, unbelieving heart that turns away from the living God."

4:1 "Therefore, since the promise of entering [God's] rest still stands, let us be careful that none of you be found to have fallen short of it."

4:11 "Let us, therefore, make every effort to enter that rest, so that no one will fall by following their example of disobedience."

The terrifying consequences of living a life of intentional sin ought to be mentioned in sermons. In Hebrews we read that every believer has the responsibility to seek the spiritual welfare of his fellow Christians. We may call this corporate responsibility because it is our mutual task. And pastors may refer to hellfire in their sermons, for such a warning also belongs to the full message of God's revelation.

As the pastor warns the wayward, so he encourages the faint-hearted. A believer may lack the assurance of salvation, fearing that he has committed the sin against the Holy Spirit. But the unpardonable sin cannot be attributed to a person who doubts his or her salvation. Only the person who demonstrates an open and deliberate hatred toward God, divine revelation, and Christ's accomplished work of salvation has committed that sin. The doubter, then, needs words of encouragement. He should be invited to repeat the reassuring words of Paul, "Yet I am not ashamed, because I know whom I have believed, and am convinced that he is able to guard what I have entrusted to him for that day" (II Tim. 1:12).

Greek Words, Phrases, and Constructions in 10:26–31

Verse 26

ἑκουσίως—an adverb derived from the adjective ἑκών (voluntary, willing, of one's own free will).

ἁμαρτανόντων—the genitive absolute construction with a present active participle denoting a condition. The first person plural pronoun ἡμῶν completes the construction. Note that the present participle (indicating duration) and not the aorist participle (depicting a single occurrence) is used.

τὴν ἐπίγνωσιν—the compound noun is preceded by the definite article and has a perfective connotation; that is, the compound noun is more precise than the noun γνῶσις (knowledge). ἐπίγνωσιν has the meaning *recognition, acknowledgment.*

Verse 27

τις—this indefinite pronoun, usually translated "someone" or "something," should be taken with the adjective φοβερά. It strengthens the adjective and means "a *very* fearful expectation."[33]

---

33. Robertson, *Grammar*, p. 743. Italics his.

ἐκδοχή—the noun has its origin in the verb ἐκδέχομαι (I expect, await). It appears only here in the New Testament. The noun controls two objects in the genitive case: judgment and fire.

ζῆλος—although translations treat this word as an adjective (raging; NIV, JB), it is a noun that means "jealousy"; that is, the fierceness of fire.

Verse 28

ἀθετήσας—the aorist active participle from ἀθετέω (I nullify, reject) conveys the idea of annulling the law of Moses, resulting in a complete break with the old covenant.

ἐπί—this preposition may be translated "in the presence of."

Verse 29

ποσῷ—the dative case points out the degree of difference between physical death and eternal punishment. It introduces the hermeneutical rule of contrast "from the lesser to the greater."

ἀξιωθήσεται—the future passive of ἀξιόω (I consider worthy) controls the genitive case τιμωρίας (punishment). The verb usually has the positive connotation of receiving rewards; here it means deserving punishment.

ἡγησάμενος—the aorist middle participle of ἡγέομαι (I think, regard) and ἡγιάσθη (the aorist passive of ἁγιάζω, I make holy) are a play on words in the Greek text.

Verse 31

τὸ ἐμπεσεῖν—an aorist infinitive of the directive compound ἐμπίπτω (I fall into). The aorist shows single occurrence. It is succeeded by the preposition εἰς (into).

ζῶντος—the present active participle from the verb ζάω (I live) describes God as distinct from manmade idols that are dead.

---

32 Remember those earlier days after you had received the light, when you stood your ground in a great contest in the face of suffering. 33 Sometimes you were publicly exposed to insult and persecution; at other times you stood side by side with those who were so treated. 34 You sympathized with those in prison and joyfully accepted the confiscation of your property, because you knew that you yourselves had better and lasting possessions.

35 So do not throw away your confidence; it will be richly rewarded. 36 You need to persevere so that when you have done the will of God, you will receive what he has promised. 37 For in just a very little while,

"He who is coming will come and not delay.
38 But my righteous one will live by faith.
And if he shrinks back,
I will not be pleased with him."
39 But we are not of those who shrink back and are destroyed, but of those who believe and are saved.

C. A Reminder to Continue
10:32–39

1. As in the Past
10:32–34

As a pastor sensitive to the needs to his people, the author changes his remarks from admonition to praise, from reproof to commendation. He heartily approves of the works of love and mercy they showed to those who were persecuted and those who lost their possessions. The writer draws a parallel to his warning against falling away (6:4–6) and to his tribute to the readers for their demonstration of love and their willingness to help (6:9–11).

32. Remember those earlier days after you had received the light, when you stood your ground in a great contest in the face of suffering.

Times of hardship, persecution, and suffering remain indelibly fixed in man's memory. Memories come to mind with the simple question, "Do you recall?" Yes, the readers vividly remembered those early days when at first they had professed their faith and received the sacrament of baptism. In those days they received the light (6:4). But as soon as they had become Christians, they faced hostility.

Especially in Jewish circles the sign of Christian baptism indicates the breaking point, and Jewish converts to the Christian religion are excommunicated and subject to abuse and insult, if not persecution. The recipients of the Epistle to the Hebrews had experienced first hand suffering for their faith in Jesus. And they had not forgotten this "great contest," even though the present was calm and peaceful. They recalled the intensity and the duration of this difficult period in their lives.[34] Their faith was tested, and they emerged victoriously in spite of and because of the suffering they endured. Not only had they personally endured hardship, but also they had reached out in love to others who experienced similar treatment.

33. Sometimes you were publicly exposed to insult and persecution; at other times you stood side by side with those who were so treated.

The readers of this epistle knew what it meant to be objects of public ridicule and persecution. The text indicates that these conditions persisted for an extended period. Wherever the church begins to develop and grow, opposition can be expected. The "Hebrews," who were known as traitors to the Jewish faith, had become the target of abuse. In effect, they were treated as outlaws. As aliens in a foreign land, they were deprived of legal protection. Persecution was their lot. To them the Beatitudes of Jesus were especially meaningful. "Blessed are those who are persecuted because of righteousness, for theirs is the kingdom of heaven. Blessed are you when people insult you, persecute you and falsely say all kinds of evil against you because of me" (Matt. 5:10–11).

They stood side by side with those who endured the same hostility. They demonstrated the love of Christ to fellow church members who faced harassment, maltreatment, and deprivation. The members of the congregation stood together in aiding one another in the hour of need.

34. You sympathized with those in prison and joyfully accepted the confiscation of your property, because you knew that you yourselves had better and lasting possessions.

Christians are expected to visit the prisoners. Jesus commends the righteous for having visited the captives: "I was in prison and you came to visit

34. Michel, *Hebräer,* p. 239.

me" (Matt. 25:36; also see vv. 39, 43, 44). Prisoners depended on relatives, friends, and acquaintances for food, clothing, and other needs (see, for example, Acts 23:16; 24:23; 27:3; II Tim. 4:13). The writer of Hebrews exhorts his readers to "remember those in prison as if you were their fellow prisoners" (13:3).

Moreover, the readers of the epistle were obedient to the words of Jesus, "Do not store up for yourselves treasures on earth. . . . But store up for yourselves treasures in heaven" (Matt. 6:19, 20). Cheerfully they gave up their property when, presumably, governmental authorities confiscated their goods. Their lasting possession was stored up for them in heaven, and in that knowledge they rejoiced. These readers lived in harmony with the precepts that Jesus taught in the gospel (Matt. 5:12; Luke 6:23; James 1:2).

The author of Hebrews seems to develop a sequence of the events that had occurred in the lives of his readers. First, they had endured a period of suffering when they "had received the light" (v. 32). Then they were exposed to public insult and persecution (v. 33). Also, they supported fellow believers who suffered similar abuse. And last, they had lost their property, perhaps in a time of political or religious turmoil (v. 34).

We would appreciate seeing a chronicle of events with exact dates and places. But the writer of Hebrews provides no historical information on when and where events took place. Therefore, we can work only with hypotheses that by nature are quite subjective.

The author's remark that the readers were in the category of second-generation Christians (2:3) makes an early date for persecution somewhat difficult to accept. For example, the persecution following the death of Stephen (Acts 8:1) may have occurred in A.D. 32. And the persecution that resulted in the death of James, brother of John, and the imprisonment of Peter (Acts 12:1–3) can be dated rather accurately for April A.D. 44. Both Stephen and James died in Jerusalem.

Rome witnessed the expulsion of the Jews in A.D. 49 during the reign of Emperor Claudius.[35] We can be reasonably sure that Jewish Christians were involved in this persecution—Luke mentions Aquila and Priscilla (Acts 18:1–2).[36] How severe the terms of this edict may have been is not known. Eventually those who were expelled returned to Rome (Rom. 16:3).

Then, following the burning of Rome in A.D. 64, Nero instigated severe persecutions directed primarily against the Christians.[37] Christians were

---

35. Suetonius, *Claudius,* 25.4 (LCL). "Since the Jews constantly made disturbances at the instigation of Chrestus [another form of Christus], he expelled them from Rome."

36. F. F. Bruce, *New Testament History* (Garden City, N.Y.: Doubleday, 1980), p. 297.

37. Tacitus, *Annals* 15.44 (LCL). Bruce, *Hebrews,* p. 267, rules out identifying the persecution of the Hebrews with the Neronian persecution. Says he, "It could never have been said to Roman Christians after A.D. 64 that they had 'not yet resisted unto blood, striving against sin'; that is precisely what they had done, and right nobly." Bruce, then, links the Hebrew persecution to the decree of Claudius. However, the clause "you have not yet resisted to the point of shedding your blood" (Heb. 12:4) must be seen in the context of the imagery used in verses 1–3. The clause should not be taken out of context and applied to historical references of an earlier chapter.

publicly oppressed when they faced wild animals in the arena or were burned at the stake. Because the author of Hebrews fails to provide any hints when the recipients of his letter endured persecution and loss of property, we assume that the events resulting from Claudius's decree and from Nero's cruel tactics mark the background of 10:32–34. As I already noted, the writer appears to develop somewhat of a sequence in these verses. The one event follows the other. Now he looks back into history and asks his readers to recall the hardships they had experienced.

2. So in the Present
10:35–39

35. So do not throw away your confidence; it will be richly rewarded.
If the readers suffered for their Christian faith in earlier days, will they at present throw away the confidence they showed in the face of persecution? Apparently time has elapsed, and the believers are living in a period of peace and safety. Their boldness in confessing their faith in Christ has fallen into disuse. And because they have not exercised their gift of confidence, they are ready to discard it.

Faith must be confessed boldly and confidently. In difficult circumstances the believer puts his faith in God and readily confesses the name of his Lord and Savior. But in a time of ease the Christian faces no necessity of taking a stand. His faith wavers and declines. Writes the author of Hebrews, "And without faith it is impossible to please God, because anyone who comes to him must believe that he exists and that he rewards those who earnestly seek him" (11:6). The confidence he expresses does not relate to the freedom we have in coming to God in prayer (4:16) or with a sincere heart (10:19, 22). Rather, the author wants the readers to exhibit their confidence or courage toward man (see also 3:6).

God will richly reward the believer who courageously confesses his faith. He rewards the Christian not because he has deserved the reward in the sense of having merited or earned it. God dispenses his gifts to those who earnestly seek him, not in terms of counting "human values and achievements, but [in terms of] a joyful hopefulness" that God has promised.[38]

36. You need to persevere so that when you have done the will of God, you will receive what he has promised.
The writer shows tact and pastoral concern. He exhorts the readers to persevere; as in the past they stood their ground in the face of suffering (10:32), so now they ought to persevere in doing the will of God. When he writes the phrase *the will of God,* he immediately reminds the recipients of the obedience of Christ, who came to do the will of God (10:7, 9–10). The exhortation, then, is to follow Christ in obediently keeping the commandments. And when they persevere in faithfulness to God's will, they will "receive what he has promised."

---

38. Paul Christoph Böttger, *NIDNTT,* vol. 3, p. 143.

The expression *promise* is a key word in the Epistle to the Hebrews.[39] It stands for forgiveness of sins, in terms of the new covenant, but especially for complete salvation in Jesus Christ.[40] God's promise to man is unbreakable. What God has promised, the believer will receive.

37. For in just a very little while,
"He who is coming will come and not delay.
38. But my righteous one will live by faith.
And if he shrinks back,
I will not be pleased with him."

Steeped in the Old Testament Scriptures, the author cites prophecy to support his exhortation to persevere. Whether the introduction to the quotation, that is, the words "in just a very little while," was purposely taken from Isaiah 26:20 is debatable. Isaiah 26 is a song of praise that was chanted or read in the worship services of the ancient synagogue and of the early Christian church.[41] However, the phrase "in just a very little while" also appears in nonbiblical Greek literature and may simply be a colloquial expression. The meaning of the phrase expresses the thought that the period of waiting will not be long. In fact, the adverb *very* makes the phrase all the more pointed.

The author of Hebrews has taken a quotation from the prophecy of Habakkuk and has given it a decidedly messianic interpretation. He follows not the Hebrew text but the Septuagint translation, and for his own purposes introduces some changes. A comparison of the passage in parallel columns is helpful:

Habakkuk 2:3b, 4	*Hebrews 10:37b, 38*
3b. Though it [the revelation] linger, wait for it; it will certainly come and will not delay.	37b. He who is coming will come and will not delay.
4. "See, he is puffed up; his desires are not upright—[Septuagint: And if he shrinks back I will not be pleased with him.] but the righteous will live by his faith."	38. But my righteous one will live by faith. And if he shrinks back, I will not be pleased with him.

Although the text of Habakkuk relates to the revelation, the writer of Hebrews makes the wording personal and applies it to the Messiah. The phrase *he who is coming* is a descriptive title of Christ (see Matt. 11:3; Luke

---

39. The noun *promise* occurs fifty-three times in the New Testament, fourteen of which are in Hebrews (4:1; 6:12, 15, 17; 7:6; 8:6; 9:15; 10:36; 11:9 [twice], 13, 17, 33, 39). The verb appears fifteen times, four of which are in Hebrews (6:13; 10:23; 11:11; 12:26).

40. Ernst Hoffmann, *NIDNTT,* vol. 3, p. 73.

41. Ernst Werner, *The Sacred Bridge* (London: D. Dobson, 1959), p. 140. The early church used nine songs taken from the Old Testament and five from the New Testament. See Kistemaker, *Psalm Citations,* p. 47.

7:20; Rev. 1:4, 8; 4:8). Christ comes quickly and will not delay. When the time arrives for his return, God's revelation will be fulfilled.

Habakkuk prophesies against the Babylonians and portrays them as haughty people who are ruthless and a law unto themselves (Hab. 1:6–7). He refers to them collectively and says, "See, he is puffed up; his desires are not upright." In the Septuagint the reading is, "And if he shrinks back I will not be pleased with him." The contrast is between the godless Babylonian and the righteous Israelite who put his faith in God.

The writer of Hebrews turns the two sentences around. He inserts the personal pronoun *my* and writes, "But my righteous one shall live by faith." Because Paul also uses this line, although without the pronoun (Rom. 1:17; Gal. 3:11), we assume that these words were familiar to the early Christians. The author adds the second part—"and if he shrinks back, I will not be pleased with him." The order, therefore, is reversed.

The difference between Habakkuk's prophecy and the wording of Hebrews is that in the prophecy the Babylonian is contrasted with the Israelites: the one is godless; the other, a devout believer. In Hebrews, "my righteous one" is the same person who shrinks back. In rearranged form the quotation addresses the recipient of the epistle.

The righteous person who perseveres does not receive God's promise on the basis of keeping the law and doing the will of God. He receives the promise by faith.[42] The object of faith, of course, is understood. The believer places his faith in Jesus Christ. Out of a relationship of trust and confidence, the believer lives.[43]

In the face of opposition, persecution, and temptation, the believer ought to stand firm in his faith. Should he shrink back in fear, should he abandon his faith, and should he eventually turn away, God "will not be pleased with him." Instead God's displeasure will rest upon him because he has forsaken the author of his salvation.

The quotation from Habakkuk, then, contains a warning to remain true to God. That does not mean that the recipients of Hebrews are forsaking their Lord. On the contrary, the author encourages them by writing reassuring words.

39. But we are not of those who shrink back and are destroyed, but of those who believe and are saved.

As in many other passages, the author identifies himself with the readers. He places himself on their level when he uses the personal pronoun *we*. He points out two classes: "those who shrink back" and "those who believe." The first group perishes; the second is saved.

The pastor-writer encourages his people. He gives them words of comfort

---

42. Grosheide, *Hebreeën*, p. 253. The writer of Hebrews avoids advocating works righteousness whereby man earns his salvation. Man is declared righteous on the basis of faith in Christ.

43. A few manuscripts have transposed the personal pronoun and have the reading, "But the righteous will live by faith in me."

and assurance. He says, "We belong to those people who believe and are saved." He knows the readers of his epistle and is confident that they will continue to believe. And the people realize that the person who shrinks back faces eternal condemnation, whereas he who believes obtains salvation. The contrast is clearly delineated. No one can plead ignorance, for the one road leads to destruction; the other, to life.

In the concluding verses of chapter 10, the author introduces the concept *faith*. He sets the tone for a lengthy discussion about the heroes of faith by tracing sacred history from Abel to the prophets.

Practical Considerations in 10:32–39

"You . . . joyfully accepted the confiscation of your property." This statement seems incongruous, unreal. All of us have a natural inclination to cherish and protect our own belongings. We are not unwilling to help people in need. Indeed we give cheerfully. But we certainly do not shout for joy when our possessions are taken from us.

When Jesus asks us to love our enemies, to do good to those who hate us, to bless those who curse us, and to pray for those who mistreat us (Luke 6:27–28), we readily consent. And when he continues and asks us to turn the other cheek when someone strikes us (Luke 6:29), we nod our heads and are willing to endure physical abuse. But when Jesus says, "Give to everyone who asks you, and if anyone takes what belongs to you, do not demand it back" (Luke 6:30), we object. Our belongings are valuable to us, and we certainly make our unhappiness known when someone takes them from us. Jesus, however, wants us to cling not to earthly but to heavenly possessions. Treasures laid up in heaven are lasting; those on earth are fleeting.

The recipients of Hebrews understood and applied the words of Jesus. When their possessions were taken away and when their property was confiscated, they realized they "had better and lasting possessions" in heaven.

When a member of the Jewish community converts to Christianity, a period of conflict begins in his family, household, and locale. The Hebrew or Jew who becomes a Christian faces alienation, especially when he receives the sacrament of baptism. The temptation to renounce Christ and return to the fold of Judaism is real, for being surrounded once more by relatives and friends signifies an end to persecution and hardship. The Epistle to the Hebrews is a letter of encouragement and admonition to all those who have confessed Christ as their Savior. Let no one shrink back and renounce Christ. Turning one's back on him leads to condemnation and destruction. Do true believers fall away? No. By his Word and Spirit, God enables them to remain faithful to the end.

Greek Words, Phrases, and Constructions in 10:32–39

Verse 32

τὰς πρότερον ἡμέρας—the use of the definite article and the position of the adverb πρότερον (earlier) reveal that much time has elapsed since the occurrence of events to which the author alludes.

φωτισθέντες—the aorist passive from φωτίζω (I bring light to) may be understood spiritually to refer to accepting the truth of the gospel and being baptized (see John 1:9; Eph. 1:18; Heb. 6:4).

Verse 34

δεσμίοις—this noun has been subject to change. Writes Bruce M. Metzger: "The reading that best explains the origin of the others is δεσμίοις [prisoners], which is supported by good representatives of both the Alexandrian and the Western types of text, as well as several Eastern witnesses. Through transcriptional oversight the first iota was omitted, resulting in the reading δεσμοῖς [bonds]. Then, in order to improve the sense, copyists added a personal pronoun, either αὐτῶν [their], referring to those mentioned in ver[se] 33b, or μου [my], in imitation of the statements of Php 1:7, 13, 14, 17; Col 4:18."[44]

ὕπαρξιν—the collective noun is actually the equivalent of the more common ὑπάρχοντα (property).

Verse 35

μὴ ἀποβάλητε—the aorist subjunctive preceded by the negative particle conveys the idea that the readers of the epistle were not throwing away their confidence. The writer only warns them never to think about doing this. The aorist subjunctive as imperative is balanced by the present imperative ἀναμιμνήσκεσθε (v. 32).

ἥτις—as an indefinite relative pronoun it has a causal connotation.

Verse 36

ὑπομονῆς—the noun derived from the verb ὑπομένω (I remain, endure) is introduced by ὑπεμείνατε (v. 32).

κομίσησθε—in 6:15 the synonym ἐπέτυχεν appears (also see 11:33). The verb κομίζω (in the middle: I receive, obtain) has the meaning of personally appropriating the promise. Its synonym ἐπιτυγχάνω (I attain, obtain) is a more general term.

Verse 39

ἡμεῖς—this personal pronoun stands first in the sentence, receives all the emphasis, and supports the verb ἐσμέν that is understood in the second part of the verse. The sentence is perfectly balanced to feature the opposites in the contrast.

ὑποστολῆς—a noun derived from ὑποστέλλω (in the middle: I shrink) has its counterpart in πίστεως. And the noun ἀπώλειαν (destruction) from ἀπόλλυμι (I destroy) is balanced by περιποίησιν ψυχῆς (saving of the soul).

Summary of Chapter 10

The first section of chapter 10 is actually a continuation of the theme and content of the preceding chapter. In chapter 9 the author writes of the

---

44. Bruce M. Metzger, *A Textual Commentary on the Greek New Testament* (London and New York: United Bible Societies, 1975), p. 670.

unique sacrifice of Christ, and in the first eighteen verses of chapter 10 he summarizes the teachings concerning this unique sacrifice. That is, Christ came to set aside the shadows of the Levitical priestly service. By his death he established the era of the new covenant.

Quoting Psalm 40:6–7, the writer of Hebrews underlines the significance of Christ's sacrifice over against animal sacrifices. Christ came to do the will of God. That is important, for God takes no pleasure in sacrifices and offerings of animals that were devoted to God as substitutes to atone for man's disobedience.

The difference between the sacrificial system of the old covenant and that of the new covenant is the repetitive nature of presenting sacrifices in the one, and the once-for-all offering in the other. The sacrifice of Christ is sufficient to sanctify his people. They have God's law written on their hearts and minds. And they know that because of Christ's perfect sacrifice, their sins have been forgiven.

The second part of chapter 10 is also the beginning of the second part of the epistle. This segment features exhortations and admonitions. The readers are exhorted to enter the presence of God because Christ has opened the way by shedding his blood.

The writer encourages the believers to remain true to their confession; he challenges them to demonstrate their love in word and deed; and he admonishes them to seek the fellowship of the saints at worship.

He calls their attention once more (see 3:16–19; 6:4–6) to the sin of falling away from God. He describes the horrible consequences of deliberately sinning against God. The warning against unbelief, "See to it, brothers, that none of you has a sinful, unbelieving heart that turns away from the living God" (3:12), is a recurring refrain in the epistle. In the present section the same warning, although in different wording, is given twice.

But besides warning the people, the author also encourages them. As a loving pastor, he tells them that God will richly reward their faith. They ought to persevere in doing the will of God and live by faith. Because of their faith in God, they are saved.

The chapter ends with the introduction of the concept *faith*. And faith is the subject of the next chapter.

11

The Heroes of Faith

11:1–40

Outline

11 1 Now faith is being sure of what we hope for and certain of what we do not see. 2 This is what the ancients were commended for.

3 By faith we understand that the universe was formed at God's command, so that what is seen was not made out of what was visible.

A. A Definition of Faith
11:1–3

The writer delights in recounting the history of the heroes of faith recorded in Scripture. Before he cites examples, however, he composes a brief definition of faith. He does not write a dogmatic exposition. Instead he formulates a few clear, straightforward sentences.

1. Now faith is being sure of what we hope for and certain of what we do not see.

As we study this verse, let us note the following points:

a. *Faith.* The word *faith* in the New Testament has many aspects. For example, when the Judean Christians, whom Paul had sought to destroy, spoke of their belief in Christ, they said, "The man who formerly persecuted us is now preaching the faith he once tried to destroy" (Gal. 1:23). Faith, then, is a confession, much the same as we call the Apostles' Creed the articles of our Christian faith. However, this is not the meaning of faith that the writer of Hebrews conveys.

For the evangelists who wrote the Gospels, Jesus Christ is the object of faith. John summarizes this emphasis when he states the purpose of his Gospel, namely, "that you may believe that Jesus is the Christ, the Son of God, and that by believing you may have life in his name" (John 20:31). Also, the Acts show that in the first century, "a personal faith in Jesus was a hallmark of the early Christians."[1]

Still another aspect of faith is Paul's emphasis on appropriating, that is, claiming salvation in Jesus Christ. Paul contends that God puts the sinner right with him through faith: "This righteousness from God comes through faith in Jesus Christ to all who believe" (Rom. 3:22). And Paul explains that faith comes from hearing the Word proclaimed (Rom. 10:17).

---

1. Donald Guthrie, *New Testament Theology* (Downers Grove, Ill.: Inter-Varsity, 1981), p. 588.

The author of Hebrews recognizes these same aspects of faith featured by other writers of the New Testament. However, his use of the concept *faith* must be understood primarily in the context of the eleventh chapter of his epistle. The heroes of faith have one thing in common: they put their undivided confidence in God. In spite of all their trials and difficult circumstances, they triumphed because of their trust in God. For the author, faith is adhering to the promises of God, depending on the Word of God, and remaining faithful to the Son of God.

When we see chapter 11 in the context of Hebrews, the author's design to contrast faith with the sin of unbelief (3:12, 19; 4:2; 10:38–39) becomes clear. Over against the sin of falling away from the living God, the writer squarely places the virtue of faith.[2] Those people who shrink from putting their trust in God are destroyed, but those who believe are saved (10:39).

b. *Assurance.* What is true faith? In 1563 a German theology professor, Zacharias Ursinus, formulated his personal faith:

> True faith—
>   created in me by the Holy Spirit through the gospel—
> is not only a knowledge and conviction
>   that everything that God reveals in his Word is true,
> but also a deep-rooted assurance
>   that not only others, but I too,
>   have had my sins forgiven,
>   have been made forever right with God,
>   and have been granted salvation.
>   These are gifts of sheer grace
>   earned for us by Christ.[3]

The author of Hebrews expresses that same assurance in much more concise wording: "Faith is being sure of what we hope for." The expression *being sure of* is given as "substance" in other translations.[4] The difference between these translations arises from understanding the original Greek word *hypostasis* subjectively or objectively. If I am sure of something, I have certainty in my heart. This is a subjective knowledge because it is within me. Assurance, then, is a subjective quality. By contrast, the word *substance* is objective because it refers to something that is not part of me. Rather, sub-

---

2. F. W. Grosheide, *De Brief aan de Hebreeën en de Brief van Jakobus* (Kampen: Kok, 1955), p. 255.

3. Heidelberg Catechism, answer 21.

4. See, for example, the KJV, NKJV, and NEB. Other translations have "confidence" (*Phillips*, Lenski), "we are confident" *(Moffatt)*, or "guarantee" (JB). The RV, ASV, RSV, NASB, NAB, and MLB have "assurance." Helmut Köster, in *TDNT,* vol. 8, pp. 586–87, argues that the term *hypostasis* (substance) refers to "the reality of the goods hoped for, which have by nature a transcendent quality." Or, "among the meanings that can be authenticated the one that seems to fit best here is *realization . . . in faith things hoped for become realized,* or *things hoped for become reality.*" See Bauer, p. 847. Both Köster and Bauer favor understanding *hypostasis* subjectively.

stance is something on which I can rely. As one translation has it, "Faith is the title-deed of things hoped for."[5] That, in fact, is objective.

To come to a clear-cut choice in the matter is not easy, for the one translation does not rule out the other. The translation *confidence* or *assurance* has gained prominence, perhaps because 3:14 also has the same word: "We have come to share in Christ if we hold firmly till the end the confidence we had at first." In the case of 11:1, even though the objective sense has validity, the subjective meaning is commended.

The author teaches the virtue of hope wherever he is able to introduce the topic (3:6; 6:11, 18; 7:19; 10:23). Hope is not an inactive hidden quality. Hope is active and progressive. It relates to all the things God has promised to believers: "all things of present grace and future glory."[6]

c. *Certainty.* Although the brief statement on faith consists of only two phrases, they are perfectly balanced. Note the structure:

	Faith
	is
being sure of	certain of
what we hope for	what we do not see

In short, assurance is balanced by certainty. These two nouns are in this text synonymous. Certainty, then, means "inner conviction."[7] The believer is convinced that the things he is unable to see are real. Not every conviction, however, is equal to faith. Conviction is the equivalent of faith when certainty prevails, even though the evidence is lacking. The things we do not see are those that pertain to the future, that in time will become the present. Even things of the present, and certainly those of the past, that are beyond our reach belong to the category of "what we do not see." Comments B. F. Westcott, "Hope includes that which is internal as well as that which is external."[8] Hope centers in the mind and spirit of man; sight relates to one of his senses (Rom. 8:24–25).

Faith, therefore, radiates from man's inner being where hope resides to riches that are beyond his purview. Faith demonstrates itself in confident assurance and convincing certainty.

2. This is what the ancients were commended for.

A somewhat literal translation of this verse reads, "It is for their faith that

---

5. James Hope Moulton and George Milligan, *The Vocabulary of the Greek Testament Illustrated from the Papyri and Other Non-Literary Sources* (London: Hodder and Stoughton, 1930), pp. 659–60.

6. John Owen, *An Exposition of Hebrews,* 7 vols. in 4 (Evansville, Ind.: Sovereign Grace, 1960), vol. 7, p. 7.

7. Bauer, p. 249.

8. B. F. Westcott, *Commentary on the Epistle to the Hebrews* (Grand Rapids: Eerdmans, 1950), p. 350.

the men of old [the elders] stand on record" (NEB).[9] The faith demonstrated by the ancients gained them God's approval. The term *ancients,* more literally "elders," refers to the same group of people listed as "forefathers" in 1:1. All of them have one thing in common: their faith. For that faith they are commended by God.

The writer of Hebrews begins his list of the heroes of faith with Abel and Enoch. For both of these illustrations, he uses the verb *to commend.* In verse 4 we read, "By faith [Abel] was commended as a righteous man," and in verse 5, "For before [Enoch] was taken, he was commended as one who pleased God." It would not be necessary for the author to say that everyone mentioned in the list was commended. All the ancients whose names are recorded in sacred history experienced God's favor because of their faith. For their faith they were recognized by God and by his people.

3. By faith we understand that the universe was formed at God's command, so that what is seen was not made out of what was visible.

At first sight we are inclined to read verse 3 with verse 1 and consider verse 2 the logical heading of the list of the men of faith. But we have no justification for rearranging the author's design. He begins his illustrations of demonstrating faith with a comment about creation. No one was present at creation to observe the formation of the world. "Where were you when I laid the earth's foundation?" God asks Job (38:4). By using the plural *we understand,* the author includes himself and all his readers in the confession that God created the world.

The first declaration in the long list of the verses beginning with "by faith" is so rich in meaning that we do well to discuss this verse phrase by phrase. Before we enter upon a full discussion, however, we should note that verse 3b is translated in two ways. That is, the negative adverb *not* is placed either before the verb *to make* or before the word *appear*—apart from variations in translating this verse. The verse can be translated either "so that what is seen was not made out of what was visible"[10] or "so that what is seen was made out of things which do not appear."[11] Translators are about equally divided on this particular issue. We shall discuss the matter as it presents itself in the sequence of the verse.

a. "By faith." This is the first occurrence in a series of twenty-one uses of the phrase *by faith.* After these the author tells the readers that he lacks the time to write about additional Old Testament saints who also showed their faith (11:32–38). "These were all commended for their faith" (11:39).

b. "We understand." The author and his readers are able to understand

---

9. The expression *elder* describes a person who is both aged and dignified. Spanish-speaking people honor a gentleman by calling him "don." Not every gentleman, however, receives this title; it is given to him who has gained the respect of the community.

10. Among the translations that negate the verb *to make* are the KJV, NKJV, RV, ASV, NASB, NIV, and JB.

11. The translations that negate "to appear" include the RSV, NEB, NAB, GNB, MLB, *Phillips,* and *Moffatt.*

God's creation by faith. Although we are unable to observe that which is invisible, in our minds we recognize the power of God. Understanding creation—even in a limited sense—means that we reflect in faith on the relationship of Creator to creation.[12] In Romans 1:20 Paul provides a striking parallel that even in translation is close.

Romans 1:20	*Hebrews 11:3*
For since	By faith we understand
the Creation of the world	that the universe was formed
God's invisible qualities...	at God's command,
have been clearly seen, being understood from what has been made	so that what is seen, was not made out of what was visible

c. "The universe was formed." Translations vary from "world" or "worlds" to "universe" (see Heb. 1:2). The concept includes "the whole scheme of time and space" *(Phillips).* Moreover, God gave form, shape, and order to the universe. According to the creation account in Genesis, "God created the heavens and the earth" (1:1) and then proceeded to give structure and variety to a formless and empty earth.

d. "At God's command." We are immediately reminded of the six commands God spoke at the time of creation (Gen. 1:3, 6, 9, 14, 20, 24). "By the word ⌐f ⌐he LORD were the heavens made," says the psalmist (Ps. 33:6). Purposely God created the world in such a manner that man can understand its origin only by faith. God made the world by his command. "For he spoke, and it came to be; he commanded, and it stood firm" (Ps. 33:9).

e. "So that what is seen." The author of Hebrews refers to that which visibly exists in God's creation—that is, light, sky, stars, earth, and countless other things.[13] Man is able to see all these entities with his physical eyes. These things, however, have not been made of what can be observed.

f. "Was not made out of what was visible." Because no one was present at the time of creation, eyewitness reports do not exist. Man must rely on what God has revealed to him about the creation of the universe and the formation of the world. And by faith man ascertains that creation originates with God.

How should verse 3 be translated? I have adopted the translation that negates the verb *to make,* for this translation appears to favor the flow of the argument. The word *visible* implies that at one time this creation did not exist and therefore is not eternal. Creation has a beginning. Moreover, prior to creation, the invisible prevailed.[14] We would have been happy to receive more revelation concerning this point, but the author of Hebrews

12. Günther Harder, *NIDNTT,* vol. 3, p. 128.

13. John Albert Bengel, *Gnomon of the New Testament,* ed. Andrew R. Fausset, 7th ed., 5 vols. (Edinburgh: Clark, 1877), vol. 4, p. 445.

14. Grosheide, *Hebreeën,* p. 260.

provides no further information where God's revelation is silent. We do well not to speculate (Deut. 29:29).

Practical Considerations in 11:1-3

Chapter 11 is the chapter about faith in the Epistle to the Hebrews. Earlier in the letter the author introduces the concept *faith* when he speaks of the disobedient Israelites. These people heard the message of the gospel, but they "did not combine it with faith" (4:2). They persevered not; instead they followed their own willful way. The writer stresses the aspect of perseverance of faith (10:36) and places faith conspicuously over against unbelief. Faith, then, is the confidence the believer expresses when he faces blatant unbelief.

This unbelief surrounds the believer especially when the origin of the world becomes the topic of discussion. Modern man refuses to accept the creation account recorded in Genesis. For him the teaching of evolution solves problems and answers questions. Because this doctrine is a substitute for the biblical account of creation, man rejects God and his Word. Countering unbelief, the Christian unwaveringly maintains his faith. He confidently teaches the creation account that God has revealed in Scripture.

Greek Words, Phrases, and Constructions in 11:1-3

Verse 1

ἐλπιζομένων—this present passive participle in the plural lacks the definite article to give the participle a broader range. The case is genitive—not subjective but objective. The present tense implies continued activity.

ὑπόστασις—a compound noun, derived from ὑπό (under) and ἵστημι (I stand), it has been translated as "substance," "being" (Heb. 1:3), or "confidence" (Heb. 3:14).

οὐ βλεπομένων—the present passive participle is preceded by the negative particle οὐ, not μή. The use "of οὐ with the participle means that the negative is clearcut and decisive."[15] The present tense is descriptive. The genitive case is objective.

Verse 3

νοοῦμεν—closely linked to πίστις, the verb νοέω (I perceive with my mind) discloses that faith is not blind assent but engages man's intellect and mind.

ῥήματι θεοῦ—both nouns appear without a definite article. In the following passages the definite article occurs: Luke 22:61; John 3:34; 8:47; Acts 11:16. The absence of the article, the use of ῥῆμα instead of λόγος, and the reference to the creation account make the translation *at God's command* unique.

εἰς τὸ μὴ . . . γεγονέναι—"we have a clear example of result,"[16] not of purpose. The use of the perfect infinitive shows permanence. That which has been created has lasting validity and stability. The definite article need not precede the infinitive without any intervening words (see, for example, Mark 5:4; Acts 8:11; I Peter 4:2).

---

15. A. T. Robertson, *A Grammar of the Greek New Testament in the Light of Historical Research* (Nashville: Broadman, 1934), pp. 1137–38.

16. Ibid., p. 1003.

For this reason, the negative particle μή fits in better with the infinitive construction than with the preposition and participle ἐκ φαινομένων.

---

4 By faith Abel offered God a better sacrifice than Cain did. By faith he was commended as a righteous man, when God spoke well of his offerings. And by faith he still speaks, even though he is dead.

5 By faith Enoch was taken from this life, so that he did not experience death; he could not be found, because God had taken him away. For before he was taken, he was commended as one who pleased God.   6 And without faith it is impossible to please God, because anyone who comes to him must believe that he exists and that he rewards those who earnestly seek him.

7 By faith Noah, when warned about things not yet seen, in holy fear built an ark to save his family. By his faith he condemned the world and became heir of the righteousness that comes by faith.

B. Three Examples of Faith: Abel, Enoch, and Noah
11:4–7

The contrast between faith and unbelief is exemplified in the lives of the forefathers. The writer presents the positive element *faith;* nevertheless, by mentioning the name *Cain,* he introduces an example of disobedience and unbelief.

4. By faith Abel offered God a better sacrifice than Cain did. By faith he was commended as a righteous man, when God spoke well of his offerings. And by faith he still speaks, even though he is dead.

The author places the name of Abel, and by implication that of Adam, at the beginning of his list of Old Testament saints. Adam's son Abel occupies a special place in sacred history, for even Jesus calls him righteous (Matt. 23:35; Luke 11:51).

With reference to Abel, note the following points:

a. Abel presented a "better sacrifice" than did his brother Cain. As a tiller of the soil, Cain brought some of its fruits. Abel, the shepherd, sacrificed the fat of "some of the firstborn of his flock" (Gen. 4:4). Is the word *better* (literally, "greater") an indication that animal sacrifices were more acceptable to God than were the fruits of the field? No. We should look not at the gifts but at the giver. The historical context is quite explicit. In Genesis 4:6–7 we read: "Then the LORD said to Cain, 'Why are you angry? Why is your face downcast? If you do what is right, will you not be accepted? But if you do not do what is right, sin is crouching at your door; it desires to have you, but you must master it.' "

The Septuagint version of verse 7 reads, "Did you not sin when you offered [your sacrifice] correctly, but did not divide it correctly?"[17] Throughout his epistle the author of Hebrews shows that he depends on this Greek

---

17. Clement of Rome says the same thing: "If thou offeredst rightly, but didst not divide rightly, didst thou not sin?" *The Apostolic Fathers*, vol. 1, I Clem. 4:4 (LCL).

translation of the Old Testament. But the author's choice of version is not at issue. The fact remains that Cain's attitude toward God was sinful. In effect, God pleaded with him to repent, to change his way of life, and to conquer sin. However, the writer introduces Cain's name only for contrast; he is interested in Abel's faith. Notice, for example, that the expression *by faith* occurs three times in this verse (NIV).

b. Abel was a "righteous man." He lived in harmony with God and man and therefore became known as a righteous man. How God communicated with Abel is not known. One assumes that as God spoke directly with Cain, so he addressed Abel. There is no reason to resort to interpretations that hold that God communicated through symbols, such as fire that came down from heaven to consume Abel's sacrifice or smoke that ascended from this sacrifice.[18] The Genesis account provides no further information on how God "looked with favor on Abel and his offering" (4:4). God looked on Abel's heart and was pleased with the motives of the giver. As Paul puts it, "God loves a cheerful giver" (II Cor. 9:7).

c. Even after his death, Abel is a constant witness. The text ("he still speaks, even though he is dead") can be interpreted to refer to Abel's blood. God says to Cain, "Your brother's blood cries out to me from the ground" (Gen. 4:10; see also Matt. 23:35; Luke 11:51; Heb. 12:24). But the writer of Hebrews stresses the concept *faith,* not the avenging of Abel's blood. The difficulty of relating faith to blood that has been shed ought not be bolstered by a quick reference to Revelation 6:10, where the souls under the altar cry out, "How long, Sovereign Lord, holy and true, until you judge the inhabitants of the earth and avenge our blood?" Not the blood of Abel, but the faith of Abel is important; therefore, the reference to the souls under the altar is of little consequence. The author places Abel before the readers as a righteous man who lived by faith (Heb. 10:38). Abel is at the top of the list of the Old Testament heroes of faith. Even after his death, his example encourages people to seek the Lord, because he rewards those who earnestly seek him. Abel, then, is the father of believers of the time before Abraham. His faith in God still speaks as a constant witness.

5. By faith Enoch was taken from this life, so that he did not experience death; he could not be found, because God had taken him away. For before he was taken, he was commended as one who pleased God.

As Abel showed his love toward God, so Enoch, a member of the seventh generation in the family of Adam (Gen. 5:1–24; Jude 14), served the Lord. The writer of Hebrews chooses Enoch as the next person who exemplified a life of true dedication to God. The Genesis account is rather brief:

---

18. Speculation about why Abel's sacrifice was better than Cain's has occupied numerous commentators from ancient times to the present. One of Rembrandt's paintings portrays the two brothers as they present their offerings to God. The smoke of Abel's sacrifice spirals heavenward; that of Cain's fails to ascend.

When Enoch had lived 65 years, he became the father of Methuselah. And after he became the father of Methuselah, Enoch walked with God 300 years and had other sons and daughters. Altogether, Enoch lived 365 years. Enoch walked with God; then he was no more, because God took him away. [5:21–24]

Whereas the information about Abel comes to us in the form of a historical account, the details concerning Enoch are recorded in a genealogy. Yet the facts are sufficiently clear. All the other people mentioned in the genealogy are described by the same refrain, "and then he died." But "Enoch was taken from this life, so that he did not experience death." And the writer introduces this sentence with the expression *by faith*. Because of his faith, Enoch did not face death but was translated to glory.

When the author says, "Enoch was taken from this life," he actually repeats the conclusion of the Genesis account. The conclusion rests on the clause *Enoch walked with God,* which appears twice in his genealogy.[19] What does the phrase *walk with God* mean? It means that a person lives a spiritual life in which he tells God everything (see Gen. 6:9). Enoch lived a normal life of rearing sons and daughters, but his entire life was characterized by his love for God. For this reason God took him to heaven.

Note that the author writes the phrase *was (or: had) taken* three times. Enoch's faith was so strong and his relationship to God so close that he was kept from dying. The curse of death pronounced upon Adam and his descendants did not prevail against Enoch, for God transformed him. Enoch "was commended as one who pleased God."[20]

6. And without faith it is impossible to please God, because anyone who comes to him must believe that he exists and that he rewards those who earnestly seek him.

This text teaches a spiritual truth that touches the spiritual life of every believer. It is one of the most eloquent expressions of faith and prayer in the Epistle to the Hebrews. By comparison, Paul's declaration that "everything that does not come from faith is sin" (Rom. 14:23) is short. In one beautifully constructed verse, the writer of Hebrews communicates the method of pleasing God, the necessity of believing his existence, and the certainty of answered prayer.

a. How do we please God? By walking with him in faith! We must fully trust God and confide in him as our closest friend. "Without faith it is impossible to please God." The word *impossible* is a reminder of Hebrews 6:4. It conveys the idea that faith is the indispensable ingredient for pleasing God.

---

19. In the intertestamental period, several writers mentioned Enoch. For example, in Sir. 44:16 we read, "Enoch pleased the Lord, and was taken up; he was an example of repentance to all generations" (RSV). See the extracanonical books Wis. 4:10; Jub. 4:17–21; 10:17; I En.
20. The author of Hebrews takes the Old Testament quotation of Gen. 5:24 not from the Hebrew text but from the Greek translation.

b. Why do we pray to God? When the believer prays to God, he must believe that God exists. Although God's existence is an established truth for the believer, repeatedly he will ignore God by failing to pray to him. God, however, desires that the believer pray continually.

c. How do we seek God in prayer? Earnestly, in full confidence! The sinner receives pardon; the suppliant, mercy; and the righteous, peace. God invites us to come to him in full assurance that he will hear and answer prayers. "So," says the writer, "do not throw away your confidence; it will be richly rewarded" (10:35).

Rewards can never be earned. In his sovereign goodness, God grants rewards not in terms of payments, but as blessings on his people. God grants us the gift of life eternal. "No human action can in any way counterbalance this in value."[21] God's rewards to us are free, for he is sovereign.

7. By faith Noah, when warned about things not yet seen, in holy fear built an ark to save his family. By his faith he condemned the world and became heir of the righteousness that comes by faith.

One person demonstrated his faith in God in a world of unbelief, and that person was Noah. In the historical account of the flood, we read that God told Noah about an impending flood that would destroy life because of man's great wickedness. God warned Noah that he would wipe out men, animals, and birds when a period of 120 years had ended (Gen. 6:1–7). Noah found favor in God's eyes, for "he walked with God" (Gen. 6:8–9). Like his ancestors, Abel and Enoch, he put his full trust in God.

God instructed Noah to build an ark of specific and adequate size to hold his family and all the animals and birds that God wanted to keep alive. God informed Noah "about things not yet seen" (see Heb. 11:1).

Although the Scripture bears no record of the ridicule, the harassment, and the delays Noah had to endure while he built a huge ship, presumably on dry land, we can be sure that he felt the rough edge of unbelief. Jeers, taunts, and scorn constituted his daily diet of opposition.

Noah stood alone in the midst of a hostile world. Apart from the immediate members of his family, he could not find any support. To believe in God amid fellow believers is relatively easy. But to have no one to lean on except God is the true test of faith. Noah believed and "in holy fear built an ark to save his family." On the one hand he expressed deep reverence to God, and on the other hand he was terrified because of the coming destruction. He was filled with holy fear at the prospect of God's judgment on the sinful world. For if he had not believed God's warning, he would not have been afraid. His faith drove him to fear and to build. Obediently he followed the instructions God gave him. He constructed the ark and by doing so demonstrated his firm confidence in God. His faith became his testimony

---

21. Paul Christoph Böttger, *NIDNTT,* vol. 3, p. 143. Also see John Calvin, *Epistle to the Hebrews* (Grand Rapids: Eerdmans, 1949), p. 272.

that condemned the unbelieving world around him. Noah's faith stood dia-
metrically opposed to the unbelief of the world.

Scripture describes Noah as a righteous man (Gen. 6:9). Ezekiel writes of
the possibility that God would send a famine to a country that sins against
him; should Noah, Daniel, and Job be in that country, "they could save only
themselves by their righteousness" (Ezek. 14:14, 20). And Peter calls Noah
"a preacher of righteousness" (II Peter 2:5). The writer of Hebrews says that
Noah "became heir of the righteousness that comes by faith." No prophet
ever preached such a message of doom as Noah did for such an extended
time—120 years. Moreover, Noah preached to the entire world of that day.

By his faith Noah inherited the gift of righteousness. His ancestor Abel
"was commended as a righteous man" (Heb. 11:4). Noah, however, became
the possessor of righteousness; that is, his way of life was a pattern of righteousness always in opposition to unbelief. His life was a constant example
of obedience to God's will. Throughout his righteous life, Noah found God's
favor. By faith he pleased God.

Practical Considerations in 11:4–7

The heroes of faith who preceded Abraham were true pioneers: Abel, Enoch,
and Noah. These men stood virtually alone in their contest of faith; unbelief and
disobedience surrounded them and a believing community to support them did
not exist.

Consider Abel, for instance. His father and mother had fallen into disobedience
and were driven out of Paradise. His brother refused to listen to the voice of God
and became a servant of sin (Gen. 4:7). Abel, by contrast, desired to serve God and
to do God's will. He put his trust in the Lord. He was a solitary figure, a true
pioneer, a child of God.

We know very little about the world in which Enoch lived. The writer places
Enoch's name in a genealogy and refrains from writing historical details. Nevertheless, he singles out Enoch's characteristic: Enoch walked with God. All the other
persons mentioned in the genealogy (Gen. 5:3–32) lack this description. Only
Enoch is known as a man of faith.

And last, Noah walked with God (Gen. 6:9). He, too, stood (with his own family)
as a pioneer of faith. The world forsook him, yet he remained faithful.

Note the following:

For his faith Abel paid the price of his life.

Because of his faith Enoch was taken from this life.

By faith Noah saved his own family's life.

Greek Words, Phrases, and Constructions in 11:4–7

Verse 4

πλείονα—the accusative singular, masculine and feminine, comparative adjective
of πολύς (much, many) signifies not quantity but rather quality. The translation
better is therefore preferred.

αὐτοῦ τοῦ θεοῦ—a variant of this reading (αὐτοῦ τῷ θεῷ), in spite of its manu-script support, "provides no satisfactory sense."[22] The genitive τοῦ θεοῦ and the present active participle μαρτυροῦντος form the genitive absolute construction.

δι' αὐτῆς—this feminine singular pronoun can refer to either the antecedent πίστις (faith) or θυσία (sacrifice). Because of the writer's emphasis on faith, the New International Version and the New English Bible relate both δι' ἧς and δι' αὐτῆς to πίστις.

Verse 5

ηὑρίσκετο—the imperfect passive of εὑρίσκω (I find) expresses repeated action in the past. That is, the people kept on looking for Enoch.

μεμαρτύρηται—the use of the perfect tense reveals continued action from the past to the present.

Verse 7

βλεπομένων—artistically the author of Hebrews links this verse to the introductory statement (v. 1). Note, however, that in verse 1 the negative particle precedes the participle, whereas here it is μηδέπω (not yet).

δι' ἧς—three antecedents in the feminine precede the relative pronoun ἧς. They are πίστις, κιβωτός, and σωτηρία. As in verse 4, the context favors the word *faith*.

---

8 By faith Abraham, when called to go to a place he would later receive as his inheritance, obeyed and went, even though he did not know where he was going.   9 By faith he made his home in the promised land like a stranger in a foreign country; he lived in tents, as did Isaac and Jacob, who were heirs with him of the same promise.   10 For he was looking forward to the city with foundations, whose architect and builder is God.

11 By faith Abraham, even though he was past age—and Sarah herself was barren—was enabled to become a father because he considered him faithful who had made the promise.   12 And so from this one man, and he as good as dead, came descendants as numerous as the stars in the sky and as countless as the sand on the seashore.

13 All these people were still living by faith when they died. They did not receive the things promised; they only saw them and welcomed them from a distance. And they admitted that they were aliens and strangers on earth.   14 People who say such things show that they are looking for a country of their own.   15 If they had been thinking of the country they had left, they would have had opportunity to return.   16 Instead, they were longing for a better country—a heavenly one. Therefore God is not ashamed to be called their God, for he has prepared a city for them.

17 By faith Abraham, when God tested him, offered Isaac as a sacrifice. He who had received the promises was about to sacrifice his one and only son,   18 even though God had said to him, "It is through Isaac that your offspring will be reckoned."   19 Abraham reasoned that God could raise the dead, and figuratively speaking, he did receive Isaac back from death.

---

22. Bruce M. Metzger, *A Textual Commentary on the Greek New Testament* (London and New York: United Bible Societies, 1975), pp. 671–72.

C. The Faith of Abraham
11:8–19

1. The Promised Land
11:8–10

Abraham is known as the father of believers, and thus the writer of Hebrews devotes much time and space to this patriarch. Abraham lived with promises God had given him, and in faith he accepted their reality.

8. By faith Abraham, when called to go to a place he would later receive as his inheritance, obeyed and went, even though he did not know where he was going. 9. By faith he made his home in the promised land like a stranger in a foreign country; he lived in tents, as did Isaac and Jacob, who were heirs with him of the same promise. 10. For he was looking forward to the city with foundations, whose architect and builder is God.

Abraham's faith triumphed in at least three different instances. First, God asked him to go to a land that he would show Abraham and give to him as an inheritance. Yet of that land, which proved to be Canaan, Abraham never owned a foot of ground except the burial plot he bought for Sarah, his wife (Gen. 23:3–20; Acts 7:5). Second, God promised that he would make of Abraham a great nation. When he reached his one hundredth birthday, his son Isaac was born; and fifteen years before Abraham's death, his grandsons Jacob and Esau entered the world. But Abraham never saw "descendants as numerous as the stars in the sky and as countless as the sand on the seashore" (Heb. 11:12). Also, God called Abraham to sacrifice his son Isaac, for God wanted to test Abraham's faith. And that faith triumphed.

One other observation. Noah received instructions to build an ark to save his family from impending doom. Although he had to wait for 120 years before the flood came, he nevertheless saw the fulfillment of God's warning and the result of his own faith. Abraham, however, received two promises— the inheritance of the Promised Land and the formation of a mighty people as his descendants. But he never saw these promises fulfilled in his lifetime, even though he lived for 175 years. Abraham, to be sure, lived by faith.

As we consider Abraham's faith in respect to the Promised Land, we note:

a. *A place.* A more literal translation of the first part of verse 8 is, "By faith, while he was being called, Abraham obeyed to go out to a place which he was about to receive as an inheritance." As soon as God called, Abraham responded obediently and was ready to do the Lord's bidding. "Leave your country, your people and your father's household and go to the land I will show you" (Gen. 12:1). In faith Abraham left, not knowing where the Lord would lead. What a break with his kinsfolk! Abraham could not even inform his relatives where he was going, because he did not know.

What were the reasons for Abraham's departure? God wished to fulfill his promise to Abraham to make him into a great nation, to bless him, and to

321

make Abraham's name great (Gen. 12:2–3). God also called Abraham to make his own name great. Through the patriarch, God revealed himself as the faithful covenant God who keeps his promises.

b. *A land.* Abraham received God's promise that he would become heir of a place God would give him. That place was the land of Canaan, the land of the promise. Abraham traveled from Haran to Canaan, leaving his relatives behind in Paddan Aram. He lived in the southern part of Canaan in tents. He remained an alien and in a sense an outsider who had little in common with the local population.[23] That Abraham lived in a tent indicated that he was a wandering herdsman who possessed countless animals, but no land.

Yet God had promised the land to Abraham, and he repeated the promise to Isaac and to Jacob. For three generations the heirs of the land lived in faith with a promise. Not until the twelve tribes of Israel entered the land under the leadership of Joshua were they able to claim the promise and make the land their own.

c. *A city.* Abraham's stay in Canaan was as temporary as the pegs he drove into the ground to keep his tents pitched. He constantly moved from place to place, and so did his son and his grandson. His stay may have been temporary, but his faith was enduring.

Abraham's faith in God reached beyond the promise of a place or a land, even though God had promised the land to him and his descendants. Abraham knew that earthly possessions are temporary; he always kept his eye of faith on "the city with foundations, whose architect and builder is God."

> In the land of fadeless day
> Lies the city foursquare;
> It shall never pass away,
> And there is no night there.
> —John R. Clements

The father of believers walked with God; "he was called God's friend" (James 2:23). In faith he knew that the city God had designed and built has everlasting foundations (Rev. 21:14, 19). He looked forward to the new Jerusalem, "the city of the living God" (Heb. 12:22), to which all believers come to find accommodation.

Abraham knew that his earthly dwelling could not be compared with the heavenly city of which God himself was architect and builder. In faith he envisioned the eventual gathering of all believers for the feast of redemption. He anticipated the coming and the work of the Christ, for in him all believers are one with the Son and the Father.

By faith Abraham, although living in tents, looked to the permanent city. For him this city marked the fulfillment of the promises God had made.

---

23. Hans Bietenhard, *NIDNTT,* vol. 1, p. 690, defines an alien as "one who lives among resident citizens without having citizen rights yet enjoying the protection of the community."

Therefore Abraham looked not at the process of salvation, but at its conclusion.

2. The Promised Son
11:11–12

The author of Hebrews follows the historical sequence of the Genesis account. He moves from the promise of the land to the promise of the son.

11. By faith Abraham, even though he was past age—and Sarah herself was barren—was enabled to become a father because he considered him faithful who had made the promise. 12. And so from this one man, and he as good as dead, came descendants as numerous as the stars in the sky and as countless as the sand on the seashore.

The translation of the New International Version differs sharply from others. At first sight the reader may regard the translation of verse 11 as a radical departure from the well-known wording of that text. The Revised Standard Version provides a representative reading of verse 11: "By faith Sarah herself received power to conceive, even when she was past the age, since she considered him faithful who had promised." The New American Standard Bible has "ability to conceive" instead of "power to conceive," but adds this informative marginal note, "Literally, *power for the laying down of seed*" (italics in original). That literal translation is the essence of the problem because the italicized phrase "is used of the sexual function of the male."[24] In other words, the subject of verse 11 is Abraham, not Sarah.

Explanations for this curious problem are numerous, and the translations themselves reflect them. Here are a few explanations:

a. The writer of Hebrews places the expression *and Sarah herself* near the beginning of the original Greek sentence, immediately after the phrase *by faith.* He seems to indicate, by the nominative case, that Sarah is the subject of the sentence. The translators of the New International Version and the Good News Bible have inserted the name *Abraham* to show that the patriarch is the logical subject and that the name *Abraham* suits the broader context.

b. The Greek idiom, translated literally and modestly as "power for the laying down of seed," always refers to the male and not to the female. Therefore, to translate the idiom as "power to conceive" is contrary to linguistic usage. It fails to do justice to the original text and appears to be an accommodation to the presence of the name *Sarah.*

c. Many commentators take the approach that as husband and wife are one so Abraham and Sarah should be mentioned together. They contend that the original Greek for the words *Sarah herself* may be read as a dative. The reading then is, "By faith he [Abraham] also, together with Sarah,

---

24. Friedrich Hauck, *TDNT,* vol. 3, p. 621. Also see Joseph H. Thayer, *A Greek-English Lexicon of the New Testament* (New York, Cincinnati, and Chicago: American Book Company, 1889), p. 330.

received power to beget a child."[25] Plausible as this explanation may be, the fact remains that manuscript evidence cannot provide definite proof for this reading.

d. Still others suggest that the subject of verse 11 is Sarah and that the idiom "power for the laying down of seed" actually means "she received power to establish a posterity."[26] The difficulty this suggestion meets is that Abraham, not Sarah, is the father and founder of the nation Israel.

e. Perhaps we should understand the words "and Sarah herself was barren" to be a parenthetical thought of the author. If the words referring to Sarah had not been in the text, no one would have difficulty translating and interpreting the text. Verse 11 expresses the thought that Abraham "was enabled to become a father" and is a natural introduction to verse 12. To delete the clause about Sarah is unthinkable because of manuscript support for these words. But to understand it as a parenthetical comment is feasible and sensible.[27]

Also Paul comments on Abraham's faith in God, who would make him "the father of many nations." Says Paul, "Without weakening in his faith, he faced the fact that his body was as good as dead—since he was about a hundred years old—and that Sarah's womb was also dead" (Rom. 4:19). Abraham trusted that God would honor his promise. God is faithful.

The result of Abraham's faith is that from one man numerous descendants were born. The author of Hebrews knows that his readers are fully acquainted with the history of the patriarch. Therefore, he minimizes his allusions to that history. He says that Abraham was "as good as dead" and that his offspring were "as numerous as the stars in the sky and as countless as the sand on the seashore" (Gen. 15:5; 22:17; 32:12; Exod. 32:13; Deut. 1:10; 10:22).

Both Abraham and Sarah were well advanced in age—Sarah considered herself "worn out" and her husband "old" (Gen. 18:12). That Abraham married after Sarah's death and had six children (Gen. 25:1–2) has no bearing on this matter. The author of Hebrews is interested in the fulfillment of the promise of God: Isaac, the son of the promise (Gen. 21:12; Rom. 9:7; Heb. 11:18).

---

25. F. F. Bruce, *The Epistle to the Hebrews,* New International Commentary on the New Testament series (Grand Rapids: Eerdmans, 1964), p. 302. Also see R. C. H. Lenski, *The Interpretation of the Epistle of the Hebrews and of the Epistle of James* (Columbus: Wartburg, 1946), p. 393; Otto Michel, *Der Brief an die Hebräer,* 10th ed. (Göttingen: Vandenhoeck and Ruprecht, 1957), p. 262; and Leon Morris, *The Expositor's Bible Commentary,* vol. 12, *Hebrews* (Grand Rapids: Zondervan, 1981), p. 119.

26. Thomas Hewitt, *The Epistle to the Hebrews* (Grand Rapids: Eerdmans, 1960), p. 175. Also see Philip Edgcumbe Hughes, *Commentary on the Epistle to the Hebrews* (Grand Rapids: Eerdmans, 1977), p. 473; and Bauer, p. 409.

27. Metzger, *Textual Commentary,* p. 672, reports on the deliberations of the Editorial Committee: "Appreciating the lexical difficulty, but unwilling to emend the text, a majority of the Committee understood the words [and Sarah herself was barren] to be a Hebraic circumstantial clause, thus allowing [Abraham] (ver. 8) to serve as subject of [he received] ('by faith, even though Sarah was barren, he [Abraham] received power to beget. . . .')."

Countless descendants of Abraham formed the nation Israel. And through Abraham all nations on earth were blessed (Gen. 12:3; Gal. 3:8). But more significantly, Abraham's descendants ultimately are all believers (Rom. 9:6–8; Gal. 3:7–9, 16, 29; 4:28). All believers in Christ call Abraham their father, for in effect, the promised Son is the Christ, not Isaac.

3. The Promise
11:13–16

In Old Testament times believers looked for the coming of Christ. These believers lived by faith, not by sight, for they were the recipients of the promise.

13. All these people were still living by faith when they died. They did not receive the things promised; they only saw them and welcomed them from a distance. And they admitted that they were aliens and strangers on earth.

When the author says "all these people," he means the people who were recipients of the promise, namely, Abraham, Sarah, Isaac, and Jacob. God gave Abraham the promise about the land and repeated it to Isaac and to Jacob. Yet the patriarchs remained tent-dwellers who lived in the land as "aliens and strangers." They received the promise of innumerable offspring; yet when they died, the patriarchs had only sons and grandsons. In short, "they did not receive the things promised." Their faith, however, sustained them, for they believed that God would honor his word and eventually fulfill the promises he had made.

The patriarchs discerned the fulfillment of God's promises in the future. In faith they welcomed this fulfillment, although from a distance. That is, with their eyes of faith, they saw God's goodness in fulfilling promises in his time. But with their physical eyes they saw "that they were aliens and strangers on earth." The list of those believers who considered themselves "aliens and strangers on earth" is extensive. For example, Moses received the promise that the nation Israel would possess Canaan, but he himself never entered the land; he was permitted to see it from one of the mountaintops of Moab (Num. 27:12; Deut. 3:27; 32:49; 34:1–4). Throughout his life Moses was a wanderer who moved from Egypt to Midian and eventually to the border of Canaan. Moses "persevered because he saw him who is invisible" (Heb. 11:27). To the day of his death, he remained an alien and a stranger.

14. People who say such things show that they are looking for a country of their own.

Believers know that this earthly scene is transitory and their heavenly home abiding. Therefore, they fully recognize their temporary stay on earth and long for their eternal dwelling in heaven. Believers do not flee this world (John 17:11, 14). This world, redeemed by Christ, is the Christian's workshop. And whatever honest and honorable occupation the believer pursues, God will bless. Nevertheless, this present earth shall pass away, but according to God's promise, "we are looking forward to a new heaven and a new earth, the home of righteousness" (II Peter 3:13).

15. If they had been thinking of the country they had left, they would have had opportunity to return. 16. Instead, they were longing for a better country—a heavenly one. Therefore God is not ashamed to be called their God, for he has prepared a city for them.

The author of Hebrews intimates that the patriarchs would have had many opportunities to return to their country of origin; to be sure, Abraham had left Ur of the Chaldeans, "the land of his birth" (Gen. 11:28). They could have retraced their steps and moved from Canaan via Haran to Mesopotamia.

Had the patriarchs indeed contemplated returning to their native country, they would have broken faith with God and would have lost the promise God had given them. Abraham had been called away from the land of his father and forefathers, who "worshiped other gods" (Josh. 24:2). He could not return because he had responded in faith to God. Therefore, for Abraham and his son and grandson to retrace their steps to the land of Abraham's origin was unthinkable. In obedience to God's call, the patriarch had entered Canaan, and in full reliance upon his God, he stayed in the Promised Land. Isaac and Jacob showed the same obedience, for Jacob, after spending a number of years in Paddan Aram, returned to the southern part of Canaan. Also, Abraham, Sarah, Isaac, Jacob, and Joseph were buried in the land of the promise.

The other side of the proverbial coin is that the patriarchs sought not an earthly heritage but a heavenly one. Says the writer of Hebrews, "They were longing for a better country." They had their sight set, in faith, on a heavenly country. They looked for life eternal with God who had given them the promises. And their faith was rewarded, for Jesus himself, in answering the Sadducees' question about the resurrection, said, "But about the resurrection of the dead—have you not read what God said to you, 'I am the God of Abraham, the God of Isaac, and the God of Jacob'? He is not the God of the dead but of the living" (Matt. 22:31–32; and see Mark 12:26–27; Luke 20:37–38; Exod. 3:6; 4:5).

God is God of the living. Everyone who puts his faith in God enters that heavenly country mentioned by the author of the epistle. And God is not ashamed to be his God. What an honor to be called children of God! God permits us to bear his name, for he already has prepared a place for us. We are privileged above all others because "our citizenship," as Paul puts it, "is in heaven" (Phil. 3:20). All who in faith long for the heavenly city that God has prepared receive celestial citizenship (John 14:2; Rev. 21:2). "We are hence to conclude, that there is no place for us among God's children, except we renounce the world, and that there will be for us no inheritance in heaven, except we become pilgrims on earth."[28]

---

28. Calvin, *Hebrews*, p. 285.

4. The Test of Faith
11:17–19

After departing somewhat from his theme of Abraham's faith with the introduction of a few verses as a parenthetical thought (vv. 13–16), the writer of Hebrews returns to this theme. He summarizes and concludes his remarks on Abraham's faith on the basis of a vividly historical incident: Abraham's willingness to sacrifice his son Isaac.

17. By faith Abraham, when God tested him, offered Isaac as a sacrifice. He who had received the promises was about to sacrifice his one and only son, 18. even though God had said to him, "It is through Isaac that your offspring will be reckoned." 19. Abraham reasoned that God could raise the dead, and figuratively speaking, he did receive Isaac back from death.

Genesis 22 contains the story of Abraham's greatest test of faith. This story reveals Abraham's readiness to obey God at the expense of Isaac, to cling to God's promises even though obedience to God's command would nullify it, and to believe that God would raise Isaac from the dead. We note three points.

a. *Obedience.* Abraham's faith had triumphed when God directed him to the land of the promise and when God gave him Isaac, the son of the promise. But had Abraham reached a plateau of faith? Was his faith dormant and inactive?[29] Would Abraham be able to submit to a much greater test of faith? Would he be willing to offer his son Isaac as a sacrifice to God?

The writer of Hebrews says that God tested Abraham and implies that the test lasted from the moment God called him to sacrifice Isaac on one of the mountains of Moriah until the angel of the Lord stopped him from slaying Isaac. God tested Abraham to see whether the patriarch's love for God was stronger than his fatherly love for his son Isaac. Therefore, God asked Abraham to sacrifice his son at a place far removed from where they lived. Presumably Sarah may not have been informed about God's command to sacrifice Isaac.

If God had taken Isaac's life by natural or even accidental death, Abraham's faith would have been severely tested. But God asked Abraham to take Isaac and with his own hands kill his son for a sacrifice to God. Job could say, "The LORD gave and the LORD has taken away" (1:21); but Abraham would have to say, "The Lord has given me a son and wants me to give him back as a sacrifice."

Abraham obeyed. He fully complied with God's request. In fact, if God had not intervened, Isaac would have been killed. Abraham showed his unwavering faith in God in humble obedience to God's word. He demonstrated his love for God above anyone else, even his son Isaac.

b. *Promise.* That Abraham responded not in blind faith and slavish obe-

---

29. Ceslaus Spicq, *L'Épître aux Hébreux,* 3d ed., 2 vol. (Paris: Gabalda, 1953), vol. 2, p. 352.

dience is clear from the second part of verse 17 and verse 18. Abraham had received God's promises, especially this word: "It is through Isaac that your offspring will be reckoned" (Gen. 21:12; also see Rom. 9:7). Abraham knew that in Isaac the promise of the multitude of descendants would be fulfilled. Descendants of Isaac would include all the spiritual offspring of Abraham.[30] Thus, with the death of Isaac, the line of believers would be terminated.

The author of Hebrews writes that Abraham "was about to sacrifice his one and only son" (v. 17). Certainly Abraham had Ishmael, but this son belonged to the Egyptian servant Hagar. Isaac, not Ishmael, was the heir, the son of the promise.[31] If Isaac's life were to end, the salvation of the world would not take place. For through Isaac, God's promise of salvation would come to realization. Actually, the promise remained in effect, for God prevented Abraham from terminating Isaac's life and from nullifying the promise. Abraham was about to kill his son, but God said, "Do not lay a hand on the boy. Do not do anything to him. Now I know that you fear God, because you have not withheld from me your son, your only son" (Gen. 22:12).

c. *Power.* In genuine faith Abraham believed that God would raise Isaac from the dead. He knew that God's power is unlimited and that God can make that which is dead come back to life. Abraham himself had experienced that: he who was "as good as dead" (Heb. 11:12) was able to procreate a son through God's power. Abraham's faith reached a mountaintop of trust in God when he said to his servants, "Stay here with the donkey while I and the boy go over there. We will worship and then we will come back to you" (Gen. 22:5). He knew that Isaac would return with him. He believed that God would give life to the dead (Rom. 4:17), even though no one as yet had been raised from death.

Of course, Isaac did not die, someone may say, and therefore a resurrection from the dead did not take place. The author of Hebrews anticipates this observation, and to avoid any misunderstanding he adds the phrase that is translated as "and figuratively speaking." Because Abraham's obedience was complete, Isaac had no way of escape. Only God's direct intervention saved his life, and thus "figuratively speaking" he was brought back to life.

What is the meaning of the expression *figuratively speaking?* Is Isaac a figure of Jesus Christ? Both have the designation *one and only son.* Both were appointed to be a sacrifice, except that for Isaac a ram served as substitute. Commentators in the early church and the Middle Ages were apt to see a parallel between Isaac and Christ and to say that Isaac prefigured Christ.[32]

However, a word of caution is in order. The writer of the Epistle to the Hebrews nowhere regards "the sacrifice and salvation of Isaac as a type of

---

30. James Swetnam, *Jesus and Isaac: A Study of the Epistle to the Hebrews in the Light of the Aqedah* (Rome: Biblical Institute Press, 1981), pp. 95–96, 128. Says Swetnam, "The spiritual 'seed' is composed of all those who believe that God can give eternal life" (p. 129).

31. James M. Bulman, "The Only Begotten Son," *CTJ* 16 (1981): 64.

32. Hughes in *Hebrews*, pp. 484–85, tabulates the christological interpretations from the first century through the sixteenth.

Christ's death and resurrection," and "the idea is nowhere found in the New Testament."[33] No one disputes the well-known truth that the New Testament is the fulfillment of the Old Testament. But we ought to avoid making a writer say more than he intends to convey.

The conclusion of this matter is that the author of Hebrews stresses the unique faith of Abraham. By faith Abraham offered his son Isaac and received him back from the dead. The writer implies that Isaac actually never died, and therefore the incident must be understood figuratively and not literally. In this sense Abraham received Isaac back from death.

Practical Considerations in 11:8-19

God called Abraham "to go to a place he would later receive as his inheritance" (v. 8). That was not easy for Abraham, for he had to leave his relatives and go to an unknown land. The patriarch believed God and obeyed his Word. God still calls men and women to leave their loved ones and their familiar surroundings to bring the gospel to people living in other lands. These men and women serve "in the army of the Lord." Obediently they respond to God's call and give their time and talent in complete dedication to God. These "soldiers of the cross" are indeed aliens and strangers in foreign lands.

In a sense, all Christians are strangers on this earth. The Bible warns us not to attach ourselves too firmly to this earthly scene. Scripture tells us that this earth really is not our home. The Christian looks and longs for his eternal home. He sings,

> I am a stranger here,
> within a foreign land;
> My home is far away,
> upon a golden strand;
> Ambassador to be
> of realms beyond the sea,
> I'm here on business
> for my King.
> —E. T. Cassel

Faith has its counterpart in obedience. Faith and obedience are two sides of the same coin. Abraham learned that faith and obedience go together, especially at the time when God called him to sacrifice his son Isaac.

Note this sequence: Abraham believed and loved God, who promised him a son. After many years of waiting, Abraham received this promised son and loved him. Then God called Abraham to sacrifice Isaac. If Abraham sacrificed Isaac, he would keep God but lose his son. If he disobeyed God, Abraham would keep his son but

---

33. Hugh Montefiore, *The Epistle to the Hebrews* (New York and Evanston: Harper and Row, 1964), p. 200. Swetnam in *Jesus and Isaac* speaks of a foreshadowing (p. 123). He adds, however, that "Abraham was not aware of the Christological aspects of his actions" (p. 127). And Bauer explains the offering of Isaac "as a type (of the violent death and of the resurrection of Christ)," p. 612.

lose God. Abraham chose to obey God, and thus he placed the problem of losing his son of the promise in the hands of God. He believed that God could raise Isaac from death. In short, Abraham's life with God bore the motto *Trust and Obey*.

Greek Words, Phrases, and Constructions in 11:8–19

Verse 8

καλούμενος—this present passive participle of καλέω (I call) depends on the main verb ὑπήκουσεν, which is the aorist active of ὑπακούω (I obey). The present tense shows duration; the aorist, single occurrence. At the time God was calling, Abraham obeyed.

Verse 9

παρῴκησεν—both this verb in the aorist active and the aorist active participle κατοικήσας derive from the verb οἰκέω (I dwell, inhabit). The prepositions παρά and κατά modify the meaning of the verb. The first one expresses a temporary idea; the second one denotes permanence.

Verse 10

ἐξεδέχετο—the preposition ἐκ in this compound verb indicates direction. The verb in the imperfect middle (deponent) exhibits continued action in the past. Abraham was constantly "looking forward" to the heavenly city God had prepared for him.

δημιουργός—derived from δήμιος (public) and ἔργον (work), this compound rises above the interpretation *public worker;* it means "builder, designer, architect." It is synonymous with κτίστης (creator). Writers of both the Old Testament and the New Testament prefer to use the verb *to create* and derivatives rather than the term employed in this verse, a fact that is evident from the single occurrence of this compound noun in the entire New Testament.

Verse 11

στεῖρα—numerous Greek texts and translations omit this adjective (barren). The Editorial Committee of the United Bible Societies' Greek New Testament, however, by majority vote regarded the deletion as an omission caused by a scribe who was copying an earlier manuscript that had the adjective.[34] Therefore, the text of the United Bible Society and Nestle-Aland include this adjective.

Verse 12

νενεκρωμένου—from the verb νεκρόω (I put to death), the participle in the genitive case is appositive to ἑνός (one) and in the perfect tense shows duration of time.

---

34. Metzger, *Textual Commentary,* p. 673.

Verse 13

κατὰ πίστιν—only twice (11:7, 13) in the entire epistle does this construction occur. The author of Hebrews used these two instances as synonyms of the expression πίστει.

λαβόντες—the aorist active participle is one of four aorist participles in verse 13. They are "receiving," "seeing," "greeting," and "admitting." The main verb ἀπέθανον (they died) attains significance.

Verse 15

εἰ μέν—the contrary to fact conditional sentence with the imperfect conveys the meaning "of an unreal hypothesis in the past of a continuous nature."[35] That is, if the patriarchs had kept on thinking of their fatherland, they would have had ample opportunity to return. Verse 15 shows contrast with verse 16 in the use of μέν . . . δέ. These two verses comprise one unit. The adverb νῦν (now) "serves to contrast the real state of affairs with an unreal conditional clause."[36] The translation *instead* serves verse 16 well.

Verse 17

προσενήνοχεν—this perfect active verb from προσφέρω (I offer) is followed by the imperfect active προσέφερεν. The perfect tense reveals that the sacrifice actually took place in the demonstration of Abraham's willingness and obedience. The imperfect, by contrast, points to Abraham's attempt to sacrifice Isaac.

πειραζόμενος—the present passive participle of the verb πειράζω (I try) has the meaning of being put to the test to prove a person's faith (see John 6:6).

Verse 19

ὅθεν—an adverb from the relative pronoun ὅ and the enclitic θεν indicating motion away from a place or a deduction on the basis of reality. The adverb occurs six times in Hebrews (2:17; 3:1; 7:25; 8:3; 9:18; 11:19) and conveys the meaning *therefore*.

ἐκομίσατο—the aorist middle of κομίζω (I carry away) is much more precise than a form of the verb λαμβάνω (I receive), for it signifies recovering something that is one's possession. In a sense, Isaac belonged to Abraham.

---

20 By faith Isaac blessed Jacob and Esau in regard to their future.

21 By faith Jacob, when he was dying, blessed each of Joseph's sons, and worshiped as he leaned on the top of his staff.

22 By faith Joseph, when his end was near, spoke about the exodus of the Israelites from Egypt and gave instructions about his bones.

---

35. Robertson, *Grammar,* pp. 921, 1015. Robertson calls the construction "a classical idiom, though uncommon."
36. Bauer, p. 546.

D. The Faith of Isaac, Jacob, and Joseph
11:20–22

The son, grandson, and great-grandson of Abraham span the generations and centuries by faith. In their old age, with death approaching, the patriarchs Jacob and Joseph passed on blessings and instructions concerning the Promised Land.

20. By faith Isaac blessed Jacob and Esau in regard to their future.

In this verse and the next two verses, the author unfolds an interesting description of the patriarchal blessings. Note that in the case of Abraham's sons, not Ishmael but Isaac received the blessing. Isaac was the son of the promise. In the next generation, not Esau, the first-born, but Jacob received the covenant blessing that God had given to Abraham and his descendants. Next, not Reuben, Jacob's first-born, but Joseph received the blessings in his sons Manasseh and Ephraim. And last, not Manasseh, Joseph's first-born, but Ephraim received the choice blessing. God's electing love is independent of the rules and regulations concerning the right of the first-born (Deut. 21:15–17). The reason that the names of the patriarchs Isaac, Jacob, and Joseph appear in the list of the heroes of faith is that they exhibited their faith in God.

Isaac knew that he was the recipient of God's favor. God appeared to him and repeated the promise he had made to Abraham: "I will make your descendants as numerous as the stars in the sky and will give them all these lands, and through your offspring all nations on earth will be blessed" (Gen. 26:4). And when Isaac sent Jacob on his way to Paddan Aram, he blessed his son with a similar blessing. Said he, "May God Almighty bless you and make you fruitful and increase your numbers until you become a community of peoples. May he give you and your descendants the blessing given to Abraham, so that you may take possession of the land where you now live as an alien, the land God gave to Abraham" (Gen. 28:3–4). Isaac virtually repeated the words of the ancient promise first given to Abraham. For this reason the author of Hebrews lists Isaac among the men of faith. Isaac blessed Jacob and Esau in faith (Gen. 27:27–28, 39–40). Jacob, not Esau, however, continued in the line of faith, as the writer notes afterward (Heb. 12:16–17).

Even though Isaac was an old man when he blessed his sons, his hour of death came more than forty years later (Gen. 27:2; 35:28–29). He lived to be 180 years old. His son Jacob pronounced the patriarchal blessing on the sons of Joseph when he was ill and expected the end of his life (Gen. 48:1, 21).

21. By faith Jacob, when he was dying, blessed each of Joseph's sons, and worshiped as he leaned on the top of his staff.

The writer of Hebrews omits any reference to the blessings that Jacob pronounced on his sons as the patriarch predicted the future (Gen. 49). Instead he selects the incident when Jacob blessed Joseph's sons as a demonstration of Jacob's faith. That historic moment was indeed significant. Note these points:

a. In his first act of blessing, Jacob addressed Joseph and repeated the words of the promise God had given to Abraham, Isaac, and Jacob. God had told Jacob, "I am going to make you fruitful and will increase your numbers. I will make you a community of peoples, and I will give this land [of Canaan] as an everlasting possession to your descendants after you" (Gen. 48:4). This was the patriarchal blessing passed on from one generation to the next.

b. When Joseph with his two sons came to Jacob, he received the blessing of the first-born. He received a double portion not of Jacob's herds and flocks, but of the promised land of Canaan. Not Joseph himself, but each of his two sons Manasseh and Ephraim received this blessing. They became two tribes in Israel because Jacob accepted Manasseh and Ephraim as his own sons (Gen. 48:5).

c. Blessing the two sons of Joseph, Jacob functioned as king of the Promised Land. The patriarch crossed his arms and granted the blessing of the first-born not to Manasseh but to Ephraim (Gen. 48:12–20). In the course of time, the tribe of Ephraim indeed became a leader in Israel. In faith, Jacob looked into the future and was given prophetic insight. He knew that God would fulfill the patriarchal blessing in the sons of Joseph.

d. Convinced that God would fulfill his promise, Jacob gave Joseph instructions to bury him in the cave of Machpelah in the land of Canaan (Gen. 47:29–31; 50:12–14). Jacob's grave in the Promised Land would serve as a testimony and an encouragement to his descendants that they, too, would enter their inheritance.

e. Jacob worshiped his God as he leaned on his staff.[37] He fully acknowledged God's power and presence in the development of the patriarchal blessing. He worshiped in faith.

22. By faith Joseph, when his end was near, spoke about the exodus of the Israelites from Egypt and gave instructions about his bones.

Of all Joseph's earlier trials and experiences in which his faith had been tested, the writer of Hebrews selects none. He is interested in the promise of God that Abraham's descendants would inherit the land of Canaan. Therefore, the words Joseph spoke to his brothers at the end of his life are important. He said, "I am about to die. But God will surely come to your aid and take you up out of this land to the land he promised on oath to Abraham, Isaac and Jacob" (Gen. 50:24). The golden thread of the promise binds the patriarchs in faith that transcends the generations.

At the age of seventeen (Gen. 37:2), Joseph was sold to Midianite mer-

---

37. The sentence "and [he] worshiped as he leaned on the top of his staff" is a quotation from Gen. 47:31. The NIV at this verse has the word *staff* in the text with the footnote, "Israel bowed down at the head of his bed." The difference in wording centers on one Hebrew noun which, with the same consonants but with varying vowels, can mean either "staff" or "bed." The Septuagint features the term *staff*. As he does elsewhere, the writer of Hebrews follows this translation.

chants who took him from his native land to Egypt. Joseph returned briefly to Canaan for the burial of his father Jacob (Gen. 50:4–14). He had lived at the court of Pharaoh, had married an Egyptian, and had the Egyptian name *Zaphenath-Paneah*. Nevertheless, Joseph remained true to the God of his fathers, and when he knew that the end of his life was near, he prophesied concerning the patriarchal blessing. He predicted the exodus of Jacob's descendants from Egypt. And in faith he told these descendants to carry his bones from Egypt to Canaan (Gen. 50:25). When the exodus occurred, "Moses took the bones of Joseph with him" (Exod. 13:19). "And Joseph's bones, which the Israelites had brought up from Egypt, were buried at Shechem" (Josh. 24:32) within the land allotted to the tribe of Ephraim.

Joseph's command to bury his bones in Canaan was not an act of nostalgia or superstition, but an act of faith. Prophetically he spoke of the exodus and in faith saw that his remains would be carried to the Promised Land. He believed that God would fulfill his word.

Practical Considerations in 11:20–22

What a joy to see the "faith of our fathers" spanning the generations! The author of Hebrews lists the names of Isaac, Jacob, and Joseph. Each belonged to the covenant that God had made with Abraham when God said, "I will establish my covenant as an everlasting covenant between me and you and your descendants after you for the generations to come, to be your God and the God of your descendants after you" (Gen. 17:7). God keeps his word throughout the generations.

When parents see the love of the Lord in their children, who express a desire to do his will, their hearts are filled with gratitude to God. To see the next generation take up the torch of faith is an evident sign of God's faithfulness.

But when parents see their sons and daughters turn away from God and his Word, in spite of the training in home, church, and perhaps school, their parental hearts grieve. Isaac and Rebekah endured constant grief when Esau lived a life of disobedience (Gen. 26:34–35). And on his deathbed Jacob pronounced a curse on Simeon and Levi (Gen. 49:7). Salvation cannot be inherited; it is a gift of God. Parents of spiritually wayward sons and daughters need to pray that God in his grace will give them this gift. By exercising their faith, they trust in God's unlimited power to save their prodigal son or daughter.

Greek Words, Phrases, and Constructions in 11:20–22

Verse 20

καί—although some leading manuscripts omit this conjunction, external textual evidence for its inclusion is strong. The translators of the New International Version have omitted it. Other translations include it and take it either as a connective or as an emphatic: "By faith Isaac blessed Jacob and Esau, even regarding things to come" (NASB).

Verse 22

τῆς ἐξόδου—the writer of Hebrews employs this noun with the definite article as a technical term for the exodus of the Israelites. The term occurs frequently in the Septuagint as a designation for Israel's departure from Egypt. In the New Testament it appears in three places: in Luke 9:31 and II Peter 1:15, it refers to death; and in Hebrews 11:22, to the exodus.

---

23 By faith Moses' parents hid him for three months after he was born, because they saw he was no ordinary child, and they were not afraid of the king's edict.

24 By faith Moses, when he had grown up, refused to be known as the son of Pharaoh's daughter. 25 He chose to be mistreated along with the people of God rather than to enjoy the pleasures of sin for a short time. 26 He regarded disgrace for the sake of Christ as of greater value than the treasures of Egypt, because he was looking ahead to his reward. 27 By faith he left Egypt, not fearing the king's anger; he persevered because he saw him who is invisible. 28 By faith he kept the Passover and the sprinkling of blood, so that the destroyer of the firstborn would not touch the firstborn of Israel.

29 By faith the people passed through the Red Sea as on dry land; but when the Egyptians tried to do so, they were drowned.

E. The Faith of Moses
11:23–29

1. Moses' Childhood and Position
11:23–26

Abraham is the father of believers, but Moses is the father of the nation of Israel. The author of Hebrews devotes five sections that begin with the formula *by faith* to Moses (vv. 23, 24, 27, 28, 29). The first of these instances relates to Moses' parents; the last, the people of Israel.

23. By faith Moses' parents hid him for three months after he was born, because they saw he was no ordinary child, and they were not afraid of the king's edict.

The writer of Hebrews opens the Book of Exodus and reads about the cruel command of Pharaoh to kill all the Hebrew male children at birth. A Levite and his fianceé, Amram and Jochebed, decide to get married. Subsequently they are blessed with the birth of a son. Now they face the possibility of losing their child. They act boldly in faith. Seeing that their son is a most attractive child, they defy the king's command. What gives Amram and Jochebed the courage to disobey? Most likely, they see in their strikingly handsome son a sign of God's approval (see Exod. 2:2; Acts 7:20).[38] And because of God's favor they continue to exercise their faith. They hide Moses

---

38. Josephus in his *Antiquities of the Jews* 2.201–16 (LCL) relates that Moses' father had a vision. God exhorted him not to despair, because Moses would deliver the Hebrew race from Egyptian bondage. John Brown in *An Exposition of Hebrews* (Edinburgh: Banner of Truth Trust, 1961), p. 539, asserts that the writer of Hebrews concurs with the Jewish belief of a special revelation to which Josephus refers.

for three months until necessity dictates that they devise new ways to protect him. Unafraid of the king and his men, they decide to hide Moses among the reeds of the Nile River.[39] God protects Moses royally when the daughter of Pharaoh tells Jochebed to nurse the child and pays her for the service. When Moses is old enough to leave his parental home, he enters the royal palace of Pharaoh. God honors the faith of Moses' parents, because he protects Moses by having him live in the palace of Pharaoh who had given orders to destroy the male babies of the Hebrews.

24. By faith Moses, when he had grown up, refused to be known as the son of Pharaoh's daughter.

Stephen relates that Pharaoh's daughter took Moses "and brought him up as her own son." He concludes, "Moses was educated in all the wisdom of the Egyptians and was powerful in speech and action" (Acts 7:21–22). Apparently Stephen had access to a source of oral tradition, for he states that Moses was forty years old when he decided to throw in his lot with the Hebrew slaves. In spite of his training at Pharaoh's court, Moses put his faith in Israel's God and severed his ties with Pharaoh's daughter. He refused to be recognized as an Egyptian prince, for he knew himself to be a descendant of Abraham, a son of the covenant that God had made with the patriarch, and a Hebrew who longed to be free. He identified with the oppressed Hebrew slaves.

The author of Hebrews writes that Moses *by faith* "refused to be known as the son of Pharaoh's daughter." The title *son of Pharaoh's daughter* was prestigious in Egypt and entailed power and privileges. To break the tie with the daughter of Pharaoh and to choose to be identified with the mistreated Hebrew slaves called for faith and courage. Moses acted not rashly in youthful fervor but maturely as a man who at the age of forty was fully educated. Deliberately he associated with "the people of God," the Hebrews.

25. He chose to be mistreated along with the people of God rather than to enjoy the pleasures of sin for a short time.

In God's providence, Moses received training that enabled him to become a leader of a nation. He was uniquely qualified to lead the nation Israel out of Egypt to the Promised Land. Thus he regarded himself as God's appointed deliverer of Israel. Says Stephen, "Moses thought that his own people would realize that God was using him to rescue them, but they did not" (Acts 7:25). Although Moses had been trained, he was not yet ready to govern the nation Israel. His own people were not yet ready to accept him.

Moses, however, had cast his lot with the Israelites. His people, not the Egyptians, were the recipients of God's promises to Abraham, Isaac, and Jacob. Should he have sided with the Egyptians and turned his back on the

---

39. In his commentary on the faith of Moses' parents, Calvin writes, "We must, however, remark, that the faith here praised was very weak; for after having disregarded the fear of death, they ought to have brought up Moses; instead of doing so, they exposed him" (*Hebrews*, p. 293). I cannot agree with this observation, for it appears to militate against the concluding part of Heb. 11:23, "they were not afraid of the king's edict." Faith banishes fear.

people of God, he would have committed the sin of apostasy. In the words of the writer of Hebrews, he would have turned "away from the living God" (3:12). The choice Moses faced, then, was not so much between either being mistreated or enjoying the pleasures of Egypt as between either associating with the people of God or falling into the sin of apostasy.[40] Moses chose mistreatment and identified himself with God's people.

Moses could have taken a halfway position. As the son of Pharaoh's daughter, he might have said that his influence would be incalculable in setting the Israelites free. In earlier times Joseph had wielded his power and authority in the interest of Jacob and his descendants. No one would have chided Moses if he had stayed in Egypt. But Joseph by faith predicted the exodus and made his brothers promise to take his bones with them for burial in Canaan. Likewise Moses sided with the Hebrew slaves and renounced his royal title *son of Pharaoh's daughter.*

26. He regarded disgrace for the sake of Christ as of greater value than the treasures of Egypt, because he was looking ahead to his reward.
This verse relates three main thoughts.

a. *Christ.* The writer is rather explicit in his wording, for he refers to *the* Christ, in the original Greek. Elsewhere in his epistle he says, "Jesus Christ is the same yesterday and today and forever" (13:8). Because Christ transcends the centuries, the author of Hebrews confidently asserts that Moses endured disgrace for the sake of Christ. Moses considered disgrace for Christ of greater significance than all the glittering riches of Egypt. The writer, therefore, implies that even though Moses never used the name *Messiah,* he was fully aware of his presence and his coming.

Nevertheless, the reader of this passage faces some problems in interpreting it. For instance, Moses had no idea of the person and work of Christ as we know Jesus from the pages of the New Testament. Moses had the promises God had given to his ancestors, Abraham, Isaac, and Jacob. These promises related to the growth of the nation Israel, the inheritance of Canaan, and the coming of the Christ. Moses saw the fulfillment of the promise that Abraham's descendants would be "as numerous as the stars in the sky and as countless as the sand on the seashore" (Heb. 11:12; see also Gen. 15:5; 22:17; 32:12). And he realized that the time for the exodus and the return to Canaan was imminent. That he believed in the coming Deliverer is not in question. The problem of understanding the meaning of the word *Christ* centers on Christ's place in the context of the Old Testament.

Some commentators seek an explanation in symbolism. They point to the fulfillment of the prophecy in which God says, "out of Egypt I called my son" (Hos. 11:1) and see an identification of Christ with the nation Israel. Both of them came forth out of Egypt. Others understand the expression *the Anointed* (the Messiah) to refer in a collective sense to Israel (Ps. 89:50–51). Still others think that Christ accompanied the Israelites during the time of

---

40. Spicq, *Hébreux,* vol. 2, p. 357.

the exodus and the journey to the Promised Land (I Cor. 10:4). Based on Scripture, all these comments are helpful in understanding the text at hand. However, we ought not expect more from a text than the author intends to convey.[41]

b. *Comparison.* The emphasis falls on this comparison: "disgrace for the sake of Christ as of greater value than the treasures of Egypt." This is a comparison of spiritual riches and earthly treasures. The words of the Beatitudes readily come to mind: "Blessed are you when people insult you, persecute you and falsely say all kinds of evil against you because of me. Rejoice and be glad, because great is your reward in heaven" (Matt. 5:11–12).

To insult is a passion that originates in man's sinful heart. Man directs this passion against his fellow man, especially the person who is righteous. And insult directed against man is ultimately directed against God. We know that the Israelites endured daily abuse from their ruthless Egyptian taskmasters (Exod. 1:11–14). God saw the misery of the Israelites, heard their cries, and was concerned about their suffering (Exod. 3:7). Moses deliberately sought identity with these Hebrew slaves because he believed that God would set his people free and fulfill his promises. Moses knew that gaining spiritual objectives for the cause of God's people was incomparably better than becoming heir to the riches of Egypt. He pursued his spiritual objectives, even though that pursuit resulted in scorn, derision, abuse, and disgrace. Moses, however, "was looking ahead to his reward."

c. *Compensation.* Although Scripture clearly teaches that no man is able to earn salvation, the term *reward* (for example, see Heb. 10:35; 11:6) appears repeatedly. That is, God rewards man on the basis of divine sovereignty and not because of merit. "Every claim to one's deserts must fall silent in the face of the demand for total obedience."[42] But Jesus' word is reassuring to every believer who seeks to do God's will. Jesus said, "And if anyone gives even a cup of cold water to one of these little ones because he is my disciple, I tell you the truth, he will certainly not lose his reward" (Matt. 10:42). In his sovereign grace God rewards anyone who diligently seeks him in faith. And that is exactly what Moses did in Egypt. He looked to God for his reward.

2. Moses' Leadership
11:27–29

27. By faith he left Egypt, not fearing the king's anger; he persevered because he saw him who is invisible.

What does the writer mean when he writes "he left Egypt"? Moses left Egypt twice. The first time he fled because he feared for his life after he

---

41. Hewitt, *Hebrews*, p. 181. Johannes Eichler and Colin Brown suggest that Moses identified himself with Israel's lot and considered Israel God's anointed. "This interpretation has the further advantage of being compatible with all the other instances of faith in Heb. 11 drawn from OT history." *NIDNTT,* vol. 2, p. 835.

42. Böttger, *NIDNTT,* vol. 3, p. 141.

had killed an Egyptian (Exod. 2:14–15). Between the first and the second time lies a forty-year period (Acts 7:30).

Considering the flow of the author's thought in respect to the flight of Moses in chapter 11, we note that he selects significant incidents that underscore Moses' faith. He begins with the act of faith exercised by Moses' parents (v. 23). In the next section he presents Moses as a man of faith at Pharaoh's court. The summary of this period of Moses' life begins with the formula *by faith*. Then, describing Moses' faith in three sentences, the author mentions Moses' refusal to be called son of Pharaoh's daughter, his choice to identify with the people of God, and his decision to endure disgrace rather than enjoy royal treasures (vv. 24–26). Next the writer selects Moses' departure from Egypt as an example of an act of faith (v. 27). Also, the account of the institution of the Passover, whereby the first-born of Israel were saved, depicts Moses as a man of faith (v. 28). And last, the crossing of the Red Sea represents the faith of Moses and the Israelites (v. 29). The writer of Hebrews, then, enumerates specific events from the life of Moses in which his faith triumphed.

Was Moses' flight from Egypt after he killed an Egyptian an act of faith? The Exodus account relates that Moses was afraid and that Pharaoh tried to kill him (Exod. 2:14–15). If Moses left Egypt in fear, we have difficulty believing that his flight was an act of faith. Why would the author of Hebrews select this incident as an example of Moses' trust in God? Moreover, the writer adds that Moses did not fear the anger of the king. This observation makes the interpretation of Moses' flight to Midian rather complicated.

By contrast, after Moses had waited forty years in Midian, God called him and spoke to him from the burning bush. He instructed Moses to go to Pharaoh and to bring the people of Israel out of Egypt (Exod. 3:10). This was an assignment that demanded faith. Moses repeatedly objected until God reassured him that the elders of Israel would listen to him (v. 18), that God would "make the Egyptians favorably disposed" to the Israelites (v. 21), that Moses would perform miracles (Exod. 4:1–9), and that Moses' brother Aaron would accompany him (vv. 14–16). After receiving these divine instructions, Moses became a man of faith who was unafraid of Pharaoh. The responsibility of leading the people of Israel out of Egypt was assigned to Moses in his capacity of Israel's leader. Furthermore, the entire verse—"By faith he left Egypt, not fearing the king's anger; he persevered because he saw him who is invisible"—refers to all the confrontations Moses had with Pharaoh in his effort to gain freedom for God's people.[43] That "he left Egypt" is then the culmination of a series of events. One of these events is the institution of the Passover, to which the author of Hebrews pays par-

---

43. Spicq, *Hébreux*, vol. 2, p. 359. Lenski in *Hebrews*, p. 411, notes that Moses' fearlessness toward Pharaoh is described in Exod. 10:28–29.

ticular attention in the next verse.[44] And the clause "not fearing the king's anger" covers the period of the ten plagues and Pharaoh's pursuit of the Israelites to the waters of the Red Sea (Exod. 14:5–28).[45] Moses is the man of faith, who tells the people not to be afraid, to stand firm, and to see the Lord fight for them (vv. 13–14). By faith Moses was unafraid, for he knew that God was on his side.

The words "he persevered because he saw him who is invisible" take on added meaning against the setting of Moses' experience of seeing the burning bush in Midian. Also, God spoke to Moses repeatedly in Egypt. During the wilderness journey, "the LORD would speak to Moses . . . , as a man speaks with his friend" (Exod. 33:11; also see Num. 12:7–8). Although Moses was not permitted to see the face of God, he did see his back (Exod. 33:23). The abiding presence of God, especially during Moses' trying days in Egypt, strengthened Moses' faith. Because of God's instructions, Moses was able to persevere in faith and accomplish his task to lead the people of Israel out of Egypt.

From the general context of the account in Exodus, the author of Hebrews moves to a specific incident: the institution of the Passover celebration.

28. By faith he kept the Passover and the sprinkling of blood, so that the destroyer of the firstborn would not touch the firstborn of Israel.

"By faith," writes the author of Hebrews. In selecting the mountaintop experiences of Moses' life of faith, the author takes the incident of the institution of the Passover feast. This experience was different from the preceding instances. For the first time the Israelites themselves were involved, for they with Moses had to exercise their faith in God. Second, this experience was essentially spiritual. In the days of Abraham, God instituted the sacrament of circumcision. When the Israelites were about to leave Egypt, God inaugurated the Old Testament sacrament of the Passover. And he appointed Moses to instruct the people of Israel to implement this sacrament. Moses' task of instructing a nation of slaves in the meaningful celebration of the Passover was an act of faith. To understand the meaning of the phrase *by faith,* we must note the following points:

a. *Institution of Passover.* God told Moses to keep the Passover and to sprinkle the blood of the lamb that was slain. The word *Passover* is a popular translation of the Hebrew original which may mean "to pass over by sparing" someone.[46] Obviously, the word relates to the Exodus account, where Moses

---

44. Some commentators find the order of events in Heb. 11:27–28 difficult to explain because the Passover observance (v. 28) took place before the actual departure from Egypt (v. 27). Grosheide in *Hebreeën,* p. 274, remarks that the writer of Hebrews departs from a strict chronological order more often (see 11:21).

45. The NEB translation is, "By faith he left Egypt, and not because he feared the king's anger." In their respective commentaries on this verse, Bruce and Hughes favor the NEB translation and apply it to Moses' flight from Egypt into Midian.

46. Thayer, *Lexicon,* p. 493. However, Ludwig Koehler points out that the meaning of the Hebrew original is "not yet etymologically explained at all satisfaction [sic]." *Lexicon in Veteris Testamenti Libros* (Leiden: Brill, 1953), p. 769.

instructs the elders of Israel to slaughter the Passover lamb. They had to put some of the blood of the lamb on the top and sides of the doorframe of the houses of the Israelites. "When the LORD goes through the land to strike down the Egyptians," said Moses, "he will see the blood on the top and sides of the doorframe and will pass over that doorway, and he will not permit the destroyer to enter your houses and strike you down" (Exod. 12:23).

Moses instituted the festival of Passover as an annual event. On the four-teenth day of the month Nisan (approximately March-April), each family had to select and kill a year-old male lamb, without blemish, at sundown (Exod. 12:5; Lev. 23:5; Deut. 16:6). The blood of the lamb had to be smeared on the doorposts and lintel of the house. The lamb was roasted and eaten with unleavened bread and bitter herbs. Everything had to be eaten that evening. If food was left, it had to be burned (Exod. 12:10; 34:25). The meal had to be eaten in haste. And the festival had to be observed as "a lasting ordinance" (Exod. 12:14).[47]

b. *Sprinkling of blood.* Before the Israelites were to leave Egypt, they had to sacrifice a lamb and put some of its blood on the doorposts and lintel of their house. God would go throughout the land of Egypt and strike down every first-born of man and animal. But if a house had the blood of a lamb on its doorpost and lintel, God would spare its inhabitants. Moses listened obediently to God's instructions and in faith passed them on to the Israelites. Could he expect the Israelites to obey the command of God? If they failed to listen, they would suffer the death of their first-born. And Moses himself put full confidence in God. If the blood of the lamb proved to be ineffective in protecting the first-born from the destructive power of the angel of death, his role as leader of the people would end abruptly. To establish Moses' authority in spiritual matters, the people of Israel would have to see that not one first-born died in those houses where the blood of a lamb had been sprinkled. How many first-born among the Israelites were spared? We know that the nation numbered 603,550 men who were twenty years or older (Num. 1:45). Moses' faith stood the test when numberless first-born of man and animal were saved.

c. *Salvation of first-born.* Why would God strike down the first-born of the Egyptians and protect those of the Israelites? Certainly not because of any merit in the nation Israel. Within a relatively short time, all the Israelites of twenty years and older would hear the verdict: all of them would perish in the wilderness, except Joshua and Caleb (Num. 14:29–30). God spared the first-born because the Israelites believed God and obeyed his word. Their first-born were spared because the atoning blood of the Passover lamb was

---

47. Literature on the subject of Passover is extensive. A few representative studies are Judah Benzion Segal, *The Hebrew Passover from the Earliest Times to A.D. 70* (London: Oxford University Press, 1963); Jakob Jocz, "Passover," *ZPEB*, vol. 4, pp. 605–11; Joachim Jeremias, "Pascha," *TDNT*, vol. 5, pp. 896–904; and Bernd Schaller, "Passover," *NIDNTT*, vol. 1, pp. 632–34.

sprinkled on the entrance of their homes. The Israelites had to see physically and spiritually that salvation comes from the Lord.

The festival of Passover became the sacrament of the Lord's Supper. The Passover lamb in the New Testament times was Jesus Christ, who gave his life as the Lamb of God to take away the sin of the world (John 1:29, 36; I Peter 1:19). Christ Jesus "gave himself as a ransom for all men" (I Tim. 2:6).

The author of Hebrews says nothing about the work of Christ at this point. He depicts the life of faith of Moses and the Israelites. Their keeping of the Passover feast was the beginning of an observance that would lead to and end in the sacrifice of the Lamb of God. Covered by his blood, countless believers are saved.

29. By faith the people passed through the Red Sea as on dry land; but when the Egyptians tried to do so, they were drowned.

In the eighth century John of Damascus composed a hymn in which he gave expression to the joy the Israelites experienced after crossing the Red Sea.

> Come, ye faithful, raise the strain
> Of triumphant gladness;
> God hath brought his Israel
> Into joy from sadness;
> Loosed from Pharaoh's bitter yoke
> Jacob's sons and daughters;
> Led them with unmoistened foot
> Through the Red Sea waters.
> —translated by John Mason Neale

Israel expressed joy and gladness in the so-called Song of Moses (Exod. 15:1–18), and no wonder—faith had triumphed. The Israelites looked back upon the waters of the Red Sea and saw that the Lord had fought for them and had given them the victory (Exod. 14:14).

But what of Israel's faith in crossing the Red Sea? Instead of acting in faith they cowered in fear. No faith is evident in their complaint against Moses: "Was it because there were no graves in Egypt that you brought us to the desert to die? What have you done to us by bringing us out of Egypt? Didn't we say to you in Egypt, 'Leave us alone; let us serve the Egyptians'? It would have been better for us to serve the Egyptians than to die in the desert!" (Exod. 14:11–12). And the fact that the Israelites, except Joshua and Caleb, died in the desert because of their lack of faith in God makes the phrase *by faith* rather general.

The writer of Hebrews has already spoken about the lack of faith of the Israelites. Candidly he asks, "Who were they who heard and rebelled? Were they not all those Moses led out of Egypt?" (3:16). But because of the faith of those who genuinely believed in the promise that God would save the nation Israel from the imminent attack of the Egyptian military forces, God led his people safely to the other side of the Red Sea. From the Exodus account we learn that Moses' faith was undaunted. By faith he knew that the Lord would deliver the Israelites and the Egyptians would meet defeat (14:13–14).[48]

The contrast with respect to faith and unbelief is not between the faithful minority and the complaining, terrified Israelites. Rather, the contrast is between the nation Israel that expressed faith in God and thus was victorious and the unbelieving king and army of Egypt who perished in the waters of the Red Sea. The Israelites listened to Moses' instructions; they saw the Red Sea divided and the path through the sea as dry land; they noticed that the pillar of cloud had shifted from being in front of them to being behind them; and in the light of that cloud they reached the other shore. The Egyptians tried to do exactly the same thing. But it was not the same.[49] The Egyptian army spent the night in darkness; they followed the Israelites into the sea; they experienced difficulties in driving their chariots; and they suddenly saw the waters of the Red Sea rising. All of them drowned; "not one of them survived" (Exod. 14:28). They had entered the Red Sea without faith in Israel's God. When they realized that the Lord was fighting for the Israelites, it was too late.

The Israelites were victorious because they had listened to the instructions God had given to Moses. They had acted in faith. But this act of faith is indeed the only one recorded. The writer of Hebrews chooses this act in view of Moses' trust in God. The next act relates to the fall of Jericho's walls, but that happened forty years later when the next generation had taken the places of their parents. This generation differed from the one that left Egypt. Whereas the people leaving Egypt failed to trust the Lord, the new generation faithfully executed divine instructions.

Practical Considerations in 11:23–29

Among the heroes of faith stand Amram and Jochebed, the father and mother of Moses. They put their full confidence in God when they married, when children were born, and when hiding the infant Moses became an impossible task. Moses' resourceful parents exercised their faith, used their imagination, and demonstrated their courage when they constructed a simple basket made of papyrus reeds, tar, and pitch. They placed the three-month-old Moses in the basket, had Moses' sister watch him, and put the basket among the reeds of the Nile. Undoubtedly they knew that Pharaoh's daughter would bathe along the riverbank. When Pharaoh's daughter found the infant, Moses' sister offered to find a nurse for the child. Thus Jochebed was asked to nurse the child, was paid for her services, and was assured of Moses' safety.

---

48. In his commentary on Hebrews, Brown queries whether the faith of the Israelites when they crossed the Red Sea was saving faith. He writes "that the faith of the revelation made to Moses respecting the Israelites obtaining a safe passage through the Red Sea, was not what we ordinarily term saving faith" (p. 566).
49. Bengel, *Gnomon*, vol. 4, p. 454; "when two do the same thing, it is not the same thing."

By faith parents are able to protect their children from the constant attack of evil in our society. They realize that Satan "prowls around like a roaring lion" seeking to destroy their children (I Peter 5:8). Parents resist the devil by standing firm in their faith. They build spiritual homes in which they train their children to fear and love the Lord. With their children, they faithfully attend the worship services of a church true to Scripture. And with ingenuity, wherever God gives opportunity and occasion, they provide Christian day school education for their children. And, of course, they spend much time in prayer in behalf of their sons and daughters.

The first few years of his life Moses spent in the slave hut of his godly parents. Amram and Jochebed taught him to fear God. But when the day came to take Moses to the royal palace, they knew that he would be educated in the culture of the Egyptians and in a pagan religion. Humanly speaking, they had lost a son to the secular world of that day. But the amazing fact is that Moses loved God and "chose to be mistreated along with the people of God" (Heb. 11:25). Instead of being called "son of Pharaoh's daughter," he was called "friend of God."

What happened? Joseph had been the second-in-command in Egypt (Gen. 41:43). In a similar fashion, Moses faced the prospect of ascending the Egyptian throne. Instead Moses associated with God's people and turned his back upon the "treasures of Egypt." Why? Because Moses believed God! In faith he accepted God's promises. In every situation he sought God, trusted him, and knew that God "rewards those who earnestly seek him" (Heb. 11:6). As a child of God, Moses talked to and trusted in his heavenly Father. And God blessed him.

Although times, customs, and circumstances today differ from those of Moses' day, spiritual choices are the same. Young people today must make the same choice Moses made in ancient Egypt. Earnestly and sincerely they ought to seek God in prayer, strive to do his will, ask for wisdom, and cling to his promises.

After the exodus, the people of Israel knew God not only as the God of Abraham, Isaac, and Jacob, but as the Lord God, who had brought them out of Egypt, the land of slavery (see Exod. 20:2). Today God's people know him as the Father of the Lord Jesus Christ (Rom. 15:6; II Cor. 1:3; 11:31; Eph. 1:3; I Peter 1:3). That is, because of his Son Jesus Christ, God is the Father of everyone who believes in Jesus.[50] Moses "regarded disgrace for the sake of Christ as of greater value than the treasures of Egypt, because he was looking ahead to his reward" (Heb. 11:26). In the New Testament we have received God's complete revelation and know that "Jesus Christ is the same yesterday and today and forever" (Heb. 13:8).

Greek Words, Phrases, and Constructions in 11:23–29

Verse 23

ἀστεῖον—this two-ending adjective is a derivative of the noun ἄστυ (city) and is the opposite of the adjective ἄγροικος (rustic).[51] It occurs in the Septuagint text of Exodus 2:2; Judges 3:17; Judith 11:23; and Susanna 7; and in the New Testament text of Acts 7:20 and Hebrews 11:23. The adjective has perplexed translators, as

---

50. Herman Veldkamp, *Zondagskinderen,* 2 vols. (Franeker: Wever, n.d.), vol. 1, p. 113.
51. Thayer, *Lexicon,* p. 81.

is evident from the many translations: "proper child" (KJV), "goodly child" (RV, ASV), "fine child" (JB, NEB), "beautiful child" (RSV, NAB, GNB, MLB, NASB, *Moffat*, NKJV), and "no ordinary child" (NIV). The word may designate someone who is "fair to look on and comely."[52]

Verse 24

υἱὸς θυγατρὸς Φαραώ—the phrase is devoid of definite articles to emphasize the dignity of Moses' status. He bore the title *son of Pharaoh's daughter.*

Verse 25

ἑλόμενος—as a second aorist middle participle from αἱρέω (I take; in the middle: I choose, prefer), this form is modified by the adverb μᾶλλον (rather). The adverb is somewhat redundant with the participle in the middle voice, not in the active voice. The aorist tense of the participle coincides with that of the main verb ἠρνήσατο (he refused) in the preceding verse. The contrast with the aid of μᾶλλον ... ἤ features the durative present infinitives συγκακουχεῖσθαι (to suffer with) and ἔχειν (to have).

The durative idea is expressed in the adverb πρόσκαιρον (for a while) and the noun ἀπόλαυσις (enjoyment), which shows progression in the -σις ending. The noun ἁμαρτίας is an objective genitive; it is descriptive of the noun *enjoyment* and is the equivalent of "*sinful* enjoyment."

Verse 26

ἡγησάμενος—from the verb ἡγέομαι (I consider), this aorist middle participle expresses action that is simultaneous with that of the main verb ἠρνήσατο in verse 24.

The Greek word order is significant because it shows emphasis. The words *of greater value* stand first, and the phrase in opposition, "disgrace for the sake of Christ," appears last in this part of the sentence. The genitive of τοῦ Χριστοῦ is objective.

μισθαποδοσίαν—the noun occurs three times in Hebrews (2:2; 10:35; 11:26). Only in this verse does it have the definite article which takes the place of a possessive pronoun: *his* reward.

Verse 27

κατέλιπεν—the compound in the second aorist active is directive. The verb is often used to indicate abandoning a heritage, giving up riches, and leaving one's native land.[53]

μὴ φοβηθείς—the aorist passive participle denotes cause. The New English Bible even inserts the conjunction *and,* an addition which has no manuscript support: "By faith he left Egypt, and not because he feared the king's anger."

ὁρῶν—although the main verb ἐκαρτέρησεν (he persevered) is in the aorist, the participle from ὁράω (I see) is in the present tense.

---

52. R. C. Trench, *Synonyms of the New Testament* (Grand Rapids: Eerdmans, 1953), p. 388.
53. Spicq, *Hébreux,* vol. 2, p. 359.

Verse 28

πεποίηκεν—this verb from ποιέω (I make, do), in combination with the word πάσχα, means "to keep the Passover" (see Exod. 12:48, LXX; Matt. 26:18; and the expression τοῦτο ποιεῖτε in Luke 22:19; I Cor. 11:24, 25). The verb, however, in the perfect active indicative, has two objects ("Passover" and "the sprinkling of blood"). Admittedly, the verb suits the first object better than the second.[54] The perfect tense, to be sure, relates to the institution of the Passover feast that was celebrated annually afterward and became the sacrament of the Lord's Supper in New Testament times.

τὰ πρωτότοκα—by using the neuter plural, the author indicates that he wants the noun, preceded by the definite article, understood in the widest possible sense to include male and female, man and animal.

θίγῃ—the verb θιγγάνω (I touch) appears three times in the New Testament (Col. 2:21; Heb. 11:28; 12:20). In these passages it occurs as the aorist active subjunctive. The verb governs the genitive case.

Verse 29

διέβησαν—the subject of the verb must be supplied; it is intimated by the use of αὐτῶν in the preceding verse. The verb derives from διαβαίνω (I go through), is a directive compound, and is culminative aorist.

ἧς πεῖραν λαβόντες—although the feminine relative pronoun in the genitive case follows the noun γῆς (land), it finds its antecedent in θάλασσαν (sea). The noun πεῖραν (attempt) and the aorist participle of λαμβάνω (I take) are an idiomatic expression for "experiencing."

---

30 By faith the walls of Jericho fell, after the people had marched around them for seven days.
31 By faith the prostitute Rahab, because she welcomed the spies, was not killed with those who were disobedient.

F. Faith at Jericho
11:30–31

The writer of Hebrews deliberately by-passes the forty-year journey from Egypt to Canaan. He wants to indicate that the people of Israel refused to exercise faith and that, devoid of faith, they perished in their disobedience. Except for Joshua and Caleb, all the Israelites who were twenty years or older died in the desert. Their sons and daughters demonstrated faith in Israel's God when they conquered the fortress city of Jericho.

30. By faith the walls of Jericho fell, after the people had marched around them for seven days.

The story of Jericho's fall is well known (Josh. 6:1–24). Joshua, the successor of Moses, received God's promise: he and all the Israelites would take possession of the land from Lebanon to the Negev desert, and from the river

---

54. Lenski, *Hebrews*, p. 412.

Euphrates to the Mediterranean Sea. Repeatedly God instructed Joshua to be strong and courageous (see Josh. 1:6–7, 9).

Joshua and the Israelites put their faith in God, and because of their faith they were prosperous and successful. Whereas their fathers had refused to follow the pillar of cloud into the Promised Land (Deut. 1:32–36), they, by contrast, trusted the Lord God, crossed the Jordan, and conquered Jericho.

Jericho was strategically located on the eastern flank of Canaan. Nomadic tribes from the desert to the east would cross the Jordan and invade the land. The heavily-walled city of Jericho filled with mighty warriors prevented the invaders from entering the main valleys that provided access to the central part of Canaan.[55] The city itself was comparatively small; it had a circumference of 600 meters and measured approximately 225 by 80 meters.[56]

Because of their access to fresh water and storehouses of food, the people of Jericho could bide their time behind the massive city walls. However, the people of Israel received God's promise to Joshua: "See, I have delivered Jericho into your hands, along with its king and its fighting men" (Josh. 6:2). God told the Israelites to march around the city once every day for six days and on the seventh day seven times. And on that last day, when the priests sounded their trumpets on the seventh time around, Joshua commanded the people to shout, "for the LORD has given you the city!" (6:16). They had to devote the city to God as a first-fruit offering of their conquest. God brought down the walls of Jericho, which was situated on a volcanic rift prone to earthquakes.[57] Regardless of the means by which God destroyed Jericho, the fact remains that Joshua and the people of Israel put their faith in him. That is the point the writer of Hebrews makes: "By faith the walls of Jericho fell." Faith in God can move mountains.

The writer of Hebrews could have chosen to recount the incident in which the sun stood still in the middle of the sky for a full day (Josh. 10:13) at the request of Joshua. That feat was an act of faith. Says the writer of Joshua, "There has never been a day like it before or since, a day when the LORD listened to a man" (10:14). But the author of Hebrews excludes this incident and mentions the destruction of Jericho instead. By implication he cites the faith of the people of Israel. Purposely, however, he places the faith of the

---

55. Howard M. Jamieson highlights the commercial interests of Jericho's citizenry. Because of their proximity to the Dead Sea, the citizens traded salt, bitumen, and sulphur. Also, agricultural products abounded because of the fresh water available in the area. See his article "Jericho" in *ZPEB*, vol. 3, pp. 451–55.

56. Marten H. Woudstra, *The Book of Joshua*, New International Commentary on the Old Testament series (Grand Rapids: Eerdmans, 1981), p. 109. Also see Martin Noth, *The Old Testament World*, trans. Victor I. Gruhn (Philadelphia: Fortress, 1966), p. 147.

57. John J. Bimson, *Redating the Exodus and Conquest* (Sheffield: Journal for the Study of the Old Testament, 1978), p. 129. Archaeologists have discovered debris of walls that resemble those of medieval castles and of brown, black, and red-colored ashes of burnt material (see Josh. 6:24). Bimson concludes that the excavated city "would fit excellently as the large walled city which the biblical narrative says Joshua faced on crossing the Jordan" (p. 128).

immoral and pagan prostitute Rahab next as a contrast to the faith of the Israelites.

31. By faith the prostitute Rahab, because she welcomed the spies, was not killed with those who were disobedient.

Both James and the author of Hebrews refer to Rahab and call her forth-rightly "the prostitute" (James 2:25). Matthew lists her name as the mother of Boaz in Jesus' genealogy (Matt. 1:5). She was one of Jesus' forebears because she believed in Israel's God.[58]

Faith knows no barriers. Consider the evidence against Rahab, for she was

> a pagan Canaanite,
> a prostitute, and
> a woman.

Rahab's faith triumphed. Her fellow citizens were destroyed, but she and her extended family lived because of her faith in Israel's God (Josh. 2:8–13; 6:25). God did not condone her sinful practice of prostitution; instead he granted her grace and salvation. And although in Israel the man, not the woman, was heir of God's promises, in matters of faith distinctions disappear (Gal. 8:28).

Rahab believed Israel's God. She received no promise of salvation, no gospel of faith and repentance, and no assurance of acceptance. She had heard the reports about the exodus from Egypt, the conquest of the land east of the Jordan, and the destruction of the Amorites. Her confession of faith was based on the works of God. She said, "The LORD your God is God in heaven above and on the earth below" (Josh. 2:11). Hers was a simple but basic confession. She believed in God and trusted in him to deliver her from the impending destruction of her people and her city.

The author of Hebrews writes, "By faith the prostitute Rahab . . . was not killed with those who were disobedient." By using the expression *disobedient,* the writer places the inhabitants of Jericho on the same level as the rebellious Israelites who perished in the desert. He asks, "And to whom did God swear that they would never enter his rest if not to those who disobeyed?" (3:18). Unbelief results in disobedience; faith in obedience. Rahab believed and welcomed the spies into her home. At great personal risk she protected them from the king's soldiers, who knew that the spies were in Rahab's house. Rahab not only believed; she also put her faith to work in the interest of God's people (James 2:25). And last, she trusted God that at the time of the siege of Jericho her life and those of the members of her family would

---

58. Donald J. Wiseman, "Rahab of Jericho," *Tyn H Bul* 15 (1964): 8–10. Woudstra, in *The Book of Joshua,* mentions that the Targums call Rahab an innkeeper. This expression "in the Targums always receives an unfavorable sense" (p. 69, n. 7). Also see Josephus, *Antiquities* 5.7–9 (LCL).

be spared (Josh. 2:14–21).[59] We see somewhat of a parallel in the case of the Philippian jailer who asked Paul and Silas, "Men, what must I do to be saved?" They replied, "Believe in the Lord Jesus, and you will be saved— you and your household" (Acts 16:30–31).

Joshua spared the life of Rahab's family and placed them "outside the camp of Israel" (Josh. 6:23). Nevertheless, because of her faith, Rahab was welcomed by the Israelites, married Salmon, and became the mother of Boaz, who was the great-grandfather of David (Ruth 4:21; Matt. 1:5–6).

---

32 And what more shall I say? I do not have time to tell about Gideon, Barak, Samson, Jephthah, David, Samuel and the prophets, 33 who through faith conquered kingdoms, administered justice, and gained what was promised; who shut the mouths of lions, 34 quenched the fury of the flames, and escaped the edge of the sword; whose weakness was turned to strength; and who became powerful in battle and routed foreign armies. 35 Women received back their dead, raised to life again. Others were tortured and refused to be released, so that they might gain a better resurrection. 36 Some faced jeers and flogging, while still others were chained and put in prison. 37 They were stoned; they were sawed in two; they were put to death by the sword. They went about in sheepskins and goatskins, destitute, persecuted and mistreated— 38 the world was not worthy of them. They wandered in deserts and mountains, and in caves and holes in the ground.

39 These were all commended for their faith, yet none of them received what had been promised. 40 God had planned something better for us so that only together with us would they be made perfect.

G. Known and Unknown Heroes of Faith
11:32–40

1. Those Who Triumphed
11:32–35a

The list of individuals mentioned as heroes of faith is coming to a close, but not because the author has depleted his sources. He simply lacks the time to enumerate additional heroes. Instead of describing their deeds of faith, the writer merely records the names of those stalwarts known from Scripture.

32. And what more shall I say? I do not have time to tell about Gideon, Barak, Samson, Jephthah, David, Samuel and the prophets.

Ever since the beginning of the epistle, the author modestly refrained from mentioning himself. Here, however, for the first time he uses the first person singular pronoun *I*. In the concluding part of his epistle, he refers to himself again in the first person singular (13:19, 22, 23).

---

59. Clement of Rome refers at length to Rahab and the spies. However, when he comments on the scarlet cord (Josh. 2:21), he gives it New Testament fulfillment. He writes, "And [the spies] proceeded to give her a sign, that she should hang out a scarlet thread from her house, foreshowing that all who believe and hope on God shall have redemption through the blood of the Lord. You see, beloved, that the woman is an instance not only of faith but also of prophecy" (*The Apostolic Fathers*, vol. 1, I Clem. 12:7–8, LCL).

"What more shall I say?" He hesitates in view of the numberless examples of men and women who lived by faith. He takes a sample of names: some of them belong to the period of the judges; others, to that of the kings. To be sure, the author fails to present the names in chronological order. He should have said Barak (Judges 4–5), Gideon (Judges 6–8), Jephthah (Judges 11–12), Samson (Judges 13–16), Samuel (I Sam. 1–16), and David (I Sam. 16–31; II Sam.; I Kings 1–2:12). But the writer of Hebrews has no intention of listing the names chronologically. In effect, he follows the order Samuel gave in his farewell speech to the people of Israel: "Then the LORD sent Jerub-Baal [also called Gideon], Barak, Jephthah and Samuel, and he delivered you from the hands of your enemies on every side, so that you lived securely" (I Sam. 12:11). We have no indication why Samuel and the author of Hebrews follow a sequence differing from the chronological one.

The names appear in the sequence of three pairs: Gideon before Barak, Samson before Jephthah, and David before Samuel. The first one named in each set seems to be the more popular.[60]

a. Gideon fought with only three hundred men against the multitude of Midianite soldiers. By following faithfully the instruction from God, Gideon became a hero of faith. With his God Gideon was always in the majority (Judges 7:7).

b. Barak refused to do battle with Sisera and Jabin's army unless the prophetess Deborah went with him (Judges 4:8). With the prophetess to guide him, Barak fought the Canaanites and defeated them (Judges 4:16; and see 5:1).

c. Samson captures the imagination of everyone relishing physical prowess. But his love affair with Delilah not only deprived him of his strength; it also placed a permanent blot on his name. Yet Samson displayed unshakable faith in Israel's God when he prayed for strength to mete out justice to his enemies. God heard his prayer. "Thus [Samson] killed many more when he died than while he lived" (Judges 16:30).[61]

d. Jephthah's name is indissolubly tied to his rash vow that compelled him to sacrifice his only daughter (Judges 11:39–40). Nevertheless, Jephthah was filled with the Spirit of God. God used him to defeat the Ammonites and to punish the tribe of Ephraim. He was a man of faith.

e. David stands at the head of the kings of Israel. Because he trusted God, David was enabled to conquer his enemies, build his kingdom, and strengthen the people of Israel. He was Israel's statesman and spiritual leader.

f. Samuel was a prophet, who was called a seer (I Sam. 9:9). He stands

---

60. Henry Alford, *Alford's Greek Testament: An Exegetical and Critical Commentary,* 4 vols. (Grand Rapids: Guardian, 1976), vol. 4, pt. 1, p. 228.

61. James C. Moyer evaluates Samson: "His life is a negative example of a charismatic leader who came to a tragic, yet heroic, end. Nevertheless, his partial victory over the enemy was reason to be named with the heroes of the faith (Heb. 11:32)." *ZPEB*, vol. 5, p. 252.

first among the prophets and was an outstanding leader in Israel. The people turned to him, for they knew that God's favor rested on him.[62] God answered his prayers offered in faith. Said Samuel, "As for me, far be it from me that I should sin against the LORD by failing to pray for you" (I Sam. 12:23).

The author no longer provides a commentary on the lives of the heroes of faith. Instead he summarizes categories of deeds of faith.

**33. Who through faith conquered kingdoms,
administered justice, and
gained what was promised.[63]**

Although the author omits details, the common denominator he supplies is the expression *through faith*. This expression is a slight variant of the constantly recurring term *by faith*. The writer seems to intimate that the readers themselves ought to furnish details from their own knowledge of the Bible.

a. Who "conquered kingdoms"? Certainly Joshua did when he took possession of the Promised Land. The description is even more apt for David. He conquered the nations surrounding Israel and thus extended the borders of the Promised Land in fulfillment of God's sacred oath. God had sworn that he would give the land to the descendants of Abraham, Isaac, and Jacob. He had promised Moses that this land would extend from Lebanon in the north to the Negev in the south, and from the river Euphrates in the east to the Mediterranean Sea as the western border (Deut. 1:7–8). David fulfilled that promise through faith.

b. Who "administered justice"? The names of the judges in Israel come to mind, especially the name of Samuel. The people of Israel said that Samuel had not cheated or oppressed anyone (I Sam. 12:4). Kings of Israel and Judah administered justice in behalf of the people, as Scripture attests:

David reigned over all Israel, doing what was just and right for all his people. [II Sam. 8:15]

When all Israel heard the verdict [Solomon] had given, they held the king in awe, because they saw that he had wisdom from God to administer justice. [I Kings 3:28]

Jehoshaphat, king of Judah, appointed judges in the land and told them, "Consider carefully what you do, because you are not judging for man but for the LORD, who is with you whenever you give a verdict. Now let the fear of the LORD be upon you. Judge carefully, for with

---

62. Samuel J. Schultz, *The Old Testament Speaks* (New York: Harper and Row, 1960), p. 122.

63. Westcott in *Hebrews*, p. 377, neatly categorizes verses 33–34 into the literary symmetry of three triplets. The first triplet includes "material victory, moral success in government, spiritual reward." The second triplet describes personal escape from "wild beasts, physical forces, human tyranny." The last triplet describes the characteristics of "strength, the exercise of strength, the triumph of strength."

the Lord our God there is no injustice or partiality or bribery." [II Chron. 19:6–7]

c. Who "gained what was promised"? Because the expression *promises* is in the plural, I think that the author intends to call to mind numerous promises God had made to his people. Already the writer spoke of Abraham, who after waiting for the son of the promise received Isaac (Gen. 21:1–2; Heb. 6:15). At the end of his life, Joshua said to the elders, leaders, judges, and officials of Israel, "You know with all your heart and soul that not one of all the good promises the Lord your God gave you has failed. Every promise has been fulfilled; not one has failed" (Josh. 23:14). Indeed, God's promises to his people are innumerable, as the Scriptures themselves testify.

The author continues to enumerate the deeds of faith performed by his people. They are the heroes of faith,

who shut the mouths of lions,
34. quenched the fury of the flames,
and escaped the edge of the sword.

a. Among the biblical examples of people who fought lions is Samson, who tore a lion to pieces with his bare hands because "the Spirit of the Lord came upon him in power" (Judges 14:6). Also, David told Saul that while David was keeping the sheep of his father Jesse, he would rescue a sheep from the mouth of a lion or a bear and kill the wild beast (I Sam. 17:34–37). David testified that God delivered him from the paw of the lion. And from the lions' den, Daniel answered King Darius: "O king, live forever! My God sent his angel, and he shut the mouths of the lions" (Dan. 6:21–22). Centuries later Paul wrote, "But the Lord stood at my side . . . and I was delivered from the lion's mouth" (II Tim. 4:17).

b. The three friends of Daniel withstood the heat of the fiery furnace. Shadrach, Meshach, and Abednego, accompanied by someone who looked "like a son of the gods" (Dan. 3:25), walked around in the fire.[64] Nebuchadnezzar confessed that God "sent his angel and rescued his servants! They trusted in him" (v. 28).[65]

c. Who escaped the edge of the sword? On numerous occasions David fled to safety when he was pursued by Saul. Elijah fled the murderous Jezebel and went to Mount Horeb in the Sinai Peninsula (I Kings 19:8–10). Elisha heard that the king of Israel wanted to kill him during the famine in besieged Samaria (II Kings 6:31–32).

---

64. Edward J. Young, *The Prophecy of Daniel: A Commentary* (Grand Rapids: Eerdmans, 1949), p. 94. Also see John F. Walvoord, *Daniel: The Key to Prophetic Revelation* (Chicago: Moody, 1971), p. 191.

65. Mattathias, the father of Judas Maccabeus, addressed his sons when he was about to die. He enumerated the heroic deeds of many persons who are also mentioned by the author of Hebrews; for example, he referred to Abraham, Joseph, Joshua, and David. Says Mattathias, "Hananiah, Azariah, and Mishael [the Hebrew names for Shadrach, Meshach, and Abednego] believed and were saved from the flame" (I Macc. 2:59, RSV).

Still other heroes of faith received divine aid in overcoming weaknesses. They were the people

**whose weakness was turned to strength;
and who became powerful in battle
and routed foreign armies.**

a. Who was weak and became strong? Of course, Samson. Just before he died, God strengthened him to execute the superhuman feat of pushing the pillars of the temple of Dagon from their places (Judges 16:29–30). Hezekiah prayed to God when Isaiah told him that he would die. God answered his prayer and granted Hezekiah fifteen additional years (Isa. 38:1–8; II Kings 20:1–6; II Chron. 32:24). And when the weak remnant of the exiles returned from Babylonian captivity, God gave the leaders Nehemiah and Ezra and the people strength to rebuild the city of Jerusalem and the temple.

b. Who were the mighty in battle? And who put foreign armies to flight? Here are a few names and examples:

So David triumphed over the Philistine with a sling and a stone; without a sword in his hand he struck down the Philistine and killed him. [I Sam. 17:50]

Jehoshaphat, king of Judah, faced a vast army from Edom. The king defeated the enemy because God fought for his people (II Chron. 20:1–30).

Hezekiah, king of Judah, knew that a mighty Assyrian army had taken all the fortified cities of Judah and was marching toward Jerusalem. Because of Hezekiah's faith in God, an angel of the Lord struck down 185,000 Assyrian soldiers in one night (II Kings 19:35; II Chron. 32:21). Sennacherib, king of Assyria, withdrew his army and returned to Nineveh.

35a. Women received back their dead, raised to life again.
In the Old Testament we read that both Elijah and Elisha raised boys from the dead and gave them back to their mothers. The widow of Zarephath, who was not of Israel, believed. When she received her son from Elijah, she said, "Now I know that you are a man of God and that the word of the LORD from your mouth is the truth" (I Kings 17:24). The Shunammite woman came to Elisha because she knew that this "man of God" would be instrumental in raising her son from the dead (II Kings 4:8–37).

The New Testament provides the example of the widow of Nain who received her son when Jesus raised him from the dead (Luke 7:11–15). Mary and Martha received their brother Lazarus when Jesus called him forth from the grave (John 11:1–44). And the widows in Joppa welcomed Dorcas back when Peter raised her to life (Acts 9:36–41).

2. Those Who Suffered
11:35b–38

In the next few verses the author summarizes the physical suffering that the heroes of faith endured. They were martyrs for God's cause. By faith they conquered even though they lost their lives.

35b. Others were tortured and refused to be released, so that they might gain a better resurrection.

The instrument on which people were tortured in ancient times was called the *tympanum*. Presumably it consisted of a large wheel on which victims were stretched out. Then they were beaten to death.[66] In the Maccabean period during the first part of the second century before Christ, an almost ninety-year-old scribe named Eleazar was put on the rack and endured blows that led to his death. Said Eleazar, "It is clear to the Lord in his holy knowledge that, though I might have been saved from death, I am enduring terrible sufferings in my body under this beating, but in my soul I am glad to suffer these things because I fear him" (II Macc. 6:30, RSV). In this same period seven brothers and their mother were tortured by King Antiochus Epiphanes. They were put to death one after the other. One theme of this gruesome tale is that the martyrs believed in the "everlasting renewal of life" (II Macc. 7:9; also see vv. 14, 23, 29, 36).[67]

Accounts from the dark days of persecution that led to the Maccabean revolt were well known to the Jewish people whom the author of Hebrews addressed. These martyrs suffered and died because of their faith. They looked for a better resurrection. That is, they did not expect to return to this earthly life. A better resurrection, however, is an everlasting renewal of life in the presence of God.

Saints of the Old Testament era had a vague idea about the doctrine of the resurrection. But during the immediate centuries before Christ's coming to earth, the teaching of a resurrection after this life developed. And later when Jesus was about to raise Lazarus, Martha expressed this doctrine when she said, "I know he will rise again in the resurrection at the last day" (John 11:24). By faith believers endured suffering and hoped for a better resurrection in the life hereafter.

36. Some faced jeers and flogging, while still others were chained and put in prison.

The author of Hebrews moves from specific incidents to the more general occurrences of jeering, flogging, and being chained and imprisoned. From the New Testament we learn that jeering, flogging, and imprisonment were rather common. Jesus had to endure the sneers of Jews and soldiers. He suffered flogging during his trial at the court of Pontius Pilate. The apostles repeatedly spent time in prison. For example, Paul writes to the Corinthians, "I have worked much harder, been in prison more frequently, been flogged more severely, and been exposed to death again and again" (II Cor. 11:23).

The recipients of the Epistle to the Hebrews had experienced public insult and persecution. They themselves had seen the inside walls of a prison (10:33–34). They knew that their trust in God would be richly rewarded.

---

66. Thayer, *Lexicon*, p. 632.

67. Bruce M. Metzger, *An Introduction to the Apocrypha* (New York: Oxford University Press, 1957), p. 147.

Old Testament examples of people who were mocked, scourged, or imprisoned include the prophet Michaiah, who was slapped in the face and sent to prison for predicting the future (I Kings 22:24–28). Jeremiah was beaten by the officials of King Zedekiah and placed in prison for a long time (Jer. 37:14–21; also see 20:1–3; 38:1–13). And at the time of the Maccabean revolt, King Antiochus Epiphanes had the seven brothers and their mother tortured "with whips and cords" (II Macc. 7:1, rsv).

Once again the writer of Hebrews becomes specific in listing the types of suffering that believers had to bear. He puts three of them in brief succession.

37a. They were stoned;
they were sawed in two;
they were put to death by the sword.

a. Because stones are plentiful in Israel, the practice of throwing stones to kill someone was common. The law of Moses specified that a blasphemer had to be stoned by the community (Lev. 24:14–23). Naboth the Jezreelite, although he was innocent, was put to death by the scheming Jezebel (I Kings 21:10–15). Also, prophets of the Lord God met a similar fate. Zechariah, son of Jehoiada the priest, died in the courtyard of the Lord's temple during the reign of Joash, king of Judah (II Chron. 24:21–22; Matt. 23:35; Luke 11:51). That the practice of stoning the prophets had been quite prevalent in ancient Israel is evident from Jesus' remark in his discourse of the seven woes. "O Jerusalem, Jerusalem, you who kill the prophets and stone those sent to you, how often I have longed to gather your children together" (Matt. 23:37).[68]

b. Nowhere in Scripture is there a parallel to the clause "they were sawed in two." Tradition is strong that the prophet Isaiah was cut in half with a wooden saw.[69] This happened during the reign of King Manasseh. The Old Testament has no record of this incident.

c. Prophets who were killed by the sword are the contemporaries of Elijah. Complains the prophet to God, "The Israelites have rejected your covenant, broken down your altars, and put your prophets to death with the sword" (I Kings 19:10). King Jehoiakim in the days of Jeremiah struck down with the sword the prophet Uriah. This prophet prophesied in the name of the Lord and predicted the destruction of Jerusalem (Jer. 26:20–23). And John the Baptist died at the hand of Herod's executioner because he had told Herod, "It is not lawful for you to have your brother's wife" (Mark 6:14–29).

Many of the unknown heroes of faith were living in miserable conditions

68. Jews in Egypt, objecting to Jeremiah's admonitions, stoned him to death. Consult Tertullian, *Scorpion Antidote 8;* and Jerome, *Against Jovinian* 2.37.
69. Captives were put to work and cut wood and stone (II Sam. 12:31; I Chron. 20:3). But the cruelty of cutting a person in two seems to have been inflicted only on Isaiah. For Jewish sources see Yebamoth 49b and Sanhedrin 103b, *Talmud.* Early Christian references are Justin Martyr, *Dial.* 120; Tertullian, *Of Patience* 14; also see the apocryphal book the Ascension of Isaiah.

and sordid circumstances. **37b. They went about in sheepskins and goatskins, destitute, persecuted and mistreated— 38a. The world was not worthy of them.** The prophet Elijah is an example of those servants of God who lived in abject poverty. His lifestyle became a message of God's impending judgment on Israel. Elijah's appearance suited his prophetic calling. He was depicted as "a man with a garment of hair and with a leather belt around his waist" (II Kings 1:8). His successor Elisha inherited his coat, and in successive generations a garment of hair was the distinctive attire of a prophet (Zech. 13:4). With this apparel the prophet proclaimed a message of repentance and faith in God. John the Baptist, dressed in "clothing made of camel's hair, with a leather belt around his waist" (Mark 1:6), preached "a baptism of repentance" (v. 4). The darker hair of a camel or of a goatskin gave the prophet's garment more of a mournful appearance than did the lighter colored sheepskins.[70]

These prophets of old, persecuted and mistreated, were the world's refugees. Their adversaries denied them bread to eat and water to drink. Consider the plight of Elijah. He depended on the ravens to supply him with bread and meat, and he obtained drinking water from the brook Kerith (I Kings 17:2–6). King Ahab sent search parties to every nation and kingdom to find Elijah, so that he might put the prophet to death (I Kings 18:9–10). In the eyes of Ahab, Elijah was not worthy to live on the face of the earth.

The text, however, says the exact opposite: "the world was not worthy of them." That is, God's enemies cannot be compared with God's servants. These servants are great in honor and stature. King Ahab cannot be measured against Elijah, and King Herod is no match for John the Baptist. By their faith, believers tower above an unbelieving world in which God has placed them for man's benefit.

Referring to the prophets of the Old Testament era, the writer of Hebrews says, **38b. They wandered in deserts and mountains, and in caves and holes in the ground.** Obadiah, in charge of King Ahab's palace, "hid a hundred of the LORD's prophets in two caves, fifty in each, and supplied them with food and water" (I Kings 18:13; and see v. 4). Elijah fled into the Negev desert (I Kings 19:4). For him the land of Israel was no longer safe.

Caves were rather numerous in Israel (I Sam. 13:6). As fugitives, David and his men had no difficulty finding shelter from their pursuers or from the elements of nature (I Sam. 24:1–13). Constantly they endured the hostilities of Saul and his soldiers.

The believer is always surrounded by an unbelieving world. He is often lonely but never alone, for Jesus is his faithful companion in life. Confesses Henry F. Lyte,

---

70. Franz Delitzsch, *Commentary on the Epistle to the Hebrews*, 2 vols. (Edinburgh: Clark, 1877), vol. 2, p. 289.

Man may trouble and distress me,
'Twill but drive me to Thy breast;
Life with trials hard may press me,
Heaven will bring me sweeter rest.

3. Commendation
11:39–40

The author has come to the end of his discourse on the heroes of faith. Throughout the chapter the expression *by faith* is the golden thread that characterizes the life and deeds of God's people. He concludes this chapter by commending these heroes of faith and by including the readers of his epistle in God's blessing.

39. These were all commended for their faith, yet none of them received what had been promised.

In this text the writer stresses a positive element and a negative. We consider them in sequence.

a. *Positive.* The word choice in the first part of this verse reminds us of the beginning of the chapter. After the brief definition of faith, the author writes, "This is what the ancients were commended for" (11:2). Then he provides examples of those who have been commended: Abel (v. 4) and Enoch (v. 5). He seems to imply that all the other people he mentions are commended for their faith—all the known and unknown believers. And who commends these saints? God, of course.[71] God forgets none of his children. He recognizes everyone who acts in faith, because he has promised to be the God of his people (see, for instance, 8:10). As Father of his children, he expects them to put their trust in him. Instinctively a child puts full confidence in his parents and sometimes expects a parent to perform impossible feats. So God wants the believer to come in faith and ask for seemingly impossible things. Why? Because God takes pleasure in commending the believer for his faith.

b. *Negative.* Although believers in Old Testament times received words of praise for exercising their faith, and although many promises that God had given them were fulfilled in their lifetime, they failed to obtain that which had been promised. They saw some promises come true, but not the one promise of the coming of Christ. The writer of Hebrews already stated that the Old Testament believers saw and welcomed the promises in Christ from a distance (11:13). These believers looked forward to a heavenly country where God himself had prepared a place for them. At the conclusion of this chapter, the author once more testifies that although the saints received divine approval for their faith, they did not obtain that which had been promised.[72]

---

71. Lothar Coenen, *NIDNTT*, vol. 3, p. 1047.

72. The RSV expresses the concessive idea in verse 39 more directly: "And all these, *though* well attested by their faith, did not receive what was promised" (italics added).

What, precisely, did these Old Testament believers not receive? They had the promise of the coming of the Messiah and salvation in him. They were the heirs of the messianic prophecies (Gen. 3:15; 49:10; Num. 24:17; II Sam. 7:13; Job 19:25; Ps. 2:6–12; 16:10; 22:1; 45:6–8; 110:1; and numerous passages in the books of the prophets). But all these believers died before Jesus appeared on earth. To be sure, they died in faith and entered heaven. Nevertheless, they entered the presence of God with the promise that they had received and in expectation of its fulfillment. Their understanding of the plan of salvation was vague and incomplete. With the revelation God had given them, they tried to understand the mystery of redemption.[73] Peter testifies to this when he writes, "Concerning this salvation, the prophets, who spoke of the grace that was to come to you, searched intently and with the greatest care, trying to find out the time and circumstances to which the spirit of Christ in them was pointing when he predicted the sufferings of Christ and the glories that would follow" (I Peter 1:10–11).

The author of Hebrews ends the chapter by including the readers of his epistle in the discussion of faith and the promise of salvation in Christ. Before he began this discussion, he already had exhorted his readers to persevere in faith, "so that when you have done the will of God, you will receive what he has promised" (10:36). He brings the Old Testament saints and New Testament believers together in Jesus Christ. He considers them one family, and "a family is not complete unless all its members are present."[74]

40. God had planned something better for us so that only together with us would they be made perfect.

Here the pastor speaks not with words of exhortation or admonition. Rather, he teaches his readers the unity and continuity of the believers of both the Old Testament and New Testament eras.[75] He is saying that they (the heroes of faith) and we (believers in Jesus Christ) are one. In the next chapter the writer brings the "great cloud of witnesses" and the readers of his epistle together in Jesus (12:1–2). Jesus is the originator, the author, and the captain of faith. He leads the believer to perfection.

Says the writer, "God had planned something better for us." In view of its repeated use in Hebrews, we know that the word *better* relates to the era of fulfillment in Jesus Christ.[76] That is, believers who belong to the Christian era have become recipients of the promised salvation in Christ. The Old Testament believers look forward to this fulfillment. Because we look back

---

73. Owen, *Hebrews,* vol. 7, p. 215. Also consult Brown, *Hebrews,* p. 593.

74. Montefiore, *Hebrews,* p. 212.

75. Consult Hughes, *Hebrews,* p. 517. He quotes Moffatt, who writes, "The conclusion of the whole matter rather is (vv. 39, 40) that the reward of their faith had to be deferred till Christ arrived in our day. The [perfection] is entirely wrought out through Christ, and wrought out for all. It covers all God's People (compare 12:23), for now the Promise has been fulfilled to these earlier saints."

76. In the original Greek, the comparative adjective *better* appears nineteen times in the New Testament, thirteen of which are in the Epistle to the Hebrews (1:4; 6:9; 7:7, 19, 22; 8:6 [twice]; 9:23; 10:34; 11:16, 35, 40; 12:24).

upon the accomplished work of Christ, by faith we are able to appropriate the fullness of salvation. In other words, we are privileged above the saints who had only the promise.

What is the significance of Christ's coming for the Old Testament believers? The author puts it this way: "Only together with us would they be made perfect." During the time of the old covenant (Heb. 8:6–7), believers were unable to reach perfection. With his coming, Christ brought "many sons to glory" (2:10) and made them perfect (10:14). Through his atoning work, Christ caused Old Testament and New Testament believers to share in his perfection (12:23).[77]

Christ, then, perfects believers, for he is the perfecter of their faith (12:2). No believer can ever make himself perfect, because this work belongs to Christ. However, this does not mean that man should remain idle. Not at all. The author of Hebrews spurs his readers on to perseverance in the faith. Both Old and New Testament believers not only share the perfection Christ provides; they also have a common faith. And as the heroes of faith diligently exercised their faith, so the readers of the Epistle to the Hebrews must persevere. The saints of the Old Testament era serve the New Testament believers as incentives to persevere in faith. In the unity we have with them, we know that through faith we inherit the promise of salvation (6:12; 13:7).

Practical Considerations in 11:32–40

The word *saint* makes us think of a person who walks around with hands folded, with eyes turned heavenward, and with a halo around his head. Somehow we get the impression that he is not one of us. But when the author of Hebrews takes us to the art gallery of the Old Testament and shows us the portraits of Gideon, Barak, Samson, Jephthah, David, Samuel, and numerous other people, he confronts us with paintings of people in action. These saints are our brothers and sisters in faith. The paintings are scenes of battles, feats of courage, and instances of suffering. The dominant people in these portraits are ordinary men and women. They have one thing in common, and that is faith.

These people are saints, and because of this common faith, we are intimately related. We belong to the same family, for their trials and triumphs are ours, too. And just as they depended on divine help, we also trust in the Lord for aid. They spent their time in prayer; so do we. We pray and work for the coming of Christ's kingdom; as the second petition of the Lord's prayer has it, "your kingdom come" (Matt. 6:10). And thus as prayer partners and coworkers for God (I Cor. 3:9), we ourselves are saints who put faith into practice.

Ever since childhood we have been told not to boast about ourselves. Solomon said it well: "Let another praise you, and not your own mouth; someone else, and not your own lips" (Prov. 27:2). But we must not only listen to what the author of Hebrews tells about our spiritual possessions; we must also tell everyone about

---

77. Reinier Schippers, *NIDNTT*, vol. 2, p. 64. Also see Guthrie, *New Testament Theology*, p. 597.

them. In fact, we have to brag about them because they are so much better than the possessions of the Old Testament believers. We have a better salvation (6:9), a better hope (7:19), a better covenant (7:22), better promises (8:6), and better and lasting possessions (10:34). We are privileged sons and daughters of God, heirs and coheirs with Christ (Rom. 8:17). We may not keep silent. God wants us to talk about our riches in Christ, so that others, too, may share our spiritual wealth.

By contrast, the Old Testament believers, mentioned in Hebrews 11, had only fragments of God's revelation. With these bits and pieces, they persevered in faith. We, who have God's full revelation in Jesus Christ, ought to strive more earnestly to do the will of God (Heb. 10:35). "A small spark of light led them to heaven; when the sun of righteousness shines over us, with what pretence can we excuse ourselves if we still cleave to the earth?"[78]

Greek Words, Phrases, and Constructions in 11:32-40

Verse 32

λέγω—an instance of the deliberative subjunctive in a rhetorical question.

διηγούμενον—the present middle participle (from διηγέομαι, I relate) modifies the accusative singular personal pronoun με. The gender of the participle is masculine.

Verse 33

διὰ πίστεως—this construction is a variant of πίστει, much the same as κατὰ πίστιν (v. 13). Compare also δι᾽ ἧς (vv. 4, 7) and δι᾽ αὐτῆς (v. 4).

κατηγωνίσαντο—derived from καταγωνίζομαι (I overcome), this verb in the aorist middle is a compound with perfective force.[79] The compound consists of κατὰ (down) and ἀγωνίζομαι (I fight).

ἐπέτυχον—a verb in the aorist active from ἐπιτυγχάνω (I obtain) governs a genitive case.

Verse 34

παρεμβολάς—the accusative plural of the compound noun παρεμβολή derives from παρά (along), ἐν (in), and βάλλω (I throw). Here it refers to an army that is placed in line of battle.

ἀλλοτρίων—from ἄλλος (another), with the meaning *belonging to another*. The secondary meaning is "foreign," that is, "enemy."

Verse 36

ἕτεροι—in verse 35 the term ἄλλοι occurs. Although the two words are quite often differentiated, here they are synonymous.

πεῖραν ἔλαβον—see verse 29.

---

78. Calvin, *Hebrews*, p. 308.
79. Robertson, *Grammar*, p. 606.

Verse 37

ἐπρίσθησαν—from πρίζω (I cut in two with a saw), the aorist passive form perhaps has led to dittography in the word ἐπειράσθησαν (they were tempted). But the expression *they were tempted,* sometimes appearing before the verb *they were sawed in two* and sometimes after it, breaks the sequence of those verbs used for describing the administration of the death penalty. In short, ἐπειράσθησαν does not fit the context. Conjectural emendations of this form are numerous.[80]

Verse 39

μαρτυρηθέντες—the aorist passive participle of μαρτυρέω (I testify) has a concessive denotation.

διὰ τῆς πίστεως—see verse 33. The definite article takes the place of the possessive pronoun *their.*

τὴν ἐπαγγελίαν—some manuscripts, perhaps because of verse 13, have the plural. The singular also appears in 9:15 and 10:36.

Verse 40

προβλεψαμένου—the aorist middle participle from the compound πρό (before) and βλέπω (I see) is with τοῦ θεοῦ a genitive absolute construction and has a causal meaning. In the middle voice the verb means "to provide."

ἵνα—the conjunction seems to introduce a result clause instead of a purpose clause.

τελειωθῶσιν—from τελειόω (I complete), this form is the aorist passive subjunctive. The verb occurs nine times in Hebrews out of a total of twenty-three times in the New Testament. The negative μή appears to negate χωρὶς ἡμῶν more than the verb itself.

Summary of Chapter 11

What is faith? The author answers this question by giving the readers first a brief definition and then the application of faith in the lives of many believers. The definition is not designed to be comprehensive; rather, it is introductory in nature. Using examples taken from life, the writer demonstrates the characteristics and qualities of faith.

After an initial reference to the origin of the world, the author chooses his illustrations from specific periods of history. First, from the period between creation and the flood he selects the names of Abel, Enoch, and Noah. These people lived by faith and experienced intimate fellowship with God. With these examples, the writer depicts a gradual progression: Abel's faith

---

80. Metzger, *Textual Commentary,* p. 674. The editions of the United Bible Society and Nes-Al delete the word; many translations (RSV, GNB, JB, NAB, NEB, NIV, and *Moffatt*) do the same. Editions that retain the word are TR, Bover, Merk, BF, and Nes-Al (25th ed.); so do the KJV, NKJV, RV, ASV, NASB, and MLB. J. B. Phillips expands the verb into a clause: "they were tempted by specious promises of release."

eventually resulted in physical death; Enoch's faith brought translation to glory; and Noah's faith provided salvation for him, his family, and the animals.

Then, from the period of the patriarchs, the author selects incidents from the life of Abraham. He shows Abraham's obedience relative to traveling to the land of Canaan, the birth of a son, and the sacrifice of Isaac. The patriarchs died without seeing the promises of God fulfilled: they longed for life eternal in a heavenly city. Also, Isaac, Jacob, and Joseph looked to the future.

From the time of the exodus from Egypt to the conquest of Canaan, the writer gleans events from the life of Moses: his birth, childhood, education, and departure from Egypt. He also relates the faith of the Israelites in crossing the Red Sea and in marching around Jericho's walls. A brief remark on Rahab's faith concludes his comments about that era.

When the author comes to the period of the judges, kings, and prophets, he lists only some representative names. He summarizes the types of trials and triumphs that believers endured and enjoyed. Although he refrains from providing details, he intimates a relation between these persons and deeds of faith.

In his conclusion, the writer discloses that the Old Testament saints and the readers of his epistle share a common faith and together reap the benefits of a fulfilled promise. Believers are made perfect through the work of Christ.

12

Admonitions and Exhortations, *part 1*

12:1–29

Outline

12 1 Therefore, since we are surrounded by such a great cloud of witnesses, let us throw off everything that hinders and the sin that so easily entangles, and let us run with perseverance the race marked out for us. 2 Let us fix our eyes on Jesus, the author and perfecter of our faith, who for the joy set before him endured the cross, scorning its shame, and sat down at the right hand of the throne of God. 3 Consider him who endured such opposition from sinful men, so that you will not grow weary and lose heart.

4 In your struggle against sin, you have not yet resisted to the point of shedding your blood. 5 And you have forgotten that word of encouragement that addresses you as sons:

"My son, do not make light of the Lord's discipline,
and do not lose heart when he rebukes you,
6 because the Lord disciplines those he loves,
and he punishes everyone he accepts as a son."

7 Endure hardship as discipline; God is treating you as sons. For what son is not disciplined by his father? 8 If you are not disciplined (and everyone undergoes discipline), then you are illegitimate children and not true sons. 9 Moreover, we have all had human fathers who disciplined us and we respected them for it. How much more should we submit to the Father of our spirits and live! 10 Our fathers disciplined us for a while as they thought best; but God disciplines us for our good, that we may share in his holiness. 11 No discipline seems pleasant at the time, but painful. Later on, however, it produces a harvest of righteousness and peace for those who have been trained by it.

12 Therefore, strengthen your feeble arms and weak knees. 13 "Make level paths for your feet," so that the lame may not be disabled, but rather healed.

A. Divine Discipline
12:1–13

1. Look to Jesus
12:1–3

Using a series of examples taken from the history of God's people, the author continues to exhort his readers. Earlier he exhorted them to persevere in doing the will of God (10:36); now he tells them to run the race with perseverance and to look to Jesus. Believers in the Old Testament era had only the promise. In New Testament times believers have the fulfillment of the promise and therefore see Jesus.

1. Therefore, since we are surrounded by such a great cloud of witnesses, let us throw off everything that hinders and the sin that so easily entangles, and let us run with perseverance the race marked out for us.

The contemporaries of the first readers of Hebrews had developed an interest in sports. Athletes contended in a local stadium, while spectators sat on the tiered seats around the arena. Although Christians perhaps were not fully involved (because the games provided an excuse for pagan excesses), they were thoroughly familiar with the sports of their day. From the world of sports, the author borrows the imagery of spectators, apparel and condition of contestants, and the contest itself.

Note these points:

a. *Cloud.* The author places himself on the same level as that of the readers. He is one with them, for he is a contestant, too. With his fellow contestants, he looks up at the stands and sees a multitude of spectators. The writer of Hebrews calls them "a great cloud of witnesses." This may be an idiomatic expression that means the same as our term *a host of people.* The word *witness,* however, has two meanings. First, it refers to a person who watches the scene before him; his eyes and his ears tell him what is happening. Next, the word means that a person is able to talk about what he has seen and heard.

The witnesses are not silent. In fact, the writer of Hebrews says of Abel, "And by faith he still speaks, even though he is dead" (11:4). The heroes of faith mentioned in chapter 11 speak, but they do so through the pages of Scripture.[1] They cheer us on, so to speak, for the race we run concerns the cause of Christ. Through their biblical voices they encourage us in our contest of faith.[2] The witnesses surround us, for they have an interest in our achievement (11:40).

b. *Hindrance.* "Let us throw off everything that hinders," writes the author. He looks at the clothes we wear and the physical condition we are in. When we run a race, we dress in suitable sportswear designed to provide minimum weight and maximum comfort. And to qualify as runners, we strive to lose extra body fat by strengthening our muscles. That which is bulky in our bodies must disappear, for it hinders us in the race that we run.

What are the impediments that hinder us? Jesus says, "Be careful, or your hearts will be weighed down with dissipation, drunkenness and the anxieties of life" (Luke 21:34). Paul instructs, "But now you must rid yourselves of all such things as these: anger, rage, malice, slander, and filthy language from your lips" (Col. 3:8; also see James 1:21; I Peter 2:1).[3]

---

1. R. C. H. Lenski, *The Interpretation of the Epistle to the Hebrews and of the Epistle of James* (Columbus: Wartburg, 1946), p. 424.

2. Scripture teaches elsewhere (Rev. 7:9, for example) that the saints in heaven surround the throne of the Lamb. From the term *witness,* however, we cannot exclude the idea *spectator,* although the emphasis may be more on testifying than on viewing. Says B. F. Westcott, "They are spectators who interpret to us the meaning of our struggle, and who bear testimony to the certainty of our success if we strive lawfully (II Tim. 2:5)." *Commentary on the Epistle to the Hebrews* (Grand Rapids: Eerdmans, 1950), p. 391. Also consult F. W. Grosheide, *De Brief aan de Hebreeën en de Brief van Jakobus* (Kampen: Kok, 1955), p. 283. And see Hermann Strathmann, *TDNT,* vol. 4, p. 491.

3. That the impediment hindering the athlete has general significance is evident from the wording "*everything* that hinders" (italics added).

c. *Sin.* A hindrance in itself is not a sin, but because it impedes a contestant a hindrance can become sin. Sin entangles, much as a flowing robe that reaches down to the ground would entangle a runner in ancient times. Put this impediment aside, says the author of Hebrews. "Let us strip off anything that slows us down or holds us back, and especially those sins that wrap themselves so tightly around our feet and trip us up."[4]

The writer is rather specific. He calls sin *the* sin. What does he mean? He refrains from answering this question, but other passages of Scripture suggest that the sin of covetousness ranks chief among man's transgressions. Remember that Eve fell into sin because she *desired* to gain wisdom (Gen. 3:6). The last commandment in the Decalogue forbids covetousness (Exod. 20:17; Deut. 5:21). And this commandment actually serves as a summary to point out that the preceding commandments implicitly are directed against man's covetousness. In his letter to the Colossians, Paul calls evil desires and greed idolatry (3:5; also see Eph. 4:22). Even though the author of Hebrews refers to *the* sin, he himself leaves the precise meaning an open question. The intent of his exhortation is that we ought to avoid sin, for it impedes our movement in the race that we must run.

d. *Race.* When the writer exhorts us to "run with perseverance the race marked out for us," he echoes the words of Paul: "I have fought the good fight, I have finished the race, I have kept the faith" (II Tim. 4:7). Paul spoke these words at the end of his life when he knew he was approaching the finish line and the "crown of righteousness" waiting for him.[5]

We, the contestants, must run the race with perseverance. Our objective is to come to the finish line. But as we keep on running the course that God laid out before us, we keep our eye of faith fixed on Jesus. He encourages us to persevere in the contest, for he himself has run the same race. Jesus is the one who strengthens the runner and enables him to endure.

2. Let us fix our eyes on Jesus, the author and perfecter of our faith, who for the joy set before him endured the cross, scorning its shame, and sat down at the right hand of the throne of God.

The main emphasis in this verse lies in the opening clause. All the other clauses describe Jesus in respect to his work, endurance, and position.[6] Notice that the author introduces the name *Jesus* so the readers will concentrate on his earthly life.

a. "Fix our eyes on Jesus." Immediately the refrain of the invitational hymn composed by Helen H. Lemmel comes to mind:

---

4. The paraphrase of Kenneth Taylor (LB) is quite descriptive at this point.

5. In his epistles Paul frequently employs the imagery of a race (I Cor. 9:24–26; Gal. 2:2; Phil. 2:16).

6. In his article "Chiasmus, Creedal Structure, and Christology in Hebrews 12:1–2" (*Biblical Research* 23 [1978]: 37–48), E. B. Horning examines the structure of verses 1 and 2 and concludes that the passage shows an inverse parallelism with nine clauses, of which the center line is "keeping our eyes on Jesus the pioneer and perfecter of the faith."

Turn your eyes upon Jesus,
Look full in his wonderful face;
And the things of earth will grow strangely dim
In the light of his glory and grace.

As contestants engaged in running the race, we have no time to look around. We must keep our eyes focused on Jesus and must do so without distraction. The writer of Hebrews does not place the name *Jesus* among those of the heroes of faith; he gives him special recognition, for he calls him "the author and perfecter of our faith." Jesus is "the author of [our] salvation" (2:10), who as forerunner has entered the heavenly sanctuary (6:19–20) and has opened "a new and living way" for us that leads to this sanctuary (10:20).[7] He is the Beginning and the End, the Alpha and the Omega (Rev. 1:17; 21:6; 22:13). And he whom God perfected through suffering (Heb. 2:10) perfects his brothers and sisters who have placed their trust in him. As originator and perfecter of our faith, Jesus has laid its foundation in our hearts and in time brings faith to completion. He can do this because he is able, and he will do this because he is our brother (Heb. 2:11–12). In a similar vein, Paul encourages the Philippians when he says that God "who began a good work in you will carry it on to completion until the day of Christ Jesus" (1:6). Therefore, "turn your eyes upon Jesus."

b. "Joy set before him." How do we interpret the word *joy*? Does the writer mean that Jesus exchanges heavenly joy for earthly sorrow? Or does he mean that because of the joy awaiting Jesus after his death, Christ willingly "endured the cross"? Some scholars think that Jesus chose death on the cross in place of the joy of heavenly bliss he enjoyed in the presence of God (II Cor. 8:9; Phil. 2:6–7). They are of the opinion that this is what the author means to say.[8] Other scholars disagree. They believe that the intent is to convey this message: To obtain the joy God had planned for him, Jesus obediently suffered the agony of death.[9]

The evidence appears to favor the second interpretation. The context in general and the phrase *set before him* in particular support this approach. That is, God destined the path of suffering for Jesus (Isa. 53:4–6) and afterward filled him with joy (Ps. 16:11; Acts 2:28). The clause "for the joy set before him" seems to point to the future. It relates to Jesus' exaltation when he was glorified after his death on the cross.

c. "Endured the cross." In his epistle the author seldom speaks directly

---

7. Otto Michel, *Der Brief an die Hebräer,* 10th ed. (Göttingen: Vandenhoeck and Ruprecht, 1957), p. 291.

8. Consult, for example, Westcott, *Hebrews,* p. 397; Grosheide, *Hebreeën,* p. 286; John Calvin, *Epistle to the Hebrews* (Grand Rapids: Eerdmans, 1949), p. 313; Murray J. Harris, *NIDNTT,* vol. 3, p. 1180; and P. Andriessen and A. Lenglet, "Quelques passages difficiles de l'Épître aux Hébreux (5:7, 11; 10:20; 12:2)," *Bib* 51 (1970): 215–20.

9. For instance, refer to Ceslaus Spicq, *L'Épître aux Hébreux,* 3d ed., 2 vols. (Paris: Gabalda, 1953), vol. 1, p. 387; Lenski, *Hebrews,* p. 428; and Philip Edgcumbe Hughes, *Commentary on the Epistle to the Hebrews* (Grand Rapids: Eerdmans, 1977), pp. 523–24.

about the earthly life of Jesus. In fact, this is the only time he mentions the word *cross*. That term, together with the verb *endured,* mirrors the entire passion narrative of Jesus' trial and death. Jesus stood alone during his trial before the high priest and before Pontius Pilate. Jesus endured the agony of Gethsemane alone. And he alone bore the wrath of God at Calvary. In his suffering Jesus visibly demonstrated his faith in God. In obedience he sustained the anguish of death on the cross.

d. "Scorning its shame." The Jews who demanded Jesus' crucifixion wanted to place him under the curse of God. They knew that God had said, "Anyone who is hung on a tree is under [my] curse" (Deut. 21:23; see also Gal. 3:13). They wanted Jesus to experience the utmost shame. He took the curse upon himself to set his people free and to experience with them the joy God had set before him. Indeed, the author and perfecter of our faith triumphed when he sat down at God's right hand.

e. "And sat down." With a few strokes of his pen, the writer provides an account of Jesus' life, death, resurrection, and ascension. The crowning point, of course, is Jesus' enthronement at the right hand of God. That place of honor belongs to him and will be his for all eternity. The author repeatedly quotes and alludes to Psalm 110:1: "Sit at my right hand until I make your enemies a footstool for your feet" (1:13). He develops a definite progression of thought.[10] Note these verses:

1:3 "he sat down at the right hand of the Majesty in heaven"
8:1 "who sat down at the right hand of the throne of the Majesty in heaven"
10:12 "he sat down at the right hand of God"
12:2 "sat down at the right hand of the throne of God"

Jesus accomplished his task on earth, assumed his place in heaven, and now assures the believer of divine assistance in the race marked out for him.

3. Consider him who endured such opposition from sinful men, so that you will not grow weary and lose heart.

Look carefully at the entire life of Jesus, says the author of Hebrews to his readers, and consider what he had to encounter. He literally tells them to compare their lives with that of Jesus and to take careful note of all that Jesus had to endure. Jesus came to fulfill the messianic prophecies, and therefore he came to his own people; "but his own did not receive him" (John 1:11). Instead, Jesus met willful unbelief and unmitigated opposition. He endured the hatred of a sinful world set against the truth of God. If, then, Jesus experienced such opposition, would not his followers share the same lot (John 17:14)?

The writer reveals himself to be an excellent pastor. He knows the tendency to look at the Christian and not at the Christ. Introspection causes spiritual weariness and discouragement, but looking at Jesus renews the

---

10. Westcott, *Hebrews,* p. 396.

Christian's strength and boosts his courage. Therefore, directing attention to Jesus, the author exhorts the Christian to consider the suffering Christ sustained not only on the cross but throughout his ministry. When the Christian realizes that Jesus withstood the hatred of sinful men for the sake of the believer, the Christian ought to take courage. Then his own problems become easier to bear, and he, too, will be able to continue and eventually complete the race marked out for him.[11]

Practical Considerations in 12:1–3

We are individualists who take pride in our achievements. But sometimes this attitude, commendable as it is, can develop into a complex. That is, we think that we are alone in this world, for we are the only Christians who have kept the faith. We feel somewhat like the prophet Elijah, who complained that he was the only one left (I Kings 19:10). As a consequence, discouragement sets in.

We are not alone, however. First, consider the countless multitudes that have kept the faith and have been translated into glory. The writer of Hebrews describes them as "a great cloud of witnesses." Next, we must look to Jesus, the author and perfecter of our faith. He is always near us and ready to help. And last, we are part of the body of Christ, the church. We have numberless brothers and sisters who are fighting the good fight of faith.

Yet, as runners engaged in a race, we are individuals. Every believer must run the race that God has set out for him. And everyone has his own set of obstacles, his own track, and his own capabilities. To run the race God has given us, we must put aside everything that hinders us. The clothing of a long-distance runner consists of shirt, shorts, and shoes, and weighs less than a pound. On the track of faith, we are told to travel far. Therefore we must travel light.

The Christian's life of faith is more than one outstanding feat, a single accomplishment, and a sudden burst of spiritual energy. The believer looks to Jesus without distraction, for then he perseveres and lives a life of holiness. Then he progresses as he travels the road of sanctification.

We bear our cross, but we do not carry the cross Jesus bore. He carried the cross alone. We carry ours by unwaveringly looking at him. From his exalted position in heaven at God's right hand, Jesus enables us to persist, to endure, and to be faithful to God and his Word.

Greek Words, Phrases, and Constructions in 12:1–3

Verse 1

τοιγαροῦν—a combination of τοί (or τῷ), γάρ, and οὖν that functions as "a particle introducing a conclusion with some special emphasis or formality, and gen-

---

11. Apparently the words *grow weary* and *lose heart* were current in the world of sports. Writes James Moffatt, "Aristotle uses both to describe runners relaxing and collapsing, once the goal has been passed." See his *Epistle to the Hebrews*, International Critical Commentary series (Edinburgh: Clark, 1963), p. 199.

erally occupying the first place in the sentence."[12] It means "therefore," "consequently," "then."

καὶ ἡμεῖς—although translations fail to render the exact equivalent of the Greek, the combination of these words is emphatic: we ourselves, too.

τοσοῦτον—this correlative adjective denotes quantity. By contrast, the adjective τοιαύτην (v. 3) denotes quality.

ἔχοντες—denoting cause, this is a present active participle.

νέφος—literally the word means "cloud," but as an idiom we may translate it as "throng" or "host."

μαρτύρων—besides the double meaning the expression μάρτυς has (witnessing by eye or ear; and testifying God's truth), in the New Testament it conveys the idea *martyr* (Acts 22:20; Rev. 2:13; 17:6).

ὄγκον—apparently derived from φέρω (I carry) in the aorist ἐνεγκεῖν.[13]

ἀποθέμενοι—the aorist middle participle from the compound verb ἀπό (away) and τίθημι (I place) means "laying aside from yourselves every weight."[14]

εὐπερίστατον—because this verbal adjective appears once in the New Testament, a modification (εὐπερίσπαστον, easily distracting) occurs in two major manuscripts. The compound derives from εὖ (well), περί (around), and ἵστημι (I stand).

τὴν ἁμαρτίαν—even though the author uses the definite article, places a verbal adjective between the definite article and the noun, and gives the noun in the singular, he fails to communicate the nature of ἁμαρτία; instead, he points to sin itself.

τρέχωμεν—the hortatory subjunctive, because of the present active first person plural, reveals that the readers already are engaged in the race.

Verse 2

ἀφορῶντες—the compound present active participle from ἀπό (away) and ὁράω (I see) signifies that we ought to look to Jesus without distraction; that is, everything else takes second place. The present tense is durative.

ἀρχηγόν—in the New Testament the noun occurs four times (Acts 3:15; 5:31; Heb. 2:10; 12:2) and in each passage refers to Jesus. He is the ruler, leader, author, prince. The genitive τῆς πίστεως is objective.

κεκάθικεν—although manuscript P[46] has the aorist active indicative ἐκάθισεν, the perfect active indicative appears to be the original reading. The perfect tense relates the action that happened in the past and is effective for the present and future.

Verse 3

τοιαύτην—it denotes quality (cf. v. 1).

τὸν ὑπομεμενηκότα—the use of the definite article directs attention to Ἰησοῦν (v. 2). The participle, from ὑπομένω (I remain), is the perfect active; it reveals that

---

12. Joseph H. Thayer, *A Greek-English Lexicon of the New Testament* (New York, Cincinnati, and Chicago: American Book Company, 1889), p. 627.

13. Ibid., p. 437. Also refer to Philo, *Allegorical Interpretation* 3.45 (LCL); and Josephus, *Jewish Wars* 4.319; 7.443 (LCL).

14. A. T. Robertson, *A Grammar of the Greek New Testament in the Light of Historical Research* (Nashville: Broadman, 1934), p. 810. Also see Robert Hanna, *A Grammatical Aid to the Greek New Testament* (Grand Rapids: Baker, 1983), p. 412.

Jesus endured opposition in the past, but that even in the present the effects are evident.

ἑαυτόν—the manuscript evidence favors the reading αὐτόν or even αὐτούς. However, the reading of the reflexive pronoun in the singular, although poorly supported by manuscripts, fits the context of the passage.[15]

ἐκλυόμενοι—the present passive participle, denoting manner, depends on the aorist active subjunctive κάμητε (from κάμνω, I am weary). The expression ταῖς ψυχαῖς (your souls), as a dative of respect, must be construed with the participle, not the verb.

---

2. Accept Correction
12:4–6

Sin is a power that is universal in its opposition to God and his revelation. The writer of Hebrews portrays it as a personified force that man confronts and fights. Sin affects everyone and everything. Jesus is the only one who was not influenced by sin, for he conquered sin. The author exhorts his readers to look at Jesus (v. 2) and to strive against sin.

4. In your struggle against sin, you have not yet resisted to the point of shedding your blood.

The metaphor in this verse—"resisted to the point of shedding your blood"—comes from the sports arena. The author goes from one sport to the other, from the imagery of the race to that of boxing.[16] In boxing, blood flows from the faces of the contestants when they withstand vicious blows. At times serious injuries result in death.

The imagery of withstanding the opponent to the point of shedding blood serves as a parallel to the readers' struggle against sin. No specific sin is mentioned. Sin, however, with its mysterious power is a formidable opponent that must be resisted unto death. Martin Luther, who frequently encountered the power of Satan and sin, exhorts the Christian in his well-known hymn:

> Let goods and kindred go,
> This mortal life also;
> The body they may kill,
> God's truth abideth still,
> His kingdom is forever.

The text itself reveals nothing about the political world in which the readers lived. In earlier days they had stood their ground when they had been

---

15. Bruce M. Metzger, *A Textual Commentary on the Greek New Testament* (London and New York: United Bible Societies, 1975), p. 675.

16. John Albert Bengel, *Gnomon of the New Testament*, ed. Andrew R. Fausset, 7th ed., 5 vols. (Edinburgh: Clark, 1877), vol. 4, p. 462. The paragraph division differs in Bible translations; for example, JB places verse 4 with the preceding verses to show continuation of the imagery from sports. The GNB, NKJV, RSV, NEB, and TR include verse 3 with the following section on discipline. The NIV, Nes-Al, and the United Bible Societies editions begin a new paragraph at verse 4.

publicly insulted, had been persecuted, and had seen their property confiscated (Heb. 10:32–34). But those days belonged to the past, and the writer repeatedly indicates that the recipients of the epistle were enjoying a period of rest and ease that had caused spiritual relaxation.

The writer admonishes rather than exhorts the readers that they should resist sin to the point of shedding blood. The possibility of persecution on account of their faith in Jesus was real. If Jesus endured the persecution and shed his blood, his followers ought not entertain illusions of being exempt.

> Our fathers, chained in prisons dark,
> Were still in heart and conscience free;
> How sure will be their children's peace
> If they, like them, contend for thee!
> —Frederick W. Faber

5. And you have forgotten that word of encouragement that addresses you as sons:

"My son, do not make light of the Lord's discipline,
and do not lose heart when he rebukes you,
6. Because the Lord disciplines those he loves,
and he punishes everyone he accepts as a son."

Believers in the first century had access to the Scriptures when they attended the worship services. There they memorized passages from the Old Testament, especially those from the Psalter, Proverbs, and Prophets. The New Testament reveals that Proverbs 3 was well known; writers quote from and allude to it more than any other chapter of this book.[17] When the author of Hebrews calls to mind Proverbs 3:11–12, he refers to a text that was basic to training believers in the church. But the readers were slow to learn (Heb. 5:11) and had forgotten the passage from Proverbs 3. The writer, then, spells it out for them.

We note the following points:

a. *Jesus.* The readers ought to recall the word of encouragement from Proverbs 3 that addresses them as sons. They are sons because of Jesus, the Son of God. Throughout his epistle the writer of Hebrews has indicated the importance of the Son and its implications for the sons (see especially 2:10–11). The one exists for the others. As Son of God, Jesus had to suffer, learn obedience, and become "the source of eternal salvation for all who obey him" (5:8–9). To be sure, the suffering of Christ is unique; it cannot and need not be repeated by his followers. However, the principle of discipline remains the same. Scripture addresses the followers of Jesus as sons, and thus they can expect correction and rebuke.

b. *Sons.* The writer says that the Word of God addresses God's children

---

17. Simon J. Kistemaker, *The Psalm Citations in the Epistle to the Hebrews* (Amsterdam: Van Soest, 1961), p. 51. Also refer to Nes-Al, Appendix 3; Philo, *Preliminary Studies* 175 (LCL); I Clem. 56:2 (*The Apostolic Fathers*, vol. 1, LCL); and SB, vol. 3, p. 747.

and encourages them. God speaks to his sons and daughters through his Word. He says, "My son, do not make light of the Lord's discipline, and do not lose heart when he rebukes you." That is, believers should see and feel the hand of God in their difficulties. The use of the expression *not make light of* suggests that they ought to view discipline as coming directly from God. If the readers of the epistle take discipline lightly, they will also think lightly of the suffering Jesus had to endure. However, they have to take God's corrective measures most seriously and understand that God gives his children adversities for their spiritual well-being. When they accept good as well as trouble from God (Job 2:10), they will not become discouraged and lose heart. Then they know that God is their Father.

c. *Father.* God, as our heavenly Father, "disciplines those he loves, and he punishes everyone he accepts as a son." The last part of this quotation comes from the Septuagint. The Old Testament reads, "Because the LORD disciplines those he loves, as a father the son he delights in" (Prov. 3:12). The variation affects the wording but not the intent of the verse.

Discipline, then, is a privilege that God extends to those he loves. This almost sounds contradictory until we see that discipline is not extended to the ungodly. They receive his judgment. God disciplined his people Israel as a consequence of their transgressions, but he displays patience and forebearance with his enemies until the measure of their iniquity is full (Gen. 15:16; Matt. 23:32; I Thess. 2:16). Discipline is a sign that God accepts us as his children.

Does God punish his children? He does send us trials and hardships designed to strengthen our faith in him. Adversities are aids to bring us into a closer fellowship with God. But God does not punish us. He punished the Son of God, especially on Calvary's cross, where he poured out his wrath on Jesus by forsaking him (Ps. 22:1; Matt. 27:46; Mark 15:34). As sin-bearer, Jesus bore God's wrath for us, so that we who believe in him will never be forsaken by God. God does not punish us, because Jesus received our punishment. We are disciplined, not punished.

Moreover, we should accept God's rebuke, discipline, and castigation as evidence of his love to us. If we do this, we demonstrate that we indeed are his children and as a result grow in faith and trust.

Practical Considerations in 12:4–6

Jesus employs a metaphor about tending a vineyard when he says that he is the true vine and his Father the gardener (John 15:1). What is the work of this gardener? "He cuts off every branch in me that bears no fruit, while every branch that does bear fruit he prunes so that it will be even more fruitful" (v. 2). When a gardener has finished pruning, a vine has only its essential branches left. At the end of the next growing season, the gardener reaps an abundant harvest.

God plunged Job into grief when he allowed Satan to take the lives of Job's ten children. Job lost all his earthly possessons. His wife told him to curse God and die, and his friends proved to be the world's most wretched comforters. Yet Job's faith triumphed; he knew that his Redeemer lived; and he received from God "twice as much as he had before" (Job 42:10).

In a time of permissiveness, Solomon's proverb points out a basic flaw: "He who spares the rod hates his son" (Prov. 13:24). The reverse is that "he who loves him is careful to discipline him." God loves us and therefore disciplines us. He removes hindrances to our spiritual development to make us partakers of his holiness and sharers in his rewards.

Greek Words, Phrases, and Constructions in 12:4–6

Verse 4

ἀντικατέστητε—the second aorist indicative, second person plural, is composed of two prepositions, ἀντί (against) and κατά (down), and the verb ἵστημι (I stand). Followed by the prepositional phrase πρὸς τὴν ἁμαρτίαν the verb is directive as well as intensive. The aorist is ingressive. Note the assonance in this verse: four words begin with the vowel ἀ.

ἀνταγωνιζόμενοι—in the main verb (ἀντικατέστητε) and in this participle the preposition ἀντί appears. The author has chosen these two forms to express the seriousness of fighting sin. The participle in the present middle (deponent) signifies continuity.

Verse 5

ἐκλέλησθε—from the verb ἐκλανθάνομαι (I forget), the perfect tense reveals that not a temporary loss of memory but an inability to recall is meant. The perfect expresses that an act accomplished in the past has lasting results. Verbs of forgetting (and remembering) have a direct object in the genitive case.[18]

ἥτις—an indefinite relative pronoun, although used as a relative pronoun, has its antecedent in παρακλήσεως.

ὀλιγώρει—the verb in the present active imperative has the participle μή. This combination means that the action is in progress but must be discontinued.

Verse 6

παιδεύει—the present active indicative form exhibits progress in the activity of training a child (παῖς).

μαστιγοῖ—derived from the verb μαστιγόω (I scourge), the present active indicative implies that God indeed strikes with a whip.

3. Endure Hardship
12:7–11

How does the writer of Hebrews apply the quotation from Proverbs 3:11–12? He knows that every son and daughter of God endures periods

---

18. Robertson, *Grammar*, p. 508.

of hardship. Whether God's children experience the pain of accident, misfortune, or loss, they need encouragement.

7a. Endure hardship as discipline; God is treating you as sons.

In times of affliction, says the author, keep in mind that all your setbacks come from God; he is training you in godliness and has accepted you as sons. The adversities you encounter are blessings in disguise, for behind your difficulties stands a loving Father who is giving you what is best. God's children, then, must always look beyond their trials and realize that God himself is at work in their lives.

Translators differ in their reading and understanding of the Greek text of this verse. Here are the three representative translations:

KJV "If ye endure chastening, God dealeth with you as with sons."

RSV "It is for discipline that you have to endure. God is treating you as sons."

NIV "Endure hardship as discipline; God is treating you as sons."

The King James Version, based on a variant Greek reading, translates this verse as a conditional sentence. The evidence for the reading is rather weak.

A common translation is that given by the Revised Standard Version. The verse is a statement of fact and informs the reader that the recipients of Hebrews endured suffering as discipline.

The New International Version renders the verse as a command. The author-pastor tells his readers what they must do. The choice is difficult, but the general context of the first part of this chapter features many sentences as commands (imperatives).

7b. For what son is not disciplined by his father?

The question is rhetorical. Of course a son submits to his father's rule; otherwise he would not be a true son.

The concept *discipline* in ancient Israel was not limited to describing physical punishment but included the concept *education*.[19] That is, the father as head of the household taught his children the law of God, the tradition of the elders, and the skills of a trade. Education was meant to inculcate obedience to God's law, respect for authority, and a love for their national heritage.

The point of verse 7 is that God himself is educating his children. The writer employs the illustration of a human father teaching his son. In a similar way God himself is giving his children moral and spiritual training. In the case of the recipients of Hebrews, the writer relates that they made light of the training God gave them. Therefore, the readers needed a pastoral admonition to submit to discipline. God trains them as sons, so that they may take their place next to the Son of God.

8. If you are not disciplined (and everyone undergoes discipline), then you are illegitimate children and not true sons.

---

19. Georg Bertram, *TDNT*, vol. 5, p. 604; and Dieter Fürst, *NIDNTT*, vol. 3, pp. 776–77. Also consult Günther Bornkamm, "Sohnschaft und Leiden," *Judentum, Urchristentum, Kirche* (1960): 188–98.

This verse can be interpreted to mean that the readers were illegitimate children, spiritually. But that is not the case, because the writer has already stated that they are sons of God (vv. 5–7). He presents his argument in the form of a simple conditional sentence that expresses reality. He rebukes the people on account of their carelessness in accepting divine discipline. Certainly God gave them spiritual training, but they had failed to pay attention to what God was teaching them. This careless attitude toward discipline placed them in the same category as illegitimate children. These children had no claim to inheritance; they were a source of shame and embarrassment to their father; and they were denied the discipline, coaching, and grooming that true sons received.

Careful training within a family setting has always been an accepted norm, and people are expected to receive training as part of their development in social graces. Not to accept discipline is a mark of rebellion against authority. The readers of the epistle, however, had shown disregard for this norm and had slighted God who disciplined them. They had to be told to observe the norm, accept discipline, and behave like sons. Should they continue to neglect God's teaching, they would be regarded as illegitimate children. These children have no claim to spiritual sonship and to a spiritual inheritance— that is, salvation—to which the writer of Hebrews repeatedly refers (1:14; 6:12; 9:15; 12:17). In short, sons need instruction.

9. Moreover, we have all had human fathers who disciplined us and we respected them for it. How much more should we submit to the Father of our spirits and live!

In the preceding verse the author addresses the readers directly by using the second person plural pronoun *you.* In verse 9 the wise counselor includes himself and says "we." Again he introduces an illustration from family life. He does so by comparing human fathers with God, the heavenly Father. Thus we note two parts:

a. "We have all had human fathers." The writer speaks in general terms and refrains from mentioning exceptions, for example, orphans. In family circles the head of the household is the father; he trains the children to behave and to conduct themselves properly.

Reflecting on his own youth, the author declares that children accept discipline without question. Did we resist our fathers when they corrected us? Of course not! We respected them in harmony with the commandment, "Honor your father and your mother" (Exod. 20:12; Deut. 5:16). As the time-worn saying has it, "A father is someone you look up to—no matter how tall you grow."

b. "We submit to the Father of our spirits and live." As he has done many times in his epistle, the writer employs the expression *how much more* to illustrate the extent of his comparison (2:2–3; 9:14; 10:29; 12:25). He follows the teachings of Jesus, who compared human fathers' giving good gifts with the heavenly Father's giving good gifts (Matt. 7:11; Luke 11:13).

The contrast is explicit and implicit in the last part of the verse:

human fathers—Father
bodies—spirits
death—life

We ought to avoid reading too much into verse 9, for the author wishes only to convey that he is comparing the human with the divine, and mortality with immortality. He intimates that obedience to God results in eternal life, for he is our heavenly Father. Comments F. F. Bruce, "As 'the fathers of our flesh' are our physical (or earthly) fathers, so 'the Father of (our) spirits' is our spiritual (or heavenly) Father."[20]

10. Our fathers disciplined us for a little while as they thought best; but God disciplines us for our good, that we may share in his holiness.

The comparison continues. Children are in their parental home for the time of childhood and adolescence. The years in which they receive parental discipline are relatively few; they end when the child becomes an adult. Fathers (and mothers) seek that which is best for their children, but often make mistakes. Their skills in rearing sons and daughters are limited, for they have to learn by doing. With the best of intentions, they sometimes fail in either method or purpose. In disciplining their children, parents frequently lack wisdom; corrective measures are at times too severe, and at other times are abandoned. Punishment is administered in many instances not in love but in anger. Parents who are honest with themselves and with their children admit their shortcomings.

What a difference when we consider God's discipline! He never makes a mistake, always chastens in love, scourges us, and at the same time comforts us. His discipline does not end when we have reached adulthood. Throughout our earthly life he trains us; although we often disappoint him, he never forsakes us. His patience toward us seems unlimited in spite of our lack of progress.

God has a definite purpose in mind for disciplining us. He wants us to "share in his holiness." Whereas human fathers train their children to conduct themselves appropriately, God disciplines us for holiness. That is, he wants us to become like him, perfect and holy (Matt. 5:48; Lev. 11:44–45; 19:2; 20:7; I Peter 1:15–16). God prepares us for life eternal. Therefore, we cheerfully accept God's discipline, for we know that the adversities we experience are for our spiritual welfare. As Paul says to the Corinthian believers, "For our light and momentary troubles are achieving for us an eternal glory that far outweighs them all" (II Cor. 4:17).

11. No discipline seems pleasant at the time, but painful. Later on, however, it produces a harvest of righteousness and peace for those who have been trained by it.

---

20. F. F. Bruce, *The Epistle to the Hebrews,* International Commentary on the New Testament series (Grand Rapids: Eerdmans, 1964), pp. 359–60. For the expression *Father of our spirits,* compare Num. 16:22; 27:16; Rev. 22:6.

Once more the author uses the device of contrast. This time he contrasts discipline of the present with results garnered in the future. Whatever discipline you experience at the moment, he tells his readers, whether it is physical, psychological, or spiritual discipline administered by God or man, it does not seem to be pleasant.

We do not relish correction, even though we readily acknowledge that discipline is a necessary part of our development. Discipline that is painful comes in many forms: spankings, suspension of privileges, loss of possession, departure of a loved one, serious injury, illness, unemployment, and persecution. When these adversities strike, we experience pain; our first reaction to affliction is not one of joy. We know that James writes, "Consider it *pure joy*, my brothers, whenever you face trials of many kinds" (1:2, italics added). But joy arrives later when we are able to look back and see the benefits we have received from these trials.

The message of Hebrews is the same. The suffering you encounter is painful, says the writer, but when the period of distress has ended, you will be able to see results: "a harvest of righteousness and peace." Your reward will be a right relationship with God and man in which peace reigns supreme. You are the peacemakers. Says James, "Peacemakers who sow in peace raise a harvest of righteousness" (3:18).

Who receives these blessings? They are "for those who have been trained by" discipline. Those who willingly have endured hardship as discipline and who have submitted themselves to the will of God in their lives are the recipients of righteousness and peace. They have been trained, writes the author. At the conclusion of this section he employs the expression *train*. He borrowed the word from the world of sports to remind the readers that they are engaged in a contest that demands perpetual training.

Practical Considerations in 12:7–11

To be sure, the addressees are sons, for this is the term the author uses. His intention, however, is not to give the impression that daughters are excluded from discipline. Rather, he employs the terminology of his day and expresses himself according to the norms of his culture. By addressing the men, he includes the women. They, too, are the recipients of God's discipline.

When God sends sorrow or sickness, we often hear those afflicted ask, "Why me?" They search their hearts and minds and try to find out why God is displeased with them, why he sends them adversity. Scripture speaks directly to these questions and gives this answer: "Because the Lord disciplines those he loves."

Guido de Brès, author of the Belgic Confession of Faith, was executed on the last day of May 1567, in Belgium. Just before he was brought to the gallows, he wrote a letter to his wife in which he said, "O my God, now the time has come that I must leave this life and be with you. Your will be done. I cannot escape from your hands. Even if I could, I would not do it, for it is my joy to conform to your will." This martyr had learned to endure hardship as discipline by submitting joyfully to God's will.

379

"Spare the rod, and spoil the child." Some fathers may have the mistaken notion that they need not discipline their offspring. In their view discipline is the opposite of love and thus should never be applied. When a lack of discipline leads to licentiousness, the results can be tragic for the child, for his parents, and for society. God, however, disciplines his sons and daughters because he loves them. He trains them in this earthly life and prepares them for eternity. Already in this life they harvest the fruits of righteousness and peace, and in the life to come they share God's holiness.

Greek Words, Phrases, and Constructions in 12:7-11

Verse 7

εἰς—with the accusative this preposition denotes cause.

παιδεύει—this verb (third person singular, present active indicative) has the synonym διδάσκω (I teach). The verb παιδεύειν "suggests moral training, disciplining the powers of man, while διδάσκειν expresses the communication of a particular lesson."[21]

Verse 8

εἰ—the force of the conditional sentence with the present indicatives ἐστε (in the protasis and apodosis clauses) is strong. The simple fact condition states reality that is tempered by the phrase ἧς μέτοχοι γεγόνασιν πάντες. The perfect tense of γεγόνασιν (from γίνομαι, I become) expresses the general truth of the statement.

ἄρα—introducing a conclusion, this conjunction is emphatic.

Verse 9

μὲν ... δέ—in verses 9, 10, and 11 the author uses this literary device to show contrast.

εἴχομεν—the imperfect tense from ἔχω (I have) is best translated in the perfect: "have had."

πολὺ μᾶλλον—the combination of the accusative singular πολύ with the adverb μᾶλλον is akin to the expression πολλῷ μᾶλλον—the dative of degree of difference.

Verse 10

ὀλίγας ἡμέρας—the accusative of time answers the question, "How long?"

εἰς τὸ μεταλαβεῖν—with the preposition εἰς and the definite article, the aorist infinitive connotes purpose. The infinitive has a synonym in μέτοχοι (v. 8).

Verse 11

εἰρηνικόν—adjectives with the suffix -ικος convey the idea *"belonging to, pertaining to, with the characteristics of."*[22] The adjective εἰρηνικός therefore pertains to peace, but also means "bringing peace."

---

21. Westcott, *Hebrews*, p. 400.
22. Bruce M. Metzger, *Lexical Aids for Students of New Testament Greek* (Princeton, N.J.: published by the author, 1969), p. 43. His italics.

γεγυμνασμένοις—the perfect middle participle in the dative plural derives from γυμνάζω (I exercise). The perfect tense indicates progress that was initiated in the past and continues to the present. The dative is the indirect object.

---

4. Be Strong
12:12–13

This section about discipline is now coming to an end. With a pastoral exhortation and additional imagery about athletics, the author concludes his remarks. As in many other passages, he supports his teaching by alluding to the Scriptures.

12. Therefore, strengthen your feeble arms and weak knees. 13. "Make level paths for your feet," so that the lame may not be disabled, but rather healed.

On the basis of what he wrote in the preceding verses, the writer says conclusively, "Therefore." This is what you must do, he exhorts: "Strengthen your feeble arms [literally, hands] and weak knees." Apparently he employs a proverbial saying, because the expression *feeble hands and weak knees* occurs elsewhere. First, in the messianic passage that describes the joy of the redeemed, Isaiah jubilantly encourages the believers: "Strengthen the feeble hands, steady the knees that give way; say to those with fearful hearts, 'Be strong, do not fear; your God will come, he will come with vengeance; with divine retribution he will come to save you' " (35:3–4). I assume that this messianic chapter of Isaiah's prophecy was well known to the people who worshiped in the synagogues or churches of the first century.[23]

Second, Eliphaz the Temanite reminds Job of his influence. "Think how . . . you have strengthened feeble hands. Your words have supported those who stumbled; you have strengthened faltering knees" (Job 4:3–4). And third, the writer of Ecclesiasticus describes the life of an unhappy husband: "Drooping hands and weak knees are caused by the wife who does not make her husband happy" (Sir. 25:23, RSV).

The author of Hebrews speaks as a coach to the members of a sports team, and he uses sayings that are familiar to them. Although the race is not yet finished, the runners are tired. They need an encouraging word from their coach, who utters the proverbial saying, "Strengthen your feeble arms and weak knees."

The coach continues and says, "Make level paths for your feet." This is a quotation from Proverbs 4:26 that is completed with the parallel statement "and take only ways that are firm." However, the writer of Hebrews adds his own rejoinder to the line from Proverbs. Says he, the reason for making the track level for the footrace is "that the lame may not be disabled, but rather healed." Before a runner sets himself to a footrace, he examines the track

---

23. Isa. 35 was understood as a messianic prophecy (see Matt. 11:5; Mark 7:37; Luke 7:22).

carefully. He realizes that unevenness can make him vulnerable to a fall. He is in danger of spraining his ankle and consequently of being disqualified from the race. Especially when fatigue sets in, the possibility of sustaining injury is real. For that reason, the paths should be leveled.

Not all the runners are in perfect physical condition. Some are handicapped—that is, lame. Yet in spite of their condition—whether this condition arose before or during the race is of no account—they must persist, continue, and eventually complete the race.[24] By encouraging these handicapped runners and by removing dips and bumps in the road, the able-bodied athletes perform a distinct service. The result will be that the weak also reach the finish line.[25] If the paths are not leveled, the lame will be disqualified.

What idea is the author conveying with these illustrations from the world of sports? He stresses the necessity and obligation of corporate responsibility that the believers have. In earlier passages he instructed the readers to take this responsibility seriously:

3:13 "But encourage one another daily, as long as it is called Today, so that none of you may be hardened by sin's deceitfulness."
4:1 "Therefore, since the promise of entering his rest still stands, let us be careful that none of you be found to have fallen short of it."
4:11 "Let us, therefore, make every effort to enter that rest, so that no one will fall by following their example of disobedience."
6:11 "We want each of you to show this same diligence to the very end, in order to make your hope sure."

The body of Christ consists of many parts, as Paul reminds us (I Cor. 12:12–27). All the parts of the body form a unit, and no part exists for itself. As a result, each part is accountable to the whole, and the whole takes care of the individual parts. The "strong ought to bear with the failings of the weak" (Rom. 15:1).

Greek Words, Phrases, and Constructions in 12:12–13

Verse 12

διό—this inferential conjunction contracted from διά (because of) and ὅ (which) occurs nine times in Hebrews (3:7, 10; 6:1; 10:5; 11:12, 16; 12:12, 28; 13:12).

τὰς παρειμένας χεῖρας—the perfect passive participle in the feminine plural (from παρίημι, I relax, loosen) is used as a descriptive adjective and modifies the

---

24. Donald A. Hagner suggests, "Where there is weakness and drooping limbs there may also be lameness." See his *Hebrews*, Good News Commentary series (New York: Harper and Row, 1983), p. 205.
25. Hughes chooses the translation of the KJV, "lest that which is lame be turned out of the way." He interprets the clause by applying it to Hebrew Christians who might turn from the true path and thus commit "themselves to the irremediable sin of apostasy" (*Hebrews*, p. 535).

noun χείϱ (hand). In this instance, the part stands for the whole—that is, the word *hand* may mean "arm."[26]

παϱαλελυμένα—this perfect passive participle derived from the compound παϱά (on the side of) and λύω (I loose) as a descriptive adjective qualifies the noun γόνυ (knee). Both this participle and the one preceding are in the perfect tense, signifying a completed action with lasting effect.

ἀνοϱθώσατε—a first aorist active imperative, second person plural (from the compound verb ἀνοϱθόω, I erect, restore strength) strictly speaking applies better to γόνατα than χεῖϱας.

Verse 13

τϱοχιάς—from the verb τϱέχω (I run), this noun in the accusative plural signifies wheel tracks or paths. A related noun is τϱοχός (wheel).

ποιεῖτε—the external and internal evidence favors the present active imperative, not the aorist active imperative ποιήσατε.

ἐκτϱαπῇ—in the aorist passive subjunctive, third person singular, this verb derived from ἐκτϱέπω (I turn away) "is often taken here, because of the context, as a medical technical term *be dislocated*."[27] The combination ἵνα μή with the subjunctive expresses negative purpose.

ἰαθῇ—the aorist passive subjunctive, third person singular (from ἰάομαι, I heal, cure) is indeed passive in spite of the deponent.

---

14 Make every effort to live in peace with all men and to be holy; without holiness no one will see the Lord. 15 See to it that no one misses the grace of God and that no bitter root grows up to cause trouble and defile many. 16 See that no one is sexually immoral, or is godless like Esau, who for a single meal sold his inheritance rights as the oldest son. 17 Afterward, as you know, when he wanted to inherit this blessing, he was rejected. He could bring about no change of mind, though he sought the blessing with tears.

18 You have not come to a mountain that can be touched and that is burning with fire; to darkness, gloom and storm; 19 to a trumpet blast or to such a voice speaking words that those who heard it begged that no further word be spoken to them, 20 because they could not bear what was commanded: "If even an animal touches the mountain, it must be stoned." 21 The sight was so terrifying that Moses said, "I am trembling with fear."

22 But you have come to Mount Zion, to the heavenly Jerusalem, the city of the living God. You have come to thousands upon thousands of angels in joyful assembly, 23 to the church of the firstborn, whose names are written in heaven. You have come to God, the judge of all men, to the spirits of righteous men made perfect, 24 to Jesus the mediator of a new covenant, and to the sprinkled blood that speaks a better word than the blood of Abel.

25 See to it that you do not refuse him who speaks. If they did not escape when they refused him who warned them on earth, how much less will we, if we turn away from him who warns us from heaven? 26 At that time his voice shook the earth, but now he has promised, "Once more I will shake not only the earth but also the heavens." 27 The words "once more" indicate the removing of what can be shaken—that is, created things—so that what cannot be shaken may remain.

---

26. Bauer, p. 880.
27. Ibid., p. 246.

28 Therefore, since we are receiving a kingdom that cannot be shaken, let us be thankful, and so worship God acceptably with reverence and awe,　29 for our God is a consuming fire.

B. A Divine Warning
12:14–29

1. Live in Peace
12:14–17

In clear speech and in direct commands, the pastor-author tells the readers how to live holy lives before God. In fact, he tells them what to do, what to avoid, and what to learn from history. Besides, his remarks are echoing teachings from many parts of Scripture.

14. Make every effort to live in peace with all men and to be holy; without holiness no one will see the Lord.

This verse sets a positive tone and is introductory to the rest of the passage. Let us look at this passage point by point.

a. *What to do.* The first command is: pursue peace! Keep on pursuing one goal—that is, peace; do not rest until you have attained it. When spiritual life flourishes in the family circle and in the congregation, peace holds the members together. But when disharmony stunts the spiritual life of family or congregation, peace has left, just as a fleeting shadow skips across the fields. Pursuing peace implies banning quarrels. "Live in peace with all men," says the writer. What do the words *all men* mean? Do they include enemies? According to Jesus' teaching, the answer is yes. Jesus said, "Love your enemies and pray for those who persecute you, that you may be sons of your Father in heaven" (Matt. 5:44–45). And they who are called sons of God are the peacemakers (Matt. 5:9). "The peace makers are the true Israel and acknowledged by God as His children."[28]

A recurring refrain in the Old Testament as in the New is the command to live at peace with one another. David exhorts the Israelites, "Turn from evil and do good; seek peace and pursue it" (Ps. 34:14; see also I Peter 3:11). In his Epistle to the Romans, Paul stresses the pursuit of peace twice: "If it is possible, as far as it depends on you, live at peace with everyone" (12:18) and "Let us therefore make every effort to do what leads to peace" (14:19).[29] Peace is attained through close communion with Jesus Christ, the Prince of Peace (Isa. 9:6; Col. 3:15).

The second command is: pursue holiness. Peace and holiness are two sides of the same coin. Holiness is not the state of perfection already attained. Rather, the word in the original Greek refers to the sanctifying process that occurs in the life of the believer. To put it differently, the believer reflects

---

28. T. W. Manson, *The Sayings of Jesus* (London: SCM, 1950), p. 151.

29. Additional passages that refer to pursuing peace are Mark 9:50; II Cor. 13:11; I Thess. 5:13; II Tim. 2:22. Also consult Hartmut Beck and Colin Brown, *NIDNTT,* vol. 2, pp. 780–83; and Werner Foerster, *TDNT,* vol. 2, pp. 411–17.

God's virtues. In so doing, he becomes more and more like Christ who through the Holy Spirit continues to work in the believer's heart. As the writer of Hebrews says, Jesus is the one who makes the believer holy (2:11). Therefore, we as believers must do everything in our power to obtain holiness.

The conclusion to these two commands is this: without peace and holiness no one will see the Lord. Only the pure in heart, says Jesus, will see God (Matt. 5:8; compare I John 3:2). A holy God can have communion only with those who are at peace with him (Rom. 5:1) and those who have been made holy through the work of Christ (Heb. 2:10; 10:10, 14; 13:12). God's holy wrath is directed against those who are unholy (Heb. 10:29). The unrighteous person cannot stand the sight of Christ's appearance, for his wrath is terrible (Rev. 6:15–17). Isaiah says that angels cover their faces in the presence of God (6:2); how then could an unholy person see God?

15. See to it that no one misses the grace of God and that no bitter root grows up to cause trouble and defile many.

Now comes the warning; the author instructs us what not to do.

b. *What to avoid.* First, the writer reasserts the corporate responsibility of the believers. "See to it that no one misses the grace of God" (compare 3:12; 4:1, 11). As members of the body of Christ we are responsible for each other. We have the task of overseeing one another in spiritual matters, so that we may grow and flourish in the grace of God and not come short of it. That is, no one should be allowed to straggle, for if this happens he becomes Satan's prey and will miss God's grace (II Cor. 6:1; Gal. 5:4). Mutual supervision within the entire body stimulates the spiritual health of the individual members. Avoid, therefore, the indifference to one another manifested by Cain, who asked, "Am I my brother's keeper?" (Gen. 4:9). Instead we should ask each other about our spiritual well-being, although perhaps not in the quaint wording of the Methodist preacher who inquired, "How is it with thy soul, brother?" But certainly as members of Christ's body we must put similar questions to our brothers and sisters in the Lord.

Second, if mutual oversight is neglected, other problems arise. Missing the grace of God becomes falling into apostasy. And falling into apostasy is equivalent to serving other gods. The author of Hebrews more or less quotes from the Septuagint version of Deuteronomy 29:18 (v. 17, LXX), where Moses tells the Israelites: "Make sure there is no man or woman, clan or tribe among you today whose heart turns away from the LORD our God to go and worship the gods of those nations; make sure there is no root among you that produces such bitter poison."

The roots of many weed plants spread rapidly and produce plants in all the places where the roots grow. These roots develop undetected; the resultant rapid multiplication of plants is quite unsettling. Roots and plants spell trouble for crop-producing plants that are then deprived of necessary nutrients and as a result yield a reduced harvest.

With this picture borrowed from the world of agriculture, the author of Hebrews looks at the church and compares a person who has missed the grace of God (and has fallen away) with a bitter root. Such a person causes trouble among God's people by disturbing the peace. With his bitter words, he deprives the believers of holiness. Says the writer, he defiles many. The verb *defile* actually conveys the idea of giving something color by painting or staining it.[30] Avoid such bitterness, for it will defile you. "To the pure, all things are pure, but to those who are corrupted and do not believe, nothing is pure" (Titus 1:15).

16. See that no one is sexually immoral, or is godless like Esau, who for a single meal sold his inheritance rights as the oldest son.

Third, the author tells the readers to avoid immorality. He uses the example of Esau and calls him a godless person. Esau was trained in the godly home of Isaac and Rebekah, but he deliberately chose to live a life that grieved his parents. He married two Canaanite women who were a source of grief to his parents (Gen. 26:35). Scripture does not condemn Esau for marrying these women and does not call him a fornicator. Instead the Bible reports that when Esau noticed his father's grief, he married a daughter of Ishmael son of Abraham (Gen. 28:9).

How do we interpret the term *immoral*? Some commentators understand it literally and argue that Esau's married life was tantamount to fornication.[31] But Scripture fails to provide the evidence. Others understand the word *immoral* spiritually and say that Esau committed spiritual adultery. But Scripture teaches that spiritual adultery is committed by the nation Israel, not by individuals. And still others hold that Jewish tradition and legend affirm that Esau was a fornicator.[32] However, we do well to rely on the information in Scripture, even though tradition has a value all its own.

The New International Version solves the problem by separating the two adjectives *immoral* and *godless*. The first adjective applies to the readers, for in the next chapter the writer repeats his admonition. Says he, "Marriage should be honored by all, and the marriage bed kept pure, for God will judge the adulterer and all the sexually immoral" (Heb. 13:4). The author describes Esau not as an immoral but as a godless person. The second adjective, then, applies to Esau who had no regard for God's blessing and promise which he, as the first-born, would receive. He despised his birthright and displayed utter indifference to the spiritual promises God had given to his grandfather Abraham and his father Isaac.[33] He refused to follow in the footsteps of his forefathers, and thus his name is omitted from the list of

---

30. R. C. Trench, *Synonyms of the New Testament* (Grand Rapids: Eerdmans, 1953), p. 110; J. I. Packer, *NIDNTT*, vol. 1, p. 447; and Friedrich Hauck, *TDNT*, vol. 4, pp. 644–46.

31. Hughes, *Hebrews*, p. 540. Also consult Franz Delitzsch, *Commentary on the Epistle to the Hebrews*, 2 vols. (Edinburgh: Clark, 1877), vol. 2, pp. 333–34; and Spicq, *Hébreux*, vol. 2, p. 401.

32. SB, vol. 3, pp. 748–49.

33. Esau's indifference to God's promise can be seen in his remark to Jacob, "Look, I am about to die. What good is the birthright to me?" (Gen. 25:32). His only concern was for temporal matters. See Gerhard Charles Aalders, *Bible Student's Commentary: Genesis*, 2 vols. (Grand Rapids: Zondervan, 1981), vol. 2, p. 82.

the heroes of faith. His brother Jacob, however, is mentioned because he blessed Joseph's sons and transmitted God's promises to them.

What does the writer of Hebrews teach? Simply this: abstain from immorality and avoid godlessness.

17. Afterward, as you know, when he wanted to inherit this blessing, he was rejected. He could bring about no change of mind, though he sought the blessing with tears.

In the conclusion of the passage the author reminds the readers of what they should learn from history.

c. *What to know.* Throughout his epistle, the writer has warned the readers not to turn away from the living God (3:12), for the result of such a deed is disastrous. He used two examples, one from Old Testament history and one from his own time. First he took the illustration of the rebellious Israelites who because of their unbelief died in the desert (3:16–19). Next he pointed to some of his own contemporaries who had heard the Word preached and had received the sacraments of baptism and the Lord's Supper, but had fallen away of their own accord. For these people, said the author, repentance is impossible (6:4–6; compare 10:26–31).

Now once more the writer returns to this subject. Taking the example of Esau, he shows that Esau deliberately rejected the faith of his father and his grandfather by despising his birthright; therefore, he himself was rejected. God rejected him. Moreover, that rejection was final and irrevocable. Years after he had sold his birthright, his father Isaac wanted to give him the blessing, but was unable to do so (Gen. 27:30–40). Suddenly Esau realized that God had by-passed him, but his heart had hardened so much that "he could bring about no change of mind." Repentance was impossible for him. The author adds that Esau "sought the blessing with tears." According to the Genesis account, Esau showed no sign of penitence, only anger toward his brother Jacob. Hence with his tears he sought not repentance, but only the blessing.[34]

The lesson is obvious. We must know that unbelief leads to hardening of the heart and to apostasy. He who has fallen away from the living God finds that God has rejected him. Therefore, we must strive for peace and holiness, avoid immorality and godlessness, and know that falling into the hands of the living God is most dreadful (Heb. 10:31).

Practical Considerations in 12:14–17

Society today fosters individualism, and this trait, unfortunately, has also taken hold in the church. Even though we lustily sing, "We are not divided, all one body we," each one goes his own way.

Scripture teaches that the church members need spiritual care and oversight.

---

34. The KJV has this reading: "though he sought *it* carefully with tears" (italics added). The term *it* can refer to repentance or to the blessing. The historical context favors the latter.

The pastor is called overseer and shepherd of God's flock (Acts 20:28; I Peter 5:2–3). He needs to know us personally and somewhat closely. I favor the practice of the pastor who, accompanied by an elder or a deacon, visits every family and every individual once a year. The pastoral visit, then, is strictly for the purpose of helping one another spiritually. The intent is not to embarrass anyone or to meddle in someone's private business, but to inquire tactfully about spiritual needs, to speak a word of encouragement, to help and support. These annual visits strengthen the bond of unity in the church.

As every farmer knows, neglect causes weeds to grow and multiply. Similarly, neglect of pastoral duties in a congregation causes church members to drift away. And a member who is drifting eventually separates himself from the church. The truth of the matter is that separation from the church inevitably leads to separation from God.

The message of the Epistle to the Hebrews is relevant today. As members of the body of Christ, we must do everything in our power to prevent fellow members from drifting away from God and his Word. We have the solemn responsibility to guard against signs of unbelief and disobedience, to promote peace and holiness, and to further the cause of unity and harmony in the church. Peter puts it succinctly: "But grow in the grace and knowledge of our Lord and Savior Jesus Christ" (II Peter 3:18).

Greek Words, Phrases, and Constructions in 12:14–17

Verse 14

διώκετε—the second person plural, present active imperative exhorts the readers to actively continue their pursuit of peace.

τὸν ἁγιασμόν—preceded by the definite article, this noun as direct object of the main verb expresses the process of sanctification, not the state or the fact of sanctification. Nouns ending in -μος describe action.[35]

Verse 15

ἐπισκοποῦντες—derived from ἐπισκοπέω (I oversee), the present active participle functions in an imperatival construction. The word itself has derivatives in English: "episcopal" and "bishop."

ἐνοχλῇ—the present active subjunctive from ἐνοχλέω (I cause trouble) is part of a negative purpose clause. The compound consists of ἐν (in) and ὄχλος (crowd). The form ἐν χολῇ as an alternative reading is a conjecture.

μιανθῶσιν—the aorist passive subjunctive, third person plural (from μιαίνω, I stain, paint; pollute) suggests finality because of the aorist tense.

Verse 17

ἴστε—although this form may be either imperative or indicative, the context favors the indicative. The form itself is a literary term from οἶδα (I know) in the second person plural. It occurs three times in the New Testament (Eph. 5:5; Heb. 12:17; James 1:19).

---

35. Metzger, *Lexical Aids,* pp. 42–43.

ἀπεδοκιμάσθη—the author seems to take pleasure in word play: in verse 16 Esau sold (ἀπέδετο) his inheritance; in verse 17 he was rejected (ἀπεδοκιμάσθη) by God. The form is the aorist passive, third person singular, from ἀποδοκιμάζω (I reject).

ἐκζητήσας—the participle in the aorist active from ἐκζητέω (I seek out, search for) is intensive because of the compound form.

---

2. Consider Mount Sinai
12:18–21

At first appearance, it seems the author introduces an entirely new topic: the contrast between Mount Sinai and Mount Zion. But this is not quite the case, for the topic is already introduced in elementary form in the brief clause "without holiness no one will see the Lord" (12:14). As the readers strive for peace and holiness, they ought to know the difference between the time of the old covenant and that of the new covenant. They are different from the Israelites who received the Ten Commandments at Mount Sinai. Therefore, the writer says, **18. you have not come to a mountain that can be touched and that is burning with fire; to darkness, gloom and storm.**

The context of the word choice and the contrast with verse 22 demand that the concept *Mount Sinai* be understood. In the better Greek manuscripts, the term *mountain* is omitted, and many translations show this omission.[36] However, similarity with Deuteronomy 4:11 is telling. Moses reflects on the experience at Sinai and recalls for the benefit of the Israelites, "You came near and stood at the foot of the mountain while it blazed with fire to the very heavens, with black clouds and deep darkness" (see also Exod. 19:18; Deut. 5:22–23).

The focus is not so much on the place itself as on the appearance of God who revealed his majesty and power. The Israelites had consecrated themselves outwardly by washing their clothes (Exod. 19:10–11). Inwardly they trembled with fear when they looked at the mountain, for they had come to "darkness, gloom and storm." In these awesome aspects of nature, God appears to his people and expects them to increase their reverence for him.[37] The author of Hebrews confirms this point when at the conclusion of this passage he writes, "Let us be thankful, and so worship God acceptably with reverence and awe, for our God is a consuming fire" (12:28–29).

The Israelites saw the spectacle of fire, smoke, clouds, and an electrical storm; they also were witnesses **19a. to a trumpet blast or to such a voice**

---

36. Despite the weak manuscript attestation, TR includes the word *mountain*. Translations vary: the RSV, JB, *Moffatt*, and *Phillips* omit it; the RV, ASV, and NASB print the word *mount* or *mountain* in italics to indicate that the Greek text provides no (or insufficient) support; the MLB, NAB, NKJV, and NIV have the word *mountain* ("mount," KJV) without notation; the NEB is rather expansive and approaches a paraphrase: "Remember where you stand: not before the palpable, blazing fire of Sinai." And the GNB has, "You have not come, as the people of Israel came, to what you can feel, to Mount Sinai."

37. John Owen, *An Exposition of Hebrews*, 7 vols. in 4 (Evansville, Ind.: Sovereign Grace, 1960), vol. 7, p. 311.

speaking words. They fully understood that the fiery storm raging at the top of Mount Sinai was much more than a display of natural forces. God himself was present and made himself heard by the sound of the trumpet (Exod. 19:16; 20:18).[38] Then God spoke to the people and gave them the Decalogue—that is, the covenant (Deut. 4:13). God came to the Israelites with this covenant so that the fear of God himself might reside in his people to keep them from sinning (Exod. 20:20). The overwhelming sight and the thunderous voice of God struck mortal fear into the hearts of the people, so **that those who heard it begged no further word be spoken to them** (see also Exod. 20:19; Deut. 5:25–26).

Scripture reveals that the people at Mount Sinai heard the voice of God, but the words he spoke failed to penetrate the hearts and minds of the Israelites. They asked Moses to listen to all that God would tell him and then relay the commandments to them. They were willing to listen and obey, but the spectacle was too much for them (Deut. 5:27–28).

The Israelites were awestruck, **20. because they could not bear what was commanded: "If even an animal touches the mountain, it must be stoned."** The author of Hebrews chose this particular passage from Exodus 19:13, that renders the general meaning but not the exact wording, to demonstrate the majesty of God's holiness. No one might touch God's holy mountain, not even an animal that strayed near it. Should man or animal touch the mountain, God said, "he shall not be permitted to live"(Exod. 19:13). The Israelites had to execute the person or animal by stoning him to death or by shooting him with arrows. They were not allowed to touch him.

The stress, then, is on God's holiness. God wanted the people to be aware of his sacred majesty. The Israelites were filled with fear and terror. Even Moses, to whom God would speak as to a friend, was afraid (Exod. 33:11). **21. The sight was so terrifying that Moses said, "I am trembling with fear."** Moses was the intermediary between God and man, for he was God's spokesman. Nevertheless, at the sight of God's majesty and on hearing God's voice utter the Ten Commandments, Moses was one with the people and shook with fear.

The accounts recorded in Exodus 19–20 and Deuteronomy 4–5 are silent about the fear of Moses. And Moses' statement on being afraid ("I feared," Deut. 9:19) occurs partially in the context of God's anger expressed against the Israelites when they had worshiped the golden calf. Possibly the author of Hebrews had access to an oral tradition, much the same as Stephen had received the information that "Moses trembled with fear" at the sight of the burning bush (Acts 7:32). And Paul, in mentioning Jannes and Jambres, may have used the same tradition (II Tim. 3:8).[39] When God reveals his

---

38. At the time of Christ's return, the trumpet will sound from the heavens (see Matt. 24:31; I Cor. 15:52; I Thess. 4:16).

39. According to Shabbath 88b, *Talmud,* Moses ascended Mount Sinai and feared the consuming breath of the angels. Michel, *Hebräer,* p. 315, refers to rabbinic traditions. Haggadic formulations similar to Heb. 12:21 appear in I En. 89:30 and I Macc. 13:2. Consult Kistemaker, *Psalm Citations,* p. 53.

holiness to man, fear and trembling result. Isaiah saw the Lord God "seated on a throne, high and exalted," and cried out, "Woe to me! I am ruined! For I am a man of unclean lips, and I live among a people of unclean lips, and my eyes have seen the King, the LORD Almighty" (6:1, 5). So Moses trembled with fear at Mount Sinai when he saw God's majesty and glory in awesome display.

Greek Words, Phrases, and Constructions in 12:18–21

Verse 18

οὐ—as the first word in the sentence, this negative particle receives emphasis, especially with the contrast of ἀλλά (v. 22).

προσεληλύθατε—derived from the compound προσέρχομαι (I approach), the perfect active indicative, second person plural is repeated in verse 22. The perfect shows lasting results. The word *proselyte* derives from this verb form.

γνόφῳ καὶ ζόφῳ καὶ θυέλλῃ—the lack of definite articles in this verse emphasizes the characteristics of the nouns. Note the use of rhyme in the first two nouns γνόφος (darkness) and ζόφος (gloom). A θύελλα is a whirlwind.

Verse 19

σάλπιγγος ἤχῳ καὶ φωνῇ ῥημάτων—the absence of definite articles for these four nouns is designed to stress their characteristics. The nouns are placed in chiastic order. Also note that the term ῥῆμα "usually relates to individual words and utterances" and λόγος "can often designate the Christian proclamation as a whole in the N[ew] T[estament]."[40]

ἧς—this feminine singular relative pronoun in the genitive has its antecedent in φωνή and is construed with οἱ ἀκούσαντες. The use of the genitive with the verb ἀκούω depicts the *hearing,* not the *understanding* of the voice that spoke.

Verse 20

ἔφερον—the imperfect active tense of φέρω (I bear) is descriptive.

κἄν—as a contraction of καὶ ἐάν, the word introduces the future more vivid condition that has the aorist active subjunctive θίγῃ (from θιγγάνω, I touch) in the first clause and the future passive indicative λιθοβοληθήσεται (from λιθοβολέω, I stone) in the second.

τοῦ ὄρους—the genitive case depends upon the preceding verb.

3. Look at Mount Zion
12:22–24

The author is a literary artist who develops his argument with contrast and balanced clauses. Although the two sections (vv. 18–21 and 22–24) of the argument fail to correspond at every point, the second portion itself consists of seven parts (two in verse 22, three in verse 23, and two in verse 24).

---

40. Otto Betz, *NIDNTT,* vol. 3, p. 1121.

22. But you have come to Mount Zion, to the heavenly Jerusalem, the city of the living God. You have come to thousands upon thousands of angels in joyful assembly,   23. to the church of the firstborn, whose names are written in heaven. You have come to God, the judge of all men, to the spirits of righteous men made perfect,   24. to Jesus the mediator of a new covenant, and to the sprinkled blood that speaks a better word than the blood of Abel.

a. "Mount Zion, . . . the heavenly Jerusalem." What a difference between the description of Mount Sinai and that of Mount Zion! What a contrast! The first scene is one of doom and dread; the second scene portrays life and joy. In the first portion of the argument Mount Sinai is not even mentioned, for the Israelites were not to stay there. In the second part, Mount Zion is described as "the heavenly Jerusalem" and as "the city of the living God."

The verb *have come* intimates that the readers of Hebrews have arrived at a permanent place. That is, the temporary conditions of the old covenant have ended, and the everlasting terms of the new covenant now prevail. That the expression *Mount Zion* ought to be understood spiritually and not literally is evident from the explanation "the heavenly Jerusalem, the city of the living God." The new Jerusalem is the place where Jesus, the mediator of the new covenant, dwells.[41]

> Zion, founded on the mountains,
> God, thy Maker, loves thee well;
> He has chosen thee, most precious,
> He delights in thee to dwell;
> God's own city,
> Who can all thy glory tell?
> —*Psalter Hymnal*

Mount Zion is the highest elevation in the city of Jerusalem. As a fortress it was fiercely defended by the Jebusites, who were defeated at last by David. In time, the fortress, including the surrounding area, was called the city of David, but poets and prophets used the name *Zion* and designated it God's dwelling place (see, for instance, Ps. 2:6; 20:2; 99:2; 135:21; Isa. 4:3–5; Jer. 8:19).

The writer of Hebrews employs the adjective *heavenly* to signify that the place he mentions is not the southeast corner of Jerusalem, but the heavenly Zion where God dwells with all the saints (Rev. 14:1; 21:2). The citizens of the heavenly Jerusalem are known as sons and daughters of Zion. It is the place where "God himself will be with them and be their God" (Rev. 21:3). The heavenly Jerusalem excels its earthly counterpart, for sin and death are banished eternally in heaven; the city has no need of sun or moon, "for the glory of God gives it light, and the Lamb is its lamp" (Rev. 21:23). The living God lives among his people forever.

---

41. Eduard Lohse, *TDNT,* vol. 7, p. 337. Also consult Helmut Schultz, *NIDNTT,* vol. 2, p. 329.

What an honor to live in that city! Consider this: Moses was given the honor of climbing Mount Sinai and being with God for forty days and forty nights (Exod. 34:28). We shall be with him in heaven always. Mount Sinai is a windswept, uninhabited mountain; the new Jerusalem is a city populated by the saints who dwell permanently in Zion with their living God (Gal. 4:26; Phil. 3:20).

b. "Thousands upon thousands of angels." Already Abraham looked "forward to the city with foundations, whose architect and builder is God" (Heb. 11:10; cf. 13:14). That city is the habitation of countless angels as well. Certainly the New International Version has the translation "thousands upon thousands of angels," but this is an expression that appears in Revelation 5:11 and stands for countless thousands.[42] "Then I looked and heard the voice of many angels," says John, "numbering thousands upon thousands, and ten thousand times ten thousand." This "joyful assembly" of angels sings a song of glory, honor, and praise to the Lamb (see also Dan. 7:10).

Translations differ on the exact position of the Greek word translated as "assembly." Depending on the placing of a comma, the word *assembly* or its equivalent is taken either with angels or with "the church of the firstborn" in the next verse (v. 23).[43] Commentators are divided on this matter. However, it appears that the translation "thousands upon thousands of angels in joyful assembly" is preferred because the author of Hebrews "perhaps intended to offset any thought that angels were angels of judgment."[44] Angels were commissioned to deliver the law at Mount Sinai (Acts 7:53; Gal. 3:19; cf. Deut. 33:2; Ps. 68:17); by contrast, they constitute a joyful assembly at Mount Zion, the heavenly Jerusalem (see Rev. 5:11–13). In heaven angels rejoice when they see that one sinner repents (Luke 15:10). They are sent out to serve all those who inherit salvation (Heb. 1:14).

c. "Church of the firstborn." When the writer of Hebrews says to the readers, "You have come to Mount Zion, to the heavenly Jerusalem, the city of the living God," and then mentions the festive gathering of an immense number of angels, he could be misunderstood. Because he places the scene in heaven, the readers might say that they as yet have not come to the heavenly Jerusalem. But when he says, "[You have come] to the church of the firstborn, whose names are written in heaven," he definitely addresses the readers. They are the ones who belong to the new covenant, and their names already have been recorded in the Book of Life (see also Luke 10:20; Phil. 4:3; Rev. 3:5; 13:8; 20:12).

---

42. Bauer, p. 529.

43. Editors of Greek New Testament editions put a comma after the word *angels* and therefore show that the expression *assembly* ought to be part of the following verse. These translations have adopted the punctuation of the Greek editions of the New Testament: KJV, NKJV, RV, ASV, NASB, GNB, NEB, and *Phillips*. Translators of the RSV, NAB, JB, MLB, NIV, and *Moffatt*, however, take the term *assembly* or *festal gathering* (or a variant) with the phrase *thousands upon thousands of angels*.

44. Donald Guthrie, *Hebrews*, Tyndale New Testament Commentary series (Grand Rapids: Eerdmans, 1983), p. 261. Also consult Lenski, *Hebrews*, p. 456.

That the believers belong to the church on earth is evident from the clause "the spirits of righteous man made perfect." They are still sinners, and their spirits have not yet been glorified to join the church in heaven. They are on earth; their names, however, are written in heaven.

What is meant by the expression *first-born?* The New Testament shows repeatedly that Jesus is the first-born. Of the nine occurrences of this word (Matt. 1:25; Luke 2:7; Rom. 8:29; Col. 1:15, 18; Heb. 1:6; 11:28; 12:23; Rev. 1:5), seven refer to Jesus. One passage (Heb. 11:28) relates to Egypt's first-born slain by the angel of death, and the other passage (Heb. 12:23) concerns believers. The privilege of the first-born is that he is able to lay claim to the inheritance. Christ is therefore the heir, and we are coheirs with him (Rom. 8:17). We value our birthright, whereas Esau despised it (Heb. 12:16). We are first-born because of Christ who makes us holy, and we who are made holy belong to the same family (Heb. 2:11).[45]

Recording the names of the first-born males in Israel was done at God's command. Moses counted all their names and made a list (Num. 3:40). In heaven all the names of those believers included in the new covenant are written in the Book of Life.[46]

d. "God, the judge." God is judge of all men, and no one is higher than God. At Mount Sinai he came to Israel to give the people his law and to make a covenant with them. There he did not appear as judge, only as lawgiver.

Here the readers of Hebrews learn that God is judge of all men, and (by implication) that everyone must appear before him. Seated at Mount Zion, the heavenly Jerusalem, God summons his people to the judgment seat, not to condemn them, but to justify them. God declares them righteous because of his Son who paid their debt (II Tim. 4:8). God's right hand is filled with righteousness, says the psalmist (Ps. 48:10). God rewards his people by renewing them after his image of true righteousness, holiness, and knowledge (Eph. 4:24; Col. 3:10).

e. "Spirits of righteous men." Who are these "spirits of righteous men made perfect"? Some commentators are of the opinion that these spirits belong to Old Testament believers; others think that the writer refers to New Testament saints who have died.[47] But all believers of both Old Testament and New Testament times, who have been translated to glory, are declared righteous. They have been made perfect on the basis of Jesus' work; he is "the author and perfecter of our faith" (Heb. 12:2).

---

45. Karl Heinz Bartels, *NIDNTT,* vol. 1, p. 669. Also see Wilhelm Michaelis, *TDNT,* vol. 6, p. 881.

46. Although the writer has the readers of his epistle in mind, he has not excluded those saints who died before the coming of Christ (see Heb. 11:39–40).

47. Bruce, *Hebrews,* p. 378, for example, argues that "they are surely believers of pre-Christian days." By contrast, Bengel in *Gnomon,* vol. 4, p. 473, asserts that they "are New Testament believers."

What then is the relation between the saints on earth and the saints in heaven? The saints in glory have been perfected, for they are set free from sin. Their souls are perfect; their bodies wait for the day of resurrection. In principle, the believers on earth share in the perfection Christ gives his people. They enjoy the prospect of joining the assembly of the saints in heaven. Only death separates the church below from the church above. When death occurs the believer obtains the fulfillment of Christ's atoning work (Heb. 2:10).

f. "Jesus the mediator." In earlier chapters the writer explained the covenant (7:22; 8:6, 8–12; 9:4, 15–17, 20; 10:16, 29); once more he reminds the readers that Jesus is the mediator of a new covenant. He purposely uses the name *Jesus* to bring into focus the suffering, death, resurrection, and ascension of Jesus.

At Mount Sinai Moses served as mediator between God and man; and with respect to the covenant God made with his people, Moses was the intermediary. But Mount Sinai represents that which is temporary: Moses died, and the first covenant eventually came to an end. To be sure, God replaced it with a new covenant (Jer. 31:31–34; Heb. 8:8–12), and Jesus became the mediator of it. The readers of the epistle observed that the establishing of a new covenant was relatively recent. It occurred when Jesus died on Calvary's cross (also see Matt. 26:28). Moreover, the readers ought to look not to Moses, who mediated the old covenant, but to Jesus. As mediator of the new covenant, he calls the believer to joyful and thankful obedience; he removes the burden of guilt and cleanses the sinner's conscience; he grants him the gift of eternal life; and he functions as intercessor in behalf of his people.

g. "Sprinkled blood." When Moses formally confirmed the first covenant at Sinai, he sprinkled blood on the altar, the scroll, the people, and even the tabernacle (Exod. 24:6–8; Heb. 9:17–22). Sprinkled blood signified forgiveness of sin, for "without the shedding of blood there is no forgiveness" (Heb. 9:22). Jesus inaugurated the new covenant by shedding his blood once for all at Golgotha. Because of that sprinkled blood, believers enter the presence of God as forgiven sinners (Heb. 10:22; I Peter 1:2).

You have come, says the author, "to the sprinkled blood that speaks a better word than the blood of Abel." The comparison is somewhat unequal. The blood of Abel called for revenge, and God placed a curse upon Cain for killing his brother Abel (Gen. 4:10–11). The blood of Christ removed the curse placed upon fallen man and effected reconciliation and peace between God and man. Abel's blood is the blood of a martyr that evokes revenge. The blood of Jesus is the blood of the Lamb of God who "takes away the sin of the world" (John 1:29).

The deliberate contrast accentuates the significance of Jesus' blood that proclaims the gospel of redemption. The blood of Jesus sets the sinner free. And that is the better word the author wishes to convey.

Practical Considerations in 12:22–24

"Why do you go to church on Sunday?" Your answer may be: "Because I want to worship the Lord my God together with his people." You may also say: "I attend the worship services because the blood of Jesus shed for me has cleansed me from all my sins. I enter the very presence of God as a forgiven sinner cleansed by the blood of the Lamb."

Sermons about the blood of Jesus are few. Certainly on Good Friday pastors describe the suffering and death of Christ, and the people sing "Alas! and did my Savior bleed." But neither preacher nor parishioner dwells on the concept *Jesus' blood*. The thought of blood is too gruesome. The repulsiveness of blood causes us to turn to pleasantries instead, and thus we miss the message of Jesus' "blood that *speaks* a better word than the blood of Abel" (italics added).

What is the message of the blood? It tells me that Jesus removed the curse, lifted the burden of guilt, and forgave my sins. It assures me that I have peace with God and that I have been set free to live a life of obedience. It tells me that God loved me so much that he had his Son die for me.

I go to church not to hear a theological lecture or to receive some pastoral advice on how to avoid conflict, but to learn that the blood of Jesus daily speaks to me and brings me the message of salvation. I have been delivered from the bondage of sin because of Jesus' blood. Throughout the week, but especially on Sundays, I am reminded of the words of an Italian hymn, translated by Edward Caswall,

> Grace and life eternal
> In that blood I find;
> Blest be his compassion,
> Infinitely kind!

Greek Words, Phrases, and Constructions in 12:22–24

Verse 22

ὄρει καὶ πόλει—in this passage (vv. 22–24) the author omits the definite articles before the nouns to stress their characteristics and qualities instead of categorical designations. The noun πόλει stands in apposition to ὄρει and describes permanence. The datives are the dative of place.

Verse 23

ἀπογεγραμμένων ἐν οὐρανοῖς—the noun ἀπογραφή appears in Luke 2:2 and Acts 5:37, where it means "census." Derived from the compound verb ἀπογράφω (I register), the perfect passive participle shows that the registration has taken place and that its effect continues to remain valid. Note the use of the plural οὐρανοῖς (see also 1:10; 4:14; 7:26; 8:1; 9:23; 12:25).

καὶ κριτῇ θεῷ πάντων—word order rules that the translation should be "and to a judge who is God of all" (rsv) instead of "to God, the judge of all" (niv). Arguments for one or the other translation divide commentators and translators. For the phrase *judge of all*, see Genesis 18:25.

τετελειωμένων—the perfect tense in the passive participle from τελειόω (I complete) discloses lasting effect. This is the last time the writer uses a form (noun, verb, or adjective) from this verb family. The perfect tense appears in three verses (7:28; 10:14; 12:23).

Verse 24

νέας—in preceding passages (8:8, 13; 9:15), the writer described the covenant as καινή. Here it is νέα. Writes R. C. Trench, "νέος refers to time, καινός to the thing."[48] The covenant that is καινή originates in the old covenant, whereas the covenant that is νέα can be described as recent.

ῥαντισμοῦ—literally translated, the expression is "to the blood of sprinkling." The noun occurs twice in the New Testament (Heb. 12:24; I Peter 1:2). Of the six instances the verb ῥαντίζω (I sprinkle) appears in the New Testament, four are in Hebrews (9:13, 19, 21; 10:22).

---

4. Apply the Prophecy
12:25-27

The Epistle to the Hebrews displays one overriding characteristic: contrast. At times the author employs the comparison "how much more" or "how much less" (see, for instance, 9:14; 12:9). In this particular passage he contrasts earth with heaven, the old revelation with the new revelation, and "they" and "them" with "we" and "us."

25. See to it that you do not refuse him who speaks. If they did not escape when they refused him who warned them on earth, how much less will we, if we turn away from him who warns us from heaven?

Note that the writer addresses three groups of people: you (the readers), they (the Israelites), and we (the author and the readers).

a. Throughout this epistle, the warning against turning a deaf ear to God has sounded clearly in the ears of the addressees. Think, for example, of the direct warning: "See to it, brothers, that none of you has a sinful, unbelieving heart that turns away from the living God" (3:12). This admonition has been repeated in various forms in the letter, and every time it calls the readers to pay close attention.

The writer does not accuse the readers of rebellion. He does not say that they are guilty of refusing to listen to God's voice. Rather, he addresses them pastorally and exhorts them to heed the Word of God when they hear it. He reminds them of how the Israelites died in the desert.

b. Avoiding details, the author selects a few key words to describe the plight of the Israelites. They received their just punishment when they rebelled against God (2:2; 3:16–19; 4:2; 10:28). They could not escape when they refused to heed God's warnings. The time came when God pronounced the verdict that every person who was twenty years old and older would die

---

48. Trench, *Synonyms of the New Testament*, p. 225. The French language makes the distinction between novelty and new: "une invention est *nouvelle,* une expression *neuve*" (Trench's italics).

in the desert (Num. 14:29). Escape was impossible. As God's representative, Moses had warned the Israelites repeatedly, but they had repudiated the spoken word. They failed to realize that rejecting God's Word is tantamount to rejecting God.[49] If then history reveals the dire consequences of Israel's rebellion in the desert, how much less will we escape?

c. The author includes himself in the comparison. He conveys the thought in the form of a condition, "if we turn away from him who warns us from heaven" (see 10:26 for a similar inclusion). If we do not listen to the voice of Jesus who warns us from heaven, escape is even less possible than it was for the Israelites. The contrast is between the piecemeal revelation of God, communicated to the people by Moses on earth, and the full revelation in Jesus Christ that "was first announced by the Lord" (Heb. 2:3). Indeed, "how shall we escape if we ignore such a great salvation?" Jesus continues to speak to his people through his servants, the ministers of the gospel, for "in these last days [God] has spoken [and continues to speak] to us by his Son" (1:2).

26. At that time his voice shook the earth, but now he has promised, "Once more I will shake not only the earth but also the heavens."

Again the writer reminds the readers of the experience at Mount Sinai. From numerous places throughout the Old Testament Scriptures, they learned that the shaking of the mountains when God gave his people the Decalogue was an extraordinary event.[50] The speaker obviously is God, whose voice shook the mountain and made the people tremble with fear. But the same voice also utters a promise that has recurring and lasting significance. Through the prophet Haggai, God spoke to the Israelites concerning the rebuilt temple and said, "In a little while I will once more shake the heavens and the earth, the sea and the dry land. I will shake all nations, and the desired of all nations will come, and I will fill this house with glory" (2:6–7). From the literature of the Jewish rabbis, we learn that this particular passage was considered to be messianic.[51]

The prophet predicted a shaking of the heavens and the earth. The writer transposes the terms *heaven* and *earth* to show the sequence of the effect of Christ's work. The earth shook when Jesus died and when he arose (Matt. 27:51; 28:2), but more importantly the preaching of the gospel and the outpouring of the Holy Spirit shook the entire world. The heavens also experienced change: the angelic hosts sing Christ's praises (Rev. 5:12); angels rejoice when one sinner repents (Luke 15:10); angels are sent out to minister to the needs of the believers on earth (Heb. 1:14); and angels long to look

---

49. Hagner, *Hebrews*, p. 216. Because the writer of Hebrews uses the expression *on earth*, he seems to say that it was Moses who warned the Israelites. This is the view, for instance, of Moffatt, *Hebrews*, p. 220, and Hugh Montefiore, *The Epistle to the Hebrews* (New York and Evanston: Harper and Row, 1964), p. 234. Some commentators, including Bruce, *Hebrews*, p. 381, assert that God is the speaker. Apart from the divine appearance at Mount Sinai, God speaks to the people through Moses.

50. Consult Exod. 19:18; Judges 5:4–5; Ps. 68:7–8; 77:18; 114:4, 7.

51. See the *Talmud*, Sanhedrin 97b, p. 659; SB, vol. 3, p. 749; Kistemaker, *Psalm Citations*, p. 54.

into the mystery of salvation (Eph. 3:10; I Peter 1:12). It is Christ, therefore, who is at the center of this upheaval on earth and in heaven. He will cause heaven and earth to shake when he appears a second time (Matt. 24:29; II Peter 3:10).

27. The words "once more" indicate the removing of what can be shaken—that is, created things—so that what cannot be shaken may remain.

Every now and then, the writer provides somewhat of a commentary on Old Testament quotations he cites. Here he lifts out the expression *once more* and explains it by saying that created things can be shaken and thus are temporary. They will be removed. Permanent things are those that cannot be shaken.

What kind of a commentary is this? In fact, the reader needs a commentary on the author's explanation before he is able to understand the intent. First, the writer comments on the entire quotation from Haggai 2:6, not just the expression *once more*. Next, in the original Greek he reminds the reader that he used the term *removing* earlier (7:12), where it is translated as "change." "For when there is a change of the priesthood, there must also be a change of the law." An example, then, of temporary things is the Levitical priesthood that came to an end when it was replaced by the eternal priesthood of Christ. Also, the prophet Isaiah foresees the end of this present world when he transmits what the Sovereign Lord says: "Behold, I will create new heavens and a new earth. The former things will not be remembered, nor will they come to mind" (65:17; also see 66:22). And last, the only things that survive this world are those that are unshakable and eternal. The kingdom of Jesus Christ cannot be shaken.

Greek Words, Phrases, and Constructions in 12:25–27

Verse 25

βλέπετε—the present active imperative, second person plural of βλέπω (I see) introduces a negative command.

παραιτήσησθε—the negative particle μή with the aorist passive subjunctive from παραιτέομαι (I reject, refuse) denotes a command not to begin to reject God. By contrast, μή with a present imperative implies that an action that must be stopped is already in progress.

τὸν λαλοῦντα—the present active participle preceded by the definite article in the masculine accusative singular refers to God (see Heb. 1:1–2). The present tense signifies repeated and continued speech. Attention is drawn to the fact that God speaks (λαλεῖν), not to the content of his words, for then the verb λέγειν is used.[52]

εἰ—this particle introduces a simple fact condition that expresses reality. To make the reality even more certain and vivid, the author writes the negative particle οὐκ (not). Normal usage demands the word μή.

---

52. Trench, *Synonyms of the New Testament,* p. 287.

ἐξέφυγον—the compound form intensifies the meaning of the verb φεύγω (I flee). The aorist tense reveals single occurrence.

ἐπὶ γῆς—this prepositional phrase has its counterpart in ἀπ' οὐρανῶν and relates to the present active participle χρηματίζοντα. The participle is understood in the second part of the verse.

ἀποστρεφόμενοι—from ἀποστρέφω (I turn away), the participle is in the present middle and denotes condition: "if we turn away."

Verse 26

τότε, νῦν δέ—contrast is the author's penchant. Here it is the *then* over against the *now*.

ἐπήγγελται—the perfect middle from ἐπαγγέλλομαι (I promise) connotes that the promise, although made in the past, is valid for the present. Therefore, the writer introduces the verb with the phrase νῦν δέ.

Verse 27

τὸ δέ—the neuter nominative singular article takes the quotation ἔτι ἅπαξ as its noun (see also Eph. 4:9). The writer has commented on quotations in numerous places (see 2:8-9; 3:15; 4:3-7; 10:8-10).

μετάθεσιν—derived from the verb μετατίθημι (I change), the word has a -σις ending that signifies process.

ὡς πεποιημένων—this phrase is actually an explanatory note. The particle ὡς means "that is," and the perfect passive participle is in apposition to σαλευομένων, which is the present passive participle.

---

5. Worship God
12:28-29

The last two verses of the chapter flow forth from the immediately preceding paragraph. At the same time, however, they form the conclusion.

28. Therefore, since we are receiving a kingdom that cannot be shaken, let us be thankful, and so worship God acceptably with reverence and awe.

What a statement! "We are receiving a kingdom." If there is a kingdom, there is also a king. And a king makes his rule known to his subjects, for they are part of the kingdom. We are receiving the governing rule, the administration, so to speak, of Jesus Christ. The writer of Hebrews already mentioned that we have come "to Jesus the mediator of a new covenant" (12:24). That covenant relation becomes reality when we receive the kingdom, the rule of Christ. As a trustworthy saying has it, "If we endure, we will also reign" with Christ (II Tim. 2:12). That is not at all surprising, for both the Old Testament and the New reveal that "the saints of the Most High will receive the kingdom and will possess it forever" (Dan. 7:18; see also Rev. 1:6; 5:10). Jesus confers a kingdom on us and grants us the honor of sitting on thrones (Luke 22:29-30; Rev. 20:4-6).

The kingdom we receive is unshakable; it remains forever; it is eternal (Dan. 7:14). Those in the kingdom, then, cannot be shaken, remain forever, and partake of eternity. The privileges Christ grants his people are unbelievably rich. God told the Israelites at Mount Sinai that if they kept his covenant, they would be for him "a kingdom of priests and a holy nation" (Exod. 19:5–6). That kingdom, however, came to an end because it was temporary. How different for us, the New Testament believers, who are in the new covenant! We receive "a kingdom that cannot be shaken."

Moreover, we are in the process of receiving an unshakable kingdom. Jesus taught us to pray for the coming of his kingdom (Matt. 6:10; Luke 11:2). His kingdom is here; at the same time we admit that it has not yet come. Hence we pray the well-known petition of the Lord's Prayer, "your kingdom come."

Because of the royal recognition we receive, we are exhorted to give thanks—"let us be thankful." The literal translation of this clause is, "let us have grace."[53] However, usage indicates that the words *have grace* form an idiomatic expression that means "give thanks."[54] Luke uses this idiom in relating the parable of the farmer and his servant (Luke 17:9), and Paul employs it in his pastoral Epistles (I Tim. 1:12; II Tim. 1:3).

Let us live a life of thankfulness, says the author of Hebrews, and by doing so let us worship God. Giving thanks in word and deed and worshiping God are two sides of the same coin. Worship is not limited to a formal worship service on Sunday. Horatius Bonar understood this when he wrote,

> So shall no part of day or night
> From sacredness be free,
> But all my life, in every step,
> Be fellowship with Thee.

How do we worship God acceptably? The writer reminds us of Enoch who walked with God, pleased him, and was commended for his faith (11:5; also see 13:21). Our worship must be pleasing to God on the one hand, and on the other we must approach him with reverence and awe (5:7). And the reason for serving God with reverence and fear is expressed in the concluding verse of this chapter.

29. For our God is a consuming fire.

These words were spoken by Moses when he exhorted the Israelites not to serve idols. "For the LORD your God is a consuming fire, a jealous God" (Deut. 4:14; see also 9:3). Even though Christ has granted us unusual privileges, we must be aware of God's awesomeness and holiness. Therefore we worship him with reverence and awe.

---

53. This is the translation in the KJV, NKJV, RV, and ASV. The JB has "let us therefore hold on to the grace"; and the NAB, "we . . . should hold fast to God's grace."

54. With variations, numerous translations have this reading. Consult John Brown, *An Exposition of Hebrews* (Edinburgh: Banner of Truth Trust, 1961), p. 668. Also see Bauer, p. 878.

Practical Considerations in 12:28–29

The author of Hebrews tells us to worship God acceptably with reverence and awe. But if we take note of worship conducted throughout the world, we conclude that God cannot be averse to variety because he is worshiped in numerous ways. This observation is correct only inasmuch as we worship God in harmony with his Word.

The Word of God ought to take the central place in a worship service, for through the reading and the preaching of his Word God makes his will known to his people. The sermon, then, is the main part of worship. God speaks, and we listen. Preaching must be the proclamation of God's Word and should never be replaced by discourses on unrelated topics. The preacher as Christ's ambassador delivers the message his sender has entrusted to his care. When preaching takes place, God's people worship.

Greek Words, Phrases, and Constructions in 12:28–29

Verse 28

βασιλείαν—without the definite article the noun expresses the qualities and characteristics of the kingdom.

ἀσάλευτον—as a verbal adjective the word modifies the noun βασιλείαν, expresses inability, and serves as a passive.

παραλαμβάνοντες—this present active participle must be understood in the causal sense. The present indicates continued action.

ἔχωμεν . . . λατρεύωμεν—although textual evidence supports either the indicative or the subjunctive reading, the context favors the subjunctive which then is translated as a hortatory subjunctive.

Verse 29

καὶ γάρ—five times the author uses this combination to show emphasis (4:2; 5:12; 10:34; 12:29; 13:22).

καταναλίσκον—a present active participle from the compound verb κατά (down) and ἀναλίσκω (I consume, destroy). The compound exhibits intensity.

Summary of Chapter 12

This is a chapter of exhortations, commands, and applications. It is a rather practical chapter in which the pastor exhorts us, the believers, to live a Christian life. In his own direct manner, the writer exhorts us to stimulate our Christian hope by enduring hardship and affliction. He begins by encouraging us to exercise perseverance, to look to Jesus, to struggle against sin, to submit to discipline, and to overcome weakness.

He encourages us to pursue peace and holiness and warns us against apostasy, immorality, and godlessness. Esau serves as an example, for as Isaac's first-born he should have received the birthright with its spiritual implications. Instead he despised this right and consequently rejected God.

Before he continues to write about the subject of apostasy, the author contrasts the fear and dread of the Israelites who received the law at Mount Sinai with the joy and perfection of believers who come to the city of God at Mount Zion.

Once again he exhorts us to listen to the voice of God. Failure to heed his Word results in punishment. As the Israelites who rejected God did not escape, so we who have God's revelation through Jesus will not escape if we fall away.

Therefore, the writer says, we ought to live thankful lives because we are part of the everlasting kingdom of Jesus Christ. By living thankfully, we serve God in acceptable worship with deep respect and veneration.

13

Admonitions and Exhortations, *part 2*

13:1–25

Outline

13 1 Keep on loving each other as brothers. 2 Do not forget to entertain strangers, for by so doing some people have entertained angels without knowing it. 3 Remember those in prison as if you were their fellow prisoners, and those who are mistreated as if you yourselves were suffering.

4 Marriage should be honored by all, and the marriage bed kept pure, for God will judge the adulterer and all the sexually immoral. 5 Keep your lives free from the love of money and be content with what you have, because God has said,

"Never will I leave you;
never will I forsake you."

6 So we say with confidence,

"The Lord is my helper; I will not be afraid.
What can man do to me?"

C. Communal Obligations
13:1–6

The sequence of exhortations which the author began in the preceding chapter continues. Some commentators are of the opinion that the exhortations in this section are unrelated.[1] Others see the hand of a literary artist at work in the construction of this passage.[2] The writer mentions the topic *love* in its expression in society: among the brothers, for strangers, for prisoners, and for the underprivileged. The second topic concerns the home, in which marriage and morality are upheld; and the third subject is contentment based on confidence in God.

1. Keep on loving each other as brothers. 2. Do not forget to entertain strangers, for by so doing some people have entertained angels with-

---

1. James Moffatt refers to them as "a handful of moral counsels." See his *Epistle to the Hebrews,* International Critical Commentary series (Edinburgh: Clark, 1963), p. 224. Looking at the entire chapter, Donald Guthrie labels its content "a series of apparently disconnected exhortations and other incidental teaching." See his commentary on *The Letter to the Hebrews,* Tyndale New Testament Commentary series (Grand Rapids: Eerdmans, 1983), p. 266.

2. Otto Michel, *Der Brief an die Hebräer,* 10th ed. (Göttingen: Vandenhoeck and Ruprecht, 1957), pp. 328–29. Michel detects four sets of admonitions: showing brotherly love and hospitality (vv. 1–2), visiting prisoners and those who are mistreated (v. 3), honoring marriage and wedding vows (v. 4), avoiding greed and fostering contentment (vv. 5–6). Albert Vanhoye, in "La question littéraire de Hébreux 13:1–6" (*NTS* 23 [1977]: 121–39), sees a much more elaborate threefold structure in the first six verses (vv. 1–3, 4, 5–6).

out knowing it. 3. Remember those in prison as if you were their fellow prisoners, and those who are mistreated as if you yourselves were suffering.

The practical application of Christian love in the context of the society in which the readers lived is fourfold.

a. In the Christian community brothers and sisters care for one another, and a spirit of brotherly love and affection prevails. In a world rife with hostility against the Christian church, love for each other within the community needs constant encouragement. B. F. Westcott makes this telling observation: "The love of the Jew for his fellow Jew, his 'brother,' was national: the Christian's love for his fellow-Christian is catholic. The tie of the common faith is universal."[3] Christians recognize each other as brothers and sisters in the Lord, for together they form the worldwide community of believers. The writers of the New Testament repeatedly admonish the Christians to cultivate brotherly love (Rom. 12:10; I Thess. 4:9; Heb. 13:1; I Peter 1:22; II Peter 1:7). To express the concept *brotherly love,* they use the word *philadelphia.* The members of the church in Philadelphia in effect demonstrated this love (Rev. 3:7–13).

b. The writer of Hebrews counsels the readers to extend their love from their own circle to all men. They are to entertain strangers; that is, by opening their homes to travelers, they show the love of Christ. In ancient times, hotels as we know them today were nonexistent, and the inns had the reputation of being unsafe.[4] Travelers were dependent on local residents to provide lodging and offer hospitality.

The readers of Hebrews have apparently become indifferent to the needs of the traveler; however, the writer exhorts them to be mindful of their fellow man who needs a roof over his head. He reminds them of Abraham, Lot, Gideon, and the parents of Samson, who entertained angels (Gen. 18:1–15; 19:1–22; Judges 6:11–23; 13:3–21). Providing food and accommodation for a stranger is an act of kindness. Furthermore, Christians who entertain a stranger in their own home have an opportunity to introduce him to the gospel of Christ. If the traveler accepts Christ in faith, he will spread the good news along the way.

Providing hospitality was considered a virtue in the first-century Christian church. In his letter to the Romans, Paul writes, "Practice hospitality" (12:13). And in his pastoral Epistles Paul stipulates that an overseer in the church must be hospitable (I Tim. 3:2; Titus 1:8; also see I Peter 4:9) and that among their good deeds widows must be able to list hospitality (I Tim. 5:10).[5]

c. "Remember those in prison as if you were their fellow prisoners." Earlier in his epistle, the writer commends the readers for their loving care of

---

3. B. F. Westcott, *Commentary on the Epistle to the Hebrews* (Grand Rapids: Eerdmans, 1950), p. 429.
4. "It is common knowledge that inns existed in Greek times and throughout the period of the Roman empire. Generally they were considered bad, the traveler being subject not only to discomfort, but also robbery and even death." Robert C. Stone, "Inn," *ZPEB,* vol. 3, p. 280.
5. Hans Bietenhard, *NIDNTT,* vol. 1, p. 690.

prisoners (10:34). Visiting prisoners was a common practice in ancient times. Jesus refers to it in his discourse on the sheep and the goats: "I was in prison and you came to visit me" (Matt. 25:39, 43). And Luke writes about Paul's imprisonment in Caesarea and in Rome (Acts 24:23; 28:16). Paul was given much freedom, was allowed to have his own rented house in Rome, "and welcomed all who came to see him" (Acts 28:30).

Prisoners depended on relatives and friends to provide food, clothing, and other necessities. The numerous references to Paul's experiences as a prisoner reveal that his friends came to take care of his needs (Acts 24:23; 27:3; 28:10, 16, 30; Phil. 4:12; II Tim. 1:16; 4:13, 21). Prisoners, then, had to be remembered; otherwise they suffered hunger, thirst, cold, and loneliness.

Travelers came to the homes of the recipients of Hebrews and received hospitality. By contrast, the author now admonishes his readers to leave their homes, go to the prisoners, and empathize with them. The writer tells them to take care of these prisoners "as if you were their fellow prisoners." Show them the love of Christ by ministering to their needs!

d. The last exhortation is to remember the people who are mistreated. The words remind us of another passage: "Sometimes you were publicly exposed to insult and persecution; at other times you stood side by side with those who were so treated" (10:33). The admonition need not refer only to what the readers of Hebrews had done in the past. The suffering of the underprivileged is universal. Does the author leave the impression that the unity of the Christians is all-important? A more literal translation of the text—remember "those who are ill-treated, since you yourselves also are in the body" (NASB)—perhaps supports this interpretation. And a cross-reference to Paul's discourse on the unity of the body of Christ points in that direction (I Cor. 12:26). However, it is better to think especially of the physical body, because mistreatment pertains to physical suffering. Therefore, the translation "as if you yourselves were suffering" is appropriate.

The admonitions to extend a helping hand to the stranger, the traveler, the prisoner, and the sufferer actually are exhortations to fulfill the command to "love your neighbor as yourself" (Lev. 19:18; Matt. 22:39; Mark 12:33; Luke 10:27; Rom. 13:9; Gal. 5:14; James 2:8).

4. Marriage should be honored by all, and the marriage bed kept pure, for God will judge the adulterer and all the sexually immoral.

From the second part of the summary of the law ("Love your neighbor as yourself"), the writer proceeds to the commandment "You shall not commit adultery" (Exod. 20:14; Deut. 5:18). Moreover, he moves from the social sphere to the private circle of husband and wife. Love for the neighbor, whoever he may be, most effectively flows forth from a home in which husband and wife work together in mutual love. When marriage is honored in the home, love emanates to society in numerous ways. For this reason the author stresses the necessity of maintaining the sanctity of married life.

In the New Testament nearly every writer discusses marriage, because a stable marriage is a building block in the structure of society. Also, in this chapter of exhortations, the author of Hebrews instructs the readers concerning holy living within the bonds of marriage.[6] He is actually saying, "Let marriage be precious to all of you." Marriage is a treasure we receive from God who has instituted it. Therefore, marriage must be honored by all.

The clause "and the marriage bed kept pure" is a euphemism. The author warns the people not to break the marriage vow by committing adultery. Marriage is sacred, and defilement of it is sin. Why is having sexual relations outside the bonds of matrimony sin? Here is the answer: "God will judge the adulterer and all the sexually immoral."

The world in which we live considers loose living inconsequential: sex is fun, not sin. But in God's eyes illicit sex is sin that deserves punishment.[7] The writer of Hebrews clearly speaks to offenders and warns them of God's judgment (10:30–31). What kind of punishment does God administer? Scripture says that "neither the sexually immoral nor idolaters nor adulterers nor male prostitutes nor homosexual offenders . . . will inherit the kingdom of God" (I Cor. 6:9–10; Eph. 5:5; Rev. 21:8; 22:15). They perish in their sin. Christians, then, must set the example of living sexually pure lives (I Thess. 4:7) and keep the commandment "You shall not commit adultery."

5a. Keep your lives free from the love of money and be content with what you have.

The next commandments in the Decalogue are "You shall not steal" and "You shall not covet" (Exod. 20:15, 17; Deut. 5:19, 21). In a sense the commandments to which the author alludes are closely related; they uncover man's desire for someone's wife, possessions, and property.[8] The Christian must uproot "the love of money," because it leads to all kinds of evil (I Tim. 6:10). Paul counsels Timothy in these pithy words, "But godliness with contentment is great gain" (I Tim. 6:6). And he himself confesses: "I have learned to be content whatever the circumstances. I know what it is to be in need, and I know what it is to have plenty. I have learned the secret of being content" (Phil. 4:11–12). Certainly Scripture does not teach that the Christian ought to seek a life of poverty. God told Adam to fill the earth and subdue it (Gen. 1:28), but he warns man against the *love* of money, for that attitude leads to greed, and greed is idolatry (Col. 3:5).

5b. Because God has said,

> **"Never will I leave you;**
> **never will I forsake you."**

---

6. In the original Greek the verb *to be* is to be supplied in the first part of verse 4. Some translations supply the indicative verb *is* ("Marriage is honorable," KJV, NKJV, NEB); others have the translation "Let marriage be held in honor" or a variant (RSV, ASV, NASB, NAB, JB, MLB, GNB, NIV). The latter is preferred because the general context has many verbs in the imperative mood.

7. John Albert Bengel, *Gnomon of the New Testament,* ed. Andrew R. Fausset, 7th ed., 5 vols. (Edinburgh: Clark, 1877), vol. 4, p. 494. Says Bengel, "He most of all punishes them, whom man does not punish."

8. Paul discloses that immoral people commit sexual sins, as well as sins of theft and greed (Rom. 1:26–29; I Cor. 5:10–11; 6:9–10; Eph. 5:3–5; Col. 3:5–6).

The choice is simple: either love the Lord your God or love money. "You cannot serve both God and Money" (Matt. 6:24; Luke 16:13). Instead of worshiping that which is created (money), Christians are exhorted to worship the Creator and to put their trust in him.

Introducing an Old Testament quotation with the words *God has said,* the author is true to form. For him God is the author of Scripture, and the voice that speaks is the voice of God. To find the exact wording of the quotation in the Old Testament, however, is not easy. Rather, the text itself appears in varying form in many places, and always signals God's faithfulness and assurance. Jacob fled from his brother Esau and in a dream heard God say to him, "I am with you . . . I will not leave you" (Gen. 28:15). Near the end of his life, Moses encouraged the Israelites and said, "For the Lord your God goes with you; he will never leave you nor forsake you" (Deut. 31:6, 8). When Joshua began his work as leader of the Israelites, God said, "I will never leave you nor forsake you" (Josh. 1:5). And last, when David instructed Solomon to build the temple, he encouraged him with these words, "Do not be afraid or discouraged, for the Lord God, my God, is with you. He will not fail you or forsake you" (I Chron. 28:20).[9]

I conclude that because of its frequent usage the quotation had become proverbial. In all probability, the words were part of the liturgy in the ancient synagogue and early church. The people, then, were quite familiar with this text.[10]

6. So we say with confidence,

**"The Lord is my helper; I will not be afraid.
What can man do to me?"**

Once again the author places himself on the same level with his readers, for together they confess their confidence and trust in God. They recite the words from Psalm 118:6 and do so courageously. For them the quotation is a confession of faith. If we look at the passages liturgically, we notice that in the Old Testament text in the preceding verse, God is the speaker. The testimony of faith in the lines from Psalm 118:6 is the response of the people. Apparently this psalm citation belonged to the liturgy of synagogue and church.[11] The New Testament writers frequently quote from this psalm,

---

9. The quotation coincides to a degree with the Septuagint (Deut. 31:6). The text of Heb. 13:5b, however, appears verbatim in Philo, *Confusion of Tongues* 166 (LCL). To say that the author of Hebrews borrowed the wording from Philo does not explain why Philo's version differs from the Septuagint. Interestingly, both Philo and the author of the epistle introduce the quotation with the information that God is the speaker.

10. In his *Commentary on the Epistle to the Hebrews,* 2 vols. (Edinburgh: Clark, 1877), vol. 2, p. 374, Franz Delitzsch writes, "We may rather conclude that, in the liturgical or homiletical usage of the Hellenistic synagogues, the passage Deut. 31:6 assumed this shape." Also see Simon J. Kistemaker, *The Psalm Citations in the Epistle to the Hebrews* (Amsterdam: Van Soest, 1961), p. 56; and Gerhard Kittel, *TDNT,* vol. 1, p. 465.

11. Ernst Werner, *The Sacred Bridge* (London: D. Dobson, 1959), p. 57. Compare Michel, *Hebräer,* p. 333.

interpret it christologically, and indicate that it served as a source of joy and happiness for God's people.

"What can man do to me?" Nothing, because the Lord is my helper. The forces of unbelief cannot do anything unless the Lord gives them permission. The believer, however, need not be afraid when God is on his side. The Scottish reformer John Knox fearlessly stood his ground against formidable opposition and said, "A man with God is always in the majority."

Practical Considerations in 13:1–6

Pastors living next door to the church building often receive visits from idle wanderers who look for a quick handout of money, food, or clothing. Should the pastor supply the necessities of life and show hospitality to the outcasts of society? Scripture teaches that the apostles did not think that it was right "to neglect the ministry of the Word of God" to take care of the needy (Acts 6:2). They appointed seven men and turned the responsibility of caring for the poor over to them.

Society today differs remarkably from that of the first century when prisoners could freely receive visitors. These prisoners depended on visitors to supply them with their daily needs. Today this is no longer the case. Certainly we should still visit prisoners. However, we ought to extend and expand the concept *prisoner* to include the shut-ins and the elderly who are confined to a bed, a hospital room, or a private home. These people welcome visits, treasure moments of fellowship, and are thankful for the attention they receive.

And last, in a world saturated with sex, the Christian who lives by the commandment "You shall not commit adultery" appears to be out of touch with reality. Not so. When God created man and woman, he set the rules for marital relations. And these rules have not been invalidated. God wants his people to make his commandment known in the society in which he has placed them. The apostles faced a sexually perverted world when they began to preach the gospel of salvation. They faithfully preached and taught the rules for wholesome living. That is one of the reasons that we read so much about marriage in the New Testament, for God's Word transformed society in the first century. It will do so again in our age. Keep the commandment, and live a pure and wholesome life!

Greek Words, Phrases, and Constructions in 13:1–6

Verse 2

φιλοξενίας—this noun and the preceding φιλαδελφία are related, for both have the same base as φίλος. Hospitality is the practical result of brotherly love. The genitive case depends on the main verb.

μὴ ἐπιλανθάνεσθε—the present middle imperative preceded by the negative particle μή discloses that the readers of the epistle had become lax in showing hospitality. They no longer provided shelter for the traveler.

ἔλαθόν τινες ξενίσαντες—a Greek idiom that reveals a transposition of words in

---

12. Bengel, *Gnomon*, vol. 5, p. 412. Also consult A. T. Robertson, *A Grammar of the Greek New Testament in the Light of Historical Research* (Nashville: Broadman, 1934), p. 551.

which the main idea is conveyed in the participle and the secondary thought in the verb. The phrase stands for λαθόντες ἐξένισαν.[12]

Verse 3

μιμνῄσκεσθε—the present middle imperative governs the genitive case of τῶν δεσμίων (the prisoners). Verbs of forgetting and remembering take a genitive case as direct object.

ἐν σώματι—because of the absence of the definite article, the author does not intimate that he refers to the members of the body of Christ. Rather he is thinking of the physical bodies of believers.

Verse 4

ἐν πᾶσιν—this adjective can be either masculine or neuter in the dative plural. Even though the neuter fits the context ("in all respects"),[13] translators prefer the masculine ("by all").

ὁ θεός—these words appear last in the sentence to receive emphasis.

Verse 5

ἀφιλάργυρος—a compound verbal adjective derived from ἀ (not), φίλος (friendly), and ἄργυρος (silver).

οὐ μή σε ἀνῶ—in this particular line five negatives appear. The Greek cannot express the idea any more forcefully. In English the lines from the well-known hymn "How Firm a Foundation" come close: "That soul, though all hell should endeavor to shake, I'll never, no never, no never forsake!"

Verse 6

ὥστε—with the accusative ἡμᾶς as subject of the present infinitive λέγειν, this is a result clause.

οὐ φοβηθήσομαι—in the future passive indicative from φοβέω (I fear), this form means "I shall not be afraid" in the durative sense.

---

7 Remember your leaders, who spoke the word of God to you. Consider the outcome of their way of life and imitate their faith.   8 Jesus Christ is the same yesterday and today and forever.

9 Do not be carried away by all kinds of strange teachings. It is good for our hearts to be strengthened by grace, not by ceremonial foods, which are of no value to those who eat them.   10 We have an altar from which those who minister at the tabernacle have no right to eat.

11 The high priest carries the blood of animals into the Most Holy Place as a sin offering, but the bodies are burned outside the camp.   12 And so Jesus also suffered outside the city gate to make the people holy through his own blood.   13 Let us, then, go to him outside the camp, bearing the disgrace he bore.   14 For here we do not have an enduring city, but we are looking for the city that is to come.

15 Through Jesus, therefore, let us continually offer to God a sacrifice of praise—the fruit of lips that confess his name.   16 And do not forget to do good and to share with others, for with such sacrifices God is pleased.

17 Obey your leaders and submit to their authority. They keep watch over you as men who

---

13. R. C. H. Lenski, *The Interpretation of the Epistle to the Hebrews and of the Epistle of James* (Columbus: Wartburg, 1946), p. 471.

must give an account. Obey them so that their work will be a joy, not a burden, for that would be of no advantage to you.

D. Ecclesiastical Duties
13:7–17

1. Remember Your Leaders
13:7–8

Three times in this chapter the author stresses the word *leaders*: "remember your leaders" (v. 7), "obey your leaders" (v. 17), and "greet all your leaders" (v. 24). In the first instance, the concept *leadership* is related to Jesus Christ himself.

7. Remember your leaders, who spoke the word of God to you. Consider the outcome of their way of life and imitate their faith. 8. Jesus Christ is the same yesterday and today and forever.

The author of Hebrews employs the verb Paul uses when he writes, "Remember Jesus Christ, raised from the dead, descended from David" (II Tim. 2:8). The verb means "call back to mind that which you know about a person." The writer exhorts his people to think of those leaders whom death has taken away. The expression *leader* is rather broad and somewhat vague, so that it fails to contribute anything to our understanding of the historical background of the Epistle to the Hebrews.[14] The word itself gives no assurance that the author had apostles in mind. That probability, however, is not excluded. Whether the author referred to Paul and Peter is speculation. What we do know is that the leaders "spoke the word of God" to the people. They were, then, preachers of the gospel of Jesus Christ and had been instrumental in building the church, that is, the body of Christ. These founding fathers had passed away, but the readers still remembered their labors.

The next command is to "consider the outcome of their way of life." The verb *consider* actually means to "look at again and again," to "observe carefully."[15] The author urges the people to look attentively at the lives these leaders lived and at the totality, that is, the result, of their lives. "Observe how they closed a well-spent life" (MLB). Look at their lives from beginning to end!

And the third command follows: "Imitate their faith." The writer wishes to leave the impression that these leaders were to be considered heroes of faith, similar to those listed in chapter 11. Follow in their footsteps; perform deeds of faith, and speak words of faith. We are not told whether these leaders suffered martyrdom. That is not the point. The readers of the epistle must imitate their faith. Faith is all-important. "We more easily contemplate

---

14. Clement of Rome and the writer of Hermas feature the expression (with a slight variation) in their writings. Consult I Clem. 1:3; 21:6; 44:5, *Apostolic Fathers*, vol. 1 (LCL); and Hermas, Visions, 2.2.6; 3.5.1; 3.9.7, *Apostolic Fathers*, vol. 2 (LCL).
15. Bauer, p. 54.

and admire the happy death of godly men than imitate the faith by which they have attained to it."[16]

In this fast-changing world, nothing seems dependable and permanent. Leaders come, and leaders go. One leader, however, is unchangeable: Jesus Christ. Says the author, "Jesus Christ is the same yesterday and today and forever." More sermons have been preached on this text than on any other verse from Hebrews, so that this verse almost has attained confessional status in the church.

First, note that the writer uses both names, "Jesus" and "Christ." The name *Jesus* embraces the work and word of God's Son on earth. He has come to save his people from their sin. The name *Christ* is the official title that expresses the divinity of the Son. The double name occurs only three times in Hebrews (10:10; 13:8, 21).

Next, not only Christ's divinity but also his changelessness the author explains in the first chapter of his epistle. For instance, quoting Psalm 102:27, he says, "But you remain the same, and your years will never end" (1:12; and see 7:24).

Furthermore, note the sequence of time: past, present, and future. The term *yesterday* relates to the mediatorial work of Jesus on earth, proclaimed and confirmed to the readers by those who heard him (2:3). The expression *today* refers to the intercessory work Jesus performs in heaven, where he represents the believer in God's presence (Rom. 8:34; Heb. 7:25; 9:24). And the word *forever* pertains to the priesthood of Christ. He is priest forever (5:6; 6:20; 7:17, 21, 24, 28).

For the readers of the epistle, Jesus is the same. That implies faith on the part of the believers, for they can depend on him because he remains true to himself. He is the first and the last, the one "who is, and who was, and who is to come, the Almighty" (Rev. 1:8).

Greek Words, Phrases, and Constructions in 13:7–8

Verse 7

τῶν ἡγουμένων—the definite article designates the group of leaders. The present tense of the middle participle (from ἡγέομαι, I lead) expresses the function of the leader. The noun ἡγούμενος refers to a ruler (Sir. 17:17), prince (Sir. 41:17), governor (Acts 7:10), military leader (I Macc. 9:30), and spiritual leader (Acts 15:22).

οἵτινες—as an indefinite relative pronoun, the word connotes cause and description.

ἐλάλησαν—the aorist tense indicates action accomplished in the past. The verb λαλέω (I speak) depicts the mode of speech; the verb λέγω (I speak), its content.

ἀναθεωροῦντες—dependent on the main verb μιμεῖσθε (present middle imperative), this present active participle assumes the imperative mood. The compound

---

16. Bengel, *Gnomon*, vol. 4, p. 495.

can be either directive (to look up) or intensive (to look at again). The intensive is preferred.

Verse 8

ὁ αὐτός—with the definite article the intensive personal pronoun in the attributive position means "the same." The verb *to be* is understood in this short sentence.

---

2. Avoid Strange Teaching
13:9–11

At first glance, the exhortations and admonitions in this segment seem rather unrelated. However, the author reveals a definite sequence. Leaders proclaimed the word of God; they taught the gospel. And that word is as abiding as Jesus Christ is changeless. Therefore, do not depart from the doctrine of Christ.

9. Do not be carried away by all kinds of strange teachings. It is good for our hearts to be strengthened by grace, not by ceremonial foods, which are of no value to those who eat them.

Some of the readers were susceptible to teaching that was different from and contrary to the Word of God. Influenced by that teaching, they were "carried away," as the author says. We assume that this development had not yet become a great concern, for this is the only reference to it in the entire epistle. But because of the danger of drifting away from the moorings of the Christian faith, the writer warns the people against "all kinds of strange teachings." He does not say what these teachings are. However, from other parts of the New Testament, we learn that in the second half of the first century, traveling philosophers were influencing the people with teachings opposed to the apostolic doctrine. Paul warns the Ephesian elders to be on guard against savage wolves. Says he, "Even from your own number men will arise and distort the truth in order to draw away disciples after them" (Acts 20:30). And he rebukes the Galatians for "turning to a different gospel—which is really no gospel at all" (1:6–7). Then, he admonishes the Colossians to avoid being taken "captive through hollow and deceptive philosophy, which depends on human tradition and the basic principles of this world rather than on Christ" (2:8; compare Eph. 4:14). Moreover, these Colossians were told by some philosophers to observe self-imposed rules on food, drink, festivals, celebrations, worship, and discipline. Paul concludes, "These [rules] are all destined to perish with use, because they are based on human commands and teachings" (2:22).[17] These teachings, therefore, were varied and of foreign origin. To interpret the verse as a reference only to

---

17. For additional references to false teachings, consult Eph. 5:6; I Tim. 1:3–7; 4:1–3; 6:3–5; II Tim. 2:18; 4:3–4; Titus 3:9; II Peter 2:1–3, 9–22; II John 7–10; Jude 5–16; Rev. 2:2, 6, 14–16, 20–24.

Jewish law is unwarranted and contrary to the remainder of the verse that mentions "ceremonial foods."[18]

The contrast in the last half of the verse is between the spiritual and the material. "It is good for our hearts to be strengthened by grace, not by ceremonial foods, which are of no value to those who eat them." Grace is placed over against foods. Even though the term *grace* is not defined, we are not amiss in understanding it as the grace of God. Throughout his epistle the writer has spoken of this divine grace (2:9; 4:16; 10:29). He has even explained the term in the context of living peaceful and holy lives (12:14–15). The grace of God provides inner strength for the believer and benefits him spiritually.

But teachers of a strange philosophy think that by adhering to strict dietary regulations they are able to advance spiritually. The New International Version has rendered the last part of the verse somewhat freely, "by ceremonial foods, which are of no value to those who eat them." The original has only the noun *foods*.[19] Nevertheless, the general context allows for the explanatory adjective *ceremonial*. Also, the original has the reading "which are of no value to those who walk." That is, those who adhere to food regulations receive no benefit from them. And no wonder. Paul tells the Romans who are passing judgment on one another regarding eating habits, "Do not allow what you consider good to be spoken of as evil. For the kingdom of God is not a matter of eating and drinking, but of righteousness, peace and joy in the Holy Spirit" (14:16–17). To the Corinthians he writes, "But food does not bring us near to God; we are no worse if we do not eat, and no better if we do" (I Cor. 8:8). Philip Edgcumbe Hughes summarizes the matter cogently: "Food goes into the stomach for the strengthening of the body; but only *grace* strengthens *the heart,* that is, the vital center of man's being and personality and the source of his conduct and character."[20]

10. We have an altar from which those who minister at the tabernacle have no right to eat.

If in verse 9 the emphasis is on that which is spiritual, so much more is this the case in verse 10. The author of Hebrews speaks figuratively when he uses the word *altar*. It has a connotation that is different from the ordinary meaning of a structure made out of stones. In a sense, we do exactly the same thing when we say that at a meeting held in a stadium the evangelist extended the altar call. Now the term *altar call* in that setting has nothing to do with the altar. Rather it describes people who at the invitation of the evangelist come forward and make a decision to commit their lives to Christ.

---

18. F. F. Bruce writes, "The strange teaching which laid such insistence on food was probably some form of syncretistic gnosis, perhaps with Essene or quasi-Essene affinities." See his *Epistle to the Hebrews,* New International Commentary on the New Testament series (Grand Rapids: Eerdmans, 1964), p. 398.

19. Johannes Behm, *TDNT,* vol. 1, p. 643; Hans Kropatschek, *NIDNTT,* vol. 2, p. 268.

20. Philip Edgcumbe Hughes, *Commentary on the Epistle to the Hebrews* (Grand Rapids: Eerdmans, 1977), p. 574. His italics.

For the writer, the altar is the cross on which Jesus offered himself as a sacrifice to God.[21] And to the Christian the cross is a symbol that represents the completed work of redemption. As the author of Hebrews repeatedly confirms, Christ offered his sacrifice once for all (9:25, 26, 28; 10:9, 12, 14). The clause *we have an altar*, then, stands for the cross, which symbolizes the redemption Christ offers his people.

The second part of the verse—"from which those who minister at the tabernacles have no right to eat"—is open to interpretation. First, the reference is to the Levitical priests who were told to take the "hides, flesh and offal" of a bull and a goat and burn them outside the camp (Lev. 16:27). But this reference is too restrictive, for the phrase "those who minister at the tabernacle" seems to include all Jewish worshipers who came to the tabernacle. Note that the writer says *at*, not *in*, the tabernacle. Next, Christians could be accused of having no altar and hence no real religion.[22] But after the destruction, the Jews no longer had an altar either. Nevertheless, the writer of Hebrews can say, "We have an altar, that is, spiritually speaking, the cross of Jesus Christ." Then, does the author intimate that only Christians can partake of the holy elements at the celebration of Communion, from which Jews are excluded? If this is true, we in effect make the Christian communion table the equivalent of the altar. Certainly the believer partakes spiritually of the Lord's body and blood when he eats and drinks the holy elements. And the identification of the celebration of the Lord's Supper with the altar is most attractive. By doing so, however, we affirm that we have a visible and tangible altar. This is not what the author of Hebrews means. He places the sacrificial work of Christ over against the animal sacrifices of Old Testament times. In 13:10, when we consider it in the light of the entire epistle, the writer's intent is to show the superiority of Christ's work to that of the Aaronic priesthood.[23]

11. The high priest carries the blood of animals into the Most Holy Place as a sin offering, but the bodies are burned outside the camp.

Repetition is one of the trademarks of Hebrews. In earlier chapters the author writes about the Day of Atonement when the high priest sacrifices a bull and a goat and takes their blood into the inner sanctuary of the tabernacle (5:3; 7:27; 9:7). In his description of the duties performed on the Day of Atonement, the writer explains the purpose of these sacrifices. These

---

21. A. Snell, "We Have an Altar," *Reformed Theological Review* 23 (1964): 16–23. John Owen asserts, "The altar which we now have is *Christ alone,* and his sacrifice. For he was both priest, altar, and sacrifice, all in himself" (his italics). See his *Exposition of Hebrews,* 7 vols. in 4 (Evansville, Ind.: Sovereign Grace, 1960), vol. 7, p. 438.

22. Irenaeus, *Heresies* 4.17–18. Also consult Bruce, *Hebrews,* p. 400.

23. Donald Guthrie, *New Testament Theology* (Downers Grove, Ill.: Inter-Varsity, 1981), p. 781. Roman Catholic scholars identify the altar with the celebration of the Eucharist. Also, Michel advocates that the words *eat, body,* and *altar* can best be understood within the context of the Eucharistic liturgy. See his *Hebräer,* p. 343.

animals were slaughtered as a sin offering for the people. The removal of sin is the dominant feature of the religious duties the high priest and his helpers carried out on that special day.

The high priest offered a "bull for his own sin offering to make atonement for himself and his household" (Lev. 16:6). Then he sacrificed one goat as a sin offering for the people, and the other goat he sent away "into the desert as a scapegoat" (vv. 10, 22). He sprinkled the blood of the bull on the ark inside the Most Holy Place for his own sin and the blood of the goat for the sin of the people.

Sent into the desert, the live goat carried all the sins of the people (v. 22). The man who released the goat had to wash his clothes and take a bath before entering the camp (v. 26). The bodies of the bull and the goat had to be taken outside the camp and burned (v. 27). The person who burned the hides, flesh, and offal of these animals had to wash his clothes and take a bath before he could return to camp (v. 28). All this was done to point out that sin pollutes. The sacrifices themselves were considered polluted, even though the blood of these animals was sprinkled on the ark in the Most Holy Place. Hence, the priests were not allowed to eat the flesh of these sacrifices because these animals represented sin.

The implied contrast is that the sacrifice of Christ on the cross has removed sin once for all for all his people. By his death he ended the ceremonial rituals of the Day of Atonement, because he entered the heavenly sanctuary to represent the believer in the presence of God.

Practical Considerations in 13:9–11

Any gardener knows that after he has prepared his garden and has sown vegetable or flower seeds, the weed seeds germinate, grow, and develop much faster. Weeds flourish while the garden plants cope with setbacks of weather and disease.

This simple illustration aptly portrays the religious scene today. Evangelical churches are growing, but their growth seems insignificant compared with that of sects and cults. Sects have often been called "the unpaid bills of the Christian church." They prosper and develop; nothing seems to hinder them: they have their origin in Christianity, but they refuse to have anything to do with the church. Their message is no longer the direct teaching of the Old and New Testaments. Additional teaching or "revelation" is not only central; it also serves to reinterpret the Bible and is even called Scripture in some instances. Cults, of course, have their roots in movements other than the Christian faith. Adherents teach philosophies and modes of life that are unrelated and foreign to the Christian. Therefore, the admonition of the author of Hebrews is as relevant today as when he wrote it: "Do not be carried away by all kinds of strange teachings."

What then is basic? God's revealed Word stands forever. As Peter says, it is "the living and enduring word of God" (I Peter 1:23) that is preached. Furthermore, throughout the centuries the Holy Spirit has led the church in understanding God's truth revealed in Scripture. Differences do exist and doctrinal emphases vary, but those believers who hold to the historic Christian faith confess that their faith is rooted in God's abiding and changeless Word. Christians form the body of the Lord Jesus Christ and find their common unity in him. Anticipating differences of opinion in the church, Paul writes to the Philippians and to us, "All of us who are mature should take such a view of things. And if on some point you think differently, that too God will make clear to you" (3:15).

Greek Words, Phrases, and Constructions in 13:9-11

Verse 9

ξέναις—as an adjective in the dative plural modifying the noun διδαχαῖς (teachings), it relates to something that is new, in the sense of foreign (see Acts 17:18). The dative case is the dative of means.

μὴ παραφέρεσθε—the present passive imperative preceded by the negative particle μή shows that some people were indeed being carried away by strange teachings. The present tense is iterative; that is, the phenomenon occurred more often.

οἱ περιπατοῦντες—from the verb περιπατέω (I walk), the present active participle with the definite article represents a group of people other than the readers of the epistle. In context the term is idiomatic and can best be paraphrased in translation.

Verse 11

ζῴων—this noun in the genitive plural (from ζῷον, animal) is preceded by the relative pronoun ὧν. The word itself is unique in referring to the animals (bull and goat) that were sacrificed on the Day of Atonement.

περί—the sequence of the prepositions is noteworthy in this verse: περί (for; almost in the sense of "for the sake"), εἰς (into), and διά (by, through [agency]).

κατακαίεται—the use of the compound verb is to stress the intensive idea (to consume, burn up). The present tense in this verb with the preceding εἰσφερέται is a literary device of the author (compare 9:6-7).

---

3. Strive for Holiness
13:12-16

Paragraph divisions are somewhat difficult to determine, as a cursory comparison of translations reveals. Whatever the division, the flow of thought from verses 9-16 is continuous. I have separated verses 9-11 from 12-16 to emphasize the theme of holiness.

12. And so Jesus also suffered outside the city gate to make the people holy through his own blood.

On the basis of the preceding verse the author of Hebrews makes a comparison. He compares the implied purpose of the sacrifices made on the Day of Atonement to the suffering Jesus experienced on the cross. As he explains in earlier parts of his epistle, Jesus' sacrifice is once for all and incomparably superior. To speak, then, of a parallel in these verses is only partly accurate; only the phrase *outside the city gate* is equivalent to "outside the camp." The comparison in general points to Jesus' work to make his people holy.

The writer assumes that the readers are fully acquainted with the gospel. In his epistle he seldom alludes to Jesus' life on earth (5:7–8; 10:12; 12:2). Here he describes the place where Jesus suffered—outside the city of Jerusalem. He writes that Jesus suffered; he implies the agony Jesus endured on Calvary's cross.

The high priest annually entered the Most Holy Place, sprinkled animal blood, and atoned for the sin of the people. Jesus became sin for us (II Cor. 5:21), bore the curse that rested upon us (Gal. 3:13), and according to the law was condemned to die outside the city gate (John 19:17–18).[24] For instance, the son of the Israelite woman who blasphemed the name of the Lord had to be taken outside the camp, and the people were to stone him to death (Lev. 24:11–16, 23; also see Num. 15:35). Achan was taken outside the camp to the valley of Achor where the Israelites stoned him (Josh. 7:24–26; cf. Acts 7:58).[25] Because of man's sin, Jesus had to suffer outside the city gate where he endured God's wrath.

Outside the city gate of Jerusalem, Jesus paid for our sins by suffering the agony of hell on the cross when he cried, "My God, my God, why have you forsaken me?" (Matt. 27:46; Mark 15:34). Through the shedding of his blood, Jesus removed the sin of his people and made them holy. That is, by fulfilling the stipulations concerning the removal of sin on the Day of Atonement (Lev. 16:26–28), Jesus cleansed his people and sanctified them. The author of Hebrews briefly summarizes the purpose of Jesus' suffering: "to make the people holy through his own blood." In many places he has explained this point and therefore has no need to elaborate on it now (see 2:11; 10:10, 14; 12:14).

13. Let us, then, go to him outside the camp, bearing the disgrace he bore. 14. For here we do not have an enduring city, but we are looking for the city that is to come.

Statement after statement in this particular section is conclusive ("and so," v. 12; "then," v. 13; "for," v. 14; "therefore," v. 15). On the basis of this teach-

24. If Golgotha is located at the present-day cemetery where, according to tradition, Jesus was crucified, we can see an interesting confirmation of the parallel "outside the city gate" and "outside the camp." Michel, *Hebräer*, p. 345. However, we cannot be absolutely certain about the location of Golgotha.

25. Bruce, in his commentary on Hebrews (p. 403), makes the interesting observation that because the people worshiped the golden calf, sin had defiled the camp of the Israelites. Moses, therefore, would pitch a tent outside the camp where God would meet him and speak to him face to face (Exod. 33:7–11). Hughes also mentions this incident. See his *Hebrews*, p. 581. And consult Helmut Koester, "Outside the Camp: Hebrews 13:9–14," *HTR* 55 (1962): 299–315.

ing in general and the message of the preceding verses in particular, the author exhorts the readers to go to Jesus "outside the camp."

First, we look at the exhortation from a Jewish point of view. The Jewish Christian must leave the family structure in which he learned the precepts and commandments, the ceremonies and traditions, the prejudice and pride of the Jew. He is asked to go to Jesus upon whom the Jewish people invoked God's curse by hanging him on a cross (Deut. 21:23). To go to one who bears the curse of God is to share "the disgrace he bore."[26] By choosing for Christ, the Jew rejects Judaism and thus faces expulsion, alienation, and at times persecution. The author of Hebrews reminds the readers of the suffering, public insult, and persecution they had endured in earlier days when they became Christians (10:33).

Next, every reader is exhorted to go to Jesus who was cursed by God, because through Jesus we have access to God.[27] We identify with him, for through him we are made holy (Isa. 52:11; Ezek. 20:41; II Cor. 6:17). He bore disgrace to set us free from the guilt of sin and to remove the curse from us. That means that the world of sin vents its hatred against us for going to Jesus (John 17:14). Christians are not taken out of the context of a sinful world but are placed in it to be witnesses for Christ. In his list of the heroes of faith, the writer notes that Moses "regarded disgrace for the sake of Christ as of greater value than the treasures of Egypt, because he was looking ahead to his reward" (11:26). Christians bear the name of Christ and are commanded by him to deny themselves, take up their cross, and follow him (Matt. 10:38; 16:24). The Christian keeps his eye of faith fixed on Jesus (12:2). He knows that this present world will not remain unchanged, but will pass away.

"For here we do not have an enduring city." The words echo an earlier statement of the author when he discussed those people who lived by faith but who did not see the promises fulfilled in their lifetime. "And they admitted that they were aliens and strangers on earth" (11:13). They longed for a better country, a heavenly country, much the same as Abraham looked forward to a heavenly city (11:10; and see 12:22). Thus, the writer repeats his former remarks, by saying conclusively, "We are looking for the city that is to come." Do Christians live in an ethereal world detached from the pressing realities of everyday life? Certainly not! Christians are to be "the salt of the earth" and "the light of the world" (Matt. 5:13, 14). Wherever God in his providence has placed them, they are to be Christ's ambassadors (II Cor. 5:20). They are to represent Christ by boldly speaking the Word he has given them. Yet they know the brevity of life and the fleeting nature of this

---

26. Colin Brown says that the author "sees a heightened symbolism in the crucifixion of Jesus outside Jerusalem." See *NIDNTT*, vol. 3, p. 965. Also consult David Hill, *NIDNTT*, vol. 2, p. 29; and Joachim Jeremias, *TDNT*, vol. 6, p. 922.

27. F. W. Grosheide, *De Brief aan de Hebreeën en de Brief van Jakobus* (Kampen: Kok, 1955), p. 314.

world. Therefore, they look and long for their eternal dwelling: "a city that is to come."

15. Through Jesus, therefore, let us continually offer to God a sacrifice of praise—the fruit of lips that confess his name.

First in the sentence stands the phrase *through Jesus*. That is significant. Because of the once-for-all sacrifice of Jesus, the need for offering sacrifices to God had ended. Are Christians, then, without sacrifices and without a priest to present these offerings to God? No.

We are exhorted to go to Jesus outside the camp. He is our eternal, faithful, and merciful high priest. He represents us in the presence of God, and he prays for us. To come to God the Father we must go through the Son (John 14:6). Set free from the burden of guilt and sin, we want to express our thanks to God. This we do through Jesus. We offer to God not the material sacrifices that Christ made superfluous but the continual confession of praise and thanks. Whereas Jesus offered himself once, we present our praises continually. Our entire life ought to be a song of adulation expressed in words and deeds.

The Israelites expressed their thankfulness by offering cakes of bread to the Lord as a sacrifice of thanksgiving (Lev. 7:12). But Christians show by a dedicated life of obedience their thankfulness to God. The Ten Commandments are not a set of dos and don'ts; rather, for the Christian, they are rules for thankful living.

How then do we live before God? Paul and Peter have something to say on this subject:

> Therefore, I urge you, brothers, in view of God's mercy, to offer your bodies as living sacrifices, holy and pleasing to God. [Rom. 12:1]

> Give thanks in all circumstances, for this is God's will for you in Christ Jesus. [I Thess. 5:18]

> You also, like living stones, are built into a spiritual house to be a holy priesthood, offering spiritual sacrifices acceptable to God through Jesus Christ. [I Peter 2:5]

The author of Hebrews specifies what the sacrifice of praise should be: "the fruit of lips that confess his name." The expression *fruit of lips* comes from Hosea 14:2, where the prophet urges the people of Israel to return to the Lord and pray, "Forgive all our sins and receive us graciously, that we may offer the fruit of our lips." And the phrase *confess his name* may be taken from the Septuagint translation of Psalm 54:6, "I will praise [confess] your name, O LORD." God reveals himself in his name, and therefore his name is revelation. The psalmist makes God's revelation known to the people. Similarly the author of Hebrews intimates that a life of praise should be a continual confession of God's name.

16. And do not forget to do good and to share with others, for with such sacrifices God is pleased.

Living a holy life consists of loving the Lord with heart, soul, and mind, and of loving one's neighbor as oneself. The early Christians illustrated their love for the Lord by devoting themselves to the teaching of the gospel, the worship services, communion, and prayer (Acts 2:42). But they also showed their love for their fellow man by sharing everything they had (Acts 4:32). In fact, they took care of the poor so that "there were no needy persons among them" (v. 34). Love for the Lord has its counterpart in love for the neighbor. These two go hand in hand. When we say that we love the Lord, we must be ready to help our neighbors in need. This is what the Macedonian believers did. Says Paul, "Entirely on their own, they urgently pleaded with us for the privilege of sharing in this service [showing generosity] to the saints" (II Cor. 8:3–4).

The readers of the Epistle to the Hebrews had neglected their ministry to the needy (see also 13:2). Praising God in the local worship service they observed, even though some people stayed away (10:25). But praise and love were not always put to practice in relieving the needs of the poor (6:10; 10:33–34). The writer tells the readers "to do good and to share with others." He sees these deeds of love and mercy as sacrifices of praise. And with these sacrifices God is pleased.

When the author says that God is pleased with good deeds, he reminds us of his description of Enoch's life. Enoch was commended for his intimate fellowship with God (11:5). Also we are reminded of our duties to care for the needy, for if we keep the royal law—"Love your neighbor as yourself" (James 2:8)—we do well and please God.

Practical Considerations in 13:12–16

"Do good," says the writer of Hebrews. Do we have to be reminded to do good? Doing good ought to be the Christian's way of life. But, sad to say, at times we forget, and our worship becomes lip service and not life commitment. If our Christian religion is nothing more than talk, it is dead. Words and deeds are two sides of the same coin. God wants us to praise him with both lips and life.

In a word game, arranging the letters *g o o d* is relatively simple. The same set of letters, however, can also be divided into two words that read, "Go do!" That means translating the word into deed. I must go and do to be good in the sight of God.

When I attended elementary school, the teacher used to mark my papers with the comment *good*. Of course, that meant I had learned my lesson well but not well enough to receive the comment *excellent*. Scripture does not use that remark.[28] When the servants appeared before the master with ten and four talents respectively, they heard him say, "Well done, you *good* and faithful servant!" (Matt. 25:21, 23, italics added). Being good Christians means that we look for opportunities to do the things that please God and that bring joy to our fellow man.

---

28. Herman Veldkamp, *Zondagskinderen,* 2 vols. (Franeker: Wever, n.d.), vol. 1, p. 32.

Greek Words, Phrases, and Constructions in 13:12–16

Verse 12

ἁγιάσῃ—the aorist active subjunctive from the verb ἁγιάζω (I make holy) has been occasioned by τὰ ἅγια (the Most Holy Place) in the preceding verse. The subjunctive stands in a purpose clause. The aorist is constative.

τὸν λαόν—this is the last time in the epistle that the author uses the expression *the people.* In the thirteen times it occurs, it refers to God's people.

Verse 15

οὖν—this inferential conjunction is "absent from several early and important witnesses. It is difficult to decide whether copyists added the word, which seems to be needed at this point, or whether it was accidentally omitted in transcription."[29]

αἰνέσεως—the noun derived from the verb αἰνέω (I praise) shows by its nominative singular ending αἴνεσις that this is an action noun that denotes progress. This feature is amplified by the prepositional phrase διὰ παντός (continually).

ὁμολογούντων—as a present active participle, the word stands in apposition to χειλέων (lips), from which it takes the genitive case. It is followed by the dative case τῷ ὀνόματι (his name), which is the direct object of the participle. The difference between the simple verb ὁμολογέω and the compound verb ἐξομολογέω is insignificant.

Verse 16

τῆς δὲ εὐποιΐας καὶ κοινωνίας—although a few manuscripts have a definite article before κοινωνίας, the preferred reading omits it. Because the article is not repeated, the second noun is descriptive of the first.[30]

τοιαύταις—an adjective in the dative plural feminine, describing quality. The dative expresses cause.[31]

ὁ θεός—note the position of the noun. It stands last for emphasis.

---

4. Obey Your Leaders
13:17

This verse has no connection with the preceding verses. We need to go back to verse 7 where the same expression *your leaders* occurs. And in verse 24 the writer once more employs that expression.

17. Obey your leaders and submit to their authority. They keep watch over you as men who must give an account. Obey them so that their work will be a joy, not a burden, for that would be of no advantage to you.

---

29. Bruce M. Metzger, *A Textual Commentary on the Greek New Testament* (London and New York: United Bible Societies, 1975), p. 676.

30. Henry E. Dana and Julius R. Mantey, *A Manual Grammar of the Greek New Testament* (New York: Macmillan, 1957), p. 147.

31. Robertson, *Grammar,* p. 532.

In this particular verse, the author emphasizes three points.

a. *Obedience demanded.* Those leaders who had spoken the Word of God in earlier days were no longer present. They must be remembered for their conduct and faith, says the author of Hebrews (13:7). Successive leaders have taken their place. The writer is not interested in the status of these leaders— he gives no hint whether they were elders, overseers, preachers, or teachers. Rather, he asks the reader to obey them.

A lack of obedience prevailed among some of the readers. Note, for example, the author's admonition not to "be carried away by all kinds of strange teachings" (13:9). The leaders needed help and encouragement. Thus the appeal to obey them and to submit to their authority is timely. Of course, the readers could question whether this authority was self-imposed by the leaders or delegated to them by Christ. If a leader is a dedicated minister of the Word of God, he proves thereby that Christ has given him authority. And if Christ has entrusted him with the task of assuming leadership, the people need not question his authority (Acts 20:28; Eph. 4:11; I Peter 5:1–3).

b. *Care provided.* The leaders have taken their God-given task seriously. "They keep watch over you." They literally lost sleep over the spiritual welfare of the believers. They know the word God spoke to the prophet Ezekiel: "Son of man, I have made you a watchman for the house of Israel; so hear the word I speak and give them warning from me. When I say to a wicked man, 'You will surely die,' and you do not warn him or speak out to dissuade him from his evil ways in order to save his life, that wicked man will die for his sin, and I will hold you accountable for his blood" (3:17–18).

The leaders stay with the congregation, are vigilant in caring for the members, nurture them spiritually, ward off deceitful attacks, and administer discipline when necessary. Writes John Calvin, "The heavier the burden they bear, the more honour they deserve; for the more labour any one undertakes for our sake, and the more difficulty and danger he incurs for us, the greater are our obligations to him."[32] These leaders are accountable to God, for he is their overseer. That is not to say that the members are not held accountable. Certainly they are. They, too, are told to work together harmoniously so that the task of the leaders is a joy and not a burden.

c. *Joy experienced.* Throughout his epistle the author has stressed the corporate responsibility of the believers. To mention one example, he exhorts the readers to encourage one another, "so that none of you may be hardened by sin's deceitfulness" (3:13). In a similar fashion, as a body they are to respond to their leaders, for then there is joy in the interpersonal relationships in the church. They receive the Lord's blessings by obeying the leaders God has given them. If they all respond favorably the work of their leaders becomes increasingly joyful.

When the members refuse to obey and fail to respect their leaders, the work in the church becomes burdensome. The members ought to realize

---

32. John Calvin, *Epistle to the Hebrews* (Grand Rapids: Eerdmans, 1949), p. 353.

that neither they nor the leaders own the church. The church belongs to Jesus Christ, to whom the readers are responsible. Should they make the work and life of the leaders difficult, they would be the losers. The leaders can testify before the Lord that they warned the wayward person who chose not to turn from his sin. That person will die in his sin, but the leaders are free from blame (Ezek. 3:19). Ultimately, then, the Lord avenges and judges his people (Heb. 10:30; Deut. 32:35–36; Ps. 135:14). Pastorally and prudently the writer of Hebrews observes that a sad instead of a glad report on the spiritual conduct of the readers will not be advantageous to them.

Greek Words, Phrases, and Constructions in 13:17

Verse 17

ὑπείκετε—with πείθεσθε this form is a present imperative. It derives from the verb ὑπείκω (I submit to authority) that appears only here in the entire New Testament. The verb is classical Greek.

ἀγρυπνοῦσιν—this verb from ἀγρυπνέω (I keep awake, keep watch) occurs in the Gospels (Mark 13:33; Luke 21:36) and Paul's epistles (Eph. 6:18; as a noun in II Cor. 6:5; 11:27). The verb describes an absence of sleep due to an alert mind.

ἀποδώσοντες—preceded by the participle ὡς and the noun λόγον (account), this future active participle of ἀποδίδωμι (I render) denotes purpose.[33]

ἵνα ποιῶσιν—here is an instance of result instead of purpose.

---

18 Pray for us. We are sure that we have a clear conscience and desire to live honorably in every way. 19 I particularly urge you to pray so that I may be restored to you soon.

20 May the God of peace, who through the blood of the eternal covenant brought back from the dead our Lord Jesus, that great Shepherd of the sheep, 21 equip you with everything good for doing his will, and may he work in us what is pleasing to him, through Jesus Christ, to whom be glory for ever and ever. Amen.

E. Prayers and Benedictions
13:18–21

The conclusion to the epistle is rather personal. Earlier, in two succeeding sentences, the author refers to himself in the first person singular—"And what more shall I say? I do not have time" (11:32). Now he uses the first person plural, as well as the singular, and requests prayer.

18. Pray for us. We are sure that we have a clear conscience and desire to live honorably in every way. 19. I particularly urge you to pray so that I may be restored to you soon.

Apparently the writer was one of the leaders in the church that receives

---

33. Robertson feels that the participle "is as much cause as purpose." See his *Grammar*, p. 1128. And Robert Hanna asserts that the participle "expresses a subjective motive, meaning 'with the thought that they must.' " See his *Grammatical Aid to the Greek New Testament* (Grand Rapids: Baker, 1983), p. 414.

his epistle. Tension between him and the readers developed, perhaps because of his teachings about the priesthood of Christ. These doctrines were hard for Jewish believers to accept, for they were accustomed to thinking of the priesthood in terms of the duties of the Levitical priests only. Probably the author's direct warnings against apostasy were not readily heeded by some members of the church. The author has put his teachings and admonitions in an epistle addressed to the readers. He realizes that the letter itself will not remove tension. However, he reduces it by putting himself in debt to them.

a. *Prayer.* The request for prayer is similar to those in Paul's epistles and fits into the spiritual climate of the first century (Rom. 15:30; II Cor. 1:11–12; Eph. 6:19; Col. 4:3–4; I Thess. 5:25; II Thess. 3:1). The writer places himself in the position of one who asks a favor. He knows that if the readers pray for him, the bond of unity between himself and the recipients of his letter is strengthened. And if they pray, they indicate that the message he conveys has been well received.

The first person plural in this verse can be understood literally. However, its close connection with the next verse, where the first person singular is used, seems to favor the interpretation that *we* and *us* should be understood editorially. That is, the author speaks about himself. Also, in the broader context, he does not mention other leaders (but see 13:23).

b. *Clear conscience.* The original text has the word *for,* which links the request for prayer to the reason that prompted the request. The sentence, then, is as follows: "Pray for us, for we are sure that we have a clear conscience." The writer is trying to say to the readers that he is aware of their uneasiness about his instruction and exhortations, but he himself bears no ill will. He can understand that some of the readers are not pleased with abolishing Levitical precepts because of the tradition of the fathers. But in his own heart the writer is persuaded that his conscience is clear. He has dedicated himself to the service of the Lord and therefore he desires to live honorably in every respect. He wants to help the readers and be of service to them as a faithful pastor. In short he is saying, "Trust me." The readers can be assured that their pastor is not leading them in the wrong direction with his teachings about priesthood and covenant.

Nowhere in the New Testament is the break with the traditions of the Old Testament era spelled out so clearly as in the Epistle to the Hebrews. Whether the writer is too progressive in his teachings may have been a relevant point of discussion among the readers whose religious and cultural roots are in Jewish tradition. Certainly the letter writer is no traditionalist who upholds the practices of the past. His task is to explain God's progressive revelation to the readers. He knows that his pastoral work has been and is performed honorably. He expresses the desire that he may be permitted in the near future to continue his pastoral duties among the readers. As he sees his relationship to the readers, his conduct has been above reproach.

c. *Special request.* Once more the author asks the readers to pray for him.

But now he makes a specific request: "Pray that I may be restored to you soon." The New International Version gives the reading "I particularly urge you to pray." But this translation is open to misunderstanding. For it could be interpreted to mean that all people, particularly the writer, urge the readers to pray. The original, however, expresses a repetitive idea in the sense of *more*: "I urge you all the more" (NASB) to pray in my behalf. The writer intimates that he wishes more and more to urge communal prayer for their eventual reunion. His desire is to be with the members of the church as soon as possible.

Where is the writer? What keeps him from visiting the readers? To these and similar questions we have no answer; and we do well not to speculate. To put it differently, at one time the readers knew exactly what the writer meant. With the passing of time the explanatory comments that were needed to understand these personal remarks were lost. What is important, however, is that we realize the significance of the author's special request: he desires that the church ask God for a speedy reunion of pastor and people. When this happens, the writer knows that the bond of peace and harmony is strong. He prays for unity in the Lord. Hence he utters the pastoral benediction that is unique, for it is a summary of many elements in his epistle (see 7:14, 16, 22; 9:12, 15; 11:5–6; 12:28; 13:16).

20. May the God of peace, who through the blood of the eternal covenant brought back from the dead our Lord Jesus, that great Shepherd of the sheep, 21. equip you with everything good for doing his will, and may he work in us what is pleasing to him, through Jesus Christ, to whom be glory for ever and ever. Amen.

In the immediately preceding verses (vv. 18–19), the author requests prayer for himself. Now he offers a prayer for the people he addresses. What a moving prayer! The wealth of theology and language in this benediction that virtually concludes his epistle compares favorably with the beauty and fullness of the first few verses of the introduction with which the author begins his epistle. The author is a literary artist and a masterful theologian.

In the first part (v. 20) of the benediction, note the following points:

a. "God of peace." The writer puts the subject *God* first. He describes God as "the God of peace." That is meaningful, for he is the one who creates peace in the hearts and lives of people. Peace comes from God. Note the author does not pray, "May the peace of God," but "May the God of peace." God, then, is the peacemaker who is able to dispel distrust and dissent. And God grants the gift of peace to his people, so that they in turn are able to effect peace among their fellow men. Paul prays these words—"the God of peace"—rather frequently in benedictions at the conclusion of his epistles (see Rom. 15:33; 16:20; II Cor. 13:11; Phil. 4:9; I Thess. 5:23; II Thess. 3:16). The formula, therefore, seems to have been quite common in the early church.

b. "Brought back from the dead." God brought Jesus back from the dead, says the author of Hebrews. The doctrine of Jesus' resurrection is fundamental to the Christian faith, for one of the requirements for holding the office of apostle was to be a witness of the resurrection (Acts 1:22). In their preaching, testifying, and writing, the apostles proclaimed the resurrection of Jesus. Even though Paul was not a disciple of Jesus, as were the other apostles, he encountered the resurrected Jesus on the Damascus road. Therefore, in his writings Paul teaches the resurrection and at the same time affirms his apostleship (see Gal. 1:1).

The writer of the Epistle to the Hebrews mentions the resurrection of Jesus once, in the benediction. Indirectly he includes this doctrine when he introduces the topic of Christ's exaltation at the right hand of the Majesty in heaven (1:3). He writes about the "great high priest who has gone through the heavens" (4:14) and he supposes that the readers will understand that Jesus rose from the dead and ascended to heaven. And in his summation of fundamental Christian doctrines, he lists the resurrection of the dead (6:2). Last, he alludes to the possibility of God's raising Isaac from the dead (11:19) and the actuality of women receiving the dead who were raised to life (11:35). He cannot claim to be a witness of Jesus' resurrection. As a second-generation believer, he heard the gospel from the immediate followers of Jesus (2:3). The author, then, briefly states that God raised Jesus from the dead and links this reference to Jesus' office.

c. "Shepherd of the sheep." The words "the great Shepherd of the sheep" remind us of Jesus' teaching that he is the good shepherd who lays down his life for the sheep (John 10:11; also see Isa. 63:11). In effect, the metaphor of the shepherd who dies for his sheep is equivalent to that of the high priest who offers himself as a sacrifice for his people. Especially the adjective *great* is telling, for the writer of Hebrews calls Jesus the great high priest (4:14). The two concepts, then, complement each other, although as Guthrie observes, "There is a tender aspect to the shepherd figure which is not as vivid in the high priest."[34] Peter depicts Jesus as the Chief Shepherd (I Peter 5:4). This great shepherd shed his blood and laid down his life for his sheep—in other words, his people—to obtain for them eternal redemption and to establish with them the eternal covenant that God had promised.

d. "Blood of the eternal covenant." Through the prophets Isaiah, Jeremiah, and Ezekiel, God announces his intention to establish an everlasting covenant with his people (Isa. 55:3; 61:8; Jer. 32:40; 50:5; Ezek. 16:60; 37:26). This covenant is everlasting because it is sealed in blood—to be precise, the blood of the Messiah. In the messianic prophecy of Zion's king who enters Jerusalem on a donkey (Zech. 9:9; also see Matt. 21:5 and parallels), God promises his people deliverance "because of the blood of my covenant" (Zech. 9:11).

Two major themes dominate the epistle: the high-priestly work of Christ, summarized in the expression *blood,* and the covenant that is eternal. In this verse, once again and for the last time these themes are highlighted. God's

---

34. Guthrie, *New Testament Theology,* p. 388.

covenant with his people will remain forever. That covenant has been sealed with Christ's blood which was shed once for all (9:26; 10:10).

e. "Our Lord Jesus." These three words—four words in the original—appear last to receive all the emphasis in the verse. A literal translation of the verse is, "Now the God of peace, who brought up from the dead the great Shepherd of the sheep through the blood of the eternal covenant, even Jesus our Lord" (NASB).

In addition to using the given name *Jesus,* which calls to mind the earthly ministry and humanity of Christ, the author of Hebrews designates him "Lord" (2:3; 7:14). Although the title *Lord* occurs infrequently in Hebrews, its use in the Christian world was common, for it served as a brief confession of faith (for example, see I Cor. 12:3). In the benediction at the end of his epistle, the author wants to emphasize the sovereignty of Jesus. As in the introduction where he briefly points to the priestly and kingly offices of Christ (1:3), so in his benediction he combines in one sentence a reference to the priesthood and kingship of Jesus.

In the second part of the benediction (v. 21), we note these considerations:

a. "May God . . . equip you." The first part of the benediction consists of a summary of what God has done in Christ; the second reveals what God is doing in Christ's people. In this section the author utters a prayer in behalf of the readers and asks God to equip them to do his will. The verb *to equip* actually means to make someone complete. It connotes the act of restoring—that is, perfecting—something. Some translations have the reading "may the God of peace . . . make you perfect" (NEB; also consult KJV; RV; ASV). God strengthens man so that shortcomings may be overcome.[35] He supplies us with every good thing so that we may be able to do his will.

A plaque with simple wording adorns a wall in our family room. Every member of the family can testify to the truthfulness of the wording. Here is the text:

> The will of God
> can never lead you
> where the grace of God
> cannot keep you.

b. "May [God] work in us." In preceding verses the writer encourages the reader to live a life that is pleasing to God (11:5–6; 12:28; 13:16). A person who lives such a life is commended by God himself and is rewarded (II Cor. 5:9–10). But man looks to God for help, direction, and wisdom. And because of the eternal covenant he has made with us through Jesus Christ, he grants us assistance. The writer of Hebrews prays that God may work in us to do that which pleases him. And Paul, writing to the church in Philippi, formulates the human and the divine in salvation. Says he, "Work out your

---

35. Reinier Schippers in *NIDNTT,* vol. 3, p. 350, states that in the New Testament the meaning of the verb in question is "to prepare, establish, form, and equip."

salvation with fear and trembling, for it is God who works in you to will and to act according to his good purpose" (Phil. 2:12–13).

Why is God willing to work in us? The author is almost repetitious in the wording of this benediction. He spells out that through Jesus Christ—note the combination of the two names (also see 10:10; 13:8)—God himself works in us and equips us to do his will. Through Jesus Christ, therefore, we are in God, and God works in us (John 17:21).

c. "To whom be glory." Translations vary, because in the original Greek it is not clear whether glory ought to be attributed to God or to Jesus Christ. Some commentators think that because God is the subject in the benediction, the author means to say that God should receive the glory. Moreover, in greetings and benedictions glory is given to God (Rom. 11:36; 16:27; Gal. 1:5; Eph. 3:21; Phil. 4:20; I Tim. 1:17; Jude 25). But some of them ascribe glory to Jesus Christ (II Tim. 4:18; II Peter 3:18; Rev. 1:6; 4:11). In the benediction in Hebrews, the flow of the sentence seems to indicate that Jesus Christ should receive the glory. Obviously the formula itself is the stock phrase "glory for ever and ever. Amen." And, therefore, the writer may not have intended a clear choice. For him they are the familiar words at the conclusion of a benediction. Amen, so let it be!

Practical Considerations in 13:18–21

The psalmists teach us that prayer is praise. God is to be praised for his work in creation and redemption. But prayer also concerns the practical matters of life, as Jesus teaches us in the Lord's Prayer. After three petitions about the name, the kingdom, and the will of God, he teaches us to pray for daily bread, forgiveness of sin, victory in temptation, and deliverance from evil. God is interested in everything we do. We have the privilege of praying not only for ourselves, but also for our fellow man. We may bring all our needs to God in prayer.

> What a friend we have in Jesus,
> All our sins and griefs to bear!
> What a privilege to carry
> Everything to God in prayer!
> O what peace we often forfeit,
> O what needless pain we bear,
> All because we do not carry
> Everything to God in prayer!
> —Joseph Scriven

When someone is making a decision, we often advise him, "Let your conscience be your guide." But if a conscience is seared by sin, it is of little help in making the right choices. Jonathan Edwards compared man's conscience with a sundial: "As the sundial cannot make the hour known when the sun does not shine upon it, so conscience is not a plain or safe guide to duty unless it is enlightened by God's Word." Man's conscience should be directed to the Scriptures, much the same as the needle of a compass invariably points north.

Greek Words, Phrases, and Constructions in 13:18–21

Verse 18

προσεύχεσθε—first in the sentence, this verb is an imperative in the present tense, middle as a deponent. The present tense expresses continued action: keep on praying.

πειθόμεθα—the same verb, although in the second person plural, appeared in 13:17. There the meaning is "obey;" here it is "persuaded." Some translators (including those of the NIV) omit the postpositive conjunction γάρ in their versions. The word should be maintained, for the conjunction makes the author's intent clear.

ἔχομεν—the repeated use of the first person plural in pronoun and verb appears to be the editorial "we."[36]

ἀναστρέφεσθαι—as a present passive infinitive from ἀναστρέφω (I turn back), the verb means "to conduct oneself in life" (see Heb. 10:33).

Verse 19

τάχιον—this comparative adverb, like περισσοτέρως (all the more), "appears to have a true comparative sense in this verse, 'more quickly,' or 'sooner.' "[37]

ἀποκατασταθῶ—from the compound ἀποκαθίστημι (I restore), this verb is the aorist passive subjunctive. The subjunctive is used because of the indirect command structure of παρακαλῶ and ἵνα.

Verse 20

ὁ ἀναγαγών—the articular aorist active participle, derived from ἀνάγω (I bring up), may connote either bringing someone *up* from the dead or bringing him *back* from the dead.

τὸν μέγαν—the position of the adjective together with the definite article is rather emphatic.

ἐν αἵματι—the instrumental use of the preposition reflects Semitic form in this instance current in the Septuagint. The noun αἷμα lacks the definite article.

Verse 21

καταρτίσαι—this is one of the few occurrences of the optative mood—one of the sixty-seven instances in the New Testament. The form is the first aorist active optative of καταρτίζω (I restore). The subject of the verb is ὁ θεός. The sentence conveys a wish.

εἰς τὸ ποιῆσαι—the preposition εἰς with the articular infinitive expresses purpose. The aorist tense of the infinitive is constative.

ποιῶν—in a few major manuscripts this participle is preceded by αὐτῷ. However,

---

36. Robertson, *Grammar,* pp. 677–78.
37. Hanna, *Grammatical Aid,* p. 415. Also see Friedrich W. Blass and Albert Debrunner, *A Greek Grammar of the New Testament and Other Early Christian Literature,* rev. and trans. Robert W. Funk (Chicago: University of Chicago Press, 1961), sec. 244 (1).

the pronoun is unintelligible and "may be a homiletic expansion."[38] Therefore, we do well to delete it.

ἡμῖν—because of the preceding form ὑμᾶς, a number of Greek manuscripts have the reading ὑμῖν. By applying the rule that the more difficult reading is the more original, we are able to explain the presence of the second person plural pronoun better than that of the first person plural pronoun. Thus we favor the reading ὑμῖν.

ᾧ—the relative pronoun in the dative singular, as indirect object, has its nearest antecedent in the immediately preceding Ἰησοῦ Χριστοῦ. For this reason, we apply the words to Jesus and not to ὁ θεός, the subject of the sentence.

---

22 Brothers, I urge you to bear with my word of exhortation, for I have written you only a short letter.
23 I want you to know that our brother Timothy has been released. If he arrives soon, I will come with him to see you.
24 Greet all your leaders and all God's people. Those from Italy send you their greetings.
25 Grace be with you all.

F. Final Greetings
13:22-25

The last few verses of this epistle are too brief to tell us something about the time and circumstances in which the letter was written. The names of Timothy and of Italy, although interesting, are of very little help in this respect. The author is not giving us newsworthy items. Rather, he is writing a "word of exhortation." That is the purpose of his "short letter."

22. Brothers, I urge you to bear with my word of exhortation, for I have written you only a short letter.

In this somewhat personal section of the epistle, the author addresses the readers as brothers (3:1, 12; 10:19). He follows the custom of his day and therefore ought not be faulted for failing to mention the feminine gender.

A second time he says "I urge" (see 13:19), but now almost apologetically as he explains what he wants the readers to do. Says he, "Bear with my word of exhortation." Actually, he tells the readers to put up with his word of exhortation; or, in less colloquial terms, he is asking them to listen carefully to what he has to say.

What does the expression *word of exhortation* mean? Throughout his epistle the writer has been a faithful pastor to his people by exhorting them to listen attentively and obediently to the Word of God. Although at first glance his letter may seem to be a doctrinal treatise, the epistle consists of pastoral admonitions that are supported by teachings derived from a sound knowledge of the Old Testament. The conclusion that we draw therefore is that the Epistle to the Hebrews indeed is a word of exhortation written by a dedicated pastor who watches over the spiritual well-being of his people.

---

38. Metzger, *Textual Commentary*, p. 676.

Besides admonishing them, the pastor also teaches them new truths concerning Jesus Christ. They may have objected to these teachings and perhaps to his exhortations. Therefore he urges them to listen to him as he addresses them in this word of exhortation (compare Acts 13:15).

"For I have written you only a short letter." The tone is apologetic. A few times in the body of his letter the author shortened his remarks (5:11; 9:5; 11:32) and stated that he lacked time even though he had much to say. The letter itself can easily be read in one sitting; let us say, during a worship service. Moreover, the adjective *short* need not be taken literally.

Last, the word *letter* is significant. The writer speaks of a letter, not a theological treatise. He wants to communicate the truth and chooses the form of a letter. The exhortations, the personal remarks (especially those in the last part of chapter 13), and the greetings make this writing a letter.

23. I want you to know that our brother Timothy has been released. If he arrives soon, I will come with him to see you.

Actually this verse has the appearance of a postscript at the end of the letter. As the New English Bible has it, "I have news for you."

"Our brother Timothy has been released." Is this person Paul's faithful fellow worker? Perhaps. Certainly we do not have proof. But because the writer calls Timothy "our brother," indications are that he is Paul's companion. In early Christian literature, only the coworker of Paul bears the name *Timothy*. A few times Paul calls Timothy "our brother" (II Cor. 1:1; Col. 1:1; I Thess. 3:2; Philem. 1). He invites Timothy, a native of Lystra, to accompany him on his second missionary journey (Acts 16:1–3). Timothy traveled widely, helped Paul in writing letters (for example, II Corinthians), served as Paul's good will ambassador to Corinth, and was the pastor of the church at Ephesus. In short, Timothy was well known.

Timothy had been in Rome during Paul's first imprisonment (Phil. 1:1; Col. 1:1; Philem. 1). From Rome Paul wrote the so-called prison Epistles (Ephesians, Philemon, Colossians, and Philippians). During Paul's second imprisonment at Rome, he urged Timothy to come to him quickly (II Tim. 4:9).

We have no information about Timothy's imprisonment. The writer of Hebrews only states, "Our brother Timothy has been released." Presumably he had been imprisoned for his Christian testimony and was released. The author is not sure what plans Timothy may have, but one thing is certain: "If he arrives soon, I will come with him to see you." Where Timothy will arrive and at what place the writer resides is not known. Whether the author needed Timothy's moral support in respect to the Jewish Christians who received his letter remains an open question.

24. Greet all your leaders and all God's people. Those from Italy send you their greetings.

Three times the leaders attract attention. First, they are to be remembered and imitated (v. 7). Then they are to be obeyed because they have authority (v. 17). And now they receive greetings. At the conclusions of letters, writers

435

generally add salutations. Paul, Peter, and John in their respective epistles convey greetings.

The author of Hebrews, however, makes a distinction between leaders and God's people by repeating the adjective *all*. If he had said, "Greet all your leaders and people," he would have given the impression that the letter was addressed to one particular church. Apparently the writer sends greetings to all the church leaders, and he greets all God's people who formed a segment of the church. This segment, then, consists of a group of Jewish Christians called Hebrews.[39]

Where did the readers live? A hasty answer would be Rome. The writer says, "Those from Italy send you their greetings." If the expression *those from Italy* had only one meaning, we would be able to decide whether the readers lived in Rome or not. The expression can mean, first, that the author writes from Rome to a group of Christians living outside of Italy. He includes his Italian friends in Rome in the greetings he sends to the group. This view was commonly held by the church fathers. And numerous Greek manuscripts had a subscription at the end of the epistle that said, "Written to the Hebrews from Italy [Rome] by Timothy" (KJV).[40] Needless to say, subscriptions were added by scribes at a later date.

The second interpretation is that the author addressed his epistle to Christians at Rome from a place outside Italy. His friends who hail from Italy send greetings to their relatives and acquaintances in Rome. This seems to be an acceptable interpretation, and scholars generally advance this theory.

Whether we accept the first or the second interpretation, the fact remains that we have to work with hypotheses because the text itself is not clear.

25. Grace be with you all.

The final greeting is customary. Paul writes either "the grace of the Lord Jesus [Christ] be with you [all]" (Rom. 16:24; I Cor. 16:23; II Cor. 13:14; I Thess. 5:28; II Thess. 3:18) or "the grace of our Lord Jesus Christ be with your spirit" (Gal. 6:18; Phil. 4:23; Philem. 25), or "grace be with you [all]" (Col. 4:18; I Tim. 6:21; II Tim. 4:22; Titus 3:15). Some manuscripts add the word *Amen*; others delete it. The addition of the word is easier to explain than its deletion. Therefore, the New International Version ends the Epistle to the Hebrews with "Grace be with you all."

Greek Words, Phrases, and Constructions in 13:22–25

Verse 22

ἀνέχεσθε—instead of the infinitive ἀνέχεσθαι featured in a few manuscripts, the better reading is the present middle imperative (compare 13:19, where the infini-

---

39. Grosheide, *Hebreeën*, pp. 27–28. Westcott notes that "the letter was not addressed officially to the Church, but to some section of it." See his *Hebrews*, p. 451.

40. In his *Textual Commentary*, p. 678, Metzger lists the variant readings of the subscriptions. Some are rather lengthy. For example, here is the reading of Manuscript 431: "This Epistle to the Hebrews was written from Italy by the apostle Timothy who was sent to them by the blessed Paul in order that he might set them on a straight path."

tive occurs with παρακαλῶ). The compound verb ἀνά (up) and ἔχω (I have, hold) corresponds to the idiom *to put up with*. The verb governs the genitive case in τοῦ λόγου.

καὶ γάρ—this emphatic combination appears only five times in the entire epistle (4:2; 5:12; 10:34; 12:29; 13:22). It means "for indeed."

διὰ βραχέων—the preposition διά is followed by the plural adjective in the genitive case. The adjective actually modifies the understood noun λόγων (words). The literal translation of the idiomatic expression "in few words" is better understood adverbially—that is, "briefly."

ἐπέστειλα—from ἐπιστέλλω (I write a letter), this aorist active indicative is the so-called epistolary aorist. The writer places himself in the time of the recipient of the letter and thus views the act of writing as having taken place in the past.

Verse 23

γινώσκετε—because the word stands first in the sentence, this verb is the present active imperative, not the present active indicative. It can best be translated as "I want you to know" (NIV).

ἐὰν τάχιον ἔρχηται—the particle ἐάν introduces a conditional sentence with a subjunctive verb ἔρχηται in the protasis and a future middle indicative ὄψομαι in the apodosis. The first part of the sentence expresses uncertainty. For the comparative adverb τάχιον, see verse 19.

Verse 24

ἀσπάσασθε—the aorist middle imperative from the verb ἀσπάζομαι (I greet) derives from σπάω that is preceded by the intensive ἁ and means "I draw to myself," in the middle voice. Generally a greeting was expressed by embracing and kissing. Here the greeting is conveyed by a letter.

Summary of Chapter 13

The last chapter of the Epistle to the Hebrews gives the letter a personal touch. The writer reveals his pastoral concerns for the believers and makes his desire known to be in their midst again.

The content of this chapter does not consist of some loosely connected exhortations. The writer encourages the readers to express their Christian love in the social context of their day: love for the brothers and sisters in the Lord, love toward the traveler in need of a roof over his head at night, and loving compassion and empathy for prisoners and people who are mistreated. From the love for the neighbor in the narrow and broad senses, the writer moves to the love in the home; that is, the bond of marriage, the husband's relationship to his wife and vice versa. He includes the admonition not to love money, but to be content and trust God. The first section of this last chapter, then, delineates the requirements of the summary of the law, in reverse order: love your neighbor as yourself, and love the Lord your God.

In the second part of the chapter the author enumerates some ecclesiastical duties and concerns. He begins with an exhortation to remember those leaders whose service on earth has ended. Imitate their faith, he says, and look at the lives they lived. From the topic of church leaders the author goes to that of doctrine. Stay away from doctrines that deviate from the truth. Rather, consider the work of Jesus, who suffered and died in disgrace outside the city gate. Thankfulness for salvation comes to expression by confessing God's name, doing good deeds, and sharing with others. Church leaders and church members ought to work together harmoniously so that the obedience of the members is a source of joy to the leaders.

The last section of the chapter includes a personal request for prayer, a beautifully worded benediction, an announcement of the writer's intended visit accompanied by Timothy, greetings to leaders and people of the church, and greetings from Italian friends. The letter ends with the final greeting, "Grace be with you all."

Select Bibliography

Commentaries

Alford, Henry. *Alford's Greek Testament: An Exegetical and Critical Commentary.* 4 vols. Vol. 4, pt. 1, *Prolegomena and Hebrews.* 1875. Grand Rapids: Guardian, 1976.

Bengel, John Albert. *Gnomon of the New Testament.* Edited by Andrew R. Fausset. 7th ed. 4 vols. Vol. 4. Edinburgh: T. and T. Clark, 1877.

Bleek, F. *Der Brief an die Hebräer.* 2 vols. Berlin: F. Dummler, 1828–40.

Bristol, Lyle O. *Hebrews: A Commentary.* Valley Forge: Judson, 1967.

Brown, John. *An Exposition of Hebrews.* Edinburgh: The Banner of Truth Trust, 1961.

Bruce, F. F. *The Epistle to the Hebrews.* New International Commentary on the New Testament series. Grand Rapids: Eerdmans, 1964.

Buchanan, George W. *To the Hebrews.* Anchor Bible. New York: Doubleday, 1972.

Calvin, John. *Commentaries on the Epistle to the Hebrews.* Grand Rapids: Eerdmans, 1949.

Davidson, A. B. *The Epistle to the Hebrews.* Edinburgh: T. and T. Clark, 1882.

Davies, J. H. *A Letter to the Hebrews.* London: Cambridge University Press, 1967.

Delitzsch, Franz. *Commentary on the Epistle to the Hebrews.* 2 vols. Edinburgh: T. and T. Clark, 1877.

Gouge, William. *Commentary on Hebrews.* 1655. Grand Rapids: Kregel, 1980.

Grosheide, F. W. *De Brief aan de Hebreeën en de Brief van Jakobus.* Kampen: Kok, 1955.

Guthrie, Donald. *Hebrews.* Tyndale New Testament Commentaries series. Grand Rapids: Eerdmans, 1983.

Hagner, Donald. *Hebrews.* Good News Commentary series. San Francisco: Harper and Row, 1983.

Héring, J. *The Epistle to the Hebrews.* Translated by A. W. Heathcoat and P. J. Allock from French original of 1955. London: Epworth, 1970.

Hewitt, Thomas. *The Epistle to the Hebrews.* Tyndale New Testament Commentaries series. Grand Rapids: Eerdmans, 1960.

Hughes, Philip Edgcumbe. *A Commentary on the Epistle to the Hebrews.* Grand Rapids: Eerdmans, 1977.

Jewett, Robert. *Letter to Pilgrims: A Commentary on the Epistle to the Hebrews.* International Critical Commentary series. 1924. New York: Pilgrim, 1981.

Lang, G. H. *The Epistle to the Hebrews.* London: Paternoster, 1951.

Lenski, R. C. H. *The Interpretation of the Epistle to the Hebrews and of the Epistle of James.* Columbus: Wartburg, 1946.

Michel, Otto. *Der Brief an die Hebräer.* 10th ed. Göttingen: Vandenhoeck and Ruprecht, 1957.

Moffatt, James. *Epistle to the Hebrews.* International Critical Commentary series. Edinburgh: T. and T. Clark, 1963.

Montefiore, Hugh. *The Epistle to the Hebrews*. New York and Evanston: Harper and Row, 1964.

Neil, W. *The Epistle to the Hebrews*. Torah Commentaries. London: SCM, 1955.

Owen, John. *An Esposition of Hebrews*. 7 vols. in 4. Evansville, Ind.: Sovereign Grace, 1960.

Peake, A. S. *Hebrews*. Century Bible. New York: Henry Frowde; Edinburgh: T. C. and E. C. Jack, 1914.

Pink, Arthur W. *An Exposition of Hebrews*. 2 vols. Grand Rapids: Baker, 1954.

Riggenbach, Edward. *Der Brief an die Hebräer*. Leipzig and Erlangen: Deichert, 1922.

Schneider, Johannes. *The Letter to the Hebrews*. Grand Rapids: Eerdmans, 1957.

Snell, A. *New and Living Way*. London: Faith Press, 1959.

Strathmann, Hermann. *Der Brief an die Hebräer*. Das Neue Testament Deutsch. Göttingen: Vandenhoeck and Ruprecht, 1937.

Spicq, Ceslaus. *L'Épître aux Hébreux*. 3d ed. 2 vols. Paris: Gabalda, 1952–53.

Westcott, B. F. *Commentary on the Epistle to the Hebrews*. Grand Rapids: Eerdmans, 1950.

Windisch, J. *Der Hebräerbrief*. Tübingen: Mohr, 1931.

Studies

Berkhof, Louis. *Systematic Theology*. Grand Rapids: Eerdmans, 1953.

Bruce, F. F. "The Kerygma of Hebrews." *Interpretation* 23 (1969): 3–19.

————. "Recent Literature on the Epistle to the Hebrews." *Themelios* 3 (1966): 31–36.

Buchanan, George W. "The Present State of Scholarship on Hebrews." In *Christianity, Judaism and Other Greco-Roman Cults: Studies for Morton Smith at Sixty*, edited by J. Neusner, vol. 1, pp. 299–330. Leiden: Brill, 1975.

Deissmann, Adolf. *Bible Studies*. Winona Lake, Ind.: Alpha Publications, 1979.

Elbogen, Ismar. *Der Jüdische Gottesdienst*. Frankfurt: Kaufmann, 1931.

Guthrie, Donald. *New Testament Introduction*. Downers Grove, Ill.: Inter-Varsity Press, 1970.

————. *New Testament Theology*. Downers Grove, Ill.: Inter-Varsity, 1981.

Harrison, E. F. "The Theology of the Epistle to the Hebrews." *BS* 12 (1964): 333–40.

Hoekema, A. A. "The Perfection of Christ in Hebrews." *CTJ* 9 (1974): 31–37.

Kistemaker, Simon J. *The Psalm Citations in the Epistle to the Hebrews*. Amsterdam: Van Soest, 1961.

Ladd, George E. *A Theology of the New Testament*. Grand Rapids: Eerdmans, 1974.

Morris, Leon. *The Gospel of John*. New International Commentary on the New Testament series. Grand Rapids: Eerdmans, 1970.

Ridderbos, Herman N. *Mattheüs*. Korte Verklaring. 2 vols. Kampen: Kok, 1952.

Ridderbos, Jan. *De Psalmen*. 2 vols. Kampen: Kok, 1955.

Schürer, Emil. *A History of the Jewish People in the Time of Jesus Christ*. 5 vols. Edinburgh: T. and T. Clark, 1885.

Smalley, S. S. "Atonement in Hebrews." *Evangelical Quarterly* 33 (1961): 126–35.

Vos, Geerhardus. *Biblical Theology*. Grand Rapids: Eerdmans, 1954.

————. *The Teaching of the Epistle to the Hebrews*. Grand Rapids: Eerdmans, 1956.

Werner, Ernst. *The Sacred Bridge*. London: D. Dobson, 1959.

Tools

Aland, Kurt, et al. *The Greek New Testament.* 3d ed. United Bible Societies, 1975.

Bauer, W., W. F. Arndt, F. W. Gingrich, and F. W. Danker. *A Greek-English Lexicon of the New Testament.* 2d ed. Chicago: University of Chicago Press, 1978.

Berkhof, Louis. *Principles of Biblical Interpretation.* Grand Rapids: Baker, 1950.

Brown, Colin, ed. *New International Dictionary of New Testament Theology.* 3 vols. Grand Rapids: Zondervan, 1975–78.

Danby, H., ed. *Mishna,* Moed Yoma. London: Oxford University Press, 1967.

Epstein, I., ed. *The Babylonian Talmud.* 18 vols. London: The Soncino Press, 1948–52.

Hanna, Robert. *A Grammatical Aid to the Greek New Testament.* Grand Rapids: Baker, 1983.

Hodges, Zane C., and Arthur L. Farstad. *The Greek New Testament According to the Majority Text.* Nashville and New York: Nelson, 1982.

Josephus, Flavius. Loeb Classical Library Series. London: Heinemann; New York: Putnam, 1966–76.

Kittel, Gerhard, and Gerhard Friedrich, eds. *Theological Dictionary of the New Testament.* Translated by G. W. Bromiley. 10 vols. Vols. 1–9. Grand Rapids: Eerdmans, 1964–76.

Merk, Augustinus. *Novum Testamentum.* 9th ed. Rome: Pontifical Biblical Institute, 1964.

Metzger, Bruce M. *A Textual Commentary on the Greek New Testament.* London and New York: United Bible Societies, 1975.

Nestle, E., and Kurt Aland. *Novum Testamentum Graece.* 26th ed. Stuttgart: Deutsche Bibelstiftung, 1981.

Phillips, J. B. *The New Testament in Modern English.* New York: Macmillan, 1958.

Philo. Loeb Classical Library Series. Vol. 1–6. Cambridge, Mass.: Harvard University Press; London: Heinemann, 1966–71.

Robertson, A. T. *A Grammar of the Greek New Testament in the Light of Historical Research.* Nashville: Broadman, 1934.

Strack, H. L., and P. Billerbeck. *Kommentar zum Neuen Testament aus Talmud und Midrasch.* 5 vols. München: Beck, 1922–28.

Thayer, Joseph H. *A Greek-English Lexicon of the New Testament.* New York, Cincinnati, and Chicago: American Book Company, 1889.

Zuntz, Gunther. *The Text of the Epistles.* London: Oxford University Press, 1953.

Index of Authors

Index of Scripture

Genesis

1:1—313
1:3—313
1:6—313
1:9—313
1:11–12—165
1:14—313
1:20—313
1:24—313
1:26–27—64
1:27–30—66
1:28—65, 410
2:2—9, 107, 108, 112
3:6—367
3:8—26
3:15—358
3:17–18—165
3:17–19—67
3:19—265
3:24—240
4:3–5—276
4:4—315, 316
4:6–7—315
4:7—315, 319
4:9—385
4:10—316
4:10–11—395
5:1–24—316
5:3–32—319
5:5—185
5:21–24—317
5:24—317n
6:1–7—318
6:8–9—318
6:9—317, 319
9:1–2—64
9:29—185
11:11—187 n. 10
11:28—326
12:1—321
12:1–9—170
12:2–3—188, 322

12:3—325
12:6–7—170
13:14–17—170, 188
14—191
14:17—186
14:17–20—9
14:18—135, 184, 210
14:18–20—184, 185, 189, 193
14:19—184
14:19–20—186, 188
14:20—184
14:22—173, 186
14:22–23—184, 186
15:5—170, 324, 337
15:16—374
16:16—170
17:7—178, 334
17:21—170
18:1–15—408
18:12—324
18:25—396
19:1–22—408
21:1–2—352
21:5—170
21:12—10, 170, 324, 328
22—327
22:5—328
22:12—328
22:16—171, 201, 204
22:16–17—174, 260
22:17—9, 171, 324, 337
23:3–20—321
25:1–2—324
25:7—170, 185
25:26—170
25:32—386 n. 33
26:4—332
26:34–35—334
26:35—386
27:2—332
27:27–28—332
27:27–29—188

27:30–40—387
27:39–40—332
28:3–4—332
28:9—386
28:15—411
32:12—324, 337
35:28–29—332
37:2—333
41:43—344
47:29–31—333
47:31—333n
48:1—332
48:4—333
48:5—333
48:12–20—333
48:15–16—188
48:21—332
49—188, 332
49:7—334
49:10—358
50:4–14—334
50:12–14—333
50:24—333
50:25—334

Exodus

1:11–14—338
2:2—335, 345
2:14–15—339
3:6—326
3:7—338
3:10—339
3:18—339
3:21—339
4:1–9—339
4:5—326
4:14–16—339
4:22—36 n. 15
6:7—226
10:28–29—339n
12–20—160
12:5—341

447

459

2:1–3—416n
2:5—319
2:9–22—416n
2:13—95
3:10—151, 399
3:12—151
3:13—326
3:18—388, 432

I John

2:1—263
2:2—264
2:20—44
2:27—44
3:2—385
4:10—84
5:16—293

II John

7–10—416n

Jude

5–16—416n
9—50
11—178
14—316
25—432

Revelation

1:4—303
1:4–5—216
1:5—38, 394
1:6—221, 400, 432
1:8—303, 415
1:9—15
1:13—69
1:14—45
1:17—368
1:16—116, 120
1:18—76

2:2—416n
2:6—416n
2:11—137
2:12—120
2:13—371
2:14–16—416n
2:18—45
2:20–24—416n
2:25—128
2:26–27—36
3:2—51
3:5—393
3:7–13—408
3:11—128
3:14—29n
3:21—221
4:2—216
4:8—303
4:10—216
4:11—432
5:1—216
5:5—195
5:7—216
5:9–10—262–63
5:10—400
5:11—50, 393
5:11–13—393
5:12—398
5:13—216
6:10—316
6:14—47
6:15–17—385
6:16—119, 216
7:2—98
7:9—366n
7:10—216
7:15—216
7:15–17—216
12:5—216
13:8—393
13:16—34
13:17—34

14:1—227, 392
14:9—34
14:11—34
14:13—112
14:14—69
15:2—34
15:3—39
15:4—209
16:2—34
16:5—209
16:17—216
17:6—371
18:1—158
19:1—41
19:3—41
19:4—216
19:6—41
19:12—451
19:13—116
19:15—36, 120
19:20—34
20:4—34
20:4–6—400
20:6—137
20:12—393
20:14—137
21:2—326, 392
21:3—226, 392
21:4—50, 112
21:5—216
21:6—368
21:8—137, 410
21:14—322
21:19—322
21:23—158, 392
22:4—227
22:5—158
22:6—378n
22:13—368
22:15—410
22:20—266

Extrabiblical References

Apocrypha

Judith

11:23—345
15:7—186

I Maccabees

2:59—352n
9:30—415
13:2—390n

II Maccabees

7:1—355
7:9—354
7:14—354
7:23—354